WESTERN
CIVILIZATIONS

W · W · NORTON & COMPANY · NEW YORK · LONDON

R O B E R T E. L E R N E R
S T A N D I S H M E A C H A M
E D W A R D M C N A L L B U R N S

WESTERN CIVILIZATIONS

Their History and Their Culture

VOLUME II

ELEVENTH EDITION

For Dietlind and Olivia;
Edith, Louisa, and Samuel

Eleventh Edition 1988

First Edition, Copyright 1941
Second Edition, Copyright 1947
Third Edition, Copyright 1949
Fourth Edition, Copyright 1954
Fifth Edition, Copyright © 1958
Sixth Edition, Copyright © 1963
Seventh Edition, Copyright © 1968
Eighth Edition, Copyright © 1973
Ninth Edition, Copyright © 1980
Tenth Edition, Copyright © 1984

BY W. W. NORTON & COMPANY, INC.

Book Design by Antonina Krass
Layout by Ben Gamit

Cartography by Harold K. Faye

W. W. Norton & Company, Inc.,
500 Fifth Avenue, New York, N.Y. 10110
W. W. Norton & Company Ltd.,
37 Great Russell Street, London WC1B 3NU

ISBN 0-393-95661-X

1 2 3 4 5 6 7 8 9 0

CONTENTS

Part Five   THE FRENCH AND INDUSTRIAL REVOLUTIONS AND THEIR CONSEQUENCES

Chapter 23   NATIONALISM AND NATION-BUILDING (1815–1870)   809

Part Six   THE WEST AT THE WORLD'S CENTER

Chapter 24   THE PROGRESS OF INTERNATIONAL INDUSTRIALIZATION AND COMPETITION (1870–1914)   845

Chapter 25   THE MIDDLE CLASS CHALLENGED   875

Chapter 26   THE SEARCH FOR STABILITY (1870–1914)   903

Chapter 27   THE FIRST WORLD WAR   939

Chapter 28 THE WEST BETWEEN THE WARS   969

Chapter 29 THE SECOND WORLD WAR   1009

Part Seven THE EMERGENCE OF WORLD CIVILIZATION

Chapter 30 NEW POWER RELATIONSHIPS AND THE NEW EUROPE   1033

Chapter 31 PROBLEMS OF WORLD CIVILIZATION   1069

MAPS

PREFACE

First published in 1941 and soon approaching its fiftieth birthday, *Western Civilizations* is often deemed a "textbook classic." Most likely Edward McNall Burns, who brought out the first eight editions without collaborators between 1941 and 1973, was aiming toward this goal. Certainly Professor Burns was determined to create a history text of high literary distinction, one that provided coherence of narrative and interpretation expressed in vigorous and distinguished prose. Professor Burns recognized, moreover, that any introductory history text of quality needed to be more than a political history—or an economic or social history for that matter. Instead he firmly conceived of his book as a history of *civilizations*—an account of the changing ways in which humans have organized their lives in response to changing environments and consistent imperatives. Accordingly he chose to complement narrative passages with thoughtful discussions of ideas and societal institutions. Perhaps above all, Professor Burns wished to engage his readers' attention. As a true teacher/writer he intended to demonstrate, without resorting to the slightest meretriciousness, that "freshman history" need not be viewed as a chore but might be welcomed as a source of intellectual stimulation and perhaps even delight.

Approving of Professor Burns's strategies and sharing his goals, we have sought to retain the basic physiognomy of *Western Civilizations* in our revisions. Nevertheless the explosion of knowledge about previously neglected historical subject matters and the progress of research in more traditional areas has made it necessary to rewrite much of the work we inherited. Having redone most of the medieval and nineteenth-century material for the ninth edition, and most of the early-modern material for the tenth, we have now concentrated on overhauling the opening and the closing chapters of the book while also reexamining the entire text word by word.

Those familiar with earlier versions of *Western Civilizations* will notice right away that Part One in this eleventh edition bears minimal resemblance to its predecessors insofar as it now contains four chapters instead of five, covers several aspects of paleoanthropology hitherto ignored, treats Mesopotamia before Egypt, integrates the Hittites into the Mesopotamia chapter but removes the Persians from the same chapter, and unites the Minoans and Mycenaeans with the Hebrews in one chapter. More specifically, almost the entire contents of Chapters 1 and 2 and most of what appears in Chapter 4 is completely new. Chapter 1 now aims to present simply and coherently the latest findings in paleoanthropology (a field perhaps right behind superconductivity as one of the fastest moving areas of scientific research) and to concentrate on the most important moments of change in early human existence in western Asia—the origins of sedentary villages and the "birth of Western civilizations." Chapter 2 takes up where Chapter 1 left off (hence the new placement of Mesopotamia before Egypt) and seeks to address the flow of Mesopotamian history over the course of two and a half millennia from a more developmental perspective than before. Also new to this chapter is its emphasis on ecology and technology. The bulk of Chapter 4 consists of a fully rewritten consideration of the history and fortunes of the ancient Hebrews, stressing the magnitude of their influence on subsequent patterns of thought and behavior in the Western world.

The most extensive revision in Part Two of *Western Civilizations* lies in its treatment of the Hellenistic era. The Hellenistic chapter now opens with a consideration of the Persians (hitherto treated as a postscript to Mesopotamia) and then narrates the conquests of Alexander the Great (hitherto located in the Greek chapter); in both cases these transpositions were made in order to provide a more coherent background to the nature of Hellenistic civilization itself. In addition, the assessments of an earlier scholarly generation regarding Hellenistic economic and social "modernity" have been revised. Although less dramatic changes have been made in the respective chapters on the Greeks and the Romans, streamlining for clarity appears in both of those chapters on almost every page.

Significant revisions in Parts Three and Four include a new discussion of Jesus's career and teachings as well as a revised consideration of Augustine's *City of God;* an overhaul of the treatment of Waldensianism and of the founding of the Dominican and Franciscan Orders; and new accounts concerning Heloise and Abelard, the "Jacquerie," the reigns of Ferdinand and Isabella, and Anabaptism. Chapter 16 reformulates and expands previous treatments of the joint-stock company, the enclosure movement, rural manufacturing, and demographic trends in the early-modern era. Coverage of "The Age of Absolutism" in Chapter 17 now emphasizes the close relationship between economic innovation and the rise of the power of the state, and includes new material on the absolutism of central and eastern Europe. The treatment of Kant has been moved from the section on nineteenth-century Romanticism to the Enlightenment chapter.

In Parts Five and Six changes have similarly reflected recent scholarly perceptions and conclusions, as well as a desire to organize and present material as logically and cogently as possible. The treatment of the French Revolution in Chapter 19 contains a revised analysis of the factors that brought about the crisis of 1789, and additional material on the spread of revolutionary and Napoleonic reforms throughout the Continent. Chapter 20, "The Industrial Revolution," ties early nineteenth-century change to antecedents in what can no longer be perceived as an entirely "pre-industrial" past. Subsequent chapters on the nineteenth and early twentieth centuries contain new material on eastern Europe, on the role of women, on the meaning and importance of imperialism, and on the rise of militarism before the First World War. Revised and expanded discussion of the interwar era in Chapter 28 conveys a clearer sense of the varieties of twentieth-century totalitarianism, and, in particular, of the nature of Nazism.

In keeping with the dramatic changes in the post-Second World War era, Part Seven has been extensively reconstituted, revised, and expanded. Chapter 30 now carries forward the saga of Europe and the West well into the 1980s, treating such issues as international power relationships and class consciousness in terms of themes developed in earlier discussions. Europe's economic recovery and integration, postwar politics, and patterns of social and intellectual change are explored with a new thoroughness. The final chapter offers revised, reorganized, and updated coverage of the emergence of the Third World, the problems of international peacekeeping, ecology, population, and scientific and technological advance.

Robert Lerner has enjoyed writing and revising the material in Chapters 1 through 15 as well as Chapter 18, and Standish Meacham has enjoyed writing and revising the rest. To be sure, our enjoyment would have been greatly diminished had we not been able to draw on the criticisms and tips of a number of extremely thoughtful and helpful readers. Loretta Smith (Northwestern University) helped a Neanderthal master the material of Chapter 1 so much that she ought really to count as its coauthor. Carl Petry (Northwestern University) offered invaluable guidance on Egypt; Seymour Scheinberg (California State University at Fullerton) supplied welcome advice on all of Part One, and William V. Harris (Columbia University) and Richard Saller (University of Chicago) provided tough-minded critiques of all of Part Two. Helpful suggestions made by James Stanely and Stephen Knoble (both of Moody Bible College) were incorporated into Chapter 2, and suggestions made by Richard T. Nolan (Mattatuck Community College) were incorporated into Chapter 8. A needed fresh perspective on medieval Europe came from Stephen Ferruolo (Stanford University). A. N. Galpern (University of Pittsburgh) helped greatly to improve many passages in the early-modern chapters, and Martin Katz (University of Alberta) provided valued help on Russia in all periods. Gert Wendelborn (University of Rostock, Germany) read the entire first half of the book with extraordinary attentiveness and is responsible for numerous improvements. Later chapters received the benefit of detailed and thoughtful criticism from James J. Sheehan (Stanford University), Allen Cronenberg (Auburn University), and James Boyden (University of Texas). Peter Hayes (Northwestern University) made some valuable observations about the treatment of twentieth-century Germany. George Robb (Northwestern University) read the entire work and smoked out several errors and infelicities. Deeana Copeland won a proofreading derby by catching twice as many "typos" as did one of the authors. At W.W. Norton & Company, Ruth Mandel has gathered illustrations with her wonted tenacity, Ben Gamit has executed the page layout with imagination and flair, and Sandy Lifland has demonstrated that firm and skillful editorial commandeering can be accomplished with tact. Our greatest debt, as it has been from the start, is to Robert E. Kehoe—omnicompetent, omnipresent (New York, Indiana, Illinois, Texas, apparently all at the same time), and, if not omniscient, pretty close to it.

Robert E. Lerner
Standish Meacham

Chapter 15

A CENTURY OF CRISIS FOR EARLY-MODERN EUROPE

(c. 1560—c. 1660)

I do not wish to say much about the customs of the age in which we live. I can only state that this age is not one of the best, being a century of iron.

—R. Mentet de Salmonet, *History of the Troubles in Great Britain* (1649)

What in me is dark
Illumine, what is low raise and support.

—John Milton, *Paradise Lost*

O n the night before St. Bartholomew's Day in August of 1572 the Catholic queen mother of France, Catherine de Medici, authorized the ambush of French Protestant leaders who had come to Paris to attend a wedding. Thereupon, during the hours after midnight, unsuspecting people found themselves awakened to be stabbed in bed or thrown out of windows. Soon all the targeted Protestants were eliminated, but the killing did not stop because roving bands of Parisian Catholics seized the opportunity of licensed carnage to slaughter at will any enemies they happened upon, Protestant or otherwise. By morning the River Seine was clogged with corpses and scores of bodies hung from gibbets in witness to an event known ever since as the Massacre of St. Bartholomew's Day.

A massacre in Paris

Had this lamentable incident been an isolated event it hardly would be worth mentioning, but in fact throughout the hundred years from roughly 1560 to roughly 1660 outbreaks of religious mayhem—with Protestants the ruthless killers in certain cases as Catholics were in others—recurred in many parts of Europe. Moreover, to make matters far worse, economic hardships and prolonged wars accompanied religious riots to result in a century of pronounced crisis for European civilization.

A century of crisis

The St. Bartholomew's Day Massacre. A contemporary painting depicts the merciless slaughter of Huguenots in Paris. At the top left (in front of the large gate next to the Seine) the Queen Mother Catherine looks over a pile of naked dead bodies; to the right a Huguenot leader is being pushed out of a window.

Lack of uniformity in causes and effects

In many respects Europe's early-modern period of crisis resembled the terrible times of the late Middle Ages, but the early-modern crisis was much less uniform in its nature and extent. From the economic point of view, there were two different major difficulties—first a dramatic price inflation lasting from about 1560 to 1600 that hurt the poor far worse than it did the rich, and then a period of overall economic stagnation which was marked, however, by significant exceptions from place to place. Similarly, although the main theme of political history during the entire era was intense warfare, the causes of war differed greatly according to place and time, with some areas occasionally even managing to bask in intervals of peace. Nonetheless, seen from the broadest perspective the period from 1560 to 1660 was western Europe's "iron century"—an age of enormous turbulence and severe trials.

1. ECONOMIC, RELIGIOUS, AND POLITICAL TESTS

Impending crisis

Europe's time of troubles crept up on contemporaries unawares. For almost a century before 1560 most of the West had enjoyed steady economic growth, and the discovery of the New World seemed to harbinger even greater prosperity to come. Political trends too seemed auspicious, since most western European governments were becoming ever more efficient and providing more internal peace for their subjects. Yet around 1560 thunderclouds were gathering in the skies that would soon burst into terrible storms.

Although the causes of these storms were interrelated, each may be examined separately, starting with the great price inflation. Nothing like the upward price trend which affected western Europe in the second half of the sixteenth century had ever happened before. The cost of a measure of wheat in Flanders, for example, tripled from 1550 to 1600, grain prices in Paris quadrupled, and the overall cost of living in England advanced well over 100 percent during the same period. Certainly the twentieth century has seen even more dizzying inflations than this, but since the skyrocketing of prices in the later sixteenth century was a novelty, most historians agree on calling it the "price revolution."

Soaring prices

If experts agree on the terminology, however, very few of them agree on the exact combination of circumstances that caused the price revolution, for early-modern statistics are patchy and many areas of economic theory remain under dispute. Nonetheless, for present purposes two widely accepted dominant explanations for the great inflation may be offered with confidence. The first is demographic. Starting in the later fifteenth century, Europe's population began to mount again after the plague-induced falloff: roughly estimated, there were about 50 million people in Europe around 1450 and 90 million around 1600. Since Europe's food supply remained more or less constant owing to the lack of any noteworthy breakthrough in agricultural technology, food prices inevitably were driven sharply higher by greater demand. In contrast, the prices of manufactured goods did not rise as steeply because there was a greater match between supply and demand. Yet prices of manufactured items did rise nonetheless, especially in cases where the supply of agricultural raw materials crucial to the manufacturing process remained relatively inelastic.

*Causes of inflation: (1)
population increase*

Population trends therefore explain much, but since Europe's population did not grow nearly as rapidly in the second half of the sixteenth century as prices, complementary explanations for the great inflation are still necessary, and foremost among these is the enormous influx of bullion from Spanish America. Around 1560 a new technique of extracting silver from silver ore made the working of newly discovered mines in Mexico and Bolivia highly practical, soon transforming the previous trickle of silver entering the European economy into a flood. Whereas in the five years between 1556 and 1560 roughly 10 million ducats worth of silver passed through the Spanish entry point of Seville, between 1576 and 1580 that figure had doubled, and between 1591 and 1595 it had more than quadrupled. Inasmuch as most of this silver was used by the Spanish crown to pay its foreign creditors and its armies abroad or by private individuals to pay for

(2) influx of silver

imports from other countries, Spanish bullion quickly circulated throughout Europe, where much of it was minted into coins. This dramatic increase in the volume of money in circulation further fueled the spiral of rising prices. "I learned a proverb here," said a French traveler in Spain in 1603, "everything costs much here except silver."

Aggressive entrepreneurs and landlords profited most from the changed economic circumstances, while the masses of laboring people were hurt the worst. Obviously, merchants in possession of sought-after goods were able to raise prices at will, and landlords either could profit directly from the rising prices of agricultural produce or, if they did not farm their own lands, could always raise rents. But laborers in country and town were caught in a squeeze because wages rose far more slowly than prices, owing to the presence of a more than adequate labor supply. Moreover, because the cost of food staples rose at a sharper rate proportionately than the cost of most other items of consumption, poor people had to spend an ever-greater percentage of their paltry income on necessities. In normal years they barely managed to survive, but when disasters such as wars or poor harvests drove grain prices out of reach, some of the poor literally starved to death. The picture that thus emerges is one of the rich getting richer and the poor getting poorer—splendid feasts enjoyed amid the most appalling suffering.

Political results

In addition to these direct economic effects, the price inflation of the later sixteenth century had significant political effects as well because higher prices placed new pressures on the sovereign states of Europe. The reasons for this were simple. Since the inflation depressed the real value of money, fixed incomes from taxes and dues in effect yielded less and less. Thus merely to keep their incomes constant governments would have been forced to raise taxes. But to compound this problem, most states needed much more real income than previously because they were undertaking more wars, and warfare, as always, was becoming increasingly expensive. The only recourse, then, was to raise taxes precipitously, but such draconian measures incurred great resentments on the part of subject populations—especially the very poor who were already strapped more than enough by the effects of the inflation. Hence governments faced continuous threats of defiance and potential armed resistance.

*Economic stagnation after
1600*

Less need be said about the economic stagnation that followed the price revolution because it interfered little with most of the trends just discussed. When population growth began to ease and the flood of silver from America began to abate around 1600, prices soon leveled off. Yet because the most lucrative economic exploitation of the New World only began in the late seventeenth century and Europe experienced little new industrial development, the period from about 1600 to 1660 was at best one of very limited overall economic growth, even though a few areas—notably Holland—bucked the trend. Within this context the rich were usually able to hold their own, but the poor as a group made no advances since the relationship of prices to wages remained fixed to their disadvantage. Indeed, if anything, the lot of the poor in many places deteriorated because the mid–seventeenth century saw some particularly expensive and destructive wars, causing helpless civilians to be plundered either by rapacious tax collectors, looting soldiers, or sometimes by both.

It goes without saying that most people would have been far better off had there been fewer wars during Europe's iron century, but given prevalent attitudes, newly arisen religious rivalries made wars inevitable. Simply stated, until religious passions began to cool toward the end of the period, most Catholics and Protestants viewed each other as minions of Satan who could not be allowed to live. Worse, sovereign states attempted to enforce religious uniformity on the grounds that "crown and altar" offered each other mutual support and in the belief that governments would totter where diversity of faith prevailed. Rulers on both sides felt certain that religious minorities, if allowed to survive in their realms, would inevitably engage in sedition; nor were they far wrong since militant Calvinists and Jesuits were indeed dedicated to subverting constituted powers in areas where they had not yet triumphed. Thus states tried to extirpate all potential religious resistance, but in the process sometimes provoked civil wars in which both sides tended to assume there could be no victory until the other was exterminated. And of course civil wars might become international in scope when one or more foreign powers resolved to aid embattled religious allies elsewhere.

Religious wars

Compounding the foregoing problems were more strictly political ones: namely, while strapped by price trends and racked by religious wars, governments brought certain provincial and constitutional grievances down upon themselves. Regarding the provincial issue, most of the major states of early-modern Europe had been built up by conquests or dynastic marital accretions, with the result that many smaller territories had been subjected to absentee rule. At first some degree of provincial autonomy was usually preserved and hence the inhabitants of such territories did not object too much to their annexation. But in the iron century, when governments were making ever-greater financial claims on all their subjects or trying to enforce religious uniformity, rulers customarily moved to destroy all semblances of provincial autonomy in order to implement their financial or religious policies. Naturally the province-dwellers were usually not inclined to accept total subjugation without a fight, so rebellions might break out on combined patriotic and economic or religious grounds. Nor was that all, since most governments seeking money and/or religious uniformity tried to rule their subjects with a firmer hand than before, and thus sometimes provoked armed resistance in the name of traditional constitutional liberties. Given this bewildering variety of

Governmental crises

motives for revolt, it is by no means surprising that the century between 1560 and 1660 was one of the most turbulent in all European history.

2. A HALF CENTURY OF RELIGIOUS WARS

*Religious wars in
Germany until the Peace
of Augsburg*

Despite the multiplicity of overlapping causes for instability, the greatest single cause of warfare in the first half of Europe's iron century was religious rivalry. Indeed, wars between Catholics and Protestants began as early as the 1540s when the Catholic Holy Roman Emperor Charles V tried to reestablish Catholic unity in Germany by launching a military campaign against several German princes who had instituted Lutheran worship in their principalities. At times thereafter it appeared as if Charles was going to succeed in reducing his German Protestant opponents to complete submission, but since he was also involved in fighting against France, he seldom was able to devote concerted attention to affairs in Germany. Accordingly, religious warfare sputtered on and off until a compromise settlement was reached in the Religious Peace of Augsburg (1555). This rested on the principle of *"cuius regio, eius religio"* ("as the ruler, so the religion"), which meant that in those principalities where Lutheran princes ruled, Lutheranism would be the sole state religion, and the same for those with Catholic princes. Although the Peace of Augsburg was a historical milestone inasmuch as Catholic rulers for the first time acknowledged the legality of Protestantism, it boded ill for the future in assuming that no sovereign state larger than a free city (for which it made exceptions) could tolerate religious diversity. Moreover, in excluding Calvinism it ensured that Calvinists would become aggressive opponents of the *status quo*.

Even though wars in the name of religion were fought in Europe before 1560, those that raged afterward were far more brutal, partly because the combatants had become more fanatical (intransigent Calvinists and Jesuits customarily took the lead on their respective sides), and partly because the later religious wars were aggravated by political and economic resentments. Since Geneva bordered on France, since Calvin himself was a Frenchman who longed to convert his mother country, and since Calvinists had no wish to displace German Lutherans, the next act in the tragedy of Europe's confessional warfare was played out on French soil. Calvinist missionaries had already made much headway in France in the years between Calvin's rise to power in Geneva in 1541 and the outbreak of religious warfare in 1562. Of the greatest aid to the Calvinist (Huguenot) cause was the conversion to Calvinism of many aristocratic French women because such women often won over their husbands, who in turn maintained large private armies. The foremost example is that of Jeanne d'Albret, queen of the tiny Pyrenean kingdom of Navarre, who brought over to Calvinism

Jeanne D'Albret

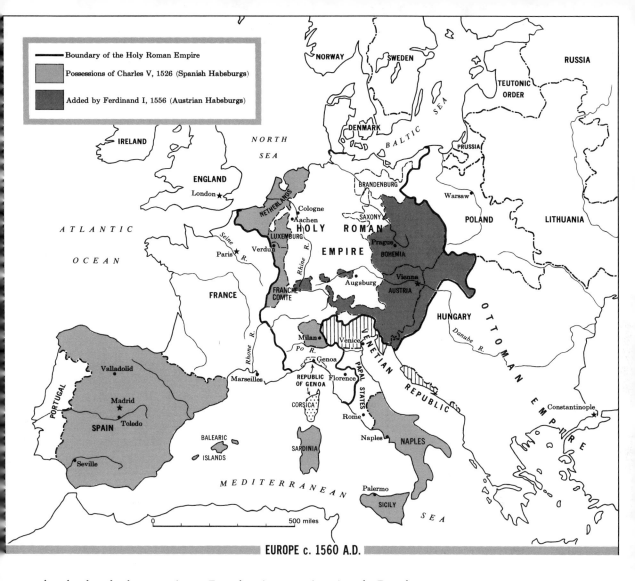

Legend:
— Boundary of the Holy Roman Empire
▨ Possessions of Charles V, 1526 (Spanish Habsburgs)
▨ Added by Ferdinand I, 1556 (Austrian Habsburgs)

EUROPE c. 1560 A.D.

her husband, the prominent French aristocrat Antoine de Bourbon, and her brother-in-law, the prince de Condé. Not only did Condé take command of the French Huguenot party when civil war broke out in 1562, but he later was succeeded in this capacity by Jeanne's son, Henry of Navarre, who came to rule all of France at the end of the century as King Henry IV. In addition to aristocrats, many people from all walks of life became Huguenots for a variety of motives, with Huguenot strength greatest in areas of the south which had long resented the dominance of northern rule from Paris. In short, by 1562 Calvinists comprised between 10 and 20 percent of France's population of roughly 16 million, and their numbers were swelling every day.

Since both Catholics and Protestants assumed that France could have

Background of the French wars of religion

only a single *roi, foi,* and *loi* (king, faith, and law), civil war was inevitable, and no one was surprised when a struggle between the Huguenot Condé and the ultra-Catholic duke of Guise for control of the government during a royal minority led in 1562 to a show of arms. Soon all France was aflame. Churches were ransacked and local scores were settled by rampaging mobs who often were incited on both sides by members of their clergy. After a while it became clear that the Huguenots were not strong or numerous enough to gain victory, but they were also too strong to be defeated. Hence, despite intermittent truces, warfare dragged on at great cost of life until 1572. Then, during an interval of peace, the cultivated queen mother Catherine de Medici, normally a woman who favored compromise, plotted with members of the Catholic Guise faction to kill all the Huguenot leaders while they were assembled in Paris for the wedding of Henry of Navarre. In the early morning of St. Bartholomew's Day (August 24) most of the Huguenot chiefs were murdered in bed and two to three thousand other Protestants were slaughtered in the streets or drowned in the Seine by Catholic mobs. When word of the Parisian massacre spread to the provinces, some ten thousand more Huguenots were killed in a frenzy of blood lust that swept through France.

The St. Bartholomew's Day episode effectively broke the back of Huguenot resistance, but even then warfare did not cease because the neurotic King Henry III (1574–1589) tried to play off Huguenots against the dominant Catholic Guise family and because die-hard Huguenots sometimes were able to ally with Catholics revolting against overburdensome taxes or inequities in tax assessments. Only when the politically astute Henry of Navarre succeeded to the French throne as Henry IV[1](1589–1610), initiating the Bourbon dynasty that would rule until 1792, did civil war finally come to an end. In 1593 Henry abjured his Protestantism in order to placate France's Catholic majority ("Paris is worth a mass") and then, in 1598, offered limited religious freedom to the Huguenots by the Edict of Nantes. According to the terms of this proclamation, Catholicism was recognized as the official religion, but Huguenot nobles were allowed to hold Protestant services privately in their castles, other Huguenots were allowed to worship at specified places (excluding Paris and all cities where bishops and archbishops resided), and the Huguenot party was permitted to fortify some towns, especially in the south, for military defense if the need arose. Thus, although the Edict of Nantes certainly did not countenance absolute freedom of worship, it nevertheless represented a major stride in the direction of toleration. With religious peace established, France quickly began to recover from decades of devastation, but Henry IV himself was cut down by the dagger of a Catholic fanatic in 1610.

[1]Here, as elsewhere, dates following a ruler's name refer to dates of reign.

The Assassination of Henry IV. This contemporary engraving shows Henry seated in an open carriage without any concern for his personal danger while his assassin climbs on the spoke of the carriage wheel to attack him. The entire composition conveys a vivid impression of early-modern Paris.

Contemporaneous with the religious warfare in France was equally bitter religious strife between Catholics and Protestants in the neighboring Netherlands, where national resentments gravely compounded religious hatreds. For almost a century the Netherlands (or Low Countries), comprising modern-day Holland in the north and Belgium in the south, had been ruled by the Habsburg family. Particularly the southern part of the Netherlands prospered greatly from trade and manufacture: southern Netherlanders had the greatest per capita wealth of all Europe and their metropolis of Antwerp was northern Europe's leading commercial and financial center. Moreover, the half-century-long rule of the Habsburg Charles V (1506–1556) had been popular because Charles, who had been born in the Belgian city of Ghent, felt a sense of rapport with his subjects and allowed them a large degree of local self-government.

Habsburg rule in the Netherlands

But around 1560 the good fortune of the Netherlands began to ebb. When Charles V retired to a monastery in 1556 (dying two years later) he ceded all his vast territories outside of the Holy Roman Empire and Hungary—not only the Netherlands, but Spain, Spanish America, and close to half of Italy—to his son Philip II (1556–1598). Unlike Charles, Philip had been born in Spain, and thinking of himself as a Spaniard, made Spain his residence and the focus of his policy. Thus he viewed the Netherlands primarily as a potentially rich source of income necessary for pursuing Spanish affairs. (Around 1560 silver was only beginning to flood through Seville.) But in order to tap the wealth of the Netherlands Philip had to rule it more directly than his father had, and such attempts were naturally resented by the local magnates who until then had dominated the government. To make matters worse, a religious storm also was brewing, for after a treaty of 1559 ended a

Philip II and the impending crisis

The Emperor Charles V. This portrait by the Venetian painter Titian depicts the emperor in a grandiloquent equestrian pose. (Another depiction of Charles V by Titian appears in the section of color plates following p. 449.)

Philip II of Spain. Titian's portrait shows Philip's resemblance to his father, Charles V, particularly in the protruding lower jaw of the Habsburgs.

long war between France and Spain, French Calvinists had begun to stream over the Netherlandish border, making converts wherever they went. Soon there were more Calvinists in Antwerp than in Geneva, a situation that Philip II could not tolerate because he was an ardent Catholic who subscribed wholeheartedly to the goals of the Counter-Reformation. Indeed, as he wrote to Rome on the eve of conflict: "rather than suffer the slightest harm to the true religion and service of God, I would lose all my states and even my life a hundred times over because I am not and will not be the ruler of heretics."

Evidence of the complexity of the Netherlandish situation is found in the facts that the leader of resistance to Philip, William the Silent, was at first not a Calvinist and that the territories which ultimately succeeded in breaking away from Spanish rule were at first the most Catholic ones in the Low Countries. William "the Silent," a prominent nobleman with large landholdings in the Netherlands, was in fact very talkative, receiving his nickname rather from his ability to hide his true religious and political feelings when the need arose. In 1566, when still a nominal Catholic, he and other local nobles not formally committed to Protestantism appealed to Philip to allow toleration for Calvinists. But while Philip momentarily temporized, radical Protestant mobs proved to be their own worst enemy—ransacking Catholic churches throughout the country, methodically desecrating hosts, smashing statuary, and shattering stained-glass windows. Though local troops soon had the situation under control, Philip II nonetheless decided to dispatch an army of ten thousand commanded by the steely

Spanish duke of Alva to wipe out Protestantism in the Low Countries forever. Alva's tribunal, the "Council of Blood," soon examined some twelve thousand persons on charges of heresy or sedition, of whom nine thousand were convicted and one thousand executed. William the Silent fled the country, and all hope for a free Netherlands seemed lost.

But the tide turned quickly for two related reasons. First, instead of giving up, William the Silent converted to Protestantism, sought help from Protestants in France, Germany, and England, and organized bands of sea rovers to harass Spanish shipping on the Netherlands coast. And second, Alva's tyranny helped William's cause, especially when the hated Spanish governor attempted to levy a repressive 10 percent sales tax. With internal disaffection growing, in 1572 William, for tactical military reasons, was able to seize the northern Netherlands even though the north until then had been predominantly Catholic. Thereafter geography played a major role in determining the outcome of the conflict. Spanish armies repeatedly attempted to win back the north, but they were stopped by a combination of impassable rivers and dikes which could be opened to flood out the invaders. Although William the Silent was assassinated by a Catholic in 1584, his son continued to lead the resistance until the Spanish crown finally agreed by a truce in 1609 to stop fighting and thus implicitly recognized the independence of the northern Dutch Republic. Meanwhile, the pressures of war and persecution had made the whole north Calvinistic, whereas the south—which remained Spanish—returned to uniform Catholicism.

The Duke of Alva. The gaunt Spanish general who attempted in vain to extirpate Calvinism in the Netherlands.

Predictably, religious strife which could take the form of civil war, as in France, or war for national liberation, as in the Netherlands, could also take the form of warfare between sovereign states, as in the

Protestants Ransacking a Catholic Church in the Netherlands. The "Protestant fury" of 1566 was responsible for the large-scale destruction of religious art and statuary in the Low Countries, provoking the stern repression of Philip II.

case of the late-sixteenth-century struggle between England and Spain. After narrowly escaping domination by the Catholic Queen Mary and her Spanish husband Philip II, English Protestants rejoiced in the rule of Queen Elizabeth I (1558–1603) and naturally harbored great antipathy for Philip II and the Counter-Reformation. Furthermore, English economic interests were directly opposed to those of the Spanish. A seafaring and trading people, the English in the later sixteenth century were steadily making inroads into Spanish naval and commercial domination, and were also determined to resist any Spanish attempt to block England's lucrative trade with the Low Countries. But the greatest source of antagonism lay in naval contests in the Atlantic, where English privateers, with the tacit consent of Queen Elizabeth, could not resist raiding silver-laden Spanish treasure ships. Beginning around 1570, and taking as an excuse Spanish oppression of Protestants in the Netherlands, English admirals or pirates (the terms were really interchangeable) such as Sir Francis Drake and Sir John Hawkins began plundering Spanish vessels on the high seas. In a particularly dramatic sailing exploit lasting from 1577 to 1580, lust for booty and prevailing winds propelled Drake all the way around the world, to return with stolen Spanish treasure worth twice as much as Queen Elizabeth's annual revenue.

All this would have been sufficient provocation for Philip II to have

Left: *The Defeat of the Spanish Armada.* Right: *Queen Elizabeth I.* The contemporary English oil painting of the great sea battle gives only a schematic idea of its turbulence. Note, however, the prominence of the papal insignia (tiara over crossed keys of St. Peter) on the ship in the middle foreground. Englishmen were convinced that had they not defeated the Spanish Armada in 1588 the pope would have planted his banner on their shores. At the right is a typically overblown portrait of Queen Elizabeth, known to her admiring subjects as "Gloriana," standing on a map of England.

retaliated against England, but because he had his hands full in the Netherlands he resolved to invade the island only after the English openly allied with the Dutch rebels in 1585. And even then Philip did not act without extensive planning and a sense of assurance that nothing could go wrong. Finally, in 1588 he dispatched an enormous fleet, confidently called the "Invincible Armada," to punish insolent Britannia. After an initial standoff in the English Channel, however, English fireships outmaneuvered the Spanish fleet, setting some Spanish galleons ablaze and forcing the rest to break formation. "Protestant gales" did the rest and a battered flotilla soon limped home with almost half its ships lost.

The defeat of the Spanish Armada

The defeat of the Spanish Armada was one of the most decisive battles of Western history. Had Spain conquered England it is quite likely that the Spanish would have gone on to crush Holland and perhaps even to destroy Protestantism everywhere. But, as it was, the Protestant day was saved, and not long afterward Spanish power began to decline, with English and Dutch ships taking ever-greater command of the seas. Moreover, in England itself patriotic fervor became intense. Popular even before then, "Good Queen Bess" was virtually revered by her subjects until her death in 1603, and England embarked on its golden "Elizabethan Age" of literary endeavor. War with Spain dragged on inconclusively until 1604, but the fighting never brought England any serious harm and was just lively enough to keep the English people deeply committed to the cause of their queen, their country, and the Protestant religion.

The salvation of Protestantism

3. YEARS OF TREMBLING

With the promulgation of the Edict of Nantes in 1598, the peace between England and Spain of 1604, and the truce between Spain and Holland of 1609, religious warfare tapered off and came to an end in the early seventeenth century. But in 1618 a major new war broke out, this time in Germany. Since this struggle raged more or less unceasingly until 1648 it bears the name of the Thirty Years' War. Meanwhile, far from returning to enduring peace, Spain and France became engaged in the Thirty Years' War and war with each other, and internal resentments in Spain, France, and England flared up in the decade of the 1640s in concurrent outbreaks of uprisings and civil turmoil. As an English preacher said in 1643, "these are days of shaking, and this shaking is universal." He might have added that while in some instances religion remained one of the contested issues, secular disputes about powers of government were now becoming predominant.

A new phase of turmoil

The clearest example is that of the Thirty Years' War, which began in a welter of religious passions as a war between Catholics and Prot-

Two Artistic Broadsides from the Thirty Years' War. On the left the German peasantry is ridden by the soldiery; on the right is an allegorical representation of "the monstrous beast of war."

The Thirty Years' War

See color map facing
page 545

*The involvement of
Sweden and France*

estants but immediately raised basic German constitutional issues and ended as an international struggle in which the initial religious dimension was almost entirely forgotten. Between the Peace of Augsburg in 1555 and the outbreak of war in 1618, Calvinists had replaced Lutherans in a few German territories, but the overall balance between Protestants and Catholics within the Holy Roman Empire had remained undisturbed. In 1618, however, when a Protestant uprising against Habsburg Catholic rule in Bohemia (not a German territory, but nonetheless part of the Holy Roman Empire) threatened to upset the balance, German Catholic forces ruthlessly counterattacked, first in Bohemia and then in Germany proper. Led by Charles V's Habsburg descendant Ferdinand II, who was archduke of Austria, king of Hungary, and from 1619 to his death in 1637, Holy Roman Emperor, a German Catholic league seized the military initiative and within a decade seemed close to extirpating Protestantism throughout Germany. But Ferdinand, who was intent on pursuing political goals as well, imposed firm direct rule in Bohemia in order to build up the strength of his own Austro-Hungarian state, and attempted to revive the faded authority of the Holy Roman Empire in whatever ways he could.

Thus when the Lutheran king of Sweden, Gustavus Adolphus, marched into Germany in 1630 to champion the nearly lost cause of Protestantism, he was welcomed by several German Catholic princes who preferred to see the former religious balance restored rather than stand the chance of surrendering their sovereignty to Ferdinand II. To make matters still more ironic, Gustavus's Protestant army was secretly subsidized by Catholic France, then governed by a cardinal of the

Church, because Habsburg Spain had been fighting in Germany on the side of Habsburg Austria and France's Cardinal Richelieu was determined to resist any possibility of being surrounded by a strong Habsburg alliance on the north, east, and south. In the event, the military genius Gustavus Adolphus started routing the Habsburgs, but when the Swedish king fell in battle in 1632, Cardinal Richelieu had little choice but to send ever-greater support to the remaining Swedish troops in Germany, until in 1639 French armies entered the war directly on Sweden's side. From then until 1648 the struggle was really one of France and Sweden against Austria and Spain, with most of Germany a helpless battleground.

The result was that Germany suffered more from warfare in the terrible years between 1618 and 1648 than it ever did before or after until the twentieth century. Several German cities were besieged and sacked nine or ten times over, and soldiers from all nations, who often had to sustain themselves by plunder, gave no quarter to defenseless civilians. With plague and disease adding to the toll of outright butchery, some parts of Germany lost more than half their populations, although it is true that others went relatively unscathed. Most horrifying was the loss of life in the last four years, when the carnage continued unabated even while peace negotiators had already arrived at broad areas of agreement and were dickering over subsidiary clauses.

The toll of warfare in Germany

Nor did the Peace of Westphalia, which finally ended the Thirty Years' War in 1648, do much to vindicate anyone's death, even though it did establish some abiding landmarks in European history. Above all, from the international perspective the Peace of Westphalia marked the reemergence of France as the predominant power on the continental European scene, replacing Spain—a position France was to hold

The Peace of Westphalia

A Swearing of Oaths at the Peace of Westphalia, 1648

for two centuries more. In particular, France moved its eastern frontier directly into German territory by taking over large parts of Alsace. As for strictly internal German matters, the greatest losers were the Austrian Habsburgs, who were forced to surrender all the territory they had gained in Germany and to abandon their hopes of using the office of Holy Roman Emperor to dominate central Europe. Otherwise, something very close to the German *status quo* of 1618 was reestablished, with Protestant principalities in the north balancing Catholic ones in the south, and Germany so hopelessly divided that it could play no united role in European history until the nineteenth century.

The decline of Spain

Still greater losers from the Thirty Years' War than the Austrian Habsburgs were their Spanish cousins, for Spain had invested vast sums in the struggle it could not afford and ceased being a great power forever after. The story of Spain's swift fall from grandeur is almost like a Greek tragedy in its relentless unfolding. Even after the defeat of the "Invincible Armada," around 1600 the Spanish empire—comprising all of the Iberian peninsula (including Portugal, which had been annexed by Philip II in 1580), half of Italy, half of the Netherlands, all of Central and South America, and even the Philippine Islands—was the mightiest power not just in Europe but in the world. Yet a bare half century later this empire on which the sun never set had come close to falling apart.

*Economic causes of
Spain's decline*

Spain's greatest underlying weakness was economic. At first this may seem like a very odd statement considering that in 1600, as in the three or four previous decades, huge amounts of American silver were being unloaded on the docks of Seville. Yet as contemporaries themselves recognized, "the new world that Spain had conquered was conquering Spain in turn." Lacking either rich agricultural or mineral resources, Spain desperately needed to develop industries and a balanced trading pattern as its rivals England and France were doing. But since the dominant Spanish nobility had prized ideals of chivalry over practical business ever since the medieval days when it was engaged in winning back Spanish territory from the Muslims, the Spanish governing class was only too glad to use American silver to buy manufactured goods from other parts of Europe in order to live in splendor and dedicate itself to military exploits. Thus bullion left the country as soon as it entered, virtually no industry was established, and when the influx of silver began to decline after 1600 the Spanish economy remained with nothing except increasing debts.

*Spain's continued
aggressiveness*

Nonetheless, the crown, dedicated to supporting the Counter-Reformation and maintaining Spain's international dominance, would not cease fighting abroad. Indeed, the entire Spanish budget remained on such a warlike footing that even in the relatively peaceful year of 1608 four million out of a total revenue of seven million ducats were paid for military expenditures. Thus when Spain became engaged in fighting France during the Thirty Years' War it fully overextended itself. The clearest visible sign of this was that in 1643 outnumbered French troops at Rocroi inflicted a stunning defeat on the famed Spanish infantry, the first time that a Spanish army had been overcome in battle since the reign of Ferdinand and Isabella. Yet worse still was the fact that by then two territories belonging to Spain's European empire were in open revolt.

In order to understand the causes of these revolts one must recognize that in the seventeenth century the real "nation of Spain" was Castile—all else was acquired territory. After the marriage of Isabella of Castile and Ferdinand of Aragon in 1469, geographically central Castile emerged as the dominant partner in the Spanish union, becoming even more dominant when Castile conquered the Muslim kingdom of Granada in southern Spain in 1492 and annexed Portugal in 1580. In the absence of any great financial hardships, semi-autonomous Catalonia (the most fiercely independent part of Aragon) endured Castilian hegemony. But in 1640, when the strains of warfare induced Castile to limit Catalonian liberties in order to raise more money and men for combat, Catalonia revolted. Immediately afterward the Portuguese learned of the Catalonian uprising and revolted as well, followed by southern Italians who revolted against Castilian viceroys in Naples and Sicily in 1647. At that point only the momentary inability of Spain's greatest external enemies, France and England, to take advantage of its plight saved the Spanish empire from utter collapse. Nothing if not determined, the Castilian government quickly put down the Italian revolts and by 1652 also brought Catalonia to heel. But Portugal retained its independence forever, and by the Peace of the Pyrenees, signed with France in 1659, Spain in effect conceded that it would entirely abandon its ambitions of dominating Europe.

Internal revolts against the Castilian government

A comparison between the fortunes of Spain and France in the first half of the seventeenth century is highly instructive because some

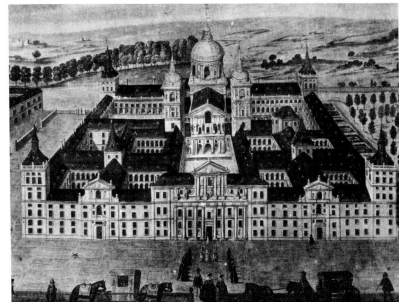

The Escorial. Philip II of Spain ordered the building between 1563 and 1584 of this somber retreat—part royal residence, part monastery—on an isolated spot, well removed from Madrid. Conceived on a gridiron plan to honor the grid-iron martyrdom of St. Lawrence (on whose feast day Philip had won a decisive victory against the French), the Escorial symbolizes for many the Spanish crown's dedication to the ideals of the Counter-Reformation as well as its attempt to impose rationalized central government on the refractory outlying provinces of the Spanish Empire.

striking similarities existed between the two countries, but in the end differences turned out to be most decisive. Spain and France were of almost identical territorial extent, and both countries had been created by the same process of accretion. Just as the Castilian crown had gained Aragon in the north, Granada in the south, and then Portugal, so the kingdom of France had grown by adding on such diverse territories as Languedoc, Dauphiné, Provence, Burgundy, and Brittany. Since the inhabitants of all these territories cherished traditions of local independence as much as the Catalans or Portuguese, and since the rulers of France, like those of Spain, were determined to govern their provinces ever more firmly—especially when the financial stringencies of the Thirty Years' War made ruthless tax-collecting urgently necessary—a direct confrontation between the central government and the provinces in France became inevitable, just as in Spain. But France weathered the storm whereas Spain did not, a result largely attributable to France's greater wealth and the greater prestige of the French crown.

In good times most French people, including those from the outlying provinces, tended to revere their king. Certainly they had excellent reason to do so during the reign of Henry IV. Having established religious peace in 1598 by the Edict of Nantes, the affable Henry, who declared that there should be a chicken in every French family's pot each Sunday, set about to restore the prosperity of a country devastated by four decades of civil war. Fortunately France had enormous economic resiliency, owing primarily to its extremely rich and varied agricultural resources. Unlike Spain, which had to import food, France normally had been able to export it, and Henry's finance minister, the duke of Sully, quickly saw to it that France became a food exporter once more. Among other things, Sully distributed throughout the country free copies of a guide to recommended farming techniques and financed the rebuilding or new construction of roads, bridges, and canals to help expedite the flow of goods. In addition, Henry IV was not content to see France rest its economic development on agricultural wealth alone; instead he ordered the construction of royal factories to manufacture luxury goods such as crystal glass and tapestries, and he also supported the growth of silk, linen, and woolen cloth industries in many different parts of the country. Moreover, Henry's patronage allowed the explorer Champlain to claim parts of Canada as France's first foothold in the New World. Thus Henry IV's reign certainly must be counted as one of the most benevolent and progressive in all French history.

Far less benevolent was Henry's *de facto* successor as ruler of France, Cardinal Richelieu (1585–1642), yet Richelieu fully managed to maintain France's forward momentum. The cardinal, of course, was never the real king of France—the actual title was held from 1610 to 1643 by Henry IV's ineffectual son Louis XIII. But as first minister from 1624 to his death in 1642 Richelieu governed as he wished, and what he

Cardinal Richelieu. A contemporary portrait emphasizing the cardinal's awesome bearing.

wished most of all was to enhance centralized royal power at home and expand French influence in the larger theater of Europe. Accordingly, when Huguenots rebelled against restrictions placed on them by the Edict of Nantes, Richelieu put them down with an iron fist and emended the Edict in 1629 by depriving them of all their military rights. Since his armed campaigns against the Huguenots had been very costly, the cardinal then moved to gain more income for the crown by abolishing the semi-autonomy of Burgundy, Dauphiné, and Provence so that he could introduce direct royal taxation in all three areas. Later, to make sure all taxes levied were efficiently collected, Richelieu instituted a new system of local government by royal officials known as *intendants* who were expressly commissioned to run roughshod over any provincial obstructionism. By these and related methods Richelieu made French government more centralized than ever and managed to double the crown's income during his rule. But since he also engaged in an ambitious foreign policy directed against the Habsburgs of Austria and Spain, resulting in France's costly involvement in the Thirty Years' War, internal pressures mounted in the years after Richelieu's death.

A reaction against French governmental centralization manifested itself in a series of revolts between 1648 and 1653 collectively known as "the slingshot tumults," or in French, the *Fronde*. By this time Louis XIII had been succeeded by his son Louis XIV, but because the latter was still a boy, France was governed by a regency consisting of Louis's mother Anne of Austria and her paramour Cardinal Mazarin. Considering that both were foreigners (Anne was a Habsburg and Mazarin originally an Italian adventurer named Giulio Mazarini), it is not surprising that many of their subjects, including some extremely powerful nobles, hated them. Moreover, nationwide resentments were greater still because the costs of war and several consecutive years of bad harvests had brought France temporarily into a grave economic plight. Thus when cliques of nobles expressed their disgust with Mazarin for primarily petty and self-interested reasons, they found much support throughout the country, and uncoordinated revolts against the regency flared on and off for several years.

France, however, was not Spain, and thus did not come close to falling apart. Above all, the French crown itself, which retained great reservoirs of prestige owing to a well-established national tradition and the undoubted achievements of Henry IV and Richelieu, was by no means under attack. On the contrary, neither the aristocratic leaders of the *Fronde* nor the commoners from all ranks who joined them in revolt claimed to be resisting the young king but only the alleged corruption and mismanagement of Mazarin. Some of the rebels, it is true, insisted that part of Mazarin's fault lay in his pursuance of Richelieu's centralizing, antiprovincial policy. But since most of the aristocrats who led the *Fronde* were merely "outs" who wanted to be "in," they often squabbled among themselves—sometimes even arranging

The case of England

*Henry VIII and
Elizabeth I increase royal
power*

agreements of convenience with the regency or striking alliances with France's enemy, Spain, for momentary gain—and proved completely unable to rally any unified support behind a common program. Thus when Louis XIV began to rule in his own name in 1651 and pretexts for revolting against "corrupt ministers" no longer existed, all opposition was soon silenced. As so often happens, the idealists and poor people paid the greatest price for revolt: in 1653 a defeated leader of popular resistance in Bordeaux was broken on a wheel, and not long afterward a massive new round of taxation was proclaimed. Remembering the turbulence of the *Fronde* for the rest of his life, Louis XIV resolved never to let his aristocracy or his provinces get out of hand again and ruled as the most effective royal absolutist in all of French history.

Compared to the civil disturbances of the 1640s in Spain and France, those in England proved the most momentous in their results for the history of limited government. Whereas all that the revolts against Castile accomplished was the achievement of Portuguese independence and the crippling of an empire that was already in decline, and all that happened in France was a momentary interruption of the steady advance of royal power, in England a king was executed and barriers were erected against royal absolutism for all time.

England around 1600 was caught up in a trend toward the growth of centralized royal authority characteristic of all western Europe. Not only had Henry VIII and Elizabeth I brought the English Church fully under royal control, but both monarchs employed so-called prerogative courts wherein they could proceed against subjects in disregard of traditional English legal safeguards for the rights of the accused. Furthermore, although Parliament met regularly during both reigns, members of Parliament were far less independent than they had been in the fifteenth century: any parliamentary representative who might have stood up to Henry VIII would have lost his head, and almost all parliamentarians felt sufficiently in rapport with Elizabeth that they were willing to abide by her policies. Thus when the Stuart dynasty succeeded Elizabeth, the last of the Tudors, it was only natural that the Stuarts would try to increase royal power still more. And indeed they might have succeeded had it not been for their ineptness and an extraordinary combination of forces ranged against them.

Lines of contention were drawn immediately at the accession of Elizabeth's nearest relative, her cousin James VI of Scotland, who in 1603 retained his Scottish crown but also became king of England as James I (1603–1625). Homely but vain, addled but erudite, James fittingly was called by Henry IV of France "the wisest fool in Christendom," and presented the starkest contrast to his predecessor. Whereas Elizabeth knew how to gain her way with Parliament without making a fuss about it, the schoolmasterish foreigner insisted on lecturing parliamentarians that he was semi-divine and would brook no resistance: "As it is atheism and blasphemy to dispute what God can do, so it is

James I. "The wisest fool in Christendom."

presumption and high contempt in a subject to dispute what a king can do." Carrying these sentiments further, in a speech to Parliament of 1609 he proclaimed that "kings are not only God's lieutenants on earth . . . but even by God Himself they are called gods."

That such extreme pretentions to divine authority would arouse strong opposition was a result even James should have been able to foresee, for the English were still intensely committed to the theory of parliamentary controls on the crown. Yet not just theory was at stake since the specific policies of the new king antagonized large numbers of his subjects. For one, James insisted upon supplementing his income by modes of money-raising which had never been sanctioned by Parliament; and when the leaders of that body remonstrated, he angrily tore up their protests and dissolved their sessions. Worse, he interfered with the freedom of business by granting monopolies and lucrative privileges to favored companies. And, worst of all in the eyes of most patriotic Englishmen, James quickly put an end to the long war with Spain and refused thereafter to become involved in any foreign military entanglements. Today many of us might think that James's commitment to peace was his greatest virtue; certainly his pacifism was well advised financially since it spared the crown enormous debts. But in his own age James was hated particularly for his peace policy because it made him seem far too friendly with England's traditional enemy, Spain, and because "appeasement" meant leaving seemingly heroic Protestants in Holland and Germany in the lurch.

Causes of antagonism to James I

Although almost all English people (except for a small minority of clandestine Catholics) objected to James I's pacific foreign policy, those who hated it most were a group destined to play the greatest role in overthrowing the Stuarts, namely, the Puritans. Extremist Calvinistic Protestants, the Puritans believed that Elizabeth I's religious compromises had not broken fully enough with the forms and doctrines of Roman Catholicism. Called Puritans from their desire to "purify" the English Church of all traces of Catholic ritual and observance, they most vehemently opposed the English "episcopal system" of church government by bishops. But James I was as committed to retaining episcopalianism as the Puritans were intent on abolishing it because he viewed royally appointed bishops as one of the pillars of a strong monarchy: "No bishop, no king." Since the Puritans were the dominant party in the House of Commons and many Puritans were also prosperous businessmen who opposed James's monopolistic policies and money-raising expediencies, throughout his reign James remained at loggerheads with an extremely powerful group of his subjects for a combination of religious, constitutional, and economic reasons.

The Puritans

Nonetheless, James survived to die peacefully in bed in 1625, and had it not been for mistakes made by his son Charles I (1625–1649), England might have gone the way of absolutistic France. Charles held the same inflated notions of royal power and consequently was quickly at odds with the Puritan leaders of Parliament. Soon after his accession

Charles I

Charles I. This portrait by Van Dyck vividly captures the ill-fated monarch's arrogance.

The Scottish uprising

The convening of Parliament

to the throne Charles became involved in a war with France and needed revenue desperately. When Parliament refused to make more than the customary grants, he resorted to forced loans from his subjects, punishing those who failed to comply by quartering soldiers in their homes or throwing them into prison without a trial. In reaction to this, Parliament forced the Petition of Right on the king in 1628. This document declared all taxes not voted by Parliament illegal, condemned the quartering of soldiers in private houses, and prohibited arbitrary imprisonment and the establishment of martial law in time of peace.

Angered rather than chastened by the Petition of Right, Charles I soon resolved to rule entirely without Parliament—and nearly succeeded. From 1629 to 1640 no Parliaments were called. During this "eleven-years' tyranny," Charles's government lived off a variety of makeshift dues and levies. For example, the crown sold monopolies at exorbitant rates, revived highly antiquated medieval financial claims, and admonished judges to collect the stiffest of fines. Though technically not illegal, all of these expedients were deeply resented. Most controversial was the collection of "ship money," a levy taken on the pretext of a medieval obligation of English seaboard towns to provide ships (or their worth in money) for the royal navy. Extending the payment of ship money from coastal towns to the whole country, Charles threatened to make it a regular tax in contravention of the Petition of Right, and was upheld in a legal challenge of 1637 brought against him on these grounds by the Puritan squire John Hampden.

By such means the king managed to make ends meet without the aid of taxes granted by Parliament. But he became ever more hated by most of his subjects, and above all the Puritans, not just because of his constitutional and financial policies but also because he seemed to be pursuing a course in religion that came much closer to Catholicism than to Calvinism. Whether the English Puritans would have risen up in revolt on their own is a moot question, but they were ultimately emboldened to do so by a chain of events beginning with a revolt in Scotland. The uprising in Scotland of 1640 against the policy of an English king was not unlike those in Catalonia and Portugal of the same year against the Spanish crown except that the Scottish rising was not just nationalistic but also explicitly religious in nature. Like his father, Charles believed in the adage "no bishop, no king" and hence foolhardily decided to introduce episcopalian church government into staunchly Presbyterian Scotland. The result was armed resistance by Charles's northern subjects and the first step toward civil war in England.

In order to obtain the funds necessary to punish the Scots, Charles had no other choice but to summon Parliament and soon found himself the target of pent-up resentments. Knowing full well that the king was helpless without money, the Puritan leaders of the House of Commons determined to take England's government into their own hands. Accordingly, they not only executed the king's first minister, the earl of Strafford, but they abolished ship money and the prerogative courts which ever since the reign of Henry VIII had served as instruments of arbitrary rule. Most significantly, they enacted a law forbidding the crown to dissolve Parliament and requiring the convening of sessions at least once every three years. After some indecision, early in 1642 Charles replied to these acts with a show of force. He marched with his guard into the House of Commons and attempted to arrest five of its leaders. All of them escaped, but an open conflict between crown and Parliament could no longer be avoided. Both parties collected troops and prepared for an appeal to the sword.

These events initiated the English Civil War, a conflict at once political and religious, which lasted from 1642 to 1649. Arrayed on the royal side were most of England's most prominent aristocrats and largest landowners, who were almost all "high-church" Anglicans. Opposed to them, the followers of Parliament included smaller landholders, tradesmen, and manufacturers, the majority of whom were Puritans. The members of the king's party were commonly known by the aristocratic name of Cavaliers. Their opponents, who cut their hair short in contempt for the fashionable custom of wearing curls, were derisively called Roundheads. At first the royalists, having obvious advantages of military experience, won most of the victories. In 1644, however, the parliamentary army was reorganized, and soon afterward the fortunes of battle shifted. The Cavalier forces were badly beaten, and in 1646 the king was compelled to surrender.

Civil war: the Cavaliers vs. the Roundheads

The struggle would now have ended had not a quarrel developed within the parliamentary party. The majority of its members, who had allied with the Presbyterian Scots, were ready to restore Charles to the throne as a limited monarch under an arrangement whereby a uniform Calvinistic Presbyterian faith would be imposed on both Scotland and England as the state religion. But a radical minority of Puritans, commonly known as Independents, distrusted Charles and insisted upon religious toleration for themselves and all other non-Presbyterian Protestants. Their leader was Oliver Cromwell (1599–1658), who had risen to command the Roundhead army. Taking advantage of the dissension within the ranks of his opponents, Charles renewed the war in 1648, but after a brief campaign was forced to surrender. Cromwell now resolved to end the life of "that man of blood," and, ejecting all the Presbyterians from Parliament by force of arms, obliged the remaining so-called Rump Parliament to vote an end to the monarchy. On 30 January 1649 Charles I was beheaded; a short time later the hereditary House of Lords was abolished, and England became a republic.

Oliver Cromwell

But founding a republic was far easier than maintaining one, and the new form of government, officially called a Commonwealth, did not last long. Technically the Rump Parliament continued as the leg-

Cromwell Felling the Royal Oak of England. A Royalist print of 1656 which portrays Oliver Cromwell as a destructive villain.

From republic to dictatorship

islative body, but Cromwell, with the army at his command, possessed the real power and soon became exasperated by the attempts of the legislators to perpetuate themselves in office and to profit from confiscating the wealth of their opponents. Accordingly, in 1653 he marched a detachment of troops into the Rump, and, saying "Come, I will put an end to your prating," ordered the members to disperse. Thereby the Commonwealth ceased to exist and was soon followed by the "Protectorate" or virtual dictatorship established under a constitution drafted by officers of the army. Called the Instrument of Government, this text was the nearest approximation of a written constitution England has ever had. Extensive powers were given to Cromwell as Lord Protector for life, and his office was made hereditary. At first a Parliament exercised limited authority in making laws and levying taxes, but in 1655 its members were abruptly dismissed by the Lord Protector. Thereafter the government became a thinly disguised autocracy, with Cromwell now wielding a sovereignty even more absolute then any the Stuart monarchs would have dared to claim.

The Stuart Restoration

Given the choice between a Puritan military dictatorship and the old royalist regime, when the occasion arose England unhesitatingly opted for the latter. Above all, years of Calvinistic austerities such as the prohibition of any public recreation on Sundays—then the workingperson's only holiday—had discredited the Puritans, making most people long for the milder Anglicanism of the original Elizabethan settlement. Thus not long after Cromwell's death in 1658, one of the deceased Protector's generals seized power and called for elections for a new Parliament which met in the spring of 1660 and proclaimed as king Charles I's exiled son, Charles II. With the reign of Charles II

(1660–1685) Anglicanism was immediately restored, but by no means the same was true for untrammeled monarchical power. Rather, stating with characteristic good humor that he did not wish to "resume his travels," Charles agreed to respect Parliament and observe the Petition of Right. Of greatest constitutional significance was the fact that all the legislation passed by Parliament immediately before the outbreak of the Civil War, including the requirement to hold Parliaments at least once every three years, remained as law. Thus in striking contrast to absolutistic France, England became a limited monarchy. Putting its constitutional struggles behind it after one brief further test in the late seventeenth century, the realm of England would soon live up to the poet Milton's prediction of "a noble and puissant nation rousing herself like a strong man after sleep."

4. QUESTS FOR LIGHT OUT OF DARKNESS

Caught up in economic uncertainty, religious rivalries, and political turmoil, many Europeans between 1560 and 1660 understandably cast about for emotional or intellectual resolutions of their most pressing problems. Sometimes, as in the case of the great witchcraft delusion, this quest led merely to an intensification of hysteria. But in the case of more dispassionate reflections, the search for ways of resolving Europe's crises led to some of the most enduring statements of moral and political philosophy of all time.

Witchcraft and philosophy

Although no one simple explanation can be offered for the outbreak of western Europe's fearful witchcraft hysteria that reached its peak between 1580 and 1660, it is certain that persecutions of witches in those years were fiercest during times of greatest disaster and that people who burned witches genuinely thought they were fighting the powers of darkness. Looking for the origins of the great early-modern witchcraft delusion, historians recognize that peasant culture throughout the Middle Ages included belief in the possibilities of sorcery. In other words, most simple rural people assumed that certain unusual individuals could practice good, or "white," magic in the form of healing, divination for lost objects, and fortune-telling, or perhaps also evil, "black" magic that might, for example, call up tempests or ravage crops. Yet only in the later Middle Ages did learned authorities begin to insist on theological grounds that black magic could be practiced only as a result of pacts with the devil. Naturally, once this belief became accepted, judicial officers soon found it urgent to prosecute all "witches" who practiced black magic because warfare against the devil was paramount to Christian society and "the evil one" could not be allowed to hold any sway. Accordingly, as early as 1484 Pope Innocent VIII ordered papal inquisitors to root out alleged witchcraft with all the means at their disposal, and the pace of witch hunts gained momentum in the following decades. Nor were witch trials curtailed

The origins of the witchcraft delusion

in areas that broke with Rome, for Protestant reformers believed in the insidious powers of Satan just as much as Catholics did. Indeed, Luther himself once threw an inkpot at a supposed apparition of the devil, and Calvin saw Satan's evil workings wherever he looked. Thus both urged that alleged witches be tried more peremptorily and sentenced with less leniency than ordinary criminals, and persecutions of innocent people continued apace in Protestant as well as Catholic lands.

Yet the outbreak of a real mania for catching and killing "witches" did not begin until about 1580. Therefore it can only be supposed that the witchcraft hysteria was connected in some way with Europe's general crisis—all the more since it continued for about as long as the age of crisis itself and was most severe in just those localities where warfare or economic dislocation was most intense. In such places, whenever crops failed or cattle sickened people assumed that a "witch"—usually a defenseless old woman—was responsible, and rushed to put her to death. If not always old, the victims were most frequently women, no doubt in part because preachers had encouraged their flocks to believe that evil had first come into the world with Eve and in part because men in authority felt psychologically most ambivalent about members of the opposite sex. Pure sadism certainly cannot have been the original motive for such proceedings, but once trials began, horrendous sadism very often was unleashed. Thus old women, young girls, and sometimes even mere children might be brutally tortured by having needles driven under their nails, fires placed at their heels, or their legs crushed under weights until marrow spurted

Supposed Witches Worshiping the Devil in the Form of a Billy-Goat. In the background other "witches" ride bareback on flying demons. This is one of the earliest visual conceptions of witchcraft, dating from around 1460.

Burning of Witches at Dernberg in 1555. From a sixteenth-century German pamphlet denouncing witchcraft.

from their bones, in order to make them confess to having had filthy orgies with demons. The final death toll will never be known, but in the 1620s there was an average of one hundred burnings a year in the German cities of Würzburg and Bamberg, and around the same time it was said the town square of Wolfenbüttel "looked like a little forest, so crowded were the stakes."

Why persecution quickly ended in the years immediately after 1660 will remain a matter for scholarly speculation. Aside from the fact that better times returned to most of Europe around then, probably the best explanation is that shortly after 1660 educated magistrates began to adhere to a mechanistic view of the universe. In other words, once the leaders of society came to believe that storms and epidemics arose from natural rather than supernatural causes, they ceased to countenance witch hunts.

The end of the witch hunts

Fortunately, other attempts of Europeans between 1560 and 1660 to master the darkness around them were not in themselves so dark. Indeed, one of the most "enlightened" of all European moral philosophers was the Frenchman Michel de Montaigne (1533–1592), who wrote during the height of the French wars of religion. The son of a Catholic father and a Huguenot mother of Jewish ancestry, the well-to-do Montaigne retired from a legal career at the age of thirty-eight to devote himself to a life of leisured reflection. The *Essays* which resulted were a new literary form originally conceived as "experiments" in writing (French *essai* simply means "trial"). Because they are extraordinarily well written as well as being searchingly reflective, Montaigne's *Essays* ever since have ranked securely among the most enduring classics of French literature and thought.

Michel de Montaigne

Although the range of subjects of the *Essays* runs a wide gamut from "The Resemblance of Children to Their Fathers" to "The Art of Conversing," two main themes are dominant. One is a pervasive skepticism. Making his motto "Que sais-je?" (What do I know?),

A *"Camel-Leopard."* In the
sixteenth century burgeoning
overseas travel led to prolifer-
ating rumors of strange sights.
This "camel-leopard" is obviously a crude conception of
what was really a giraffe. Uncertain of absolute truth and
falsity, Montaigne concluded
that what seemed true one day
might be cast into doubt tomorrow.

Jean Bodin

Montaigne decided that he knew very little for certain. According to
him, "it is folly to measure truth and error by our own capacities"
because our capacities are severely limited. Thus, as he maintained in
one of his most famous essays, "On Cannibals," what may seem
indisputably true and proper to one nation may seem absolutely false
to another because "everyone gives the title of barbarism to everything that is not of his usage." From this Montaigne's second main
principle followed—the need for tolerance. Since all people think they
know the perfect religion and the perfect government, no religion or
government is really perfect and consequently no belief worth fighting for to the death.

If the foregoing description makes Montaigne sound surprisingly
modern, it must be emphasized that he was by no means a rationalist.
On the contrary, he believed that "reason does nothing but go astray
in everything," and that intellectual curiosity "which prompts us to
thrust our noses into everything" is a "scourge of the soul." Moreover, concerning practical affairs Montaigne was a fatalist who thought
that in a world governed by unpredictable "fortune" the best human
strategy is to face the good and the bad with steadfastness and dignity.
Lest people begin to think too highly of their own abilities, he reminded
them that "sit we upon the highest throne in the world, yet we do sit
upon our own behinds." Nonetheless, despite his passive belief that
"fortune, not wisdom, rules the life of mankind," the wide circulation
of Montaigne's *Essays* did help combat fanaticism and religious intolerance in his own and subsequent ages.

If Montaigne sought refuge from the trials of his age in skepticism,
tolerance, and resigned dignity, his contemporary, the French lawyer
Jean Bodin (1530–1596), looked for more light to come out of darkness from the powers of the state. Like Montaigne, Bodin was particularly troubled by the upheavals caused by the religious wars in
France—he had even witnessed the frightful St. Bartholomew's Day
Massacre of 1572 in Paris. But instead of shrugging his shoulders about
the bloodshed, he resolved to offer a political plan to make sure turbulence would cease. This he did in his monumental *Six Books on the
Commonwealth* (1576), the earliest fully developed statement of governmental absolutism in Western political thought. According to
Bodin, the state arises from the needs of collections of families, but
once constituted should brook no opposition, for the maintenance of
order is paramount. Whereas writers on law and politics before him
had groped toward a theory of governmental sovereignty, Bodin was
the first to offer a succinct definition; for him, sovereignty was "the
most high, absolute, and perpetual power over all subjects," consisting principally in the power "to give laws to subjects without their
consent." Although Bodin acknowledged the theoretical possibility of
government by aristocracy or democracy, he assumed that the nation-
states of his day would be ruled by monarchs and insisted that such
monarchs could in no way be limited, either by legislative or judicial

bodies, or even by laws made by their predecessors or themselves. Expressing the sharpest opposition to contemporary Huguenots who were saying (in contravention of the original teachings of Luther and Calvin) that subjects had a right to resist "ungodly princes," Bodin maintained that a subject must trust in his ruler's "mere and frank good will." Even if the ruler proved a tyrant, Bodin insisted that the subject had no warrant to resist, for any resistance would open the door "to a licentious anarchy which is worse than the harshest tyranny in the world." Since in his own day Bodin knew much "licentious anarchy" but had hardly any notion of how harsh the "harshest tyranny" could be, his position is somewhat understandable. Yet in the next century his *Commonwealth* would become the point of departure for justifications of an increasingly oppressive French royal absolutism.

Quite understandably, just as the French civil wars of the sixteenth century provoked a variety of responses, so did the English Civil War of the seventeenth. Drawing on a tradition of resistance to untrammeled state power expressed by French Huguenots and earlier English parliamentarians and Puritans, the great English Puritan poet John Milton enunciated a stirring defense of freedom of the press in his *Areopagitica* (1644). Similarly bold upholders of libertarianism were a party of Milton's Puritan contemporaries known as Levellers, the first exponents of democracy since Greek times. Organizing themselves as a pressure group within Cromwell's army in the later 1640s when Charles I's monarchy seemed clearly doomed, the Levellers—who derived their name from their advocacy of equal political rights for all classes—agitated in favor of a parliamentary republic based on nearly universal manhood suffrage. For them, servants and other wage-laborers had no right to vote because they formed part of their employer's "family" and allegedly were represented by the family head. Moreover, the Levellers did not even deign to argue about women's rights. Otherwise, however, in the immortal words of one of their spokesmen, they argued that "the poorest He that is in England hath a life to live as the greatest He, and therefore . . . every man that is to live under a government ought first by his own consent to put himself under that government." But since Oliver Cromwell, who believed that the only grounds for suffrage was sufficient property, would have none of this, once Cromwell assumed virtually dictatorial powers the Leveller party disintegrated. More radical still were the communistic Diggers, so called from their attempts to cultivate common lands in 1649. Claiming to be "true Levellers," the Diggers argued that true freedom lies not in votes, but "where a man receives his nourishment," and hence argued for the redistribution of property. Cromwell, however, dispersed them quickly and thus the Diggers have merely historical interest as vanguards of movements to come.

John Milton and the Levellers

Far to the other extreme of the libertarian Puritans was the political philosopher Thomas Hobbes (1588–1679), whose reactions to the

*The Title Page of Hobbes's Le-
viathan*

Hobbes's pessimism

English Civil War led him to become the most forceful advocate of unrestrained state power of all time. Like Bodin, who was moved by the events of St. Bartholomew's Day to formulate a doctrine of political absolutism, Hobbes was moved by the turmoil of the English Civil War to do the same in his classic of political theory entitled *Leviathan* (1651). Yet Hobbes differed from Bodin in several respects. For one, whereas Bodin assumed that the absolute sovereign power would be a royal monarch, the more radical Hobbes, writing without any respect for tradition in Cromwell's England two years after the beheading of a king, thought the sovereign could be any ruthless dictator whatsoever. Then too, whereas Bodin defined his state as "the lawful government of families" and hence did not believe that the state could abridge private property rights because families could not exist without property, Hobbes's state existed to rule over atomistic individuals and thus was licensed to trample over both liberty and property.

But the most fundamental difference between Bodin and Hobbes lay in the latter's uncompromisingly pessimistic view of human nature. Whereas Bodin was pessimistic about mankind only by implication, Hobbes posited that the "state of nature" which existed before civil government came into being was a condition of "war of all against all." For Hobbes, since man naturally behaves as "a wolf" toward man and hence increasing fear of violent death in the state of nature makes human life "solitary, poor, nasty, brutish, and short," people for their own good at some purely theoretical point in time surrender their liberties to a sovereign ruler in exchange for his agreement to keep the peace. Having thus granted away their liberties, subjects have no right whatsoever to seek them back, and the sovereign can tyrannize as he likes—free to oppress his charges in any way other than to kill them, an act which would negate the very purpose of his rule. It is a measure of the relentless logic and clarity of Hobbes's abstract exposition that his *Leviathan* is widely regarded as one of the four or five greatest political treatises ever written, for practically nobody really likes what he says. Indeed, even in his own age Hobbes's views were vastly unpopular—libertarians detested them for obvious reasons, and royalists hated them as much because Hobbes was contemptuous of dynastic claims based on blood lineage and rationalized absolutistic rule not on the grounds of powers granted from God, as most royalists did, but on powers surrendered by society. Yet because many important thinkers felt compelled to argue against Hobbes, he had enormous influence, if only in provoking the responses of others.

Perhaps fittingly, the most moving and in certain ways most modern attempt to bring light out of pervasive darkness was that of the seventeenth-century French moral and religious philosopher Blaise Pascal (1623–1662). In certain superficial ways Pascal's most enduring legacy, his *Pensées* (*Thoughts*), resemble Montaigne's *Essays* because both are highly introspective collections of informal short pieces written with great literary power. But Pascal, who turned away in a conversion experience from scientific rationalism to become a firm adherent of Jansenism (the most puritanical wing of French Catholicism), was as ardent a religious believer as Montaigne was a cool skeptic. Thus while Pascal agreed with Montaigne that human life on earth was fraught with peril—he defined man as "a thinking reed"—he had no doubt that a just Providence ruled the world, and he believed as firmly as did Luther or Calvin that faith alone could show the way to salvation. Yet, recognizing that skeptics or secular rationalists could never be brought to the true faith by dogmatic authority, he hoped to convert doubters by appealing simultaneously to their intellects and their emotions in a major defense of Christianity. Unfortunately, premature death prevented him from accomplishing this ambitious goal, but the *Pensées* survive as previews of his approach. In these he conceded his own sense of terror and anguish in the face of evil and eternity, but made the awe itself a sign of the existence of God. Individuals today will be moved by Pascal's *Pensées* in varying degrees according to their own convictions, but few people of any persuasion will dispute Pascal's famous paradox that "man knows he is wretched; he is therefore wretched because he is so; but he is very great because he knows it."

Blaise Pascal

5. LITERATURE AND THE ARTS

The combined wretchedness and greatness of humanity may be taken as the theme for the extraordinary profusion of towering works of literature and art produced during western Europe's period of crisis from 1560 to 1660. Of course not every single writing or painting of the era expressed the same message. During a hundred years of extraordinary literary and artistic creativity, works of all genres and sentiments were produced, ranging from the frothiest farces to the darkest tragedies, the serenest still lifes to the most grotesque scenes of religious martyrdom. Nonetheless, the greatest writers and painters of the period all were moved by a realization of the ambiguities and ironies of human existence not unlike that expressed in different ways by Montaigne and Pascal. They all were fully aware of the horrors of war and human suffering so rampant in their day, and all were directly or indirectly aware of the Protestant conviction that men are "vessels of iniquity"; but they also inherited a large degree of Renaissance affirmativeness, and most of them accordingly preferred to view life on earth as a great dare.

From the host of remarkable writers who flourished during what was probably the most extraordinary century in the entire history of western European poetry and drama, we may take the very greatest: Cervantes, the Elizabethan dramatists—Shakespeare to the fore—and John Milton. Although Miguel de Cervantes (1547–1616) was not

Major statements concerning the human condition

Miguel de Cervantes

Miguel de Cervantes

Elizabethan drama

strictly speaking either a poet or a dramatist, his masterpiece, the satirical romance *Don Quixote,* exudes great lyricism and drama. The plot recounts the adventures of a Spanish gentleman, Don Quixote of La Mancha, who has become slightly unbalanced by constant reading of chivalric epics. His mind filled with all kinds of fantastic adventures, he sets out at the age of fifty upon the slippery road of knight-errantry, imagining windmills to be glowering giants and flocks of sheep to be armies of infidels whom it is his duty to rout with his spear. In his distorted fancy he mistakes inns for castles and serving girls for courtly ladies on fire with love. Set off in contrast to the "knight-errant" is the figure of his faithful squire, Sancho Panza. The latter represents the ideal of the practical man, with his feet on the ground and content with the modest but substantial pleasures of eating, drinking, and sleeping. Yet Cervantes clearly does not wish to say that the realism of a Sancho Panza is categorically preferable to the "quixotic" idealism of his master. Rather, the two men represent different facets of human nature. Without any doubt, *Don Quixote* is a devastating satire on the anachronistic chivalric mentality that would soon help hasten Spain's decline. But for all that, the reader's sympathies remain with the protagonist, the man from La Mancha who dares to "dream the impossible dream."

Directly contemporaneous with Cervantes were the English Elizabethan dramatists who collectively produced the most glorious age of theater known in the Western world. Writing after England's victory over the Spanish Armada, when national pride was at a peak, all exhibited great exuberance but none was by any means a facile optimist. In fact a strain of reflective seriousness pervades all their best works, and a few, like the tragedian John Webster (c. 1580–c. 1625), who "saw the skull beneath the skin," were if anything morbid pessimists. Literary critics tend to agree that of a bevy of great Elizabethan playwrights the most outstanding were Christopher Marlowe (1564–1593), Ben Jonson (c. 1573–1637), and, of course, William Shakespeare (1564–1616). Of the three, the fiery Marlowe, whose life was cut short in a tavern brawl before he reached the age of thirty, was the most youthfully energetic. In plays such as *Tamburlaine* and *Doctor Faustus* Marlowe created larger-than-life heroes who seek and come close to conquering everything in their path and feeling every possible sensation. But they meet unhappy ends because, for all his vitality, Marlowe knew that there are limits on human striving, and that wretchedness as well as greatness lies in the human lot. Thus though Faustus asks a reincarnated Helen of Troy, conjured up by Satan, to make him "immortal with a kiss," he dies and is damned in the end because immortality is not awarded by the devil or found in earthly kisses. In contrast to the heroic tragedian Marlowe, Ben Jonson wrote corrosive comedies which expose human vices and foibles. In the particularly bleak *Volpone* Jonson shows people behaving like deceitful and lustful animals, but in the later *Alchemist* he balances an attack on quackery and gullibility with admiration for resourceful lower-class characters who cleverly take advantage of their supposed betters.

Incomparably the greatest of the Elizabethan dramatists, William Shakespeare, was born into the family of a tradesman in the provincial town of Stratford-on-Avon. His life is enshrouded in more mists of obscurity than the careers of most other great people. It is known that he left his native village, having gained little formal education, when he was about twenty, and that he drifted to London to find employment in the theater. How he eventually became an actor and still later a writer of plays is uncertain, but by the age of twenty-eight he had definitely acquired a reputation as an author sufficient to excite the jealousy of his rivals. Before he retired to his native Stratford about 1610 to spend the rest of his days in ease, he had written or collaborated in writing nearly forty plays, over and above 150 sonnets and two long narrative poems.

William Shakespeare. Portrait made for the First Folio edition of his works, 1623.

As everyone knows, Shakespeare's plays rank as a kind of secular Bible wherever the English language is spoken. The reasons lie not only in the author's unrivaled gift of expression, and in his scintillating wit, but most of all in his profound analysis of human character seized by passion and tried by fate. Shakespeare's dramas fall rather naturally into three groups. Those written during the playwright's earlier years are characterized by a sense of confidence. They include a number of history plays, which recount England's struggles and glories leading up to the triumph of the Tudor dynasty; the lyrical romantic tragedy *Romeo and Juliet;* and a wide variety of comedies including the magical *Midsummer Night's Dream* and Shakespeare's greatest creations in the comic vein—*Twelfth Night, As You Like It,* and *Much Ado about Nothing.* Despite the last-named title, few even of the plays of Shakespeare's early, lightest period are "much ado about nothing." Rather, most explore with wisdom as well as wit fundamental problems of psychological identity, honor and ambition, love and friendship. Occasionally they also contain touches of deep seriousness, as in *As You Like It,* when Shakespeare has a character pause to reflect that "all the world's a stage, and all the men and women merely players" who pass through seven "acts" or stages of life.

Shakespeare's three periods: (1) confidence

Such touches, however, never obscure the restrained optimism of Shakespeare's first period, whereas the plays from his second period are far darker in mood. Apparently around 1601 Shakespeare underwent a crisis during which he began to distrust human nature profoundly and to indict the whole scheme of the universe. The result was a group of dramas characterized by bitterness, frequent pathos, and a troubled searching into the mysteries of things. The series begins with the tragedy of indecisive idealism represented by *Hamlet,* goes on to the cynicism of *Measure for Measure* and *All's Well That Ends Well,* and culminates in the cosmic tragedies of *Macbeth* and *King Lear,* wherein characters assert that "life's but a walking shadow . . .

(2) crisis

a tale told by an idiot, full of sound and fury signifying nothing," and that "as flies to wanton boys are we to the gods; they kill us for their sport." Despite all this gloom, however, the plays of Shakespeare's second period generally contain the dramatist's greatest flights of poetic grandeur.

Although *Macbeth* and *Lear* suggest an author in the throes of deep depression, Shakespeare managed to resolve his personal crisis and end his dramatic career with a third period characterized by a profound spirit of reconciliation. Of the three plays (all idyllic romances) written during this final period, the last, *The Tempest,* is the greatest. Here ancient animosities are buried and wrongs are righted by a combination of natural and supernatural means, and a wide-eyed, youthful heroine rejoices on first seeing men with the words "O brave new world, that has such people in it!" Here, then, Shakespeare seems to be saying that for all humanity's trials life is not so unrelentingly bitter after all, and the divine plan of the universe is somehow benevolent and just.

Though less versatile than Shakespeare, not far behind him in eloquent grandeur stands the Puritan poet John Milton (1608–1674). The leading publicist of Oliver Cromwell's regime, Milton wrote the official defense of the beheading of Charles I as well as a number of treatises justifying Puritan positions in contemporary affairs. But he was also a man full of contradictions who loved the Greek and Latin classics at least as much as the Bible. Hence he could write a perfect pastoral elegy, *Lycidas,* mourning the loss of a dear friend in purely classical terms. Later, when forced into retirement by the accession of Charles II, Milton, though now blind, embarked on writing a classical epic, *Paradise Lost,* out of material found in Genesis concerning the creation of the world and the fall of man. This magnificent poem, which links the classical tradition to Christianity more successfully than any literary work written before or since, is surely one of the greatest epics of all time. Setting out to "justify the ways of God to man," Milton in *Paradise Lost* first plays "devil's advocate" by creating the compelling character of Satan, who defies God with boldness and subtlety. But Satan is more than counterbalanced in the end by the real "epic hero" of *Paradise Lost,* Adam, who learns to accept the human lot of moral responsibility and suffering, and is last seen leaving Paradise with Eve, the world "all before them."

The ironies and tensions inherent in human existence also were portrayed with extraordinary eloquence and profundity by several immortal masters of the visual arts who flourished between 1560 and 1660. The dominant style in painting in Italy and Spain in the second half of the sixteenth century was Mannerism. Originally a term of opprobrium for alleged imitators—supposedly second-rate artists who painted in the "manner" of Michelangelo's late phase—the term *Mannerism* in current analysis has come to mean much more than that; indeed art historians now rank some Mannerist painters among the

John Milton. From the First Edition of his poems, 1645.

Self-Portrait, Albrecht Dürer (1471–1528). Dürer was the first major artist to paint self-portraits at different phases of his life. Here, aged twenty-eight, he makes himself seem almost Christlike. Note also the prominent initials "A.D." under the date of the painting at the upper left. (Alte Pinakothek)

Erasmus, Hans Holbein the Younger (1497–1543). This portrait is generally regarded as the most telling visual characterization of "the prince of the Christian humanists." (Louvre)

The Harvesters, Peter Brueghel (c. 1525–1569). Brueghel chose to depict both the hard work and recreation of the peasantry. (MMA)

The Crucifixion, Tintoretto (1518–1594). This Venetian master of Mannerism combined typically Venetian richness of color with an innovative concern for movement and emotion. (Scala)

Saint Andrew and St. Francis, El Greco (c. 1541–1614). A striking exemplification of the artist's penchant for elongation as well as his profound psychological penetration. (The Prado)

View of Toledo, El Greco. One of the most awesomely mysterious paintings in the entire Western tradition. (MMA)

The Maids of Honor, Diego Velásquez (1599–1660). The artist himself is at work on an idealized double portrait of the king and queen of Spain (who may be seen in the rear mirror), but reality is more obvious in the foreground in the persons of the delicately impish princess, her two maids, and a misshapen dwarf. The twentieth-century Spanish artist Picasso gained great inspiration from this work. (The Prado)

Pope Innocent X, Velásquez. A trenchant portrait of a decisive man of affairs. (Doria-Pamphili Collection)

England and Scotland Crowning Charles I, Peter Paul Rubens (1577–1640). A typical piece of Baroque propaganda, in this case painted to glorify the English monarch of the Stuart family in the years before his ill-fated demise. (Minneapolis Institute of Art)

The Horrors of War, Rubens. The war god Mars here casts aside his mistress Venus and threatens humanity with death and destruction. In his old age Rubens took a far more critical view of war than he did for most of his earlier career. (Gall. Palatina)

Aristotle Contemplating the Bust of Homer, Rembrandt van Rijn (1606–1669). One of the greatest painters' view of one of the greatest of philosophers caught up by the aura of one of the greatest poets. (MMA)

The Calling of St. Matthew, Caravaggio (1565–1609). Among the earliest of the great Baroque painters, Caravaggio specialized in contrasts of light and shade *(chiaroscuro)*, and preferred to conceive of religious scenes in terms of everyday life. Here Christ (extreme right), whose halo is the only supernatural detail in the composition, enters a tavern to call St. Matthew (pointing doubtfully at himself) to his service. (Art Resource)

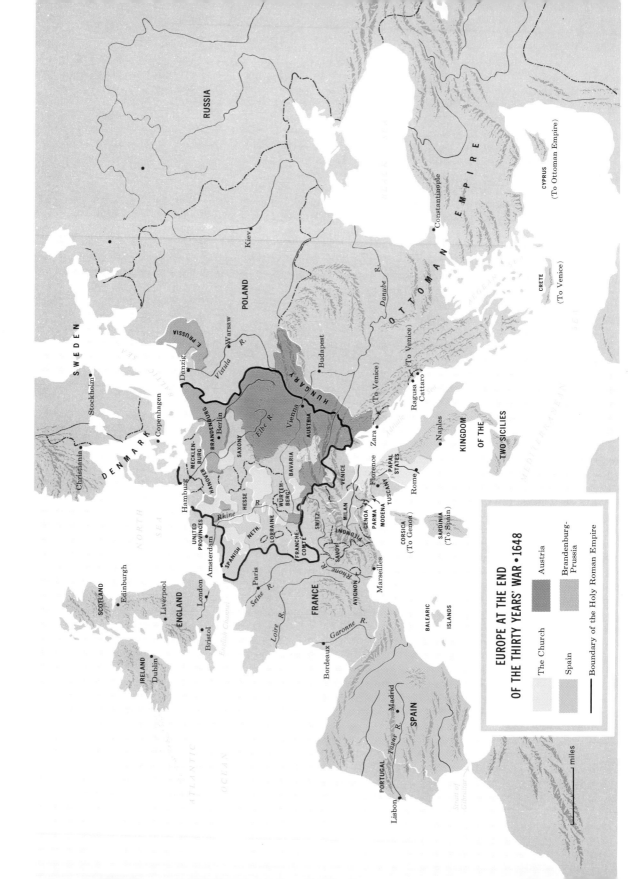

EUROPE AT THE END
OF THE THIRTY YEARS' WAR • 1648

The Church   Austria

Spain   Brandenburg-
Prussia

Boundary of the Holy Roman Empire

RUSSIA

SWEDEN

DENMARK

POLAND

E. PRUSSIA

Kiev

Warsaw

Danzig

Stockholm

Copenhagen

Christiania

Hamburg

MECKLEN-
BURG

BRANDENBURG

Berlin

HANOVER

SAXONY

HESSE

Vistula R.

Elbe R.

OTTOMAN EMPIRE

Constantinople

CYPRUS
(To Ottoman Empire)

CRETE
(To Venice)

HUNGARY

Budapest

Danube R.

Vienna

AUSTRIA

BAVARIA

WÜRTEM-
BERG

SWITZ.

VENICE

Zara
(To Venice)

Ragusa
(To Venice)

Cattaro
(To Venice)

SCOTLAND

Edinburgh

IRELAND

Dublin

ENGLAND

Liverpool

London

Bristol

NORTH
SEA

English Channel

BALTIC SEA

UNITED
PROVINCES

Amsterdam

SPANISH
NETH.

LORRAINE

FRANCHE-
COMTÉ

Rhine R.

FRANCE

Paris

Seine R.

Loire R.

Bordeaux

Garonne R.

Rhône R.

Marseilles

AVIGNON

SAVOY

PIEDMONT

MILAN

GENOA

PARMA

MODENA

TUSCANY

Florence

PAPAL
STATES

Rome

Naples

KINGDOM
OF THE
TWO SICILIES

CORSICA
(To Genoa)

SARDINIA
(To Spain)

BALEARIC
ISLANDS

PORTUGAL

Lisbon

SPAIN

Madrid

Tagus R.

ATLANTIC
OCEAN

Strait of
Gibraltar

MEDITERRANEAN SEA

ADRIATIC SEA

AEGEAN SEA

miles

West's greatest masters. Unquestionably Mannerism did take as its point of departure Michelangelo's tendency toward anticlassicism and distortion of nature for emotional effects, but Mannerist painters went so much further in emphasizing restlessness, imbalance, and distortion that they left Michelangelo far behind. Admittedly many of them lacked skill and depth of vision, contenting themselves with portraying brawn instead of muscle, melodrama instead of drama. But some others fully succeeded in balancing great artistic virtuosity with the communication of radiant inner light.

Of the latter, the two most outstanding are the Venetian Tintoretto (1518–1594) and the Spaniard El Greco (c. 1541–1614). Combining Manneristic distortion and restlessness with a traditionally Venetian taste for rich color, Tintoretto produced an enormous number of monumentally large canvases devoted to religious themes that still inspire awe with their broodingly shimmering light and gripping theatricality. More emotional still is the work of Tintoretto's disciple, El Greco. Born Domenikos Theotokopoulos on the Greek island of Crete, this extraordinary painter absorbed some of the stylized elongation characteristic of Greco-Byzantine icon painting before traveling to Italy to learn from great contemporary Mannerist painters such as Tintoretto and then finally settling in Spain, where he was nicknamed "El Greco"—Spanish for "the Greek." El Greco's paintings were too bizarre to be greatly appreciated in his own age, and even now they often appear so unbalanced as to seem the work of one almost deranged. Yet such a view slights El Greco's deeply mystical Catholic fervor as well as his technical achievements. Best known today is his transfigured landscape, the *View of Toledo,* with its somber but awe-

Fray Felix Hortensio Paravicino, by El Greco. More restrained in composition than most of the artist's other work, this portrait nonetheless communicates a sense of deep spiritual intensity.

See color plates following page 544 for the *Crucifixion* by Tintoretto and the *View of Toledo* by El Greco

The Laocoön, by El Greco. An extreme example of Manneristic stress on restlessness and distortion. Note that the Spanish painter here drew for inspiration on the famous Hellenistic sculpture group shown on p. 165.

Left: *David,* by Bernini. Whereas the earlier conceptions of David by the Renaissance sculptors Donatello and Michelangelo were reposeful (see pp. 439 and 441), the Baroque sculptor Bernini chose to portray his young hero at the peak of physical exertion. Right: *St. Theresa in Ecstasy,* by Bernini. As David is seen at the peak of bodily exertion, St. Theresa is shown at the peak of spiritual transport.

some light breaking where no sun shines, but equally inspiring are his swirling religious allegories such as *The Burial of the Count of Orgaz* (thought by the painter to be his masterpiece), and his myriad stunning portraits in which gaunt, dignified Spaniards radiate a rare blend of austerity and spiritual insight.

The dominant artistic school of southern Europe succeeding Mannerism was that of the Baroque, a school not just of painting but of sculpture and architecture lasting from about 1600 until the early 1700s. The term *Baroque* is derived from a Portuguese word for an irregular, rough pearl, and this reveals much about its meaning. Picking up where Mannerism left off, the Baroque style emphasized the emotional and the swirling as much as Mannerism, but Baroque works of art characteristically were less shrouded by somber mystery and were far more affirmative than Manneristic paintings. One major explanation for this is that Baroque art in all genres was usually semi-propagandistic. Originating in Rome as an expression of the ideals of the Counter-Reformation papacy and the Jesuit order, Baroque architecture in particular aimed to gain adherence for a specific worldview. Similarly, Baroque painting often was done in the service of the Counter-Reformation Church, which at its high tide around 1620 seemed everywhere to be on the offensive, and when Baroque painters were not celebrating Counter-Reformation ideals, most of them worked in the service of monarchs who sought their own glorification.

Indubitably the most imaginative and influential figure of the original Roman Baroque was the architect and sculptor Gianlorenzo Bernini (1598–1680), a frequent employee of the papacy who created one of the most magnificent celebrations of papal grandeur in the sweeping colonnades leading up to St. Peter's basilica. Breaking with the serene Renaissance classicism of Palladio, Bernini's architecture retained the use of classical elements such as columns and domes, but combined them in ways meant to express both aggresssive restlessness and great power. In addition Bernini was one of the first to experiment with church facades built "in depth"—building frontages, that is, not conceived as continuous surfaces but which jutted out at odd angles and seemingly invaded the open space in front of them. If the purpose of these innovations was to stir the viewer and draw him emotionally into the ambit of the work of art, the same may be said for Bernini's aims in sculpture. Harking back to the restless motion of Hellenistic statuary—particularly the Laocoön group—and building on tendencies already present in the later sculpture of Michelangelo, Bernini's statuary emphasizes drama and incites the viewer to respond to it rather than serenely observe.

Since most Italian Baroque painters lacked Bernini's artistic genius, to view the very greatest masterpieces of southern European Baroque painting one must look to Spain and the work of Diego Velásquez (1599–1660). Unlike Bernini, Velásquez, a court painter in Madrid just when Spain hung on the brink of ruin, was not an entirely typical

The Church of S. Carlo alle Quattro Fontane, Rome. Built by Bernini's contemporary Francesco Borromini in 1665, the facade of S. Carlo well exemplifies the frontage "in depth" characteristic of Baroque architecture.

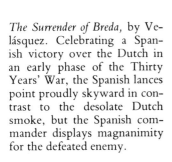

The Surrender of Breda, by Velásquez. Celebrating a Spanish victory over the Dutch in an early phase of the Thirty Years' War, the Spanish lances point proudly skyward in contrast to the desolate Dutch smoke, but the Spanish commander displays magnanimity for the defeated enemy.

A Dwarf, by Velásquez. The great Spanish artist had an enduring fascination with the less favored of the earth.

See color plates following page 544 for *Maids of Honor* and *Pope Innocent X* by Velásquez and *Harvesters* by Breughel

exponent of the Baroque style. Certainly many of his canvases display a characteristically Baroque delight in motion, drama, and power, but Velásquez's best work is characterized by a more restrained thoughtfulness than usually found in the Baroque. Thus his famous *Surrender at Breda* shows muscular horses and splendid Spanish grandees on the one hand, but un-Baroque humane and deep sympathy for defeated, disarrayed troops on the other. Moreover, Velásquez's single greatest painting, *The Maids of Honor,* done around 1656 after Spain's collapse, radiates thoughtfulness rather than drama and is one of the most probing artistic examinations of illusion and reality ever executed.

Southern Europe's main northern rival for artistic laurels in the "iron century" was the Netherlands, where three extremely dissimilar painters all explored the theme of the greatness and wretchedness of man to the fullest. The earliest, Peter Brueghel (rhymes with frugal) (c. 1525–1569), worked in a vein related to earlier Netherlandish realism. But unlike his predecessors, who favored quiet urban scenes, Brueghel exulted in portraying the busy, elemental life of the peasantry. Most famous in this respect are his rollicking *Peasant Wedding* and *Peasant Wedding Dance,* and his spacious *Harvesters,* in which guzzling and snoring fieldhands are taking a well-deserved break from their heavy labors under the noon sun. Such vistas give the impression of uninterrupted rhythms of life, but late in his career Brueghel became appalled by the intolerance and bloodshed he witnessed during the time of the Calvinist riots and the Spanish repression in the Netherlands and expressed his criticism in an understated yet searing manner. In *The Blind Leading the Blind,* for example, we see what happens when ignorant fanatics start showing the way to each other. More powerful still is Brueghel's *Massacre of the Innocents,* which from a distance looks like a snug scene of a Flemish village buried in snow. In fact, however, heartless soldiers are methodically breaking into homes and slaughter-

The Massacre of the Innocents. This painting by Brueghel shows how effectively art can be used as a means of social commentary. Many art historians believe that Brueghel was tacitly depicting the suffering of the Netherlands at the hands of the Spanish in his own day.

The Triumph of the Eucharist, by Rubens. A typical Baroque work, this painting proclaims the victory of the Cross and the Eucharistic Chalice, symbols of Counter-Reformation Catholicism.

ing babies, the simple peasant folk are fully at their mercy, and the artist—alluding to a Gospel forgotten by warring Catholics and Protestants alike—seems to be saying "as it happened in the time of Christ, so it happens now."

Vastly different from Brueghel was the Netherlandish Baroque painter Peter Paul Rubens (1577–1640). Since the Baroque, unlike Mannerism, was an international movement closely linked to the spread of the Counter-Reformation, it should offer no surprise that Baroque style was extremely well represented in just that part of the Netherlands which, after long warfare, had been retained by Spain. In fact, Rubens of Antwerp was a far more typical Baroque artist than Velásquez of Madrid, painting literally thousands of robust canvases that glorified resurgent Catholicism or exalted second-rate aristocrats by portraying them as epic heroes dressed in bearskins. Even when Rubens's intent was not overtly propagandistic he customarily revelled in the sumptuous extravagance of the Baroque manner, being perhaps most famous today for the pink and rounded flesh of his well-nourished nudes. But unlike a host of lesser Baroque artists, Rubens was not entirely lacking in subtlety and was a man of many moods. His gentle portrait of his son Nicholas catches unaffected childhood in a moment of repose, and though throughout most of his career Rubens had celebrated martial valor, his late *Horrors of War* movingly portrays what he himself called "the grief of unfortunate Europe, which, for so many years now, has suffered plunder, outrage, and misery."

In some ways a blend of Brueghel and Rubens, the greatest of all Netherlandish painters, Rembrandt van Rijn (1606–1669), defies all attempts at facile characterization. Living across the border from the Spanish Netherlands in staunchly Calvinistic Holland, Rembrandt

See color plates following page 544 for the *Horrors of War* and *England and Scotland Crowning Charles I* by Rubens

Rubens's Portrait of his Son Nicholas.

The Polish Rider, by Rembrandt. Unlike Titian's equestrian Charles V (above, p. 520), Rembrandt's rider is self-reflective and hence more humane.

See color plates following page 544 for *Aristotle Contemplating the Bust of Homer* by Rembrandt

belonged to a society which was too austere to tolerate the unbuckled realism of a Brueghel or the fleshy Baroque pomposity of a Rubens. Yet Rembrandt managed to put both realistic and Baroque traits to new uses. In his early career he gained fame and fortune as the painter of biblical scenes which lacked the Baroque's fleshiness but retained its grandeur in their swirling forms and stunning experiments with light. In this early period too Rembrandt was active as a realistic portrait painter who knew how to flatter his self-satisfied subjects by emphasizing their Calvinistic steadfastness, to the great advantage of his purse. But gradually his prosperity faded, apparently in part because he grew tired of flattering and definitely because he made some bad investments. Since personal tragedies also mounted in the painter's middle and declining years his art inevitably became far more pensive and sombre, but it gained in dignity, subtle lyricism, and awesome mystery. Thus his later portraits, including those of himself, are imbued with introspective qualities and a suggestion that only the half is being told. Equally moving are explicitly philosophical paintings such as *Aristotle Contemplating the Bust of Homer,* in which the supposedly earthbound philosopher seems spellbound by the otherworldy luminous radiance of the epic poet, and the *The Polish Rider,* in which realistic and Baroque elements merge into a higher synthesis portraying a pensive young man setting out fearlessly into a perilous world. Like Shakespeare, Rembrandt knew that life's journey is full of perils, but his most mature paintings suggest that these can be mastered with poetry and courage.

SELECTED READINGS

• *Items so designated are available in paperback editions.*

• Aston, T., ed., *Crisis in Europe: 1560–1660*, London, 1965. A collection of highly valuable essays.

• Braudel, F., *The Mediterranean and the Mediterranean World in the Age of Philip II*, 2 vols., New York, 1972. One of the most brilliant history books of our age. Treats life in the Mediterranean regions in the second half of the sixteenth century with particular emphasis on how geography determines the course of human history.

• Chute, M., *Shakespeare of London*, New York, 1949. The best popular biography.

• Dean, Leonard F., ed., *Shakespeare: Modern Essays in Criticism*, New York, 1958. A variety of scholarly appraisals.

• Dunn, Richard S., *The Age of Religious Wars, 1559–1715*, 2nd ed., New York, 1979. The best college-level text on this period. Extremely well written.

• Elliott, J. H., *Imperial Spain, 1469–1716*, London, 1963. A masterpiece of sophisticated synthesis.

• _____, *Europe Divided: 1559–1598*, London, 1968. An extremely lucid narrative of complex events.

• Elton, G. R., *England under the Tudors*, 2nd ed., London, 1977. Engagingly written and authoritative.

• Ford, Boris, ed., *The Age of Shakespeare*, Baltimore, 1955. A good shorter handbook.

• Frame, D., *Montaigne: A Biography*, New York, 1965. By far the best study in English.

• Fraser, Lady Antonia, *Cromwell: The Lord Protector*, London, 1973. A popular biography.

  Held, J. S., and D. Posner, *17th and 18th Century Art: Baroque Painting, Sculpture, Architecture*, New York, 1979. The most complete introductory review of the subject in English.

• Hibbard, Howard, *Bernini*, Baltimore, 1965. The basic study in English of this central figure of Baroque artistic activity.

• Hill, Christopher, *A Century of Revolution: 1603–1714*, 2nd ed., New York, 1982. A valuable survey of English developments that holds narrative to a minimum and stresses economic and social trends.

  Hirst, Derek, *Authority and Conflict: England, 1603–1658*, London, 1986. Integrates recent interpretations. The best survey out of several available.

• Kahr, M. M., *Velázquez: The Art of Painting*, New York, 1976.

  Kamen, Henry, *The Iron Century: Social Change in Europe, 1559–1660*, New York, 1971. One of the most detailed and persuasive statements of the view that there was a "general crisis" in many different aspects of European life.

  Le Roy Ladurie, Emmanuel, *Carnival in Romans*, New York, 1979. A closeup view of social turmoil in France in 1580.

• Mattingly, Garrett, *The Armada*, Boston, 1959. Fascinating narrative; thoroughly reliable but reads like a novel.

• Monter, E. W., ed., *European Witchcraft*, New York, 1969. Selected readings with fine introductions by one of the world's leading experts.

Parker, Geoffrey, *The Dutch Revolt,* Ithaca, N.Y., 1977. Now the standard survey in English on the revolt of the Netherlands.

• _____, *Europe in Crisis: 1598–1648,* Brighton, Sussex, 1980. A primarily political narrative of war and revolution in Europe exclusive of England.

• Pennington, D. H., *Seventeenth-Century Europe,* London, 1970. An extremely thorough and reliable survey that follows the conventional periodization of treating a century bounded by the round numbers 1600 and 1700.

Pierson, Peter, *Philip II of Spain,* London, 1975. An absorbing attempt to study Philip's personality and actions in terms of the dominant assumptions of his age.

• Rabb, T. K., *The Struggle for Stability in Early Modern Europe,* New York, 1975. A stimulating essay arguing for a shift from crisis to stability around 1660.

Roots, Ivan, ed., *Cromwell, A Profile,* New York, 1973. A collection of readings on problems in interpretation; complements Fraser.

• Rosenberg, Jakob, *Rembrandt: Life and Work,* London, 1964.

• Russell, Conrad, *The Crisis of Parliaments: English History, 1509–1660,* New York, 1971. The best survey covering this broad range of time.

• Shearman, John, *Mannerism,* Baltimore, 1967. Treats trends in late-sixteenth-century architecture and sculpture as well as Manneristic painting.

• Steinberg, S. H., *The Thirty Years' War and the Conflict for European Hegemony, 1600–1660,* New York, 1966. The best scholarly account.

• Stone, Lawrence, *The Causes of the English Revolution, 1529–1642,* New York, 1972. A judicious analysis by one of the foremost social historians of our age.

• Thomas, Keith, *Religion and the Decline of Magic,* London, 1971. A marvelously insightful study of popular belief in England.

• Trevor-Roper, H. R., *The European Witch-Craze of the Sixteenth and Seventeenth Centuries and Other Essays,* New York, 1968. A collection of path-breaking essays.

• Walzer, Michael, *The Revolution of the Saints: A Study in the Origins of Radical Politics,* Cambridge, Mass., 1965. An attempt by a political scientist to demonstrate that English Puritanism was the earliest form of modern political radicalism.

• Wedgwood, C. V., *William the Silent,* London, 1944. A laudatory and urbanely written biography.

SOURCE MATERIALS

• Cervantes, Miguel de, *Don Quixote,* tr. Walter Starkie, New York, 1957.

Hobbes, Thomas, *Leviathan,* abridged by F. B. Randall, New York, 1964.

• Montaigne, Michel de, *Essays,* tr. J. M. Cohen, Baltimore, 1958.

Pascal, Blaise, *Pensées,* French-English ed., H. F. Stewart, London, 1950.

Sprenger, Jakob, and H. Kramer, *The Malleus Maleficarum,* tr. M. Summers, 2nd ed., London, 1948. A frightful yet fascinating work, the *Malleus* ("The Hammer of Witches") was the most frequently used handbook of early-modern witchcraft prosecutors.

Chapter 16

THE ECONOMY AND SOCIETY OF EARLY-MODERN EUROPE

We ought to esteem and cherish those trades which we have in remote or far countries, for besides the increase in shipping and mariners thereby, the wares also sent thither and received from thence are far more profitable unto the kingdom than by our trades near at hand.

—Thomas Mun, *England's Treasure by Foreign Trade,* 1630

In nearly every state in Europe citizens are divided into the three orders of nobles, clergy, and people. . . . . Even Plato, although he intended all his citizens to enjoy an equality of rights and privileges, divided them into the three orders of guardians, soldiers and labourers. All this goes to show that there never was a commonwealth, real or imaginary, even if conceived in the most popular terms, where citizens were in truth equal in all rights and privileges. Some always have more, some less than the rest.

—Jean Bodin, *Six Books of the Commonwealth,* 1570

Any study of early-modern European society must concern itself with change, with the factors that in the two hundred years after 1600 were powerful enough to produce the political upheaval of the French Revolution and the economic stimulus for the Industrial Revolution. Unquestionably, the most profound change during that period was economic. By the latter part of the eighteenth century, the freebooting overseas expansionism that had begun in the sixteenth century with the Spanish conquistadors had ended with Europe at the center of a vast system of worldwide trade. Commerce on this increasingly global scale had given birth to institutions fashioned for its support, and had altered patterns of living among those caught up in its overpowering dynamic. Banks and joint-stock companies financed international commercial ventures. New urban workshops responded to the intensified demand for manufactured goods.

Economic change

As international banking developed into a highly sophisticated profession, its practitioners became powerful men. As urban workshops imposed new conditions and habits, the urban artisan was forced to bend uncomfortably to unfamiliar demands.

European society as a whole found bending no more comfortable. Change was imposed upon national communities which, in many cases, were still defined according to the hierarchies of the Middle Ages: landlord and peasant, nobleman and serf. Each order was expected to acknowledge its inherent obligations and responsibilities, as each was assumed to be part of an organic and divinely sanctioned communal whole. Where, within this preordained structure, was the independent commercial entrepreneur or the dispossessed laborer supposed to fit? Tension of this sort between old forms and new realities was further exacerbated by the general crisis that we analyzed in the preceding chapter. Change produced by economic expansion and dislocation occurred against the background of civil and religious turmoil that tore much of Europe to pieces in the seventeenth century, and against an equally disruptive cycle of demographic swings caused by warfare and disease, by good weather one year, bad weather—and hence famine—the next. Those were the changes closest to the lives of most Europeans, the men and women still bound to the land, for whom, as the French historian Pierre Goubert has observed, "death was at the center of life, just as the graveyard was at the center of the village." The concerns of this chapter are thus both the economic and social circumstances that represented change, and the habits and traditions that were making change complex and difficult.

1. CAPITALISM, MERCANTILISM, AND THE COMMERCIAL REVOLUTION

The early-modern world of commerce and industry was governed by the assumptions of capitalism and mercantilism. Reduced to its simplest terms, capitalism is a system of production, distribution, and exchange, in which accumulated wealth is invested by private owners for the sake of gain. Its essential features are private enterprise, competition for markets, and business for profit. Generally it involves the wage system as a method of payment of workers; that is, a mode of payment based not on the amount of wealth they create, but rather upon their willingness to compete with one another for jobs. Capitalism represented a direct challenge to the semi-static economy of the medieval guilds, in which production and trade were supposed to be conducted for the benefit of society and with only a reasonable charge for the service rendered, instead of unlimited profits. Capitalism is a system designed to encourage commercial expansion beyond the local level, on a national and international scale. Guildmasters had neither the money (capital) to support nor the knowledge to organize and direct commercial enterprises beyond their own towns. Activity on that wider scale demanded the resources and expertise of wealthy and experienced entrepreneurs. These men, who usually started as merchants operating over a wide area and ended as bankers, could afford to invest in large quantities of manufactured goods, and if necessary, to hold them unsold until they could command a high price. The capitalist entrepreneur studied patterns of international trade. He knew where markets were and how to manipulate them to his advantage.

Capitalism is a system designed to reward the individual. In contrast, mercantilist doctrine emphasized direct governmental intervention in economic policy to increase the general prosperity of the state. Mercantilism was by no means a new idea. It was in fact a variation on the medieval notion that the populace of any particular town comprised a community with a common wealth, and that the economic well-being of such communities depended on the willingness of that populace to work at whatever task God or their rulers assigned them to benefit the community as a whole. Membership in a particular order within the community ensured to men and women the privileges of that order. In the case of the poor, this meant no more than protection from unfair prices and from starvation. In return for such protection, members of the community willingly placed themselves under the regimentation that guild restrictions and town ordinances imposed.

*The medieval origins of
mercantilism*

The mercantilism of the seventeenth and eighteenth centuries translated this earlier concept of community as a privileged, but regimented, economic unit from the level of towns to the level of the entire state. This translation represented not so much a complete change as it did the extension and elaboration of theories and practices that had governed the policies of earlier rulers. The conquest and subsequent plundering of the New World by Spain was an instance of mercantilism at work on a grand scale. The Statute of Artificers, passed by the English Parliament in 1563, which established a customary "fair" wage scale applicable to all laborers, instituted economic privilege and regimentation at the national level.

Mercantilism and the state

Mercantile theory held that a state's power depended on its actual, calculable wealth, expressed in terms of the amount of gold and silver bullion in its possession at any given time. A state amassed bullion by ensuring itself as favorable a balance of trade as possible. Hence the degree to which a state could remain self-sufficient, importing as little as necessary while exporting as much as possible, was the clearest gauge not only of its economic prosperity but of its power. This doctrine had profound effects on state policy. First, it led to the establishment and development of overseas colonies. Colonies, mercantilists reasoned, would, as part of the national community, provide it with raw materials, including precious metals in some instances, which would otherwise have to be obtained outside the community. Second,

Definition of wealth

it inspired state governments to encourage industrial production and trade, both sources of revenue which would increase the state's income. And finally, it persuaded policy-makers to discourage domestic consumption, since goods purchased on the home market reduced the goods available for export. Government policy was thus to keep wages low, so that laborers would not have money to spend for more than it took to provide them with basic food and shelter.

Mercantilism in practice

Although most western European statesmen were prepared to endorse mercantilist goals in principle, the degree to which their policies reflected those goals varied according to national circumstance. Spain, despite its insistence on closed colonial markets and its determination to amass a fortune in bullion, never succeeded in attaining the economic self-sufficiency that mercantilist theory demanded. The Spaniards therefore found it necessary to exchange their bullion for Flemish, French, and English manufactured goods which they were unable to supply to either their home market or to their colonies. Mercantilism, which appealed at least in theory to the rulers in Madrid, had little attraction for the merchants of Amsterdam. The Dutch rejected the governmental centralization implicit in the mercantilist notion of the sovereign state as an economic unit which they associated with the hated regime of Philip II of Spain. They further recognized that the United Provinces were too small to permit them to achieve economic self-sufficiency. Throughout the seventeenth and eighteenth centuries the Dutch remained dedicated in principle and practice to free trade, often investing, contrary to mercantilist doctrine, in the commercial enterprises of other countries and promoting national prosperity by encouraging the rest of Europe to rely upon Amsterdam as a hub of international finance and trade. The Dutch commitment to free trade did not extend to their colonial preserves which remained closed to their commercial rivals. It was the French and the English who combined, in differing degrees, governmental centralization and independent commercial enterprise most consistently and effectively and who became the most successful practitioners of mercantilism in early-modern Europe.

*Capitalism and
mercantilism: a
commercial revolution*

The goal of capitalism was a commercial system that would make individuals rich. The goal of mercantilism was a system that would make the state powerful. Though they differed as to ends, the two systems functioned compatibly together for most of the early-modern period. Together, governments and entrepreneurs designed new institutions that facilitated the expansion of global commerce during the seventeenth and eighteenth centuries and effected what has come to be called a Commercial Revolution.

*Elements of the
Commercial Revolution:
(1) increased capital*

Enterprise on this new scale depended on the availability of capital for investment. And that capital was generated primarily by a gradual increase in agricultural prices throughout much of the period. Had that increase been sharp, it would probably have produced enough hunger and suffering to retard rather than stimulate economic growth.

Merchants' Houses in Seventeenth-Century Amsterdam. This engraving depicts not only the opulence of middle-class life in a thriving commercial capital, but also the spirit of civic unity, expressed by the crowds gathered for a public celebration. (Several of the principal thoroughfares of Amsterdam are canals.)

Had there been no increase, however, the resulting stagnation produced by marginal profits would have proved equally detrimental to expansion. Agricultural entrepreneurs had surplus capital to invest in trade; bankers put that surplus to use to expand their commercial enterprises. Together, capitalist investors and merchants profited.

Banks played a vital role in the history of this expansion. Strong religious and moral disapproval of lending money at interest meant that banking had enjoyed a dubious reputation in the Middle Ages. Because the Church did come to allow profit-making on commercial risks, however, banks in Italy and Germany were organized under family auspices, the most notable examples being the fourteenth- and fifteenth-century operations of the Medici in Florence and the Fuggers of Augsburg. The Fuggers lent money to kings and bishops, and served as broker to the pope for the sale of indulgences. The rise of these private financial houses was followed by the establishment of government banks, reflecting the mercantilist goal of serving the monetary needs of the state. The first such institution, the Bank of Sweden, was founded in 1657. The Bank of England was established in 1694, at a time when England's emergence as a world commercial power guaranteed that institution a leading role in international finance.

(2) the rise of banking

The growth of banking was necessarily accompanied by the adoption of various aids to financial transactions on a large scale, further evidence of a commercial revolution. Credit facilities were extended in such a way that a merchant in Amsterdam could purchase goods from a merchant in Venice by means of a bill of exchange issued by an Amsterdam bank. The Venetian merchant would obtain his money by depositing the bill of exchange in his local bank. Later, the two banks would settle their accounts by comparing balances. Among the other facilities for the expansion of credit were the adoption of a system of payment by check in local transactions and the issuance of bank notes as a substitute for gold and silver. Both of these devices were invented by the Italians and were gradually adopted in northern Europe. The system of payment by check was particularly important in increasing the volume of trade, since the credit resources of the banks could now be expanded far beyond the actual amounts of cash in their vaults.

International commercial expansion called forth larger units of business organization. The prevailing unit of production and trade in the Middle Ages was the shop or store owned by an individual or a family. Partnerships were also quite common, in spite of the grave disadvantage of unlimited liability of each of its members for the debts of the entire firm. Obviously no one of these units was well adapted to business involving heavy risks and a huge investment of capital. The attempt to devise a more suitable business organization resulted in the formation of *regulated companies*. The regulated company was an association of merchants banded together for a common venture. Members did not pool their resources but agreed merely to cooperate for their mutual advantage and to abide by certain definite regulations. Usually the purpose of the combination was to maintain a monopoly of trade in some part of the world. Assessments were often paid by the members for the upkeep of docks and warehouses and especially for protection against "interlopers," as those traders were called who attempted to break into the monopoly. A leading example of this type of organization was an English company known as the Merchant Adventurers, established for the purpose of trade with the Netherlands and Germany.

The Commercial Revolution was facilitated in the seventeenth century when the regulated company was largely superseded by a new type of organization at once more compact and broader in scope. This was the *joint-stock company,* formed through the issuance of shares of capital to a considerable number of investors. Those who purchased the shares might or might not take part in the work of the company. Whether they did or not, they were joint owners of the business and therefore entitled to share in its profits in accordance with the amount they had invested. The joint-stock company had advantages over the partnership and the regulated company. First, it was a permanent unit, not subject to reorganization every time one of its members died or withdrew. And second, it made possible a much larger accumulation of capital, through a wide distribution of shares. Its organization

The Lyons Stock Exchange. Built in 1749, the stylish and impressive facade of the structure bespeaks the prominent role of commerce in French society.

and methods resembled to a degree those of the modern corporation. Yet the joint-stock company of the early-modern period is best understood not so much as a conscious precursor of capitalist endeavor as a pragmatic attempt at commercial expansion by both individuals and the state, its structure dictated by present opportunity and circumstance. Initially, for example, the Dutch United East India Company, one of the early joint-stock ventures, had expected to pay off its investors ten years after its founding in 1602, much as regulated companies had. Yet when that time came, the directors recognized the impossibility of the plan. By 1612, the company's assets were scattered—as ships, wharves, warehouses, and cargoes—across the globe. As a result, the directors urged those anxious to realize their profits to sell their shares on the Amsterdam exchange to other eager investors, thereby ensuring the sustained operation of their enterprise and, in the process, establishing a practice of continuous financing that was soon to become common.

While most of the early joint-stock companies were founded for commercial ventures, some were organized later in industry. A number of the outstanding trading combinations were also *chartered companies.* They held charters from the government granting a monopoly of the trade in a certain locality and conferring extensive authority over the inhabitants, and were thus an example of the way capitalist and mercantilist interests might coincide. Through a charter of this kind, the British East India Company undertook the exploitation of vast territories on the Indian subcontinent, and remained virtual ruler there until the end of the eighteenth century.

A final important feature of the Commercial Revolution was the development of a more efficient money economy. Money had been used widely since the revival of trade in the eleventh century. Neverthe-

Chartered companies

(5) a money economy

The dangers of expansion

The South Sea Bubble

less, there were few coins with a value that was recognized other than locally. By 1300, the gold ducat of Venice and the gold florin of Florence had come to be accepted in Italy and also in the international markets of northern Europe. But no country could be said to have had a uniform monetary system. Coins issued by kings circulated side by side with the money of foreign states. Moreover, the types of currency were modified frequently, and the coins themselves were often debased. A common method by which kings expanded their own personal revenues was to increase the proportion of cheaper metals in the coins they minted. The growth of trade and industry in the Commercial Revolution accentuated the need for more stable and uniform monetary systems. The problem was solved by the adoption of a standard system of money by every important state to be used for all transactions within its borders. Much time elapsed, however, before the reform was complete. England began the construction of a uniform coinage during the reign of Queen Elizabeth, but the task was not finished until late in the seventeenth century. Indeed, the French did not succeed in reducing their money to its modern standard of simplicity and convenience until the early nineteenth century.

The Commercial Revolution, although it contributed to the prosperity of both individuals and states, was accompanied by serious risks and consequences occasionally disastrous to investors and to national economies. One major result of overseas expansion was the severe inflation caused by the increase in the supply of silver, which plagued Europe at the end of the sixteenth century (see above, p. 513). Price fluctuations, in turn, produced further economic instability. Businessmen were tempted to expand their enterprises too rapidly; bankers extended credit so liberally that their principal borrowers, especially noblemen, often defaulted on loans. In both Spain and Italy, failure of wages to keep pace with rising prices brought severe and continuing hardships to the lower classes. Impoverishment was rife in the cities, and bandits flourished in the rural areas. In Spain, ruined nobles found themselves compelled to join the throngs of vagrants who wandered from city to city. At the end of the fifteenth century the great Florentine bank of the Medici closed its doors. The middle of the century that followed saw numerous bankruptcies in Spain and the decline of the Fuggers in Germany, while England, Holland, and to some extent France waxed prosperous.

The period between 1540 and 1620 was characterized by an alternation of economic booms and recessions, which were followed by outbreaks of feverish speculation. These reached their climax early in the eighteenth century. The most notorious were the South Sea Bubble and the Mississippi Bubble. The former was the result of inflation of the stock of the South Sea Company in England, whose offer to assume the national debt led to unwarranted confidence in the company's future. When buoyant hopes gave way to fears, investors made frantic attempts to dispose of their shares for whatever they would bring. A crash which came in 1720 was the inevitable result.

During the years when the South Sea Bubble was being inflated in England, the French were going through a similar wave of speculative madness. In 1715 a Scotsman by the name of John Law, who had been compelled to flee from British soil for killing his rival in a love intrigue, settled in Paris, after various successful gambling adventures in other cities. He persuaded the regent of France to adopt his scheme for paying off the national debt through the issuance of paper money and to grant him the privilege of organizing the Mississippi Company for the colonization and exploitation of Louisiana. As the government loans were redeemed, those who received the money were encouraged to buy stock in the company. Soon the shares began to soar, ultimately reaching a price forty times their original value. Nearly everyone who could scrape together a bit of surplus cash rushed forward to participate in the scramble for riches. Stories were told of butchers and tailors who were supposed to have become millionaires by buying a few shares and holding them for a rise in price. But as the realization grew that the company would never be able to pay more than a nominal dividend on the stock at its inflated value, the more cautious investors began selling their holdings. The alarm spread, and soon all were as anxious to sell as they had been to buy. In 1720 the Mississippi Bubble burst in a wild panic. Thousands of people who had sold good property to buy the shares at fantastic prices were ruined.

Joint-stock companies in France were more directly dependent on the state than was the case elsewhere, a reflection of French dedication to mercantilist theory. In most cases French companies were floated under governmental auspices; courtiers—and the king himself—were heavy investors. Agents of the state played a direct role in their management, sometimes to the company's ultimate disadvantage. The French East India Company, for example, was compelled by state direction to govern its colonies in accordance with the laws of Paris, a fact which, one historian has remarked, "reminds one of the complaint that French progress in the Sahara was retarded by the refusal of the camel to accommodate its habits to administrative regulations made in Paris." [1] Even though companies elsewhere were less subject to governmental regulation than they were in France, government and commerce generally worked to promote each other's interests. In time of war, governments called upon commercial capitalists to assist in the financing of their campaigns. When England went to war against France in 1689, for example, the government had no long-range borrowing mechanism available to it; during the next quarter century the merchant community, through the Bank of England, assisted the government in raising over £170 million and in stabilizing the national

---

[1]G. N. Clark, *The Seventeenth Century* (New York, 1961), p. 39.

debt at £40 million. In return, trading companies used the war to increase long-distance commercial traffic at the expense of their French enemy, and exerted powerful pressure on the government to secure treaties that would work to their advantage.

2. COLONIZATION AND OVERSEAS TRADE

Spanish colonization

The institutions of the Commercial Revolution—banks, credit facilities, joint-stock companies, monetary systems—were designed specifically to assist both capitalist entrepreneurs and mercantilist policy-makers in the development and exploitation of overseas colonies and trading posts, the most visible evidence of the economic expansionism of early-modern Europe. Following the exploits of the conquistadors, the Spanish established colonial governments in Peru and in Mexico, which they controlled from Madrid in proper mercantilist fashion by a Council of the Indies. In return for a protection fee, as distinct from the royalty of one-fifth of all bullion extracted from the colonies, the Spanish navy attempted to protect treasure ships from attacks by the French, English, and Dutch. The mercantilist governments of Philip II and his successors were determined to defend their monopoly in the New World. They issued trading licenses to none but Spanish merchants; exports and imports passed only through the port of Seville (later the more navigable port of Cadiz), where they were registered at the government-operated Casa de Contratación, or customs house. In their heyday, Spanish traders circled the globe. Because of the lucrative market for silver in East Asia, they found it well worth their while to establish an outpost in far-off Manila in the Philippines, where Asian silk was exchanged for South American bullion. The silk was then shipped back to Spain by way of the Mexican ports of Acapulco and Veracruz.

Challenges to Spanish predominance

Spain's predominance did not deter other countries from attempting to win a share of the treasure for themselves. Probably the boldest challengers were the English, and their leading buccaneer the "sea dog" Sir Francis Drake, who three times raided the east and west coasts of Spanish America and who, in 1587, the year before the Armada set sail on its ill-fated voyage north, "singed the beard of the Spanish king" by attacking the Spanish fleet at its anchorage in Cadiz harbor. Yet despite dashing heroics of that sort, the English could do no more than dent the Spanish trade.

English colonization

Reluctantly forsaking the search for the quick profits Spain was extracting from its colonial gold and silver mines, English colonists began to establish agricultural settlements in North America and the Caribbean basin. The first permanent, though ultimately unsuccessful, colony was established at Jamestown, in Virginia, in 1607. Over the next forty years, 80,000 English emigrants founded over twenty autonomous settlements in the New World. In this instance, however,

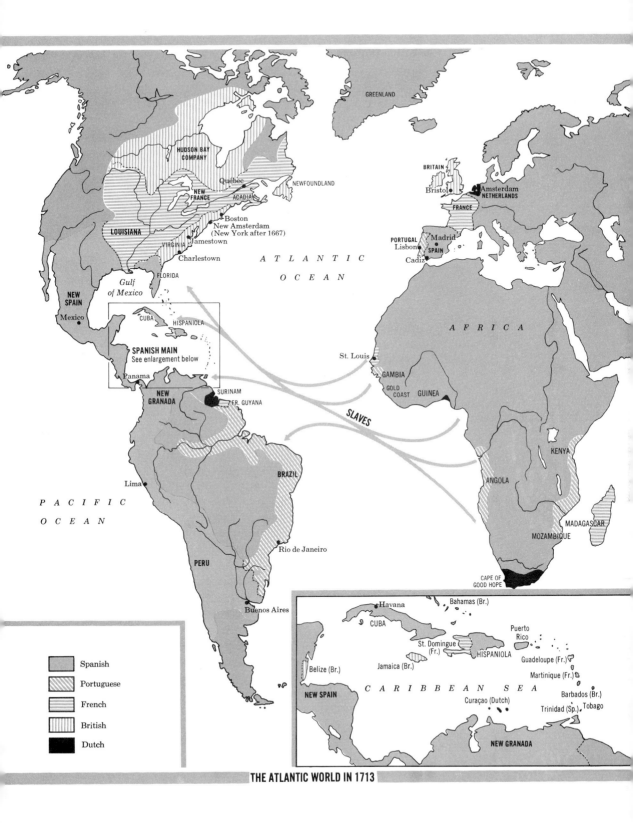

GREENLAND

HUDSON BAY
COMPANY

Québec
NEW
FRANCE   ACADIA   NEWFOUNDLAND

LOUISIANA

Boston
New Amsterdam
(New York after 1667)
VIRGINIA   Jamestown

Charlestown

FLORIDA

NEW
SPAIN

Mexico

Gulf
of Mexico

CUBA
HISPANIOLA

SPANISH MAIN
See enlargement below

Panama

NEW
GRANADA   SURINAM
FR. GUYANA

BRAZIL

Lima

PACIFIC

OCEAN

PERU

Rio de Janeiro

Buenos Aires

ATLANTIC

OCEAN

BRITAIN
Bristol   Amsterdam
NETHERLANDS
FRANCE

PORTUGAL   Madrid
Lisbon   SPAIN
Cadiz

AFRICA

St. Louis

GAMBIA
GOLD
COAST   GUINEA

ANGOLA

SLAVES

KENYA

MADAGASCAR

MOZAMBIQUE

CAPE OF
GOOD HOPE

Spanish
Portuguese
French
British
Dutch

Havana   Bahamas (Br.)

CUBA   Puerto
Rico
St. Domingue
(Fr.)
HISPANIOLA
Guadeloupe (Fr.)
Jamaica (Br.)
Martinique (Fr.)
Belize (Br.)

C A R I B B E A N   S E A   Barbados (Br.)
Curaçao (Dutch)
NEW SPAIN   Trinidad (Sp.)   Tobago

NEW GRANADA

THE ATLANTIC WORLD IN 1713

religious freedom, rather than economic gain, was often the primary motive of the settlers. The renowned band of "pilgrim fathers" that landed on the New England shores in 1620 were but one of a large number of dissident groups that sought to escape the attempts of the English Kings, James I and Charles I, to impose religious conformity on their subjects. Religion also played a role in the efforts of the French to penetrate the hinterlands of North America. Roman Catholic missionaries, intent upon the conversion of native Americans to Christianity, joined fur traders in journeys across the continent to the Great Lakes and the Mississippi.

*The growth of English
colonial regulation*

Yet both England and France were quick to extract economic profit from their expanding colonial empires. England's agricultural colonies were producing crops in high demand throughout Europe. The success of colonial planters encouraged the governments of both Oliver Cromwell and Charles II to intervene in the management of their overseas economy. Navigation Acts, passed in 1651 and 1660, and rigorously enforced thereafter, decreed that all exports from English colonies to the mother country be carried in English ships, and forbade the direct exporting of certain "enumerated" products directly from the colonies to continental ports.

Sugar and tobacco

The most valuable of those products were sugar and tobacco. Sugar, virtually unknown in Europe earlier, had become a popular luxury by the end of the sixteenth century. Where once it had been considered no more than a medicine, one observer now noted that the wealthy were "devouring it out of gluttony." Sugarcane was raised in the West Indies after 1650 in rapidly increasing amounts. In the eighteenth century, the value of the sugar that England imported from its small island colonies there—Barbados, Jamaica, St. Kitts, and others—exceeded the value of its imports from the vast subcontinents of China and India. Although the tobacco plant was imported into Europe by the Spaniards about fifty years after the discovery of America, another half century passed before Europeans contracted the habit of smoking. At first the plant was believed to possess miraculous healing powers and was referred to as "divine tobacco" and "our holy herb nicotian." (The word "nicotine" derives from the name of the French ambassador to Portugal, Jean Nicot, who brought the tobacco plant to France.) The practice of smoking was popularized by English explorers, especially by Sir Walter Raleigh, who had learned to smoke while living among the Indians of Virginia. It spread rapidly through all classes of European society. Governments at first joined the Church in condemning the use of tobacco because of its socially and spiritually harmful effects, but by the end of the seventeenth century, having realized the profits to be made from its production, they were encouraging its use.

French colonial policy matured during the administration of Louis XIV's mercantilist finance minister, Jean Baptiste Colbert (1619–1683), who perceived of overseas expansion as an integral part of

The Dutch East India Company Warehouse and Timber Wharf at Amsterdam. The substantial warehouse, the stockpiles of lumber, and the company ship under construction in the foreground illustrate the degree to which overseas commerce could stimulate economy of the mother country.

state economic policy. He organized joint-stock companies to compete with those of the English. He encouraged the development of lucrative sugar-producing colonies in the West Indies, the largest of which was St. Dominique (present-day Haiti). France also dominated the interior of the North American continent. Frenchmen traded furs and preached Christianity to the Indians in a vast territory that stretched from Acadia and the St. Lawrence River in the northeast to Louisiana in the west. Yet the financial returns from these lands were hardly commensurate with their size. Furs, fish, and tobacco were exported to home markets, but not in sufficient amounts to match the profits from the sugar colonies of the Caribbean or from the line of trading posts the French maintained in India.

> *The French in America*

The Dutch were even more successful than both the English and the French in establishing a flourishing commercial empire in the seventeenth century. Their joint-stock East India Company, founded in 1602, rivaled its English counterpart in Asia, gaining firm control of Sumatra, Borneo, and the Moluccas, or Spice Islands, and driving Portuguese traders from an area where they had heretofore enjoyed an undisturbed commercial dominion. The result was a Dutch monopoly in pepper, cinnamon, nutmeg, mace, and cloves. The Dutch also secured an exclusive right to trade with the Japanese, and maintained outposts in China and India as well. In the Western Hemisphere, their achievements were less spectacular. Following a series of trade wars with England, they surrendered their North American colony of New Amsterdam (subsequently renamed New York) in 1667, re-

> *The Dutch in the Far East*

The decline of the Spanish and Portuguese empires

taining Surinam, off the northern coast of South America, as well as the islands of Curaçao and Tobago in the West Indies in compensation.

The fortunes of these commercial empires rose and fell in the course of the seventeenth and eighteenth centuries. The Spanish, mired in persistent economic lassitude and embroiled in a succession of expensive wars and domestic rebellions, were powerless to preserve the sanctity of their empire. Their merchant marine, once a match for cunning pirate-admirals like Drake, was by the middle of the seventeenth century unable to protect itself from attack by its more spirited commercial rivals. In a war with Spain in the 1650s, the English captured not only the island of Jamaica but treasure ships lying off the Spanish harbor of Cadiz. Further profit was obtained by bribing Spanish customs officials on a grand scale. During the second half of the century, two-thirds of the imported goods sold in Spanish colonies were smuggled in by Dutch, English, and French traders. By 1700, though Spain still possessed a colonial empire, it was one which lay at the mercy of its more dynamic rivals. Portugal, too, found it impossible to prevent foreign penetration of its colonial economies. The English worked diligently and successfully to win commercial advantages. They obtained concessions to export woolens duty-free into Portugal itself in return for similar preferential treatment for Portuguese wines. (The notorious affection of the English upper class for port wine dates from the signing of the Treaty of 1703.) English trade with the mother country led in time to English trade with the Portuguese colony of Brazil, indeed to the opening of commercial offices in Rio de Janeiro.

Dutch commerce

The Dutch, whose merchant fleet of over 16,000 vessels was the largest in Europe, were the masters of world trade throughout most of the seventeenth century. Dutch ships—about half the European total—not only sailed the high seas, but dominated the coastal carrying trade as well. To reduce the time of ocean voyages, Amsterdam shipyards developed the *fluitschip*. Longer and shallower than conventional craft, it was flat-bottomed and built of lightweight fir or pine, rather than oak. The *fluitschip* required only half the crew of regular ships, and cost half as much to build. The Dutch merchant marine ensured the position of Amsterdam as the world's premier trading center, the volume of Dutch commerce allowing Amsterdam merchants to undersell their English and French rivals. During the eighteenth century a growing Anglo-French rivalry in India stole the commercial spotlight from the Dutch spice monopoly in the Far East. The French and English East India Companies employed mercenaries to establish and expand trading areas such as Madras, Bombay, and Pondichéry. By exploiting indigenous industries, European capitalists continued to increase the flow of fine cotton textiles, tea, and spices which passed through these commercial depots on their way to Europe. The struggle for economic dominance in India was resolved in mid-century in En-

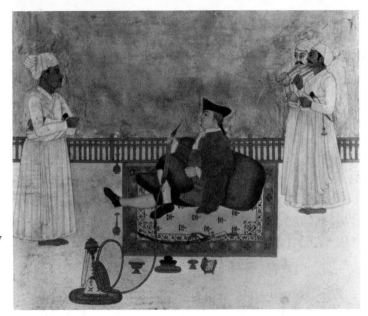

The Rewards of Commercial Exploitation. An English employee of the East India Company, enjoying his ease and his opium, as depicted by an eighteenth-century Indian artist.

gland's favor following a series of military clashes. As a sign of France's defeat, in 1769 the French East India Company was dissolved.

Despite the commercial importance of India, however, patterns of world trade came increasingly to be dominated by western routes that had developed in response to the lucrative West Indian sugar industry, and to the demand for slaves from Africa to work the plantations in the Caribbean. Here Britain, again, eventually assumed the lead. Typically, a ship might begin its voyage from New England with a consignment of rum and sail to Africa, where the rum would be exchanged for a cargo of slaves. From the west coast of Africa the ship would then cross the South Atlantic to the sugar colonies of Jamaica or Barbados, where slaves would be traded for molasses, which would make the final leg of the journey to New England, where it would be made into rum. A variant triangle might see cheap manufactured goods move from Bristol or Liverpool, in England, to Africa, where they would be traded for slaves. Those slaves would then be shipped to Virginia and exchanged for tobacco, which would be shipped to England and processed there for sale in continental markets. Other eighteenth-century trade routes were more direct: the Spanish, French, Portuguese, and Dutch all engaged in the slave trade between Africa and Central and South America; the Spanish attempted, vainly, to retain a mercantilist monopoly on direct trade between Cadiz and their South American colonies; others sailed from England, France, or North America to the Caribbean and back again. And of course trade continued to flourish between Europe and the Near and Far East. But the triangular western routes, dictated by the grim economic symbiosis of sugar and slaves, remained dominant.

Increasing dominance of western trade routes

The slave trade

The cultivation of sugar and tobacco depended on slave labor; and as demand for those products increased, so did the traffic in black slaves, without whose labor those products could not be raised or harvested. At the height of the Atlantic slave trade in the eighteenth century, somewhere between 75,000 and 90,000 blacks were shipped across the Atlantic yearly: 6 million in the eighteenth century, out of a total of over 9 million for the entire history of the trade. About 35 percent went to English and French Caribbean plantations, 5 percent (roughly 450,000) to North America, and the rest to the Portuguese colony of Brazil and to Spanish colonies in South America. Although run as a monopoly by various governments in the sixteenth and early seventeenth centuries, in its heyday the slave trade was open to private entrepreneurs, who operated ports on the West African coast. Traders exchanged cheap Indian cloth, metal goods, rum, and firearms with African slave merchants in return for their human cargo. Already disoriented and degraded by their capture at the hands of rival tribes, black men, women, and children were packed by the hundreds into the holds of slave ships for the gruesome "middle passage" across the Atlantic (so called to distinguish it from the ship's voyage from Europe to Africa, and from the slave colony back to Europe again). Shackled to the decks, without sanitary facilities, the black "cargo" suffered horribly; the mortality rate, however, remained at about 10 or 11 percent, not much higher than the rate for a normal sea voyage of one hundred days or more. Since traders had to invest as much as £10 per slave in their enterprise, they ensured that their consignment would reach its destination in good enough shape to be sold for a profit.

The ending of the trade

Not until the very end of the eighteenth century did Europeans protest this ghastly traffic. The trade was risky, dependent as it was on a good wind and fair weather, and competition was increasingly keen. Yet profits could run high, occasionally as much as 300 percent. Demand for slaves remained constant throughout the eighteenth cen-

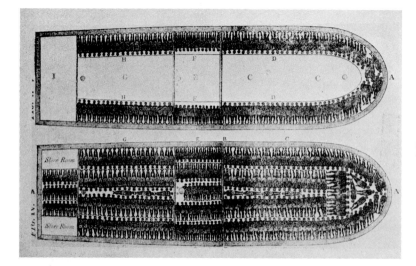

How Slaves Were Stowed Aboard Ship during the Middle Passage. Men were "housed" on the right; women on the left; children in the middle. The human cargo was jammed onto platforms six feet wide without sufficient headroom to permit an adult to sit up. This diagram is from evidence gathered by English abolitionists and depicts conditions on the Liverpool slave ship *Brookes.*

tury. By the 1780s, there were over 500,000 slaves on the largest French plantation island, St. Dominique, and 200,000 or more on the English counterpart, Jamaica. Those numbers reflected the expanding world market for slave-grown crops. As long as there was a market for the crops cultivated by slaves—as long as the economy relied to the extent it did upon slave labor—governments would remain unwilling to put an end to the system that, as one Englishman wrote in 1749, provided "an unexhaustible fund of wealth to this nation." Philosophers argued that though there was reason to rejoice that slavery had been banished from the continent of Europe (forgetting, apparently, the extent to which it continued to exist east of the Elbe in the form of serfdom), it remained a necessity in other parts of the world. Public pressure, first from Quakers and then from others motivated either by religious or humanitarian zeal, helped put an end to the trade in England in 1807, and to slavery itself in British colonies in 1833. Slavery in French colonies was abolished in 1793, but only after slaves had risen in massive revolt on St. Dominique. Elsewhere, in Latin and North America, slavery lasted well into the nineteenth century—in the United States, until the Civil War of 1861–1865.

The slave trade is an integral part of the history of the dramatic rise of English and French commerce during the eighteenth century. French colonial trade, valued at 25 million livres in 1716, rose to 263 million livres in 1789. In England, during roughly the same period, foreign trade increased in value from £10 million to £40 million, the latter amount more than twice that for France. These figures suggest the degree to which statecraft and private enterprise were bound to each other. If merchants depended on their government to provide a navy to protect and defend their overseas investments, governments depended equally on entrepreneurship, not only to generate money to build ships, but to sustain the trade upon which national power had come to rely so heavily.

The continuing rise of commerce

3. AGRICULTURE AND INDUSTRY

The pace of industrial change in early-modern Europe was not as dynamic as that of the Commercial Revolution and the expansion of overseas colonization and trade. Changes did occur, but less uniformly and dramatically than those we have been tracing. This is not surprising, since the major economic enterprise remained agricultural production, which, throughout much of the period, was generally carried on according to traditional techniques that kept the volume of production low. Yet by the end of the eighteenth century, tradition in some areas had yielded to innovation, with the result that production was increasing dramatically.

The predominance of agriculture

Most of the agricultural regions of seventeenth-century Europe consisted of open fields. In the north, these fields were usually large

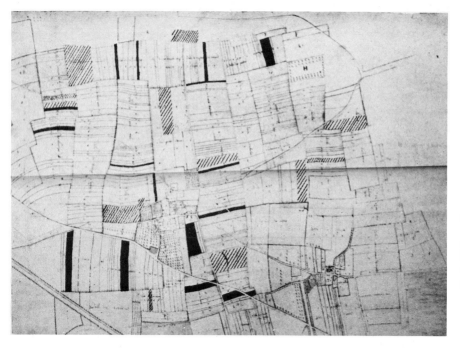

The Open-Field System in Northern France, 1738. Note the subdivision of large tracts into narrow strips, each owned by different proprietors.

sections of land, divided into long, narrow strips; in the south, the strips tended to reflect the more irregular shape of local landscapes. Although one or two rich aristocrats might own as much as three-fourths of the land in an open-field village, that land did not comprise one solid block. Instead it was made up of a great many plots, seldom contiguous, within the various open fields that surrounded the village. A large property owner's *desmesne* farm—which he worked with hired laborers for his own direct profit—and his tenant farms—those which he leased out to peasants—all consisted of these bits and pieces of land which lay alongside other bits and pieces that belonged to other landowners—very often small peasant proprietors. Each large open field thus resembled a patchwork quilt. Under these circumstances, in order for the fields to be cultivated with any degree of efficiency, all the "patches" had to be planted with the same crop, and sown, cultivated, and harvested together. Once the harvest was in, livestock was often turned into the fields to graze. One consequence of this practice was that crops were cut with a primitive sickle, which left more stubble for sheep and cattle, rather than with the far more efficient scythe. Inefficiency was indeed the hallmark of the open-field system, an inefficiency which those who owned large tracts of land grew more and more unwilling to tolerate. The Commercial Revolution encouraged landlords, particularly those in England and Holland, to compete for markets as capitalist agricultural entrepreneurs. In doing so, they looked for ways to improve the yield on their lands.

By the end of the eighteenth century a great many English and Dutch landlords had resolved the problem of low production by adopting a full range of innovative farming techniques, the most drastic of which was the enclosure of open fields to allow for more systematic and therefore more productive farming. "Enclosure" was the term for land reorganization within a traditional village community. The earliest enclosures in England took place in the fifteenth and sixteenth centuries and entailed the conversion of lands into fenced-off sheep meadows. Because of the great profits to be accrued from wool, some landlords converted common pastures that hitherto had supported peasant livestock into their own preserves for sheep-raising, thus threatening the livelihood of entire peasant communities. As Thomas More wrote in his *Utopia* (1516), "sheep that used to be so meek and eat so little now are becoming so greedy and wild that they devour men themselves . . . for they leave no land free for the plough."

Enclosure

Enclosure was more easily accomplished in those countries—England most notably—where the manorial emphasis had given way to a system of absolute property rights and wage labor. Where the tradition of "common" rights to grazing and foraging was strong, as in France, landlords found it far more difficult to impose a new economic order. Monarchs tended to oppose enclosure since it promised to enrich further a rival noble class. In seventeenth-century France the monarchy needed an economically stable peasantry to support its expanding tax programs, and therefore worked to secure peasants in the customary tenure of their farms. Thus defended, the peasants were able to resist effectively attempts at enclosure launched by large landholders. English property owners were more fortunate, taking advantage of the absence of royal opposition during the Cromwellian period to enclose on a broad scale.

Absolute vs. common property rights

The really dramatic enclosure movement in England took place between 1710 and 1810 when landlords began to engage in the practice of "scientific farming." They realized that by introducing new crops and farming methods they could reduce the amount of fallow lands and bring in higher yields, and thus higher profits. The most important new crops with which landowners experimented were clover, alfalfa, and related varieties of leguminous plants. These reduced fertility much less than cereal grains and helped to improve the quality of the soil by gathering nitrogen and making the ground more porous. Another new crop that had a similar effect was the turnip. The greatest propagandist for the planting of this unattractive vegetable was Viscount Charles Townshend (1674–1738), a prominent aristocrat and politician, who toward the end of his life gained the nickname of "Turnip" Townshend because of his dedication to the use of the turnip in new crop-rotation systems.

Scientific farming

Clover, alfalfa, and turnips not only helped do away with fallow lands; they also provided excellent winter food for animals, thereby aiding the production of more and better livestock. More livestock also meant more manure. Accordingly, intensive manuring became another way in which scientific farmers could eliminate the need for fallow land. Other improvements in farming methods introduced in

Improved farming techniques

the period were more intensive hoeing and weeding, and the use of the seed drill for planting grain. The latter eliminated the old wasteful method of sowing grain by hand, much of it remaining on top to be eaten by birds.

The process of enclosure

Scientific farming dictated the necessity of enclosures because the "improving" landlord needed flexibility to experiment as he wished. He could not plant one narrow open strip with turnips while peasants were continuing to rotate all the contiguous areas on the basis of the age-old three-field system. Instead, he had to organize his land into fenced-off compact plots, to leave no doubt as to which territory was his own, to maximize efficiency in experimentation, and to exclude stray grazing animals. The introduction of fodder crops such as clover eliminated the large landowner's need for common pastures, since he could now graze his livestock on his own fields. Hence, most eighteenth-century enclosures were of previously common land.

The social consequences of enclosure

Enclosure was a change that had major social consequences where it occurred. Village life under the open-field system was communal to the extent that decisions as to which crops were to be grown where and when had to be arrived at jointly. Common land afforded the poor, not only a place to tether a cow, to fish, or to gather firewood, but to breathe at least a bit of the air of social freedom. Enclosure cost villagers their modest freedoms, as well as the traditional right to help determine how the community's subsistence economy was to be managed. Cottagers (very small landholders) and squatters, who had over generations established a customary right to the use of common lands, were reduced to the rank of landless laborers.

The increasingly capitalistic basis of European agriculture

On the Continent, except for Holland, there was nothing comparable to the English advance in scientific farming. Nor, with the notable exception of Spain, was there a pronounced enclosure movement as in England and the Low Countries. Yet despite that fact, European food production became increasingly capitalistic in the seventeenth and eighteenth centuries. Landlords leased farms to tenants and reaped profits as rent. Often they allowed tenants to pay rent in the form of half their crops. This system of sharecropping was most prevalent in France, Italy, and Spain. Farther east, in Prussia, Poland, Hungary, and Russia, landowners continued to rely on unpaid serfs to till the land. Wherever the market economy replaced the economy of local self-sufficiency, it brought change in its wake.

Introduction of maize and potatoes

The eighteenth century saw the introduction of two crops from the New World, maize (Indian corn) and the potato, that eventually resulted in the provision of a more adequate diet for the poor. Since maize can only be grown in areas with substantial periods of sunny and dry weather, its cultivation spread through Italy and the southeastern part of the Continent. Whereas an average ear of grain would yield only about four seeds for every one planted, an ear of maize would yield about seventy or eighty. That made it a "miracle" crop, filling granaries where they had been almost empty before. The potato was an equally miraculous innovation for the European north. Its advantages were numerous: potatoes could be grown on the poorest, sandiest, or wettest of lands where nothing else could be raised; they could be fitted into the smallest of patches. Raising potatoes even in small patches was profitable because the yield of potatoes was extraordinarily abundant. Finally, the potato provided an inexpensive means of improving the human diet. It is rich in calories, and contains many vitamins and minerals. Northern European peasants initially resisted growing and eating potatoes. Clergymen taught them to fear the plant because it is not mentioned in the Bible. Some claimed that it transmitted leprosy. Still others insisted that it was a cause of flatulence, a property acknowledged by the French *Encyclopédie* in 1765, although the writers added: "What is a little wind to the vigorous organs of the peasants and workers?" Yet in the course of the eighteenth century the poor grew accustomed to the potato, although sometimes after considerable pressure. Frederick the Great compelled Prussian peasants to cultivate potatoes until the crop achieved acceptance and became a staple throughout much of northern Germany. By about 1800 the average north German peasant family ate potatoes as a main course at least once a day. In the same period the potato was also introduced into Ireland and England. In the 1840s, it was all that stood between millions of Irish and starvation.

Agriculture was not the only commercial enterprise in early-modern rural Europe. Increasingly, manufactured goods—particularly textiles—were being produced in the countryside, as entrepreneurs battled to circumvent artisanal and guild restrictions that limited production in urban manufacturing centers. Unfettered rural industry was a response to the constantly growing demand of new markets created by the increase in regional, national, and international commerce. Entrepreneurs made use of the so-called putting-out system to address this demand and to reap large profits. Unhampered by guild regulations, which in medieval times had restricted the production and distribution of textiles to maintain price levels, merchants would buy up a stock of raw material, most often wool or flax, which they would then "put out," or supply, to rural workers for carding (combing the fibers) and spinning. Once spun, the yarn or thread was collected by the merchant and passed to rural weavers, who wove it into cloth. Collected once more, the material was processed by other workers at bleaching or dyeing shops, and collected for a final time by the entrepreneur who then either sold it to a wholesaler or directly to retail customers.

Although the putting-out phenomenon occurred throughout Europe, it was usually concentrated regionally. Most industrial areas specialized in the production of particular commodities, based on the availability of raw materials. Flanders was a producer of linens; Verviers (in present-day Belgium) of woolens; Silesia of linens and coal. As markets—regional, national, and international—developed, these rural

The Title Page of One of Many Agricultural Tracts Available to Capitalist Farmers Interested in Improving Their Output

Rural manufacturing: the putting-out system

Regional specialization

manufacturing areas grew accordingly. Industries employed home-workers by the thousands. A large textile firm in Abbéville, France, provided work to 1,800 in central workshops but to 10,000 in their own homes. One of the largest woolen manufacturers in Linz, Austria, in 1786 was employing 35,000, of whom over 29,000 were domestic spinners.

Family production

Rural workers accepted the putting-out system as a means of staving off poverty, or possible starvation in years of particularly bad harvests. Domestic textile production involved the entire family. Even the youngest children could participate in the process of cleaning the raw wool. Older children carded. Wives and husbands spun or wove. Spinning, until the invention of the jenny at the end of the eighteenth century (see below, p. 731) was a far more time-consuming process than weaving, which had been speeded considerably by the invention of the fly-shuttle by the Englishman John Kay in the early eighteenth century, a mechanical device that automatically returned the shuttle to its starting place after it had been "thrown" across the loom.

Advantages of putting-out

In addition to providing extra income, the putting-out system brought other advantages to rural homeworkers. They could regulate the pace of their labor to some degree, and could abandon it altogether when farm work was available during the planting and harvest seasons. Their ability to work at home was not an unmixed blessing, for conditions in cottages that were wretchedly built and poorly ventilated were often exceedingly cramped and unpleasant, especially when workers were compelled to accommodate a bulky loom within their already crowded living quarters. But domestic labor, however unpleasant, was preferable in the minds of most to work away from home in a shop, where conditions might be even more oppressive under the watchful eye of an unsympathetic master. There were also advantages for the merchant-entrepreneur, who benefited not only from the absence of guild restrictions, but from the fact that none of his capital was tied up in expensive equipment. (Spinners usually owned their spinning wheels; weavers either owned or rented their looms.) Governments appreciated the advantages of the system too, viewing it as one way to alleviate the ever-present problem of rural poverty. The French abolished the traditional privileges of urban manufacturers in 1762, acknowledging by law what economic demand had long since established: the widespread practice of unrestricted rural domestic production. By that time, the putting-out system prevailed not only in northern France, but in the east and northeast of England, in Flanders, and in much of northern Germany—all areas where a mixed agricultural and manufacturing economy made economic sense to those engaged in it as entrepreneurs and producers.

Later generations, looking back nostalgically on the putting-out system, often compared it favorably to the factory system which displaced it. Life within the system's "family economy" was seldom other

Left: *"Rustic Courtship."* This detail from an etching (1785) by the English satirist Thomas Rowlandson suggests the advantages of doorstep domestic industry: natural lighting, improved ventilation, and a chance to converse with visitors. Work under these self-paced conditions, though usually long and hard, was carried on to a personal rhythm. Right: *Artisan and Family* by Gerard ter Borch. This seventeenth-century wheelwright, though a skilled artisan, is nevertheless depicted as living on the brink of poverty. Sickness, a bad harvest, unemployment—any of these might easily drive him and his family over the edge.

than hard, however. While workers could set their own pace to some extent, they remained subject to the demands of small, often inexperienced entrepreneurs who, misjudging their markets, might overload spinners and weavers with work at one moment, then abandon them for lack of orders the next. Though it often kept families from starvation, putting-out did little to mitigate the monotony and harshness of their lives. The pressures of the system are crudely if eloquently expressed in an English ballad, in which the weaver husband responds to his wife's complaint that she has no time to sit at the "bobbin wheel," what with the washing and baking and milking she must do. No matter, the husband replies. She must "stir about and get things done./ For all things must aside be laid,/ when we want help about our trade."

Quality of life under the family system

Textiles were not the only manufactured goods produced in the countryside. In France, for example, metal-working was as much a rural as an urban occupation, with migrant laborers providing a work force for small, self-contained shops. In various parts of Germany,

Roadside Inn by Thomas Rowlandson. Coaching inns brought the outside world into the lives of isolated villagers. Note the absence of any clearly defined roadway.

Other rural manufacturing activities

the same sort of unregulated domestic manufacturing base prevailed: in the Black Forest for clock making, in Thuringia for toys. English production of coal increased from 200,000 tons a year in the 1550s to more than 3 million tons by the end of the seventeenth century; that of iron, another essentially rural enterprise, grew fivefold in the same period.

Rudimentary transportation systems

Rural industry flourished despite the fact that for most of the early-modern period transportation systems remained rudimentary. In all but a very few cases, roads were little more than ill-defined tracks, full of holes as much as four feet deep, and all but impassable in the rain, when carts and carriages might stay mired in deep ruts for days. One of the few paved roads ran from Paris to Orléans, the main river port of France, but that was a notable exception. In general, no one could travel more than 12 miles an hour—"post haste" at a gallop on horseback—and speed such as that could be achieved only at the expense of fresh horses at each stage of the ride. A journey of 60 miles over good roads could be accomplished in twenty-four hours, provided that the weather was fair. To travel by coach from Paris to Lyons, a distance of approximately 250 miles, took ten days. Merchants ran great risks when they shipped perishable goods. Breakables were not expected to survive for more than 15 miles. Transportation of goods by boat along coastal routes was far more reliable than shipment overland. In 1675, English merchants calculated that it was cheaper to ship coal 300 miles by water than to send it 15 miles overland, so impassable were the roads to heavy transport. Madrid, without a river, relied upon mules and carts for its supplies. By the mid-eighteenth century, the city required the services of over half a million mules and 150,000 carts, all forced to labor their way into town over rugged terrain. In 1698, a bronze statue of Louis XIV was sent on its way from the river port of Auxerre, southeast of Paris, to the town of Dijon. The cart in which it was dispatched was soon stuck in the mud, however, and the statute remained marooned in a wayside shed for twenty-one years, until the road was improved to the point that it could continue its belated journey.

Gradually in the eighteenth century transportation improved. The French established a Road and Bridge Corps of civil engineers, with a separate training school, in 1747. Work began in 1777 on a series of canals which eventually linked the English Channel to the Mediterranean. By the end of the century, France was spending seven million livres a year on road construction. In England, private investors, spearheaded by that inveterate canal builder the duke of Bridgewater, constructed a network of waterways and turnpikes linking provincial towns to each other and to London. With improved roads came stagecoaches, feared at first for their speed and recklessness much as automobiles were feared in the early twentieth century. People objected to being crowded into narrow carriages designed to reduce the load pulled by the team of horses. "If by chance a traveller with a big stomach or wide shoulders appears," an unhappy passenger lamented, "one has to groan or desert." Improvements such as stagecoaches and canals, much as they might increase the profits or change the pattern of life for the wealthy, meant little to the average European. Barges plied the waterways from the north to the south of France, but most men and women traveled no farther than to their neighboring market

Transportation improvements

The Duke of Bridgewater Canal

*Urban manufacturing
centers*

town, on footpaths or on rutted cart tracks eight feet wide, which had
served their ancestors much as they served them.

That industry flourished to the extent it did, despite the hazards and
inefficiencies of transport, is a measure of the strength of Europe's
ever-increasing commercial impulse. Rural "putting-out" did not
prevent the growth of important urban manufacturing centers. In
northern France, many of the million or so men and women employed
in the textile trade lived and worked in cities such as Amiens, Lille,
and Rheims. The eighteenth-century rulers of Prussia made it their
policy to develop Berlin as a manufacturing center, taking advantage
of an influx of French Protestants to establish the silk-weaving industry there. Even in cities, however, work was likely to be carried out
in small shops, where anywhere from five to twenty journeymen
labored under the supervision of a master to manufacture the particular products of their craft. Despite the fact that manufacturing was
centered in homes and workshops, by 1700 these industries were
increasing significantly in scale as many workshops grouped together
to form a single manufacturing district. Textile industries led this trend,
but it was true as well of brewing, distilling, soap and candle-making,
tanning, and the manufacturing of various chemical substances for the
bleaching and dying of cloth. These and other industries might often
employ several thousand men and women congregated together into
towns—or larger communities of several towns—all dedicated to the
same occupation and production.

*Response to changing
machinery and techniques*

Techniques in some crafts remained much as they had for centuries.
In others, however, inventions changed the pattern of work as well
as the nature of the product. Knitting frames, simple devices to speed
the manufacture of textile goods, made their appearance in England
and Holland. Wire-drawing machines and slitting mills, the latter
enabling nail-makers to convert iron bars into rods, spread from Germany into England. Mechanically powered saws were introduced into
shipyards and elsewhere across Europe in the seventeenth century.
The technique of calico printing, the application of colored designs
directly to textiles, was imported from the Far East. New and more
efficient printing presses appeared, first in Holland and then elsewhere.
The Dutch invented a machine, called a "camel," by which the hulls
of ships could be raised in the water so that they could be more
easily repaired.

*Adverse reaction to new
machinery and processes*

Innovations of this kind were not readily accepted by workers.
Labor-saving machines such as mechanical saws threw men out of
work. Artisans, especially those organized into guilds, were by nature
conservative, anxious to protect not only their restrictive "rights,"
but the secrets of their trade. Often, too, the state would intervene to
block the widespread use of machines if they threatened to increase
unemployment. The Dutch and some German states for example,
prohibited the use of what was described as a "devilish invention," a
ribbon loom capable of weaving sixteen or more ribbons at the same

time. Sometimes the spread of new techniques was curtailed by states in order to protect the livelihood of powerful commercial interest groups. On behalf of both domestic textile manufacturers and importers of Indian goods, calico printing was for a time outlawed in both France and England. The cities of Paris and Lyons, and several German states banned the use of indigo dyes because they were manufactured abroad.

Changes that occurred in trade, commerce, agriculture, and industry, though large-scale phenomena, nevertheless touched individual men and women directly. Enclosure stripped away customary rights. Markets developed to receive and transmit goods from around the world altered the lives of those whose work now responded to their rhythms. An English cottager lost his family's age-old right to tether a cow on the common, now an enclosed and "scientifically" manured corn field. A linen weaver in rural Holland, whose peasant father had eked out a meager living from his subsistence farm, now supplemented his income by working for an Amsterdam entrepreneur, who paid progressively less for his food as a result of the cheap grain imported to the Low Countries across the Baltic Sea from eastern Europe. A carpenter in a Toulon shipyard lost his job when his employer purchased a mechanical saw that did the work of five men. A sailor on one of the ships built in that Toulon shipyard died at sea off the French colony of Martinique, an island of which he had never heard, at a distance so far from home as to be inconceivable to those who mourned his death when they learned of it months later. Meanwhile, in vast areas of southern and eastern Europe, men and women led lives that followed the same patterns they had for centuries, all but untouched by the changes taking place elsewhere. They clung to the life they knew, a life which, if harsh, was at least predictable.

The human implications of change

4. POPULATION PATTERNS

The patterns of life for most seventeenth-century Europeans centered on the struggle to stay alive. They lived and worked within a subsistence economy, considering themselves extremely fortunate if they could grow or earn what it took to survive. In most instances their enemy was not an invading army, but famine. At least once a decade, climatic conditions—usually a long period of summer rainfall—would produce a devastatingly bad harvest, which in turn would result in widespread malnutrition often leading to serious illness and death. A family might survive for a time by eating less; but eventually, with its meager stocks exhausted and the cost of grain high, the human costs would mount. The substitution of grass, nuts, and tree bark for grain on which the peasants depended almost entirely for nourishment was as inadequate for them as it appears pathetic to us.

The threat of famine

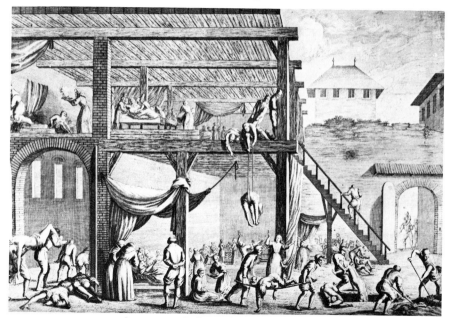

Left: *A Plague Hospital in Vienna.* The efforts to contain outbreaks of plague by gathering the sick in establishments such as this and burying the dead on the site proved unsuccessful. Right: *A Physician's Mask.* This German device containing smelling salts in its curved beak was designed to combat the plague, which physicians incorrectly believed was spread by poisonous vapors.

Population crises

Widespread crop failures occurred at fairly regular intervals—the worst in France, for example, about every thirty years (1597, 1630, 1662, 1694). They helped to produce the series of population crises that are the outstanding feature of early-modern demographic history. Poor harvests and the high prices produced by a scarcity of grain meant not only undernourishment and possible starvation, but increasing unemployment: with fewer crops to be harvested, more money was spent on food and, consequently, less on manufactured goods. The despair such conditions could easily breed would in turn contribute to a postponement of marriage and of births, and thus to a population decline. The patterns of marriages and births revealed in local parish registers indicate that throughout Europe the populations of individual communities rose and fell dramatically in rhythm with the fortunes of the harvest.

Health and sanitation

An undernourished population is a population particularly susceptible to disease. Bubonic plague had ravaged seventeenth-century Europe. Severe outbreaks occurred in Seville in 1649, in Amsterdam in 1664, and in London the following year. By 1700 it had all but disappeared; it last appeared in western Europe in a small area of southern France in 1720, though Moscow suffered an outbreak as late as 1771. Despite the gradual retreat of the plague, however, other diseases took a dreadful toll, in an age when available medical treatment was little more than crude guesswork, and in any event, beyond the reach of the poor. Epidemics of dysentery, smallpox, and typhus occurred with savage regularity. As late as 1779, over 100,000 people died of dysentery in the French province of Brittany. Most diseases attacked rich and poor impartially. Water supplies in towns and in the country were contaminated by heedless disposal of human waste and by all manner of garbage and urban filth. Bathing, feared at one time as a method of spreading disease, was by no means a weekly habit, whatever the social status of the household. Samuel Pepys, a prosperous servant of the crown in seventeenth-century London, recorded in his diary that his housemaid was in the habit of picking the lice from his scalp, that he took his first bath only after his wife had taken hers and experienced the pleasures of cleanliness, and that he had, on occasion, thought nothing of using the fireplace in his bedroom as a toilet, the maid having failed to provide him with a chamberpot. If such was Pepys's attitude toward hygiene and sanitation, imagine that of the poverty-stricken and ignorant peasant, and the threat to health implicit in such attitudes.

The precariousness of life helped encourage most men and women in early-modern Europe to wed much later than in traditional societies in Asia and Africa. This exceptional pattern found women marrying, on average, at twenty-five years of age, men at twenty-seven or twenty-eight, by which time they hoped to have accumulated sufficient resources to establish a household. Young couples lived on their own, and not, as in societies elsewhere, as part of "extended" families of three generations. In those extended families, a farm might pass from father to son before the death of the former. But in Europe this was not the custom. Since a son could not inherit until his father died, he was compelled to establish himself independently, and to postpone starting his own family until he had done so. Though historians have failed to find a clear explanation for this pattern of later marriages,

"Summer Amusement: Bugg Hunting." In this joking treatment of one of the facts of everyday life the bedbugs meet sudden death in a full chamber pot.

Implications of the European marriage pattern

Eighteenth-Century Sanitation. "Nightmen" moved through city streets after dark emptying the refuse of privies.

it may have resulted from a growing desire on the part of younger men and women for a higher standard of living. Late marriage helped to control the birth rate. Once married, however, a couple generally produced their first child within a year. Although subsequent children appeared with annual or biennial regularity, long periods of breast-feeding, which tends to reduce the mother's fertility, and community disapproval of extramarital sexual relations went some way toward limiting childbirth.

Population growth

Until the middle of the eighteenth century, populations continued to chart their rise and fall according to the outbreak of warfare, famine, and disease. From about 1750 on, however, there was a steady and significant population increase, with almost all countries experiencing major growth. In Russia, where territorial expansion added further to the increases, the population rate may have tripled in the second half of the eighteenth century. Gains elsewhere, while not usually as spectacular, were nevertheless significant. The population of Prussia and Spain doubled; Hungary's more than tripled; and England's population, which was about 5.5 million in 1700, reached 9 million in 1800. France, already in 1700 the most heavily populated country in Europe (about 20 million), added a further 6 million before 1790. Although reasons for the population increase remain something of a mystery, historians are inclined to agree that it was the cumulative result of a very gradual decline in the death rate, due in large measure to an equally gradual increase in the food supply. Better transportation facilitated the shipment of food over greater distances. Land clearances, particularly in England, and in Prussia and Russia, where territories were opened to colonization, provided an essential ingredient for increased production. New staples—the potato and maize—supplemented the diets of the very poor. And although evidence here is only fragmentary, it appears that whereas the climate of seventeenth-century Europe was abnormally bad, that of the succeeding hundred years was on the whole favorable.

New problems and attitudes

Population increase brought with it new problems and new attitudes. For example, the decline in the death rate among infants—along with an apparent increase in illegitimacy at the end of the eighteenth century—created a growing population of unwanted babies among the poor. Some desperate women resorted to infanticide, though since children murdered at birth died without benefit of baptism, the crime was stigmatized as especially heinous by the Church as well as by society in general. More often, babies were abandoned at the door of foundling hospitals. As an English benefactor of several such institutions, Jonas Hanway, remarked in 1766, "it is much less difficult to the human heart and the dictates of self-preservation to drop a child than to kill it." In Paris during the 1780s from seven to eight thousand children were being abandoned out of a total of thirty thousand new births. Paradoxically, some historians now argue that during this same period the decrease in infant and child mortality encouraged many parents to lavish care and affection on their offspring in a way that they had not when the repeated early deaths of their sons and daughters had taught them the futility of that emotional bond.

Although somewhere between 80 and 90 percent of the population lived in small rural communities, towns and cities were coming to play an increasingly important role in the life of early-modern Europe. One must speak of the "rise" of towns and cities with caution, however, since the pace of urbanization varied greatly across the Continent. Russia remained almost entirely rural: only 2.5 percent of its population lived in towns in 1630, and that percentage had risen by only 0.5 percent by 1774. In Holland, on the other hand, 59 percent of the population was urban centered in 1627 and 65 percent in 1795.

The "rise" of towns and cities

The total number of urban dwellers did not vary markedly after the end of the sixteenth century, when there were approximately 200 cities in Europe with a population of over 10,000. What did change between 1600 and 1800 was, first, the way in which those cities were distributed across the map, concentrated increasingly in the north and west; and second, the growing proportion of very large cities to the whole. The patterns of trade and commerce had much to do with these shifts. Cities like Hamburg in Germany, Liverpool in England, Toulon in France, and Cadiz in Spain grew by about 250 percent between 1600 and 1750. Amsterdam, the hub of early-modern international commerce, increased from 30,000 in 1530 to 115,000 in 1630 and 200,000 by 1800. Naples, the busy Mediterranean port, went from a population of 300,000 in 1600 to nearly half a million by the late eighteenth century. Where goods were traded, processed, and manufactured, fleets built and provisioned, people flocked to work. An eighteenth-century commentator noted that the laborers in Paris were "almost all foreigners"—that is, men and women born outside the city: carpenters from Savoy, water carriers from Auvergne, porters from Lyons, stonecutters from Normandy, .wig-makers from Gascony, shoemakers from Lorraine.

Shifts in urban population

As some cities expanded, however, others stagnated or declined as a result of commercial changes. Norwich, in England, grew at the expense of older industrial centers on the English Channel when the manufacture of woolen goods shifted north. The population of the important German market center of Frankfurt declined during and after the period of the Thirty Years' War, when difficulties of communication and the general instability caused by frequent military campaigns diverted much of its former business to Amsterdam.

Ebb and flow of urban growth

The most spectacular urban population growth occurred in the administrative capitals of the increasingly centralized nations of Europe. By the middle of the eighteenth century, Madrid, Berlin, and St. Petersburg all had populations of over 100,000. London grew from 674,000 in 1700 to 860,000 a century later. Paris, a city of approximately 180,000 in 1600, increased to over half a million by 1800. Berlin presents a particularly interesting example of urban expansion.

Growth of administrative centers

From a population of 6,500 in 1661, it swelled to 60,000 in 1721 and 140,000 in 1783. Its increase was due in part to the fact that successive Prussian rulers undertook to improve its position as a trade center by the construction of canals that linked it with Breslau and Hamburg. Its population rose as well, however, because of the marked increase in Prussian army and bureaucratic personnel based in the capital city. Of the 140,000 citizens of Berlin in 1783, approximately 65,000 were state employees or members of their families.

5. LIFE WITHIN A SOCIETY OF ORDERS

*Orders, privilege, and
freedom*

Despite the economic and demographic shifts that were occurring in early-modern Europe, it remained a society ranked in traditional orders. The changes we have been concerned with occurred against the continuity of long-accepted social divisions based upon birth and occupation. As circumstances altered, the fluid patterns of economic reorganization clashed with older, rigid assumptions about the place of men and women within a pre-ordained—to many, a divinely ordained—social hierarchy. Jean Bodin, the French philosopher, wrote in 1570 that the division of the citizenry into "the three orders of nobles, clergy and people" was no more than natural. "There never was a commonwealth, real or imaginary, where citizens were in truth equal in all rights and privileges. Some always have more, some less than the rest." And some had none. Orders were demarcated by those rights and privileges. "Freedom" was understood as one such privilege, as a benefit, bestowed not upon all men and women, but upon special groups whose position "freed" them to do certain things others could not do, or freed them from the burden of doing certain things that were required of others. An English landowner was, because of the position his property conferred upon him, privileged, and therefore "free," to participate directly in the election of his government. A French nobleman was privileged, and therefore "free," to avoid the heavy burden of taxation levied upon the unprivileged orders. A German tailor who had served out his seven-year apprenticeship was free to set up his own shop for profit, something an unapprenticed man was not traditionally "at liberty" to do, no matter what his degree of skill with needle and thread. The master tailor's position conferred his freedom, just as the position of aristocrat and property owner conferred theirs.

*The theater of a society of
orders*

The members of the higher orders attempted at all times to live their lives in a particular style which accorded with their rank. The nobility was taught from birth to consider itself a class apart. Merchants and manufacturers were just as insistent upon maintaining the traditional marks of privilege that separated them from artisans and peasants. Sumptuary laws decreed what could be worn and by whom. An edict promulgated in the German principality of Brunswick in 1738, for

Middle-Class Fashion. In this seventeenth-century portrait of a Dutch burgomaster and his family, the patriarch and his wife are wearing the costume of an earlier generation, while the children are clothed in the current style. All display the opulence characteristic of their prosperous class.

example, forbade servant girls to use silk dress materials, to wear gold or silver ornaments, or shoes of anything but plain black leather. A similar law in the Polish city of Posen prohibited the wives of burghers from wearing capes or long hair. Style was not simply a matter of current whim. It was a badge of status and was carefully adhered to as such. An aristocratic lady powdered her hair and rouged her cheeks as a sign that she was an aristocrat. Life within a society of orders demanded a certain degree of theatricality, especially from those at the top of the social hierarchy. Aristocrats "acted" their part in a calculatedly self-conscious way. Their manner of speech, their dress, the ceremonial sword they were privileged to wear, the title by which they were addressed, were the props of a performance which constantly emphasized the distinctions between those above and those below. Noble families lived in castles, chateaux, or country houses whose size and antiquity were a further proclamation of superiority. When they built new mansions, as the *nouveau riche* capitalist English gentry did in the eighteenth century, they made certain their elaborate houses and spacious private parks declared their newfound power. The English politician Robert Walpole had an entire village moved to improve the view from his grand new residence.

The vast majority of men and women defined and understood social hierarchy in terms of the rural communities in which they lived. At the head of those communities, in all likelihood, stood a representative of the noble elite. Aristocrats probably numbered about 3 percent of

Banquet Given in Paris by the Spanish Duke of Alva in Honor of the Prince of Asturias. The scene illustrates the ostentatious display this powerful nobleman believed suitable to his rank and fortune.

the total population of Europe. The percentage was higher in Russia, Poland, Hungary, and Spain; lower in Germany, France, and England. Land was the hallmark of aristocratic position. And, generally speaking, the more land one possessed, the higher one stood within the aristocracy. In Hungary, five noble families owned about 14 percent of the entire country; the greatest of these, Prince Esterházy, controlled the lives of over half a million peasants. Most noblemen were not nearly so rich and powerful. Some, indeed, could rely on little more than inherited privilege to distinguish themselves from peasants.

The nobility

The pattern of noble life varied considerably from country to country. In England and Prussia, the nobility tended to reside on its estates; in south and west Germany, and in France, aristocrats were more likely to leave the management of their estates to stewards and to live at the royal court. Despite the traditional assumption that noblemen need not, and therefore must not, soil their aristocratic reputation by commercial dealing, by the end of the eighteenth century they were involving themselves in increasing numbers in a variety of entrepreneurial enterprises. Some exploited mineral deposits on their estates; others invested in overseas trade. In France, two of the four largest coal mines were owned and operated by noblemen, while the duke of Orléans was an important investor in the newly established chemical

Nobility and commerce

dye industry. In eastern Europe, because there were few middle-class merchants, aristocrats frequently undertook to market their agricultural produce themselves.

In no country was the aristocracy a completely closed order. Men who proved of use to the crown as administrators or lawyers, men who amassed large fortunes as a consequence of judicious—and often legally questionable—financial transactions, moved into the ranks of the nobility with increasing frequency during the late seventeenth and eighteenth century. Joseph II of Austria was making financiers into noblemen by the dozen in the late eighteenth century. In France, it was possible to attain nobility through the purchase of expensive offices from the crown. There was also a growing legal nobility of the "robe," headed by members of the thirteen provincial *parlements* whose function it was to record, and thereby sanction, the laws of the kingdom.

An "open" nobility

In time, severe tensions arose, most particularly in France but elsewhere as well, between the older nobility and those much more active and frequently more intelligent men of the new nobility. Tradition had it that noble service meant military service, that the ideal of noble honor involved heroism on the battlefield, not cunning at the law courts or conniving in palace antechambers. Hence, there was conflict over the legitimacy of those in the new noble order.

Rivalry between the old and new nobility

Whether recently enobled or members of one of those ancient families that existed throughout Europe and which the French called—simply and eloquently—*les grands,* most aristocrats owned large landed estates. Land ownership helped them not only to establish their position but to define it as well, by bringing them into direct relationship with the peasants and laborers who worked that land and over whose lives the aristocracy exercised dominion. The status of the peasantry varied greatly across the face of rural Europe. In the East—Russia, Poland, Hungary, and in parts of Germany beyond the Elbe—the desire for profit in agriculture and the collusion of the state with the aristocracy led to the growth of a "second serfdom," a serf system much stronger than that which had existed during the Middle Ages. In East Prussia, serfs often had to work from three to six days a week for their lord, and some had only late evening or night hours to cultivate their own lands.

The peasantry

Peasants throughout eastern Europe found their destinies controlled in almost all respects by their masters. Noble landlords dispensed justice in manorial courts and even ruled in cases to which they were themselves interested parties. These men were a combination of sheriff, chief magistrate, and police force in one, able to sentence their "subjects" to corporal punishment, imprisonment, exile, or in many cases death, without right of appeal. Peasants could not leave their land, marry, or learn a trade unless permitted to do so by their lord. In Russia, where half the land was owned by the state, peasants were bound to work in mines or workshops if their masters so ordered,

Peasant subordination in eastern Europe

and could be sold to private owners. Although Russian peasant serfs were said to possess a "legal personality" that distinguished them from slaves, the distinction was obscured in practice. They lived as bound to their masters as had their great-grandfathers.

In western Europe, the position of the peasantry reflected the fact that serfdom had all but disappeared by the sixteenth century. Peasants might theoretically own land, although the vast majority were either tenants or laborers. Hereditary tenure was in general more secure than in the East; peasants could dispose of their land and had legal claim to farm buildings and implements. Although far freer than their eastern European counterparts, the peasantry of western Europe still lived to a great degree under the domination of landowners. They were in many cases responsible for the payment of various dues and fees: an annual rent paid to landlords by those who might otherwise own their land outright; a special tax on recently cleared land; a fee, often as much as one-sixth of the assessed value of the land, collected by the manorial lord whenever peasant property changed hands; and charges for the use of the lord's mill, bakery, or wine press. In France, peasants were compelled to submit to the *corvée,* a requirement that they labor for several weeks a year maintaining local roads. Even access to the often questionable justice meted out in the manorial courts, which endured throughout the early-modern period in almost all of western Europe, was encumbered with fees and commissions. To many peasants, however, the most galling badge of their inferiority was their inability to hunt within the jurisdiction of their landlord's manor. The slaughter of game was a privilege reserved to the nobility, a circumstance generating sustained resentment on the part of a population that looked upon deer and pheasant not as a symbol of aristocratic status but as a necessary supplement to its meager diet. Noble landlords rarely missed an opportunity to extract all the money they could from their peasants while constantly reminding them of the degree to which their destiny was controlled by the lord of the manor.

Peasant obligations

A French Peasant. Tattered and overworked, this peasant farmer is shown feeding his livestock as the tax collector at his door relieves him of all of his profits.

Despite their traditional subservience, however, western European peasants found themselves caught up directly in the process of economic change. The growth of centralized monarchies intensified the states' need for income, with the result that peasants were more burdened than ever with taxes and required services. They responded by accepting a new role as wage-earners in an expanding market economy, some as agricultural day laborers on enclosed estates, others as part of the work force in expanding rural industries. A few were genuinely independent, literate, influential members of the communities where they lived, owning not only land but considerable livestock. In France, some acted as intermediaries between their landlords, from whom they leased several large farms, and the sharecroppers who actually worked the land. Most, however, were far less fortunate. Those with claim to a small piece of property usually worked it into infertility in the course of one or two generations as they scrambled to make

Poverty and the peasantry

Market Scene by Jean Michelin. Peasant women and children bringing produce to a nearby market town.

it produce as much as possible. Each time a peasant proprietor died, his holdings were divided among his male heirs, encouraging the sort of marginal economic existence that was the fate of most rural laborers.

Poor peasants often lived, contrary to the biblical injunction, by bread alone—two pounds a day if they were lucky, the dark dough a mixture of wheat and rye flour. Bread was supplemented by peas and beans, beer, wine, or, far less often, skimmed milk. Peasant houses usually contained no more than one or two rooms, and were constructed of wood, plastered with mud or clay. Roofs were most often thatched with straw, which was used as fertilizer when replaced, and provided fodder for animals at times of scarcity. Furnishings seldom consisted of more than a table, benches, pallets for sleeping, a few earthenware plates, and simple tools—an axe, a wooden spade, a knife.

Peasant bread and board

Wives of peasants tended livestock and vegetables, and managed the dairy, if there was one. Women went out as field workers, or worked at home at knitting, spinning, or weaving in order to augment the family income. A popular seventeenth-century poem has a laborer's wife lamenting her lot with a refrain that has echoed down the ages: ". . . my labor is hard,/ And all my pleasures are debarr'd;/ Both morning, evening, night and noon,/ I am sure a woman's work is never done."

The peasant wife

The spread of the putting-out system broke down the previously sharp demarcations between town and country, between the life lived inside a city's medieval walls and that lived outside. Suburbs merged urban and rural existence. In some, textile workers labored. In others, families of fashion took their ease, creating an environment "where

Urban living conditions

the want of London smoke is supplied by the smoke of Virginia tobacco," as one Englishman remarked wryly. Houses in areas inhabited by the wealthy were increasingly built of brick and stone, which replaced the wood, lath, and plaster of the Middle Ages. This change was a response to the constant danger of fire. The great fire of London in 1666, which destroyed three-quarters of the town—12,000 houses—was the largest of the conflagrations that swept cities with devastating regularity. Urban dwellings of the laboring poor remained firetraps. Workers' quarters were badly overcrowded; entire families lived in one-room accommodations in basements and attics that were infested with bugs and fleas.

*Urban society: the
bourgeoisie*

Urban society was, like its rural counterpart, a society of orders. In capital cities, noble families occupied the highest social position, as they did in the countryside, living a parasitic life of conspicuous consumption at court. The majority of cities and towns were dominated by a nonnoble *bourgeoisie*. That French term originally designated a burgher or townsman who was a long-term, resident property owner or leaseholder and taxpayer. By the eighteenth century it had come to mean a townsman of some means who aspired to be recognized as a person of local importance, and evinced a willingness to work hard, whether at counting-house or government office, and a desire to live a comfortable, if by no means extravagant, existence. A bourgeois gentleman might derive his income from rents; he might, as well, be an industrialist, banker, or merchant, a professional, lawyer, or physician. If he served in the central bureaucracy, he would consider himself the social superior of those provincials whose affairs he administered. Yet he would himself be looked down upon by the aristocracy, who tended to think of the *bourgeoisie* as a class of vulgar social climbers. The French playwright Molière's comedy *The Bourgeois Gentleman* (1670) reflected this attitude, ridiculing the manners of the commercial class who were trying to ape their betters. "Bourgeois," another French writer observed, "is the insult given by noblemen to anybody they deem slow-witted or out of touch with the court." The *bourgeoisie* usually constituted about 20 to 25 percent of a town's population. As its economic elite, these men were almost always its governing elite as well. Municipal offices were considered a privilege of this order and were distributed accordingly.

The 'Bon Ton.' This English cartoon mocks the rage for French fashion and illustrates the affluence of a middle class able to afford the changing dictates of fashion.

Surprisingly, given the increase of commercial and industrial activity in the early-modern period, many cities witnessed a decline in the relative size of their industrial bourgeoisies. For example, Frenchmen who made their money in trade could purchase land, and by paying fees to the king, gain the right to an ennobling office. In seventeenth-century Amiens, a major textile center, the upper bourgeoisie deserted trade and derived the majority of its income from land or bonds. Where the bourgeoisie thrived, it more often than not did so as the result of a burgeoning state or regional bureaucracy.

Next within the urban hierarchy was a vast middle range of shop-keepers and artisans. Many of the latter continued to learn and then to practice their craft as members of guilds, which in turn contained their own particular ascending hierarchy of apprentice, journeyman, and master, thus preserving a society of orders. Throughout the early-modern period, however, commercial expansion threatened the rigid hierarchy of the guild structure. The expense and curtailed output resulting from restrictive guild practices met with serious opposition in big cities such as Paris and London, and in the industrial hinterlands of France and Germany, where expanding markets called for cheaper and more readily available goods. Journeymen tailors and shoemakers in increasing numbers set up shops without benefit of mastership and produced cheaper coats and shoes in defiance of guild regulations. In the silk workshops of Lyons, both masters and journeymen were compelled to labor without distinction of status for piece rates (wages paid per finished article, rather than per hour) set by merchandising middlemen and far below an equitable level in the opinion of the silk workers. Artisans like these, compelled to work for low wages at the behest of profiteering middlemen, grew increasingly restive. In France and Germany, journeymen's associations had originated as social and mutual-aid organizations for young men engaged in "tramp-ing" the country to gain experience in their trade. In some instances, however, these associations fostered the development of a trade con-sciousness that led to strikes and boycotts against masters and middle-men over the issues of wages and working conditions. An imperial law passed in Germany in 1731 deprived the associations of their right to organize, and required journeymen to carry a certificate of identification as testimony of their respectability during their travels.

At the bottom of urban society was a mass of semi-skilled and unskilled workers: carters and porters; stevedores and dockers; water carriers and sweepers; seamstresses, laundresses, cleaners, and domestic servants. These men and women, like their rural counterparts, lived on the margins of life, constantly battling the trade cycles, seasonal unemployment, and epidemics that threatened their ability to survive. A number existed in shanties on the edge of towns and cities. In Genoa, the homeless poor were sold as galley slaves each winter. In Venice, the poor lived on decrepit barges under the city's bridges. A French ordinance of 1669 ordered the destruction of all houses "built on poles by vagabonds and useless members of society." Deprived of the certainty of steady work, these people were prey not only to economic fluctuations and malevolent "acts of God," but to a social system that left them without any "privilege" or "freedom" whatso-ever.

Attitudes toward poverty varied from country to country. Most localities extended the concept of orders to include the poor: "the deserving"—usually orphans, the insane, the aged, the infirm; and

Hanging Thieves. This seventeenth-century engraving is designed to teach a lesson. Troops stand by and priests shave the heads of the condemned criminals as they are executed by the dozen. "At last," the engraver's caption reads, "these infamous lost souls are hung like unhappy fruit."

Attitudes toward poverty

"the undeserving"—able-bodied men and women who were out of work or who, even though employed, could not support themselves and their families. The authorities tended to assume in the latter case that poverty was the result of personal failings; few made a connection between general economic circumstances and the plight of the individual poor. For the deserving, private charitable organizations, such as those in France, founded by the order of St. Vincent de Paul and by the Sisters of Charity, provided assistance. For the undeserving, there was harsh treatment at the hands of the state whose concern to alleviate extreme deprivation arose more from a desire to avert public disorder than from motives of human charity. Food riots were common occurrences. In times of scarcity the French government frequently intervened to reduce the price of grain, hoping thereby to prevent an outbreak of rioting. Yet riots nevertheless occurred. When property damage resulted, the ringleaders were always severely punished, usually by hanging, The remainder of the crowd was often left untouched by the law, a fact suggesting the degree to which governments were prepared to tolerate rioting itself as a means of dealing with the chronic problem of poverty.

The treatment of paupers

Poor vagrants were perceived as a serious threat to social tranquility. They were therefore frequently rounded up at harvest time to keep them from plundering the fields. Vagrants and other chronically unemployed persons were placed in poorhouses where conditions were little better than those in prisons. Often the very young, the very old, the sick, and the insane were housed together with hardened criminals. Poor relief in England was administered parish by parish in accordance with a law passed in 1601. Relief was tied to a "law of settlement," which stipulated that paupers might receive aid only if still residing in the parish of their birth. An unemployed weaver who had migrated fifty miles in search of work could thus expect assistance only if he returned home again. In the late eighteenth century, several European countries established modest public works programs in an attempt to relieve poverty by reducing unemployment. France, for example, undertook road-building projects in the 1770s under the auspices of its progressive finance minister, Turgot. But generally speaking, indigence was perceived not as a social ill for which a remedy might be sought, but as an indelible stigma demarking the lowest of a community's social orders.

Early-modern Europe fashioned its institutions to reflect the patterns of social hierarchy. Nowhere was this more apparent than in the field of education. One barrier—a knowledge of Latin—separated aristocrats and a fair number of scholars and professionals from the commercial middle ranks; a second—the ability to read and write—separated the middle from the rest. Noblemen were generally educated by private tutors; though they might attend university for a time, they did so not in preparation for a profession but to receive further educational "finishing." Indeed during the late seventeenth and eighteenth centuries, universities more or less surrendered intellectual leadership to various academies established with royal patronage by European monarchs to enhance their own reputations as well as to encourage the advancement of science and the arts: the Royal Society of London, founded by Charles II in 1660; the French Academy of Sciences, a project upon which Louis XIV lavished a good deal of ostentatious attention; and the Berlin Royal Academy of Science and

Education in a society of orders: the nobility

Louis XIV Visiting the French Academy of Sciences. Royal patronage sustained such academies by guaranteeing members rewards suitable to their station.

Letters, patronized by Frederick the Great of Prussia in the eighteenth century. Few noblemen had the interest or the intelligence to participate in the activities of these august organizations, which were not, in any case, teaching institutions. Far better suited to their needs and inclinations was "the grand tour," often of many months' duration, which led the aristocrat through the capitals of Europe, and during which he was expected to acquire a kind of international *politesse*. One observer, commenting on the habits of young English aristocrats abroad, remarked: "they game; purchase pictures, mutilated statues, and mistresses to the astonishment of all beholders."

*Training for government
service*

Endowed, fee-charging institutions for the training of a governmental elite existed in France (the *collège*) and Spain (the *colegio mayor*) and in Germany and Austria (the *gymnasium*). Here the emphasis was by no means on "practical" subjects such as modern language or mathematics, but on the mastery of Greek and Latin translation and composition, the intellectual badge of the educated elite. An exception was the Prussian University of Halle, designed to teach a professional elite; a contemporary described that institution as teaching only what was "rational, useful, and practical."

*Education for the middle
orders*

Male children from the middle orders destined to enter the family business or profession as a rule attended small private academies where the curriculum included the sort of "useful" instruction ignored in the *collèges* and *gymnasia*. Female children, from both the upper and middle orders, were almost invariably educated at home, receiving little more than rudimentary instruction in gentlewomanly subjects such as modern language, belles lettres, and music, if from the noble ranks, and a similar, if slightly more practical training, if from the bourgeoisie.

Education for the poor

No European country undertook the task of providing primary education to all its citizens until the mid–eighteenth century, when Frederick the Great in Prussia and the Habsburg monarchs Maria Theresa and her son Joseph II in Austria instituted systems of compulsory attendance. Available evidence suggests that their results fell far short of expectation. An early–nineteenth-century survey from the relatively enlightened Prussian province of Cleves revealed dilapidated schools, poorly attended classes, and an incompetent corps of teachers. Educational conditions were undoubtedly worse in most other European communities.

Increasing literacy

Although educational opportunities for peasants and workers remained meager by modern standards, available evidence suggests that literacy rates increased considerably in the seventeenth and eighteenth centuries; in England, from one in four males in 1600 to one in two by 1800; in France, from 29 percent of the male population in 1686 to 47 percent in 1786. Literacy among women increased as well, though their rate of increase generally lagged behind that of men: only 27 percent of the female population in France was literate in 1786. Naturally, such rates varied according to particular localities and circumstances, and from country to country. Literacy was higher in urban areas which contained a large proportion of artisans. In rural eastern Europe, literacy remained extremely low (20–30 percent) well into the nineteenth century. Notwithstanding state-directed efforts in Prussia and Austria, the rise in literacy was largely the result of a growing determination on the part of religiously minded reformers to teach the poor to read and write as a means of encouraging obedience to divine and secular authority. A Sunday-school movement in eighteenth-century England and similar activities among the Christian Brotherhood in France are clear evidence of this trend.

Though the majority of the common people were probably no more than barely literate, they possessed a flourishing culture of their own. Village life, particularly in Roman Catholic countries, centered about the church, to which men and women would go on Sundays not only to worship but to socialize. Much of the remainder of their day of rest would be devoted to participation in village games. Religion provided the opportunity for association and for a welcome break from the daily work routines. Pilgrimages, for example, to a nearby shrine would include a procession of exuberant villagers led by one of their number carrying an image of the village's patron saint and accompanied by drinking, dancing, and picnicking. In towns, Catholics joined organizations, called confraternities in France, Italy, Austria, and the Netherlands, which provided mutual aid and a set of common rituals and traditions centered upon a patron saint. Religious community was expressed as well in popular Protestant movements which arose in the eighteenth century: Pietism on the Continent and Methodism in England. Both emphasized the importance of personal salvation through faith and the potential worth of every human soul regardless of station. Both therefore appealed particularly to people whose posi-

Popular culture

Cockfight by William Hogarth. This London scene suggests the degree to which men from different social orders came together for sport, drinking, and adventure. Here a clergyman and a young gentleman consort with the London riff-raff.

tion within the community had heretofore been presumed to be without any value. Though Methodism's founder, John Wesley (1703–1791), preached obedience to earthly authority, his willingness to rely on working men and women as preachers and organizers gave them a new sense of personal importance.

While much popular culture was directly linked to religious traditions and practices, much was now growing secular. Carnival, that vibrant *Carnival and other* prelenten celebration indigenous not only to Mediterranean Europe *amusements* but to Germany and Austria as well, represented an opportunity for common folk to cast aside the burdens and restraints imposed upon their order by secular authority. Performances and processions celebrated a "world turned upside down," a theme popular throughout much of Europe from the later Middle Ages, appealing to commoners for a variety of ambiguous psychological reasons, but in large part, certainly, as a way of avenging symbolically the economic and social oppression under which they lived. For a few days, the oppressed played the role of the oppressor and rulers were made to look like fools and knaves. In parades, men dressed as kings walked barefoot while peasants rode on horseback or in carriages; the poor threw pretend money to the rich. These occasions, although emphasizing social divisions, worked to hold communities to a common cultural center, since both rich and poor celebrated together, as they did on major religious holidays. Annual harvest festivals, once sponsored by the Church, were also increasingly secular celebrations of release from backbreaking labor, punctuated by feasting, drinking, sporting,

French Tavern. Often located outside the city limits so as to avoid the payment of municipal taxes, taverns such as this provided a gathering place for workers to drink, gossip, and relax after the day's labors. The tavern also served as a convenient place for public readings and for airing common grievances.

and lovemaking. Fairs and traveling circuses brought something of distant places and people into lives bound to one spot. The drudgery of everyday life was also relieved by horse races, cock fights, and bear baiting. Taverns played an even more constant role in the daily life of the village, providing a place for men to gather over tobacco and drink to gossip and gamble.

Laboring men and women depended on an oral tradition of myth, legend, and superstition to steady their lives, and give them point and purpose. Stories in books sold at fairs by peddlers were passed on by those who could read. They told of heroes and saints, and of kings like Charlemagne whose paternal concern for his common subjects led him into battle against his selfish nobility. Belief in villains matched belief in heroes. Witchcraft, as we have seen, was a reality for much of the period to superstitious men and women. So was Satan. So was any supernatural force, whether for good or evil, which could help them make sense of a world in which they, more than any, were victims of events beyond their control.

The role of the oral tradition

Though increasingly secularized, popular customs, celebrations, and beliefs remained a stabilizing force in early-modern Europe. They were the cultural expression of that social order to which the vast majority of Europeans belonged. Popular culture in the main tended to reinforce the traditions and assumptions of order and hierarchy. As such, it helped to bind men and women to what civilization had been, as capitalism and mercantilism impelled them in the direction of what it would become.

Stability and change

SELECTED READINGS

- *Items so designated are available in paperback editions.*

- Blum, Jerome, *Lord and Peasant in Russia,* Princeton, 1961. A good study of Russian society.
- Braudel, F., *Capitalism and Material Life, 1400–1800,* London, 1973. A fascinating review of evidence pertaining to the entire world.
- _____, *The Structures of Everyday Life: The Limits of the Possible,* New York, 1981. A survey of the material conditions of life; profusely illustrated.
- Burke, Peter, *Popular Culture in Early Modern Europe,* London, 1978. Synthesizes the most recent work on the period between 1500 and 1800; fascinating.
- Chambers, J. D., and G. E. Mingay, *The Agricultural Revolution, 1750–1880,* London, 1966. Now the standard work.
- Cipolla, C. M., *Before the Industrial Revolution: European Economy and Society, 1000–1700,* 2nd ed., New York, 1980. Wide-ranging and full of deft observations.
- Curtin, Philip D., *The Atlantic Slave Trade,* Madison, Wisc., 1969. Reinterprets the character of the trade.
- Darnton, Robert, *The Great Cat Massacre and Other Episodes in French Cultural History,* New York, 1984. Fascinating explorations into early-modern French mentalities.

• Davis, D. B., *The Problem of Slavery in Western Culture*, Ithaca, N.Y., 1966. A brilliant analysis of Western attitudes and assumptions.

• Davis, Natalie Z., *Society and Culture in Early Modern France*, Stanford, 1975. Eight scintillating essays by a pioneer in the use of anthropological methods for the study of early-modern European history.

Forster, Robert, *The Nobility of Toulouse in the Eighteenth Century*, Baltimore, 1960. A careful analysis of the extent and nature of aristocratic power.

• Foucault, M., *The History of Sexuality: An Introduction*, Vol. 1, New York, 1978. Useful material on the early-modern period.

Hafton, Olwen H., *The Poor of Eighteenth Century France*, Oxford, 1974. One of the first studies of a preindustrial "underclass."

Heckscher, E., *Mercantilism*, rev. ed., 2 vols., London, 1955. The most influential, but controversial, work on the subject.

Kaplow, Jeffry, *The Names of Kings. The Parisian Laboring Poor in the Eighteenth Century*, New York, 1972. A valuable study of the urban poor.

• Laslett, Peter, and Richard Wall, eds., *Household and Family in Past Times*, New York, 1972. A suggestive collection of essays.

LeRoy-Ladurie, Emmanual, *The Peasants of Languedoc*, Urbana, Ill., 1974. A classic on peasant life and demography.

Levine, David, *Family Formation in an Age of Nascent Capitalism*, New York, 1977. A thoughtful treatment of patterns of social formation.

Lougee, Carolyn C., *Le Paradis des Femmes: Women, Salons, and Social Stratification in Seventeenth-Century France*. Princeton, 1976. Women's role in the intellectual life of the old regime.

• Mousnier, R., *Peasant Uprisings in Seventeenth-Century France, Russia and China*, New York, 1970. A comparative analysis.

Parry, J. H., *Trade and Dominion: The European Overseas Empires in the Eighteenth Century*, New York, 1971. A comparative overview.

• Ranum, Orest, *Paris in the Age of Absolutism*, New York, 1968. A useful view of urban life.

Rich, E. E., and C. H. Wilson, eds., *The Cambridge Economic History of Europe*: Volume 5, *The Economic Organization of Early Modern Europe*, New York, 1977. An indispensable guide to the study of the period's economy and society.

• Stone, Lawrence, *The Family, Sex and Marriage in England, 1500–1800*, New York, 1977. An important, controversial book which argues important changes in attitudes over the course of three centuries.

• Wilson, Charles, *England's Apprenticeship, 1603–1763*, London, 1965. A reliable economic survey.

• Wrigley, E. A., *Population and History*, New York, 1969. A good introduction to family history.

SOURCE MATERIALS

Barnett, G. E., ed., *Two Tracts by Gregory King*, Baltimore, 1936. An introduction to the work of the modern world's first real statistician.

• Goubert, P., *The Ancien Régime: French Society, 1600–1750*, London, 1973. Particularly strong in its descriptions of rural life. Includes selections from illuminating documents.

Young, Arthur, *Travels in France during the Years 1787, 1788, 1789*, London, various editions. Vivid observations by an English traveler.

Chapter 17

THE AGE OF ABSOLUTISM
(1660-1789)

There are four essential characteristics or qualities of royal authority.
First, royal authority is sacred.
Second, it is paternal.
Third, it is absolute.
Fourth, it is subject to reason.

    —Jacques Bossuet, *Politics Drawn from the Very Words of Holy Scripture*

T he period from the accession to personal rule of Louis XIV of France until the French Revolution is known as the age of absolutism. The label is accurate if we define absolutism as the conscious extension of the legal and administrative power of state sovereigns over their subjects, and over the vested interests of the social and economic orders in which those subjects were ranked. The dates are suggestive in that for the period as a whole the activities of French monarchs most clearly expressed the doctrines of absolutist government. Yet both the dates and the label need to be treated with some caution. We have already noted that from about 1500 on, a general trend to make the state more powerful had manifested itself in England and on the Continent. Sixteenth-century kings saw in Protestantism a way of asserting the sovereignty of their states over the power of the papacy and the aristocracy. And political thinkers such as Jean Bodin were championing absolutist theory in their writings well before Louis XIV assumed personal rulership of France. By establishing the French monarchs as prototypical early-modern rulers, we risk ignoring other modes of centralized government instituted by the rulers of Prussia, Russia, and Austria. And we exclude the crucially important exception of England, where after 1688 absolutist tendencies gave way to oligarchy, and political power was shared among monarchy, aristocracy, and plutocracy.

Absolutism defined

The term "absolutism" needs qualification. As practiced by western European eighteenth-century rulers, absolutism was not despotism. They did not understand it as a license for untrammeled and arbitrary rule, such as that practiced by Oriental potentates. Despite the best efforts of these European monarchs to consolidate their authority, they could not issue irresponsible decrees and achieve lasting compliance. Aristocrats, churchmen, merchants, and entrepreneurs remained strong enough within their respective orders to ensure that kings and queens would need to justify the actions they took. Moreover, rulers tended to respect not only the strength of their political adversaries but the processes of law; they quarreled openly and broke with tradition only under exceptional circumstances. No matter how "absolute" monarchs might wish to be, they were limited as well by rudimentary systems of transportation and communication from interfering with any degree of consistency and efficiency in the daily lives of their subjects.

Although the emphasis in this chapter is largely upon political, diplomatic, and military events, absolutism cannot be fully understood without relating it to the commercial and industrial trends we have just analyzed. Tariff legislation, industrial regulations, wars of trade, currency manipulation, tax laws—all were useful tools in the construction of a new economic order. And all were tools that could be employed only by a strongly centralized state. Governments might take active steps to manage production and exportation, as the English did when they imposed the Navigation Acts in 1660, which restricted imports to material transported on English ships or those of their country of origin, and required colonial goods to pass through English ports before being sold elsewhere. Other governments (the French, for example), in their determination to finance expanding bureaucratic and military establishments, imposed new taxes and exacted an increasingly high price for the privileges they meted out. The state's expanding financial demands placed considerable pressure on both bourgeoisie and peasantry to make more money. And the result of that pressure, in turn, was entrepreneurship and wage labor.

Bearing in mind, then, the important symbiotic relationship between state power and economic innovation, we shall, in this chapter, measure the extent of royal power throughout Europe in the late seventeenth and eighteenth centuries, examine the varieties of absolutism as instituted and practiced by different monarchs, and take note of the way in which the centralization of power contributed to the rise of an international state system.

1. THE APPEAL AND JUSTIFICATION OF ABSOLUTISM

Absolutism appealed to many Europeans for the same reason that mercantalism did. In theory and practice, it expressed a desire for an end to the constant alarms and confusions of Europe's "iron century." The French religious wars, the Thirty Years' War in Germany, and the English Civil War all had produced great turbulence. The alternative, domestic order, absolutists argued, could come only with strong, centralized government. Just as mercantilists maintained that economic stability would result from regimentation, so absolutists contended that social and political harmony would be realized when subjects recognized their duty to obey their divinely sanctioned rulers.

Absolutist monarchs insisted, in turn, upon *their* duty to teach their subjects, even against their will, how to order their domestic affairs. As Margrave Karl Friedrich, eighteenth-century ruler of the German principality of Baden, expressed it: "We must make them, whether they like it or not, into free, opulent and law-abiding citizens." Looking back to the seventeenth-century wars that had torn Europe apart, rulers can be excused for believing that absolutism's promise of stability and prosperity—"freedom and opulence"—presented an attractive as well as an imperative alternative to disorder. Louis XIV of France remembered the *Fronde* as a threat to the welfare of the nation which he had been appointed by God to rule wisely and justly. When marauding Parisians entered his bedchamber one night in 1651 to discover if he had fled the city with Mazarin, Louis saw the intrusion as a horrid affront not only to his own person, but to the state. Squabbles among the nobility and criticisms of royal policy in the Paris Parlement during his minority left him convinced that he must exercise his powers and prerogatives rigorously if France was to survive and prosper as a great European state.

In order to achieve that objective, absolutist monarchs worked to control the disposition of the state's armed forces, the administration of its legal system, and the collection and distribution of its tax revenues. This ambitious goal required an efficient bureaucracy that owed its primary allegiance not to some particular social or economic order with interests antithetical to the monarchy, but to the institution of the monarchy itself. One hallmark of absolutist policy was its determination to construct a set of institutions strong enough to withstand, if not destroy, the privileged interests that had stood in the path of royal power in the past. The Church and the nobility, the semi-autonomous regions, and the would-be independent representative bodies (the English Parliament and the French Estates-General) were all obstacles to the achievement of strong, centralized monarchical government. And the history of absolutism is, as much as anything, the history of the attempts of various rulers to bring these institutions to heel.

In those major European countries where Roman Catholicism still remained the state religion—France, Spain, and Austria—successive monarchs throughout the eighteenth century made various attempts to "nationalize" the Church and its clergy. We have already noted the way in which in the fifteenth and sixteenth centuries, popes had conceded certain powers to the temporal rulers of France and Spain. Later absolutists, building on those earlier precedents, wrested further power from the Church in Rome. Even Charles III, the devout Spanish king who ruled from 1759 to 1788, pressed successfully for a papal concordat granting the state control over ecclesiastical appointments, and established his right to sanction the proclamation of papal bulls. Powerful as the Church was, it did not rival the aristocracy as an opponent of a centralized state. Monarchs combatted the noble orders in various ways. Louis XIV controlled the ancient French aristocracy by depriving it of political power while increasing its social prestige. Peter the Great, the talented and erratic tsar of early eighteenth-century Russia, co-opted the nobility into government service. Later in the century, Catherine II struck a bargain whereby in return for the granting of vast estates and a variety of social and economic privileges such as exemption from taxation, the Russian aristocracy virtually surrendered the administrative and political power of the state into the empress's hands. In Prussia under Frederick the Great, the army was staffed by nobles: again, as in Peter's Russia, a case of co-option. Yet in late–eighteenth-century Austria, the emperor Joseph II adopted a policy of confrontation rather than accommodation, denying the nobility exemption from taxation and deliberately blurring the distinctions between nobles and commoners.

These struggles between monarchs and nobles had implications for the additional struggle between local privileges and centralized power. Absolutists in France waged constant war against the autonomy of provincial institutions, often headed by aristocrats, much as Spanish rulers in the sixteenth century had battled independent-minded nobles in Aragon and Catalonia. Prussian rulers intruded into the governance of formerly "free" cities, assuming police and revenue powers over their inhabitants. These various campaigns, constantly waged and usually successful for a time, were evidence of the nature of absolutism and of its continuing success.

Absolutism had its theoretical apologists as well as its able practitioners. In addition to the political philosophies of men such as Bodin, defenders of royal power could rely on treatises such as Bishop Jacques Bossuet's *Politics Drawn from the Very Words of Scripture* (1708), written during the reign of Louis XIV, to sustain the case for extended monarchical control. Bossuet argued that absolute government was not the same as arbitrary government, since God, in whom "all strength and all perfection were united," was united as well with the person of the king. "God is holiness itself, goodness itself, and power itself. In these things lies the majesty of God. In the image of these things lies the majesty of the prince." It followed that the king was answerable to no one but God himself, and that the king was as far above other mortals as God was above the king. "The prince, as prince, is not regarded as a private person; he is a public personage, all the state is in him. . . .

Bishop Jacques Bossuet

As all perfection and all strength are united in God, all the power of individuals is united in the Person of the prince. What grandeur that a simple man should embody so much." What grandeur indeed! Bossuet's treatise was the most explicit and extreme statement of the theory of the divine right of kings, the doctrine that James I had tried to foist upon the English. Unlikely as it may sound to modern ears, the political philosophy of Bossuet was comforting to men and women who craved peace and stability after a century or more of international and domestic turmoil, and who found themselves embarked upon bold economic adventures that required a strong and stable polity.

2. THE ABSOLUTISM OF LOUIS XIV

Examine a portrait of Louis XIV [1] (1643–1715) in court robes; it is all but impossible to discern the human being behind the facade of the absolute monarch. That facade was carefully and artfully constructed by Louis, who recognized, perhaps more clearly than any other early-modern ruler, the importance of theater as a means of establishing authority. Well into the eighteenth century, superstitious commoners continued to believe in the power of the king's magic "touch" to cure disease. Louis and his successors used such beliefs to enhance their position as divine-right rulers endowed with God-like powers and far removed from common humanity.

Absolutism as theater: Louis XIV

The advantages of strategic theater were expressed most clearly in Louis's palace at Versailles, the town outside of Paris to which he

[1]Here, as elsewhere, dates following a ruler's name refer to dates of reign.

The Château of Versailles. Dramatically expanded by Louis XIV in the 1660s from a hunting lodge to the principal royal residence and the seat of government, the château became a monument to the international power and prestige of the Grand Monarch.

One of the 1400 Fountains in the Gardens at Versailles. The grounds as well as the palace were part of the backdrop for the theater of absolutism.

moved his court. The building itself was a stage upon which Louis mesmerized the aristocracy into obedience by his performance of the daily rituals of absolutism. The main facade of the palace was a third of a mile in length. Inside, tapestries and paintings celebrated French military victories and royal triumphs. Outside, in gardens containing 1400 fountains, statues of Apollo, god of the sun, recalled Louis's claim to be the "Sun King" of the French. Noblemen vied to attend him when he arose from bed, ate his meals (usually stone-cold, having traveled the distance of several city blocks from royal kitchen to royal table), strolled in his gardens, or rode to the hunt. As Louis called himself the Sun King, so his court was the epicenter of his royal effulgence. Its glitter, in which France's leading aristocrats were required by their monarch to share, was deliberately manufactured so as to blind them to the possibility of disobedience to the royal will. Instead of plotting some sort of minor treason on his estate, a marquis enjoyed the pleasure of knowing that on the morrow he was to be privileged to engage the king in two or three minutes of vapid conversation as the royal party made its stately progress through the vast palace halls (whose smells were evidence of the absence of sanitation facilities and of the seamy side of absolutist grandeur).

Louis understood this theater as part of his duty as sovereign, a duty which he took with utmost seriousness. Though far from brilliant, he was hard-working and conscientious. Whether or not he actually remarked "L'état, c'est moi" ("I am the State"), he believed himself personally responsible for the well-being of his subjects. "The deference and the respect that we receive from our subjects," he wrote in a memoir he prepared for his son on the art of ruling, "are not a free gift from them but payment for the justice and the protection that they expect from us. Just as they must honor us, we must protect and defend them."

Louis defined this responsibility in absolutist terms: as a need to concentrate royal power so as to produce general domestic tranquility. While taming the aristocracy, he conciliated the upper bourgeoisie by enlisting its members to assist him in the task of administration. He appointed them as intendants, responsible for the administration and taxation of the thirty-six *generalités* into which France was divided. Intendants never served in the regions where they were born, and were thus unconnected with the local elites over which they exercised authority. They held office at the king's pleasure, and were clearly "his" men. Other administrators, often from families newly ennobled as a result of administrative service, assisted in directing affairs of state from Versailles. These men were not actors in the theater of Louis the Sun King; they were the hard-working assistants of Louis the royal custodian of his country's welfare. Much of the time and energy of Louis's bureaucrats was expended on the collection of taxes, necessary above all in order to finance the large standing army on which France's

The administration of French absolutism: intendants and revenue

Louis XIV, the Sun King. This portrait by Rigaud illustrates the degree to which absolute monarchy was defined in terms of studied performance.

ambitious foreign policy depended. In addition to the *taille,* or land tax, which increased throughout the seventeenth century and upon which a surtax was levied as well, the government introduced a capitation tax, payable by all, and pressed hard for the collection of indirect taxes such as that on salt (the *gabelle*) and on wine and tobacco. Since the nobility was exempt from the *taille,* its burden fell most heavily on the peasantry, whose periodic local revolts Louis easily crushed.

Curbing regional opposition

Regional opposition—and indeed regionalism generally—was curtailed during Louis's reign. Although intendants and lesser administrators came from afar, did not speak the local dialect, ignored local custom, and were therefore despised, they were generally obeyed. The semi-autonomous outer provinces of Brittany, Languedoc, and Franche Comté (a part of that territory known collectively as the *pays d'état*) came to heel as central administration crippled their provincial Estates. To put an end to the power of regional *parlements* (the courts responsible for registering laws), Louis decreed that members of those bodies which vetoed legislation would be summarily exiled. The Estates-General, the national French representative assembly last summoned in 1614 during the troubled regency following the death of Henry IV, did not meet again until 1789.

Louis XIV's religious policies

Louis was equally determined, for reasons of state and of personal conscience, to impose religious unity upon the French. That task proved to be difficult and time-consuming. The Huguenots were not the only source of theological heterodoxy. Jesuits, Quietists, and Jansenists—all three claiming to represent the "true" Roman faith—battled among themselves for adherents to their particular brand of Catholicism. Jesuits served Louis's interests best, since they advocated obedience to the secular power of the French state. Quietists preached a retreat into personal mysticism. Jansenism—a movement named for its founder Cornelius Jansen, a seventeenth-century bishop of Ypres—was a French version of Calvinism which stressed the doctrine of original sin and rejected the belief in free will that was central to Jesuit teaching. Louis, adhering to the absolutist doctrine of *un roi, une loi, une foi* (one king, one law, one faith) which had served as a rallying cry for both Catholics and Protestants in France during the preceding century, took drastic steps to achieve religious conformity as part of his program of national unification. He persecuted Quietists and Jansenists, offering them the choice of recanting or of prison and exile. Against the Huguenots he waged an even sterner war. Protestant churches and schools were destroyed; Protestant families were forced to convert. In 1685, Louis revoked the Edict of Nantes, the legal foundation of the toleration Huguenots had enjoyed since 1598. French Protestants were thereafter denied civil rights, and their clergy was exiled. Thousands of religious refugees fled France for England, Holland, the Protestant states of Germany, and America, where their particular professional and artisanal skills made a significant contribution to economic prosperity. (The silk industry of Berlin and of Spitalfields, an urban quarter of London, was established by Huguenots.)

Louis's drive for unification and centralization was assisted by his ability to rely upon increased revenues to fuel the domestic and military machinery of his absolutist monarchy. Those revenues were largely the result of policies and programs initiated by Jean Baptiste Colbert (1619–1683), the country's finance minister from 1664 until his death. Colbert was an energetic and committed mercantilist who believed that until France could put its fiscal house in order it could not achieve economic greatness. Colbert assumed office at a time when France, because of costly wars, was deeply in debt. Although he could not rid the country of that burden, he did for a time establish an interest rate of no higher than 5 percent, significantly lower than those the government had been accustomed to paying, and began negotiating directly with major creditors, rather than relying, as in the past, on fee-charging middlemen. Meanwhile, he tightened the process of tax collection, hounding corrupt officials who skimmed off a share of the taxes for themselves. He eliminated wherever possible the practice of tax farming, the system whereby collection agents were permitted to withhold a certain percentage of what they gathered for themselves. When Colbert assumed office, only about 25 percent of the taxes collected throughout the kingdom was reaching the treasury. By the time he died, that figure had risen to 80 percent.

Jean Baptiste Colbert

But Colbert's efforts were not limited to managing the public debt and wringing the inefficiencies out of the tax system. During this period the state also perfected the merchandising of government positions and privileges. When new taxes were imposed and litigation resulted judges were appointed—for a price—to settle the disputes. Mayoralties were sold and guilds purchased the right to enforce trade regulations. The state extracted direct profit from every office it created and every privilege it controlled, demonstrating once again the way in which economy and politics were inextricably intertwined.

The sale of government positions and privileges

As a mercantilist, Colbert did all he could to increase the nation's income by means of protection and regimentation. Tariffs he imposed in 1667 and 1668 were designed to discourage the importation of foreign goods into France. He invested in the improvement of France's roads and waterways. And he used state money to promote the growth of national industry, and in particular the manufacture of goods such as silk, lace, tapestries, and glass, which had long been imported. Yet Colbert's efforts to achieve national economic stability and self-sufficiency could not withstand the insatiable demands of Louis XIV's increasingly expensive wars. Nor did his overseas trading companies ever achieve the stature of those of England and Holland. Unquestionably, however, France's economy was generally healthier as a result of his policies.

Colbert as mercantilist

3. ABSOLUTISM IN CENTRAL AND EASTERN EUROPE,
1660–1720

The degree of success enjoyed by Louis XIV as an absolutist monarch was in part the result of his own abilities, and of those of his advisors. Yet it was due as well to the fact that he could claim to stand as the supreme embodiment of the will of all of his people. Despite its internal division into territories and orders that continued to claim some right to independence, France was already unified before the accession of Louis XIV, and it was possessed of a sense of itself as a nation. In this, it differed from the empires, kingdoms, and principalities to the east, where rulers faced an even more formidable task than did Louis as they attempted to weld their disparately constructed monarchies into a united, centralized whole. The Thirty Years' War had delivered a final blow to the pretensions of the Holy Roman Empire, which the French philosopher Voltaire dubbed neither holy, Roman, nor an empire. Power, in varying degrees, passed to the over three hundred princes, bishops, and magistrates who governed the assorted states of Germany throughout the remainder of the seventeenth and eighteenth centuries.

Despite the minute size of their domains, many of these petty monarchs attempted to establish themselves as absolutists in miniature, building lesser versions of Louis XIV's Versailles. They remodeled cities to serve as explicit expressions of their power. Broad avenues led to monumental squares and eventually to the grand palace of the monarch. Medieval cities had masked the inequalities of the social order in their crowded, twisted streets and passageways, where social ranks often lived jumbled together in close physical proximity. Absolutist capital cities, in contrast, celebrated inequality, their planning and architecture purposely emphasizing the vast distance separating the ruler from the ruled. European absolutists followed the French example by maintaining standing armies, and paying for their expensive pretensions by tariffs and tolls that severely hampered the development of any sort of economic unity within the region as a whole. Although these rulers often prided themselves on their independence from imperial control, in many instances they were client states of France. A sizable portion of the money Louis devoted to the conduct of foreign affairs went to these German princelings. States like Saxony, Brandenburg-Prussia, and Bavaria, which were of a size to establish themselves as truly independent, were not averse to forming alliances against their own emperor.

Most notable among these middle-sized German states was Brandenburg-Prussia, whose emergence as a power of consequence during this period was the result of the single-minded determination of its rulers, principally Frederick William, elector of Brandenburg from

1640 to 1688, whose abilities have earned him the title of "Great Elector." The rise of Brandenburg-Prussia from initial insignificance, poverty, and devastation in the wake of the Thirty Years' War resulted from three basic achievements that can be credited to the Great Elector. First, he pursued an adroit foreign policy which enabled him to establish effective sovereignty over the widely dispersed and underdeveloped territories under his rule: Brandenburg, a large but not particularly productive territory in north-central Germany; Prussia, a duchy to the east that was dangerously exposed on three sides to Poland; and a sprinkling of tiny states—Cleves, Mark, and Ravensberg—to the west. By siding with Poland in a war against Sweden in the late 1650s, the Great Elector obtained the Polish king's surrender of nominal overlordship in East Prussia. And by some crafty diplomatic shuffling in the 1670s, he secured his western provinces from French interference by returning Pomerania, captured in a recent war, to France's Swedish allies.

Frederick William's second achievement was the establishment of a large standing army, the primary instrument of his diplomatic successes. By 1688, Brandenburg-Prussia had 30,000 troops permanently under arms. That he was able to sustain an army of this size in a state

The absolutism of Frederick William of Brandenburg

The establishment of a large standing army

Prussians Swearing Allegiance to the Great Elector at Königsberg, 1663. The occasion upon which the Prussian estates first acknowledged the overlordship of their ruler, this ceremony marked the beginning of the centralization of the **Prussian state.**

with comparatively limited resources was a measure of the degree to which the army more than repaid its costs. It ensured the elector and his successors of absolute political control by fostering obedience among the populace, an obedience they were prepared to observe if their lands might be spared the devastation of another Thirty Years' War.

Taxation and bureaucracy: bargaining with the Junkers

The third factor contributing to the emergence of the Great Elector's state as an international power was his imposition of an effective system of taxation and his creation of a government bureaucracy to administer it. Here he struck an important bargain with the powerful and privileged landlords (*Junkers*) without whose cooperation his programs would have had no chance of success. In return for an agreement which allowed them to reduce their peasant underlings to the status of serfs, the Junkers gave away their right to oppose a permanent tax system, provided, of course, that they were made immune from the payment of taxes themselves. (As in other European countries, taxes in Prussia fell most heavily on the peasantry.)

The Junkers and the army

Henceforth, the political privileges of the landlord class diminished; secure in their right to manage their own estates as they wished, the Junkers were content to surrender management of the Hohenzollern possessions into the hands of a centralized bureaucracy. Its most important department was a military commissariat, whose functions included not only the dispensing of army pay and matériel, but the development of industries to manufacture military equipment. Frederick William's success was due primarily to his ability to gain the active cooperation of the Junker class, something he needed even more than Louis XIV needed the support of the French nobility. Without it, Frederick William could never have hammered together his absolutist state from the disparate territories that were his political raw material. To obtain it, he used the army not only to maintain order, but as a way of co-opting Junker participation. The highest honor that could befall a Brandenburg squire was commission and promotion as a military servant of the state.

Absolutism in the Habsburg Empire

Like Brandenburg-Prussia, the Habsburg monarchy was confronted with the task of transforming three different regions into a cohesive state. In the case of Austria, this effort was complicated by the fact that these areas were ethnically and linguistically diverse: the southernmost Germanic lands that roughly comprised the present-day state of Austria; the northern Czech- (Slavic-) speaking provinces of Bohemia and Moravia; the German-speaking Silesia, inherited in 1527; and Hungary, where the Magyar population spoke a non-Slavic, Finno-Ugric language, also acquired in 1527 but largely lost to Turkish invasion just a few years afterward. For the next 150 years the Habsburgs and the Turks vied for control of Hungary. Until 1683 Turkish pashas ruled three-fourths of the Magyar kingdom, extending to within eighty miles of the Habsburg capital of Vienna. In 1683 the Turks beseiged

Vienna itself, but were repulsed by the Austrians, assisted by a mixed German and Polish army under the command of King John Sobieski of Poland. This victory was a prelude to the Habsburg reconquest of virtually all of Hungary by the end of the century.

The task of constructing an absolutist state from these extraordinarily varied territories was tackled with limited success by the seventeenth-century Habsburg emperors Ferdinand III (1637–1657) and Leopold I (1658–1705). Most of their efforts were devoted to the establishment of productive agricultural estates in Bohemia and Moravia, and to taming the independent nobility there and in Hungary. Landlords were encouraged to farm for export, and were supported in this effort by a government decree which compelled peasants to provide three days of unpaid *robot* service per week to their masters.[2] For this support, Bohemian and Moravian landed elites exchanged the political independence that had in the past expressed itself in the activities of their territorial legislative Estates.

Bargaining with Bohemia and Moravia

Habsburg rulers tried to effect this same sort of bargain in Hungary as well. But there the tradition of independence was stronger and died harder. Hungarian (or Magyar) nobles in the west claimed the right to elect their king, a right they eventually surrendered to Leopold in 1687. But the central government's attempts to further reduce the country by administering it through the army, by granting large tracts of land to German aristocrats and settlers, and by persecuting non-Catholics were an almost total failure. The result was a powerful nobility which, while it insisted upon its right to exploit its serfs as it saw fit, nevertheless remained fiercely determined to retain its traditional constitutional and religious "liberties." The Habsburg emperors could boast that they too, like absolutists elsewhere, possessed a large standing army and an educated (in this case German-speaking) bureaucracy. But the exigencies imposed by geography and ethnicity kept them at some distance from the absolutist goal of a unified, centrally controlled and administered state.

Problems with the Hungarian nobility

Undoubtedly the most dramatic episode in the history of early modern absolutist rule was the dynamic reign of Tsar Peter I of Russia (1682–1725). Peter's accomplishments alone would clearly have earned him his history-book title, Peter the Great. But his imposing height—he was nearly seven feet tall—as well as his mercurial personality—jesting one moment, raging the next—certainly helped. Peter is best remembered as the tsar whose policies brought Russia into the world of western Europe. Previously the country's rulers had set their faces firmly against the West, disdaining a civilization at odds with the Eastern Orthodox, semi-Oriental culture that was their heritage, while laboring to keep the various ethnic groups—Russians, Ukrainians, and a wide variety of nomadic tribes—within their ever-growing em-

Peter the Great. An eighteenth-century mosaic.

---

[2] The English usage of the term *robot* derives from the Czech designation of a serf.

pire from destroying not only each other but the tsarist state itself. Since 1613 Russia had been ruled by members of the Romanov dynasty, who had attempted with some success to restore political stability following the chaotic "time of troubles" that had occurred after the death of the bloodthirsty, half-mad Tsar Ivan the Terrible in 1584. Tsar Alexis I (1645–1676) took a significant step toward unification in 1654 when he secured an agreement with the Ukrainians to incorporate that portion of the Ukraine lying east of the Dneiper River into the Muscovy state. But the early Romanovs were faced with a severe threat to this unity and their rule between 1667 and 1671, when a Cossack leader (the Russian Cossacks were semi-autonomous bands of peasant cavalrymen) named Stenka Razin led much of southeastern Russia into rebellion. Stenka Razin's uprising found widespread support from hordes of serfs who had been oppressed by their masters as well as from non-Russian tribes in the lower Volga area who longed to cast off domination from Moscow. But ultimately Tsar Alexis and the Russian nobility whose interests were most at stake were able to raise an army capable of defeating Razin's zealous but disorganized bands. Before the rebellion was finally crushed, over 100,000 rebels had been slaughtered.

These campaigns were but a prelude to the deliberate and ruthless drive to absolutist power launched by Peter after he overthrew the regency of his half-sister Sophia and assumed personal control of the state in 1689. Within ten years he had scandalized aristocrats and churchmen alike by traveling to Holland and England to recruit highly skilled foreign workers and to study the craft of shipbuilding. Upon his return he distressed them still further by declaring his intention to Westernize Russia, and initiating this campaign by cutting off the "Eastern" beards and flowing sleeves of leading noblemen at court. Determined to "civilize" the nobility, he published a book of manners which forbade spitting on the floor and eating with one's fingers, and encouraged the cultivation of the art of polite conversation between the sexes.

Much as Peter wished to consider himself a westerner, his particular brand of absolutism differed from that of other contemporary monarchs. As we have seen, the autocracy imposed by Ivan III in the fifteenth century had a decidedly Eastern caste. Peter was the willing heir to much of that tradition. He considered himself above the law and thus his own absolute master to a degree that was alien to the absolutist theories and traditions of the Habsburgs and Bourbons. Autocrat of all the Russias, he ruled despotically, with a ferocious individual power that western European rulers did not possess. Armed with such arbitrary power in theory, and intent on realizing its full potential in practice, Peter set out to turn Russia to the West and to modernize his state. He would brook no opposition.

Confronted with a rebellion among the *streltsy*, the politically active, elite corps of the army who were most opposed to his innovations and

Peter Cutting a Nobleman's Beard. In this Russian woodcut Peter the Great is portrayed as a diminutive pest.

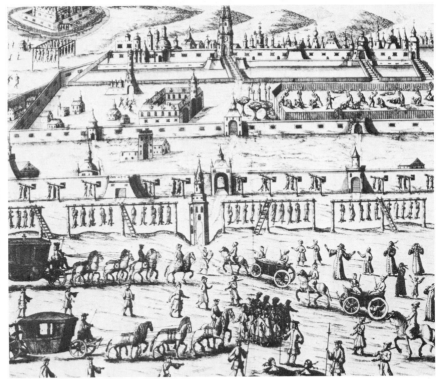

Peter the Great's Execution of the Streltsy. This contemporary print shows scores of corpses gibbeted outside the walls of the Kremlin. Peter kept the rotting bodies on display for months to discourage his subjects from opposing his efforts to Westernize Russian society.

who favored the restoration of his half-sister to the throne, Peter reacted with a savagery that astonished his contemporaries. Roughly 1200 suspected conspirators were summarily executed, many of them gibbeted outside the walls of the Kremlin, where their bodies remained for months as a graphic reminder of the fate awaiting those who would dare to challenge his absolute authority. Applying a lesson from the West, Peter proceeded to create a large standing army recruited from the ranks of the peasantry and scrupulously loyal to the tsar. One of every twenty males was conscripted for lifelong service. He financed his army, as did other absolutists, by increasing taxes, with their burden falling most heavily on the peasantry. To equip his new military force, he fostered the growth of the iron and munitions industries. Factories were built and manned by peasant laborers whose position was little better than that of slaves. Serfs were also commandeered for other public works projects, such as road and canal building, necessary for the modernization of the state.

The suppression and reconstruction of the army

In an effort to further consolidate his absolute power, he replaced the Duma—the nation's rudimentary national assembly—with a rubber-stamp senate, and appointed a procurator, dependent directly on him, to manage the affairs of the tradition-bound Russian Orthodox church, which essentially became an extension of the state. At the same time, Peter was fashioning new, larger, and more efficient administrative machinery to cope with the demands of his modernization program. Although he preferred to draw "new" men, whose

Absolutism and the new bureaucracy

*The influence of foreign
and domestic policy*

loyalty to the tsar would be unerring, into the bureaucracy, he was compelled to rely upon the services of the aristocrat—or *boyar*—class as well, rewarding them by increasing their control over their serfs. Nevertheless, membership in his new bureaucracy did not depend on birth. One of his principal advisors, Alexander Menshikov, began his career as a cook and finished as a prince. Bureaucratic status replaced noble rank as the key to power. The administrative machinery devised by Peter furnished Russia with its ruling class for the next two hundred years.

Peter the Great's Eurocentric worldview also manifested itself in his foreign policy, as witnessed by his bold drive to gain a Russian outlet on the Baltic Sea. Previous battles with the Turks to secure a port on the Black Sea, and thus a southern passage to the West, had failed. Now he engaged in a war with Sweden's meteoric soldier-king Charles XII (1697–1718), who devoted most of his reign to campaigns in the field against the Danes, the Poles, and the Russians. By defeating Charles decisively at the battle of Poltava in 1709, Peter was able to secure his window to the West. He promptly outdid his absolutist counterparts in Europe, who had moved their courts to the outskirts of their capital cities, by moving the Russian capital from Moscow to an entirely new city on the Gulf of Finland. An army of serfs was employed to erect the baroque city of St. Petersburg

The St. Petersburg Palaces. The first of six versions of the Winter Palace here depicted (left) was erected in 1711. It quickly proved to be too modest for Peter's needs. Within a decade he had created a far more elaborate complex called Peterhof (right), complete with fountains fashioned after those of Versailles.

around a palace intended to imitate and rival Louis XIV's Versailles. It was not enough that Peter looked to the West; he wanted the Russian people to share the view.

Not surprisingly, Peter's drastic programs met with concerted resistance. Resentment smoldered under his imposing hand, even within the palace. His son Alexis, who had dared to declare himself opposed to his father's innovations, became a rallying point for the forces of resistance to the tsar and his policies, and died under torture inflicted at his father's command in 1718. Upon Peter's death in 1725, *boyar* determination to undo his reforms surfaced during the succession struggle. There followed a series of ineffective tsars, creatures of the Palace guard, thus allowing the resentful nobles to rescind many of his reforms. In 1762, the crown passed to Catherine II, a ruler whose ambitions and determination were equal to those of her august predecessor.

Peter's successors

Peter the Great of Russia, Leopold I of Austria, Frederick William of Brandenburg-Prussia, and above all Louis XIV of France: these were the "great" seventeenth-century absolutists. Elsewhere, the fortunes of absolutism fared far less well. The ineffectual, weak-minded Spanish monarch Charles II found himself besieged by rebellions in Portugal and Sicily. In 1668, after years of fighting, he was forced to recognize Portuguese independence. In Sweden, Charles X and Charles XI managed to extend their territories at the expense of the Danes and to quell the independence of the aristocracy by confiscating their fiefdoms. During the reign of Charles XII, however, that legacy was dissipated by an adventurous but ultimately unproductive foreign policy. In Poland, the opposition of the landed gentry—or *szlachta*—to any form of centralized government produced a political stalemate that amounted to little more than anarchy. Foreign powers took advantage of this situation to intervene in Polish affairs and, in the eighteenth century, to carve up the country and distribute it among themselves.

The failure of absolutism to take root elsewhere

4. THE ENGLISH EXCEPTION

But what of England, which had experienced a taste of absolutist centralization under the Tudors and early Stuarts, and indeed under Oliver Cromwell, but which possessed in its Parliament the longest tradition and most highly developed form of representative government in western Europe? England's political history in the late seventeenth century provides the most striking contrast to continental absolutism. Charles II, son of the beheaded Charles I, who returned from exile and ascended the throne in 1660, was initially welcomed by most English men and women. He pledged himself not to reign as a despot, but to respect Parliament and to observe Magna Carta and the Petition of Right, for he admitted that he was not anxious to "resume his travels." His delight in the unbuttoned moral atmosphere of his court

The policies of Charles II

Charles II of England

Religion and the political reaction

James II as religious zealot

and the culture it supported (risque plays, dancing, and marital infidelity) mirrored a public desire to forget the restraints of the puritan past. The wits of the time suggested that Charles, "that known enemy to virginity and chastity," played his role as the father of his country to the fullest. However, as Charles's admiration of things French grew to include the absolutism of Louis XIV, he came to be regarded as a threat to more than English womanhood by a great many powerful Englishmen. However anxious to restore the monarchy, they were not about to surrender their traditional rights to another Stuart autocrat. By the late 1670s, the country found itself divided politically into those who supported the king (called by their opponents "Tories," a popular nickname for Irish Catholic bandits) and those opposed to him (called by *their* opponents "Whigs," a similar nickname for Scottish Presbyterian rebels).

As the new party labels suggest, religion remained an exceedingly divisive national issue. Charles was sympathetic to Roman Catholicism, even to the point of a deathbed conversion in 1685. He therefore opposed the stiff code of ecclesiastical regulations, known as the Clarendon Code, which had reestablished Anglicanism as the official state religion and which penalized Catholics and Protestant dissenters. In 1672, Charles suspended the Clarendon Code, although the public outcry against this action compelled him to retreat. This controversy, and rising opposition to the probable succession of Charles's ardent Roman Catholic brother James, led to a series of Whig electoral victories between 1679 and 1681. But Charles found that increased revenues, plus a secret subsidy he was receiving from Louis XIV, enabled him to govern without resort to Parliament, to which he would otherwise have had to go for money. In addition to ignoring Parliament, Charles further infuriated and alarmed Whig politicians by arranging the execution of several of their most prominent leaders on charges of treason, and by remodeling local government in such a way as to make it more dependent on royal favor. Charles died in 1685 with his power enhanced; but he left behind him a political and religious legacy that was to be the undoing of his successor.

James II was the very opposite of his brother. A zealous Catholic convert, he alienated his Tory supporters, all of whom were of course Anglicans, by dismissing them in favor of Roman Catholics, and by once again suspending the penal laws against Catholics and dissenters. His stubbornness, as one historian has remarked, made it all but impossible for him to take "yes" for an answer. Whereas Charles had been content to defeat his political enemies, James was determined to humiliate them. Like Charles, James interfered in local government, but his appointments were so personally distasteful and so mediocre as to arouse active opposition. James made no attempt to disguise his Roman Catholicism. He publicly declared his wish that all his subjects might be converted, and paraded papal legates through the streets of London. When, in June 1688, he ordered all Anglican clergymen to read his decree of toleration from their pulpits, seven bishops refused and were clapped into prison on charges of seditious libel. At their trial, however, they were declared not guilty, to the vast satisfaction of the English populace.

The trial of the bishops was one event that brought matters to a head. The other was the birth of a son to James and his second wife, the Roman Catholic daughter of the duke of Modena. This male infant, who was to be raised a Catholic, replaced James's much older Protestant daughter Mary as heir to the British throne. Despite a rumor that the baby boy was an imposter smuggled into the royal bedchamber in a warming pan, political leaders of both parties were prepared not only to believe in the legitimacy of the child but to take active steps to prevent the possibility of his succession. A delegation of Whigs and Tories crossed the Channel to Holland with an invitation to Mary's husband William of Orange, the *stadholder* or chief executive of the United Provinces and the great-grandson of William the Silent. William was asked to cross to England with an invading army to restore English religious and political freedom. As leader of a continental coalition determined to put a spoke in Louis XIV's expansionist policies, he accepted, welcoming the chance such a move represented to bring England into active opposition to the French (see below, p. 622).

William's conquest was a bloodless coup. James fled the country, thereby allowing Parliament to declare the throne vacant and clearing the way for the accession of William and Mary as joint sovereigns of England. A Bill of Rights, passed by Parliament and accepted by the new king and queen, reaffirmed English civil liberties such as trial by jury, habeas corpus (guaranteeing the accused a speedy trial), and the right of petition and redress, and established that the monarchy was subject to the law of the land. An Act of Toleration, passed in 1689, granted dissenters the right to worship, though not the right to full political protection. In 1701, with the son of the exiled James II now reaching maturity in France, an Act of Succession ordained that the English throne was to pass first to Mary's childless sister Anne, who ruled from 1702 to 1714, and then to George, elector of the German principality of Hanover, who was the great-grandson of James I. The connection was a distant one, but the Hanoverian dynasty was Protestant, and George reputed to be a capable enough ruler. The act was further evidence of the degree to which Parliament could dictate its terms. Henceforth, all English sovereigns were to be communicants of the Church of England. If foreign born, they could not engage England in the defense of their native land, nor leave the country, without Parliamentary consent.

William III

The events of 1688 and 1689 were soon referred to by the English as "the Glorious Revolution." Glorious for the English in that it occurred without bloodshed (although James is reputed to have been suffering from a nosebleed at the moment of crisis). Glorious, too, for defenders of Parliamentary prerogative. Although William and Mary and their royal successors continued to enjoy a large measure of executive power, after 1688 no king or queen attempted to govern without Parliament, which met annually from that time on. Parliament strengthened its control over the collection and expenditure of public money. Future sovereigns were henceforth unable to conduct the country's business without recourse to the House of Commons for the funds to do so. Glorious, finally, for advocates of the civil liberties now guaranteed within the Bill of Rights.

Yet 1688 was not all glory. It was a revolution that consolidated the position of large property holders, local magnates whose political and economic power base in their rural constituencies and on their estates had been threatened by the interventions of Charles II and James II. If it was a revolution, it was one designed to restore the *status quo* on behalf of a wealthy social and economic order that would soon make itself even wealthier as it drank its fill of government patronage and war profits. And it was a revolution that brought nothing but misery to the Roman Catholic minority in Scotland, which joined with England and Wales in the union of Great Britain in 1701, and the Catholic majority in Ireland where, following the Battle of the Boyne in 1690, repressive military forces imposed the exploitive will of a self-interested Protestant minority upon the Catholic majority.

1688 as a defense of status quo

Although the "Glorious Revolution" was an expression of immediate political circumstance, it was a reflection as well of anti-absolutist theories that had risen in the late seventeenth century to challenge the ideas of writers such as Bodin, Hobbes, and Bossuet. Chief among these opponents of absolutism was the Englishman John Locke (1632–1704), whose *Two Treatises of Civil Government* (1690) was used to justify the events of the previous two years. Locke maintained that originally all humans had lived in a theoretical state of nature in which absolute freedom and equality prevailed, and in which there was no government of any kind. The only law was the law of nature, which each individual enforced for himself in order to protect his natural rights to life, liberty, and property. It was not long, however, before men began to perceive that the inconveniences of the state of nature greatly outweighed its advantages. With individuals attempting to enforce their own rights, confusion and insecurity were the unavoidable results. Accordingly, the people agreed among themselves to establish a civil society, to set up a government, and to surrender certain powers to it. But they did not make that government absolute. The only power they conferred upon it was the executive power of the law of nature. Since the state was nothing but the joint power of all the members of society, its authority could "be no more than those persons had in a state of nature before they entered into society, and gave it up to the community." All powers not expressly surrendered were reserved to the people themselves. If the government exceeded or abused the authority explicitly granted in the political contract, it

John Locke

Defense of 1688: the political theories of John Locke

became tyrannical; the people then had the right to dissolve it or to rebel against it and overthrow it.

Locke condemned absolutism in every form. He denounced despotic monarchy, but he was no less severe in his strictures against the absolute sovereignty of parliaments. Though he defended the supremacy of the law-making branch, with the executive primarily an agent of the legislature, he nevertheless refused to concede to the representatives of the people an unlimited power. Arguing that state government was instituted among people for the preservation of property, he denied the authority of any political agency to invade the natural rights of a single individual. The law of nature, which embodied these rights, was an automatic limitation upon every branch of the government. Locke's theoretical defense of political liberties emerged in the late eighteenth century as an important element in the intellectual background of the French Revolution. In 1688, however, it served a far less radical purpose. The landed magnates responsible for the exchange of James II for William and Mary could read Locke as an apologia for their conservative revolution. James II, rather than protecting their property and liberties, had encroached upon them; hence they had every right to overthrow the tyranny he had established and to replace it with a government that would, by ensuring their rights, defend their interests.

Locke and limited sovereignty

5. WARFARE AND DIPLOMACY: THE EMERGENCE OF A STATE SYSTEM

The rise of absolutist monarchies in the late seventeenth century resulted in the emergence of an international state system. To the extent that absolutists succeeded in attaining their goals of unification and centralization, their states took shape as individual, identifiable political and economic entities. Although the achievements of various monarchs in this regard were limited, they were significant enough to encourage diplomats to speak more commonly than in the past of the "interests" of a particular state, as if that state somehow had a corporate personality of its own, and of the way in which those interests might coincide or conflict with the interests of another state. Often the interests of a monarch might clash with those of the country over which he ruled. Bourbon kings and Habsburg emperors worried about the future of their family dynasties to the detriment of the future of France or Austria. Religion, the factor that had torn Europe apart in the preceding century, remained an international issue in 1700. But increasingly, both dynasty and religion were superseded by newer "interests"—commerce and international balance and stability. The emergence of something approaching the modern state was to result, by 1715, in a significant redefinition of the aims and calculations of diplomacy and warfare.

Emergence of state interests

The organization of diplomatic bureaucracies was a major accomplishment of absolutist monarchies. Had most foreign ministers and ambassadors read the Dutchman Hugo Grotius's treatise on *The Law of War and Peace* (1625), they would have agreed with him about the necessity of establishing a body of rules that would help to bring reason and order to relations between governments. In practice, of course, reason and order gave way to bribery and improvisation. Yet the rationalization of diplomatic processes and the establishment of foreign ministries and embassies in European capitals, with their growing staffs of clerks and ministers, reflected a desire to bring order out of the international chaos that had gripped Europe during its "war century." International relations in the late seventeenth century was, among other things, a history of diplomatic coalitions, an indication of the degree to which negotiation was now a weapon in the armory of the absolutist state.

Warfare, however, continued to play an integral and almost constant role in the international arena. The armies of the period grew dramatically. When Louis XIV acceded to power in 1661, the French army numbered 20,000 men; by 1688, it stood at 290,000; by 1694, 400,000. These armies were increasingly professional organizations, controlled directly by the state, and under the command of trained officers recruited from the nobility. In Prussia, common soldiers were mostly conscripts; in other European countries they were volunteers, either native or foreign, though often "volunteers" in no more than name, having been coerced or tricked into service. Increasingly,

The Capture of Cambrai by Louis XIV in 1677. This print illustrates the tactics of siege warfare as practiced by early-modern armies. Louis is shown receiving an emissary from the city, whose walls have been breeched by siege guns.

however, enlistment was perceived by common soldiers as an avenue to a career, one which included the possibility of promotion to corporal or sergeant, and in the case of France, the promise of a small pension at the end of one's service. However recruited, common soldiers became part of an increasingly elaborate and efficient fighting force. The maneuvers of infantry, cavalry, and artillery were coordinated as never before. Soldiers were drilled with a thoroughness necessitated by tactics which depended on the accurate firepower of cannon and flintlock muskets. They were taught to stand their ground in formations of long, rigid lines in the face of direct enemy assault. They mastered the use of the bayonet (short steel spikes attached to the end of muskets, first manufactured in Bayonne, France, in the seventeenth century); the most effective procedure: stabbing the man in his left side as he raised his right arm to fire. Above all, they were made to understand the dire consequences of disobedience, breaking rank, or desertion. Soldiers were expected to obey instantly and unquestioningly. Failure to do so resulted in brutal punishment, often flogging, sometimes execution. Commissioned and noncommissioned officers carried sticks and prods with which to "encourage" correct military behavior in their men. Drill, not only on the battlefield but on the parade ground, in brilliant, elaborate uniforms and intricate formations, was designed to reduce individuals to automaton-like parts of an army whose regiments were moved across battlefields as a chess player moves pawns across the board—and with about the same concern for loss of human life.

The patterns of international relations during the period from 1660 to 1715 show European monarchs making use of the new machinery of diplomacy and warfare to resolve the conflicting interests of dynasty, stability, and commerce. At the center of that pattern, as at the center of Europe, stood Louis XIV. From 1661 until 1688, in a quest for glory, empire, and even revenge, he waged war across his northern and eastern frontiers on the pretext that the lands in question belonged both to the Bourbons and to the French by tradition, by former treaty, or by dynastic inheritance. His aggressively expansionist policies, alarming to other European rulers, led William of Orange, in 1674, to form an anti-French coalition with Austria, Spain, and various smaller German states. Yet Louis continued to push his frontiers eastward, invading territories that had been Germanic for centuries, and capturing Strassburg in 1681 and Luxembourg in 1684. Louis's seizure of Strassburg (subsequently called Strasbourg by the French), completing the conquest of the German-speaking province of Alsace begun in 1634 by Richelieu, irreversibly incorporated the seeds of a Franco-German animosity centered on this region that would bear bitter fruit in the great wars of the nineteenth and twentieth centuries. A second coalition, the so-called League of Augsburg—Holland, Austria, Sweden, and further German allies—was only somewhat more successful than the first.

The foreign policies of Louis XIV

Europe on the verge of war

These allies were concerned above all to maintain some sort of European balance of power. They feared an expansionist France would prove insatiable, as it pressed its boundaries farther and farther into Germany and the Low Countries. Louis, mistakenly expecting that William would be forced to fight an English army under James to establish his right to his new throne and would therefore be too preoccupied to devote his full attention to developments on the Continent, kept up the pressure. In September 1688 he invaded the Palatinate and occupied the city of Cologne. The following year the French armies crossed the Rhine and continued their eastward drive, burning Heidelberg and committing numerous atrocities throughout the middle Rhine area. Aroused at last to effective action, the coalition, led by William and now including in addition to its former members both England and Spain, engaged Louis in a war that was to last until 1697.

War of the League of Augsburg

The major campaigns of this War of the League of Augsburg were fought in the Low Countries. William managed to drive an army under his predecessor, James II, from Ireland in 1690; from that point on, he took command of the allied forces on the Continent. By 1694 Louis was pressed hard, not only by his allied foes, but by a succession of disastrous harvests that crippled France. Fighting remained stalemated until a treaty was signed at Ryswick in Holland which compelled Louis to return most of France's post-1679 gains, except for Alsace, and to recognize William as the rightful king of England.

The problem of the Spanish Succession

Ryswick did nothing, however, to resolve the dynastic tangle known as the Spanish Succession. Since Charles II of Spain had no direct heirs, and since he appeared to be on his deathbed in 1699, European monarchs and diplomats were obsessed by the question of who would succeed to the vast domain of the Spanish Habsburgs: not only Spain itself, but also its overseas empire, as well as the Spanish Netherlands, Naples, Sicily, and other territories in Italy. Both Louis XIV and Leopold I of Austria were married to sisters of the decrepit, unstable Charles; and both, naturally, eyed the succession to the Spanish inheritance as an exceedingly tempting dynastic plum. Yet it is a measure of the degree to which even absolutists were willing to keep their ambitions within bounds that both Leopold and Louis agreed to William's suggestion that the lion's share of the Habsburg lands should go to six-year-old Joseph Ferdinand, the prince of Bavaria, who was Charles II's grandnephew. Unfortunately, in 1699 the child died. Though the chances of war increased, William and Louis were prepared to bargain further and arranged a second treaty that divided the Spanish empire between Louis's and Leopold's heirs. Yet at the same time, Louis's diplomatic agents in Madrid persuaded Charles to sign a will in which he stipulated that the entire Spanish Habsburg inheritance should pass to Louis's grandson Philip of Anjou. This option was welcomed by many influential Spaniards, willing to endure French hegemony in return for the protection France could provide to the Spanish empire. For a time, Louis contemplated an alternative agreement which would have given France direct control of much of Italy. When Charles finally died in November 1700, Louis decided to accept the will. As if this was not enough to drive his former enemies back to war, he sent troops into the Spanish Netherlands and traders to the Spanish colonial empire, while declaring the late James II's son—the child of the warming pan myth—the legitimate king of England.

Once it was clear to the allies that Louis intended to treat Spain as if it were his own kingdom, they again united against him in the cause of balance and stability. William died in 1702, just as the War of the Spanish Succession was beginning. His position as first general of the coalition passed to two brilliant strategists, the English John Churchill, duke of Marlborough, and his Austrian counterpart, Prince Eugene of Savoy, an upper-class soldier of fortune who had been denied a commission by Louis. Under their command the allied forces engaged in battle after fierce battle in the Low Countries and Germany, including an extraordinary march deep into Bavaria, where the combined forces under Marlborough and Eugene smashed the French and their Bavarian allies decisively at Blenheim (1704). While the allies pressed France's armies on land, the English navy captured Gibraltar and the island of Minorca, thus establishing a strategic and commercial foothold in the Mediterranean, and helping to open a fourth major military theater in Spain itself.

War: the battle of Blenheim

The War of the Spanish Succession was a "professional" war that tested the highly trained armies of the combattants to the fullest. At the battle of Malplaquet in northeastern France in 1709, 80,000 French soldiers faced 110,000 allied troops. Though Marlborough and Eugene could claim to have won that battle, in that they forced the French to retreat, they suffered 24,000 casualties, twice those of the French. Neither Malplaquet nor other such victories brought the allies any closer to their final goal, which now appeared to be not the containment, but the complete destruction of the French military force. Queen Anne of England (Mary's sister and William's successor), once Marlborough's staunchest defender, grew disillusioned with the war and fired her general.

Military stalemate

More than war weariness impelled the combattants toward negotiation, however. The War of the Spanish Succession had begun as a conflict about the balance of power in Europe and the world. Yet dynastic changes had by 1711 compelled a reappraisal of allied goals. Leopold I had died in 1705. When his elder son and successor Joseph I died in 1711, the Austrian monarchy fell to Leopold's youngest son, the Archduke Charles, who had been the allies' candidate for the throne of Spain. With Charles now the Austrian and the Holy Roman Emperor as Charles VI (1711–1740), the prospect of his accession to the Spanish inheritance conjured up the ghost of Charles V and threatened to give him far too much power. International stability therefore demanded an end to hostilities and diplomatic negotiation toward a solution that would reestablish some sort of general balance.

Dynastic changes and the pursuit of peace

Treaty sites, 1697-1721
Boundary of the German Empire
Habsburg dominions

The Treaty of Utrecht

The Treaty of Utrecht settled the conflict in 1713 by redistributing territory and power in equitable portions. No one emerged a major winner or loser. Philip, Louis's grandson, remained on the throne of Spain, but Louis agreed that France and Spain would never be united under the same ruler. Austria gained territories in the Netherlands and Italy. The Dutch, victims of French aggression during the war, were guaranteed protection of their borders against future invasion. The English retained Gibraltar and Minorca, as well as territory in America: Newfoundland, Acadia, Hudson Bay, and in the Caribbean, St. Kitts. Perhaps most valuable of all, the English extracted the *asiento* from Spain which gave them the right to supply Spanish America with African slaves. The settlement reflected the degree to which new interests had superseded old. Balance of power and stability among states were the major goals of the negotiations, goals that reflected a departure from the world of seventeenth-century turmoil when religious fanaticism had been a major factor in international conflict. The eventual "winners" were undoubtedly the English, whose dynastic concerns were limited to a general acceptance of the Hanoverian settlement, and who could therefore concentrate their efforts on amassing overseas territories that would contribute to the growth of their economic prosperity and hence their international power.

6. ENLIGHTENED ABSOLUTISM AND LIMITED MONARCHY IN THE EIGHTEENTH CENTURY

Eighteenth-century absolutism was a series of variations on the dominant themes composed in the previous century by Louis XIV. That it has earned itself the historical distinction of "enlightened" absolutism suggests that those variations were of some consequence. Eighteenth-century rulers backed their sovereign claims not in the language of divine right, but in terms of their determination to act, as Frederick the Great of Prussia declared, as "first servant of the state." Enlightened rulers served their subjects by introducing reformist legislation and administration designed, at least in theory, to serve the well-being of the state community as a whole. They moved to curtail the privileges of old institutions. The Roman Catholic Church, for example, was compelled to suffer the expulsion of the Jesuits from most Catholic countries. Customary laws benefiting particular orders or interests were reformed. Serfdom was abolished or limited in some German states. Innovative policies in the areas of taxation, economic development, and education were instituted. As we shall see in Chapter 18, rational schemes of this sort reflected the spread of Enlightenment ideals as manifested in the writings of thinkers such as Beccaria, Diderot, and Voltaire. (The last was, in fact, a guest at Frederick's court for several years.) Assisting enlightened "first servants" in the implementation of these changes was a growing cadre of lesser servants: bureaucrats, often recruited from the nobility, but once recruited, expected to declare primary allegiance to their new master, the state. Despite innovation, "enlightened" absolutists continued to insist, as their predecessors had, that state sovereignty rested with the monarchy. Power remained their overriding concern, and to the extent that they combatted efforts by the estates of their realms to dilute that power, they declared their descent from their seventeenth-century forebears.

"Enlightened" absolutism

Louis XV

Louis XIV's successors, his great-grandson Louis XV (1715–1774) and that monarch's grandson Louis XVI (1774–1792), were unable to sustain the energetic drive toward centralization that had taken place under the Sun King. Indeed, during his last years, while fighting a desperate defensive war against his allied enemies, Louis XIV had seen his own accomplishments begin to crumble under the mounting pressure of military expenses. His heir was only five years old when he assumed the throne. As he grew up, Louis XV displayed little of his great-grandfather's single-minded determination to act the role of Sun King. The heroic, baroque grandeur of the main palace at Versailles

Absolutism under the successors of Louis XIV

yielded to the rococo grace of the Grand and Petit Trianons, pleasure pavillions built by Louis XV in the palace gardens. Both Louis XIV and Louis XV solaced themselves with the company of mistresses. The difference in their tastes, however, is a mark of the difference in their reigns. Madame de Maintenon, the Sun King's mistress, was a stern, devout Catholic, who interested herself directly in policies of state. Madame du Pompadour, Louis XV's favorite for many years, was a stylish, witty sensualist whose legacy was the elaborate hairstyle to which she bequeathed her name.

Resurgence of the parlements

During the minority of Louis XV, the French *parlements,* those courts of record responsible for registering and thereby legalizing royal decrees, enjoyed a resurgence of power which they retained throughout the century. No longer tame adjuncts of absolutist governmental machinery as they had been under Louis XIV, these bodies now proclaimed themselves the protectors of French "liberties." In fact they were protectors of little more than the privileges of the elite, although a growing number welcomed the *parlements'* willingness to block new taxes. In the late 1760s, hoping to emulate the success of his illustrious predecessor, and encouraged by his chancellor René Maupeou, Louis XV issued an edict effectively ending the right of *parlements* to reject decrees. Protest on the part of the magistrates resulted in their imprisonment or banishment. The *parlements* themselves were replaced by new courts charged not only with the responsibility of rubber-stamping legislation but also with administering law more justly and less expensively. When Louis XVI ascended the throne in 1774, his ministers persuaded him to reestablish the *parlements* as a sign of his willingness to conciliate his trouble-making aristocracy. This he did, with the result that government—particularly the management of finances—developed into a stalemated battle.

The achievements of Prussia

Stalemate was what the Prussian successors to Frederick William, the Great Elector, were determined to avoid. Absolutism, to thrive, needed to remain a dynamic force: precisely what it was in eighteenth-century Prussia. Frederick I (1688–1713), the Great Elector Frederick William's immediate successor, enhanced the appearance and cultural life of Berlin. As the Roman numeral by his name attests, he also succeeded in bargaining his support to the Austrians during the War of the Spanish Succession in return for the coveted right to style himself king.[3]

Frederick William I(1713–1740), cared little for the embellishments his father had made to the capital city. His overriding concern was the building of a first-rate army. So single-minded was his attention to the military that he came to be called "the sergeant king." Military display became an obsession. His private regiment of "Potsdam Giants" was comprised exclusively of soldiers over six feet in height. The king

---

[3] The Austrian monarch was the Holy Roman Emperor and therefore had the right to create kings.

traded musicians and prize stallions for such choice specimens and delighted in marching them about his palace grounds. Frederick William I's success as the builder of a military machine can be measured in terms of numbers: 30,000 men under arms when he came to the throne; 83,000 when he died twenty-seven years later, commander of the fourth-largest army in Europe, after France, Russia, and Austria. Since he could hardly count on volunteers, most of his soldiers were conscripts, drafted from the peasantry for a period of years and required to attend annual training exercises lasting three months. Conscription was supplemented by the kidnapping of forced recruits in neighboring German lands. To finance his army, Frederick William I increased taxes and streamlined their collection through the establishment of a General Directory of War, Finance, and Domains. He instituted a system of administration by boards, hoping thereby to eliminate individual inefficiency through collective responsibility and surveillance. In addition, he created an inspectorate to uncover and report to him the mistakes and inefficiencies of his officialdom. Even then, he continued to supervise personally the implementation of state policy while shunning the luxuries of court life; for him, the "theater" of absolutism was not the palace but the office, which placed him at the helm of the state and the army. Perceiving the resources of the state to be too precious to waste, he pared costs at every turn to the point where, it was said, he had to invite himself to a nobleman's table in order to enjoy a good meal.

A hard, unimaginative man, Frederick William I had little use for his son, whose passion was not the battlefield but the flute, and who admired French culture as much as his father disdained it. Not surprisingly, young Frederick rebelled; in 1730, when he was eighteen, he ran away from court with a friend. Apprehended, the companions were returned to the king, who welcomed the fledgling prodigal with something other than a fatted calf. Before Frederick's eyes, he had the friend executed. The grisly lesson took. Thenceforward Frederick, though he never surrendered his love of music and literature, bound himself to his royal duties, living in accordance with his own image of himself as "first servant of the state," and earning himself history's title of Frederick the Great.

Frederick William I's zealous austerity and his compulsion to build an efficient army and administrative state made Prussia a lean, strong state. Frederick the Great, building on the work of his father, raised his country to the status of a major power. As soon as he became king in 1740, Frederick mobilized the army his father had never taken into battle and occupied the poorly protected Austrian province of Silesia to which Prussia had no legitimate claim. Although he had earlier vowed to make morality rather than expediency the hallmark of his reign, he seemingly had little difficulty in sacrificing his youthful idealism in the face of an opportunity to make his Prussian state a leading member of the concert of nations. The remaining forty-five years of

Frederick William I

The apprenticeship of Frederick the Great

The seizure of Silesia

Frederick the Great and Voltaire. Although Frederick offered asylum to the French *philosophe,* this "enlightened despot" did not permit his intellectual pursuits to interfere with matters of state.

his monarchy were devoted to the consolidation of this first bold stroke.

Such a daring course required some adjustments within the Prussian state. The army had to be kept at full strength, and to this end, Frederick staffed its officer corps with young noblemen. In expanding the bureaucracy, whose financial administration kept his army in the field, he relied on the nobility as well, reversing the policy of his father, who had recruited his civil servants according to merit rather than birth. But Frederick was not one to tolerate mediocrity; he fashioned the most highly professional and efficient bureaucracy in all of Europe. The degree to which both army and bureaucracy were staffed by the nobility is a measure of his determination to secure the unflagging support of the most privileged order in his realm, in order to ensure a united front against Prussia's external foes.

The Prussian army and the nobility

Frederick's domestic policies reflected that same strategy. In matters where he ran no risk of offending the aristocracy, he followed his own rationalist bent, prohibiting the torture of accused criminals, putting an end to the bribing of judges, and establishing a system of elementary schools. He promoted religious toleration, declaring that he would happily build a mosque in Berlin if he could find enough Muslims to fill it. (Yet he was strongly anti-Semitic, levying special taxes on Jews and making efforts to close the professions and the civil service to them.) On his own royal estates he was a model "enlightened" monarch. He abolished capital punishment, curtailed the forced labor services of his peasantry, and granted them long leases on the land they worked. He fostered scientific forestry and the cultivation of new crops.

Frederick the Great as an enlightened absolutist

He opened new lands in Silesia and brought in thousands of immigrants to cultivate them. When wars ruined their farms, he supplied the peasants with new livestock and tools. Yet he never attempted to extend these reforms to the estates of the Junker elite, since to have done so would have alienated that social and economic group upon which Frederick was most dependent.

Although the monarchs of eighteenth-century Austria eventually proved themselves even more willing than Frederick the Great to undertake significant social reform, the energies of Emperor Charles VI (1711–1740) were concentrated on guaranteeing the future dynastic and territorial integrity of the Habsburg lineage and domain. Without a male heir, Charles worked to secure the right of his daughter Maria Theresa to succeed him as eventual empress. By his death in 1740 Charles had managed to persuade not only his subjects but all the major European powers to accept his daughter as his royal heir—a feat known as the "pragmatic sanction." Yet his painstaking efforts were only partially successful. As we have seen, Frederick the Great used the occasion of Charles's death to sieze Silesia. The French, unable to resist the temptation to grab what they could, entered the lists in this War of the Austrian Succession against the new empress, Maria Theresa (1740–1780).

*Charles VI and the
"pragmatic sanction"*

With most of her other possessions already occupied by her enemies, Maria Theresa appealed successfully to the Hungarians for support. The empress was willing to play the role of the wronged woman when, as on this occasion, it suited her interests to do so. Hungary's vital troops combined with British financial assistance helped to enable her to battle Austria's enemies to a draw, although she never succeeded in regaining Silesia. The experience of those first few years of

*Maria Theresa: Adversity
and centralization*

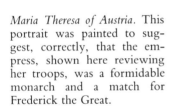

Maria Theresa of Austria. This portrait was painted to suggest, correctly, that the empress, shown here reviewing her troops, was a formidable monarch and a match for Frederick the Great.

her reign persuaded Maria Theresa, who was both capable and tenacious, to reorganize her dominions along the tightly centralized lines characteristic of absolutist Prussia and France. Ten new administrative districts were established, each with its own "war commissar" appointed by and responsible to the central administration in Vienna—an Austrian equivalent of the French intendant. Property taxes were increased to finance an expanded army, which was modernized and professionalized so as to remain on a par with the military establishments of the other great powers. Centralization, finances, army: once more those three crucial elements in the formula of absolute rule came into play.

"Enlightened" absolutism in Austria

Austrian absolutism did not stop there, however. Together Maria Theresa and her son Joseph II, with whom she ruled jointly from 1765 to 1780, and who then succeeded her for another ten years, instituted a series of social reforms which has earned them their reputation as "enlightened" absolutists. Although both mother and son were devout Roman Catholics, they moved to assert control of the Church, removing the clergy's exemption from taxation and decreeing the state's ability to block the publication of papal bulls in Austria. In 1773, following the papal suppression of the Jesuits, they used the order's assets to finance a program of state-wide primary education. Although the General Schools Ordinance of 1774 never achieved anything like a universally literate population, it did succeed in educating hundreds of thousands, and in financing not only schools for children but schools as well for those who taught the children. Joseph followed these reforms with an "Edict on Idle Institutions" in 1780, which resulted in the closing of hundreds of monastic houses, whose property went to support charitable institutions now under state control. These

Joseph II of Austria Visiting a Farm. The royal estates provided Joseph with the opportunity to experiment with agrarian reforms by raising the serfs to the status of free peasants.

reforms and others—rationalization of criminal procedures, a relaxation of censorship, and an attempt to eradicate superstition by curbing the practice of pilgrimages and celebration of saint's days—made Joseph more enemies than friends, among both the noble elite and the common people. "Enlightened" though Joseph II was, however, he nevertheless remained a staunch absolutist, as concerned with the maintenance of a strong army and an efficient bureaucracy as with the need to educate his peasantry. Joseph's brother Leopold II, who succeeded him in 1790, attempted to maintain the reformist momentum. His death two years later and the accession of his reactionary brother Francis II (1792–1835), put an end to liberalizing experiments.

Unlike Joseph II, Catherine the Great of Russia (1762–1796) felt herself compelled to curry the favor of her nobility by involving them directly in the structure of local administration, by exempting them from military service and taxation, and probably most important, by granting them absolute control over the serfs on their estates. Her policy grew out of her strong ties to powerful nobles and her involvement in the conspiracy which led to the assassination of her husband, Tsar Peter III, the last of a series of weak rulers who followed Peter the Great. Catherine was herself a German, and prided herself on her devotion to Western principles of government. Ambitious to establish a reputation as an intellectual and enlightened monarch, she corresponded with French philosophers, wrote plays, published a digest of William Blackstone's *Commentaries on the Laws of England,* and even began a history of Russia. Her contributions to social reform did not extend much beyond the founding of hospitals and orphanages, and the expression of a pious hope that someday the serfs might be liberated. Although she did summon a commission in 1767 to codify Russian law, its achievements were modest: a minor extension of religious toleration; a slight restriction of the use of torture by the state. Catherine's interest in theories of reform did, however, stimulate the development of a social conscience among certain gentry intellectuals, foreshadowing a more widespread movement in the nineteenth century.

Any plans Catherine may have had for improving the lot of the peasants, however, were abruptly cancelled after their frustration with St. Petersburg's centralization efforts erupted in a violent peasant-serf rebellion in 1773–1774. Free peasants in the Volga valley region found themselves compelled to provide labor services to nobles sent by the crown to control them, Cossacks were subjected to taxation and conscription for the first time, and factory workers and miners were pressed into service in the state's industrial enterprises. These and other disparate but dissatisfied groups, including serfs, united under the rebel banner of Emelyan Pugachev, an illiterate Cossack who claimed to be the late Tsar Peter III. The hapless Peter, who had spoken as a reformer in life, in death became a larger-than-life hero for those opposed to the determined absolutism of his successor. As Pugachev marched, he encouraged his followers to strike out not only against the empress

Catherine the Great

Catherine the Great of Russia

Emelyan Pugachev Shackled and Encaged after His Capture

but also against the nobility and the church. Over 1500 landlords and priests were murdered, and the ruling classes were terrified as the revolt spread. While Catherine's forces initially had little success against the rebel army, the threat of famine plagued Pugachev's advance and finally led to disarray among his troops. Betrayed in 1774, he was captured and taken in an iron cage to Moscow, where he was tortured and killed. Catherine responded to this uprising with further centralization and tightening of aristocratic authority over the peasantry.

The significance of Catherine the Great

The brutal suppression and punishment of the rebels reflected the ease with which the German-born Catherine took to the despotic authoritarianism that characterized Russian absolutism. She was as outsized in her tastes and personality as was Peter the Great. Her sexual appetite was voracious; her current chief officers of state as often as not were also her current lovers. But Catherine continued the work of Peter the Great in introducing Russia to Western ideas; she came to terms with the nobility in a way that brought stability to the state; and she made the country a formidable power in European affairs by extending its boundaries to include not only most of Poland but also lands on the Black Sea.

The absolutist worldview

Eighteenth-century absolutist monarchs shared a desire to pursue policies that would mark their regimes as modern, befitting a world that was leaving obscurantism and fanaticism behind. They were modern, also, in their determination to press ahead with the task, begun by their seventeenth-century predecessors, of building powerful, centralized states by continuing to eliminate or harness the ancient privileges of still-powerful noble orders and provincial estates. The notion of a limited monarchy, in which power was divided between local and central authorities and shared by monarchs, nobles, and legislative assemblies, struck them as a dangerous anachronism. Yet as the century progressed, they found that conviction challenged by the emergence of England, under limited monarchy, as the world's leading commercial and naval power.

England (or Britain, as the country was called after its union with Scotland in 1707) prospered as a state in which power was divided between the king and Parliament. This division of political power was guaranteed by a constitution which, though unwritten, was grounded in common law and strengthened by precedent and by particular legal settlements such as those that had followed the restoration of the Stuarts in 1660 and the overthrow of James II in 1688. The Hanoverians George I (1714–1727) and his son George II (1727–1760) were by no means political cyphers. Though George I could not speak English, he could converse comfortably enough with his ministers in French. The first two Georges made a conscientious and generally successful effort to govern within their adopted kingdom. They appointed the chief ministers who remained responsible to them for the creation and direction of state policy. Yet because Parliament, after 1688, retained the right

George I of England

The House of Commons. Despite its architectural division into two "sides," the House was composed of men of property whose similar economic interests encouraged them to agree on political fundamentals.

to legislate, tax, and spend, its powers were far greater than those of any European parlement, estate, or diet. During the reign of the first two Hanoverians, politics was on most occasions little more than a struggle between factions within the Whig party, composed of wealthy—and in many cases newly rich—landed magnates who were making fortunes in an expanding economy based on commercial and agricultural capitalism.

The Tories, because of their previous association with the Stuarts, remained political "outs" for most of the century. To the Whigs, national politics was no longer a matter of clashing principles. Those principles had been settled—to their satisfaction—in 1688. Nor was politics a matter of legislating in the national interest. Britain was governed locally, not from the center as in an absolutist state. Aristocrats and landed gentry administered the affairs of the particular counties and parishes in which their estates lay, as lords lieutenant, as justices of the peace, as overseers of the poor, unhampered, to a degree unknown on the Continent, by legislation imposed uniformly throughout the kingdom. The quality of local government varied greatly. Some squires were as "allworthy" as Henry Fielding's fictional character of that name in the novel *Tom Jones.* Others cared for little beyond the bottle and the chase. A French traveler noted in 1747 that the country gentleman was "naturally a very dull animal" whose favorite afterdinner toast was "to all honest fox hunters in Great Britain." These men

Local government

Left: *Sir Robert Walpole with Members of His Cabinet.* Right: *Walpole as a Roman Emperor.*

administered those general laws that did exist—the Poor Law, game laws—which were drawn in such a way as to leave their administrators wide latitude, a latitude which they exercised in order to enhance the appearance of their own local omnipotence. Thus in Britain there was no attempt to pass a law establishing a state-wide system of primary education. Centralizing legislation of that sort, the hallmark of absolutist states, was anathema to the British aristocracy and gentry. They argued that education, if it was to be provided, should be provided at their expense, in village schoolrooms by schoolmasters in their employ. Those instructors would make it their business to teach their pupils not only rudimentary reading, writing, and figuring, but the deferential behavior that bespoke the obligation of the poor to their rich benefactors. As the Church of England catechism had it, they were "to do their duty in that station of life unto which it shall please God to call them."

Politics, then, was neither first principles nor national legislation. It was "interest" and "influence," the weaving of a web of obligations into a political faction powerful enough to secure jobs and favors—a third secretaryship in the foreign office from a minister, an Act of Enclosure from Parliament. The greatest master of this game of politics was Robert Walpole (1676–1745) who was England's leading minister from the early 1720s until 1742. Walpole is sometimes called

Robert Walpole as chief minister

Britain's first prime minister, a less than entirely accurate distinction, since officially that position did not exist until the nineteenth century. Prime minister or not, he wielded great political power. He took advantage of the king's frequent absences in Hanover to assert control over the day-to-day governance of the country. He ruled as chief officer of his cabinet, a small group of like-minded politicians whose collective name derived from the small room in which they met. In time the cabinet evolved into the policy-making executive arm of the British political system; Britain is governed today by cabinet and Parliament, the cabinet composed of leading politicians from the majority party in Parliament.

Walpole was a member of a Norfolk gentry family who had risen to national prominence on the fortune he amassed while serving as paymaster-general to the armed forces during the War of the Spanish Succession. Adept at bribery and corruption, he used his ability to reward his supporters with appointments to ensure himself a loyal political following. By the end of his career, grossly fat and stuffed seemingly with the profits of his years in office, he was being depicted by cartoonists and balladeers as Britain's most accomplished robber. "Little villains must submit to Fate," lamented a typical lampoon, "while great ones do enjoy the world in state." Walpole was no more corrupt, however, than the political process over which he presided. Most seats in Parliament's lower House of Commons were filled by representatives from boroughs that often had no more than two or three dozen electors. Hence it was a relatively simple task to buy votes, either directly or with promises of future favors. Walpole cemented political factions together into an alliance that survived for about twenty years. During that time, he worked to ensure domestic tranquility by refusing to press ahead with any legislation that might arouse national controversy. He withdrew what was perhaps his most innovative piece of legislation—a scheme to increase excise taxes and reduce import duties as a means of curbing smugglers—in the face of widespread popular opposition.

Walpole and the nature of British politics

Other Whig politicians succeeded Walpole in office in the 1740s and 1750s, but only one, William Pitt, later elevated to the House of Lords as the earl of Chatham, commanded public attention as Walpole had. George III (1760–1820), who came to the throne as a young man in 1760, resented the manner in which he believed his royal predecessors had been treated by the Whig oligarchy. Whether or not, as legend has it, his mother fired his determination with the constant injunction "George, be king!" he began his reign convinced that he must assert his rightful prerogatives. He dismissed Pitt, and attempted to impose ministers of his own choosing on Parliament. King and Parliament battled this issue of prerogative throughout the 1760s. In 1770, Lord North, an aristocrat satisfactory to the king and with a large enough following in the House of Commons to ensure some measure of stability, assumed the position of first minister. His downfall occurred a

George III: the battle over prerogative

decade later, as a result of his mismanagement of the overseas war which resulted in Britain's loss of its original thirteen North American colonies. A period of political shuffling was followed by the king's appointment, at the age of twenty-three, of another William Pitt, Chatham's son, and this Pitt directed Britain's fortunes for the next twenty-five years—a political reign even longer than Walpole's. Although the period between 1760 and 1780 witnessed a struggle between crown (as the king and his political following were called) and Parliament, it was a very minor skirmish compared with the titanic constitutional struggles of the seventeenth century. Britain saw the last of absolutism in 1688. What followed was the mutual adjustment of the two formerly contending parties to a settlement both considered essentially sound.

7. WAR AND DIPLOMACY IN THE EIGHTEENTH CENTURY

Diplomacy in mid-century: the "diplomatic revolution"

The history of European diplomacy and warfare after 1715 is one in which the twin goals of international stability and economic expansion remained paramount. The fact that those objectives often conflicted with each other set off further frequent wars, in which the ever-growing standing armies of absolutist Europe were matched against each other and in which the deciding factor often turned out to be not continental military strength, but British naval power. The major conflict at mid-century, known as the Seven Years' War in Europe and the French and Indian War in North America, reflects the overlapping interests of power balance and commercial gain. In Europe, the primary concern was balance. Whereas in the past France had seemed the major threat, now Prussia loomed—at least in Austrian eyes—as a far more dangerous interloper. Under these circumstances, in 1756 the Austrian foreign minister, Prince Wenzel von Kaunitz, effected the so-called diplomatic revolution, which put an end to the enmity between France and Austria, and resulted in a formidable threat to the Prussia of Frederick the Great. Frederick, meanwhile, was taking steps to protect his flanks. While anxious not to arouse his French ally, he nevertheless signed a neutrality treaty with the British, who were concerned to secure protection for their sovereign's Hanoverian domains. The French read Frederick's act as a hostile one, and thus fell all the more readily for Kaunitz's offer of an alliance. The French indeed perceived a pressing need for trustworthy European allies, since they were already engaged in an undeclared war with England in North America. By mid-1756 Kaunitz could count France, Russia, Sweden, and several German states as likely allies against Prussia. Rather than await retribution from his enemies, Frederick invaded strategic but neutral Saxony and then Austria itself, thus once again playing the role of aggressor.

The configurations in this diplomatic gavotte are undoubtedly confusing. They are historically important, however, because they indicate the way in which the power balance was shifting, and the attempts of European states to respond to those shifts by means of new diplomatic alliances. Prussia and Britain were the volatile elements: Prussia on the Continent; Britain overseas. The war from 1756 to 1763 in Europe centered upon Frederick's attempts to prevent the dismemberment of his domain at the hands of the French-Austrian-Russian alliance. Time and again the Prussian army's superiority and Frederick's own military genius frustrated his enemies' attacks. Ultimately, Prussia's survival against these overwhelming odds—"the miracle of the House of Brandenburg"—was ensured by the death of the Tsarina Elizabeth (1741–1762), daughter of Peter the Great, and by the accession of Peter III (1762), whose admiration for Frederick was as great as was his predecessor's hostility. Peter withdrew from the war, returning the conquered provinces of East Prussia and Pomerania to his country's erstwhile enemy. The peace that followed, though it compelled Frederick to relinquish Saxony, recognized his right to retain Silesia, and hence put an end to Austria's hope of one day recapturing that rich prize.

Shifting power balances: the Seven Years' War

Overseas, battles occurred not only in North America but in the West Indies and in India, where Anglo-French commercial rivalry had resulted in sporadic, fierce fighting since the 1740s. Ultimate victory would go to that power possessing a navy strong enough to keep its supply routes open—that is, to Britain. Superior naval forces resulted in victories along the North American Great Lakes, climaxing in the Battle of Québec in 1759 and the eventual surrender of all of Canada to the British. By 1762 the French sugar islands, including Martinique, Grenada, and St. Vincent, were in British hands. Across the globe in India, the defeat of the French in the Battle of Plassey in 1757 and the capture of Pondichéry four years later made Britain the dominant European presence on the subcontinent. In the Treaty of Paris in 1763 which brought the Seven Years' War to an end, France officially surrendered Canada and India to the British, thus affording them an extraordinary field for commercial exploitation.

The British navy as key to victory

The success of the British in North America in the Seven Years' War was itself a major cause of the war which broke out between the mother country and her thirteen original colonies in 1775. To pay for the larger army the British now deemed necessary to protect their vastly expanded colonial possessions, they imposed unwelcome new taxes on the colonists. The North Americans protested that they were being taxed without representation. The home government responded that, like all British subjects, they were "virtually" if not actually represented by the present members of the House of Commons. Colonists thundered back that the present political system in Britain was so corrupt that no one but the Whig oligarchs could claim that their interests were being looked after.

"Taxation without representation . . ."

The Battle of Québec, 1759. Most often remembered for the fact that the British and French commanders, Generals Wolfe and Montcalm, were killed on the bluffs above the St. Lawrence River (the Plains of Abraham), this battle was most notable for the success of the British amphibious assault, a measure of Britain's naval superiority.

The American Revolution

Meanwhile the British were exacting retribution for rebellious acts on the part of colonists. East India Company tea shipped to be sold in Boston at prices advantageous to the company was dumped in Boston harbor. The port of Boston was thereupon closed, and democratic government in the colony of Massachusetts curtailed. The British garrison clashed with colonial civilians. Colonial "minutemen" formed a counterforce. By the time war broke out in 1775, most Americans were prepared to sever ties with Britain and declare themselves an independent nation, which they did the following year. Fighting continued until 1781 when a British army surrendered to the colonists at Yorktown to the tune of a song entitled "A World Turned Upside Down." The French, followed by Spain and the Netherlands, determined to do everything possible to inhibit the further growth of Britain's colonial empire, had allied themselves with the newly independent United States in 1778. A peace treaty signed in Paris in 1783 recognized the sovereignty of the new state. Though the British lost direct control of their former colonies, they reestablished their transatlantic commercial ties with America in the 1780s. Indeed, the brisk trade in raw cotton between the slave-owning southern states and Britain made possible the industrial revolution in textiles that began in the north of England at this time, and that carried Britain to worldwide preeminence as an economic power in the first half of the nineteenth century. This ultimately profitable arrangement lay in the future.

At the time, the victory of the American colonists seemed to contemporary observers to right the world balance of commercial power, which had swung so far to the side of the British. In this instance, independence seemed designed to restore stability.

In eastern Europe, however, the very precariousness of Poland's independence posed a threat to stability and the balance of power. As an independent state, Poland functioned, at least in theory, as a buffer among the major central European powers—Russia, Austria, and Prussia. Poland was the one major central European territory whose landed elite had successfully opposed introduction of absolutist centralization and a consequent curtailment of its "liberties." The result, however, had not been anything like real independence for either the Polish nobility or the country as a whole. Aristocrats were quite prepared to accept bribes from foreign powers in return for their vote in elections for the Polish king. And their continued exercise of their constitutionally guaranteed individual veto (the "liberum veto") in the Polish Diet meant that the country remained in a perpetual state of weakness that made it fair game for the land-hungry absolutist potentates who surrounded its borders.

Poland and the balance of power in eastern Europe

In 1764 Russia intervened to influence the election of King Stanislaus Poniatowski, an able enough nobleman who had been one of Catherine the Great's lovers. Thereafter Russia continued to meddle in the affairs of Poland—and of Turkey as well—often protecting both countries' Greek Orthodox Christian minority. When war finally broke out with Turkey in 1769, resulting in large Russian gains in the Balkans, Austria made known its opposition to further Russian expansion, lest it upset the existing balance of power in eastern Europe. In the end Russia was persuaded to acquire territory in Poland instead, by joining Austria and Prussia in a general partition of that country's lands. Though Maria Theresa opposed the dismemberment of Poland, she reluctantly agreed to participate in the partition in order to maintain the balance of power, an attitude which prompted a scornful Frederick the Great to remark that "She weeps, but she takes her share." According to the agreement of 1772, Poland lost about 30 percent of its kingdom and about half of its population.

The first partition of Poland

Following this first partition, the Russians continued to exercise virtual control of Poland. King Stanislaus, however, took advantage of a new Russo-Turkish war in 1788 to press for a more truly independent state with a far stronger executive than had existed previously. A constitution adopted in May 1791 established just that; but this rejuvenated Polish state was to be short-lived. In January 1792, the Russo-Turkish war ended and Catherine the Great pounced. Together the Russians and Prussians took two more enormous bites out of Poland in 1793, destroying the new constitution in the process. A rebellion under the leadership of Thaddeus Kosciuszko, who had fought in America, was crushed in 1794 and 1795. A final swallow by Russia, Austria, and Prussia in 1795 left nothing of Poland at all.

The second and third partitions of Poland

Dividing the Royal Cake. A contemporary cartoon showing the monarchs of Europe at work carving up a hapless Poland.

After this series of partitions of Poland, each of the major powers was a good deal fatter; but on the international scales by which such things were measured, they continued to weigh proportionately the same.

The final devouring of Poland occurred at a time when the Continent was once again engaged in a general war. Yet this most recent conflict was not just another military attempt to resolve customary disputes over commerce or problems of international stability. It was the result of violent revolution that had broken out in France in 1789, that had toppled the Bourbon dynasty there, and that threatened to do the same to other monarchs across Europe. The second and third partitions of Poland were a final bravura declaration of power by monarchs who already feared for their heads. Henceforth, neither foreign nor domestic policy would ever again be dictated as they had been in absolutist Europe by the convictions and determinations of kings and queens alone. Poland disappeared as Europe fell to pieces, as customary practice gave way to new and desperate necessity.

Though absolutism met its death in the years immediately after 1789, the relevance of its history to that of the modern world is greater than it might appear. First, centralization provided useful precedents to nineteenth-century state-builders. Modern standing armies— be they made up of soldiers or bureaucrats—are institutions whose

European upheaval

origins rest in the age of absolutism. Second, absolutism's centripetal force contributed to an economic climate that gave birth to industrial revolution. Factories built to produce military matériel, capitalist agricultural policies designed to provide food for burgeoning capital cities, increased taxes that drove peasants to seek work in rural industries: these and other programs pointed to the future. Third, in their constant struggle to curb the privileges of nobility and oligarchy, absolute monarchs played out one more act in a drama that would continue into the nineteenth century. French nobles of both sword and robe, Prussian junkers, and Russian boyars all bargained successfully to retain their rights to property and its management while surrendering to some degree their role as governors. But as long as their property rights remained secure, their power was assured. The French Revolution would curb their power for a time, but they were survivors. Their adaptability, whether as agricultural entrepreneurs or as senior servants of the state, ensured their order an important place in the world that lay beyond absolutism.

SELECTED READINGS

• *Items so designated are available in paperback editions.*

Anderson, M. S., *Historians and Eighteenth-Century Europe,* Oxford, 1979. Contains recent scholarly debate.

———, *Peter the Great,* London, 1978. A good, thorough biography.

• Avrich, Paul, *Russian Rebels, 1600–1800,* New York, 1972. A study of revolts against absolutist power.

Baxter, Stephen, *William III and the Defense of European Liberty, 1650–1702,* New York, 1965. The best study of the Dutchman who became England's king.

Bernard, Paul, *Joseph II,* New York, 1968.

• Brewer, John, *Party Ideology and Popular Politics at the Accession of George III,* Cambridge, 1976, A revisionist interpretation of political alignments and party.

Churchill, W. S., *Marlborough,* New York, 1968. An abridged edition of Churchill's magnificently written biography of his ancestor.

• Cobban, Alfred, *A History of Modern France,* New York, 1961. A survey with a point of view.

Corvisier, André, *Armies and Societies in Europe, 1494–1789,* Bloomington, Ind., 1979. Focuses on the French army.

• Dukes, Paul, *Catherine the Great and the Russian Nobility,* Cambridge, 1967. A study of the limits of absolutism.

• Dunn, Richard S., *The Age of Religious Wars, 1559–1715,* 2nd ed., New York, 1979. A detailed and up-to-date survey, useful for the history of late seventeenth- and early eighteenth-century absolutism.

Ford, Franklin, *Robe and Sword: The Regrouping of the French Aristocracy after Louis XIV,* Cambridge, Mass., 1953. An important social study of the nobility of the robe and its striving for dominance before the revolution.

- Fraser, Antonia, *Royal Charles: Charles II and the Restoration,* New York, 1979. A readable, reliable life of the king and his times.
- Goubert, Pierre, *Louis XIV and Twenty Million Frenchmen,* New York, 1972. A valuable study, the starting point for an understanding of the Sun King's reign.
- Hatton, R. H., *Europe in the Age of Louis XIV,* New York, 1969. Thoughtful interpretation of the period; excellent illustrations.
- Herr, Richard, *The Eighteenth Century Revolution in Spain,* Princeton, 1958. The best introduction to Spain in this period.
- Holborn, Hajo, *The Age of Absolutism,* New York, 1964. The best survey for Germany. Second volume of Holborn's *History of Modern Germany.*
- Krieger, Leonard, *Kings and Philosophers, 1689–1789,* New York, 1970. A thorough survey of the political and intellectual developments of this century.
- Lewis, W. H., *The Splendid Century: Life in the France of Louis XIV,* New York, 1953. A delightfully written survey.
- Palmer, R. R., *The Age of the Democratic Revolution: A Political History of Europe and America, 1760–1800,* Vol. 1, Princeton, 1964. Argues in favor of a general European aristocratic reaction prior to 1789.

  Plumb, J. H., *Sir Robert Walpole,* 2 vols., Boston, 1956, 1961. A well-written, sympathetic biography of England's leading eighteenth-century politician.
- Riasanovsky, Nicholas V., *A History of Russia,* 4th ed., Oxford, 1984. A useful introduction.
- Ritter, Gerhard, *Frederick The Great: A Historical Profile,* Berkeley, 1968. A readable biography.
- Rudé, George, *Europe in the Eighteenth Century: Aristocracy and the Bourgeois Challenge,* New York, 1972. A survey which stresses social stratification and tension.
- Speck, W. A., *Stability and Strife: England, 1714–1760,* Cambridge, Mass., 1977. A good, recent survey.

  Spielman, John P., *Leopold I of Austria,* New Brunswick, N.J., 1977. The only biography of the monarch in English.
- Wangermann, Ernst, *The Austrian Achievement, 1700–1800,* London, 1973. A suggestive introductory survey.
- Wolf, John B., *Louis XIV,* New York, 1968. The standard biography in English.

  ———, *The Emergence of the Great Powers, 1685–1715,* New York, 1951. A useful general survey of this critical period.
- Woloch, Isser, *Eighteenth Century Europe: Tradition and Progress, 1715–1789,* New York, 1982. A thoughtful, well-organized survey.

SOURCE MATERIALS

- Locke, John, *Two Treatises of Government.* (Many editions.) The argument against absolutism.

  Saint-Simon, Louis, *Historical Memoirs.* (Many editions.) A brilliant source for evidence about life at the court of Louis XIV.

Chapter 18

THE SCIENTIFIC REVOLUTION AND ENLIGHTENMENT

This is the age wherein philosophy comes in with a spring-tide. . . .
Methinks I see how all the old rubbish must be thrown away, and the
rotten buildings be overthrown, and carried away with so powerful an
inundation.

—Henry Power, *Experimental Philosophy* (1663)

Enlightenment is humanity's departure from its self-imposed immaturity. Immaturity is the inability to use one's intellect without the guidance of others. This immaturity is self-imposed when its cause is not a lack of intelligence but a failure of determination and courage to think without the guidance of someone else. Dare to know! This then is the slogan of the Enlightenment.

—Immanuel Kant, *What is Enlightenment?* (1784)

The years between roughly 1660 and 1789, which witnessed the prevalence of absolutism in western Europe, witnessed as well the most important mutation in all of European intellectual and cultural history to occur between the Middle Ages and the present. Just as the sweep of fresh winds can greatly change the weather, so in the last few decades of the seventeenth century the sweep of new ideas led to a bracing change in Europe's "climate of opinion." For purposes of analysis it is convenient to refer to two phases within the larger period: the triumph of the scientific revolution in the second half of the seventeenth century and the age of "Enlightenment" which followed for most of the eighteenth century. But without any doubt the same intellectual winds that swept into Europe during the later seventeenth century prevailed for well over a hundred years. Indeed, their influence is still felt today.

New ideas: 1660–1789

How did the new intellectual climate differ from the old? Concentrating on essentials, three points may be stressed. First, whereas medieval, Renaissance, and Reformation thinkers all assumed that past

Changes in intellectual environment

knowledge was the most reliable source of wisdom, the greatest thinkers from the seventeenth century onward rejected any obeisance to ancient authority and resolved to rely on their own intellects to see where knowledge would lead them. Making their motto "dare to know," they stressed the autonomy of science and the free play of the mind in ways unheard of in the West since the golden age of Greece. Second, the new breed of thinkers believed strongly that knowledge was valueless if it could not be put to use. For a Plato, an Aristotle, or a St. Thomas Aquinas alike, the greatest wisdom was the most abstract wisdom since such wisdom helped to turn the human mind away from all earthly "corruptibility" and supposedly brought happiness by its sheer resemblance to timeless divinity. But after the change in Europe's climate of opinion in the late seventeenth century, all knowledge without practical value was belittled and thinkers from every realm of intellectual endeavor aimed directly or indirectly at achieving "the relief of man's estate." Finally, the new climate of opinion was characterized by the demystification of the universe. Up until the mid-seventeenth century, most people, learned and unlearned, assumed that the universe was driven and inhabited by occult forces that humans could barely understand and surely never control unless they were magicians. But around 1660 a mechanistic worldview swept away occultism, and pixies became consigned to the realm of children's storybooks. Thereafter nature was believed to work like the finest mechanical clock—consummately predictable and fully open to human understanding.

Causes of change

Why such a dramatic change in basic patterns of thought took place when it did will long remain a subject for speculation. Certainly the prior Scholastic stress on human rationality and the Renaissance reacquisition of classical Greek texts helped to bring European thought to a scientific threshold. Probably the most direct causes of the intellectual mutations, however, were the twin challenges to conventional assumptions introduced in the sixteenth century by the discovery of the New World and the realization that the earth revolves around the sun rather than vice versa, for neither the Bible nor ancient science allowed room for what one bewildered contemporary called "new islands, new lands, new seas, new peoples, and what is more, a new sky and new stars." At first many thinkers, daunted by all this novelty, experienced a sense of intellectual crisis. Some took refuge in skepticism, others in relativism, and others in a return to blind faith. Speaking for several generations, the poet John Donne lamented in 1611 that "new philosophy calls all in doubt, the element of fire is quite put out, the sun is lost, and the earth, and no man's wit can well direct him where to look for it. . . . 'tis all in pieces, all coherence gone." But just as Europe surmounted its early-modern political crisis around 1660, so did it surmount its intellectual one, above all because the last stages of a profound scientific revolution gave a new, completely convincing "coherence" to things. As Alexander Pope wrote in the early eighteenth century, almost as if in response to Donne: "Nature and Nature's Law's lay hid in night:/ God said, Let Newton Be! and all was light."

I. THE SCIENTIFIC REVOLUTION

Even though Europe did not begin to resolve its intellectual crisis until about 1660, the groundwork for that resolution was prepared earlier in the seventeenth century by four great individuals—Kepler, Galileo, Bacon, and Descartes. Kepler and Galileo—both practicing scientists—have been discussed earlier; suffice it here to say that they removed all doubts about the Copernican heliocentric theory of the solar system and helped lead the way to Sir Isaac Newton's theory of universal gravitation. As for Bacon and Descartes, their main achievements were not in the realm of original scientific discovery but rather in propagating new attitudes toward learning and the nature of the universe.

Sir Francis Bacon (1561–1626), lord chancellor of England, was also an extremely influential philosopher of science. In Bacon's view, expressed most fully in his *Novum Organum* (*New Instrument*) of 1620, science could not advance unless it departed entirely from the inherited errors of the past and established "progressive stages of certainty." For Bacon this meant proceeding strictly on the basis of empirical knowledge (knowledge gained solely by the senses) and by means of the "inductive method," meaning the arrival at truth by proceeding upward from particular observations to generalizations. Insisting that "the corruption of philosophy by superstition and an admixture of theology . . . does the greatest harm," and that thinking people thus should be "sober-minded, and give to faith that only which is faith's," Bacon advocated the advancement of learning as a cooperative venture proceeding by means of meticulously recorded empirical experiments. Unlike the arid speculations of the past, collective scientific research and observation would produce useful knowledge and result in bettering the human lot. Much of Bacon's ideology is vividly evoked in the cover illustration of his *Novum Organum,* wherein intrepid ships venture out beyond the Pillars of Hercules (Straits of Gibraltar) onto a fathomless sea in pursuit of unknown but great things to come.

Bacon's later contemporary, the French philosopher René Descartes (1596–1650), agreed with him on two points: that all past knowledge should be discarded, and that the worth of any idea depended on its usefulness. Yet Descartes otherwise proposed some very different approaches to science, for unlike the empiricist Bacon, Descartes was a rationalist and an apostle of mathematics. In his *Discourse on Method* (1637), Descartes explained how, during a period of solitude, he resolved to submit all inherited doctrines to a process of systematic

Title Page of Bacon's Novum Organum. Underneath the ship sailing out into the ocean is a quotation from the Book of Daniel: "Many shall venture forth and science shall be increased."

René Descartes

*A Diagram Illustrating Cartesian
Principles.* Descartes maintained that the pineal gland,
seen here at the back of the
head, transmitted messages
from the eyes to the muscles
in purely mechanical fashion.
But the pineal gland was also
the link between the material
body and the nonmaterial human mind. From the 1677 edition of Descartes' *De Homine.*

Descartes' influence

*The English and French
traditions*

doubting because he knew that the "strangest or most incredible"
things had previously been set down in learned books. Taking as his
first rule "never to receive anything as a truth which [he] did not clearly
know to be such," he found himself doubting everything until he
came to the recognition that his mere process of thought proved his
own existence ("I think, therefore I am"). Thereupon making rationality the point of departure for his entire philosophical enterprise,
Descartes rebuilt the universe on largely speculative grounds that differed in almost every detail from the universe conceived by the Greeks,
yet conformed fully to the highest principles of human rationality as
expressed in the laws of mathematics. That most of his theories were
not empirically verifiable did not trouble him at all, because he was
confident that "natural processes almost always depend on parts so
small that they utterly elude our senses."

Predictably, the details of Descartes' scientific system are now
regarded as mere curiosities, but the French philosopher nonetheless
was enormously influential in aiding the advance of science and in
creating a new climate of opinion for several reasons. First of all, even
though his systematic doubting did not succeed in establishing any
solid new scientific truths, it did contribute to the discrediting of all
the faulty science of the ancients. Then too, Descartes' stress on
mathematics was salutary because mathematics has indeed proven to
be an indispensable handmaiden to the pursuit of natural science. But
undoubtedly Descartes' single most influential legacy was his philosophy of *dualism,* according to which God created only two kinds of
reality—mind and matter. In Descartes' view, mind belonged to man
alone, and all else was matter. Thus he insisted that all created existence
beyond man—organic and inorganic alike—operated solely in terms
of physical laws, or the interplay of "extension and motion." In other
words, for Descartes every single entity from the solar system to the
realm of animals and plants was a self-operating machine propelled by
a force arising from the original motion given to the universe by God.
Indeed, Descartes thought that man himself was a machine—although,
in this sole exception, a machine equipped with a mind. From this it
followed that the entire universe could be studied objectively, without
any aid from theology or appeals to the occult. Moreover, all apparent
atributes of matter, such as light, color, sound, taste, or smell, which
had no "extension" were to be classified as mere subjective impressions of the human mind unfit for proper scientific analysis. Based on
such assumptions the pursuit of science could be dispassionate as never
before.

Roughly speaking, for about a century after the work of Bacon and
Descartes the English scientific community was Baconian and the
French Cartesian (a name given to followers of Descartes). This is to
say that the English concentrated primarily on performing empirical
experiments in many different areas of physical science leading to concrete scientific advances, whereas the French tended to remain more

oriented toward mathematics and philosophical theory. Among the numerous great seventeenth-century English laboratory scientists were the physician William Harvey (1578–1657), the chemist Robert Boyle (1627–1691), and the biologist Robert Hooke (1635–1703). Pursuing the earlier work of Vesalius and Servetus, but daring, unlike them, to practice vivisection, Harvey was the first to observe and describe the circulation of the blood through the arteries and back to the heart through the veins. Similarly committed to empirical experiment, Boyle used the air pump to establish "Boyle's law"—namely, that under constant temperature the volume of a gas decreases in proportion to the pressure placed on it. Boyle also was the first chemist to distinguish between a mixture and a compound (wherein the chemical combination occurs), and accomplished much to discredit alchemy. As for Hooke, although he conducted research in astronomy and physics as well as biology, he is best known for having used the microscope to discover the cellular structure of plants. Meanwhile, in France, Descartes himself pioneered in analytical geometry, Blaise Pascal worked on probability theory and invented a calculating machine before his conversion to religion, and Pierre Gassendi (1592–1655) sought to demonstrate the truth of the atomic theory. Also within the French realm of thought was the Dutch Jew Baruch Spinoza (1632–1677), a philosopher who tried to apply geometry to ethics and believed that he advanced beyond Descartes by interpreting the universe as being composed of a single substance—simultaneously God and nature— instead of two.

The dichotomy between English Baconianism and French Cartesianism, however, breaks down when one approaches the man commonly considered to have been the greatest scientist of all time, Sir Isaac Newton (1642–1727). A highly unattractive personality in his daily conduct—being secretive, petty, and vindictive—Newton was nonetheless a towering genius who drew on both the Baconian and Cartesian heritages. For example, following Bacon, and in the sharpest opposition to Descartes, Newton refused to dismiss the phenomenon of light as a mere subjective impression of "mind." Instead, by means of laboratory experiments he demonstrated that light behaves differently when filtered through different media, and hence offered an interpretation of light as a stream of particles that solidly established optics as an empirical branch of physics. Yet, on the other hand, Newton thoroughly approved of Descartes' stress on mathematics, and once in a burst of purely theoretical inspiration discovered the infinitesimal calculus.

Sir Isaac Newton

Of course Newton's supreme accomplishment lay in his formulation of the law of universal gravitation, which, as expressed in his monumental Latin *Principia Mathematica* (*Mathematical Principles of Natural Philosophy*) of 1687, integrated Copernican astronomy with Galileo's physics. In the *Principia* Newton broached the two major scientific questions of his day: (1) What keeps the heavy earth in motion?

Newton's law of gravitation

(before Copernicus the earth had been thought immobile) and (2) Why do terrestrial bodies tend to fall to the earth's center whereas planets stay in orbital motion? (before Copernicus the planets were thought to be embedded in crystalline spheres moved by angels or "divine intelligences"). In the early seventeenth century Kepler had already suggested the possibility of mutual attractions between all bodies in the solar system that kept the earth and other planets moving, but the Cartesians attacked this explanation as being too occult since attraction over space left out the crucial Cartesian ingredient of matter. Disregarding these Cartesian doubts because he saw no alternative, Newton returned to consider Kepler's theory of mutual attractions, and uniting Baconian observations with Cartesian mathematics, arrived at a single law of universal gravitation according to which "every particle of matter in the universe attracts every other particle with a force varying inversely as the square of the distance between them and directly proportional to the product of their masses." Since this law was verified by experience in both terrestrial and celestial realms, there could be no doubt that it explained all motion. Indeed, Newton's law was so reliable that it was employed immediately to predict the ebb and flow of tides. Later, in 1846, astronomers, noting irregularities in the motion of the planet Uranus, were able to deduce on Newtonian grounds the presence of the more distant planet Neptune before Neptune was actually located with the aid of high-power telescopes.

The impact of Newton's
Principia

Historians of science consider Newton's law of gravity to be "the most stupendous single achievement of the human mind," finding that "no other work in the whole history of science equals the *Principia* either in originality and power of thought or in the majesty of its achievement." Certainly the publication of the *Principia* was the crowning event of the scientific revolution because it confirmed the most important astronomical and physical theories previously set forth by Copernicus, Kepler, and Galileo, and resolved beyond quarrel the major problems that Copernicus's heliocentric theory had created. Needless to say, scientific work did not thereafter come to a standstill. Quite to the contrary, since Newton's accomplishment proved inspirational to researchers in many other fields, scientific work advanced steadily after 1687. But a fundamental reconception of the nature of the physical universe had been made, and thinkers in all areas could proceed with their work confident that science rather than superstition was the new order of the day.

2. THE FOUNDATIONS OF THE ENLIGHTENMENT

Although the presuppositions for the Enlightenment were set by the triumph of the scientific revolution in the late seventeenth century, the Enlightenment itself was an eighteenth-century phenomenon, lasting for close to the entire century until certain basic Enlightenment postulates were challenged around 1790 by the effects of the French Revolution and the new movement of romanticism. Of course not every thinker who lived and worked in the eighteenth century was equally "enlightened." Some, such as the Italian philosopher of history G. B. Vico (1668–1744), were thoroughly opposed to everything the Enlightenment stood for, and others, most notably Jean Jacques Rousseau (1712–1778), accepted certain Enlightenment values but sharply rejected others. Moreover, patterns of Enlightenment ideology tended to vary from country to country and to change in each country over the course of the century. Yet, despite these qualifications, most thinkers of the eighteenth century definitely shared the sense of living in an exciting new intellectual environment in which "the party of humanity" would prevail over traditionalism and obscurantism by dint of an unflinching commitment to the primacy of the intellect.

The Enlightenment: the major pattern of eighteenth-century thought

Most Enlightenment thought stemmed from three basic premises: (1) the entire universe is fully intelligible and governed by natural rather than supernatural forces; (2) rigorous application of "scientific method" can answer fundamental questions in all areas of inquiry; and (3) the human race can be "educated" to achieve nearly infinite improvement. The first two of these premises were products of the scientific revolution and the third primarily an inheritance from the psychology of John Locke.

Premises of the Enlightenment

Regarding the substitution of a natural for a supernatural worldview, explanations must start with the euphoria which greeted Isaac Newton's discovery of a single law whereby all motion in the heavens and earth became intelligible and predictable. If Newton could deal so authoritatively and elegantly with motion, it seemed to follow that all nature is governed neither by mysterious divine intervention nor by caprice, but by humanly perceivable universal laws. Hence most serious thinkers from about 1690 to 1790 became inveterate opponents of belief in miracles, and considered all varieties of revealed religion to be not just irrelevant to the pursuit of science, but positively antithetical to it. This is not to say that the Enlightenment abandoned belief in the existence of God: to the contrary, only the smallest number of Enlightenment thinkers were atheists, and very few even were avowed agnostics. Rather, most adhered to a religious outlook known as *Deism* which assumed that God existed but, having once created a perfect universe, no longer took an active interest in it. Expressed in the language of the Deists themselves, God was the "divine clockmaker" who, at the beginning of time, constructed a perfect timepiece and then left it to run on with predictable regularity. Most Deists continued to attend the churches of their ancestors (either Protestant or Catholic) from time to time, but they made little secret of their doubts about the efficacy of ritual and spoke out against all forms of religious intolerance.

The rejection of supernaturalism

The Study of an Amateur Scientist. This late–seventeenth-century aristocratic dilettante collected all sorts of specimens from the natural world. The mounting of his crocodile must have offered some challenge.

Confidence in scientific method

As for the second Enlightenment premise, the accomplishments of the scientific revolution inspired a deep sense of assurance that "scientific method" was the only valid means for pursuing research in all areas of human inquiry. By scientific method Enlightenment thinkers usually meant the dispassionate, empirical observation of particular phenomena in order to arrive at general laws. Given the acknowledged triumph of Newtonian physics, it is not surprising that around 1700 western Europe was struck by a virtual mania for applying scientific method in studying all the workings of nature. Since most scientific work was still simple enough to be understood by amateurs without the benefit of years of specialized education, European aristocrats and prosperous people in all walks of life began to dabble in "research"—buying telescopes, chasing butterflies, or building home laboratories in the hope of participating in some new scientific breakthrough. Writing in 1710, the English essayist Joseph Addison satirized such pursuits by imagining a will written by one "Sir Nicholas Gimcrack," an earnest amateur who left his "recipe for preserving dead caterpillars" to his daughters, his "rat's testicles" to a "learned and worthy friend," and who disinherited his son for "having spoken disrespectfully of his little sister," whose mortal remains Sir Nicholas kept near his desk in "spirits of wine." Of course most of the aristocratic "Gimcracks" never progressed beyond pickling, but their enthusiasm for following the latest developments in scientific research led them to patronize the work of truly gifted scientists and contributed to creating an atmosphere wherein science was prized as humanity's greatest attainment.

Inevitably, in turn, such an atmosphere was conducive to an assumption which became dominant in the course of the eighteenth century—that scientific method was the only proper means for study-ing human affairs as well as natural phenomena. Since the world of physical nature seemed well on the way to being mastered, Enlighten-ment thinkers considered it mere common sense that the world of human nature could soon be mastered as well by scientific means. Thus students of religion started collecting myths from numerous dif-ferent traditions, not to find any occult truth in them but to classify their common traits and learn the steps by which humanity suppos-edly freed itself from superstition. Similarly, historians collected evi-dence to learn the laws governing the rise and fall of nations, and students of politics compared governmental constitutions to arrive at an ideal and universally applicable political system. In other words, as the English poet Alexander Pope stated in his *Essay on Man* of 1733, "the science of human nature [may be] like all other sciences reduced to a few clear points," and Enlightenment thinkers became deter-mined to learn exactly what those "few clear points" were.

The scientific method applied to human concerns

It must be stressed, however, that if most thinkers of the Enlighten-ment supposed that the empirical study of human conduct could reduce society's working to a few laws, most also believed that human con-duct was not immutable but highly perfectible. In this they were inspired primarily by the psychology of John Locke (1632–1704), who was not only a very influential political philosopher, as we have seen, but also the formulator of an extremely influential theory of knowl-edge. In his *Essay Concerning Human Understanding* (1690) Locke rejected the hitherto dominant assumption that ideas are innate, maintaining instead that all knowledge originates from sense perception. Accord-ing to Locke, the human mind at birth is a "blank tablet" (Latin: *tabula rasa*) upon which nothing is inscribed: not until the infant begins to experience things, that is, to perceive the external world with its senses, is anything registered on its mind. From this point of departure, Enlightenment thinkers concluded that environment determines everything. For example, in their view, if some aristocrats were any better than ordinary mortals it was not because they had inherited any special knowledge or virtues, but only because they had been better trained. It therefore followed that all people could be educated to become the equals of the most perfect aristocrats, and that there were no limits to the potentialities for universal human progress. Indeed, a few Enlightenment thinkers became so optimistic as to propose that all evil might be eradicated from the world, since whatever evil existed was not the result of some divine plan but only the product of a faulty environment that humans had created and humans could change.

John Locke's psychology and human perfectibility

3. THE WORLD OF THE PHILOSOPHES

France, the dominant country in eighteenth-century Europe, was the center of the Enlightenment movement, and thus it is customary to refer to the leading exponents of the Enlightenment, regardless of where

General characteristics of the philosophes

Voltaire

***Voltaire* by Houdon**

Voltaire's social views

they lived, by the French term *philosophe,* meaning philosopher. In fact the term philosophe is slightly misleading inasmuch as hardly any of the philosophes—with the exceptions, to be seen, of David Hume and Immanuel Kant—were really philosophers in the sense of being highly original abstract thinkers. Rather, most were practically oriented publicists who aimed to reform society by popularizing the new scientific interpretation of the universe and applying dispassionate "scientific method" to a host of contemporary problems. Since they sought most of all to gain converts and alter what they regarded as outmoded institutions, they shunned all forms of expression that might seem incomprehensible or abstruse, priding themselves instead on their clarity, and occasionally even expressing their ideas in the form of stories or plays rather than treatises.

By common consent the prince of the philosophes was the Frenchman born François Marie Arouet, who called himself Voltaire (1694–1778). Virtually the personification of the Enlightenment, much as Erasmus two centuries earlier had embodied Christian humanism, Voltaire commented on an enormous range of subjects in a wide variety of literary forms. Probably his greatest single accomplishment lay in championing the cause of English empiricism in previously Cartesian France. Having as a young man been exiled to England for the crime of insulting a pompous French nobleman, Voltaire returned after three years a thorough and extremely persuasive convert to the ideas of Bacon and Locke. Not only did this mean that he persuaded other French thinkers to accept Newton's empirically verifiable scientific system in place of Descartes' unverifiable one, but he also encouraged them to be less abstract and theoretical in all their intellectual inclinations and more oriented toward the solving of everyday problems. To be sure, throughout the eighteenth century France's intellectual world remained more rationalistic than England's, but Voltaire's lifelong campaign on behalf of empiricism nonetheless had a very salutary effect in making French thinkers more practically oriented than before.

Continually engaged in commenting on contemporary problems himself, Voltaire was an ardent spokesman for civil liberties. In this regard his battlecry was *Écrasez l'infâme*—"crush infamy"—meaning by infamy all forms of repression, fanaticism, and bigotry. In his own words, he believed that "the individual who persecutes another because he is not of the same opinion is nothing less than a monster." Accordingly, he wrote an opponent a line which forever after has been held forth as the first principle of civil liberty: "I do not agree with a word you say, but I will defend to the death your right to say it." Of all forms of intolerance Voltaire hated religious bigotry most of all because it seemed based on silly superstitions: "the less superstition, the less fanaticism; and the less fanaticism, the less misery." In addition to attacking religious repression, Voltaire also frequently criticized the exercise of arbitrary powers by secular states. In particular, he thought

that the English parliamentary system was preferable to French absolutism and that all states acted criminally when their policies resulted
in senseless wars. "It is forbidden to kill," he maintained sardonically,
"therefore all murderers are punished unless they kill in large numbers
and to the sound of trumpets."

Although Voltaire exerted the greatest effect on his age as a propagandist for the basically optimistic Enlightenment principle that by
"crushing infamy" humanity could take enormous strides forward,
the only one of his works still widely read today, the satirical story
Candide (1759), is atypically subdued. Writing not long after the disastrous Lisbon earthquake of 1755, in which over 20,000 lives were
lost for no apparent reason, Voltaire drew back in this work from
some of his earlier faith that mankind by its own actions could limit-
lessly improve itself. Lulled into false security concerning what life
has in store for him by the fatuous optimism of his tutor, Dr. Pangloss, the hero of the story, Candide, journeys through the world only
to experience one outrageous misfortune after another. Storms and
earthquakes are bad enough, but worse still are wars and rapacity
caused by uncontrollable human passions. Only in the golden never-
never land of "Eldorado" (clearly a spoof of the perfect world most
philosophes saw on the horizon), where there are no priests, law courts,
or prisons, but unlimited wealth and a "palace of sciences . . . filled
with instruments of mathematics and physics," does Candide find
temporary respite from disaster. Being a naturally restless mortal,
however, he quickly becomes bored with Eldorado's placid perfection
and leaves for the renewed buffetings of the real world. After many
more lessons in "the school of hard knocks," he finally learns one
basic truth by the end of the story: settling down on a modest farm
with his once-beautiful but now hideously disfigured wife, he shrugs
when Dr. Pangloss repeats for the hundredth time that "this is the
best of all possible worlds," and replies: "that's as may be, but we
must cultivate our garden." In other words, according to Voltaire, life
is not perfect and probably never will be, but humans will succeed
best if they ignore vapid theorizing and buckle down to unglamorous
but productive hard work.

Candide

In addition to Voltaire, the most prominent French philosophes were
Montesquieu, Diderot, and Condorcet. The baron de Montesquieu
(1689–1755) was primarily a political thinker. In his major work, *The
Spirit of Laws* (1748), Montesquieu sought to discover the ways in
which differing environments and historical and religious traditions
influence governmental institutions. Finding that unalterable differences in climates and geographic terrains affect human behavior, and
hence governmental forms, Montesquieu throughout much of *The
Spirit of Laws* seems to be saying that external conditions force humans
to behave in different ways and that there is nothing they can do about
this. But ultimately he was an idealist who preferred one particular
political system, the English constitution, and hoped that all nations

Montesquieu

might overcome whatever environmental handicaps they faced to imitate it. For him, the greatest strength of the English system was that it consisted of separate and balanced powers—executive, legislative, and judicial: thus it guaranteed liberty inasmuch as no absolute sovereignty was given to any single governing individual or group. This idealization of "checks and balances" subsequently influenced many other Enlightenment political theorists and played a particularly dominant role in the shaping of the United States Constitution in 1787.

Diderot and the Encyclopedia

Unlike Voltaire, who was not a very systematic thinker, and Montesquieu, who wrote in a somewhat ambiguous and primarily reflective mode, the most programmatic of the philosophes was Denis Diderot (1713–1784). As a young firebrand Diderot was clapped into solitary confinement for his attacks on religion and thereafter worked under the ever-present threat of censorship and imprisonment. Yet throughout his life he never shrank from espousing a fully materialistic philosophy or criticizing what he considered to be backwardness or tyranny wherever he found it. Although, like Voltaire, Diderot wrote on a wide range of subjects in numerous different forms, including stories and plays, he exerted his greatest influence as the organizer of and main contributor to an extremely ambitious publishing venture, the *Encyclopedia*. Conceived as a summation and means for dissemination of all the most advanced contemporary philosophical, scientific, and technical knowledge, with articles written by all the leading philosophes of the day (including Voltaire and Montesquieu), the *Encyclopedia* first appeared between 1751 and 1772 in installments totaling seventeen large volumes and eleven more of illustrative plates. Whereas modern encyclopedias serve primarily as reference works, Diderot thought of his *Encyclopedia* as a set of volumes that people would read at length rather than merely using to look up facts. Therefore he hoped that it would "change the general way of thinking." Above all, by popularizing the most recent achievements in science and technology, Diderot intended to combat "superstition" on the broadest front, aid the further advance of science, and thereby help alleviate all forms of human misery. Dedicated to the proposition that all traditional beliefs had to be reexamined "without sparing anyone's sensibilities," he certainly would have excoriated all "irrational" religious dogmas openly if left to himself. But since strict censorship made explicitly antireligious articles impossible, Diderot thumbed his nose at religion in such oblique ways as offering the laconic cross-reference for the entry on the Eucharist: "see cannibalism." Not surprisingly, gibes like this aroused storms of controversy when the early volumes of the *Encyclopedia* appeared. Nonetheless, the project was not only completed in the face of prominent opposition, but as time went on the complete work became so popular that it was reprinted several times and helped spread the ideas of the philosophes not just in France but all over Europe.

Diderot. A contemporary portrait by Van Loo.

A Laboratory, from Diderot's *Encylopedia.* Each printed number refers to a detailed discussion in the text. Note the far greater stress on practical instruction here than in the illustration of the amateur scientist's study shown above, p. 650.

One of the youngest of the contributors to the *Encyclopedia,* the marquis de Condorcet (1743–1794), is customarily termed "the last of the philosophes" because his career, and the philosophes' activities in general, were cut short by the excesses of the French Revolution. In his early career Condorcet gained prominence as a brilliant mathematician, but he is best known as the most extreme Enlightenment exponent of the idea of progress. Already in the late seventeenth century, particularly as the result of the triumphs of science, several thinkers began arguing that the intellectual accomplishments of their own day were superior to any of the past and that greater intellectual progress in the future was inevitable. But since it was less clear to some that modern literature was superior to the Greek and Latin classics, around 1700 an argument raged concerning the relative claims of "ancients" and "moderns" wherein so able a critic as the English writer Jonathan Swift could regard what he called the "battle of the books" as a standoff. In the eighteenth century, however, the conviction grew that the present had advanced in all aspects of human endeavor beyond the accomplishments of any earlier time, and that the future was bound to see unlimited further progress on all fronts. Condorcet's *Outline of the Progress of the Human Mind* (1794) was the ultimate expression of this point of view. According to Condorcet, progress in the past had not been uninterrupted—the Middle Ages had been an especially retrogressive era—but, given the victories of the scientific revolution and Enlightenment, indefinite and uninterrupted progress in the future was assured. Venturing into prophecy, Condorcet confidently stated not only that "as preventive medicine improves . . . the average human

Condorcet and faith in progress

life-span will be increased and a more healthy and stronger physical constitution guaranteed," but that "the moment will come . . . when tyrants and slaves . . . will exist only in history or on the stage." Ironically, even while Condorcet was writing such optimistic passages he was hiding out from the agents of the French Revolution, who in fact soon counted him among the numerous victims of their "reign of terror."

Beyond France, philosophes in other countries also made significant contributions to the Enlightenment legacy. After France, the most "enlightened" country of Europe was Great Britain, where the most noteworthy philosophes were Gibbon, Hume, and Adam Smith. *Edward Gibbon* (1737–1794) was a man of letters and historian whose *Decline and Fall of the Roman Empire* (1776–1788) remains among the two or three most widely read history books of all time. Scintillatingly written, the *Decline and Fall* covers Roman and Byzantine history from Augustus to the fall of Constantinople in 1453. According to Gibbon, the Roman Empire was brought down by "the triumph of barbarism [i.e., the Germanic invasions] and religion [i.e., Christianity]," but the Europe of his day was no longer "threatened with a repetition of those calamities." For him the rise of Christianity was the greatest calamity because "the servile and pusillanimous reign of the monks" replaced Roman philosophy and science with a credulity which "debased and vitiated the faculties of the mind." Certainly Gibbon's antireligious bias vitiated the quality of his own work, and therefore he is read today not so much for his particular opinions as for his trenchant character portrayals and above all for his devastating wit.

The Scotsman David Hume (1711–1776), on the other hand, was a truly penetrating philosopher. Dedicated like most Enlightenment thinkers to challenging preconceived opinions, Hume pushed skepticism so far in his major work, *An Enquiry Concerning Human Understanding* (1742), that he undermined all assurance that anyone knew anything for certain. Starting with the assumption that human knowledge derives from sense data alone rather than abstract reason—that "nothing is in intellect which was not first in sense"—Hume proposed that we have no way of ascertaining whether such knowledge really corresponds to objective truths lodged in the real world. Once he arrived at such extreme skepticism, Hume also proposed a philosophy of relativistic ethics: if we know nothing for certain, then there can be no absolute moral laws, and we must decide on proper courses of action from their contexts. Yet, as skeptical as Hume was, he was by no means cynical; rather, he enthusiastically joined in Voltaire's campaign to crush "infamy," or what Hume called "stupidity, Christianity, and ignorance," on the grounds that it is preferable to voyage amidst a sea of uncertainties than to dwell in a forest of supernatural shadows.

Edward Gibbon

David Hume

The most practically oriented of the leading British philosophes was the Scottish economist Adam Smith, whose landmark treatise, *The Wealth of Nations* (1776), is recognized as the classic expression of "laissez-faire" economics. Strongly opposed to mercantilism—that is, any governmental intervention in economic affairs—Smith maintained that the prosperity of all could best be obtained by allowing individuals to pursue their own interests without competition from state-owned enterprises or legal restraints. The term *laissez-faire* comes from the French expression *laissez faire la nature* (let nature take its course), and Smith's advocacy of laissez-faire economic doctrine reveals how deeply indebted he was to the Enlightenment's idealization of both nature and human nature. In other words, espousing "the obvious and simple system of natural liberty," Smith believed that just as the planets revolve harmoniously in their orbits and are prevented from bumping into each other by the invisible force of gravity, so humans can act harmoniously even while pursuing their selfish economic interests if only "the invisible hand" of competitive, free-market forces is allowed to balance equitably the distribution of wealth. Ironically, although Smith thought of himself as the champion of the poor against the economic injustices inherent in state-supported mercantile privileges, his laissez-faire doctrine later became the favored theory of private industrial entrepreneurs who exploited the poor as much if not more than mercantilistic governments ever did. Nevertheless, Smith's free-market economics, as will be seen in subsequent chapters, certainly represented the wave of the future.

Adam Smith

Elsewhere in Europe the circulation of Enlightenment ideas was by no means as widespread as in France and Britain, owing either to stiffer resistance from religious authorities, greater vigilance of state censors, or the lack of sufficient numbers of prosperous educated people to discuss and support progressive thought. Yet, aside from the Papal States, at least a few prominent philosophes flourished in virtually every country in western Europe. In Italy, for example, the Milanese jurist Cesare Beccaria (1738–1794), argued against arbitrary powers that oppressed humanity in the same spirit as the French philosophes. In his most influential writing, *On Crimes and Punishments* (1764). Beccaria attacked the prevalent view that judicial punishments should represent society's vengeance on the malefactor, asserting instead that no person has the right to punish another unless some useful purpose is served. For Beccaria, the only legitimate purpose for punishing crimes was the deterrence of other crimes. This granted, he argued for the greatest possible leniency compatible with deterrence, because enlightened humanitarianism dictated that humans should not punish other humans any more than is absolutely necessary. Above all, Beccaria eloquently opposed the death penalty, then widely inflicted throughout Europe for the most trivial offenses, on the grounds that it was no deterrent and set the bad example of public officials' pre-

Cesare Beccaria

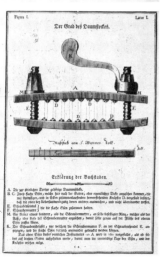

Instruments of Torture. The rack and the thumbscrew, from an official Austrian governmental handbook. Beccaria's influence helped phase out the use of such instruments by around 1800.

siding over murder rather than striving to deter it. *On Crimes and Punishments* was so favorably received that it was quickly translated into a dozen languages. Owing primarily to its influence, most European countries by around 1800 abolished torture, reserved the death penalty for capital crimes, and made imprisonment rather than any form of maiming the main form of judicial punishment.

The most representative German philosophe was the literary critic and dramatist Gotthold Lessing (1729–1781), who wrote with great eloquence of the need for tolerance. In his play *Nathan the Wise* (1779) Lessing led the audience to see that nobility of character has no relation to religious affiliations, and in his *On the Education of the Human Race* (1780) he maintained that the development of each of the world's great religions, Christianity included, was simply a step in the spiritual evolution of humanity, which would soon move beyond religion entirely toward pure rationality. The living model for Lessing's dramatic hero "Nathan the Wise" was his friend, the German Jewish sage Moses Mendelssohn (1729–1786), another philosophe who urged tolerance—in his case by writing a history of Judaism—but who also argued in favor of the immortality of the soul.

Far more difficult to classify is the greatest German philosopher of the eighteenth century—indeed one of the greatest philosophers of any nation of any time—Immanuel Kant (1724–1804). An unworldly intellectual who lived out his life far from the Enlightenment's French center of gravity in the Prussian city of Königsberg (located so far to the east that today it is part of the Soviet Union), Kant addressed his two masterworks, *The Critique of Pure Reason* (1781) and *The Critique of Practical Reason* (1790), to criticizing fashionable Enlightenment skepticism as represented most persuasively by David Hume. One of Kant's positions concerning reality and knowledge went so far against the grain of standard Enlightenment assumptions that it can hardly be called "Enlightened" at all. Namely, he maintained, in the spirit of Platonism, that the existence of a realm of absolute reality consisting of what he termed "things in themselves" cannot be doubted even though this realm remains unknowable to humans. Kant's assumption of absolute but unknowable truth, which implicitly opened philosophy to mystery, was to prove extremely attractive to his German philosophical successors in the nineteenth century, collectively known as "Idealists," but it ill accorded with his own age's stress on scientific verifiability.

In fact, however, Kant did not propose to build an action-oriented system on the basis of his assumed world of "things in themselves"; to the contrary, the bulk of his practical philosophy was more typically Enlightened. Aiming to counteract Hume's skepticism in a second way, he proposed that even though everyday knowledge begins in sense experience, the data of our senses is ordered by our rational minds in the here-and-now world of space and time in such a way as to provide us with reliable knowledge of appearances, or of what

Kant called "phenomena." In other words, Kant believed that humans could gain sufficient truth on a daily basis by a combination of sense and reason. Hence he insisted, much like Voltaire, that humans should use their learning faculties to inquire about nature, and, having done so, to improve upon it. Regarding ethics, Kant avoided the extremes of fixing upon conduct arbitrarily according to supernatural divine commandments or relativistically according to changing circumstances. Instead he maintained that if pure reason could neither prove nor disprove the existence of God, practical reason tells us that in the idea of God there exists a notion of moral perfection toward which all must strive. Thus we should always endeavor to act consistently with what Kant called the "categorical imperative": to act as if one's actions were to become a universal law of nature. Kant's principle of the categorical imperative proposed greater moral inflexibility than most philosophes thought realistic in view of the realities of everyday existence, yet it remained reconcilable with the basic Enlightenment worldview inasmuch as it rested on human rather than supernatural determinations.

Kant's practical philosophy

Immanuel Kant

In taking final stock of the Enlightenment movement, historians customarily raise two major questions. One is whether the philosophes were mere elitists who had no influence on the masses. Certainly, if one studies the sales figures of the philosophes' books or membership lists of eighteenth-century learned societies one finds that the philosophes' immediate audience consisted of aristocrats, lawyers, government officials, prosperous merchants, and a scattering of members of the higher clergy. To some degree this class bias lay beyond the philosophes' control, for many of the poorer people throughout eighteenth-century Europe remained illiterate, and most of the masses in southern and southeastern Europe—literate and illiterate alike—lived under the sway of an extremely conservative Roman Catholic hierarchy that was determined to keep them ignorant of the philosophes' ideas by means of the strictest censorship. Yet it is also true that many of the philosophes, despite their avowed commitment to clarity, wrote over the heads of most laboring people, and many did not even seek a lower-class audience because they feared that, if taken too far by the "uncouth" masses, their ideas might provoke open revolution. Typical philosophe elitism is well expressed in Gibbon's praise of imperial Roman religious policy whereby "the various modes of worship . . . were all considered by the people as equally true, by the philosopher as equally false, and by the magistrate as equally useful." Tradition also relates that whenever Voltaire discussed religion with his philosophe friends, he dismissed the servants so that they would not overhear any subversive remarks. Given this prevalent attitude, it is less surprising that Enlightenment ideas hardly percolated down to the masses than that they did have some effect on popular beliefs in France and England. For example, recent research on religious practices in southern France in the eighteenth century demonstrates

The audience of the philosophes

that from 1760 to 1790 fewer and fewer people of all classes requested that masses be said for their souls after death. Apparently, then, some servants were overhearing the philosophes' drawing-room conversations after all.

The other major question often asked about the Enlightenment is whether the philosophes were not hopelessly impractical "dreamers rather than doers." Without ignoring the clear vein of utopianism in Enlightenment thought, the answer to this must surely be no. Admittedly, most philosophes were far more optimistic about the chances of human perfectibility than most people are today, after the total wars and gas ovens of the twentieth century. Yet even the most optimistic did not expect utopian miracles to occur overnight. Rather, almost all the philosophes were committed to agitating for piecemeal social reforms which they believed would culminate, step by inevitable step, in a new world of enlightenment and virtue. Often such agitation did lead to significant changes in the conduct of practical affairs, and in at least one case, that of the American Revolution, Enlightenment ideas were the main source of inspiration for constructing a fully new political system. Moreover, sometimes even when Enlightenment propagandizing did not have any immediate practical impact, it did help to accomplish change in the future. For example, many philosophes condemned slavery on humanitarian or utilitarian grounds, thereby initiating a process of discussion that led cumulatively to the triumph of abolitionism throughout the West in the nineteenth century. In short, then, it is impossible to deny that the philosophes as a class were among the most practical-minded and influential intellectuals who ever lived.

4. THE ONWARD MARCH OF SCIENCE

Although several of the philosophes were natural scientists as well as publicists, it is preferable to treat the progress of eighteenth-century science separately because science, being highly international, is best broached by means of a topical rather than geographical method of review. The three scientific areas that witnessed the greatest progress from around the time of Newton to the end of the eighteenth century were descriptive biology, electricity, and chemistry. Regarding the first, four great pioneers in the use of newly invented high-power microscopes made enormous advances in observing small creatures and plant and cell structures during the last decades of the seventeenth century—the Italian Marcello Malpighi (1628–1694), the Englishman Robert Hooke, and two Dutchmen, Jan Swammerdam (1637–1680) and Antony van Leeuwenhoek (1632–1723). Perhaps most fundamental was the work of the last, a self-taught scientist who discovered bacteria and wrote the first description of human sperm. Building on such accomplishments as well as on numerous observations of his own, the Swedish botanist Karl von Linné (1707–1778)—commonly known by his Latinized name of Linnaeus—formulated the basic system of plant and animal classification that remains in use today. In the "Linnean Order" there are three realms—animal, vegetable, and mineral—and within the first two there are classes, "genera," and species. Furthermore, in Linnaeus's system every plant and animal is given two scientific Latin names—the first denoting the genus and the second the species. For example, robins are called *Planesticus migratorius:* the migrating species of the genus *Planesticus.*

Rivaling Linnaeus in eighteenth-century biology was the French naturalist Georges Buffon (1707–1788), whose massive *Natural History,* appearing in forty-four volumes from 1749 to 1778, was most advanced in its recognition of the close relationship between humans and other primates. Completely ignoring the biblical version of creation, yet never quite bringing himself to accept the full implications of a theory that located human origins in some form of evolution, Buffon admitted the possibility that the entire range of organic forms had descended from a single species and thus was a precursor of the evolutionism of Charles Darwin.

As opposed to developments in descriptive biology, where basic work hardly began before 1660, the "founding father" in the field of electricity was active well before the period under discussion. Around 1600 the Englishman William Gilbert discovered the magnetic properties of lodestones and introduced the word *electricity* into the language (*elektron* is the Greek word for amber, and Gilbert had observed that amber rubbed on fur will attract paper or straw). Yet because Gilbert worked before the triumph of mechanistic thought, he believed magnetism to be a purely occult force and therefore did not even dream of machines that could generate or harness electricity. Starting in the late seventeenth century, on the other hand, scientists from many different countries progressively began to master the science of electricity as we now know it. In 1672 the German Otto von Guericke published results of experiments wherein he generated electricity; in 1729 the Englishman Stephen Gray demonstrated that electricity could be conducted by means of threads and that certain other substances resisted conducting; and in 1745 a team of scientists at the Dutch University of Leyden invented a method for storing electricity in the "Leyden jar." In 1749 by using a kite-string to conduct lightning the American Benjamin Franklin charged a Leyden jar from a thunderstorm and thus was able to conclude that lightning and electricity are identical. This recognition allowed Franklin to invent the lightning rod, which saved houses from being destroyed in storms and is one of the best examples of the link between scientific theory and life-enhancing practice.

Probably the greatest theoretical breakthrough made in the second half of the eighteenth century lay in the field of chemistry, which had been languishing for about a century after the work of Robert Boyle.

Georges Buffon

Electricity

Benjamin Franklin as the God of Electricity by Benjamin West

The reason for this delay lay mostly in the wide acceptance of errors concerning such matters as heat, flame, air, and the phenomenon of combustion. The most misleading error was the so-called phlogiston theory, based on the idea that "phlogiston" was the substance of fire— i.e., when an object burned, phlogiston was supposed to be given off. The remaining ash was said to be the "true" material. In the second half of the eighteenth century important discoveries were made which discredited this theory and cleared the way for a real understanding of basic chemical reactions. In 1766 the Englishman Henry Cavendish reported the discovery of a new kind of gas obtained by treating certain metals with sulfuric acid. He showed that this gas, now known as hydrogen, would not of itself support combustion and yet would be rapidly consumed by a fire with access to the air. In 1774 oxygen was discovered by another Englishman, the Unitarian minister Joseph Priestley. He found that a candle would burn with extraordinary vigor when placed in the new gas—a fact which indicated clearly that combustion was not caused by any mysterious principle or substance in the flame itself. A few years after this discovery, Cavendish demonstrated that air and water, long supposed to be elements, are respectively a mixture and a compound, the first being composed principally of oxygen and nitrogen and the second of oxygen and hydrogen.

The final blow to the phlogiston theory was administered by the Frenchman Antoine Lavoisier (1743–1794), widely regarded as the greatest scientist of the eighteenth century, who lost his life in the French Revolution. Lavoisier proved that both combustion and respiration involve oxidation, the one being rapid and the other slow. He provided the names for oxygen and hydrogen, demonstrated that the diamond is a form of carbon, and argued that life itself is essentially a chemical process. But undoubtedly his greatest accomplishment was his discovery of the law of the conservation of mass. He found evidence that "although matter may alter its state in a series of chemical actions, it does not change in amount; the quantity of matter is the same at the end as at the beginning of every operation, and can be traced by its weight." This "law" has, of course, been modified by later discoveries regarding the structure of the atom and the conversion of some forms of matter into energy. It is hardly too much to say, however, that as a result of Lavoisier's genius chemistry became a true science.

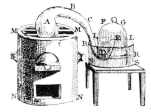

Lavoisier's Apparatus for the Decomposition of Air

Despite the notable scientific advances of the seventeenth and eighteenth centuries, the development of physiology and medicine progressed rather slowly during the same period for several reasons. One was the inadequate preparation of physicians, many of whom had begun their professional careers with little more training than apprenticeship under an older practitioner. Another was the common disrepute in which surgery was held as a mere trade, like that of a barber or blacksmith. Perhaps the most serious of all was the prejudice against dissection of human bodies for use in anatomical study. As late as 1750 medical schools which engaged in this practice were in danger of destruction by irate mobs. Despite these obstacles some progress was still possible. About 1670 Malpighi and Leeuwenhoek confirmed William Harvey's discovery of the circulation of the blood by observing the actual flow of blood through the network of capillaries connecting the arteries and veins. At approximately the same time an eminent physician of London, Thomas Sydenham, proposed a new theory of fever as a natural process by which diseased material is expelled from the system.

Medical progress during the eighteenth century was somewhat more rapid. Among the noteworthy achievements were the discovery of blood pressure, the founding of histology or microscopic anatomy, and the development of the autopsy as an aid to the study of disease. But the chief milestones of medical advancement in this period were the adoption of inoculation and the development of vaccination for smallpox. Knowledge of inoculation came originally from the Near East, where it had long been employed by the Muslims. Information concerning its use was relayed to England in 1717 through the letters of Lady Mary Wortley Montagu, wife of the British ambassador to Turkey. The first systematic application of the practice in the Western world, however, was due to the efforts of the American Puritan leader Cotton Mather, who implored the physicians of Boston to inoculate their patients in the hope of curbing an epidemic of smallpox which had broken out in 1721. Thereafter inoculation had some success in saving lives, but the practice understandably was widely resisted because smallpox inoculation guaranteed the patient one bout with the disfiguring disease before inducing further immunity to it. Only in 1796 did the Englishman Edward Jenner, noticing that milkmaids always seemed to have clear complexions, conclude that in contracting the virus of cowpox from their daily occupation, milkmaids gained immunity to smallpox. Hence inoculation of humans with the deadly smallpox virus appeared unnecessary, and Jenner introduced *vaccination* (from *vacca*—Latin for cow), employing the mild cowpox virus instead. Once vaccination proved both harmless and marvelously effective, the vast possibilities opened up for the elimination of contagious diseases appeared to confirm the Enlightenment belief in the ability of science to make nature's laws work for the betterment of the human condition.

*Inoculation and
vaccination*

5. CLASSICISM AND INNOVATION IN ART AND LITERATURE

Although the spirit of the scientific revolution and Enlightenment was reflected in certain great artistic monuments, there were no simple, one-to-one correspondences between intellectual and artistic trends in the late seventeenth and eighteenth centuries. Artists and writers

*Manifold influences on
artistic trends*

The Finding of Moses by Poussin. The artist has included a pyramid in the background (right) as a token of verisimilitude, but otherwise his scene appears to be set in ancient Rome. Note the stress on monumentality and perpendicular lines.

responded to a great variety of influences in addition to the new scientific view of the universe: national stylistic traditions, religious demands, differing political and sociological contexts, and, not least, the internal dynamics of artistic evolution within any given creative field. It is best, then, to look at certain major trends without forcing the explanations for them all to fit the same mold.

As we have seen earlier, the dominant style in European art between about 1600 and the early 1700s was the Baroque. But a few countries resisted the dominance of Baroque influences—particularly France, Holland, and England. The French resistance was primarily nationalistic in inspiration. Since Baroque style was closely associated with the tastes of the Spanish and Austrian Habsburgs, against whom the French were continually fighting throughout most of the seventeenth and early eighteenth centuries, it seemed inappropriate for France to admit cultural inferiority by imitating the style of its political rivals. In opposition to the exuberant Baroque, then, French artists and architects cultivated restrained classicism. Some of the best earlier examples of this are the canvases of seventeenth-century France's greatest painter, Nicolas Poussin (1594–1665), whose reposeful scenes from classical mythology, governed by the artist's programmatic commitment to "things well ordered," stand in the sharpest contrast to the swirling contortions of Poussin's Baroque contemporary, Rubens.

"Well-ordered" classicism continued to be the preferred style in France during the reign of Louis XIV (1651–1715) for three reasons. First of all, Louis in particular was determined to make sure that France cultivated its own characteristic national style for reasons of state. Second, Louis's own stylistic preferences tended toward the grand and

French classicism

See color plates facing page 672 for *Landscape with the Burial of Phocion* by Poussin sober. And third, the symmetrical qualities of classicism seemed to complement best the highly symmetrical natural order then being posited in France by Cartesian philosophers and scientists. Thus when Louis XIV decided to renovate his palace of the Louvre, the leading Baroque architect of the day, Bernini, submitted plans, but these were rejected in favor of those of a native Frenchman who emphasized severe classical monumentality. Later, when Louis erected his splendid new palace at Versailles, Baroque architectural features were introduced. Yet the Baroque of Versailles was a very restrained Baroque that emphasized massive symmetry rather than the jutting angles and startling curves favored by Bernini.

As classicism was the prevalent style in seventeenth-century French art, so too did it prevail in literature. This can be seen most clearly in the tragedies of Pierre Corneille (1606–1684) and Jean Racine (1639–1699). Both of these playwrights took as their subjects the heroes and heroines of classical mythology and history such as Medea, Pompey, Andromache, and Phaedra, and both strove as well to imitate the theoretical and structural principles of the classical Greek tragedians. Similarly, the great French writer of comedies, Jean Baptiste Molière (1622–1673), took the Roman comedies of Terence and Plautus for his models and was so committed to symmetrical formalism as to have his characters speak in rhyming couplets. Yet, unlike Corneille and Racine, Molière did set the action of his plays in the present because he believed that "the business of comedy is to represent in general all the defects of men and especially of the men of our time." Accordingly, his work was also highly satirical. In *Tartuffe,* for example, he

East Entrance of the Louvre, Paris. Built by the French architect Charles Perrault between 1667 and 1670, this facade is an excellent example of the rigorously classical style patronized by Louis XIV.

The Painter in his Studio by Vermeer. The model is posing as Clio, the muse of history, and thus stands for the timeless fame of painting. The fact that the source of light is concealed by the curtain may perhaps be understood to mean that the artist works essentially by the interior illumination of his mind.

pilloried religious hypocrisy, and in *The Bourgeois Gentleman* he mocked the vulgar pretentiousness of the social climber. Yet for all his satire, Molière had a measure of sympathy for the trials of human existence, rising to his greatest profundity in *The Misanthrope,* a play which pokes fun at a person who hates society but which also shows that the character has excellent reasons for his alienation. Thus mixing sympathy and occasional melancholy with wit and searing scorn, Molière was probably the most gifted European dramatic genius after Shakespeare.

In the other leading countries that resisted the Baroque, Holland and England, there can be little doubt that artistic preferences had religious as well as nationalistic causes. Since Holland and England were Protestant, they naturally preferred to limit Baroque influences emanating from Rome and the Catholic Spanish Netherlands. We have seen that the greatest seventeenth-century Dutch painter, Rembrandt, developed his own highly personal style which employed Baroque elements whenever he deemed them appropriate. Rembrandt's slightly later Dutch contemporary, Jan Vermeer (1632–1675), however, eliminated the Baroque entirely in painting the serenest realistic indoor genre scenes, as did most other seventeenth-century Dutch genre, landscape, and portrait painters. Similarly, the dominant stylistic commitment in England, after a brief flirtation with the Baroque dur-

Left: *St. Peter's Basilica with Colonnade, Rome.* Right: *St. Paul's Cathedral, London.* The sweeping colonnade in front of St. Peter's was designed by the Baroque architectural master Bernini in 1656. Such showy effects were not to the taste of the English architect Christopher Wren, who in designing St. Paul's hewed more closely to the classicism implicit in the Renaissance style of the Vatican Basilica itself. Wren's "English answer to St. Peter's," however, makes classical columns even more prominent than they were in the Vatican. Note how Wren drew inspiration from Perrault's classical Louvre facade (above, p. 665) in designing St. Paul's second-level elevation.

Chiswick House. Built near London around 1725, this country house initiated an English Palladian fad that had its echoes in Thomas Jefferson's Monticello, and later still in the Jefferson Memorial. Note how the design imitates Palladio's Villa Rotonda (above p. 442), just as that building itself was modeled on the Roman Pantheon (above, p. 194).

ing the reign of the Catholic-leaning Charles I, was to a classicizing restraint. Thus the most prominent of all English architects, Christopher Wren (1632–1723), did not hesitate to borrow Baroque elements when fitting, but emphasized classicism in his columns and domes, most notably in his masterwork, St. Paul's Cathedral (built from 1675 to 1710). More classical still was the "Palladian revival" which dominated English architecture in the first half of the eighteenth century. In this period numerous country houses commissioned by the landed gentry imitated the Renaissance master Palladio's serenely classical and highly symmetrical Villa Rotonda, just as that building had imitated the Roman Pantheon. Indeed, so many English town houses built in the fashionable resort spa of Bath around 1740 imitated Palladian models that Bath was soon called, after Palladio's main area of activity, "the English Vicenza."

Parallel to the artistic classicism of Wren and the English Palladians was the literary classicism which flourished in England from about 1660 to 1760. In fact, the writers of this period expressly called themselves "Augustans." This they did for two reasons: first, the restoration of royalty in 1660 after the English Civil War seemed to presage an age of peace and civility similar to the one installed by Augustus after civil war in ancient Rome; and second, the favored poetic models of the English Augustans were the Augustan Romans—Virgil, Horace, and Ovid. Still another reason why English literary taste became resolutely classical in the later seventeenth century was that the France of Louis XIV had enormous influence in setting fashions throughout Europe, and the English did not wish to be the slightest bit out of date in following the French lead. Finally, as in France, classicism appeared to be the one available style that came closest to being dispassionately "scientific." In other words, just when the English leisured classes were celebrating the triumphs of Newtonianism and endeavoring to

The English Augustans

The Embarkation for Cythera by Watteau. This epoch-making painting broke with the severity of Poussin in favor of a greater stress on motion and lushness. No two art historians agree upon exactly what it means, but the evocation of dreamy pleasure is unmistakable.

make their own contribution to scientific advance by collecting natural specimens or gazing through telescopes, they patronized a form of writing which seemed to resemble Newtonian methods and laws in stressing simplicity, clarity, and symmetry.

Jonathan Swift and Alexander Pope

Of the numerous members of the English Augustan school, the most outstanding were the prose writer Jonathan Swift (1667–1745) and the poet Alexander Pope (1688–1744). The former, a scathing satirist, was atypical of Augustan thinking in his pessimism concerning the potentialities of human nature: in Swift's masterpiece, *Gulliver's Travels,* humans at one point are dismissed as "the most pernicious race of little odious vermin that nature ever suffered to crawl upon the surface of the earth." Yet Swift's prose is fully Augustan in its economy and clarity; as opposed to earlier flowery stylists, Swift insisted on locating, as he said, "proper words in proper places." As for Pope, he was thoroughly Augustan in both style and thought—almost to a fault. A consistent exponent in highly regular rhyming verse of the naturalistic doctrines of the Enlightenment, Pope in such didactic poems as his *Essay on Man* and his *Essay on Criticism* held that humans must study and imitate nature if they were to bring any semblance of order into their affairs. Most necessary for mankind, in Pope's view, was unblinking self-knowledge, which the poet believed could be obtained entirely apart from theology or metaphysics. Summing up the secularistic spirit of his age, Pope responded to Milton's earlier poetic resolve to "justify the ways of God to man" in his most famous couplet: "Know then thyself, presume not God to scan;/ the proper study of Mankind is Man."

As impressive as numerous artistic and literary productions of French and English classicism may have been, the classical movement self-evidently was not highly innovative. Two entirely separate developments of the eighteenth century, on the other hand, emphasized greater originality—namely, the emergence of the continental Rococo style in art, and the rise of the English novel. Regarding the former, the basic explanation for the emergence of Rococo art and architecture was the sense of relaxation experienced in France at the coming of peace and at the death of Louis XIV in 1715. Whereas the prolonged War of the Spanish Succession had begun to exhaust the country, and whereas Louis in his declining years had become ever more puritanical and ever more determined to enforce his own severe tastes and standards on everyone else, around 1715 the leisured classes of the nation breathed a deep sigh of relief. This reaction, not surprisingly, resulted in an artistic pendulum swing from classical severity to a cheerful abandonment which goes by the name of Rococo style. In painting, the earliest and most gifted Rococo artist was Antoine Watteau (1684–1721), who was influenced more by the Baroque artist Rubens than by any other single source, but who replaced Rubens's massiveness with airy French elegance and grace. Watteau was admitted into the French Academy of Fine Arts in 1717 for his masterpiece, *The Embarkation for Cythera,* even though none of the members would have dreamed of admitting him two years earlier. Moreover, since the Academy had no formal classification for the *Embarkation*—which merely showed graceful people having a dreamily good time—it invented one for the purpose: *"fêtes galantes,"* best translated as stylish revels. At least Watteau's revellers were clothed, but the figures in the paintings of his Rococo successors François Boucher (1703–1770) and J. H. Fragonard (1732–1806) were usually half naked and displayed in postures that went well beyond sensuality in the direction of frank eroticism.

Most of the rest of Europe was too straitlaced to imitate the las-

Rococo painting

See color plates following page 672 for *Le Mezzetin* by Watteau and *Madame de Pompadour* by Boucher

A Reclining Nude by Boucher. The viewer is left to ponder the significance of the fallen flower.

French Rococo architecture

Rococo and Baroque compared

civiousness of French Rococo painting, but French Rococo architecture soon became the dominant style throughout the Continent and remained such for most of the eighteenth century. The reasons for this were, first, that the French architects who pioneered in Rococo building in the years shortly after 1715 took Baroque principles for their standards in replacing classical ones, thereby setting themselves in tune with the rest of their continental contemporaries, and second, that Rococo building design featured curvaceous elegance and thus appealed greatly to the vain European aristocrats who commissioned the major architectural projects of the day.

Perhaps the easiest way to characterize the Rococo building style is to call it the "champagne of Baroque" or "Baroque with a French accent." Both Baroque and Rococo buildings emphasize dynamic movement, but whereas Baroque style exudes force and passion, the Rococo communicates a sense of delicacy and playfulness. Most amazing to initial viewers of Rococo interiors is how light and airy they are: as opposed to Baroque interiors, which are generally sombre, Rococo ones have walls and ceilings painted in white, gold, and pink. Among the leading European Rococo buildings are the Hôtel de Soubise in Paris, the pavilion known as the Zwinger in Dresden, the jewel-box Vierzehnheiligen church in Bavaria (near Bamberg), and the Cuvillies theater in Munich, which is still used for performances of eighteenth-century operas and plays. Although Rococo art and

Two German Rococo Interiors. The Vierzehnheiligen Church near Bamberg (left) and the Wieskirche near Munich (right) are the two foremost works of German Rococo interior decoration.

architecture unquestionably allowed great play for the imagination, from the long-term perspective of art history the Rococo style was an end rather than a beginning inasmuch as it represented the final phase of the Baroque.

In contrast, the only really new development in the artistic and literary history of the Enlightenment period that had a promising future was the emergence of the novel. In treating the rise of the novel in eighteenth-century England it must be stressed that the English novel was not invented out of nothing. To the contrary, works of prose fiction known as romances had been composed in classical antiquity and throughout western Europe from the twelfth century onward. Indeed, one European romance—Cervantes's *Don Quixote*—atypically had many of the characteristics of the modern novel. Moreover, in France, where the word *roman* means both romance and novel, prose fictions were written without interruption from the Middle Ages to the recognizably modern novels of the nineteenth-century writers Balzac and Flaubert. Nevertheless, there were such major differences between the best English prose fictions of the eighteenth century and all that came before (other than *Don Quixote*) as to make it possible to say that the modern novel was invented in eighteenth-century England.

Uniqueness of the novel

The best way of characterizing the difference between the romance and the novel is that the former is patently a fabrication, whereas the latter (allowing a few inevitable exceptions) purports to be a reliable account of how humans behave. Assuming that a judge in a court of law were asked to accept the testimony of a romance as evidence for trying a case, he would have to throw it out and declare a mistrial because romances generally have little sense of verisimilitude, being written in an ornate style and recounting the adventures of clearly imaginary characters—usually from the mythical or semi-mythical past—who find themselves in preposterous situations. But a modern novel might stand up as excellent legal evidence, for in the novel, from the eighteenth-century English examples onward, experiences seem unique, plots and settings fully believable, and the manner of presentation dispassionately straightforward.

Novelistic realism

Two explanations may be offered for the emergence of the novel in eighteenth-century England. One is that the ideals of the Enlightenment unquestionably created the most conducive atmosphere for novel writing insofar as the "scientific," methodical study of human experience was widely regarded as the order of the day. Yet, because Enlightenment thinking predominated in France even more than in England, it remains to ask why England in particular was the modern novel's first home. The answer to this appears to relate to the distinctive nature of the English reading public. Specifically, England had a much larger nonaristocratic reading audience than France because of England's greater involvement in trade and industry; this class preferred novels to romances because novels were written in a gripping

*Reasons for the rise of the
novel*

rather than "elevated" style and the action of the novel's more prosaic characters seemed more relevant to common, nonaristocratic experience. As will also presently be seen, it was by no means irrelevant to the novelistic form in England that the majority of novel readers were not men but women.

*Defoe, Richardson, and
Fielding*

By common consent the three most influential novelists of eighteenth-century England were Daniel Defoe (1660–1737), Samuel Richardson (1689–1761), and Henry Fielding (1707–1754). All three portrayed recognizable, nonaristocratic characters doing their best to make their way in a perilous world, unaffected by any hint of divine intervention for good or ill. In the novels of Defoe and Richardson the narrator is usually a character who participates in the action and thus knows the "truth" of one side directly, but of course cannot be expected to understand every other character's point of view. On the other hand, in Fielding's *Tom Jones* an "omnipotent narrator" stands apart from the action, and accordingly has a fuller view of it, but seems by his obtrusive presence to be creating a rather more artificial fiction.

*Jane Austen and the
perfection of the novel*

Tom Jones is the only eighteenth-century English novel universally considered to be an enduring classic of world literature, but at the very beginning of the next century the technical achievements of Defoe, Richardson, and Fielding were consolidated by Jane Austen (1775–1817), whose *Pride and Prejudice* and *Emma* represent for many readers the heights of novelistic perfection. That a woman should emerge around 1800 as a greater writer of novels than most men was almost inevitable, above all because early-modern European fiction writing was one of the very few areas of creative expression wherein society easily tolerated female contributions. Indeed, in seventeenth-century France the most widely read authors of romances—Madeleine de Scudéry (1607–1701) and the countess de La Fayette (1634–1692)—were women, and later in England Fanny Burney (1752–1840), Ann Radcliffe (1764–1823), and Maria Edgeworth (1767–1849) all wrote novels of great popularity and considerable distinction before Jane Austen went to work. Moreover, since the English novel-reading public was predominantly female, women readers understandably were particularly interested in characteristically female problems as seen from a feminine angle, a subject matter and perspective that Jane Austen bountifully provided. But of course Austen would not rank, as she does, among the handful of greatest novelists who ever lived had she been narrowly parochial in her views and lacking in extraordinary artistic skill. Rather, men as well as women can delight in her dry, ironic wit and admire her insight into human nature. Moreover, Jane Austen's technical accomplishments may well represent novelistic skills at their pinnacle. In particular, in compromising between Defoe's and Richardson's first-person narrator and Fielding's omnipotent third-person one by the use of a third-person narrator who remains unobtrusive and pursues events primarily from the point of view of a cen-

Landscape with the Burial of Phocion, Nicolas Poussin (1594–1665). An outstanding example of the classical style in painting. As opposed to the Baroque stress on swirling movement, here there is practically no movement at all. Instead, nature is conceived in rigorously geometrical terms to convey a sense of permanence. Note too the presence of ancient classical buildings, making it seem as if the past is enduring. (Louvre)

A Dutch Interior, Pieter de Hooch (c. 1629–c. 1679). Seventeenth-century Dutch painters excelled at indoor genre compositions bathed in light. The restraint of the scene itself stands in contrast to the melodramatic Baroque painting in the background. (National Gallery, London)

Le Mezzetin, Antoine Watteau (1684–1721). Mezzetin was a popular character from Italian comedy. In portraying him in a relaxed pose Watteau succeeded in conveying a sense of dreamy elegance. (MMA)

The Blue Boy, Thomas Gainsborough (1727–1788). Gainsborough, eighteenth-century England's greatest portrait painter, combined Watteau's lushness with more traditional English gravity. (Huntington Library)

Madame de Pompadour, François Boucher (1703–1770). A characteristically frilly French Rococo portrait. Madame de Pompadour, King Louis XV's mistress, was a patroness of arts and letters, and for a time the virtual ruler of France. (The Wallace Collection, London)

The Stonemason's Yard, Canaletto (1697–1768). A quiet scene of everyday life, in strong contrast to the scene below. (National Gallery, London)

Marriage à la Mode, William Hogarth (1697–1764). A satirical look at the arranged marriage: the financial needs of the nobleman and the social aspirations of his middle-class counterpart dominate the negotiations. (National Gallery, London)

Sarah Siddons as the Tragic Muse, Sir Joshua Reynolds (1723–1792). Mrs. Siddons, a famous actress of the seventeenth century, is here portrayed as the Queen of Tragedy, in accordance with Reynolds's habit of depicting wealthy patrons in impressive classical poses. (Huntington Library)

Madame Recamier, Jacques Louis David (1748–1825). David was the exponent of a new classicism during and after the French Revolution. The couch, the lamp, and the costume are copied from Rome and Pompeii. (Louvre)

tral character, Jane Austen created a delicate balance between subjectivity and objectivity that may well never have been surpassed.

6. BAROQUE AND CLASSICAL MUSIC

The title of one of the most genial of eighteenth-century symphonic compositions, Haydn's *Surprise Symphony,* can be applied to the music of the entire age, for eighteenth-century music is continually full of surprises. Indeed, in contrast to developments in contemporary art and literature, where innovation was comparatively rare, the eighteenth century was the most fertile period of invention in all of western European musical history. Probably the major explanation for this is that early-modern composers, unlike artists and writers, did not have to concern themselves about how much they would borrow from the music of classical antiquity because the principles of ancient musical composition were virtually unknown. More free than painters and poets to strike out on their own, early-modern composers invented form after form in two successive major styles, the Baroque and the so-called classical, treating their listeners to surprise after surprise.

Innovation in Baroque and Classical music

Baroque music, like Baroque art and architecture, emerged around 1600 in Italy as an artistic expression of the Counter-Reformation. Yet from the beginning Baroque composers were perforce more inventive than their artistic counterparts, having no equivalent of columns and domes with which to work. The first important figure in the history of Baroque music was the Italian Claudio Monteverdi (1567–1643), who reacted against the highly intricate Renaissance polyphonic style of his major predecessor, Palestrina. Pursuing the Baroque goal of dramatic expressiveness, Monteverdi found that deep human emotions were difficult to convey when members of a chorus were singing against each other as they did in the music of the late Renaissance, and that dramatic intensity becomes greatest when music is combined with theater. Having no classical models to draw upon, Monteverdi thus virtually single-handedly invented a new musical form, that of opera. In addition, to lend his opera singers greater emotional power than they would have had if they had sung alone, Monteverdi wrote instrumental accompaniments so forceful that they have earned him the title of "the father of instrumentation." Since Monteverdi's new form of opera fully suited the spirit of his times, within a generation operas were performed in all the leading cities of Italy. Staged within magnificent settings, and calling upon the talents of singers, musicians, dramatists, and stage designers, opera expressed as clearly as any art form the dedication of Baroque artistic style to grandeur, drama, and display.

Claudio Monteverdi

With the notable exception of the Englishman Henry Purcell (1659–

Later Baroque music: Bach and Handel

1695), there were no enduringly great Baroque composers in the second half of the seventeenth century. Nonetheless, many imaginative musicians began to create new forms during this period, most notably the instrumental forms of the sonata and the concerto. Moreover, whatever lull there may have been in the composition of masterpieces was more than compensated for in the last phase of the Baroque era by the appearance of Bach and Handel, two of the greatest composers of all time. Born in the same year very near each other in northern Germany, Johann Sebastian Bach (1685–1750) and George Frederick Handel (1685–1759) had very different musical personalities and very different careers. Bach was an intensely pious introvert who remained in the backwaters of provincial Germany all his life and wrote music of the utmost individuality, whereas Handel was a public-pleasing cosmopolitan whose music is more accessible than Bach's in its robust affirmativeness. Despite these differences, however, both Bach and Handel were distinctly late-Baroque stylists in their commitment to writing music of the deepest expressiveness.

Bach

Anyone who has any familiarity with classical music can identify in a moment a work of Bach even if he or she has never heard it before because Bach's music is so extraordinarily individualistic. This, however, does not mean that it is in any way predictable, for part of Bach's individuality lay in his very unpredictability. Combining an uncanny imagination and capacious intellect with heroic powers of discipline and an ability to produce music of the greatest genius on demand, Bach was an extremely prolific composer in the entire gamut of contemporary forms (excluding opera), from unaccompanied instrumental pieces to enormous works for vocal soloists, chorus, and orchestra. As a church musician in Leipzig for most of his mature career, Bach's professional duty was to provide new music regularly for Sunday and holiday services. Therefore much of his work consists of religious cantatas (over two hundred surviving), motets, and passions. One might think that the mere requirement to write such music on schedule might have made it routine and lifeless, but Bach, an ardent Protestant who was entirely unaffected by the secularism of the Enlightenment, seems to have written each one of his church pieces with such fervor that the salvation of the world appears to hang on every note. Not content with expressing himself in spiritual music alone, Bach also gloried in creating joyous concertos and suites for orchestra, and succeeded in composing the purest of "pure music"— extraordinarily subtle and complex fugues for keyboard in which the capacity of the human mind for apprehending abstraction appears to approach the celestial.

Johann Sebastian Bach

Handel

Much unlike the provincial, inner-directed Bach, Handel was a man of the world who sought primarily to establish rapport with large, secular audiences. After spending his early creative years in Italy, where he mastered Italian Baroque compositional techniques, Handel established himself in London. There he tried at first to make a living by composing Italian operas, but since the highly florid Baroque operatic style proved too foreign for more staid English tastes, Handel eventually realized that he would never survive unless he turned to some more salable genre. This he found in the oratorio—a variety of music drama intended for performance in concert form. Marking a transition from the spiritual to the secular, Handel's oratorios were usually set to biblical stories but featured very worldly music, replete with ornate instrumentation and frequent flourishes of drums and trumpets. (Some music historians refer to Handel's "big bow-wow" manner.) These highly virile and heroic works succeeded in packing London's halls full of prosperous English people who interpreted the victories of the ancient Hebrews in such oratorios as *Israel in Egypt* and *Judas Maccabaeus* as implicit celebrations of England's own burgeoning national greatness. Of course Handel's music was not for one time but for all, as is demonstrated by the fact that his greatest oratorio, *The Messiah,* is sung widely throughout the English-speaking world every Christmas and its stirring "Hallelujah Chorus" certainly remains the most popular single choral piece in the entire classical repertory.

Although only a few decades separated the activity of Bach and Handel from that of their greatest eighteenth-century successors, the Austrians Franz Joseph Haydn (1732–1809) and Wolfgang Amadeus Mozart (1756–1781), the two pairs appear worlds apart because their compositional styles are utterly different. This is to say that whereas Bach and Handel were among the last and certainly the greatest composers of Baroque music, Haydn and Mozart were the leading representatives of the succeeding "classical" style. The latter term is slightly confusing because classicism in music had nothing to do with imitating music written in classical antiquity. Rather, the musical style that prevailed in Europe in the second half of the eighteenth century is called classical because it sought to imitate classical principles of order, clarity, and symmetry—in other words, to sound as a Greek temple looked. Moreover, composers of the classical school innovated in creating music that adhered rigorously to certain structural principles. For example, all classical symphonies have four movements, and all open with a first movement in "sonata form," characterized by the successive presentation of themes, development, and recapitulation. Undoubtedly the spread of the ideals of the Enlightenment influenced the development of the classical style, yet there were elements of elegant aristocratic Rococo influence at work as well, for the music of the classical era customarily has a lightness and gaiety about it that is most reminiscent of Rococo pastels.

Certainly the tastes of the same European aristocrats who commissioned Rococo buildings determined the personal fortunes of most composers in the second half of the eighteenth century because these men no longer had any interest in gaining a livelihood by writing church music as Bach had done, and as yet had no large concert-hall public (Handel's London audience being exceptional). The perils of

"The Charming Brute." A contemporary caricature of Handel, engraved by Joseph Groupy, 1754.

The classical style in music

Three Contemporary Impressions of Mozart. At the left is the child prodigy, aged seven, seated at a keyboard. The first name given as "Theoph." is not a mistake but is Greek for Mozart's real middle name, Amadeus, meaning "who loves God." The drawing of the mature Mozart in the middle is a highly idealized conception; no doubt the painting on the right comes closest to conveying what the composer really looked like.

Mozart's career

struggling for a living by composing music in the later eighteenth century can be seen best in the sad career of the sublime genius Mozart. As a phenomenal child prodigy, the young Mozart—who began composing at four, started touring Europe as a keyboard virtuoso at six, and wrote his first oratorio at eleven—was the darling of the aristocracy. The Austrian empress Maria Theresa embraced him and the pope made him "Knight of the Golden Spur." But as soon as Mozart reached puberty he was no longer a curiosity and, owing partly to his rather cantankerous personality, proved unable to gain steady employment in the service of any single wealthy aristocrat. In lieu of that, he strove to support himself as a freelance composer and keyboard performer in Vienna, but could make ends meet only with the greatest difficulty. Although he spent every year of his mature life in bountiful productivity, he had to live from hand to mouth until he died at the age of thirty-five from the effects of an undiagnosed wasting disease. Only a handful of people attended the funeral of one of the greatest creative artists of all time, and he was buried in a pauper's grave. Given these appalling circumstances, it is perfectly amazing that Mozart's music is characteristically sunny and serene. Only rarely did he write in a minor key, and even when he did so, he usually paired a melancholy work with an exuberantly joyful one, as if to demonstrate almost defiantly that the trials of his personal life had no effect on his art.

Haydn's career

Haydn's career provides an instructive contrast. Knowing much better how to take care of himself, "Papa Haydn" spent most of his life in the comfortable employment of the Esterházys, an extremely wealthy Austro-Hungarian aristocratic family that maintained its own private orchestra. But this security entailed the indignity of wearing the Esterházy livery, like any common butler. Only toward the end of his life, in 1791, did Haydn, now famous, strike out on his own by traveling to London, where for a year and a half he supported himself handsomely by writing for a paying public, as Handel once did, rather than for private patrons. The fact that London alone was able to provide opportunities for earning a commercial livelihood to two foreigners is clearly indicative of the city's unusual status in the eighteenth century as one of the few localities where there was a mass market for culture. In this regard London represented the wave of the future, for in the nineteenth century serious music would definitely leave the aristocratic salon for the urban concert hall all over Europe. It may also be noted that whereas in deeply aristocratic Austria Haydn was obliged to wear servants' livery, in London he was greeted as a creative genius—one of the earliest composers to be regarded as such even though poets and painters had been celebrated as geniuses long before. Thus Haydn's *Miracle* Symphony, written for performance in a London concert hall, is so called because during one performance a chandelier came crashing down and many would have been killed had it not been for the fact that the entire audience had moved up as close as possible to get a better view of the "genius" Haydn who was conducting.

Top: *Haydn in Livery*. Bottom: *The Composer in London*. While he worked in the pay of the Esterházy family, Haydn was little more than a high-level servant. In London, on the other hand, he was portrayed as an inspired genius with a far-away look in his eye and a sheet of his own music in his hand.

Haydn's stay in London foreshadowed the future in still another way, for the music he wrote on that occasion was wholly secular, as opposed to the semi-religious oratorios of Handel. Indeed, the music of the entire classical era was predominantly secular, as most music would remain until the present, and this secular writing advanced primarily on three fronts—opera, chamber music, and orchestral composition. In the field of opera, an important innovator of the classical period was Christoph Willibald von Gluck (1714–1787), who emphasized the necessity for dramatic action at a time when Monteverdi's many successors had made opera much too static. But by far the greatest operatic composer of the era was Mozart, whose *Marriage of Figaro, Don Giovanni,* and *The Magic Flute* remain among the most magnificent and best loved operas of all time. As for the realm of chamber music (music written for small instrumental ensembles), the classical era was the most fertile age of chamber music origins, for the genre of the string quartet was invented at the beginning of the period and was soon brought to the fullest fruition in the quartets of both Haydn and Mozart.

Yet probably the most impressive invention of the classical era was the symphony—so to speak the novel of music—for the symphony has since proven to be the most fertile and popular of all classical musical forms. Although not the very first writer of symphonies, Haydn is nonetheless usually termed the "father of the symphony" because in over one hundred works in the symphonic form—and preeminently in his last twelve symphonies, which he composed in London—Haydn formulated the most enduring techniques of symphonic composition and demonstrated to the fullest extent the symphony's creative potential. Yet Mozart's three last symphonies (out of that composer's total of forty-one) are generally regarded as greater even than those of Haydn, for the grace, variety, and utter technical perfection of these works are beyond comparison. Mere words cannot do justice to any of the marvelous musical creations of the eighteenth century, yet it may confidently be stated in conclusion that if just one or two of Mozart's musical compositions had survived instead of literally hundreds, they alone would be enough to place the century among the most inspired ages in the entire history of the human creative imagination.

SELECTED READINGS

• *Items so designated are available in paperback editions.*

Baker, Keith, *Condorcet: From Natural Philosophy to Social Mathematics,* Chicago, 1975. Advances the view that Condorcet's greatest significance lies in his attempt to create a quantifiable social science rather than in his theory of historical progress.

Baumer, Franklin L., *Modern European Thought: Continuity and Change in Ideas, 1600–1950,* New York, 1977. An extraordinarily fine intellectual history, organized around major themes rather than the work of individuals.

• Becker, Carl, *The Heavenly City of the Eighteenth-Century Philosophers,* New Haven, 1932. Advances the thesis that the philosophes were just as impractical in their commitment to abstract secular rationalism as the medieval Scholastics were in their theological rationalism. Witty and stimulating but widely regarded as out of date in its views.

Briggs, Robin, *The Scientific Revolution of the Seventeenth Century,* New York, 1969. A very brief but extremely valuable survey, with a documentary appendix.

• Bronowski, J., and B. Mazlish, *The Western Intellectual Tradition,* New York, 1960. A superb, old-fashioned intellectual history which serves as an excellent complement to Baumer for the seventeenth and eighteenth centuries.

Bukofzer, M. F., *Music in the Baroque Era,* New York, 1947.

• Butterfield, H., *The Origins of Modern Science,* London, 1949. As important for its discussion of Newton's breakthrough regarding gravity and the impact of the scientific revolution on the Enlightenment as it is for its discussion of the Renaissance period.

Darnton, Robert, *The Business of Enlightenment: A Publishing History of the Encyclopédie, 1775–1800,* Cambridge, Mass., 1979. A masterful and fascinating blend of intellectual, social, and business history.

• Gay, Peter, *The Enlightenment: An Interpretation;* Vol. 1, *The Rise of Modern Paganism;* Vol. 2, *The Science of Freedom,* New York, 1966–1969. A cross between an interpretation and a survey. Emphasizes the philosophes' sense of identification with the classical world and takes a generally positive

view of their accomplishments. Contains extensive annotated bibliographies.
- Hall, Alfred R., *The Scientific Revolution, 1500–1800*, 2nd. ed., Boston, 1956. The best place to look for clear accounts of specific scientific accomplishments.
- Hampson, Norman, *The Enlightenment*, Baltimore, 1968. Probably the best shorter introduction.
- Hazard, Paul, *The European Mind: The Critical Years (1680–1715)*, New Haven, 1953. A basic and indispensable account of the changing climate of opinion which preceded the Enlightenment.
- Hildesheimer, W., *Mozart*, New York, 1982. Widely regarded as the most literate and thought-provoking biography now available of any major musical figure.
- Kimball, F., *The Creation of the Rococo Decorative Style*, Philadelphia, 1943.

  Levey, Michael, *Rococo to Revolution: Major Trends in 18th Century Painting*, New York, 1966.

  Manuel, Frank E., *A Portrait of Isaac Newton*, Cambridge, Mass., 1968. A provocative psychobiography.

  Shackleton, Robert, *Montesquieu: A Critical Biography*, London, 1961. The standard work on the man and his thought.
- Shryock, Richard H., *The Development of Modern Medicine: An Interpretation of the Social and Scientific Factors Involved*, London, 1948. Fascinating reading and still the basic work on the subject.
- Summerson, John, *Architecture in Britain, 1530–1830*, 6th ed., Baltimore, 1977. The best introduction to Wren and English Palladianism.
- Wade, Ira O., *The Intellectual Development of Voltaire*, Princeton, 1969. A magnificent synthesis which stresses how Voltaire's "English experience" provided the cornerstone for all his subsequent thought.
- Waterhouse, Ellis K., *Painting in Britain, 1530–1790*, 4th ed., Baltimore, 1979. Very good on eighteenth-century developments.
- Watt, Ian, *The Rise of the Novel*, London, 1957. The basic work on the innovative qualities of the novel in eighteenth-century England.
- Westfall, R. S., *Never at Rest: A Biography of Isaac Newton*, New York, 1980. Illuminates all aspects of Newton's scientific accomplishment.

SOURCE MATERIALS

- Beccaria, Cesare, *An Essay on Crimes and Punishments, with a Commentary by M. de Voltaire*, Stanford, 1953. A reprint of the original English translation of 1767.
- Gibbon, Edward, *The Portable Gibbon: The Decline and Fall of the Roman Empire*, ed. D. A. Saunders, New York, 1952. A convenient abridgment.
- Voltaire, *The Portable Voltaire*, ed. Ben Ray Redman, New York, 1949. An excellent anthology including the complete *Candide*.

Part Five

THE FRENCH AND INDUSTRIAL REVOLUTIONS AND THEIR CONSEQUENCES

No two events more profoundly altered the shape of Western civilization than the French and Industrial Revolutions. "Modern" history begins with their occurrence. The major happenings of the nineteenth and early twentieth centuries—the spread of middle-class liberalism and economic success; the decline of the old, landed aristocracies; the growth of class consciousness among urban workers—all had their roots in these two revolutions.

The French and Industrial Revolutions took place at about the same time and affected many of the same people—though in different ways and to varying degrees. Together they resulted in the overthrow of absolutism, mercantilism, and the last vestiges of manorialism. Together they produced the theory and practice of economic individualism and political liberalism. And together they ensured the growth of class consciousness, and the culmination of those tensions between the middle and working classes that imparted new vitality to European history after 1800.

Each revolution, of course, produced results peculiarly its own. The French Revolution encouraged the growth of nationalism and its unattractive step-child, authoritarianism. The Industrial Revolution compelled the design of a new, urban social order. Yet despite their unique contributions, the two revolutions must be studied together and understood as the joint progenitors of Western history in the nineteenth and early twentieth centuries.

The French and Industrial Revolutions and Their Consequences

POLITICS	SCIENCE & INDUSTRY

1770

James Watt's steam engine, 1763
Spinning jenny patented, 1770

American War of Independence, 1775–1783

Beginning of factory system, 1780s

French Revolution begins, 1789

Lavoisier discovers the indestructibility of matter, 1789

France declared a republic, 1792
Declaration of Pillnitz, 1792
Reign of Terror, 1793–1794

Cotton gin invented, 1793
Edward Jenner develops smallpox vaccine, 1796

Treaty of Campo Formio, 1797

Napoleon, first consul of France, 1799

1800

Treaty of Lunéville, 1801
Napoleon declared first consul for life, 1802
Napoleon crowns himself emperor of the French, 1804
Continental System established, 1806

Reforms of Hardenberg and Stein, Prussia, 1808

Napoleon's invasion of Russia, 1812
Congress of Vienna, 1814–1815

Battle of Waterloo, 1815

"Peterloo Massacre," England, 1819
Congress of Verona, 1822
Monroe Doctrine, 1823

1825

Louis Pasteur, 1822–1895

"Decembrist" Revolt, Russia, 1825
Greek Independence, 1829
Revolution in France, 1830
"Young Italy," 1831
Reform Bill of 1832, England
Slavery abolished, British colonies, 1833
Poor Law reform, England, 1834
Chartist movement, England, 1838–1848

First railway, England, 1825

Corn Laws repealed, England, 1846
Revolutions in Europe, 1848
Karl Marx, *Communist Manifesto,* 1848
Second Republic, France, 1848
Frankfurt Assembly, Germany, 1848–1849
Reign of Louis Napoleon, 1851–1870

Great Exhibition, London, 1851
Invention of the sewing machine, 1850s

1850

Crimean War, 1854–1856

Invention of the Bessemer process, 1856

Unification of Italy, 1858–1866

Charles Darwin, *Origin of Species,* 1859

Civil War, United States, 1861–1865
Otto von Bismarck's accession to power, 1862
First International, 1864

Parliamentary Reform Bill, England, 1867

Suez Canal opened, 1869
Union Pacific railroad, United States, 1869

Franco-Prussian War, 1870

ECONOMICS & SOCIETY	ARTS & LETTERS	
		1770
Jean-Jacques Rousseau, *The Social Contract*, 1762		
	Ludwig van Beethoven, 1770–1827	
Adam Smith, *Wealth of Nations*, 1776		
	Immanuel Kant, *Critique of Pure Reason*, 1781	
Jeremy Bentham, *The Principles of Morals and Legislation*, 1789		
Utilitarianism, 1790–1870	Johann von Goethe, *Faust*, 1790–1808	
	Romantic movement, 1790–1850	
Tom Paine, *The Rights of Man*, 1791–1792		
Thomas Malthus, *An Essay on the Principle of Population*, 1798	William Wordsworth, *Lyrical Ballads*, 1798	
		1800
	G. W. Hegel, *Phenomenology of the Spirit*, 1807	
	J. G. Fichte, *Addresses to the German Nation*, 1808	
Louis Blanc, 1811–1882		
	Francisco Goya, *The Executions of the Third of May*, 1814	
Founding of Prussian Zollverein, 1818		
		1825
	Honoré de Balzac, *The Human Comedy*, 1829–1841	
	Eugène Delacroix, *Liberty Leading the People*, 1830	
	Realism in literature and art, 1840–1870	
Friedrich Engels, *The Condition of the Working Class*, 1844		
John Stuart Mill, *Principles of Political Economy*, 1848	Pre-Raphaelite Brotherhood formed, 1848	
		1850
	Giuseppe Verdi, *Il Trovatore*, 1853	
	Richard Wagner, *The Ring of the Nibelung*, 1854–1874	
	Charles Dickens, *Hard Times*, 1854	
	Gustave Flaubert, *Madame Bovary*, 1857	
Emancipation of the serfs, Russia, 1861		
	Leo Tolstoy, *War and Peace*, 1866–1869	
Karl Marx, *Capital*, 1867		
	Pope Pius IX, *Syllabus of Errors*, 1869	

Chapter 19

THE FRENCH REVOLUTION

Men are born, and always continue, free and equal in respect of their
rights. Civil distinctions, therefore, can be founded only on public utility.
The nation is essentially the source of all sovereignty; nor can any individual, or any body of men, be entitled to any authority which is not
expressly derived from it.

—*The Declaration of the Rights of Man and of the Citizen,* 1789

In 1789, one European out of every five lived in France. And
most Europeans, French or not, who thought beyond the boundaries of their own immediate concerns, perceived of France as
the center of European civilization. It followed, therefore, that a revolution in France would immediately command the attention of Europe,
and would from the first assume far more than mere national significance. Yet the French Revolution attracted and disturbed men and
women for reasons other than the fact that it was French. Both its
philosophical ideals and its political realities mirrored attitudes, concerns, and conflicts that had occupied the minds of Europeans for
several decades. When the revolutionaries pronounced in favor of
liberty, they spoke not only with the voice of the eighteenth-century
philosophes, but with those of the English aristocracy in 1688 and
the American revolutionaries of 1776. Absolutism was the bane of
continental noblemen, jealous to preserve their ancient freedoms from
monarchical inroads. It was also increasingly the bane of continental
entrepreneurs who had welcomed mercantilist interference on their
behalf in the past, but now found themselves chafing under absolutist
constraints to their economic independence. Across Europe, monarch,
nobility, and middle class confronted each other in uneasy hostilities
that varied in intensity, but reflected common mistrust and uncertainty.

The era of revolution

1. THE COMING OF THE REVOLUTION

Why a revolution?

Historians continue to ask why revolution broke out in France in 1789. They have provided a number of answers to a question that will probably never be wholly resolved. Those men and women involved in the struggle believed they were striking a blow against tyranny. Yet why did the government of Louis XVI appear to them to be so much more tyrannous than that of Louis XIV had seemed to their great-grandfathers?

(1) The persistence of privilege

There appear to have been several major factors that contributed to the breakdown that produced revolution. The first was the persistence of privilege, which we have seen as a continuously vexing problem for eighteenth-century absolutist monarchs. The various regions and orders continued to press for what they called their "liberties"— that is, their right to conduct their affairs without interference from the state. During the eighteenth century the efficacy of the intendant system declined in direct proportion to the crown's failure to keep the nobility isolated and impotent. By the 1780s intendants were themselves often noblemen, prepared to sacrifice state interests to those of their own privileged station.

Resurgence of the parlements

As we have noted, the *parlements,* France's powerful courts of record, had reasserted their privileged independence during the early years of the reign of Louis XV. Throughout the century they had grown increasingly insistent upon what they began to call their "constitutional" rights—in reality, their traditional habit of opposing any legislation that did not serve the interests of their aristocratic members. When Louis XVI had pressed for new taxes to be levied on the nobility as well as the rest of the community after the expensive Seven Years' War, the *parlements* successfully blocked the proposal, insisting upon their right to exemption from major national taxes. In the mid-1770s this episode was reenacted when Anne Robert Jacques Turgot (1727–1781), Louis XVI's principal financial minister, attempted to combat the government's indebtedness through a series of reforms that included the curtailing of court expenses, the abolition of the *corvée* (forced labor by the peasants on the royal roads) in favor of a small tax on landowners, and the abolition of certain guild restrictions in order to stimulate manufacturing. These innovations were steadfastly and successfully opposed by the Paris *parlement,* whose members claimed that Turgot was trampling upon ancient prerogatives and privileges— as indeed he was.

(2) Antagonisms among the social orders: the Church

This continued insistence on privilege was a symptom of the second major factor contributing to the outbreak of revolution: growing antagonism within and between the various social orders that composed French society. There was tension within the Roman Catholic church, the so-called first estate of the realm. Its rulers—bishops, archbishops, and cardinals—were in the main recruited from the aristocracy. They enjoyed large incomes, derived from property that had been willed to the Church over the centuries and that the Church successfully continued to claim was exempt from taxation by the state. In addition, the Church collected a tax—the tithe—on all land under cultivation, an average of between one-tenth and one-fifteenth of the annual harvest. Income from both property and tithe was inequitably distributed among the ranks of the clergy. The princes of the Church, along with the leading monastic orders, took the lion's shares. Parish priests received very little. This imbalance in the distribution of revenues was resented not only by the priests, but by peasant tithepayers, who hated to see their taxes spent to support a distant and haughty ecclesiastical hierarchy, rather than their own, often very deserving, local clergy.

The ranks of the aristocracy, France's second estate, were also divided. Many determined reformers were themselves noblemen, but they were nobles of the robe, men who had, often by purchase, acquired administrative or judicial office (hence the "robe") which conferred a title of nobility, as well as the opportunity to amass a substantial fortune in land and other property. Included in this group were talented men such as the philosopher the baron de Montesquieu, the lawyer the comte de Mirabeau, and the statesman the marquis de Lafayette, who had represented France in America at the time of the Revolutionary War. Among these nobles of the robe were men who would play prominent roles in the French Revolution.

nobles of the robe

In contrast to this group stood the nobles of the sword—or *noblesse de race,* as the group enjoyed calling itself—whose titles extended back to the Middle Ages. These aristocrats regarded the nobles of the robe as upstarts. In general, they lived at the royal court at Versailles, where they enjoyed making political mischief, leaving the management of their estates to bailiffs. In 1781, they pressed successfully for a law that restricted the sale of military commissions to men whose aristocratic lineage extended back at least four generations. If they could not prevent the general debasing of their order, they reasoned, they could at least ensure that the army remained their preserve. The tensions between the nobles of the robe and the sword kept the aristocracy fragmented and at odds with itself, and hence unable to form together into anything more than a negative and potentially destructive force.

nobles of the sword

The disdain of the *noblesse de race* for the nobility of the robe was mild compared with the contempt in which haughty aristocrats held the urban middle orders. This large group was by no means homogeneous. At the top stood government officials, talented professionals, and large-scale financiers and merchants. Lesser notables were to be found throughout the ranks of the third estate. For every major entrepreneur there were scores of small-scale masters, lodged in their workshops yet removed from the artisans and laborers below them by virtue of their ownership of those shops.

the third estate

Movement from the upper ranks of the third estate into the nobility

A Gentleman of the Third Estate with His Family.
A contemporary engraving which illustrates the respectability the third estate wished to see translated into political power.

Social mobility

had been possible in the past for wealthy, ambitious members of the middle orders. The appointment or purchase of position—the route favored by nobles of the robe—or the marriage of a wealthy financier's daughter to the son of an impoverished aristocrat were the most common means of upward mobility. Yet to increasing numbers of the urban bourgeoisie it appeared by about 1780 that the nobility of the sword was intent upon closing off the avenue of social advancement. Their discontent would not have been so great had their birth and position within the third estate not excluded them from participation in the political life of the nation. No matter how much money a merchant, manufacturer, banker, or lawyer might acquire, he was still excluded from political privileges. He had almost no influence at the court; he could not hold high political office; and except in the choice of a few petty local officers, he could not even vote. As the middle orders achieved affluence and greater self-esteem, their members were bound to resent such discrimination.

Not a bourgeois revolution

Powerful as this resentment was, however, it was not, as some historians have insisted, the primary motivating force behind revolution. They have argued that a self-consciously articulate entrepreneurial middle class, driven by a desire to achieve political power commensurate with its already established economic supremacy, made the revolution. This position overlooks the fact that though the social membrane separating nobility from upper bourgeoisie was hardening, it was by no means impermeable. The barrier between an aristocrat and a businessman was not as great as that between a businessman and an artisan or peasant. This theory also ignores the role played in the first phase of the revolution by noblemen such as Lafayette, and the fact that middle-class revolutionaries were far more likely to be lawyers than businessmen. Most important, such an explanation fails to account for the bitter hatred felt by rural peasants for their overlords—monarchical, aristocratic, and clerical.

We have seen how absolutist government imposed increasingly heavy financial burdens on the peasantry. No where was this truer than in late eighteenth-century France. Those peasants who owned property, as well as those who worked the land as tenant-farmers or laborers, were bound by numerous obligations: a tithe and levy on farm produce owed to the Church; fees, called *banalités,* for the use of a landlord's facilities—a mill, a wine press; fees, as well, to the nobility when land changed hands. In addition, peasants were forced to pay a disproportionate share of both direct and indirect taxes— the most onerous of which was the *gabelle* or salt tax—levied by the government. (For some time the production of salt had been a state monopoly; every individual was required to buy at least seven pounds a year from the government works. The result was a commodity whose cost was often as much as fifty or sixty times its actual value.) Further grievances stemmed from the requirement that peasants work to maintain public roads (the *corvée*) and from the hunting privileges accorded the aristocracy, which for centuries had regarded the right

Peasant obligations

Pre-Revolutionary Propaganda, 1788–1789. These prints support the popular view that the third estate was carrying the burden of national taxation on its shoulders while the privileged orders enjoyed the fruits of the peasant's labors, tax-free.

to indulge in the diversions of the chase, to the exclusion of all others, as a distinctive badge of their order.

The effects of enclosure

The vestiges of manorial custom were not the only sources of peasant discontent. During the eighteenth century they also came under pressure as a result of the increasingly frequent enclosure of what had been common land. Fields allowed to lie fallow, together with those tilled only infrequently, were considered "common," land on which all persons might graze their livestock. These common lands, particularly extensive in the west of France, were an important resource for the peasants. In addition to the right to pasturage, they enjoyed that of gathering wood and of gleaning cultivated fields following a harvest. Now the king's economic advisors declared these collective rights to be obstacles in the path of agricultural improvement. Anxious to increase their income by increasing the efficiency of their estates, the landlords attempted to enclose these common lands, thereby depriving the peasants of the open pasturage they had come to depend on.

(3) The role of ideas

A third important cause of revolution was intellectual. No event so all-encompassing occurs in an intellectual vacuum. Although ideas may not have "caused" the revolution, they played a critical role in giving shape and substance to the discontent experienced by so many, particularly among the literate middle orders. The political theories of Locke, Voltaire, Montesquieu, and Condorcet appealed to both discontented nobility and bourgeoisie: Voltaire, because of his general execration of the privileged institutions of church and absolute monarchy; Condorcet because of his belief in progress; Locke and Montesquieu because of their defense of private property and limited sovereignty. Montesquieu's ideas were especially congenial to aristocrats, who read his doctrine of checks and balances as a defense of their ancient privileges—now elevated to the status of "liberties." The *parlements* and provincial Estates, or governing assemblies, were the constituted bodies that would provide a check to royal power.

The physiocrats

The bourgeoisie also welcomed theoretical support from Enlightenment thinkers in its campaign for political recognition and against monarchical absolutism. That campaign was fueled as well by another group of libertarian thinkers, economic theoreticians called physiocrats in France, whose most influential member was Turgot, a contributor to the *Encyclopedia* as well as an experienced fiscal administrator, intendant, and royal minister. Their proposals were grounded in the ideas of the Enlightenment, particularly the notion of a universe governed by mechanistic laws. They argued that production and distribution of wealth were subject to laws as predictable and ultimately salutary as the laws of physics. Those laws would function beneficially, however, only if agriculture and trade were freed from mercantilist regulations. They urged the government to lift its controls on the price of grain, for example, which had been imposed to keep the cost of bread low, but which had not accomplished that goal. By allowing the laws of supply and demand to determine the market price, the government would encourage farmers to grow a crop that was more profitable to them, and an increase in supply would thus eventually reduce the cost to consumers.

The theories of one further thinker, Jean-Jacques Rousseau (1712–1778), played an important part in shaping the ideas and attitudes of French revolutionaries. The most significant of his writings on politics were *Discourse on the Origin of Inequality* (1753) and *Social Contract* (1762), the latter published in many editions before the revolution. Rousseau agreed with Locke that society had its origins in a state of nature. In contrast with Locke, however, he regarded the state of nature as a virtual paradise. Eventually, however, evils had arisen there, due primarily to quarrels over property rights which in turn produced social and economic inequality. To ensure general security, therefore, a civil society was established in which, according to Rousseau, individuals surrendered their rights to the community. This change was accomplished by means of a social contract, in which each person agreed to submit to the will of the majority. In the state that then emerged— characterized by small-scale institutions in Rousseau's vision—citizens were leveled by their contract into democratic equality.

Jean-Jacques Rousseau

Rousseau developed an altogether different conception of sovereignty from that of other Enlightenment political theorists. Whereas Locke and his followers had argued that only a portion of sovereign power is surrendered to the state, the rest being retained by the people themselves, Rousseau contended that sovereignty is indivisible, and that all of it became vested in the community when civil society was formed. He insisted further that individuals in becoming a party to the social contract gave up their rights and agreed to submit absolutely to the general will. The sovereign power of the state was thus subject to no theoretical limitations.

Rousseau vs. the Enlightenment

Rousseau's appeal, though great, was not so much to those men whose thoughts and actions dominated the first stage of the revolution. Although they might have agreed with Rousseau's opposition to hereditary privilege, they were, as convinced individualists, unmoved by arguments in favor of surrender to a general will. Rousseau's influence upon the revolution was greater during its second stage, when a more democratic and radical coterie emerged to lead events, first in the direction of democracy and then toward a new kind of "democratic absolutism" that accorded with Rousseau's notions of the sovereign state.

Rousseau's influence

A fourth important factor making for revolution was the continuing and deepening financial crisis of the 1770s and 1780s, brought on by years of administrative improvidence and ineptitude. This crisis was compounded by a general price rise during much of the eighteenth century, which permitted the French economy to expand by providing capital for investment, but also worked hardship on the peasantry and urban artisans and laborers, who found their purchasing power considerably reduced. Their plight deteriorated further at the end of

(4) The financial crisis

the 1780s when poor harvests encouraged landlords to extract even larger sums from their dependents in order to compensate for a sharp decline in profits, and when the high price of bread generated desperation among the urban poor. In 1788; families found themselves spending more than 50 percent of their income on bread, which comprised the bulk of their diet; the following year the figure rose to as much as 80 percent. Poor harvests contributed to a marked reduction in demand for manufactured goods; families had little money to spend for anything other than food. Peasants could no longer rely on the system of domestic industry to help them make ends meet, since they were receiving so few orders for the textiles and other articles they were accustomed to making at home. Many left the countryside for the cities, hoping to find work there, only to discover that unemployment was far worse than in rural areas. Evidence indicates that between 1787 and 1789 the unemployment rate in many parts of urban France was as high as 50 percent. The financial despair produced by this unemployment fueled resentment and turned peasants and urban workers into potential revolutionaries.

Administrative inefficiency: tax collection and dispersal

The country's financial position was further weakened by an inefficient system of tax collection and disbursal. Not only was taxation tied to differing social status, it varied as well from region to region— some areas, for example, subject to a much higher *gabelle* than others. The myriad special circumstances and exemptions that prevailed made the task of collectors all the more difficult. Those collectors were in many cases so-called tax farmers, members of a syndicate that loaned the government money in return for the right to collect taxes and to keep for itself the difference between the amounts it took in and the amounts it loaned. The system of disbursal was at least as inefficient as was revenue collection. Instead of one central agency there were several hundred private accountants, a fact which made it impossible for the government to keep accurate track of its assets and liabilities. The financial system all but broke down completely under the increased expenses brought on by French participation in the American war. The cost of servicing the national debt of four million livres in the 1780s consumed 50 percent of the nation's budget. By 1788 the chaotic financial situation, together with severe social tensions and an inept monarch, had brought absolutist France to the edge of political disaster.

(5) The character of Louis XVI

Finally, in attempting to explain the revolution, one must acknowledge the character of the monarch, Louis XVI. Faced with serious challenges to centralized power from resurgent noble elites as well as popularly based political movements in the eighteenth century, only the ablest absolutist ruler, possessing in equal measure the talents of administrative ability and personal determination and vision, could hope to rule successfully. Louis XVI possessed neither of these talents. He came to the throne in 1774 at the age of twenty, a well-intentioned but dull-witted and ineffectual monarch, far more devoted to his hobbies—hunting and lock-making—than to the business of absolutist kingship. On July 14, 1789, when mobs stormed the Bastille, he wrote in his diary "Nothing." Fortunate at the outset of his reign in that he had as his principal financial minister the extremely able Turgot, Louis lost that advantage two years after his accession when he dismissed Turgot rather than press ahead with Turgot's suggested economic reforms, which were strongly opposed by the nobility. From that time, national policy traced an unstable course, uncontrolled by the king and influenced by self-interested courtiers. As responsible as any for the king's indecisive misrule was the queen, Marie Antoinette, daughter of Austria's monarch Maria Theresa. Vain and strong-willed, fond of court entertainments and palace intrigue, she inspired the dedicated hatred of reformers, intellectuals, and the common people. Her reputation was completely dashed when it became apparent that she would even bestow her favors upon a cardinal of the church for the price of a diamond necklace. Both became the butt of jokes at court.

Louis XVI

2. THE DESTRUCTION OF THE ANCIEN RÉGIME

The French revolution thus resulted from the various factors outlined above: the continuing existence of privilege; widespread and debilitating social tensions; the spread of ideas subversive to the theory and practice of absolutism; a deepening financial crisis; and the ineptitude of Louis XVI. But the specific events of the revolution occurred in 1789 because of the inability of the king and his government to resolve the country's immediate financial crisis. When the king's principal ministers, Charles de Calonne and Loménie de Brienne, attempted in 1787 and 1788 to institute a series of financial reforms in order to stave off bankruptcy, they encountered not just opposition but entrenched aristocratic determination to extract further governmental concessions from the monarch. To meet the mounting deficit, the ministers proposed new taxes, notably a stamp duty and a direct tax on the annual produce of the soil. The king summoned an assembly of notables from among the aristocracy, in the hope of persuading the nobles to agree to his demands. Far from acquiescing, however, the nobles insisted that to institute a general tax such as the stamp duty the king would first have to call together the Estates General, representative of the three estates of the realm.

The crisis of 1789

The summoning of this body, which had not met for over a century and a half, seemed to many the only solution to France's deepening problems. No doubt most of those aristocrats who argued for its calling did so from short-sighted and selfish motives. Yet the politically conscious population as a whole agreed with the idea in an unreasonable and desperate hope that this unusual event might, because of its very strangeness, work a miracle and save the country from ruin.

FRANCE UNDER THE ANCIEN RÉGIME

The Estates General

During the period before the rise of monarchical absolutism, when the Estates General was convened more or less regularly, the representatives of each estate had met and voted as a body. Generally this meant that the first and second estates combined against the third. By the late eighteenth century the third estate had attained such importance that it was not willing to tolerate such an arrangement. Consequently its leaders demanded that the three orders should sit together and vote as individuals. More important, it insisted that the representatives of the third estate should be double the number of the first and second. Leaving this issue unresolved, Louis XVI, in the summer of 1788, yielded to popular clamor and summoned the Estates General to meet in May of the following year.

In the ensuing months the question of "doubling the third" was fiercely debated. After having opposed the reform initially, in December 1788 the king agreed to it. His unwillingness to take a strong stand from the first, and his continuing vacillation on the matter of voting procedures, cost him support he might otherwise have obtained from the bourgeoisie. Shortly after the opening of the Estates General at Versailles in May 1789, the representatives of the third estate, angered by the king's attitude, took the revolutionary step of leaving the body and declaring themselves the National Assembly. "What is the third estate?" asked the radical clergyman Abbé Emmanuel Sieyès, one of the most articulate spokesmen for a new order, in his famous pamphlet of January 1789. The answer he gave then—"everything"—was the answer the third estate itself gave when it constituted itself the National Assembly of France. Sieyès, unlike most other revolutionaries at this point, derived his argument from Rousseau, and claimed that the third estate was the nation and that as the nation it was its own sovereign. Now the middle-class lawyers and businessmen of the third estate acted on that claim. Locked out of their meeting hall on June 20, the commoners and a handful of sympathetic nobles and clergymen moved to a nearby indoor tennis court.

Here, under the leadership of the volatile, maverick aristocrat Honoré Riqueti, comte de Mirabeau, and Sieyès, they bound themselves by a solemn oath not to separate until they had drafted a constitution for France. This Oath of the Tennis Court, on June 20, 1789, was the real beginning of the French Revolution. By claiming the authority to remake the government in the name of the people, the Estates General

The National Assembly

Abbé Emmanuel Sieyès

The Tennis Court Oath by David. In the hall where royalty played a game known as *jeu de paume* (similar to tennis) leaders of the revolution swore to draft a constitution. In the center of this painting, with his arm extended, is Jean Bailly, president of the National Assembly. Seated at the table below him is Abbé Sieyès. Somewhat to the right of Sieyès, with both hands on his chest, is Robespierre. Mirabeau, with a hat in his left hand and wearing a black coat, stands somewhat farther to the right.

was not merely protesting against the rule of Louis XVI but asserting its right to act as the highest sovereign power in the nation. On June 27 the king virtually conceded this right by ordering the remaining delegates of the privileged classes to meet with the third estate as members of the National Assembly. The advocates of drastic change were inspired not only by the rhetoric of their leaders, but by the political debates which had occurred during the course of the preceding year. In preparation for the meeting of the Estates, the king had instructed local electoral assemblies to draw up *cahiers de doléances*— lists of grievances. Delegates took these instructions seriously. And the grievances they aired—financial chaos; aristocratic and clerical privileges; denial of political power to the third estate—became the basis for the radical reforms of the assembly in its initial weeks.

The course of the French Revolution was marked by three stages, the first of which extended from June 1789 to August 1792. During most of this period the destiny of France was in the hands of the National Assembly. In the main, this stage was moderate, its actions dominated by the leadership of liberal nobles and equally liberal men of the third estate. Yet three events in the summer and fall of 1789 furnished evidence that the revolution was to penetrate to the very heart of French society, ultimately touching both the urban populace and the rural peasants.

News of the events of late spring 1789 had spread quickly across France. From the very onset of debates on the nature of the political crisis, public attention was high. It was roused not merely by interest in matters of political reform, however, but also by the economic crisis that, as we have seen, brought the price of bread to astronomical heights. Belief was widespread that the aristocracy and king were together conspiring to punish an upstart third estate by encouraging scarcity and high prices. Rumors circulated in Paris during the latter days of June 1789 that the king was about to stage a reactionary coup d'état. The electors of Paris (those who had voted in the third estate) feared not only a counterrevolution but the actions of the Paris poor, who had been parading through the streets and threatening violence. These electors were workshop masters, craftspeople, shopkeepers, petty tradespeople, the men and women who would soon come to be called sans-culottes—so called because the men did not wear upper-class breeches. They formed a provisional municipal government and organized a militia of volunteers to maintain order. Determined to obtain arms, they made their way on July 14 to the Bastille, an ancient fortress where guns and ammunition were stored. Built in the Middle Ages, the Bastille had served as a prison for many years, but was no longer much used. However, it symbolized hated royal authority. When crowds demanded arms from its governor, he at first procrastinated and then, fearing a frontal assault, opened fire, killing ninety-eight of the attackers. The crowd took revenge, capturing the fortress (which contained only seven prisoners—five common criminals and

The Fall of the Bastille, July 14, 1789. A contemporary engraving celebrating the heroic actions of the citizenry of Paris.

two lunatics) and decapitating the governor. At the same time the sans-culottes were establishing a revolutionary municipal government in Paris, similar groups assumed control in other cities across France. This series of events—dramatized by the fall of the Bastille—was the first to demonstrate the commitment of the common people to revolutionary change.

The second popular revolt occurred in the countryside, where the peasants were suffering the direct effects of economic privation. They too feared a monarchical and aristocratic counterrevolution. Eager for news from Versailles, their anticipation turned to fear when they began to understand that the revolution might not address itself to their problems. Frightened and uncertain, peasants in many areas of France panicked in July and August, setting fire to manor houses and the records they contained, destroying monasteries and the residences of bishops, and murdering some of the nobles who offered resistance.

The "Great Fear"

The third instance of popular uprising, in October 1789, was also brought on by economic crisis. This time women, angered by the price of bread and fired by rumors of the king's continuing unwillingness to cooperate with the assembly, marched to Versailles on October 5 and demanded to be heard. Not satisfied with its reception by the assembly, the crowd broke through the gates to the palace, calling for the king to return to Paris. On the afternoon of the following day the king yielded. The National Guard, sympathetic to the agitators, led the crowd back to Paris, the procession headed by a soldier holding aloft a loaf of bread on his bayonet.

The "October Days"

In each of the three cases, these popular uprisings produced a decided effect on the course of political events as they were unfolding at Ver-

Achievements of the first stage: (1) the destruction of privilege

(2) the Declaration of the Rights of Man

(3) secularization of the Church

sailles. The storming of the Bastille helped persuade the king and nobles to treat the National Assembly as the legislative body of the nation. The "Great Fear" inspired an equally great consternation among the debaters in the assembly. On August 4, with one sweep, the remnants of manorialism were largely obliterated. Ecclesiastical tithes and the *corvée* were formally abolished. The hunting privileges of the nobles were ended. Exemption from taxation and monopolies of all kinds were eliminated as contrary to natural equality. While the nobles did not surrender all of their rights, the ultimate effect of these reforms of the "August Days" was to annihilate distinctions of rank and class and to make all French citizens of an equal status in the eyes of the law.

Following the destruction of privilege the assembly turned its attention to preparing a charter of liberties. The result was the Declaration of the Rights of Man and of the Citizen, issued in September 1789. Property was declared to be a natural right as well as liberty, security, and "resistance to oppression." Freedom of speech, religious toleration, and liberty of the press were declared inviolable. All citizens were guaranteed equality of treatment in the courts. No one was to be imprisoned or otherwise punished except in accordance with due process of law. Sovereignty was affirmed to reside in the people, and officers of the government were made subject to deposition if they abused the powers conferred upon them.

The king's return to Paris during the October Days confirmed the reforms already underway and guaranteed further liberalization along lines decreed by the middle-class majority in the assembly. In November 1789, the National Assembly resolved to confiscate the lands of the Church and to use them as collateral for the issue of *assignats,* or paper money, which, it was hoped, would resolve the country's inflationary economic crisis. In July of the following year the Civil Constitution of the Clergy was enacted, providing that all bishops and priests should be elected by the people and should be subject to the au-

Depart des Heroines de Paris pour Versailles le 5 Octobre 1789.

The Departure of the Women of Paris for Versailles, October 1789. Note that the contemporary caption refers to the "heroines of Paris." An early example of revolutionary propaganda.

thority of the state. Their salaries were to be paid out of the public treasury, and they were required to swear allegiance to the new legislation. The secularization of the Church also involved a partial separation from Rome. The aim of the assembly was to make the Catholic Church of France a truly national institution with no more than a nominal subjection to the papacy.

An Assignat

Response to this clerical revolution was mixed. Because the Church had enjoyed a privileged position during the Old Regime, it had earned itself the hatred of many who resented its tolerance of clerical abuses and its exploitation of vast monastic land holdings. Bishops and other members of the higher clergy had often held several ecclesiastical appointments at the same time, had paid scant attention to their duties, and had led far from spiritual lives. Exempt from taxes itself, the Church had not hesitated to extract all it could from the peasantry. And its control of the country's educational system made it a target for those men and women who, influenced by Englightenment thinkers like Voltaire, had turned against the doctrines of Roman Catholicism. On the other hand, the practice of centuries had made the parish church and priest into institutions of great local importance. Peasants found it very difficult to shed habits of deference and respect overnight. The dramatic changes embodied in the Civil Constitution of the Clergy thus encountered considerable resistance in some parts of rural France, and eventually helped to strengthen the forces of counterrevolution.

Response to secularization

Not until 1791 did the National Assembly manage to complete its primary task of drafting a new constitution for the nation. The constitution as it finally emerged gave eloquent testimony to the dominant position now held by the wealthier elements of the third estate. The government was converted into a limited monarchy, with the supreme power virtually a monopoly of the well-to-do. Although all citizens possessed the same civil rights, the vote was allowed only to those who paid a certain amount in taxes. About half the adult males in France made up this latter category of "active" citizen. Yet even their political power was curtailed, for they were to vote for electors, whose property ownership qualified them for that position. Those electors, in turn, chose department officials and delegates to the National—or, as it was henceforth to be called, Legislative—Assembly. The king was deprived of the control he had formerly exercised over the army and local governments. His ministers were forbidden to sit in the assembly, and he was shorn of all powers over the legislative process except a suspensive veto, which in fact could be overridden by the issuance of proclamations.

(4) constitution of 1791

The economic and governmental changes the National Assembly adopted were as much a reflection of the power of rich commoners as were its constitutional reforms. To raise money, it sold off Church lands, but in such large blocks that peasants seldom benefited by the sales as they had expected to. In opposition to the interests of the peasantry, the assembly proceeded with the enclosure of common

(5) economic and governmental changes

lands in order to facilitate the development of capitalist agriculture. To ecourage the growth of unfettered economic enterprise, guilds and trade unions were abolished. To rid the country of authoritarian centralization and of aristocratic domination, local governments were completely restructured. France was divided into eighty-three equal departments. All towns henceforth enjoyed the same form of municipal organization. All local officials were locally elected. This reorganization and decentralization expressed a belief in the necessity of individual liberty and freedom from ancient privilege. As such these measures proclaimed, as did all the work of the assembly, that the "winners" of this first stage of the revolution were the men and women of the upper middle class.

3. A NEW STAGE: RADICAL REVOLUTION

The second stage: (1) disappointment of the common people

Their triumph did not go unchallenged, however. In the summer of 1792, the revolution entered a second stage, which saw the downfall of moderate middle-class leaders and their replacement by radical republicans claiming to rule on behalf of the common people. Three major reasons accounted for this abrupt and drastic alteration in the course of events. First, the politically literate lower classes grew disillusioned as they perceived that the revolution was not benefiting them. The uncontrolled free-enterprise economy of the government resulted in constantly fluctuating and generally rising prices. These increases particularly exasperated those elements of the Parisian population that had agitated for change in preceding years. Urban rioters demanded cheaper bread, while their spokesmen called for governmental control of the ever-growing inflation. Their leaders also articulated the frustrations of a mass of men and women who felt cheated by the constitution. Despite their major role in the creation of a new regime, they found themselves deprived of any effective voice in its operation.

(2) lack of leadership

A second major reason for the change of course was a lack of effective national leadership during the first two years of the revolution. Louis XVI remained the weak, vacillating monarch he had been prior to 1789. Though outwardly prepared to collaborate with the leaders of the assembly, he remained essentially a victim of events. He was compelled to support measures personally distasteful to him, in particular the Civil Constitution of the Clergy. He was thus sympathetic to the plottings of the queen, who was in correspondence with her brother Leopold II of Austria. Urged on by Marie Antoinette, Louis agreed to attempt an escape from France in June 1791, in hopes of rallying foreign support for counterrevolution. The members of the royal family managed to slip past their palace guards in Paris, but were apprehended near the border at Varennes and brought back to the capital. Though the Constitution of 1791 declared France a monarchy, after Varennes that declaration was more fiction than fact. From that point on, Louis was little more than a prisoner of the assembly. The leadership of that body remained in the hands of Honoré Gabriel Riquetti, comte de Mirabeau, until his death in 1791. Yet he was a less than satisfactory leader. An outstanding orator, possessed of the insight of a statesman, he was nevertheless mistrusted by many revolutionaries because of his dissolute, aristocratic youth and his notorious venality. Nor, despite his continued support of a strong constitutional monarchy, did he enjoy the confidence of the king. Even with his shortcomings, Mirabeau was the most effective leader among the moderate constitutionalists, a group that generally failed to capitalize on its opportunities.

The third major reason for the dramatic turn of affairs was the fact that after 1792 France found itself at war with much of the rest of Europe. From the outset of the revolution, men and women across Europe had been compelled, by the very intensity of events in France, to take sides in the conflict. In the years immediately after 1789, the revolution in France won the enthusiastic support of a wide range of politically committed intellectuals, businessmen, and artisans. The English poet William Wordsworth, later to become disillusioned by the subsequent course of revolutionary events, recalled the rapture of his initial mood: "Bliss was it in that dawn to be alive. . . ." His sentiments were echoed across the continent by poets and philosophers, among the latter the German Johann Gottfried von Herder, who declared the revolution the most important historical moment since the Reformation. Political societies in England proclaimed their allegiance to the principles of the new revolution, often quite incorrectly seeing it as nothing more than a French version of the far less momentous events of 1688. In the Low Countries, a "patriot" group organized strikes and plotted a revolution of its own against dominant merchant oligarchies. Political revolutionaries in western Germany and anticlericals in Italy welcomed the possibility of invasion by the French as a means of achieving radical change within their own countries.

Others opposed the course of the revolution from the start. Exiled nobles, who had fled France for the haven of sympathetic royal courts in Germany and elsewhere, did all they could to stir up counterrevolutionary sentiment. The distressed clamoring of these emigrés, along with the plight of Louis XVI and his family, aroused the sympathy, if not, at first, the active support, of European defenders of absolutism and privilege. In England the cause was strengthened by the publication in 1790 of Edmund Burke's *Reflections on the Revolution in France*. A Whig politician who had sympathized with the American revolutionaries, Burke nevertheless attacked the revolution in France as a monstrous crime against the social order. He argued that by remodeling their government as they had, the French had turned their backs on both human nature and history. Men and women were not consti-

(3) The revolution abroad

Counterrevolution: Burke

Edmund Burke

Thomas Paine

Declaration of Pillnitz

tutional abstractions, endowed with an objective set of natural rights, as the Declaration of the Rights of Man had insisted. Rights—and duties as well—were the consequence of the individual histories of the countries into which men and women were born. Those histories bound people to the past and entailed a commitment to the future, as well as the present. Hence they had no right to remake their country and its institutions without reference to the past or concern for the future, as Burke insisted the French had. Their failure to pay proper respect to tradition and custom had destroyed the precious fabric of French civilization woven by centuries of national history.

Burke's famous pamphlet, in which he painted a romantic and highly inaccurate picture of the French king and queen, helped arouse sympathy for the counterrevolutionary cause. It is questionable, however, whether that sympathy would have turned to active opposition, had not the French soon appeared as a threat to international stability and the individual ambitions of the great powers. It was that threat which led to war in 1792, and which kept the Continent in arms for a generation. This state of war had a most important impact on the formation of political and social attitudes during this period in Europe. Once a country declared war with France, its citizens could no longer espouse sympathy with the revolution without paying severe consequences. Those who continued to support the revolution, as did a good many among the artisan and small tradespeople class, were persecuted and punished for their beliefs. To be found in Britain, for example, possessing a copy of Tom Paine's revolutionary tract, *The Rights of Man* (1791–1792), a prorevolutionary response to Burke's *Reflections,* was enough to warrant imprisonment. As the moderate nature of the early revolution turned to violent extension, entrepreneurs and businessmen eagerly sought to live down their radical sentiments of a few years past. The wars against revolutionary France came to be perceived as a matter of national survival; to ensure internal security, it seemed that patriotism demanded not only a condemnation of the French but of French ideas as well.

The first European states to express public concern about events in revolutionary France were Austria and Prussia. They were not anxious to declare war; their interests at the time centered upon the division of Poland between themselves. Nevertheless, they jointly issued the Declaration of Pillnitz in August 1791, in which they avowed that the restoration of order and of the rights of the monarch of France was a matter of "common interest to all sovereigns of Europe." The leaders of the French government at this time were a moderate faction, the Girondists, so called because many of them came from the mercantile Gironde district. Afraid of losing political support in France, they pronounced the Declaration of Pillnitz a threat to national security, hoping that enthusiasm for a war would unite the French and result also in enthusiasm for their continued rule. They were aided in their scheme by the activities of monarchists, both within and outside France, whose plottings and pronouncements could be made to appear an additional threat, though to a greater extent than they actually were. On April 20, 1792, the assembly declared war against Austria and Prussia.

Almost all of the various political factions in France welcomed the war. The Girondists expected that their aggressive policy would solidify the loyalty of the people to their regime. Reactionaries hailed the intervention of Austria and Prussia as the first step in the undoing of all that had happened since 1789. Extremists hoped that initially the French would suffer reverses that would discredit the moderate Girondists and the monarchy, and thus hasten the advent of a more radical regime in France, and the triumph of people's armies and revolutionary ideals across Europe. As the radicals hoped, the forces of the French met serious reverses. By August 1792 the allied armies of Austria and Prussia had crossed the frontier and were threatening the capture of Paris. A fury of rage and despair seized the capital. The belief prevailed that the military disasters had been the result of treasonable dealings with the enemy on the part of the king and his conservative followers. On August 10 Parisian rioters, organized by their radical leadership, attacked the royal palace, slaughtering the king's guards and driving him to seek refuge in the meeting hall of the assembly. At the same time, radicals seized the municipal government in Paris, replacing it with a revolutionary Commune under their control. The Commune successfully demanded that the assembly suspend the king from his duties and hand him and his family over for imprisonment.

From this point, the country's leadership passed into the hands of an equalitarian-minded segment of the third estate. These new leaders called themselves Jacobins, after the political club to which they belonged, whose headquarters was in Paris, but whose membership extended throughout France. Like the Girondists, the Jacobins were mostly members of the bourgeoisie, professionals and businessmen, though an increasing number of artisans joined the club as it grew. They differed from the Girondists in their political philosophy, however. Girondists were loud in their defense of liberty, by which they often meant no more than freedom to pursue their own economic interests without state regulation. Because their political base was in the provinces, they tended to mistrust Parisians and were alarmed by the extremism of the Commune. Jacobins, in contrast, were the masterminds of the Commune. They were vigorous proponents of equality. They supported the elimination of remaining civil and political distinctions, favored universal suffrage, and state programs for the maintenance of the poor. The Jacobins differed as well from the Girondists in that they were a tightly organized party. As such, again unlike the Girondists, they were able to move decisively and prepared to act ruthlessly in defense of their programs and their leadership.

One of the Jacobins' first actions was to call for an election by uni-

Jacobins. Contemporary drawings by Heuriot.

versal suffrage of delegates to a national convention, whose task would be to draft and enact a new and republican constitution. This convention became the effective governing body of the country for the next three years. It was elected in September 1792, at a time when disturbances across France reached a new height. The so-called September

massacres occurred when patriotic Paris mobs, hearing a rumor that political prisoners were plotting to escape from their prisons, responded by hauling them before hastily convened tribunals and sentencing them to swift execution. Over one thousand supposed enemies of the revolution were killed in less than a week. Similar riots engulfed Lyons, Orléans, and other French cities.

When the newly elected convention met in September, its membership was far more radical than that of its predecessor, the Legisla-

tive Assembly, and its leadership was determined to demand an end to the monarchy and the death of Louis XVI. On September 21, the convention declared France a republic. In December it placed the king on trial and in January he was condemned to death by a narrow margin. The heir to the grand tradition of French absolutism met his end bravely as "Citizen Louis Capet," beheaded by the guillotine, the frightful mechanical headsman that had become the symbol of revolutionary fervor.

Meanwhile, the convention turned its attention to the enactment of further domestic reforms. Among its most significant accomplish-

ments over the next three years were the abolition of slavery in French colonies; the prohibition of imprisonment for debt; the establishment of the metric system of weights and measures; and the repeal of primogeniture, so that property might not be inherited exclusively by the oldest son, but be divided in substantially equal portions among all immediate heirs. The convention also supplemented the decrees of the assembly in abolishing the remnants of manorialism and in providing for greater freedom of economic opportunity for the commoner. The property of enemies of the revolution was confiscated for the benefit of the government and the lower classes. Great estates were broken up and offered for sale to poorer citizens on easy terms. The indemnities hitherto promised to the nobles for the loss of their privileges were abruptly cancelled. To curb the rise in the cost of living, maximum prices for grain and other necessities were fixed by law, and merchants who profiteered at the expense of the poor were threatened with the guillotine. Still other measures of reform dealt with religion. An effort was made to abolish Christianity and to substitute the worship of Reason in its place. In accordance with this purpose a new calendar was adopted, dating the year from the birth of the republic (September 22, 1792) and dividing the months in such a way as to eliminate the Christian Sunday. Later, this cult of Reason was replaced by a Deistic religion dedicated to the worship of a Supreme Being and to a belief in the immortality of the soul. Finally, in 1794, the convention decreed simply that religion was a private matter, that church and

The Execution of Louis XVI. A revolutionary displays the king's head moments after it had been severed by the guillotine in January 1793.

state would therefore be separated, and that all beliefs not actually hostile to the government would be tolerated.

While effecting this political revolution in France, the convention's leadership at the same time accomplished an astonishingly successful reorganization of its armies. By February 1793, Britain, Holland, Spain, and Austria were in the field against the French. Britain's entrance into the war was dictated by both strategic and economic reasons. The English feared French penetration into the Low Countries directly across the Channel; they were also concerned that French expansion might pose a serious threat to Britain's own growing economic hegemony around the globe. The allied coalition ranged against France, though united only in its desire to contain this puzzling, fearsome revolutionary phenomenon, was nevertheless a formidable force. To counter it, the French organized an army that was able to win engagement after engagement during these years. In August 1793, the revolutionary government imposed a levy on the entire male population capable of bearing arms. Fourteen hastily drafted armies were flung into battle under the leadership of young and inexperienced officers. What they lacked in training and discipline, they made up for in improvised organization, mobility, flexibility, courage, and morale. (In the navy, however, where skill was of paramount importance, the revolutionary French never succeeded in matching the performance of the British.) In 1793–1794, the French armies preserved their homeland. In 1794–1795, they occupied the Low Countries, the Rhineland, parts of Spain, Switzerland, and Savoy. In 1796, they invaded and occupied key parts of Italy and broke the coalition that had arrayed itself against them.

The revolutionary wars

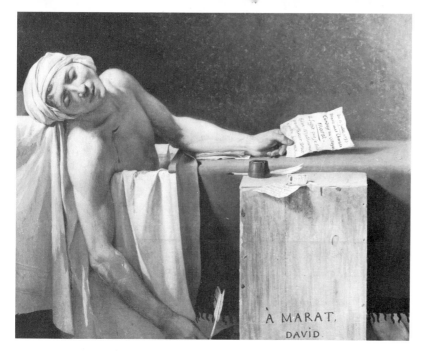

The Death of Marat. This painting by the French artist David immortalized Marat. The bloody towel, the box, and the tub were venerated as relics of the revolution.

The dictatorship of the Committee of Public Safety

These achievements were not without their price, however. To ensure their accomplishment, the rulers of France resorted to a bloody authoritarianism that has come to be known as the Terror. Although the convention succeeded in 1793 in drafting a new democratic constitution, based upon manhood suffrage, it deferred its introduction because of wartime emergency. Instead, the convention prolonged its own life year by year, and increasingly delegated its responsibilities to a group of twelve leaders known as the Committee of Public Safety. By this time the moderate Girondists had lost all influence within the convention. Complete power had passed to the Jacobins, who continued to proclaim themselves disciples of Rousseau and champions of the common man.

Foremost among the members of the Committee of Public Safety were Jean Paul Marat, Georges Jacques Danton, and Maximilien Robespierre. Jean Paul Marat (1743–1793) was educated as a physician, and by 1789 had already earned enough distinction in that profession to be awarded an honorary degree by St. Andrews University in Scotland. Almost from the beginning of the revolution he stood as a champion of the common people. He opposed nearly all of the assumptions of his more moderate colleagues in the assembly, including the idea that France should pattern its government after that of Great Britain, which he recognized to be oligarchic in form. Soon made a victim of persecution and forced to take refuge in unsanitary sewers and dungeons, he persevered in his efforts to rouse the people to a defense of their rights. His exposure to infection left him with a chronic skin affliction from which he could find relief only through frequent bathing. In 1793 he was stabbed through the heart during one of

Georges Jacques Danton

these soothing respites by Charlotte Corday, a young woman fanatically devoted to the Girondists. In contrast with Marat, Georges Jacques Danton (1759–1794) did not come into prominence until the revolution was three years old; but, like Marat, he directed his activities toward goading the masses into rebellion. Elected a member of the Committee of Public Safety in 1793, he had much to do with organizing the Terror. As time went on, however, he wearied of ruthlessness and displayed a tendency to compromise that gave his opponents in the convention their opportunity. In April 1794 Danton was sent to the guillotine. Upon mounting the scaffold he is reported to have said: "Show my head to the people; they do not see the like every day."

The most famous and perhaps the greatest of the extremist leaders was Maximilien Robespierre (1758–1794). Born of a family reputed to be of Irish descent, Robespierre was trained for the law and speedily achieved a modest success as an advocate. In 1782 he was appointed a criminal judge, but soon resigned because he could not bear to impose a sentence of death. Of a nervous and timid disposition, he was a less than able administrator, but made up for this lack of talent by fanatical devotion to principle. He adopted the belief that the philosophy of Rousseau held the one great hope of salvation for all mankind. To put this philosophy into practice he was ready to employ any means that would bring results, regardless of the cost to himself or to others. This passionate loyalty to a gospel that exalted the masses eventually won him a following. Indeed, he was so lionized by the public that he was allowed to wear the knee breeches, silk stockings, and powdered hair of the old society until the end of his life. In 1791 he was accepted as the oracle of the Jacobin Club. Later he became president of the National Convention and a member of the Committee of Public Safety. Though he had little or nothing to do with originating the Terror, he was nevertheless responsible for enlarging its scope. He came to justify ruthlessness as a necessary and therefore laudable means to revolutionary progress. In the last six weeks of his government, no fewer than 1,285 heads rolled from the scaffold in Paris.

Maximilien Robespierre

The years of the Terror were years of ruthless dictatorship in France. Pressed by foreign enemies from without, the committee faced sabotage from both the political Right and Left at home. In 1793, a royalist counterrevolution broke out in the western area of the Vendée. The peasantry there had remained generally loyal to Church and king. Government attempts to conscript troops into the revolutionary armies fanned long-smoldering resentments into open rebellion. By the summer, the peasant forces there, led by noblemen in the name of a Royal Catholic Grand Army, posed a serious threat to the convention. Meanwhile, Girondist fugitives helped fuel rebellions in the great provincial cities of Lyon, Bordeaux, and Marseilles. This harvest of the decentralizing policies of the National Assembly was bitter fruit to the

The ruthless suppression of enemies of the state

Meeting of a Revolutionary Committee of Surveillance during the Terror

committee. At the same time they met with the scornful criticism of revolutionaries even more radical than themselves. This latter group, known as the *enragés,* was led by the journalist Jacques Hébert, and threatened to topple not only the government but the country itself by its extremist crusades. Determined to stabilize France, whatever the necessary cost, the committee dispatched commissioners into the countryside to suppress the enemies of the state. During the period of the Terror, from September 1793 to July 1794, the most reliable estimates place the number of executions as high as twenty thousand in France as a whole. The victims were by no means all aristocrats. Anyone who appeared to threaten the republic, no matter what his or her social or economic position, was at risk. Far more peasants and laborers than noblemen and women were killed. Among those executed was Marie Antoinette ("The Widow Capet"). When some time later the Abbé Sieyès was asked what he had done to distinguish himself during the Terror, he responded dryly, "I lived."

The achievements of the committee

Three points need to be made with regard to the Committee of Public Safety. First, it dramatically reversed the trend toward decentralization that had characterized the reforms of the assembly. In addition to dispatching its own commissioners from Paris to quell provincial insurrection, the committee published a *Bulletin des loix,* to inform all citizens what laws were to be enforced and obeyed. And it replaced local officials, some of them still royalist in sympathy, with "deputies on mission," whose task was to conscript troops and generate patriotic fervor. When these deputies appeared too eager to act independently, they were in turn replaced by "national agents," with instructions to report directly to the committee. Second, by fostering the interests of the less economically powerful the committee significantly retarded the pace of industrial transformation in France. Through policies which assisted the peasant, the small craftsman, and the shop-keeper to acquire property, the government during this "second" revolution encouraged the entrenchment of a class at once devoted to the principle of republicanism while unalterably opposed to a large-scale capitalist transformation of the economy of France. Third, the ruthless Terror of the committee undoubtedly achieved its end by saving France from defeat at the hands of the coalition of European states. Whether the human price extracted in return for that salvation was worth the paying is a matter historians—and indeed all thoughtful human beings—may well never finally resolve.

The Committee of Public Safety, though able to save France, could not save itself. It failed to put a stop to inflation, thereby losing the support of those commoners whose dissatisfactions had helped bring the convention to power. The long string of military victories convinced growing numbers that the committee's demands for continuing self-sacrifice, as well as its insistence upon the necessity of the Terror, were no longer justified. By July 1794, the committee was virtually without allies. On July 27 (9 Thermidor, according to the new calendar) Robespierre was shouted down by his enemies while attempting to speak on the floor of the convention. Desperate, he tried to rally loyal Jacobins to his defense and against the convention. Discovered in the thick of this plot by convention troops, Robespierre tried unsuccessfully to shoot himself. The following day, along with twenty-one fellow conspirators, he met his death as an enemy of the state on the guillotine. Now the only remaining leaders in the convention were men of moderate sympathies, who, as time went on, inclined toward increasing conservatism. Gradually, the revolution came once more to reflect the interests of the wealthier bourgeoisie. Much of the extremist work of the radicals was undone. The law of maximum prices and the law against "suspects" were both repealed. Political prisoners were freed, the Jacobins driven into hiding, and the Committee of Public Safety shorn of its absolute powers. The new situation made possible the return of priests, royalists, and other emigrés from abroad to add the weight of their influence to the conservative trend.

The third stage: the Thermidorian reaction

In 1795 the National Convention adopted a new constitution, which lent the stamp of official approval to the victory of the prosperous classes. The constitution granted suffrage to all adult male citizens who could read and write. They were permitted to vote for electors, who in turn would choose the members of the legislative body. In order to be an elector, one had to be the proprietor of a farm or other establishment with an annual income equivalent to at least one hundred days of labor. The drafters of the constitution thus ensured that the authority of the government would actually be derived from citizens of considerable wealth. Since it was not practicable to restore the monarchy, lest the old aristocracy also come back into power, executive authority was vested in a board of five men known as the Directory, chosen by the legislative body. The new constitution in-

The 1795 constitution

The Fashionable Mama, 1796. An English cartoon lampooning the extreme style of dress adopted by the newly rich throughout Europe during the Directory period.

cluded not only a bill of rights but also a declaration of the *duties* of the citizen. Conspicuous among the latter was the obligation to bear in mind that "it is upon the maintenance of property . . . that the whole social order rests."

The reign of the Directory has not enjoyed a good historical press. The collection of *nouveau riche* speculators and profiteers who rose to prominence as they labored to make a good thing for themselves out of the war was not a particularly attractive crew. They were lampooned as ostentatious and vulgar *"merveilleuses"*—outrageously overdressed men and underdressed women. But however anxious they were to live down the self-denying excesses of the past several years by self-indulgent excesses of their own, they were in no mood to see the major accomplishments of the revolution undone. They had no difficulty in disposing of threats from the Left, despite their failure to resolve that bugbear of all revolutionary governments, inflation and rising living costs. When in 1796 the radical "Gracchus" Babeuf[1] launched a campaign to abolish private property and parliamentary government, his followers were arrested, and either executed or deported.

To dispatch threats from the Right was not so easy. Elections in March 1797—the first free elections held in France as a republic—returned a large number of constitutional monarchists to the councils of government. Leading politicians, among them some who had voted for the execution of Louis XVI, took alarm. With the support of the army, the Directory in September 1797 annulled most of the election results of the previous spring. Its bold coup did little, however, to end the nation's political irresolution. Two years later, after a series of further abortive uprisings and purges, and with the country still plagued by severe inflation, the Directors were desperate. This time they called their brilliant young general, Napoleon Bonaparte (1769–1821), to their assistance.

The plight of the Directory

Bonaparte's first military victory in 1793, the recapture of Toulon from royalist and British forces, had earned him promotion from captain to brigadier general at the age of twenty-four. Though arrested as a terrorist following the fall of Robespierre, he was subsequently patronized by Viscount Paul Barras, a Directory politician. Bonaparte had gained further public fame and the gratitude of the Directory when on October 4, 1795 (13 Vendémiaire, new calendar), he had delivered the "whiff of grapeshot" that saved the convention from attack by opponents of the new constitution. Since that time he had registered a remarkable series of victories in Italy, which had resulted in Austria's withdrawal from the war. Most recently, he had attempted to defeat Britain by attacking its colonies in Egypt and the Near East. Despite initial successes on land, Bonaparte eventually found himself trapped by the British, following the defeat of the French fleet by Admiral

---

[1] Called "Gracchus" after the Roman tribune Gaius Gracchus, a hero of the people.

Horatio Nelson at Abukir Bay in 1798. A year of further fighting had brought Bonaparte no nearer decisive victory in North Africa.

It was at this point that the call came from the Directory. Bonaparte slipped away from Egypt and appeared in Paris, already having agreed to participate in a coup d'état with the leading director, that former revolutionary champion of the third estate, the Abbé Sieyès. On November 9, 1799 (18 Brumaire), Bonaparte was declared a "temporary consul." He was the answer to the prayers of the Directory: a strong, popular leader who was not a king. Sieyès, who had once declared for revolution in the name of the third estate, now declared for counterrevolution in the name of virtual dictatorship: "Confidence from below, authority from above." With those words Sieyès pronounced the end of the revolutionary period.

4. NAPOLEON AND EUROPE

Few men in Western history have compelled the attention of the world as Napoleon Bonaparte did during the fifteen years of his rule in France. And few men have succeeded as he has in continuing to live on as myth in the consciousness, not just of his own country, but of all Europe. Without doubt, part of the success of the Napoleonic myth can be credited to the fact that Napoleon never attempted to disguise his less-than-gentlemanly background. Although born in Corsica into a family that held a title of nobility from the Republic of Genoa, he cultivated the rude manners of an *arriviste*, losing his temper, cheating at cards, taking what he could get without regard to the conventions of polite society. As such, he appealed to the new citizens of a triumphantly middle-class Europe. In the minds of his admirers he would remain the "little corporal" who, without the privileges of the aristocrat, had made it to the top on his own.

The Eighteenth Brumaire. A detail from a painting by Bronchet depicting Napoleon as the man of the hour.

*The character of
Napoleon Bonaparte*

Yet the myth was also grounded in the important fact of Bonaparte's undoubted abilities. Schooled in France and at the military academy in Paris, he possessed a mind congenial to the ideas of the Enlightenment—creative, imaginative, and ready to perceive things anew. His primary interests were history, law, and mathematics. His particular strengths as a leader lay in his ability to conceive of financial, legal, or military plans and then to master their every detail; his capacity for inspiring others, even those initially opposed to him; and his belief in himself as the destined savior of the French. That last conviction eventually became the obsession that led to Napoleon's undoing. But supreme self-confidence was just what the French government had recently lacked. Napoleon believed both in himself and in France. That latter belief was the tonic France now needed, and Napoleon proceeded to administer it in liberally revivifying doses.

His abilities

During the years from 1799 to 1804, Napoleon ruled under the title of first consul, but in reality as a dictator. Once again, France

Napoleonic reforms

was given a new constitution. Though the document spoke of universal male suffrage, political power was retained, by the now familiar means of indirect election, in the hands of entrepreneurs and professionals. Recognizing, however, that his regime would derive additional substance if it could be made to appear the government of the people of France, Bonaparte instituted what has since become a common authoritarian device: the plebiscite. The voters were asked to approve the new constitution and did so by the loudly proclaimed vote of 3,011,107 in favor, 1,567 opposed.

(1) Centralization and finance

Although the constitution provided for a legislative body, that body could neither initiate nor discuss legislation. The first consul made use of a Council of State to draft his laws; but in fact the government depended on the authority of one man. Bonaparte had no desire to undo the major egalitarian reforms of the revolution. He reconfirmed the abolition of estates, privileges, and local liberties, thereby reconfirming as well the notion of a meritocracy, of "careers open to talent," dear to the hearts of the bourgeoisie. Through centralization of the administrative departments, he achieved what no recent French regime had yet achieved, an orderly and generally fair system of taxation. His plan, by prohibiting the type of exemptions formerly granted the nobility and clergy, and by centralizing collection, enabled him to budget rationally for expenditures and consequent indebtedness. In this way he reduced the inflationary spiral that had entangled so many past governments. Napoleon's willingness to proceed against the decentralizing tendencies of the earlier years of the revolution marked him as a student of the absolutist policies of the Bourbons as well as an admirer of the egalitarian reforms of his more immediate predecessors. He replaced the elected officials and local self-government instituted in 1789 with centrally appointed "prefects" and "subprefects" whose administrative duties were defined in Paris, where local government policy was made as well.

(2) education and law

Napoleon's most significant accomplishment was his completion of the educational and legal reforms begun during the revolutionary period. He ordered the establishment of *lycées* (high schools) in every major town and a school in Paris for the training of teachers. To supplement these changes, Napoleon brought the military and technical schools under state control and founded a national university to exercise supervision over the entire system. Like almost all his reforms, this one proved of particular benefit to the middle class; so did the new legal code promulgated in 1810. The Code Napoleon, as the new body of laws was called, reflected two principles which had threaded their way through all the constitutional changes since 1789: uniformity and individualism. The code made French law uniform, declaring past customs and privileges forever abolished. By underscoring in various ways a private individual's right to property, by authorizing new methods for the drafting of contracts, leases, and stock companies, and by once again prohibiting trade unions, the code worked to the benefit of individually minded entrepreneurs and businessmen.

FRANCE: THE REVOLUTIONARY DEPARTMENTS AFTER 1789

To accomplish these reforms Napoleon called upon the most talented men available to him, regardless of their past political affiliations. He admitted back into the country emigrés of all political stripes. His two fellow consuls—joint executives, but in name only—were a regicide of the Terror and bureaucrat of the Old Regime. His minister of police had been an extreme radical republican; his minister of foreign affairs was the opportunist aristocrat Talleyrand. The work of political reconciliation was assisted by Napoleon's 1801 concordat with the pope, which reunited Church and state. Though the action disturbed former anti-Church Jacobins, Napoleon, ever the pragmatist, believed the reconciliation of Church and state necessary for reasons both of domestic harmony and of interna-

(3) reconciliation

tional solidarity. According to the terms of the concordat, the pope received the right to depose French bishops and to discipline the French clergy. At the same time, the Vatican agreed to lay to rest any claims against the expropriation of former Church lands. Hereafter, that property would remain unchallenged in the hands of its new middle-class rural and urban proprietors. In return, the clergy was guaranteed an income from the state. The concordat did nothing to revoke the principle of religious freedom established by the revolution. Although the Roman Catholic clergy received state money, so did Protestant clergy.

Napoleon crowned emperor

Napoleon's agreement won him the support of those conservatives who had feared for France's future as a godless state. To prove to the old Jacobins, in turn, that he remained a child of their revolution, he invaded the independent state of Baden in 1804 to arrest and then execute the duke of Enghien, a relative of the Bourbons, whom Napoleon falsely accused of a plot against his life. (Three years before he had deported over one hundred Jacobins on a similar charge, but with no permanent political repercussions.) The balancing act only served to increase Napoleon's general popularity. By 1802 the people of France were prepared to accept him as "consul for life." In 1804, they rejoiced when, in the cathedral of Notre Dame, in Paris, he crowned himself Emperor Napoleon I.

Across the boundaries of France, the nations of Europe had watched, some in admiration, others in horror, all in astonishment, at

Left: *Coronation of Napoleon and Josephine* by David. Napoleon crowned himself and his wife and assumed the title of Napoleon I, emperor of the French. Right: *Napoleon I* by Jean A. D. Ingres. This celebratory portrait incorporates stage props that echo the grandeur of imperial Rome, thereby suggesting the extent to which Napoleon wanted Europe to regard him as its supreme ruler.

the phenomenon that was Napoleon. They had fought France since 1792 in hopes of maintaining European stability. Now they faced the greatest threat to that stability yet to arise. The detailed history of the wars fought to contain the French is complex, and of little direct relevance to the patterns of ideas, institutions, and societies we are tracing. Suffice it to say that from 1792 until 1795 France had been at war with a coalition of European powers—principally Austria, Prussia, and Britain. In 1795, Prussia retired from the fray, financially exhausted and at odds with Austria. In 1797, the Austrians, defeated by Bonaparte in northern Italy, withdrew as well, signing the Treaty of Campo Formio, which ceded to France territories in Belgium, recognized the Cisalpine Republic which Bonaparte had established in Italy, and agreed to France's occupation of the left bank of the Rhine.

Anti-French alliances

By the following year, Britain was left to fight the French alone. In 1798 it formed a second coalition against the French, this one with Russia and Austria. The results did not differ significantly from those of the first allied attempt to contain France. Russia and Austria had no success in driving the French from Italy; the French likewise failed to break Britain's advantage at sea. By 1801, the coalition was in tatters, Russia having withdrawn two years previously. The Treaty of Lunéville, signed by France and Austria, confirmed the provisions of Campo Formio; in addition the so-called Batavian, Helvetian, Cisalpine, and Ligurian republics—established by Napoleon from territories in the Low Countries, Switzerland, Italy, and Piedmont—were legitimized. The Austrians also acquiesced to a general redrawing of the map of Germany, which resulted eventually in an amalgamation of semi-independent states under French domination into the Confederation of the Rhine. The following year Britain, no longer able to fight alone, settled with the French as well, returning all the territories it had captured in overseas colonial engagements except Trinidad and Ceylon.

Treaty of Lunéville

Under Napoleon's reign, the territories of central Europe underwent a revolution. This revolution was a thorough governmental reorganization, one which imposed the major egalitarian reforms of the French Revolution upon lands outside the borders of France, while building a French empire. Most affected were territories in Italy (the "Kingdom of Italy" as it was now called); Germany (the Confederation of the Rhine, including the newly formed Kingdom of Westphalia); Dalmatia (the Illyrian provinces); and Holland. (Belgium had been integrated directly into the empire.) Into all these territories Napoleon introduced a carefully organized, deliberate system of administration, based upon the notion of careers open to talent, equality before the law, and the abolition of ancient customs and privileges. The Napoleonic program of reform in the empire represented an application of the principles that had already transformed postrevolutionary France. Manorial courts were liquidated, and Church courts abolished. Provinces were joined into an enormous bureaucratic network

Napoleon's reforms in Europe

See color map facing page 736

that reached directly back to Paris. Laws were codified, the tax system modernized, and everywhere individuals were freed to work at whatever trade they chose. The one freedom denied throughout this new grand hegemony was that of self-government: i.e., all governmental direction emanated from Paris, and therefore from Napoleon.

The impact of these changes upon the men and women who experienced them was clearly enormous. In those principalities previously ruled by petty princelings and minor despots—the patchwork states of Germany, for example, or the repressive Kingdom of Naples—reforms that provided for more efficient, less corrupt administration, a more equitable tax structure, and an end to customary privileges were welcomed by the majority of inhabitants. Business and professional men, who had chafed against economic restrictions, were quick to appreciate the license given them to trade and practice with a new degree of freedom. Yet the Napoleonic presence was by no means an unmixed blessing. Vassal states shared the task of contributing heavily to the maintenance of the emperor's war machine. Levies of taxes and of manpower, and the burden of supporting armies of occupation in their own countries, constantly reminded Germans, Italians, and Dutch that the price of reform was high. Nor were the changes shaped to accommodate local tradition. When Napoleon received complaints that his legal code ran counter to customary practices in Holland, he haughtily retorted: "The Romans gave their laws to their allies; why should not France have hers adopted in Holland?" It was this arrogance, symbolized in the eyes of many by the self-coronation of 1804, that led the German composer Ludwig van Beethoven to revoke the dedication of his *Eroica* Symphony to Napoleon, declaring, "Now he, too, will trample on all the rights of man and indulge only his ambition."

The Continental System

Napoleon's motives in introducing radical political and administrative changes were by no means altruistic. He understood that the defense of his enormous domain depended on efficient government and the rational collection and expenditure of funds for his armies. His boldest attempt at consolidation, however, a policy forbidding the importation into the Continent of British goods, proved a failure. This "Continental System," established in 1806, was designed as a strategic measure in Napoleon's continuing economic war against Britain. Its purpose was to destroy Britain's commerce and credit—to starve it economically into surrender. The system failed for several reasons. Foremost was the fact that throughout the war Britain retained control of the seas. The British naval blockade of the Continent, implemented in 1807, served, therefore, as an effective counter to Napoleon's system. While the empire labored to transport goods and raw materials overland to avoid the British blockade, the British worked with success to develop a lively trade with South America. Internal tariffs were a second reason for the failure of the system. Napoleon was unable to persuade individual territories to join a tariff-

The Handwriting on the Wall. This English cartoon conjures up the biblical Feast of Belshazzar with a vice-ridden Paris, as the new Babylon, doomed to destruction. Headed by a crazed Napoleon and a grotesque Josephine, the banquet table offers a meal including the head of George III, the Tower of London, and the Bank of England.

free customs union. As a result Europe remained divided into economic camps, fortified against each other by tariffs, and at odds with each other as they attempted to subsist on nothing more than what the Continent could produce and manufacture. The final reason for the system's collapse was the fact that the Continent had more to lose than Britain. Trade stagnated ports and manufacturing centers grumbled as unemployment rose.

The Continental System was Napoleon's first serious mistake. As such it was one of the causes of his ultimate downfall. A second cause of Napoleon's decline was his constantly growing ambition and increasing sense of self-importance. Napoleon's goal was a united Europe modeled after the Roman Empire. The symbols of his empire—reflected in painting, architecture, and the design of furniture and clothing—were deliberately Roman in origin. But Napoleon's Rome was without question imperial, dynastic Rome. The triumphal columns and arches he had erected to commemorate his victories recalled the ostentatious monuments of the Roman emperors. He made his brothers and sisters the monarchs of his newly created kingdoms, which Napoleon controlled from Paris while their mother allegedly sat at court, anxiously wringing her hands and repeating to herself, "If only it lasts!" He divorced his first wife, the Empress Josephine, alleging her childlessness, and ensured himself a successor of royal blood by marrying into the monarchically respectable house of Habsburg. Even his admirers began to question if Napoleon's empire was not simply a larger, more efficient, and, therefore, ultimately more dangerous absolutism than the monarchies of the eighteenth century. War again broke out in 1805, with the Russians, Prussians, and Aus-

Reasons for Napoleon's fall

The Empress Josephine

trians joining the British in an attempt to contain France. But to no avail; Napoleon's military superiority led to defeats, in turn, of all three continental allies. Ultimately only the emperor's own unwillingness to recognize that his supply of men, matériel, and good fortune was not limitless brought military defeat upon him.

Invasion of Spain

In 1808, Napoleon invaded Spain as a first step toward the conquest of Portugal, which had remained a stalwart ally of the British. Napoleon was determined to bring the Iberian peninsula into the Continental System. Although he at first promised the senile Spanish king Charles IV that he would cede a part of Portugal to Spain, Napoleon proceeded to overthrow Charles and installed his brother Joseph Bonaparte on the throne. Napoleon then imposed a series of reforms upon the Spanish, similar to those he had instituted elsewhere in Europe. But he reckoned without two factors that led to the ultimate failure of his Spanish mission: the presence of British forces under Sir Arthur Wellesley (later the duke of Wellington), and the determined resistance of the Spanish people. They particularly detested Napoleon's interference in the affairs of the Church, actively opposing his ending of the Inquisition and his abolition of a number of monastic establishments. Together with the British, the Spanish maintained a concerted effort to drive Napoleon from their country, often employing guerrilla warfare to do so. Though at one point Napoleon himself took charge of his army, he could not achieve anything more than temporary victory. The campaign dragged on until 1813, when the French forces were finally driven back across the border. The Spanish campaign was the first indication that Napoleon could be beaten. As such, it helped to promote a spirit of anti-Napoleonic defiance that encouraged resistance elsewhere.

The Russsian debacle

A second stage in Napoleon's downfall began with the disruption of his alliance with Russia. As an agricultural country, Russia had suffered a severe economic crisis when it was no longer able, as a result of the Continental System, to exchange its surplus grain for British manufactures. The consequence was that Tsar Alexander began to wink at trade with Britain and to ignore or evade the protests from Paris. By 1811 Napoleon decided that he could endure this flouting of the Continental System no longer. Accordingly, he collected an army of 600,000 (only a third of whom were native Frenchmen) and set out in the spring of 1812 to punish the tsar. The project ended in disaster. The Russians refused to make a stand, drawing the French farther and farther into the heart of their country. They permitted Napoleon to occupy their ancient capital of Moscow. But on the night of his entry, a fire of suspicious origin broke out in the city, leaving little but the blackened walls of the Kremlin palaces to shelter the invading troops. Hoping that the tsar would eventually surrender, Napoleon lingered amid the ruins for more than a month, finally deciding on October 22 to begin the homeward march. The delay was a fatal blunder. Long before he had reached the border, the terrible Russian

The Retreat from Russia. In this painting by Charlet the horrors of the Russian winter can be seen.

winter was upon his troops. Swollen streams, mountainous drifts of snow, and bottomless mud slowed the retreat almost to a halt. To add to the miseries of bitter cold, disease, and starvation, mounted Cossacks rode out of the blizzard to harry the exhausted army. Each morning the miserable remnant that pushed on left behind circles of corpses around the campfires of the night before. On December 13 a few thousand broken soldiers crossed the frontier into Germany— a small fraction of what had once been proudly styled the *Grande Armée.* The lives of nearly 300,000 men had been sacrificed in Napoleon's Russian adventure.

Until the debacle of the Russian campaign, Napoleon's armies had enjoyed a striking series of victories. The Battle of Austerlitz, in December 1805, a mighty triumph for the French against the combined forces of Austria and Russia, had remained a symbol of the emperor's apparent invincibility. Subsequent victories in the following years—against the Prussians at Jena in 1806, the Russians at Friedland in 1807, and the Austrians at Wagram in 1809—increased the conviction on the part of Europe that it had no choice but to acquiesce in Napoleon's grand continental design. The great British naval victory at Trafalgar in 1805, which broke the maritime power of France, was perceived at the time by Napoleon's friends and foes alike as no more than a temporary check to his ambitions.

Napoleon's supposed invincibility

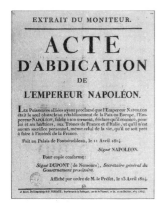

Napoleon's Abdication Proclamation, 1814

Now, however, following the retreat from Russia, the anti-Napoleonic forces took renewed hope. United by a belief that they might at last succeed in defeating the emperor, Prussia, Russia, Austria, and Britain renewed their attack. Most of the fighting during this so-called war of liberation took place in Germany. The climax of the campaign occurred in October 1813 when, at what was thereafter known as the Battle of the Nations, fought near Leipzig, the allies handed the French a resounding defeat. Meanwhile, allied armies won significant victories in the Low Countries and Italy. By the beginning of 1814, they had crossed the Rhine into France. Burdened with an inexperienced army of raw youths, Napoleon retreated to Paris, continuing, despite constant setbacks, to urge the French people to further resistance. On March 31, Tsar Alexander I of Russia and King Frederick William III of Prussia made their triumphant entry into Paris. Napoleon was forced to abdicate unconditionally, and was sent into exile on the island of Elba, off the Italian coast.

Napoleon's return and final defeat

Less than a year later he once more set foot on French soil. The allies had in the interim restored the Bourbon dynasty to the throne, in the person of Louis XVIII, brother of Louis XVI.[2] Any sovereign would have suffered in the eyes of the French by comparison with Napoleon; Louis was particularly ill suited to fill a space far too great for his mediocre talents. The French rallied enthusiastically to the former emperor. By the time he reached Paris, he had generated enough support to cause Louis to flee the country. The allies, meeting in Vienna to conclude peace treaties with the French, were stunned by the news of Napoleon's return. They dispatched a hastily organized army to counter the emperor's typically bold offensive push into the Low Countries. There, at the battle of Waterloo, fought on June 18, 1815, Napoleon suffered defeat for the final time. Shipped off to the bleak island of St. Helena in the South Atlantic, the once-mighty emperor, now the exile Bonaparte, lived out a dreary existence writing self-serving memoirs until his death in 1821.

Napoleon's legacy

Napoleon's legacy was an impressive one. His administrative and legal reforms remained in place after his fall. The Napoleonic legal code persisted not only in France but in the Low Countries, Prussia, and various other German states. The institutions introduced during his reign—centralized bureaucracy, police and educational systems—became part of the machinery of government and society in many parts of nineteenth-century Europe.

The legacy of the revolution and the Napoleonic era

To appreciate the larger impact of the revolution and the Napoleonic era on Western civilization, one must trace the ideas and institutions it fostered as they worked their way into the history of nineteenth- and twentieth-century Europe and America. Liberty—the right to act within the world with responsibility to no one but one-

[2]Louis XVII, the young son of the executed king and queen, had died under mysterious circumstances in the hands of his revolutionary captors in 1795.

self—was a notion dear to those who made the French Revolution, and one which remained embodied in the reforms it produced. So was equality—the notion of rational laws applied evenhandedly to all, regardless of birth or position. National pride, the era's third legacy, was bred in the hearts of the French people as they watched their citizen armies repel attacks against their newly won freedoms. It was instilled, as well, into those whose opposition to the French made them more conscious of their own national identity. The three concepts—liberty, equality, and nationality—were now no longer merely ideas; as laws and as a new way of addressing life, they rested at the center of European reality.

5. THE VIENNA SETTLEMENT

The European powers that met at the Congress of Vienna in 1814 to draw up a permanent peace settlement for Europe labored to produce an agreement that would as nearly as possible guarantee international tranquility. At the same time, however, they were by no means unwilling to advance the claims of their own countries to new territories, though such claims threatened conflict, or even war. Although the principal decisions of the congress were made by representatives of the major powers, it was attended by an array of dignitaries from almost all the principalities of Europe. No fewer than six monarchs attended: the tsar of Russia, the emperor of Austria, and the kings of Prussia, Denmark, Bavaria, and Württemberg. Great Britain was represented by Lord Castlereagh and the duke of Wellington. From France came the subtle intriguer Talleyrand, who had served as a bishop under Louis XVI, as foreign minister at the court of Napoleon, and who now stood ready to espouse the cause of reaction.

The Congress of Vienna

The dominant roles at the Congress of Vienna were played by Tsar Alexander I (1801–1825) and by the Austrian diplomat Klemens von Metternich (1773–1859).

The dynamic but baffling tsar played a leading role in the negotiations because Napoleon's defeat had left Russia the most powerful continental state. Reared at the court of Catherine the Great, he had imbibed the doctrines of Rousseau from a French Jacobin tutor, along with notions of absolutist authority from his military-minded father, Tsar Paul. In 1801 he succeeded his murdered father and for the next two decades disturbed the dreams of his fellow sovereigns by becoming the most liberal monarch in Europe. After the defeat of Napoleon in the Russian campaign, Alexander's mind turned more and more to mystical channels. He conceived of a mission to convert the rulers of all countries to the Christian ideals of justice and peace. But the chief effect of his voluble expressions of devotion to "liberty" and "enlightenment" was to frighten conservatives into suspecting a plot to extend his power over all of Europe. He was accused of intriguing

Tsar Alexander I

Klemens von Metternich

Barriers to French expansion

The German settlement

with Jacobins everywhere to substitute an all-powerful Russia for an all-powerful France.

The most commanding figure at the congress was Metternich, born at Coblenz in the Rhine valley, where his father was Austrian ambassador at the courts of three small German states. As a student at the University of Strassburg the young Metternich witnessed mob violence connected with the outbreak of the French Revolution, and to this he attributed his lifelong hatred of political innovation. He had been active in fomenting discord between Napoleon and Tsar Alexander, after the two became allies in 1807, and had played some part in arranging the marriage of Napoleon to the Austrian archduchess, Marie Louise. Metternich once declared himself an admirer of the spider, "always busy arranging their houses with the greatest of neatness in the world." At the Congress of Vienna, he attempted at every turn to arrange international affairs with equal neatness, to suit his own diplomatic designs. His two great obsessions were hatred of political and social change and fear of Russia. Above all, he feared revolutions inspired by the tsar for the sake of establishing Russian supremacy in Europe. For this reason he favored moderate terms for France in its hour of defeat, and was ready at one time to sponsor the restoration of Napoleon as emperor of the French under the protection and overlordship of the Habsburg monarchy.

The basic idea that guided the work of the Congress of Vienna was the principle of *legitimacy*. This principle was invented by Talleyrand as a device for protecting France against drastic punishment by its conquerors, but it was ultimately adopted by Metternich as a convenient expression of the general policy of reaction. Legitimacy meant that the dynasties of Europe that had reigned in prerevolutionary days should be restored to their thrones, and that each country should regain essentially the same territories it had held in 1789. In accordance with this principle Louis XVIII was recognized as the "legitimate" sovereign of France; the restoration of Bourbon rulers in Spain and the Two Sicilies was also confirmed. France was compelled to pay an indemnity of 700 million francs to the victorious allies, but its boundaries were to remain essentially the same as in 1789.

To ensure that the French would not soon again overrun their boundaries, however, a strong barrier was erected to contain them. The Dutch Republic, conquered by the French in 1795, was restored as the Kingdom of the Netherlands, with the house of Orange as its hereditary monarchy. To its territory was added that of Belgium, formerly the Austrian Netherlands, with the hope that this now substantial power would serve to discourage any future notions of French expansion. For the same reason the German left bank of the Rhine was ceded to Prussia, and Austria was established as a major power in northern Italy.

The principle of legitimacy was not extended to the German principalities, however. There, despite pleas from rulers of the sovereign

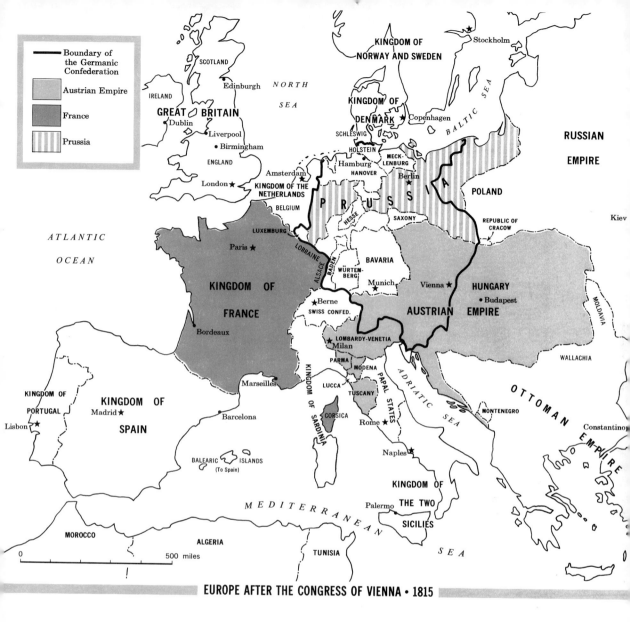

EUROPE AFTER THE CONGRESS OF VIENNA · 1815

bits and pieces that had existed before 1789, the great powers agreed to
retain the boundaries as redrawn by Napoleon. Fear of an aggressive
Russia led the other European nations to support the maintenance—as
an anti-Russian bulwark—of the Napoleonic kingdoms of Bavaria,
Württemberg, and Saxony. At the same time, however, Tsar Alexander was demanding that Poland, partitioned into virtual extinction
by Russia, Austria, and Prussia in the 1790s, be reconstituted a kingdom with himself as its constitutional monarch. Prussia was prepared
to agree with this scheme, provided that it be allowed to swallow Saxony. National avarice for territorial expansion rapidly eclipsed legitimacy as a guiding principle in these negotiations. Metternich, hor-

"Dividing the Cake." A contemporary cartoonist's impression of the work of the congress diplomats.

rified at the double threat thus presented to Austria by Prussia and Russia, allied himself with Talleyrand and Castlereagh, both of whom secretly agreed to go to war against Russia and Prussia, if necessary, in order to prevent them from consumating their Polish-Saxon deal. A compromise was eventually reached, allowing to Russia the major part of Poland and to Prussia a part of Saxony. Britain, no less anxious than the other victorious powers to gain compensation for its long years at war, received territories principally under French dominion in South Africa and South America and the island of Ceylon, thus adding further to its commercial empire.

Triumph of the state system

Legitimacy, as expressed in the treaties that concluded the Congress of Vienna, emerged as the latter-day expression of the principles of balance and stability that had shaped diplomacy during the eighteenth century. The age of absolutism had witnessed the emergence of an international state system dedicated to those principles. By enshrining them in their settlement, the diplomats at Vienna ensured that such a state system would be part of the legacy passed to their nineteenth-century successors.

SELECTED READINGS

• *Items so designated are available in paperback editions.*

• Arendt, Hannah, *On Revolution,* New York, 1963. An analysis of the American and French Revolutions and their meaning for modern man.
• Bergeron, Louis, *France under Napoleon,* Princeton, 1981. Concentrates on the era of Napoleon rather than the man.
  Bosher, J. F., *French Finances, 1770–1790: From Business to Bureaucracy,* Cambridge, 1970. An impressive study concerned with the financial apparatus of Old Regime and revolutionary France.

- Breunig, C., *The Age of Revolution and Reaction, 1789–1850*, 2nd ed., New York, 1989. A well-written survey.
- Brinton, Crane, *Anatomy of Revolution*, rev. ed., New York, 1961. Attempts to create a general model of revolutions by comparing the English, American, French, and Russian Revolutions.
- ———, *A Decade of Revolution, 1789–1799*, New York, 1934. An excellent European survey.
- Bruun, Geoffrey, *Europe and the French Imperium, 1799–1814*, New York, 1938. Describes the impact of Napoleon upon Europe.
- Cobb, R. C., *The Police and the People: French Popular Protest, 1789–1820*, New York, 1970. A survey of peasants and sans-culottes.
- Cobban, Alfred, *The Social Interpretation of the French Revolution*, Cambridge, 1964. A penetrating critique of the radical interpretation of the revolution, more important for its questions than its conclusions.
   Egret, Jean, *The French Pre-Revolution, 1787–1788*, Chicago, 1977. Describes the collapse of the Old Regime.
- Gershoy, Leo, *The French Revolution and Napoleon*, rev. ed., New York, 1964. A good survey with annotated bibliography.
   Geyl, Pieter, *Napoleon: For and Against*, rev. ed., New Haven, 1964. The ways in which Napoleon was interpreted by French historians and political figures.
   Goodwin, Albert, *The Friends of Liberty: The English Democratic Movement in the Age of the French Revolution*, Cambridge, Mass., 1979. Detailed, subtle analysis of English reform movements.
   Greer, Donald, *The Incidence of the Terror during the French Revolution: A Statistical Interpretation*, Cambridge, Mass., 1935. An important study which reveals that the lower classes suffered most during the Terror, rather than the nobility or the clergy.
- Hampson, Norman, *A Social History of the French Revolution*, London, 1963. Deals with institutional development.
- Herold, J. Christopher, *The Age of Napoleon*, New York, 1968. A well-written popular history.
- Kissinger, Henry, *A World Restored: Metternich, Castlereagh, and the Problems of Peace, 1812–1822*, Boston, 1957. By the former U.S. secretary of state, an admirer of Metternich.
- Lefebvre, Georges, *The Coming of the French Revolution*, Princeton, 1947. An excellent study of the causes and early events of the revolution.
- ———, *The French Revolution*, 2 vols., New York, 1963–64. An impressive synthesis by the greatest modern scholar of the revolution.
   ———, *The Great Fear of 1789*, New York, 1973. The best account of the rural disturbances.
   McManners, John, *The French Revolution and the Church*, New York, 1969. Describes the impact of revolutionary anticlericalism upon the French Church.
- Markham, Felix, *Napoleon*, New York, 1966. An excellent study.
- Nicolson, Harold, *The Congress of Vienna: A Study in Allied Unity*, New York, 1946. An excellent and very readable history, written by a British diplomat.
- Palmer, R. R., *The Age of the Democratic Revolution: A Political History of Europe and America, 1760–1800*, 2 vols., Princeton, 1964. Impressive for its scope; places the French Revolution in the larger context of a worldwide revolutionary movement.

- ———, *Twelve Who Ruled,* Princeton, 1958. Excellent biographical studies of the members of the Committee of Public Safety; demonstrates that Robespierre's role has been exaggerated.
- Rudé, George, *The Crowd in the French Revolution,* Oxford, 1959. An important monograph which analyzes the composition of the crowds that participated in the great uprisings of the revolution.
- Soboul, Albert, *The Sans-Culottes: The Popular Movement and Revolutionary Government, 1793–1794,* Garden City, N.Y., 1972. An outstanding example of "history from below"; analyzes the pressures upon the convention in the year of the Terror.

  Thompson, J. M., *Napoleon Bonaparte: His Rise and Fall,* Oxford, 1958. The standard work.
- ———, *Robespierre and the French Revolution,* London, 1953. An excellent short biography.
- Tilly, Charles, *The Vendée: A Sociological Analysis of the Counter-Revolution of 1793,* Cambridge, Mass., 1964. An important economic and social analysis of the factors that led to the reaction in the Vendée.
- Tocqueville, Alexis de, *The Old Regime and French Revolution.* Originally written in 1856, this remains a classic analysis of the causes of the French Revolution.
- Williams, Gwyn A., *Artisans and Sans-Culottes,* New York, 1969. Comparative history of English and French popular movements.

SOURCE MATERIALS

- Burke, Edmund, *Reflections on the Revolution in France,* London, 1790. (Many editions). The great conservative statement against the revolution and its principles.
- Montesquieu, Baron de. *The Spirit of the Laws,* 1748. (Many editions). See especially Books I, II, III, XI.
- Paine, Thomas, *The Rights of Man,* 1791. (Many editions). Paine's eloquent response to Burke's *Reflections* resulted in his conviction for treason and banishment from England.
- Pernoud, G., and S. Flaisser, eds., *The French Revolution,* New York, 1960. Contains eyewitness reports.
- Rousseau, Jean-Jacques, *Discourse on the Origin of Inequality,* 1754. (Many editions).
- ———, *The Social Contract,* 1762. (Many editions). These two tracts provided a philosophical justification for both the American and French Revolutions.

  Sieyès, Abbé, *What Is the Third Estate?,* 1789. (Many editions). The most important political pamphlet in the decisive year 1789.

  Steward, John Hall, *A Documentary Survey of the French Revolution,* New York, 1951.

  Thompson, J. M., *French Revolution Documents, 1789–1794,* Oxford, 1948.
- Walzer, Michael, ed., *Regicide and Revolution: Speeches at the Trial of Louis XVI,* 1974. Contains a thoughtful introduction.
- Young, Arthur, *Travels in France during the Years 1787, 1788, 1789,* New York, 1972. France on the eve of revolution, as seen by a perceptive English observer.

Chapter 20

THE INDUSTRIAL REVOLUTION

Providence has assigned to man the glorious function of vastly improving
the productions of nature by judicious culture, of working them up into
objects of comfort and elegance with the least possible expenditure of
human labor—an undeniable position which forms the basis of our Factory System.

—Andrew Ure, *The Philosophy of Manufactures*

There have been many revolutions in industry during the history of Western civilization, and there will undoubtedly be
many more. Periods of rapid technological change are often
called revolutions, and justifiably so. But, historically, there is one
Industrial Revolution. Occurring during the hundred years after 1780,
it witnessed the first breakthrough from a rural, handicraft economy
to one dominated by urban, machine-driven manufacturing.

The uniqueness of the revolution

The fact that it was a European revolution was not accidental. Although in the mid-eighteenth century Europe was a continent still
predominantly agricultural, although the majority of its people remained illiterate and destined to live out impoverished lives within
sight of the place they were born—despite these conditions, which in
our eyes might make Europe appear "underdeveloped," it was of
course no such thing. European merchants and men of commerce
were established as the world's foremost manufacturers and traders.
Rulers relied upon this class of men to provide them with the wherewithal to maintain the economy of their states, both in terms of
flourishing commercial activity and of victorious armies and navies.
Those men, in turn, had for the most part extracted from their rulers
the understanding that the property they possessed, whether invested
in land, or commerce, or both, was theirs outright. That understanding, substantiated by the written contracts that were replacing
unwritten, long-acknowledged custom, helped persuade merchants,
bankers, traders, and entrepreneurs that they lived in a world that was
stable, rational, and predictable. Believing the world was so, they

Why a European revolution? (1) the commercial class

moved out into it with self-confidence and in hopes of increasing their own, and their country's, prosperity. Only in Europe does one find these presuppositions and this class of men in the eighteenth century; only through the activities of such people could the Industrial Revolution have taken place.

These capitalists could not have prospered without an expanding market for their goods. The existence of this market explains further why it was in Europe that the Industrial Revolution took place. Ever since the beginning of the seventeenth century, overseas commercial exploration and development had been opening new territories to European trade. India, Africa, North and South America—all had been woven into the pattern of European economic expansion. The colonies and commercial dependencies took economic shape at Europe's behest. Even the new United States had not been able to declare its economic independence. Whatever commercial and industrial design Europe might devise, all would be compelled to accommodate themselves to Europe's demands.

A third factor helping to ensure that the revolution would occur in Europe was the population growth that occurred throughout western Europe in the eighteenth century (see above, p. 582). Increasing populations, along with overseas expansion, provided an ever-growing market for manufactured goods. It furnished, as well, an adequate pool—eventually a surplus—of laboring men, women, and children to work in the manufacture of those goods either at home or in factories.

Two important facts have inclined historians to qualify the concept of "revolutionary" industrial change. First, the existence of a thriving commercial class, expanding markets, and increasing populations prior to the Industrial Revolution suggest that the changes we are about to analyze had important antecedents. We have already noted, for example, the manner in which the putting-out system was transforming rural areas into sizable manufacturing regions in the seventeenth and eighteenth centuries (see above, p. 573). Second, the Industrial Revolution did not take place everywhere in Europe at the same time and at the same pace. Beginning in England in the late eighteenth century, it spread gradually region by region, country by country across Europe. Unlike the French Revolution whose history can be measured by a decade, the Industrial Revolution occurred over the span of at least a century.

See color map facing
page 737

1. THE INDUSTRIAL REVOLUTION IN ENGLAND

It was in England that the Industrial Revolution first took hold. England's economy had progressed further than that of any other country in the direction of abundance. In simplest terms: fewer people had to struggle just to remain alive; more people were in a position to sell a surplus of the goods they produced to an increasingly expanding market; and more people had money enough to purchase the goods that market offered. English laborers, though poorly enough paid, enjoyed a higher standard of living than their continental counterparts. They ate white bread, not brown, and meat with some regularity. Because a smaller portion of their income was spent on food, they might occasionally have some to spare for articles that were bought rather than homemade.

Further evidence of this increasing abundance was the number of bills for the enclosure of agricultural land passed by an English Parliament sympathetic to capitalism during the last half of the eighteenth century. The enclosure of fields, pasture, and waste lands into large fenced tracts of land under the private ownership and individual management of capitalist landlords meant an increased food supply to feed an increasing and increasingly urban population. Yet another sign of England's abundance was its growing supply of surplus capital, derived from investment in land or commerce, and available for further employment to finance new economic enterprises. London, already a leading center for the world's trade, served as a headquarters for the transfer of raw material, capital, and manufactured products. Portugal alone channeled as much as £50,000 in Brazilian gold per week into London. Thus English capitalists had enough money on hand to underwrite and sustain an industrial revolution.

Abundance: food and capital

But the revolution required more than money. It required habits of mind that would encourage investments in enterprises that were risky, but that represented an enormous potential for gain. In England, far more than on the Continent, the pursuit of wealth was perceived to be a worthy end in life. The aristocracy of Europe had, from the period of the Renaissance, cultivated the notion of "gentlemanly" conduct, in part to hold the line against social encroachments from below. The English aristocrats, whose privileges were meager when compared with those of continental nobles, had never ceased to respect men who made money; nor had they disdained to make whatever they could for themselves. Far more than their continental counterparts, they invested and speculated. Their scramble to enclose their lands reflected this sympathy with aggressive capitalism. Below the aristocracy, there was even less of a barrier separating the world of urban commerce from that of the rural gentry. Most of the men who pioneered as entrepreneurs in the early years of the Industrial Revolution sprang from the minor gentry or yeoman farmer class. To a degree unknown on the Continent, men from this sort of background felt themselves free to rise as high as their abilities might carry them on the social and economic ladder.

(2) climate of opinion

Eighteenth-century England was not by any means free of social snobbery: lords looked down upon bankers, as bankers looked down upon artisans. But a lord's disdain might well be tempered by the fact of his own grandfather's origins in the counting house. And the banker would gladly lend money to the artisan if convinced that the

Respect for financial success

artisan's invention might make them both a fortune. The English, as a nation, were not afraid of business. They respected the sensible, the practical, and the financially successful. Robinson Crusoe, that desert island entrepreneur, was one of their models. In the novel (1719) by Daniel Defoe, the hero had used his wits to master nature and become lord of a thriving economy. His triumph was not diminished because it was a worldly triumph; far from it. "It is our vanity which urges us on," the economist Adam Smith, defender of capitalism, declared. And thank God, Smith implied, for our blessed vanity! An individual's desire to show himself a wordly success worked to produce prosperity for the country as a whole.

(3) increasing markets.

England's eighteenth-century prosperity was based upon an expanding market for whatever goods it manufactured. The English were voracious consumers. By the mid-eighteenth century, yearly fashions were setting styles not only for the very rich but for a growing middle-class clientele as well. "Nature may be satisfied with little," one London entrepreneur declared. "But it is the wants of fashion and the desire of novelties that causes trade." The country's small size and the fact that it was an island encouraged the development of a nationwide domestic market that could respond to increasing demand. The absence of a system of internal tolls and tariffs, such as existed on the Continent, meant that goods could be moved freely to the place where they could fetch the best price. This freedom of movement was assisted by a constantly improving transportation system. Parliament in the years just before the Industrial Revolution passed acts to finance turnpike building at the rate of forty per year; the same period saw the construction of canals and the further opening up of harbors and navigable streams. Unlike the government of France, whose cumbrous mercantilist adventures as often as not thwarted economic growth, the English Parliament believed that the most effective way in which it could help businessmen was to assist them in helping themselves.

Overseas expansion

Parliament's members had every reason to promote England's economic fortunes. Some were businessmen themselves; others had invested heavily in commerce; hence their eagerness to encourage by statute the construction of canals, the establishment of banks, and the enclosure of common lands. And hence their insistence, throughout the eighteenth century, that England's foreign policy respond to its commercial needs. At the end of every major eighteenth-century war, England wrested overseas territories from its enemies. At the same time, England was penetrating hitherto unexploited territories, such as India and South America, in search of further potential markets and resources. In 1759, over one-third of all British exports went to the colonies; by 1784, if we include the newly established United States, that figure had increased to one-half. The English possessed a merchant marine capable of transporting goods across the world, and a navy practiced in the art of protecting its commercial fleets. By 1780 England's markets, together with its fleet and its established position at the center of world trade, combined to produce a potential for expansion so great as to compel the Industrial Revolution.

English entrepreneurs and technicians responded to the compulsion by revolutionizing the production of cotton textile goods. Although fewer cotton goods were made in eighteenth-century England than woolen goods, the extent of cotton manufacture by 1760 was such as to make cotton more than an infant industry. Tariffs prohibiting the importation of East Indian cottons, imposed by Parliament to stimulate the sale of woolen goods, had instead served to spur the manufacture of domestic cotton goods. Thus the revolution, when it did occur, took place in an already well-established industry. Yet without the invention of some sort of machinery that would improve the quality and at the same time dramatically increase the quantity of spun cotton thread, the necessary breakthrough would not have come. The invention of the fly-shuttle, which greatly speeded up the process of weaving, only made the bottleneck in the prior process of spinning more apparent. The problem was solved by the invention of a series of comparatively simple mechanical devices, the most important of which was the spinning jenny, invented by James Hargreaves, a carpenter and hand-loom weaver, in 1767 (patented 1770). The spinning jenny, named after the inventor's wife, was a compound spinning wheel, capable of producing sixteen threads at once. The threads it spun were not strong enough, however, to be used for the longitudinal fibers, or warp, of cotton cloth. It was not until the invention of the water frame by Richard Arkwright, a barber, in 1769, that quantity production of both warp and woof (latitudinal fibers) became possible. This invention, along with that of the spinning

The cotton industry

The Spinning Jenny. Invented by James Hargreaves in 1767

mule, conceived of by Samuel Crompton in 1779, and combining the features of both the jenny and the frame, solved the problems that had heretofore curtailed the output of cotton textiles. They increased the mechanical advantage over the spinning wheel enormously. From six to twenty-four times the amount of yarn could be spun on a jenny as on the wheel, by the end of the century two to three hundred times as much on the mule. Just as important, the quality of the thread improved not only in terms of strength but also of fineness.

Once these machines came into general use, the revolution proceeded apace. Cotton suited the mule and the jenny because it was a tougher thread than wool; as such cotton was a fiber that could withstand the rough treatment it received at the mechanical hands of the crude early machines. In addition, the supply of cotton was expandable in a way that the supply of wool was not. The cotton gin, invented by the American Eli Whitney in 1793, separated seeds from fiber mechanically, thereby making cotton available at a lower price. The invention kept America's slave plantations profitable, and meant that supply would meet increased demand.

The first machinery was cheap enough to allow spinners to continue to work at home. But as it increased in size, it was more and more frequently housed not in the cottages of individual spinners, but in workshops or mills located near water that could be used to power the machines. Eventually, with the further development of steam-driven equipment, the mills could be built wherever it might suit the entrepreneur—frequently in towns and cities in the north of England.

Eli Whitney

Growth of factories

The transition from home to factory industry was of course not accomplished overnight. Cotton yarn continued to be spun at home at the same time that it was being produced in mills. Eventually, however, the low cost of building and operating a large plant, plus the efficiency realized by bringing workers together under one roof, meant that larger mills more and more frequently replaced smaller workshops. By 1851, three-fifths of those employed in cotton manufacture worked in medium- to large-size mills. Weaving remained a home industry until the invention of a cheap, practical power loom convinced entrepreneurs that they could save money by moving the process from home to mill. Hand-loom weavers were probably ·the most obvious victims of the Industrial Revolution in England. Their unwillingness to surrender their livelihood to machinery meant that they continued to work for less and less—by 1830, no more than a pitiful six shillings a week. In 1815 they numbered about 250,000; by 1850, there remained only 40,000; by 1860, only 3,000.

The extent of the cotton trade

English cotton textiles flooded the world market from the 1780s. Here was a light material, suitable for the climates of Africa, India, and the more temperate zones of North America. Here was a material cheap enough to make it possible for millions who had never before enjoyed the comfort of washable body clothes to do so. And here was material fine enough to tempt the rich to experiment with muslins and calicos in a way they had not done before. Figures speak eloquently of the revolutionary change wrought by the expanding industry. In 1760, England exported less than £250,000 worth of cotton goods; by 1800 it was exporting over £5 million worth. In 1760, England imported 2.5 million pounds of raw cotton; in 1787, 22 million pounds; in 1837, 366 million pounds. By 1800, cotton accounted for about 5 percent of the national income of the country; by 1812, from 7 to 8 percent. By 1815, the export of cotton textiles amounted to 40 percent of the value of all domestic goods exported from Great Britain. Although the price of manufactured cotton goods fell dramatically, the market expanded so rapidly that profits continued to increase.

Unlike the changes in the textile industry, those occurring in the manufacture of iron were not great enough to warrant their being labeled revolutionary. Yet they were most significant. Britain's abundant supply of coal, combined with its advanced transportation network, allowed the English, from the middle of the eighteenth century, to substitute coal for wood in the heating of molten metal. A series of discoveries made fuel savings possible, along with a higher quality of iron and the manufacture of a greater variety of iron products. Demand rose sharply during the war years at the end of the century. It remained high as a result of calls for plant machinery, agricultural implements, and hardware; it rose dramatically with the coming of railways in the 1830s and 1840s. Britain was exporting 571,000 tons of iron in 1814; in 1852, it exported 1,036,000 tons out of a world total of almost 2,000,000—more iron than was made by all the rest of the world combined.

The need for more coal required the mining of deeper and deeper veins. In 1712, Thomas Newcomen had devised a crude but effective steam engine for pumping water from mines. Though of value to the

The iron industry

The steam engine

Aqueduct in Wales. The 124-foot-high span carried water in a 10-foot wide cast iron trough over the River Dee. Designed by Thomas Telford, this "stream in the sky" was one of the most impressive engineering feats of the early Industrial Revolution.

Old Hetton Colliery, Sunderland, England. Designed by the engineer Thomas Hair about 1840, this large mine was typical of those built to meet the increased demand for coal. Note the railways that connected the mines with the sea.

coal industry, it was of less use in other industries, since it was wasteful of both fuel and power. In 1763, James Watt, a maker of scientific instruments at the University of Glasgow, was asked to repair a model of the Newcomen engine. While engaged in this task he conceived the idea that the machine would be greatly improved if a separate chamber were added to condense the steam, so as to eliminate the necessity of cooling the cylinder. He patented his first engine incorporating this device in 1769. Watt's genius as an inventor was not matched by his business ability. He admitted that he would "rather face a loaded cannon than settle a disputed account or make a bargain." As a consequence, he fell into debt in attempting to place his machines on the market. He was rescued by Matthew Boulton, a wealthy hardware manufacturer of Birmingham. The two men formed a partnership, with Boulton providing the capital. By 1800 the firm had sold 289 engines for use in factories and mines. The steam engine replaced water as the principle motive force in industry slowly. In 1850 more than a third of the power used in woolen manufacture and an eighth of that used in cotton was still produced by water. Nevertheless, there is no question that without the steam engine there could have been no industrial expansion on the scale that we have described.

Other advances   Other industries experienced profound changes during the hundred years of the Industrial Revolution. Many of those changes came in response to the growth of textile manufacture. The chemical industry, for example, developed new methods of dyeing and bleaching, as well as improved methods of production in the fields of soap and glassmaking. Production of goods increased across the board, as profits from the boom in manufacturing increased the demand for new and more sophisticated articles. Such trades as pottery and metalware expanded to meet demands, in the process adopting methods that in most instances reduced cost and speeded manufacture.

To understand fully the nature of the Industrial Revolution in England one must not lose sight of two important factors: the first is that dramatic as the revolution was, it happened over a period of two or three generations, at varying paces in different industries. Some men and women continued to work at home, much as their grandfathers and grandmothers had. Old tools and old methods were not immediately replaced by new ones, any more than populations fled the countryside overnight for the city. Second, the revolution was accomplished from a very limited technological and theoretical base. Except in the chemical industry, change was not the result of scientific research. It was the product of empirical experimentation—in some cases, of little more than creative tinkering. To say this is not to disparage the work of men such as Arkwright, Hargreaves, Watt, and their like. It is to suggest, however, the reason why England, without a national system of education on any level, was nonetheless able to accomplish the revolution it did. Nor are these remarks intended to belittle the magnitude of the change. What occurred in England was a revolution because of the way in which it reshaped the lives, not just of the English, but of people across the globe. By responding as it did to the demands of its apparently insatiable markets, England made a revolution every bit as profound and long-lasting as that which occurred simultaneously in France.

2. THE INDUSTRIAL REVOLUTION ON THE CONTINENT

The Industrial Revolution came in time to the Continent, but not to any important degree before about 1830. As we have seen, manufacturing in eighteenth-century France and Germany clustered in regions whose proximity to raw materials, access to markets, and traditional attachment to particular skills had resulted in their development as industrial centers. Flanders and Normandy in France, and Saxony in Germany were centers for the manufacture of woolen cloth; Switzerland, southern Germany, and Normandy, of cottons; Wallonia (the area around Liège in Belgium), the Marne valley, and Silesia in Germany, of iron. Yet for a variety of reasons, these areas failed to experience the late-eighteenth-century breakthrough that occurred in Britain. Nor were they capable at first of imitating Britain's success, once they began to perceive the great economic advantages that Britain's pronounced lead was bringing it. There were a number of reasons for the delay of continental industrialization. Whereas England's transportation system was highly developed, those of France and Germany were not. France was far larger than England, its rivers were not as easily navigable, its seaports were farther apart. Central Europe was so divided into tiny principalities, each with its own set of tolls and tariffs, as to make the transportation of raw materials or manufactured

See color map facing page 737

(2) lack of entrepreneurial spirit

goods over any considerable distance impractical. Nor was France itself free of the sorts of regulations that thwarted easy shipments. In addition, the Continent was not as blessed with an abundance of raw materials as England. France, the Low Countries, and Germany imported wool. Europe lacked an abundant supply of the fuel that was the new source of industrial energy. Few major coal deposits were known to exist, while the ready availability of timber discouraged exploration that might have resulted in its discovery.

Distances and distinctions between social and economic ranks were far greater on the Continent than in England. Money was not the social solvent in France and Germany that it was across the Channel. Before the French Revolution, continental aristocrats hesitated before investing in commercial enterprises they believed would damage their social standing. In some countries, laws prevented aristocrats from engaging in business. After the revolution, middle-class Frenchmen, though free in theory to rise as high on the social and economic ladder as they might aspire, appear largely to have remained content to make only enough money to sustain a modest-size business. The motivation of the middle class was as often social as it was economic: to ensure the continuity of a family rather than to produce increasing quantities of goods. Furthermore, capital was not as readily available on the Continent as in England. In France, again, the retarded development of agricultural capitalism, due to the tenacious economic perseverance of small peasant landholders, limited the supply of savings, both for investment in industry and for expenditure on manufactured goods. Nor was the entrepreneurial spirit that compelled Englishmen to drive competitors to the wall as highly developed in France and Germany in the years after 1815. Exhausted by the competitiveness of war, and fearful of the disruptions that war brought in its train, continental

A Swedish Mining Town, 1790

THE EMPIRE OF NAPOLEON
AT ITS GREATEST EXTENT · 1812

French territory

French dependencies

Allied with Napoleon

Independent states

NORWAY

SWEDEN

RUSSIA

Moscow

Borodino

NAPOLEON 1812

Tilsit

Friedland

DENMARK • Copenhagen

BALTIC SEA

PRUSSIA

• Berlin

DUCHY OF WARSAW

• Warsaw

NORTH SEA

HOLLAND

Amsterdam •

Rhine R.

LEIPZIG •

Elbe R.

CONFEDERATION OF THE RHINE

AUSTRIAN EMPIRE

• Vienna

Austerlitz •

ENGLAND

London •

English Channel

Brussels •

Waterloo •

★ Paris

FRENCH EMPIRE

Bordeaux •

Ulm •

HELVETIC REPUBLIC

KINGDOM OF ITALY

Po R.

ILLYRIAN PROVINCES

ADRIATIC SEA

BLACK SEA

OTTOMAN EMPIRE

AEGEAN SEA

IRELAND

ATLANTIC OCEAN

Marseilles •

CORSICA

PAPAL STATES

Rome •

KDM. OF SARDINIA

KINGDOM OF NAPLES

Naples •

KDM. OF SICILY

MEDITERRANEAN SEA

KDM. OF PORTUGAL

Lisbon •

SPAIN

Madrid •

0   500 miles

THE INDUSTRIAL REVOLUTION

Percent of population living in cities of 100,000 or more

5% or less
6-10%
20% or more

Iron ore deposits
Coal and lignite deposits
Centers of industry
Railroads in 1850

0   300 miles

RUSSIAN EMPIRE

St. Petersburg

Moscow

NORWAY

Uppsala
Stockholm

SWEDEN

BALTIC SEA

DENMARK

GERMAN EMPIRE

Warsaw

Lodz

Posen

Breslau

SILESIA

Cracow

Lemberg

AUSTRIAN EMPIRE

Berlin

Hamburg

Bremen

Leipzig

Dresden

Prague

Pilsen

Vienna

Budapest

Steyr

Kassel

Eisenach

Zwickau

Chemnitz

Nuremberg

Munich

RUHR

Essen

Cologne

Frankfurt

Stuttgart

Karlsruhe

SAAR

Strasbourg

Mulhouse

Basel

Zurich

SWITZERLAND

ITALY

Milan

Turin

Florence

Livorno

Rome

Naples

NORTH SEA

Amsterdam

Rotterdam

NETHERLANDS

Brussels

BELGIUM

Liège

Lille

Amiens

Le Havre

Paris

Orleans

FRANCE

Tours

Nantes

Limoges

Lyons

Avignon

Marseilles

ATLANTIC OCEAN

KINGDOM OF GREAT BRITAIN

Glasgow

Dublin

Darlington

Leeds

Liverpool

Manchester

Sheffield

Birmingham

London

Cardiff

Gijon

Oviedo

Santander

Bilbao

Madrid

Barcelona

Seville

Jerez

Granada

SPAIN

MEDITERRANEAN SEA

OTTOMAN EMPIRE

BLACK SEA

businessmen remained far more willing than the English to keep on manufacturing and selling on the same scale they always had.[1]

The Contient did not simply stand idle, however, as England assumed its industrial lead. The pace of mechanization was increasing in the 1780s. But the French Revolution and the wars that followed disrupted growth that might otherwise have taken place. Battles fought on French, German, and Italian soil destroyed factories and machinery. Although ironmaking increased to meet the demands of the wars, techniques remained what they had been. Commerce was badly hurt both by British destruction of French merchant shipping and by Napoleon's Continental System. Probably the revolutionary change most beneficial to industrial advance in Europe was the removal of previous restraints on the movement of capital and labor; for example, the abolition of trade guilds, and the reduction in the number of tariff barriers across the Continent. On balance, however, the revolutionary and Napoleonic wars clearly thwarted industrial development on the Continent, while at the same time intensifying it in England.

(3) effect of wars

A number of factors combined to produce a climate more generally conducive to industrialization on the Continent after 1815. Population continued to increase, not only throughout Europe, but in those areas now more and more dependent upon the importation of manufactured goods—Latin America, for example (see below, p. 747). European increases, which doubled the populations of most countries between 1800 and 1850, meant that the Continent would be supplied with a growing number of producers and consumers. More people did not necessarily mean further industrialization. In Ireland, for example, where other necessary factors were absent, more people meant less food. But in those countries with an already well-established commercial and industrial base—France and Germany, for example—increased population did encourage the adoption of the technologies and methods of production that had transformed Britain.

Increases after 1815; (1) population rise

Transportation improved in western Europe both during and following the Napoleonic wars. The Austrian Empire added over 30,000 miles of roads between 1830 and 1847; Belgium almost doubled its road network in the same period; France built, in addition to roads, 2,000 miles of canals. In the United States, where industrialization was occurring at an increasingly rapid rate after 1830, road mileage jumped from 21,000 miles in 1800 to 170,000 in 1856. When these improvements were combined with the introduction of rail transport in the 1840s, the resulting increase in markets available to all Western countries encouraged them to introduce methods of manufacturing that would help meet new demands. The effect of railways on regional manufacturing, however, was not always positive. Clearly, they were a means of moving manufactured goods from a given region to more

(2) improved transportation

[1] On this point, see David S. Landes, *The Unbound Prometheus*, pp. 132–33.

widely dispersed markets. But they also brought competition in the form of an influx of goods from outside to challenge local industries. The case of the Dijon area southeast of Paris illustrates the problem. With the coming of the railway, brewers and winegrowers there expanded their trade for a time. Eventually, however, they lost business when railways made possible the transportation of beer and wine over longer distances, from Alsace and the south of France.

(3) centralization

Governments played a more direct role in the process of industrialization on the Continent than in Britain. Napoleon's rationalization of French and imperial institutions had introduced Europe to the practice of state intervention. His legal code, which guaranteed freedom of contract and facilitated the establishment of joint-stock enterprises, encouraged other rulers to provide a similar framework for commercial expansion. In Prussia, lack of private capital necessitated state operation of a large proportion of that country's mines. In no European country but Britain would railways be built without the financial assistance of the state. In the private sector, as well, more attention was given on the Continent than in England to the need for artificial stimulation to produce industrial change. It was in Belgium that the first joint-stock investment bank—the Société Générale—was founded, an institution designed to facilitate the accumulation of ready capital for investment in industry and commerce. Europeans were also willing for the state to establish educational systems whose aim, among others, was to produce a well-trained elite capable of assisting in the development of industrial technology. What Britain had produced almost by chance, the Europeans began to reproduce by design.

(4) the lack of technicians

Until the Continent produced its own technicians it was compelled to rely on British expertise. But the pace of continental, and also American, industrialization, even after 1815, remained far slower than in Britain because of Britain's natural reluctance to see its methods of production pirated by others. British industrialists believed it their patriotic duty to prevent the exportation of their techniques, although they were more than willing to raid the Continent for technological experts: Matthew Boulton imported skilled workers from Vienna and Sweden. Continental entrepreneurs likewise argued that it was patriotism, not profit, that inspired them to compete with the British. "Our reasons for building our factory were exactly those which made you oppose it," a German firm wrote to Boulton; "that is patriotic zeal." Until 1825, British artisans were forbidden to emigrate; until 1842, much innovative machinery could not be exported. Laws did not, however, prevent the movement of creative technician-entrepreneurs and their particular skills; many Englishmen, during the first part of the nineteenth century, made fortunes as they taught others in Europe and America to do what they had taught themselves. One such man was William Cockerill, who began his career in England as a carpenter. He and his sons built cotton-spinning equipment on the Continent during the revolutionary wars. In 1817, they purchased the palace of the former bishops of Liège, converting it to a factory producing machinery and steam engines. Yet despite the presence of entrepreneurs like the Cockerills, or of continental counterparts such as the Westphalian Fritz Harkort, who built and sold steam engines across Europe in the 1820s and 1830s, the general lack of large numbers of European technicians, experts, and entrepreneurs undoubtedly hampered rapid industrial expansion in France, Germany, and elsewhere.

The growth of the textile industry in Europe was patterned by the circumstances of the Napoleonic wars. The supply of cotton to the Continent had been interrupted, thanks to the British blockade, but the military's greater demand for woolen cloth meant that expansion occurred more rapidly in the latter than in the former industry. By 1820, the spinning of wool by machine was the common practice on the Continent; weaving, however, was still accomplished largely by hand. Regional centers for the production of wool were located around Rheims and in Alsace in France; in what is now Belgium; and in Saxony and Silesia in Germany. All possessed, at least in some measure, the various elements necessary to the successful growth and development of a regional economic system: transportation, resources, markets, technology, and labor supply. Mechanization was retarded because manual labor was cheap, and by the important fact that since Britain's market was so large, continental profits too often depended upon the manufacture of some particular specialty not made in England, and therefore without broad commercial appeal. Cotton manufacture was curtailed by the same circumstances. In France, as a result, mechanization occurred first in the silk industry and those sections of the cotton industry which produced finer specialty materials—lace, for example. A tradition of prestige associated with the production of

Textiles

Silk Weavers of Lyon, 1850. The first significant working-class uprisings in nineteenth-century France occurred here in 1831 and 1834. Note the domestic character of the working conditions.

A German Textile Factory, 1848. This is an unusually large manufacturing facility for this period on the Continent.

luxury goods, dating back to the reign of Louis XIV, encouraged entrepreneurs to invest in this branch of the textile industry. They were willing to forgo mass markets in the hope that their products would not meet with British competition. France nevertheless remained the largest continental producer of cotton goods, followed by Belgium and the German territories of the Rhine valley—Saxony, Silesia, and Bavaria.

Heavy industry In the area of heavy industry on the Continent, the picture was much the same as in textiles: i.e., gradual advances in the adoption of technological innovation against a background of more general resistance to change. Here, however, because change came later than in Britain, it coincided with an increased demand for various goods that had come into being as a result of industrialization and urbanization: iron pipe, much in use by mid-century in cities for gas, water, and drainage; metal machinery, now replacing earlier wooden prototypes. Consequently, the iron industry took the lead over textiles on the Continent, accompanied by an increase, where possible, in the production of coal. Coal was scarce, however; in the Rhineland, wood was still used to manufacture iron. The result was an unwillingness on the part of entrepreneurs to make as extensive use of the steam engine as they might have otherwise; it used too much fuel. In France, as late as 1844, hydraulic (i.e., water-driven) engines were employed far more often for the manufacture of iron than were steam engines. One further problem hampered the development of continental heavy industry during the first half of the nineteenth century. British competition forced continental machine construction firms to scramble for whatever orders they could get. This need to respond to a variety of requests meant that it was difficult for firms to specialize in a single product. The result was a lack of standardization, and continued production to order, when rationalization and specialization would have resulted in an increased volume of production.

3. THE COMING OF RAILWAYS

By about 1840, then, continental countries, and to some degree the United States, were moving gradually along the course of industrialization traced by Britain, producing far more than they had, yet nothing like as much as their spectacular pace setter. Within the next ten years, the coming of the railways was to alter that situation. Though Britain by no means lost its lead, the stimulus generally provided to Western economies by the introduction of railway systems throughout much of the world carried the Continent and America far enough and fast enough to allow them to become genuine competitors with the British.

Railways as a stimulus to the European and American economies

Railways came into being in answer to two needs. The first was the obvious desire on the part of entrepreneurs to transport their goods as quickly and cheaply as possible across long distances. Despite already mentioned improvements in transportation during the years before 1830, the movement of heavy materials, particularly coal, remained a problem. It is significant that the first modern railway was built in England in 1825 from the Durham coal field of Stockton to Darlington, near the coast. "Tramways"—parallel tracks along which

Railways as goods carriers

See color map facing page 737

The New Railway Age. Left: Stephenson's *Rocket.* A reconstruction of the railway engine built by George Stephenson in 1829. Right: "The Railway Juggernaut of 1845." A cartoon from the English humor magazine *Punch* satirizing speculation—often financially disastrous—in railway stocks.

coal carts were pulled by horses—had long been in use at pitheads to haul coal short distances. The Stockton to Darlington railway was a logical extension of this device, designed to answer the transportation needs produced by constantly expanding industrialization. The man primarily responsible for the design of the first steam railway was George Stephenson, a self-made engineer who had not learned to read until he was seventeen. He talked a group of northern England investors into the merits of steam traction and was given full liberty to carry out his plans. The locomotives on the Stockton-Darlington line traveled at fifteen miles per hour, the fastest rate at which human beings had yet moved overland.

Railways were also built in response to other than purely industrial needs: specifically, the need for capitalists to invest their money. Englishmen such as those who had made sizable fortunes in textiles, once they had paid out workers' wages and plowed back substantial capital in their factories, retained a surplus profit for which they wanted a decent yet reliable return. Railways provided them with the solution to their problem. Though by no means as reliable as had been hoped, railway investment proved capable of more than satisfying the capitalists' demands. No sooner did the first combined passenger and goods service open in 1830, on the Liverpool to Manchester line, than plans were formulated and money pledged to extend rail systems throughout Europe, the Americas, and beyond. In 1830, there were no more than a few dozen miles of railway in the world. By 1840, there were over 4,500 miles; by 1850, over 23,000. The English contractor, Thomas Brassey, the most famous, but by no means the only one of his kind, built railways in Italy, Canada, Argentina, India, and Australia.

Railways as an investment opportunity

Thomas Brassey

The railway boom accelerated industrialization generally. Not only did it increase enormously the demand for coal and for a variety of heavy manufactured goods—rails, locomotives, carriages, signals, switches; by enabling goods to move faster from factory to salesroom, railways decreased the time it took to sell those goods. Quicker sales meant, in turn, a quicker return on capital investment, money which could then be reinvested in the manufacture of more goods. Finally, by opening up the world market as it had never been before, the railway boom stimulated the production of such a quantity of material goods as to ensure the rapid completion of the West's industrialization.

Size and scope of the railway construction industry

The building of a railway line was an undertaking on a scale infinitely greater than the building of a factory. Railway construction required capital investment beyond the capacity of any single individual. In Britain, a factory might be worth anything from £20,000 to £200,000. The average cost of twenty-seven of the more important railway lines constructed between 1830 and 1853 was £2 million. The average labor force of a factory ranged from 50 to 300. The average labor force of a railway, after construction, was 2,500. Because a railway crossed the property of a large number of individual landowners, each of whom would naturally demand as much remuneration as he thought he could get, the planning of an efficient and economical route was a tricky and time-consuming business. The entrepreneur and contractor had to concern themselves not only with the purchase of right-of-way. They also contended with problems raised by the destruction of sizable portions of already existing urban areas, to make room for stations and switching yards. And they had to select a route that would be as free as possible of the hills and valleys that would necessitate the construction of expensive tunnels, cuts, and embankments. Railway-builders ran tremendous risks. Portions of most lines were subcontracted at fixed bids to contractors of limited experience. A spate of bad weather might delay construction to the point where builders would be lucky to bring in the finished job within 25 percent of their original bid. Of the thirty major contractors on the London to Birmingham line, ten failed completely.

If the business of a contractor was marked by uncertainty, that of the construction worker was characterized by back-breaking labor. The English "navvies," who built railways not only throughout Britain but around the world, were a remarkable breed. Their name derived from "navigator," a term applied to the construction workers on England's eighteenth-century canals. The work that they accomplished was prodigious. Because there is little friction between a train's wheels and its tracks, it can transport heavy loads easily. But lack of friction ceases to be an advantage when a train has to climb or

An American Proposal for a Steam-Driven Trolley. The application of the steam engine to transportation inspired inventors to devise novel solutions to perceived problems. This particular steam engine was disguised so as not to frighten horses on crowded city streets.

The "navvies"

Construction of the London to Birmingham Railway, London, 1838. This drawing of the building of retaining walls in a new railway cut evokes the chaos created by railway construction within urban areas.

descend a grade, thereby running the risk of slippage. Hence the need for comparatively level roadbeds; and hence the need for laborers to construct those tunnels, cuts, and embankments that would keep the roadbeds level. Navvies worked in gangs, whose migrations throughout the countryside traced the course of railway development. They were a rough lot, living in temporary encampments, often with women who were not their wives. The Irish navvies were a particularly tough breed. A sign posted by local residents in Scotland in 1845 warned that if all the Irish navvies were not "off the ground and out of the country" in a week, they would be driven out "by the strength of our armes and a good pick shaft."

The magnitude of the navvies' achievement

The magnitude of the navvies' accomplishment was extraordinary. In England and in much of the rest of the world, mid–nineteenth-century railways were constructed almost entirely without the aid of machinery. An assistant engineer on the London to Birmingham line, in calculating the magnitude of that particular construction, determined that the labor involved was the equivalent of lifting 25 billion cubic feet of earth and stone one foot high. This he compared with the feat of building the Great Pyramid, a task he estimated had involved the hoisting of some 16 billion tons. But whereas the building of the pyramid had required over 200,000 men and had taken twenty years, the construction of the London to Birmingham railway was accomplished by 20,000 men in less than five years. Translated into individual terms, a navvy was expected to move an average of twenty tons of earth per day. Railways were laid upon an almost infinite base of human muscle and sweat.

Railway Navvies. Without the aid of machinery, the burden of building Britain's railways fell on the backs of men such as these.

The Dresden Railway Station. Railways had the power to alter the architecture of the city, producing new and dramatic urban spaces.

4. INDUSTRIALIZATION AFTER 1850

In the years between 1850 and 1870, Britain remained very much the industrial giant of the West. But France, Germany, Belgium, and the United States assumed the position of challengers. In the iron indus- *Britain still the leader* try, Britain's rate of growth during these years was not as great as that of either France or Germany (5.2 percent for Britain, as against 6.7 percent for France and 10.2 percent for Germany). But in 1870 Britain was still producing half the world's pig iron; 3.5 times as much as the United States, more than 4 times as much as Germany, and more than 5 times as much as France. Although the number of cotton spindles increased from 5.5 to 11.5 million in the United States between 1852 and 1861, and by significant but not as spectacular percentages in European countries, Britain in 1861 had 31 million spindles at work in comparison with France's 5.5 million, Germany's 2 million, Switzerland's 1.3 million, and Austria's 1.8 million.

Most of the gains experienced in Europe came as a result of continuing changes in those areas we have come to recognize as important for sustained industrial growth. The improved transportation systems *Continuing European* that resulted from the spread of railways helped encourage an increase *advance* in the free movement of goods. International monetary unions were established, and restrictions removed on international waterways such as the Danube. The Prussian *Zollverein,* or tariff union, an organization designed to facilitate internal free trade, was established in 1818 and was extended over the next twenty years to include most of the German principalities outside Austria. Free trade went hand in hand with further removal of barriers to the freedom to enter trades and to practice business unhampered by restrictive regulation. Control of guilds and corporations over artisan production was abolished in Austria in 1859 and in most of Germany by the mid-1860s. Laws against usury, most of which had ceased to be enforced, were officially abandoned in Britain, Holland, Belgium, and in many parts of Germany. Governmental regulation of the operation of mines was surrendered by the Prussian state in the 1850s, freeing entrepreneurs to develop resources as they saw fit. The formation of investment banks proceeded apace, encouraged by an important increase in the money supply, and therefore an easing of credit, following the opening of the California gold fields in 1849.

Increased trade in raw materials

A further reason for increased European production was the growing trade in raw materials. Wool and hides imported from Australia helped diminish the consequences of the cotton shortage suffered after the outbreak of the United States Civil War and the Union blockade of the American South. Other importations—guano from the Pacific, vegetable oils from Africa, pyrites (sulfides) from Spain—stimulated the scale of food production and both altered and increased the manufacture of soap, candles, and finished textiles. Finally, discoveries of new sources of coal, particularly in the Pas-de-Calais region of France and in the Ruhr valley in Germany, had dramatic repercussions. Production of coal in France rose from 4.4 million to 13.3 million tons between 1850 and 1869; during the same years, German production increased from 4.2 million to 23.7 million tons.

The slower pace of industrialization in eastern and southern Europe

Industrialization in eastern and southern Europe after mid-century proceeded at a much slower pace than in western Europe. This was in part a result of the fact that many Eastern regions played an increasingly specialized role in the economy of the Continent, providing food and agricultural materials to the West. The constantly growing demand for agricultural products from the East resulted in the development of agriculture as a major capitalist industry there. As they rationalized their operations so as to make them more efficient and hence more profitable, entrepreneurs recognized the degree to which they were hampered by the outmoded economic practices of serfdom, a system which prevented the mobility of labor and thus the formation of an effective agricultural work force. Serfdom was abolished in most parts of eastern and southern Europe by 1850, and in Poland and Russia in the 1860s.

The fact that industry continued to take a back seat to agriculture does not mean, however, that eastern Europe was without important manufacturing regions. By the 1880s, the number of men and women employed in the cotton industry in the Austrian province of Bohemia exceeded that in Saxony. In the Czechoslovakian region, textile industries, developed in the eighteenth century, continued to thrive. By the 1830s, there were machine-powered Czech cotton mills, and iron works. In Russia, a factory industry producing coarse textiles—mostly linens—had grown up around Moscow. At mid-century, Russia was purchasing 24 percent of the total British machinery exports to mechanize its own mills. Many workers in Russian industry remained serfs until the 1860s—about 40 percent, a number of them employed in mines. Of the over 800,000 Russians engaged in manufacturing by 1860, however, most labored not in factories but in very small workshops, where average employment numbered about 40 persons.

Pockets of industrialization in the East

By 1870 Europe was by no means a fully industrialized continent. Fifty percent of France's labor force remained on farms. Agricultural laborers were the single largest occupational category in Britain during the 1860s. Great stretches of the Continent—Spain, southern Italy, eastern Europe—were almost untouched by the Industrial Revolution. And in the industrialized countries, much work was still accomplished in tiny workshops or at home. Yet if Europe was by no means wholly industrial, it was far and away the most industrially advanced portion of the globe—and not by accident. In order to maintain its position of producer to the world, Europe, and Britain particularly, made certain that no other areas stood a chance to compete. Europe used its economic and, when necessary, its military strength to ensure that the world remained divided between the producers of manufactured goods—Europe itself—and suppliers of the necessary raw materials—everyone else. Often this arrangement suited those in other parts of the world who made their money by providing the raw materials that fueled the European economy. Cotton-growers in the southern United States, sugar-growers in the Caribbean, wheat-growers in the Ukraine—all remained content with arrangements as dictated by the industrialized West. Those countries which expressed their discontent—Egypt, for example, which in the 1830s attempted to establish its own cotton textile industry—were soon put in their place by a show of force. Western Europeans, believing in their right to industrial leadership in the world, saw nothing wrong with employing soldiers, if they had to, to make others understand their destiny.

Europe's economy within the world

SELECTED READINGS

• *Items so designated are available in paperback editions.*

• Ashton, T. S., *The Industrial Revolution, 1760–1830,* London, 1948. A standard short introduction.

Cameron, R. E., *France and the Industrial Development of Europe.* Princeton, 1968. Valuable material on the Industrial Revolution outside Britain.

Checkland, S. G., *The Rise of Industrial Society in England, 1815–1885,* New York, 1965. Emphasizes the economic organization of England.
- Deane, Phyllis, *The First Industrial Revolution,* Cambridge, 1965.

Henderson, W. O., *The Industrialization of Europe, 1780–1914,* New York, 1969.

———, *The State and the Industrial Revolution in Prussia, 1740–1870,* Liverpool, 1958. A biographical approach. Good on technical education.
- Hobsbawn, Eric, *Industry and Empire: 1750 to the Present Day,* New York, 1968. A general survey of industrialization in Britain, written from a Marxist perspective.
- Landes, David S., *Revolution in Time: Clocks and the Making of the Modern World,* Cambridge, Mass., 1983. The social and economic changes wrought by the advent of cheap and accurate time-keeping.
- ———, *The Unbound Prometheus,* London, 1969. An excellent treatment of the technological innovations and economic results of the Industrial Revolution.

McManners, John, *European History: Men, Machines and Freedom,* New York, 1967.
- Mantoux, Paul, *The Industrial Revolution in the Eighteenth Century,* rev. ed., New York, 1961. The beginnings of the modern factory system in England.

Schofer, L. *The Formation of a Modern Labor Force,* Berkeley, 1975. Analyzes industrialization and its social consequences in Silesia.
- Taylor, George Rogers, *The Transportation Revolution, 1815–1860,* New York, 1968.

SOURCE MATERIALS

Dodd, George, *Days at the Factories; or the Manufacturing Industry of Great Britain Described, and Illustrated by Numerous Engravings of Machines and Processes,* Totawa, N.J., 1975. A reprint of the 1850 edition.

Mitchell, Brian R., and Phyllis Deane, *Abstract of British Historical Statistics,* Cambridge, 1962. The single best source for statistics on population, trade, manufacturing, etc.
- Smith, Adam, *An Inquiry into the Nature and Causes of the Wealth of Nations,* Chicago, 1977. Written in 1776, this revolutionary work called for the end of mercantilism.

Ward, J. T., *The Factory System, 1830–1855,* New York, 1970. Excerpts from contemporary documents describing, defending, and criticizing the factory system and industrialization.

Chapter 21

CONSEQUENCES OF INDUSTRIAL-IZATION: URBANIZATION AND CLASS CONSCIOUSNESS (1800–1850)

What Art was to the ancient world, Science is to the modern: The distinctive faculty. In the minds of men the useful has succeeded the beautiful. Yet rightly understood, Manchester is as great a human exploit as Athens.

—Benjamin Disraeli, *Coningsby*

The Industrial Revolution was more than an important event in the economic and technological history of the West. It helped to reshape the patterns of life for men and women, first in Britain, then in Europe and America, and eventually throughout much of the world. By increasing the scale of production, the Industrial Revolution brought about the factory system, which in turn compelled the migration of millions from the countryside and small towns into cities. Once in those cities, men and women had to learn a new way of life, and learn it quickly: how to discipline themselves to the factory whistle and survive in a slum, if they were first-generation urban workers; how to manage a work force and achieve respectable prominence for themselves in the community, if they were businessmen and their wives. One particular lesson that industrialization and urbanization taught was that of class consciousness. Men and women, to a far greater degree than heretofore, began to perceive themselves as part of a class with interests of its own, and in opposition to the interests of men and women in other classes.

Consequences of the Industrial Revolution

We shall examine this range of social and cultural changes as they occurred during the first fifty years or so of the nineteenth century, after looking briefly first at the condition of the bulk of the population, which, despite industrialization, remained on the land. Since the Industrial Revolution came first to Britain, our focus will be on that country. Yet the pattern set by the British was one that was repeated to a great extent in other European countries, as industrialization came to them in time.

1. PEOPLE ON THE LAND

Population patterns

The dramatic story of the growth of industrialization and urbanization must not be allowed to obscure the fact that, in 1850, the population of Europe was still overwhelmingly a peasant population. While in England, by 1830, a sizable minority lived in towns and cities, elsewhere society remained predominantly or overwhelmingly rural. In France and Italy, 60 percent lived in the country; in Prussia, over 70 percent; in Spain, over 90 percent; in Russia, over 95 percent. Demographic pressures, which helped produce chaos in the cities, likewise caused severe hardship in the countryside. The populations of the predominantly agricultural nations lept forward with those that were industrializing. The population of Europe as a whole, estimated roughly at 205 million by 1800, had risen to 274 million by 1850, and to 320 million by 1870. In Britain, with its comparatively high standard of living, the numbers increased from 16 million to 27 million. Yet the rural Irish, despite their periodic famines, increased too, from 5.5 to 8 million, and the Russians from 39 to 60 million, in the same period.

Causes of continuing population expansion

The causes of this continuing population explosion remain obscure. The notion that the explanation can be traced to a desire on the part of parents in industrial counties to produce more family wage-earners is now downplayed by scholars, given the fact that increases occurred in rural regions as well. One contributing factor to this continued growth may have been a decline in the virulence of certain fatal diseases as a result of the cyclical potency of microbes. Certainly the curbing of cholera, through the adoption of sanitary reforms, and smallpox, as Edward Jenner's technique of vaccination gained gradual acceptance after 1796, help to explain the population trend. The increasing ability and desire of governments to monitor and improve the lives of their subjects had a direct effect on the decline of the death rate. At the same time the availability of less expensive foods of high nutritional value—most notably the potato— and the ability to transport foodstuffs cheaply by rail meant European populations would not suffer as much from undernourishment as in the past, and that they would thus be less susceptible to debilitating illness. Other plausible explanations suggest that the population increase was the result of rising birth rates caused by earlier marriages. As serfdom declined, peasants tended to set up households at a younger age. A relatively small expansion in the population of a region in one generation would result in a far

Interior of an English Farm Laborer's Cottage, 1846. Note the wooden crate used as an infant's cradle.

greater one in the next. As the population grew, the number of young and fertile people grew faster, thereby significantly increasing the ratio of births to total population.

Whatever the reasons for the population increase, conditions remained such as to make the life of the poorer rural inhabitants of Europe seldom more than bleak. Overpopulation brought underemployment, and hence poverty, in its train. Millions of tiny holdings produced a bare subsistence living, if that. Farmers still sowed and harvested by hand. Conditions in rural areas deteriorated sharply whenever there was a bad harvest. The average daily diet for an entire family in a "good" year might amount to no more than two or three pounds of bread—a total of about 3,000 calories. Hunger—often near-starvation—as well as epidemic disease were still common occurrences. The result was a standard of living—if one can dignify the condition with that name—that for many rural inhabitants of many areas in Europe actually declined in the first half of the nineteenth century, although not enough to reverse general population growth. Governments in some countries attempted to solve the related problems of population pressure and impoverishment by passing laws raising the age of marriage. In some of the states of southern and western Germany, as well as in Austria, men were forbidden to marry before the age of thirty, and were also required to prove their ability to support a family. Governments did their best to encourage emigration to ease the overcrowding, the majority of emigrants relocating in the Americas. Emigration from England rose from 57,000 in 1830, to 90,000 in 1840, to 280,000 in 1850. Ireland, in the early years of the nineteenth century, witnessed the departure of over 1.5 million before the great potato famine of 1846, when approximately three

Wretched rural conditions

out of every four acres of potatoes were blighted. After the potato famine, the flow of emigrants increased to a flood.

Even had such policies acted as an effective curb on population growth—which, in the main, they did not—they would nevertheless have failed to prevent the rural stresses that resulted from the continuing

Agricultural capitalism

spread of agricultural capitalism. The pace of this change varied across Europe; it was furthest advanced in England and Prussia. Wherever landed proprietors determined to meet increased demand for food by farming large areas as a capital investment, they imposed a series of transformations that were bound to affect the lives of agricultural laborers. First, land must be made a negotiable commodity. It must not, therefore, be tied to ancient customs which clouded its title—as was the case, for example, with common land, to which the poor within a community might have some right of access or cultivation. Second, land must be in the hands of those with capital enough to improve it, in order to make of it a profitable investment. It must be enclosed—"regulated" was the term in Prussia—so that, as we have seen, it could be properly fertilized and drained, or, if it was grazing land, so that breeds might be scientifically improved without fear of mongrelization. Finally, a mobile force of agricultural laborers must be available to work at the capitalists' behest. They must not be "tied" to a particular piece of land, either through systems of customary rights or bondage. They must be free to go where they were told to go, to work whatever land would bring most profit to its owners.

Its results

These requirements, as they were imposed, produced dislocation and hardship. In Scotland, workers were cleared from land which they had farmed as tenants, in order to provide pasturage for the more profitable sheep. In Germany, those serfs emancipated by a reform-minded government in 1807 were compelled to forfeit somewhere between a third to a half of their land in return for their freedom; those who were able to retain small holdings were in most cases pressured to sell out to larger landholders. Not all landlords were ruthless. "Model" improvers among the wealthiest of the English landowners adjusted to capitalist competition without entirely forswearing traditional responsibilities. They built houses for tenants and laborers, and provided them with schools and churches. In eastern Europe there were among the Prussian landlords (Junkers) pietists who acknowledged obligations to their tenants as well as to the market.

Variations in the pattern of agricultural development

The speed with which agricultural change occurred in various parts of Europe depended upon the nature of particular governments. Those more sympathetic to new capitalist impulses facilitated the transfer and reorganization of land by means of enabling legislation. They encouraged the elimination of small farms and an increase in larger, more efficient units of production. In England, over half the total area of the country, excluding waste land, was composed of estates of a thousand acres or more. In Spain, the fortunes of agricultural

A Mowing Team in England, c. 1870. Roughly twenty men and boys wielding scythes were required for work that would shortly be accomplished by a single machine. The scythes, which only achieved widespread use in the nineteenth century, had replaced the sickle, a much more primitive and physically taxing tool.

capitalism fluctuated with the political tenor of successive regimes: with the coming of a liberal party to power in 1820 came a law encouraging the free transfer of land; with the restoration of absolutism in 1823 came a repeal of the law. Russia was one of the countries least affected by agricultural change in the first half of the nineteenth century. There land was worked in vast blocks; some of the largest landowners possessed over half a million acres. Until the emancipation of the serfs in the 1860s, landowners claimed the labor of dependent peasant populations for as much as several days per week.

European serfdom, which bound hundreds of thousands of men, women, and children to particular estates for generations, prohibited the use of land as a negotiable commodity and therefore prevented the development of agricultural entrepreneurship. In France, despite the fact that manorialism had been abolished by the revolution, there was no rapid movement toward large-scale capitalist farming. An army of peasant proprietors, direct beneficiaries of the Jacobins' democratic constitution, continued to work the small farms they owned. The fact that France suffered far less agricultural distress, even in the 1840s, than did other European countries, and the fact that there was less migration in France from the country to the city and overseas than there was in Germany and England, are marks of the general success of this rural lower middle class in sustaining itself on the land. Its members were content to farm in the old way, opposed agricultural innovation, and, indeed, innovation generally. Despite

The legacy of manorialism

their veneration of the revolution, they were among the most conservative elements in European society.

Rural populations, despite their isolation from urban centers, found themselves directly affected by the events of the Industrial Revolution. Factories brought about a decline in cottage industry and a consequent loss of vital income, especially during winter months. Improved communication networks not only afforded rural populations a keener sense of events and opportunities elsewhere, but also made it possible for governments to intrude upon the lives of these men and women to a degree previously impossible. Central bureaucracies now found it easier to collect taxes from the peasantry, and to conscript its sons into their armies.

Country people responded with sporadic violence against these and other harsh intrusions upon their lives. In southern England in the late 1820s, small farmers joined forces to burn barns and hayricks in protest to the introduction of thrashing machines, a symbol of the new agricultural capitalism. They masked and otherwise disguised themselves, riding out at night under the banner of their mythical leader, "Captain Swing." Their raids were preceded by anonymous threats such as the one received by a large-scale farmer in the county of Kent: "Pull down your threshing machine or else [expect] fire without delay. We are five thousand men [a highly inflated figure] and will not be stopped." Other major rural disturbances occurred in Ireland, Silesia, and Galicia in the 1830s and 1840s, and indeed, to a lesser degree, right across Europe. In no country, however, was the agrarian population a united political force. Those who owned land, those who leased it as tenants, and those who worked it as laborers had interests as different from each other as from those of the urban populations.

Rural societies and industrialization

Rural disturbances

2. URBANIZATION AND THE STANDARD OF LIVING

Reasons for the growth of cities

If the countryside continued to hold the bulk of Europe's population in the years between 1800 and 1850, the growth of cities nevertheless remains one of the most important facts in the social history of that period. Cities grew in size and number once the steam engine made it practical to bring together large concentrations of men, women, and children to work in factories. Steam engines freed entrepreneurs from their dependence on water power and allowed them to consolidate production in large cities. In cities, transportation was more accessible than in the countryside. Hence it was less costly to import raw materials and ship out finished goods. Workers were more readily available in cities, as well, attracted as they were in large numbers in the hope— often false—of finding steady work at higher wages than those paid agricultural laborers. Industrialization was not the only reason for the growth of cities in the early nineteenth century, however. General population growth combined with industrialization forced cities to expand at an alarming rate.

In the ten years between 1831 and 1841 London's population grew by 130,000, Manchester's by 70,000. Paris increased by 120,000 between 1841 and 1846. Vienna grew by 125,000 from 1827 to 1847, into a city of 400,000. Berlin had as large a population by 1848, having increased by 180,000 since 1815. The primary result in these and other fast-growing centers was dreadful overcrowding. Construction lagged far behind population growth. In Vienna, though population rose 42 percent during the twenty years before 1847, the increase in housing was only 11.5 percent. In many of the larger cities, old and new, working men and women lived in lodging houses, apart from families left behind in the country. The poorest workers in almost all European cities dwelt in wretched basement rooms, often without any light or drainage.

With cities as overcrowded as they were, it is no wonder that they were a menace to the health of those who lived within them. The middle classes moved as far as possible from disease and factory smoke, leaving the poorest members of the community isolated and a prey to the sickness which ravaged working-class sections. Cholera, typhus, and tuberculosis were natural predators in areas without adequate sewerage facilities and fresh water, and over which smoke from factories, railroads, and domestic chimneys hung heavily. A local committee appointed to investigate conditions in the British manufacturing town of Huddersfield—not by any means the worst of that country's urban centers—reported that there were large areas without

Urban population increases

Cities as a health menace

Women and Boys Fetching Water from a Standpipe in Fryingpan Alley, London. Not until the beginning of the twentieth century did major European cities begin to provide poorer residents with an adequate water supply.

Manchester, England at Mid-Century. This powerful photograph evokes the dreary, prison-like atmosphere of the new industrial city.

paving, sewers, or drains, "where garbage and filth of every description are left on the surface to ferment and rot; where pools of stagnant water are almost constant; where dwellings adjoining are thus necessarily caused to be of an inferior and even filthy description; thus where disease is engendered, and the health of the whole town perilled." Measures were gradually adopted by successive governments in an attempt to cure the worst of these ills, if only to prevent the spread of catastrophic epidemics. Legislation was designed to rid cities of their worst slums by tearing them down, and to improve sanitary conditions by supplying both water and drainage. Yet by 1850, these projects had only just begun. Paris, perhaps better supplied with water than any European city, had enough for no more than two baths per capita per year; in London, human waste remained uncollected in 250,000 domestic cesspools; in Manchester, fewer than a third of the dwellings were equipped with toilets of any sort.

The standard of living debate

Conditions such as these are important evidence in the debate that has occupied historians for the past several decades. The question is: Did the standard of living rise or fall in Europe during the first half century of the Industrial Revolution? One school, the "optimists," argues that workers shared in the more general increase in living standards which occurred throughout Europe from 1800 onward. A variation on this optimistic theme maintains that whatever the hardships workers were compelled to suffer during the period of intense industrialization after 1800, they represent the necessary and worthwhile price society had to pay before it could "take off" into a period of "sustained economic growth." Sacrifices, in terms of standard of living, were required to permit accumulation of a capital base sufficient to guarantee economic expansion and an eventual level of general prosperity higher than any civilization had hitherto achieved. Other historians insist that such an analysis encourages one to ignore the evidence of physical squalor and psychological disruption that men, women, and children suffered as they provided the statistical "base" for future economic historians' abstract calculations.

The debate is hampered by an absence of reliable evidence about wage levels, hours of work, and cost of living. Some skilled workers within the new factories, along with some artisans in older trades as yet unaffected by industrialization, appear to have benefited from a slight rise in wages and a decline in living costs. But regional variables, along with a constantly fluctuating demand for labor in all countries, suggest that the more lowly paid, unskilled worker, whether in England or on the Continent, led a thoroughly precarious existence. Textile workers in England, if guaranteed something like full employment, could theoretically earn enough to support a family. Such was not the case in Switzerland, however, where similar work paid only half what was necessary, or in Saxony, where a large portion of the population was apparently dependent upon either poor relief or charity. One of the most depressing features of working-class life in these years was its instability. Economic depressions were common occurrences; when they happened, workers were laid off for weeks at a time, with no system of unemployment insurance to sustain them. Half the working population of England's industrial cities were out of work in the early 1840s. In Paris, 85,000 went on relief in 1840. One particularly hard-pressed district of Silesia reported 30,000 out of 40,000 citizens in need of relief in 1844. Nor should one overlook the plight of those whose skills had been replaced by machinery—the hand-loom

Soup Kitchen Run by Quakers, Manchester, England, 1862. Enterprises of this sort, which doled out charity "indiscriminately"—that is, without investigating the recipient's character — were condemned by many members of the middle class as encouraging the "worst" elements — idlers and loafers — among the poor.

weavers being the most notable examples. In the English manufacturing town of Bolton, a hand-loom weaver could earn no more than about three shillings per week in 1842, at a time when experts estimated it took at least twenty shillings a week to keep a family of five above the poverty line. On that kind of pay, workers were fortunate if they did not starve to death. Forced to spend something like 65 percent of their income on food, the per capita meat consumption of the average worker declined to about forty pounds per year in the early nineteenth century.

The quality of life

Such figures make the optimists' generalizations hard to countenance. Figures of whatever sort fail to take into account the stress that urban factory life imposed upon the workers. Even workers making thirty shillings a week might well wonder if they were "better off," forced as they were to come to terms with the factory disciplines and living conditions imposed upon them. Of the more than 3 million men, women, and children living in England's sixty largest towns and cities in 1850, less than half had been born there. Though most migrated but a short distance from their place of birth, the psychological distance they traveled was tremendous. These qualitative factors, admittedly difficult to assess, must be weighed along with more easily quantifiable evidence before reaching any conclusion as to the increased standard of living in early-nineteenth-century cities. Whether or not life in cities was pleasant or ghastly, however, it was, for rapidly increasing numbers, a fact of life. Once we examine that life we will better understand the full impact of industrialization and urbanization upon those who first experienced it.

3. THE LIFE OF THE URBAN MIDDLE CLASS

The urban middle class which emerged during this period was by no means one homogeneous unit, in terms of occupation or income. In a general category that includes merchant princes and humble shopkeepers, subdivisions are important. The middle class included families of industrialists, such as the Peels (cotton) in England and, at a later period, the Krupps (iron) in Germany. It included financiers like the internationally famed Rothschilds, and, on a descending scale of wealth and power, bankers and capitalists throughout the major money markets of Europe: London, Brussels, Paris, Berlin. It included entrepreneurs like Thomas Brassey, the British railway magnate, and John Wilkinson, the English ironmaster, who had himself buried in an iron coffin, and technicians, like the engineer Isambard Kingdom Brunel, designer of the steamship *The Great Western*. It included bureaucrats, in growing demand when governments began to regulate the pace and direction of industrialization, and to ameliorate its harshest social and economic results. It included those in the already established professions—in law particularly, as lawyers put

Isambard Kingdom Brunel. Behind him are lengths of anchor chain from the steamship *The Great Western*.

their expertise to the service of industrialists. It included the armies of managers and clerks necessary to the continuing momentum of industrial and financial expansion, and the equally large army of merchants and shopkeepers necessary to supply the wants of an increasingly affluent urban middle-class population. Finally, it included the families of all those who lived their lives in the various subcategories we have listed.

Movement within these ranks was often possible, in the course of one or two generations. Movement from the working class into the middle class, however, was far less common. Most middle-class successes originated within the middle class itself—the children of farmers, skilled artisans, or professionals. Upward mobility was almost impossible without education; education was an expensive, if not unattainable luxury for the children of a laborer. Careers open to talents, that goal achieved by the French Revolution, frequently meant middle-class jobs for middle-class young men who could pass exams. The examination system was an important path for ascendancy within governmental bureaucracies.

Young Gentlemen, 1834. It was to models such as these that the young men of the middle class aspired.

If passage from working class to middle class was not common, neither was the equally difficult social journey from middle class to aristocratic, landed society. This was particularly the case on the Continent, where the division between noble and commoner had traditionally been most pronounced. In Britain, mobility of this sort was easier. Children from wealthy upper-middle-class families, if they were sent, as occasionally they were, to elite schools and universities, and if they left the commercial or industrial world for a career in politics, might effect the change. William Gladstone, son of a Liverpool merchant, attended the exclusive educational preserves of Eton, a private boarding school, and Oxford University, married a connection of the aristocratic Grenville family, and became prime minister of England. Yet Gladstone was an exception to the rule in Britain, and Britain was an exception to the Continent. Movement, when it occurred, generally did so in less spectacular degrees.

Movement from the middle class to the aristocracy

Nevertheless, the European middle class helped sustain itself with the belief that it was possible to get ahead by means of intelligence, pluck, and serious devotion to work. The Englishman Samuel Smiles, in his extraordinarily successful how-to-succeed book *Self Help*, preached a gospel dear to the middle class. "The spirit of self-help is the root of all genuine growth in the individual," Smiles wrote. "Exhibited in the lives of many, it constitutes the true source of national vigor and strength." Although Smiles's gospel declared that anyone willing to exert himself could rise to a position of responsibility and personal profit, however, and although some men actually did so, the notion remained no more than myth for the great majority.

Self-help

Seriousness of purpose was reflected in the middle-class devotion to the ideal of family and home. A practical importance attached to the institution of the family in those areas in England, France, and Ger-

Left: *A Salon in Vienna, 1830s*. A representation of middle-class home life on the Continent. Right: *A Victorian Family at Tea, 1860s*

Family and home

many where sons, sons-in-law, nephews, and cousins were expected to assume responsibility in family firms when it came their turn. Yet the worship of family more often ignored those practical considerations and assumed the proportions of sacred belief. Away from the business and confusion of the world, sheltered behind solid masonry and amid the solid comfort of their ornate furnishings, middle-class fathers retired each evening to enjoy the fruits of their daily labors. Inside the home, life was enclosed in a hierarchical and ritualistic system under which the husband and father was master. His wife was called his help-mate, and very occasionally within the middle class—especially in France—a wife might serve as shopkeeper or business associate with her husband. Far more frequently, however, a middle-class wife was treated by her spouse as a kind of superior servant. Her task was to keep the household functioning smoothly and harmoniously. She maintained the accounts and directed the activities of the servants—usually two or three women. Called in Victorian England the "Angel in the House," the middle-class woman was responsible for the moral education of her children. Yet she probably spent no more than two or three hours a day at most with her offspring. Until sent to school, they were placed in the custody of a nursemaid or governess. Much of a middle-class woman's day was spent in the company of other women from similar households. An elaborate set of social customs involving "calls" and "at homes" was established in European middle-class society. Women were not expected to improve their minds. They were not expected to be the intellectual companions of their husbands. Rather, they were encouraged to be dabblers, education for them usually consisting of little more beyond reading and writing, a smattering of arithmetic, geography, history, and a foreign language, embellished with lessons in drawing, painting in watercolor, singing, or piano-playing.

Queen Victoria, who ascended the British throne in 1837, labored to make her solemn—occasionally almost stolid—public image reflect the feminine middle-class virtues of moral probity and dutiful domesticity. Her court was eminently proper and preeminently bourgeois, a marked contrast to that of her uncle George IV, whose fleshly and unbuttoned ways had set the style for high life a generation before. Though possessing an imperious temper, Victoria trained herself to curb it in deference to her ministers and her public-spirited, ultra-respectable husband, Prince Albert of Saxe-Coburg. She was a successful queen because she embodied the traits dearest to the middle class, whose triumph she seemed to epitomize and whose habits of mind we have come to call Victorian.

Queen Victoria as prototype

Middle-class wives were indoctrinated to believe that they were superior to their husbands in one area only. A wife was "the better half" of a middle-class marriage because she was deemed pure—the untainted Vestal of the hearth, unsullied by cares of the world outside her home, and certainly untouched by those sexual desires which marked her husband, her natural moral inferior. A wife's charge was to encourage her husband's "higher nature." She must never respond to his sexual advances with equal passion; passion was, for her, a presumed impossibility. If she *was* passionate, and private diaries sug-

Sexuality

Prince Albert and Queen Victoria. In this photograph by Roger Fenton the royal couple is depicted not as monarch and consort but as a conventional upper-middle-class married couple.

gest, not surprisingly, that many middle-class women were, she would find it hard not to feel guilty about the pleasures she was presumed too pure to taste. Contraception, other than withdrawal, was not common practice among the middle classes. The result was that for women, sexual intercourse was directly related to the problems of frequent pregnancies. (Victoria, who had nine children, declared that childbirth was "the shadow side" of marriage.)

Prostitution

The middle-class wife was expected to persuade her husband to seek, through love of home and family, a substitute for the baser instincts with which nature had unhappily endowed the male. Should she fail, she must accept the fact of her "failure" as she was bound to accept the rest of her life: uncomplainingly. That she often did fail was evidenced by the brisk trade in prostitution that flourished in nineteenth-century cities. In all European cities, prostitutes solicited openly. At mid-century the number of prostitutes in Vienna was estimated to be 15,000; in Paris, where prostitution was a licensed trade, 50,000; in London, 80,000. London newspaper reports of the 1850s catalogued the vast underworld of prostitutes and their followers: those who operated out of "lodging houses" run by unsavory entrepreneurs whose names—Swindling Sal, Lushing Loo—suggest their general character; the retinue of procurers, pimps, panderers, and "fancy men" who made the lives of common prostitutes little better than slavery; the relatively few "prima donnas" who enjoyed the protection of rich, upper-middle-class lovers, who entertained lavishly and whose wealth allowed them to move on the fringes of more respectable high society. The heroines of Alexandre Dumas's novel *La Dame aux Camilles,* and of Giuseppe Verdi's opera *La Traviata*—"the lost one"—were prototypes of women of this sort.

If a middle-class wife should herself succumb to "unwomanly desires" by taking a lover, and be discovered to have done so, she could expect nothing less than complete social banishment. The law tolerated a husband's infidelity and at all times respected a husband's rights both to his wife's person and to her property. It made quick work of an "unfaithful" wife, granting to her husband whatever he might desire in terms of divorce, property, and custody, to make him amends for the personal wrongs and embarrassments he had suffered at the hands of his "unnatural" spouse.

Middle-class family rituals helped to sustain this hierarchy. Daily meals, with the father at the head of the table, were cooked and brought to each place by servants, who were a constant reminder of the family's social position. Family vacations were a particularly nineteenth-century middle-class invention. Thanks to the advent of the railways, excursions of one or two weeks to the mountains or to the seashore were available to families of even moderate means. Entrepreneurs built large, ornate hotels, adorned with imposing names—Palace, Beau Rivage, Excelsior—and attracted middle-class customers

Prostitution. A contemporary comment bearing the title "That girl seems to know you, George!" intimates that, as the wife surmises, the flower girl has more to sell than her posies.

The Middle Class at Leisure. The "morning lounge" at Biarritz, a French resort on the Atlantic coast.

by offering them on a grander scale exactly the same sort of comfortable and sheltered existence they enjoyed at home.

The houses and furnishings of the middle class were an expression of the material security the middle class valued. Solidly built, heavily decorated, they proclaimed the financial worth and social respectability of those who dwelt within. In provincial cities they were often free-standing "villas." In London, Paris, Berlin, or Vienna, they might be rows of five- or six-story townhouses, or large apartments. Whatever particular shape they took, they were built to last a long time. The rooms were certain to be crowded with furniture, art objects, carpets, and wall hangings. Chairs, tables, cabinets, and sofas might be of any or all periods; no matter, so long as they were adorned with their proper complement of fringe, gilt, or other ornamentation. The size of the rooms, the elegance of the furniture, the number of servants, all depended, of course, on the extent of one's income. A bank clerk did not live as elegantly as a bank director. Yet in all likelihood both lived in obedience to the same set of standards and aspirations. And that obedience helped bind them, despite the differences in their material way of life, to the same class.

The European middle class had no desire to confront the unpleasant urban by-products of its own success. Members of the middle class saw to it that they lived apart from the unpleasant sights and smells of industrialization. Their residential areas, usually built to the west of

Houses

See color plates following page 800 for *The Movings* by Boilly

Cities and the middle class

the cities, out of the path of the prevailing breeze, and therefore of industrial pollution, were havens from the congestion for which they were primarily responsible. When the members of the middle class rode into the urban centers they took care to do so over avenues lined with respectable shops, or across railway embankments that lifted them above monotonous working-class streets en route to their destination. Yet the middle class, though it turned its face from what it did not want to see, did not turn from the city. Middle-class men and women celebrated the city as their particular creation and the source of their profits. They even praised its smoke—as a sign of prosperity—so long as they did not have to breathe it night and day. For the most part, it was they who managed their city's affairs. And it was they who provided new industrial cities with their proud architectural

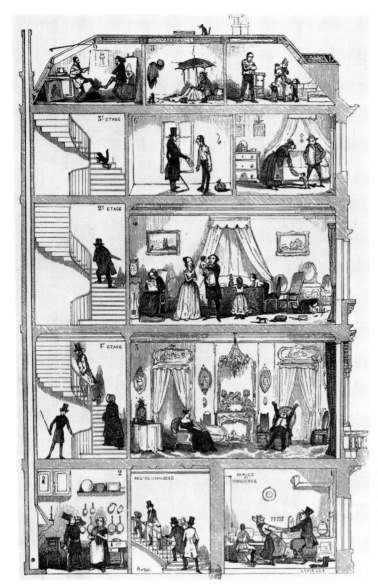

Apartment Living in Paris. This print shows that on the Continent rich and poor often lived in the same buildings, the rich on the lower floors, the poor at the top. This sort of residential mixing was unknown in Britain.

The Paris Opera. An exterior view of the Opera. Designed by Charles Garnier, it was constructed between 1861 and 1875. This grandiose display of wealth and luxury epitomized the taste of the new industrial middle class.

landmarks: city halls, stock exchanges, opera houses. These were the new cathedrals of the industrial age, proclamations of a triumphant middle class.

4. THE LIFE OF THE URBAN WORKING CLASS

Like the middle class, the working class was divided into various subgroups and categories, determined in this case by skill, wages, and workplace. The working class included skilled workers in crafts that were centuries old—glassblowing and cabinetmaking, for example. It included as well mechanics equally skilled in new industrial technology. It included the men who built textile machinery and the women and children who tended it. It included the men, women, and children who together worked in mines and quarries. And it included the countless millions who labored at unskilled jobs—dock workers, coal porters, cleaning women, and the like. The nature of workers' experiences naturally varied, depending upon where they worked, where they lived, and, above all, how much they earned. A skilled textile worker lived a life far different from that of a ditch digger, the former able to afford the food, shelter, and clothing necessary for a decent existence, the latter so busy trying to keep himself and his family alive that he would have little time to think about anything but the source of their next meal.

Ranks within the working class

Some movement from the ranks of the unskilled to the skilled was possible, if children were provided, or provided themselves, with at least a rudimentary education. Yet education was considered by many parents a luxury, especially since children could be put to work at an early age to supplement a family's meager earnings. There was movement from skilled to unskilled also, as technological change—

Social mobility

the introduction of the power loom, for example—drove highly paid workers into the ranks of the unskilled and destitute. Further variations within the working class were the result of the fact that though every year more men, women, and children were working in factories, the majority still labored either in workshops or at home. These variations mean that we cannot speak of a common European working-class experience during the years from 1800 to 1850. The life we shall be describing was most typical of English workers, during the first half century of their exposure to industrialization. Only in the years 1850–1900 did continental workers undergo this harsh process of urban acclimatization.

Housing

Life in industrial cities was, for almost all workers, uncomfortable at best and unbearably squalid at worst. Workers and their families lived in housing that failed to answer the needs of its inhabitants. In older cities single-family dwellings were broken up into apartments of often no more than one room per family. In new manufacturing centers, rows of tiny houses, located close by smoking factories, were built back-to-back, thereby eliminating any cross-ventilation or space for gardens. Whether housing was old or new, it was generally poorly built. Old buildings were allowed by landlords to fall into disrepair; new houses, constructed of cheap material, decayed quickly. Water often came from an outdoor tap, shared by several houses and adjacent to an outdoor toilet. Crowding was commonplace. Families of as many as eight lived in two or, at the most, three rooms. A newspaper account from the 1840s noted that in Leeds, a textile center in northern Britain, an "ordinary" worker's house contained no more than 150 square feet, and that in most cases those houses were "crammed almost to suffocation with human beings both day and night." When, after 1850, governments began to rid cities of some of their worst slums, many working-class men and women discovered that urban "improvement" meant relocation into dreary "model" tenements whose amenities were matched by their barracklike anonymity; or removal from one dilapidated structure to another in the wake of a clearance scheme—the nineteenth century called it "ventilation"—that replaced ancient, overcrowded housing with a more sanitary—and, for the landlord, more profitable—railway switching yard.

The life of women

The life of working-class wives and mothers was hard. Lack of cheap contraceptive devices and a belief that these devices were immoral helped to keep women pregnant through most of their childbearing years, thus endangering their general health and adding to the burden of their lives. Wives were usually handed a portion of the weekly wage packet by their husbands, and were expected to house, feed, and clothe the family on the very little they were given. Their daily life was a constant round of cooking, cleaning, shopping, and washing—in a tiny space and without enough money. Housewives could not rely, as in the country, on their own gardens to help supply them with

Nineteenth-Century Working-Class Housing. Faced with insatiable demands for urban accommodations, developers responded in a variety of ways. In Oldham (top left), a textile manufacturing center in the north of England, the answer was street after street of row houses; in Glasgow, Scotland (top right), it was multistory tenements; and in the suburbs of Paris (lower right), it was shanties. In all three settings, the result was essentially the same: a bleak existence born of overcrowding and squalor.

food. Instead, they went to markets that catered to their needs with cheap goods, often stale or nearly rotten, or dangerously adulterated. Formaldehyde was added to milk to prevent spoilage. Pounded rice was mixed into sugar. Fine brown earth was introduced into cocoa. A woman's problems were compounded, of course, when she had to work, and therefore had far less time to accomplish the household tasks she was still expected to perform.

Women were employed in growing numbers—along with children—in factories during the nineteenth century. Yet many more

A Laundress and Her Children. Note the cramped and cluttered living quarters.

Women workers

labored at home or in small workshops—"sweatshops," as they came to be called—for wretchedly low wages based not on the hours they worked but on the amount of work they did: so much per shirt stitched or matchbox glued. By far the greatest number of unmarried working-class young women worked as domestic servants, often a lonely occupation and one that occasionally trapped female servants into undesired sexual relationships with their male employers or their sons.

Sexuality

Female sexuality within the working classes of western Europe was acknowledged in a way that it was not within the middle class. Demographic evidence reveals a sharp rise in illegitimacy between 1750 and 1850. In Frankfurt, Germany, for example, where the illegitimacy rate had been a mere 2 percent in the early 1700s, it reached 25 percent in 1850. In Bordeaux, France, in 1840, one-third of the recorded births were illegitimate. Reasons for this increase are difficult to establish. Illegitimacy in Germany may have been the result of laws forbidding the poor to marry. Certainly, increased mobility meant weaker family ties, less parental supervision, and greater opportunity for an unrestricted life. This is not to say that the majority of working-class women were sexually promiscuous. Premarital intercourse was an accepted practice in preindustrial villages, but, because of the social controls that dominated village life, it was almost always a precursor to marriage. In the far more anonymous setting of a factory town, such control often did not exist. In addition, the economic uncertainties of the early industrial age meant that a young workingman's promise of marriage based on his expectation of a job might frequently be difficult to fulfill. The same economic uncertainty led some young working-class women to a career—usually temporary—as prostitutes. The anonymity of city life encouraged prostitution. Middle-class men, prepared to postpone marriage until they could afford a house and furnishings reflecting the social position to which they aspired, turned to the sexual underworld to satisfy their desires. Class consciousness encouraged them to regard working-class women— prostitutes or not—as easy prey, possessed of coarser natures and therefore a lesser breed of womankind than the middle-class "ladies" they intended eventually to marry.

New cities could be lonely places, particularly for working-class men and women struggling to cope with an alien environment. If possible, they would live near relatives who had already made the transition and who could assist the newcomers in adjusting to their very different existence. In many cities working-class families lived in districts inhabited primarily by others working at the same trade— weavers in one place, miners in another—and in this way achieved some sense of commonality.

Loneliness

Adjustment to the demands of the factory was every bit as difficult for workers as was acceptance of urban living patterns. The factory system, emphasizing as it did standard rather than individual work patterns, denied skilled laborers the pride in craft that had previously been theirs. Many workers found themselves stripped of the reassuring protection of guilds and formal apprenticeships which had bound their predecessors to a particular trade or place, and which were outlawed or sharply curtailed by legislation in France, Germany, and Britain in the first half of the nineteenth century. Factory hours were long, before 1850 usually twelve to fourteen hours a day. Conditions were dirty and dangerous. Textile mills remained unventilated, so that bits of material lodged in workers' lungs. Machines were unfenced and were a particular danger to child workers, often hired, because of their supposed agility, to clean under and around the moving parts. Manufacturing processes were unhealthy. The use of poison lead in the making of glazed pottery, for example, was a constant hazard to men and women workers in that industry. Surveys by British physicians in the 1840s catalogued the toll that long factory hours and harsh working conditions were taking, particularly on young workers. Spinal curvature and other bone malformations resulted from standing hour after hour in unnatural positions at machines. Varicose veins and fallen arches were also common. One concerned doctor stated his belief that "from what I saw myself, a large mass of deformity has been produced by the factory system." And what was true of factories was true as well of mines, in which over fifty thousand children and young people were employed in Britain in 1841. Children were used to haul coal to underground tramways or shafts. The youngest were set to work—often for as long as twelve hours at a stretch—operating doors which regulated the ventilation in the mines. When they fell asleep, which, because of long hours, they frequently did, they jeopardized the safety of the entire workforce. Women—sometimes pregnant women—were employed to haul coal and perform other strenuous underground tasks. Lung diseases—popularly known as "black spit-

*Conditions in factories and
mines*

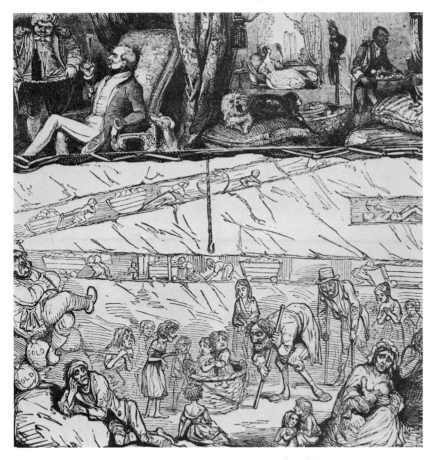

"Capital and Labour." In its earliest years, *Punch,* though primarily a humorous weekly, manifested a strong social conscience. In this 1843 cartoon, the capitalists are seen revelling in the rewards of their investments while the workers— men, women, and children— who toiled in the mines under cruel and dangerous conditions are found crippled and starving.

tle"—and eye infections, not to mention the constant danger of explosions caused by trapped gas, were constant threats to life and limb in the mines.

Daily routine

As upsetting as the physical working conditions was the psychological readjustment demanded of the first-generation workers in the factories. Preindustrial laborers had to work long hours and for very little monetary reward. Yet, at least to some degree, they were free to set their own hours and structure their own activities, to move from their home workshops to their small garden plots and back again as they wished. In a factory, all "hands" learned the discipline of the whistle. To function efficiently, a factory demanded that all employees begin and end work at the same time. Most workers could not tell time; fewer possessed clocks. None was accustomed to the relentless pace of the machine. In order to increase production, the factory system encouraged the breaking down of the manufacturing process into specialized steps, each with its own assigned time, an innovation that upset workers accustomed to completing a task at their own pace. The employment of women and children was a further disturbing innovation. In preindustrial communities, women and children had worked, as well as men, but more often than not, all together and at home. In factory towns women and children were frequently hired instead of men: they could be paid less and were declared to be easier to manage. When this happened, the pattern of family life was severely disrupted, and a further break with tradition had to be endured. It is no wonder that workers began to see machinery itself as the tyrant that had changed their lives and bound them to a kind of industrial slavery. A radical working-class song written in Britain in the 1840s expressed the feeling: "There is a king and a ruthless king;/ Not a king of the poet's dream;/ But a tyrant fell, white slaves know well,/ And that ruthless king is steam."

Faced with a drastic reordering of their lives, working-class men and women reacted in various ways. Some sought "the shortest way out of Manchester" by taking to drink (there were 1,200 public houses in that city in 1850). Many more men and women struggled to make some sort of community out of the street where they lived or the factory where they worked. It was a long and discouraging process. Yet by mid-century their experiences were beginning to make them conscious of themselves as different from and in opposition to the middle class that was imposing a new way of life on them.

Escape

5. THE MIDDLE-CLASS WORLDVIEW

The middle class was not unaware of the many social problems it was generating as it created an industrial society. Despite its confidence that the world was progressing—and at its own behest—the middle class was beset by uncertainties. Its belief in its own undoubted abilities was shadowed by concern as to whether its particular talents might ultimately prove irrelevant to the preservation of prosperity. Self-assurance could dissolve in the face of bankruptcy, and prosperity vanish in the abyss of economic catastrophe. Those who had risen by their own exertions might fall victim to someone else's ambitions. Nor was it always a simple matter for the middle class to reconcile its own affluence with the poverty of the thousands of workers exploited under its aegis. The middle class was responsible for having wrenched European society out of old patterns of living and thrust it into new ones. To those willing to acknowledge that responsibility, the realization was enough to temper confidence with apprehension. No one was certain what the factory system and urbanization might eventually produce. Evidence drawn from the reports of various official commissions and from the intentionally lurid writings of sensational journalists suggested that city life was already spawning an underclass of men and women who preferred a life of promiscuity and criminality to one of honest toil. French novelists began to use the sewers as a metaphor to describe the general condition of urban existence for what was assumed to be a vast number of Parisians. Poverty and crime were linked together in the public—middle-class—mind, until poverty itself began to be defined as criminal. All this was part of a middle-class

Uncertainty and the need for reassurance

The Interior of the Crystal Palace. This building of iron and glass was constructed to house exhibits sent to the Exhibition of the Works of Industry of All Nations, held in London in 1851. The exhibition celebrated the triumph of middle-class industrialization.

compulsion to rationalize its own prosperity, and to legitimize its ascendancy over the urban working poor.

To assist themselves in constructing this congenial worldview, the members of the new industrial middle class made use of the theories of a number of political economists. It is important to recognize that a factory-owner or a banker was not likely to have read the works of these theorists. He might, however, have encountered popular journalistic condensations of their ideas, or have participated in discussions at which the conclusions, if not the reasoned arguments, of the economists were aired. Because those conclusions supported his own interests, he grew familiar with them, until, in time, he could talk of the ideas of these men as if they were his own.

Political economics and the worldview

We have noted already the manner in which the ideas of the economist Adam Smith sustained middle-class respect for individual enterprise. Enlightenment thought in general had extolled the virtues of individualism. John Locke, for example, celebrated the reason in men and women that allowed them to make intelligent choices based upon their own enlightened self-interest. Arguments such as these were reinforced by a second generation of economists—particularly the Englishmen Thomas Malthus (1766–1834)and David Ricardo (1772–1823)—whose writings embodied principles appealing to businessmen who desired a free hand to remake the economies of their countries. The chief elements in the theories of these economists were:

Classical economics

(1) Economic individualism. Individuals are entitled to use for their own best interests the property they have inherited or acquired by any legitimate method. People must be allowed to do what they like so

long as they do not trespass upon the equal right of others to do the same.

(2) Laissez-faire. The functions of the state should be reduced to the lowest minimum consistent with public safety. The government should shrink itself into the role of a modest policeman, preserving order and protecting property, but never interfering with the operation of economic processes.

(3) Obedience to natural law. There are immutable laws operating in the realm of economics as in every sphere of the universe. Examples are the law of supply and demand, the law of diminishing returns, and so on. These laws must be recognized and respected; failure to do so is disastrous.

(4) Freedom of contract. Individuals should be free to negotiate the best kind of contract they can obtain from any other individual. In particular, the liberty of workers and employers to bargain with each other as to wages and hours should not be hampered by laws or by the collective power of labor unions.

Thomas Malthus

(5) Free competition and free trade. Competition serves to keep prices down, to eliminate inefficient producers, and to ensure the maximum production in accordance with public demand. Therefore, no monopolies should be tolerated, nor any price-fixing laws for the benefit of incompetent enterprises. Further, in order to force each country to engage in the production of those things it is best fitted to produce, all protective tariffs should be abolished. Free international trade will also help to keep prices down.

Businessmen naturally warmed to theories so congenial to their own desires and intentions. But Malthus and Ricardo made further contributions to the middle-class worldview, based upon their perceptions of conflicting interests within society. Malthus, in his controversial *Essay on Population,* first published in 1798, argued that nature had set stubborn limits to the progress of mankind. Because of the voracity of the sexual appetite there was a natural tendency for population to increase more rapidly than the supply of food. To be sure, there were powerful checks, such as war, famine, disease, and vice; but these, when they operated effectively, further augmented the burden of human misery. It followed that poverty and pain were inescapable. Even if laws were passed distributing all wealth equally, the condition of the poor would be only temporarily improved; in a very short time they would begin to raise larger families, with the result that the eventual state of their class would be as bad as the earlier. In the second edition of his work, Malthus advocated postponement of marriage as a means of relief, but he continued to stress the danger that population would outrun any possible increase in the means of subsistence.

Malthus on population

Malthus's arguments allowed the middle class to acquiesce in the destruction of an older society which had made some attempt to care for its poor. In England, for example, officials in rural parishes had instituted a system of doles and subsidized wages to help sustain laborers and their families when unemployed. The attempt failed to prevent distress and was met with increasing resistance by taxpayers. Now Malthus told taxpayers that schemes designed to help the poor damaged both rich and poor alike. Poor relief took money, and therefore food, from the mouths of the more productive members of society and put it into the mouths of the least productive. Malthus helped shift the responsibility for poverty from society to the individual, a shift appealing to the middle class, which wished to be freed from the burden of supporting the urban unemployed.

Malthusian assumptions played a large role in the development of the theories of the English economist Ricardo. According to Ricardo, wages seek a level which is just sufficient to enable workers "to subsist and perpetuate their race, without either increase or diminution." This Ricardo held to be an inescapable iron law. If wages should rise temporarily above the subsistence standard, men and women would be encouraged to marry earlier and produce more children, the population would increase, and the ensuing competition for jobs would quickly force the rate of pay down to its former level. Ricardo devised a law of rent as well as a law of wages. He maintained that rent is determined by the cost of production on the poorest land that must be brought under cultivation, and that, consequently, as a country's population increases and more land is cultivated, and higher rents charged for more productive land, an ever-increasing proportion of the national income is absorbed by landlords.

Here again, a theorist provided arguments useful to the middle class in its attempt to define and defend itself within a new social order. The law of wages gave employers a useful weapon to protect themselves from their workers' petitions for higher pay. The law of rent justified middle-class opposition to the continuing power of landed interests: a class which derived its income not from hard work but simply from its role as rent-collector was profiting unfairly at the expense of the rest of society and deserved to have its profit-making curtailed.

As soon as the middle class began to argue in this fashion, however, it betrayed its devotion to the doctrine of laissez-faire. Businessmen and entrepreneurs vehemently opposed to government intervention, which might deny them the chance to make as much money as they could, were nevertheless prepared to see the government step in and prevent profiteering landlords from making what *they* could from their property. How could this apparent inconsistency be justified? The answer lay in the theories of the Englishman Jeremy Bentham (1748–1832), without doubt among the most influential of middle-class apologists. Bentham, whose major work, *The Principles of Morals and Legislation,* was published in 1789, argued against the eighteenth-century notion that a satisfactory theory of social order could be grounded in a belief in the natural harmony of human interests. Men and women were basically selfish beings. To suppose that a stable and beneficent society could emerge unassisted from a company of self-interested egos was, Bentham believed, to suppose the impossible. Society, if it was to function properly, needed an organizing principle that would both acknowledge humanity's basic selfishness and at the same time compel people to sacrifice at least a portion of their own interests for the good of the majority. That principle, called utilitarianism, stated that every institution, every law, must be measured according to its social usefulness. And a socially useful law was one that produced the greatest happiness of the greatest number. If a law passed this test, it could remain on the books; if it failed, it should be abandoned forthwith, no matter how venerable. A selfish man would accept this social yardstick, realizing that in the long run he would do himself serious harm by clinging to laws that might benefit him, but produce such general unhappiness as to result in disruptions detrimental to his own interests as well as to those of others.

Jeremy Bentham

In what ways did this philosophy particularly appeal to the industrial middle classes? First, it acknowledged the importance of the individual. The interests of the community were nothing more than the sum of the interests of those selfish egos who lived within it. Each individual best understood his or her own interests, and was therefore best left free, whenever possible, to pursue those interests as he or she saw fit. Only when they conflicted with the interests—the happiness—of the greatest number were they to be curtailed. Entrepreneurs could understand this doctrine as a license to proceed with the business of industrialization, since, they argued, industrialization was so clearly producing happiness for the majority of the world's population. At the same time, Bentham's doctrines could be used to justify those changes necessary to bring an industrial world into being. Was the greatest happiness produced, English factory-owners might ask, by an antiquated electoral system that denied representation to growing industrial cities? Obviously not. Let Parliament reform itself so that the weight of the manufacturing interests could be felt in the drafting of legislation.

Utilitarianism's appeal to the middle class

Utilitarianism was thus a doctrine that could be used to cut two ways—in favor of laissez-faire; in favor of governmental intervention. And the middle class proceeded to cut both ways at once. Benthamite utilitarianism provided the theoretical basis for many of the middle-class interventionist reforms, such as a revised poor law in Britain and an expanded educational system in France, achieved between 1815 and 1848.[1] At the same time utilitarianism, combined with the theories of Malthus and Ricardo, fortified the position of those businessmen who believed that unfettered individualism had produced the triumphs of the Industrial Revolution. To restrain that individualism was to jeop-

Individualism and intervention

[1] These and other similar reforms will be discussed in the following chapter.

ardize the further progress of industrialization and hence the greatest happiness of the greatest number.

In arguing as it did, the middle class relied upon the conviction that industrialization and the factory system were together showering benefits on all—not just themselves. As we shall see, there were those who disagreed, who pressed, for example, for regulation of factory wages and hours. But the capitalists claimed intervention would inhibit the distribution of those benefits, and hence the proliferation of general happiness. In their support they could cite the English economist Nassau Senior, who claimed that the net profit of any industrial enterprise was derived solely from its last hour of daily operation. Reduce working hours, said Senior, and you eliminate profits, thereby compelling factories to close and workers to starve. The members of the middle class believed Senior because it was clearly in their interest to do so. They also believed him because the enterprise upon which they were embarked was so new and so uncharted that it was hard to prove him wrong. Their uncertainty led them to believe those theories that provided them with the most reassurance and encouraged them to think that what they were doing was of benefit to their fellow men.

Political economists and philosophers in France as well as in England helped provide the new middle class with a congenial worldview. Count Claude de Saint-Simon (1760–1825), while a proponent of utopian schemes for social reorganization, nevertheless preached the gospel of "industrialism" and "industrialists" (two words which he coined). Disciples of Saint-Simon were among the leading proponents in France of industrial entrepreneurship and a standardized and centralized financial system.

Auguste Comte

Far more generally influential was the Positivist philosophy of Auguste Comte (1798–1857). Comte's philosophy, like utilitarianism, insisted that all truth is derived from experience or observation of the physical world. Comte rejected metaphysics as utterly futile; no one can discover the hidden essences of things—why events happen as they do, or what is the ultimate meaning and goal of existence. All one can really know is how things happen, the laws that control their occurrence, and the relations existing between them. Positivism derived its name from the assertion that the only knowledge of any current value was "positive," or scientific, knowledge. Comte argued that humankind's ability to analyze society scientifically and to predict its future had reached a point that would soon enable Europe to achieve a "positive" society, organized not in terms of belief but in terms of facts. Such an achievement would not be a simple matter, however; "positive" attitudes and institutions could not replace those of the "metaphysical" stage through which Europe had just passed without a struggle. By dividing the history of the world into progressive stages (a "religious" stage had preceded the "metaphysical"), and by declaring that the achievement of the highest stage was not possible without the turmoil of industrialization, Comte assured the middle class of its leading role in the better world that was to be.

6. EARLY CRITICS OF THE MIDDLE-CLASS WORLDVIEW

The middle-class worldview did not go unchallenged. Many writers deplored the social disintegration they saw as the legacy of the Industrial Revolution. Others criticized the materialism and hypocrisy they saw as the hallmarks of the middle class. The Scot Thomas Carlyle (1795–1881), though a defender of the French Revolution and a believer in the need for a new aristocracy of industrialists ("captains of industry"), had nothing but contempt for the theories of the utilitarians. In Carlyle's view, they did no more than excuse the greed and acquisitiveness of the new middle class. Equally scathing in his attacks on the middle class was the English novelist Charles Dickens (1812–1870). In such novels as *Oliver Twist, Hard Times,* and *Dombey and Son,* he wrote with sympathy of the tyrannization of industrial workers by the new rich. In France, the Abbé Felicité Lamennais (1782–1854), though preaching respect for private property, nevertheless attacked self-interest. He argued, in his *Book of the People,* that the "little people" of the world enjoyed far too small a share in the direction of their lives. Honoré de Balzac (1799–1850) wrote *The Human Comedy* to expose the stupidity, greed, and baseness of the middle class. Gustave Flaubert (1821–1880), in his foremost novel *Madame Bovary,* depicted the banal, and literally fatal, nature of bourgeois existence for women.

One of the most trenchant critics of early industrialization was the English philosopher and economist John Stuart Mill (1806–1873). Mill's father had been a close disciple of Bentham, and his son began his adult life a convinced utilitarian. A severe psychological crisis in early manhood compelled him to modify his acceptance of classical economic theory. First, he rejected the universality of economic laws. Though he admitted that there are unchangeable laws governing production, he insisted that the distribution of wealth could be regulated by society for the benefit of the majority of its members. Second, he advocated radical departures from the doctrine of laissez-faire. He favored legislation, under certain conditions, for shortening the working day, and he believed that the state might properly take preliminary steps toward the redistribution of wealth by taxing inheritances and by appropriating the unearned increment of land. In the fourth book of his *Principles of Political Economy* he urged the abolition of the wage system and looked forward to a society of producers' cooperatives in which the workers would own the factories and elect the managers to run them. On the other hand, Mill was no socialist. He distrusted the state; his real reason for advocating producers' cooperatives was not to exalt the power of the workers but to give them the fruits of

John Stuart Mill

The Greek Slave by Hiram Powers. The art of the bourgeoisie: titilation combined with a moral lesson.

See color plates facing page 801 for *The Gleaners* by Millet and the *Funeral at Ornans* by Courbet

their labor. In 1859 he wrote what many consider the classic defense of individual freedom, *On Liberty,* in which he attacked what he called "the tyranny of the majority." Yet his ringing defense of individualism was as much a treatise against middle-class conformism as it was against the threat of state control. "If all mankind were of one opinion," Mill wrote, "and only one person were of the contrary opinion, mankind would be no more justified in silencing that one person than he, if he had the power, would be justified in silencing mankind." Those sentiments were not the sort to appeal particularly to a society determined to define itself in accordance with rigid behavioral patterns and codes of conduct.

Artists, too, attacked the values of industrial society in their painting and sculpture. The art preferred by the European middle class in the nineteenth century was that which in some way either told a story or, better still, preached a message. Beauty was surface decoration, which could be admired for its intrinsic richness and for what it therefore declared about its owner's wealth. Or beauty was a moralism, easily understood and, if possible, reassuring. When the Great Exhibition of the Works of Industry in All Nations was held at the Crystal Palace in London in 1851 to celebrate the triumph of industrialism, one of the most popular exhibits was *The Greek Slave,* a statue by the American sculptor Hiram Powers. Depicting a young Christian woman stripped bare and standing, according to the catalogue, before the gaze of an Eastern potentate, the work allowed its Victorian male admirers a chance to relish its salaciousness, while at the same time profiting from its depiction of the woman's righteous disdain for her captor.

Some of the artists most critical of the middle class, while repudiating the artificial and decorative, nevertheless reflected the middle-class obsession with art as morality. The self-designated Pre-Raphaelite Brotherhood of English painters was a group of men and women, led by the painter-poet Dante Gabriel Rossetti (1828–1882), determined to express its disdain for contemporary values. They called themselves Pre-Raphaelites as a way of announcing their admiration for the techniques of early Renaissance artists, untainted, supposedly, by corrupted artistic taste. Yet the works of the leading members of the Brotherhood exuded a degree of sentimentality that compromised their rebel nature and rendered them conventionally pietistic and ultimately innocuous as social protest. The same can be said, to a lesser degree, of the work of the Frenchman Jean-François Millet (1814–1875). His *Man with the Hoe* is a stark, bitter statement about peasant life; his *The Angelus* softens the statement to sentiment. In both England and France, however, some of the most talented painters seriously questioned many of the values the middle class revered. Gustave Courbet (1819–1877) and Honoré Daumier (1808–1879) both expressed sympathy toward the plight of the French working class, contrasting scenes of rural and urban misfortune with unflattering caricatures of the bourgeoisie. Daumier, in particular, was a powerful satirist of social

The Angelus by Jean-François Millet. The artist's peasants accept their humble lot in this sentimental portrayal.

and political evils, ridiculing the corruption of petty officials and the hypocritical piety of the rich. There was a harsh bite to most of the work of Daumier and Courbet that proscribed sentimentalizing.

These writers and artists, while critical of the Industrial Revolution and middle-class values, proposed nothing very tangible in the way of radical reform. If they opposed the triumph of a materialistic middle class, they opposed, as well, the idea of complete democracy. Carlyle, in particular, criticized the present by comparing it with a rosy past that had never been. In this he was like one of the doughtiest critics of the new middle-class society, the Englishman William Cobbett (1763–1835). Cobbett, in his newspaper the *Political Register,* argued against industrialization itself as well as its effects. His propaganda mirrored the dilemma most critics had to face, in asking the question: Granted industrialization has brought great social and economic hardship in its train, does this mean that we should try to return to the life of preindustrial society, also often harsh, and always confining, though probably more secure?

Past or present?

For some time, a small band of thinkers had been answering that question with a resounding "no." They argued that there could be no return to old times and old ways, but that society could be at the same time both industrial and humane. These radical thinkers were often explicitly utopian. Two of the most persuasive were the Englishman Robert Owen (1771–1858) and the Frenchman Charles Fourier (1772–1837). Owen, himself the proprietor of a large cotton factory at New Lanark in Scotland, argued against the middle-class belief that the profit motive should be allowed to shape social and economic organization. Having reorganized his own mills to provide free schooling and a system of social security for his workers, he proceeded to advocate a general reorganization of society on the basis of

Utopian thinkers

The Third Class Carriage by Honoré Daumier. Daumier's realism did not mask his sympathy with the condition of the common people of France.

Louis Blanc

cooperation, with communities rewarding workers solely as a result of their actual labor. Fourier urged an even more far-reaching reconstitution, including the abolition of the wage system and the complete equality of the sexes. The numerous followers of Owen and Fourier sought escape from the confusions of the contemporary world in idealist communities founded according to the principles of their leaders. All these attempts failed after a time, victims of faulty leadership and, in the case of Fourierist communities in France, of charges of moral turpitude resulting from Fourier's revolutionary sexual doctrines.

Less utopian radical theories were proposed during the 1840s, years which witnessed recurring economic depressions and their horrifying consequences. The French politician and journalist Louis Blanc (1811–1882), stood, like many contemporary critics, against the competitiveness of the new industrial society and particularly opposed the exploitation of the working class. His solution was to campaign for universal male suffrage, which would give working-class men control of the state. Following their triumph, these workers would make the state the "banker of the poor" and institute "Associations of Production"—actually a system of workshops governed by workers—which would guarantee jobs and security for all. Once these associations became established, private enterprise would wither through competition, and with it the state, for which there would no longer be any need. As we shall see, these workshops were briefly instituted in Paris during the Revolution of 1848. Another Frenchman, Pierre Proudhon (1809–1865), condemned the profits accruing to employers at the expense of their employees. He, too, proposed new institutions, which he argued could be made to produce goods at a price fairer to the worker, a price based solely on the amount of labor devoted to the manufacture of any particular product.

The theories of the writers and thinkers whom we have been considering—both the defenders and the opponents of the middle-class industrial world—are historically important for two reasons. First, their ideas helped men and women better understand the new social order that had sprung up following the French and Industrial Revolutions, and the part they might play, as members of a class, in that new order. Second, the ideas themselves helped inspire the concrete political, social, and economic changes and events that are the subject of the next two chapters.

SELECTED READINGS

• *Items so designated are available in paperback editions.*

Banks, J. A., *Prosperity and Parenthood: A Study of Family Planning among the Victorian Middle Classes,* London, 1954. Relates middle-class financial pressures to family limitation.

Bridenthal, Renate, and Claudia Koonz, eds., *Becoming Visible: Women in European History,* Boston, 1976. Essays on the slowly changing role of women in society.

Briggs, Asa, *Victorian Cities,* New York, 1963. A survey of British cities, stressing middle-class attitudes toward the new urban environment.

• Burn, W. L., *The Age of Equipoise,* London, 1964. A charming account of the mid-Victorian years.

• Chevalier, Louis, *Laboring Classes and Dangerous Classes During the First Half of the Nineteenth Century,* New York, 1973. An intriguing though controversial study of the quality of life in Paris between 1815 and 1848 which concludes that social mobility was downward and that fear of crime dominated middle-class social consciousness.

• Halévy, Elie, *The Growth of Philosophic Radicalism,* rev. ed., London, 1949. The best introduction to the thought of Malthus, Ricardo, Bentham, and their philosophical heirs.

———, *England in 1815,* London, 1949. The classic work by the greatest historian of nineteenth-century England.

• Hammond, J. L., and Barbara Hammond, *The Town Labourer, 1760–1832,* London, 1917. An impassioned account of the economic changes that affected the quality of life of the English worker.

Heilbroner, Rober L., *The Worldly Philosophers,* New York, 1967. An introduction to the thought of economic liberals.

Hobsbawn, Eric, *The Age of Capital, 1848–1875,* London, 1975. A perceptive world survey which traces the global triumph of capitalism and its impact on the working class, written from a Marxist perspective.

———, *Labouring Men: Studies in the History of Labour,* London, 1964. A series of essays on workers and the working class in England.

• Hobsbawn, Eric, and George Rudé, *Captain Swing: A Social History of the Great English Agricultural Uprising of 1830,* New York, 1975. Analyzes the formation of a rural working-class consciousness.

• Houghton, Walter, *The Victorian Frame of Mind, 1830–1870,* New Haven, 1957. An outstanding synthesis of Victorian middle-class mentality.

• Langer, William L., *Political and Social Upheaval, 1832–1852,* New York,

1969. Comprehensive survey of European history, with excellent analytical chapters and thorough bibliographies.

McLaren, Angus, *Sexuality and Social Order: The Debate over the Fertility of Women and Workers in France,* New York, 1982. Examines the relationship between private and public morality.

Manuel, Frank E., *The Prophets of Paris,* Cambridge, Mass., 1962. An entertaining introduction to the philosophers of progress, from Turgot to Comte.

• Rostow, W. W., *The Stages of Economic Growth,* rev. ed., Cambridge, 1971. A synthesis by the exponent of the "take-off" theory of economic development.

• Rudé, George, *The Crowd in History, 1730–1848,* New York, 1964. A study of popular disturbances in France and England.

• Sewell, William, *Work and Revolution in France: The Language of Labor from the Old Regime to 1848,* Cambridge, 1980. Examines the mentalities of workers' organizations.

• Taylor, A. J. *The Standard of Living in Britain in the Industrial Revolution,* New York, 1975. A good introduction to the debate on the effects of industrialization.

Tilly, Charles, and Edward Shorter, *Strikes in France, 1830–1848,* New York, 1974. A valuable study of early continental class consciousness.

Tilly, Louise, and Joan W. Scott, *Women, Work and Family,* New York, 1978. Deals with women in nineteenth-century France and England.

• Thompson, E. P., *The Making of the English Working Class,* London, 1963. Argues that the coincidence of the French and Industrial Revolutions fostered the growth of working-class consciousness. A brilliant and important work.

Walker, Mack, *German Home Towns: Community, State and General Estate, 1648–1871,* Ithaca, N.Y., 1971. Attempts to explain the absence of a strong middle class in Germany.

• Zeldin, Theodore, *France, 1848–1945,* 2 vols., Oxford, 1973–1977. A highly individualistic synthesis of French history, remarkable for its scope and insight.

SOURCE MATERIALS

• Engels, Friedrich, *The Condition of the Working Class in England,* New York, 1958. A much criticized but reliable firsthand account by the later collaborator of Marx, written in 1844. Presents a devastating portrait of living and working conditions, especially in Manchester.

• Malthus, Thomas R., *An Essay on the Principle of Population,* London, 1798 and 1803. Malthus's famous essay relating population growth and food production.

• Mayhew, Henry, *London Labor and the London Poor,* New York, 1968. A reprint of the 1851 edition; provides a fascinating view of the population and trades of London. A good factual companion to Dickens.

• Mill, John Stuart, *Autobiography,* London, 1873. The intellectual coming-of-age of one of England's major nineteenth-century figures.

• ———, *On Liberty,* London, 1859. The classic defense of individual freedom.

Owen, Robert, *A New View of Society,* London, 1813. A proposed utopian society based on cooperative villages by the founder of British socialism.

Chapter 22

THE RISE OF LIBERALISM (1815–1870)

The general thought, the hope of France, has been order and liberty reuniting under constitutional monarchy.

— François Guizot, "Speech on the State of the Nation," 1831

The history of nineteenth-century Europe was to a great extent shaped by the interplay of the forces of liberalism and nationalism. The middle classes of France and England, where liberalism was strongest, espoused a set of doctrines reflecting their concerns and interests. Liberalism to them meant (1) an efficient government prepared to acknowledge the value of commercial and industrial development; (2) a government in which their interests would be protected by their direct representation in the legislature—in all probability, a constitutional monarchy, and most certainly not a democracy; (3) a foreign policy of peace and free trade; and (4) a belief in individualism and the doctrines of the classical economists.

The components of liberalism

Many middle-class men and women in other European countries shared these beliefs and assumptions, and worked diligently and with some success to carry through specific liberal reforms. But for them, an equally important and often more immediate objective was the achievement of some form of national unity. The middle classes in Germany, Italy, Poland, and the Austrian Empire, however dedicated they were to liberalism, believed that their chances of achieving liberal goals would be greatly enhanced if they could unify the patchwork of principalities that surrounded them into a vigorous, "modern" nation-state. In this chapter, we shall examine the phenomenon of liberalism, primarily as it affected the fortunes of England and France. In the following chapter, we shall describe the way in which liberalism combined with nationalism to reshape the history of central Europe.

The compulsion of nationalism

1. CONSERVATIVE REACTION, 1815–1830

The growth of liberalism occurred, in part, as a reaction to the conservative policies adopted by frightened governments anxious to restore domestic and international order following the Napoleonic wars. For a period of about fifteen years after 1815 the rulers of most European countries did their best to stem the advance of middle-class liberalism. In most instances, however, their repressive policies only made liberals more determined than ever to succeed. The primary concern of governments was to ensure that Europe would never again fall prey to the sort of revolutionary upheavals which it had experienced during the preceding quarter-century.

Following Napoleon's final defeat at Waterloo in 1815, the major powers reconfirmed the Vienna settlement in the hope that their efforts might result in a permanently stable "Concert of Europe." To further ensure an end to revolutionary disturbances, they formed the Quadruple Alliance—Britain, Austria, Prussia, and Russia; when France was admitted as a fifth member in 1818 it became the Quintuple Alliance. Its members pledged to cooperate in the suppression of any disturbances that might arise from attempts to overthrow legitimate governments or to alter international boundaries. At the same time, Tsar Alexander, his mystic nature now in the ascendant, persuaded the allies to join him in the declaration of another alliance—a "Holy Alliance"—dedicated to the precepts of justice, Christian charity, and peace. The only result of this second league was to confuse Europe's leaders as to Alexander's intentions. Was he a liberal—a Jacobin even, as Metternich feared—or a reliable conservative? The confusion was cleared away, as in one country after another, liberal uprisings were stifled by stern repressive policies of the allied governments, Alexander's among them.

Attacks against reactionary governments in Naples and in Spain brought the allies scurrying to a conference at Troppau in Austria in 1820. Secret brotherhoods of young liberals, many of them army officers, had spearheaded these revolts. These organizations, which originated in Italy, called themselves *Carbonari*. They were an active counterreactionary force, whose influence spread throughout Europe in the early 1820s. In both Naples and Spain, they succeeded in forcing the kings to take oaths to establish constitutions modeled on the liberal French constitution of 1789–1791. At Troppau, Austria, Prussia, and Russia reacted to these threats to international order and absolutism by pledging to come to each other's aid to suppress revolution. France and Britain declined to endorse the pledge, not so much because they opposed repression, but because they did not wish to curtail their freedom of action by binding themselves to detailed international treaties. Metternich nevertheless proceeded, with Russian and Prussian concurrence, in a repression of the *Carbonari* rebels through imprisonment or exile.

Two years later, in 1822, another congress was convened at Verona, this one to deal with the continuing liberal threat to stability in Spain, with the series of revolutions occurring in Spanish colonies in South America, and with an insurrection in the Near East. To resolve the Spanish problem, the French dispatched an army of 200,000 men to the Iberian peninsula in 1823. Without much difficulty, this force put an end to the Spanish liberals, who opposed King Ferdinand VII's attempt to undermine representative government. The French assisted Ferdinand in restoring his authority to rule as he pleased. Contrary to their experience in Spain, the defenders of the status quo were unable to succeed in stemming the move to independence and liberalism in the colonies of Central and South America. In 1823 President James Monroe of the United States issued the "Monroe Doctrine," which declared that attempts by European powers to intervene in the affairs of the New World would be looked upon as an unfriendly act by his government. Without British maritime support, the doctrine would have remained a dead letter. Britain was ready to recognize the independence of the South American republics, however, since as new countries they were prepared to trade with Britain instead of Spain. The British therefore used their navy to keep Spain from intervening to protect its vanishing empire.

Defying the congress system

In the Near East, a Greek soldier, Alexander Ypsilanti, was attempting to encourage the formation of a Greek "empire," to be constructed on vaguely liberal principles. In doing so, he had engaged his band of armed followers in battles against the Turks who ruled over Greece. Though Ypsilanti was soon defeated, his movement lived on. Five years later its aims had been narrowed to the more accessible goal of an independent Greece. Supported for reasons of Mediterranean naval strategy by a joint Anglo-French-Russian naval intervention, and by a Russian invasion of the Balkans, the rebels this time succeeded. Their success signaled the extent of changes that had occurred since the Congress of Verona. No longer could Metternich and other reactionaries build alliances on the assumption that, for the powers of Europe, preservation of the status quo was the major goal. Britain, in particular, could not be relied upon. There, by the late 1820s, the liberal movement was gaining momentum fast.

Rebellion in Greece

2. LIBERAL GAINS IN WESTERN EUROPE, 1815–1832

Liberal gains in Britain came after an era of reaction that paralleled that which occurred on the Continent. The conservative Tory party had enjoyed almost unbroken political supremacy since the younger William Pitt had become first minister in 1783. Though Pitt had begun

British politics

his career as something of a reformer, the French Revolution had turned him, along with his fellow Tories, into a staunch defender of the status quo. The Tories' political opponents, the Whigs, had throughout the long years of the revolutionary and Napoleonic conflicts remained to some degree conciliatory to the French. But Whigs were as unsympathetic as Tories to democratic notions and as defensive of their rights to the full fruits of their property.

Hence when rioting broke out in England after 1815 as a result of depression and consequent unemployment, there was general support among the ruling class for the repressive measures adopted by the British government. Spies were hired to ferret out evidence against popular agitators. In the industrial north, where conditions were particularly severe, radical members of the middle and working classes capitalized on the general unrest to press their demands for increased representation in Parliament. At Manchester a crowd of 80,000, demonstrating for political reform in St. Peter's Fields, was fired upon by soldiers. Eleven persons were killed and over 400 injured, including 113 women. The massacre was thereafter called "Peterloo" by British radicals: i.e., a domestic Waterloo. It was the first of several repressive measures taken by the government to stifle reform. Another was the legislation known as the Six Acts, which was passed by Parliament in 1819, and outlawed "seditious and blasphemous" literature; levied a stamp tax on newspapers; allowed the searching of houses for arms; and restricted the rights of public meeting.

Yet within a surprisingly short time British political leaders reversed their opposition to everything new. Instead, they displayed an ability to compromise which kept their country free from revolution. George Canning, the foreign minister, and Robert Peel, the home sec-

The Peterloo Massacre, 1819. A contemporary rendering of the shootings which condemned the "wanton and furious attack by that brutal armed force The Manchester & Cheshire Yeomanry Cavalry."

retary, son of a rich cotton manufacturer, were both sensitive to the interests of Britain's liberal-minded capitalist entrepreneurs. Under their direction, the government retreated from its commitment to the intransigent Quintuple Alliance; it was Canning who took the lead in recognizing the new South American republics. At home, these same politicians began to make order out of the inefficient tangle of British laws; for example, they abolished capital punishment for about a hundred different offenses. And Canning liberalized, though he did not abolish, the Corn Laws. These laws levied a tariff on the importation of cheap foreign grain. As such, they benefited English landlords, but hurt manufacturers, who had to pay higher wages to enable their workers to purchase more expensive bread. These "liberalizers" among the still essentially conservative Tories went so far as to abolish the laws that had kept both dissenting Protestants (members of Prostestant sects—Baptist, Congregationalist, Methodist—other than Anglican) and Roman Catholics from full participation in public political life.

What the conservatives would not do was reform the system of representation in the House of Commons, heavily weighted on the side of the landed interests. Here the Tories, the majority party in Parliament, drew the line and showed themselves still basically committed to the status quo. Yet members of the liberal middle class argued that such a reform was absolutely necessary before they could themselves play a constant and active role in shaping British policy to comply with their own interests. "Interest" was, indeed, the key word in the debate over parliamentary reform. For centuries Parliament had represented the interests of landowners, the major propertied class in England. About two-thirds of the members of the House of Commons were either directly nominated by or indirectly owed their election to the patronage of the richest landowners in the country. Many of the parliamentary electoral districts, or boroughs, which returned members to the House of Commons, were controlled by landowners who used the pressure of their local economic power—or, in many cases, outright bribery—to return candidates sympathetic to their interests. These were the "rotten" or "pocket" boroughs, so-called because they were said to be in the pockets of those men who controlled them. Those who favored the system as it was argued that it mattered little that electoral politics were corrupt, that electoral districts represented unequal numbers, or that very, very few (about one in a hundred) were enfranchised. What did matter, they claimed, was that the interests of the nation at large, which they perceived to coincide with the interests of landed property, were well looked after by a Parliament elected in this fashion.

Parliamentary reform

Of course the new industrial middle class did not agree with the arguments of the landowners. They insisted, for example, that the Corn Laws did not coincide with the nation's best interest. (If they were followers of the theories of Jeremy Bentham, they might argue that the Corn Laws did not produce "the greatest happiness of the

The middle class and reform

greatest number.") Rather, the Corn Laws worked only for the benefit of landlords, by keeping the price of grain high; and they worked to
the disinterest of everyone else. Therefore, said members of the middle class, Parliament must be reformed to represent not only landlords
but the interests of industrial England. It is important to note that the
liberal middle class was *not* arguing in favor of reform on the basis of a
belief in democracy. Some leaders within the emerging working class
did make this argument—and, as we shall see, continued to make it
after a reform bill was passed in 1832. Most of those who spoke in
favor of reform, however, declared that the middle class was capable
of representing the interests of the working class, as well as of itself, in
Parliament. Reformers took this position either because they believed
it, or because they were afraid of working-class representatives, or
because they realized that to favor direct representation for the working class would frighten the more timid reformers and hence defeat
their whole campaign.

A working-class alliance

Spurred by the example of liberal reformers on the Continent (see
below, p. 790) and by the oratory and organizational abilities of middle-class and artisan radicals at home, the movement for reform intensified after 1830. It was strong enough to topple the Tories and to
embolden the Whigs, under the leadership of Lord Grey, to make a
party issue of reform by introducing a bill to modify the ancient electoral structure of the country. The government was clearly frightened. Revolution, if it were ever to come in England, would come as
a result of the alliance now threatening between middle-class industrialists and the artisan/tradesman leadership of the new working class.
In Birmingham, a middle-class banker, Thomas Attwood, organized
a "Political Union of the Lower and Middle Classes of the People."
By July 1830, there were similar organizations in Glasgow, Manchester, Liverpool, Sheffield, Newcastle, and Coventry, some willing
to engage in bloody clashes with army units and police. Middle-class
shopkeepers declared their determination to withhold taxes and, if
necessary, to form a national guard. Plagued as well by an outbreak
of cholera, the country appeared to be on the verge of serious general
disorder, if not outright revolution. The king, William IV, wrote
worriedly to Lord Grey that "miners, manufacturers, colliers, and
labourers" appeared ready for some sort of open rebellion.[1] Sensing
the grave danger of a possible union of the working and middle classes,
the governing class once more accommodated to change, as it had in
the 1820s.

The Reform Bill of 1832

The Reform Bill of 1832, however, was not a retreat from the notion
of representation by interest. No attempt was made to create equal
electoral districts. The franchise, though increased, extended the vote
to no more than 3 percent of the total population. It was defined in

[1] Asa Briggs, *The Age of Improvement,* New York, 1959, p. 248.

terms of the amount of property owned and the length of time one had owned it. In the counties, for example, a man could vote if he paid at least ten pounds annual rental for land held on a long-term sixty-year lease. In other words, the vote was granted to the middle class, but to very few of the working class. Probably more significant than its extension of the franchise was the bill's scheme for a redistribution of seats. One hundred forty-three seats were reallocated, most of them from the rural south to the industrial north, thereby increasing representation in and around cities such as Manchester, Leeds, and Birmingham; and thereby increasing, in turn, the political power of the industrial middle classes. Though the bill was the product of change and itself brought change in its wake, it was understood as a conservative measure. It by no means destroyed the political strength of landed aristocratic interests, though it reduced that strength somewhat. And it preserved the notion of representation by interest. The liberal, industrial middle classes had been admitted into junior partnership with the landed oligarchy that had for centuries ruled Britain and was to rule it for at least one more generation.

Efforts to introduce liberal political reforms were not limited to Britain during this period. Across the world, in Russia, a group of army officers revolted, following the death of Tsar Alexander in 1825, in hopes of persuading his liberally minded brother, Constantine, to assume the throne and guarantee a constitution. In this case, however, the attempt at reform failed. Constantine was unwilling to usurp power from the rightful heir, a third brother, Nicholas. The officers, called Decembrists (because of the month of their rebellion) came from noble families and were members of elite regiments. Learned in the ways of the West, they had obtained a taste of life outside Russia during the Napoleonic wars, when they imbibed the ideas of the Enlightenment and the French Revolution. Politically, they ranged from constitutional monarchists to Jacobin republicans. Their failure was the consequence not only of repression by the tsar but also of their inability to attract mass support from rank and file peasant soldiers. Nicholas I (1825–1855) continued to rule in the severely autocratic ways Alexander had adopted toward the end of his life, creating the Third Section, a political police force, to prevent further domestic disorder. Nicholas's proclaimed goal of "Orthodoxy, Autocracy, and Nationality" meant simply that he would serve as god's lieutenant in an army in which the rest of his countrymen would labor as obedient foot soldiers. Yet even under Nicholas, perhaps Europe's most unremitting conservative, Russia evidenced signs of modernization. Bureaucracy, less dependent than in the past on the aristocracy, grew more centralized and more efficient. Laws were systematically codified in 1832. Stimulated by European demand for Russian grain, estates were reorganized for more effective production, and railways built to transport the grain to Western markets.

Liberalism and modernization in other parts of the West: Russia

France

For a time, autocracy threatened the liberal revolutionary and Napoleonic heritage in France. The upper middle class in France had remained generally content with the domestic settlement agreed upon by the major powers in 1814 and confirmed at the Congress of Vienna the following year. Louis XVIII, a clever yet self-indulgent man, had "granted" a "constitutional charter" upon his succession to the French throne. While refusing to deny himself absolute power in theory, in practice Louis XVIII had willingly enough agreed to support those principles most desired by French middle-class liberals: legal equality; careers open to talent; and a two-chamber parliamentary government, with the vote confined to property-holders. Yet by basing the franchise on age and property qualifications, which made it impossible for the vast majority of those born after 1789 to participate directly in the government of their country, Louis's charter divided France in a way that would contribute to eventual instability.

Charles X and the threat to liberalism

In 1824, Louis died and was succeeded by his brother Charles X (1824–1830). Charles was an honest, determined reactionary, who once declared that only he and Lafayette had not changed since 1789— Lafayette was still a liberal, Charles still a zealous monarchist. By his policies Charles immediately declared himself a foe of liberalism, modernization, and the general legacies of the revolutionary and Napoleonic eras. At his direction the French assembly voted indemnities to those aristocratic emigrés whose land had been confiscated by the state. The Church was allowed to reassert its traditionally exclusive right to teach in French classrooms. The upper middle class, strengthened by its role within the country's growing industrial economy, reacted by heading a rebellion against Charles's reactionary policies. In March 1830, members of the Chamber of Deputies, led by bankers, passed a vote of no confidence in the government. Charles dissolved the chamber, as he was constitutionally empowered to do, and called new elections for deputies. When those elections went against his candidates, Charles further retaliated by a series of ordinances, issued on his own authority, which (1) again dissolved the newly elected chamber before it had even met; (2) imposed strict censorship on the press; (3) further restricted suffrage so as to exclude the upper middle class almost completely; and (4) called for new elections.

The Revolution of 1830 in France

What Charles got in return for these measures was revolution. Led by republicans—workers, artisans, students, writers, and the like— Parisians took to the streets. For three days, in intense fighting behind hastily constructed barricades, they defied the army and the police, neither of which was anxious to fire into the crowds. Sensing the futility of further resistance, Charles abdicated. Those who had manned the barricades pressed for a genuine republic. But those with the power—bankers, merchants, and industrialists—wanted none of that. Instead they brought the duke of Orleans to the throne as King Louis Philippe (1830–1848) of *the French*—not of France—after extracting a promise from him to abide by the constitution of 1814 which had

The July Revolution of 1830 in Paris. Workers construct street barricades to ward off government troops.

so suited their particular liberal needs. The franchise was extended, from about 100,000 to 200,000 males. But the right to vote was still based upon property ownership. The major beneficiaries of the change were members of the middle class, those whose interests the Revolution of 1830 primarily served.

Other countries in Europe caught the revolutionary fever in the summer of 1830. As we have already noted, middle- and working-class radicals in England were inspired by the French to press their own case for liberal reform. In Belgium, an insurrection that combined elements of liberal and national sentiment put an end to the union of that country with the Dutch, instituted by the Congress of Vienna. The European powers strengthened Belgium's political structure, and hence its independence, by agreeing to the accession as king of Leopold of Saxe-Coburg, uncle of the future Queen Victoria of England. Once again, a middle class had succeeded in establishing a constitutional monarchy to its liking, congenial to its liberal and entrepreneurial goals. No such fate awaited the liberal nationalists in Poland, who moved at this time to depose their ruler, the Russian Tsar Nicholas, whose hegemony extended to Poland as a result of the Vienna settlement of 1815. Western Europe did not intervene; Russian troops crushed the Polish liberal rebels, and Poland was merged into the tsarist empire.

Liberal revolts elsewhere

Liberal forces in Spain enjoyed a greater success. There, middle-class liberalism was linked to the attempts of Queen Maria Christina, widow of King Ferdinand VII, to secure the throne for her daughter, Isabella. Though no liberal herself, the queen was prepared to court

Spain

the favor of urban middle-class elites to win her struggle against her late husband's brother, the reactionary Don Carlos. During the so-called Carlist Wars, which lasted from 1834 to 1840, liberals extracted from Isabella II (1833–1868) a constitution that ensured them a strong voice in the legislature, while restricting the franchise in such a way as to keep the more radical lower middle and artisan classes at bay. By mid-century, however, fear of these radicals led the middle class to acquiesce in a government that was nothing more or less than an authoritarian dictatorship, but that did not threaten directly their own economic interests.

3. LIBERALISM IN BRITAIN AND FRANCE, 1830–1848

The Revolution of 1830 in France and the Parliamentary Reform Bill of 1832 in England represented a setback for aristocratic power in both countries. Aristocrats and their supporters did not cease overnight to play an active role in politics, however. Lord Palmerston, for example, was one of England's most influential prime ministers at mid-century and one of Europe's most authoritative arbiters. But no longer would it be possible for the legislatures of France and England to ignore the particular interests of the middle class. Henceforth representatives would include members from that class in sufficient numbers to press successfully for programs that accorded with liberal beliefs.

Decline of aristocratic power

One of the major accomplishments of the first British Parliament elected after 1832 was passage of a new law governing the treatment of paupers. In accordance with the law passed in 1598 under Elizabeth I, each parish in England had been declared responsible for the maintenance of its own poor, either through accommodation in poorhouses,

Liberal legislation in Britain: the new poor law

An English Workhouse for the Able-Bodied Poor. This workhouse in the county of Devon was built in the late 1830s.

or through a system of doles, coupled with local public employment programs. This system, although it by no means eliminated the debilitating effects of poverty, did provide a kind of guarantee against actual starvation. But by 1830 the system had broken down. Population growth and economic depressions had produced a far larger number of underemployed men and women in Britain than had ever before existed, placing tremendous strain upon those funds, levied as taxes, which each parish used to provide relief. Industrialization also demanded that families move in search of employment from one part of the country to another; yet the law as it stood provided assistance only to those who applied in the parish of their birth. The old law did not accord with liberal notions of efficiency; the new Parliament set about to amend it. The result, drafted by Jeremy Bentham's former private secretary, Edwin Chadwick, and passed almost without dissent, clearly reflected the liberal, middle-class notion of how to achieve "the greatest happiness of the greatest number." Doles were to cease forthwith. Those who could not support themselves were to be confined in workhouses. Here conditions were to be made so severe as to all but compel inmates to depart and accept either whatever work they might find outside, no matter how poorly paid, or whatever charity their friends and relatives might be able to provide them. Parishes were to be grouped together into more efficient unions; the law was to be administered by a central board of commissioners in London. Inspiring this new legislation were the liberal belief that poverty was a person's own fault and the liberal assumption that capitalism, though unregulated, was capable of providing enough jobs for all who genuinely wanted them. Economic depressions in the early 1840s proved that latter assumption false, and wrecked the tidy schemes of the poor-law administrators. Doles were once more instituted, taxes once more increased. Yet the law's failure did not shake the liberal conviction that poverty was, in the end, an individual and not an institutional problem.

Even more symbolic of the political power of Britain's middle class than the new poor law was the repeal of the Corn Laws in 1846. The laws, even after their modification in the 1820s, continued to keep the price of bread artificially high, forcing employers, in turn, to pay wages high enough to allow workers to keep food on their tables. More than that, the Corn Laws symbolized to the middle classes the unwarranted privileges of an ancient and, to their minds, generally useless order: the landed aristocracy. The campaign to accomplish repeal was superbly orchestrated and relentless. The Anti–Corn Law League, an organization of middle-class industrialists and their supporters, held large meetings throughout the north of England, lobbied members of Parliament, and, in the end, managed to persuade Sir Robert Peel, now prime minister, of the inevitability of their goal. They were aided, as well, by the potato famine in Ireland, whose exis-

Robert Peel

Repeal of the Corn Laws

Humanitarian reforms

Louis Philippe

tence argued in favor of ending restrictions against the importation of cheap foodstuffs. That Peel was willing to split the Tory—or as it was now coming to be called, Conservative—party to introduce repeal suggests the power of the middle class and its belief in the gospel of free trade.

Legislation during this period reflected other middle-class concerns, and in some cases, directly conflicted with the liberal doctrine of non-intervention. Many members of the urban middle class professed devotion to the tenets of Christianity, particularly that doctrine which argued that all human beings have within themselves a soul which they must work to preserve from sin for their eternal salvation. This belief in the ability of an individual to achieve salvation, which contradicted the older Calvinist doctrine of a predestined "elect," accorded well with more general middle-class notions about the importance of individualism and the responsibility of the individual for his or her own well-being. It produced legislation such as the abolition of the slave trade in British colonies (1833), and the series of Factory Acts, which set limits on the working hours for child labor and which, in 1847, culminated in the curtailment of the workday in some trades to ten hours. Evangelicals such as William Wilberforce, who was throughout his life an eloquent spokesman for enslaved blacks, and Lord Shaftesbury, who campaigned to end the employment of women and children in mines, maintained that individual souls could not find God when imprisoned in the overworked bodies of plantation slaves or factory operatives. They were joined by others who argued, simply, that to keep people tied to their work for as long as twelve or fourteen hours a day was both inhuman and unnecessary.

The religious issue affected educational reform as well. England had no comprehensive system of state education before 1870. What state support there was came, after the 1830s, in the form of government grants to schools managed by the Church of England. Any move to increase this support, however, met with the strong opposition of middle-class dissenters, who saw it as no more than an attempt by the religious Establishment to extend its influence over the young. Middle-class liberals thus found arguments for reform confusing. The laws of classical economics clashed with other prejudices and beliefs, pulling men and women in various directions at once. Their uncertainty mirrored the extent to which no one could discern a right course in this world of new difficulties and fresh options.

The years of Louis Philippe's reign in France were not so marked as those in England with significant reforms. In the first place, France was not confronted with anything like the same degree of rapid industrialization that was compelling legislative activity on a number of fronts in England. France had nothing to compare with the problems generated by the growth of urban manufacturing centers in the north of England. Though the Chamber of Deputies contained representatives from the upper middle class, they tended to be bankers and merchants, not industrialists. Some were willing to espouse the notion of free trade, though not with the general enthusiasm of their British counterparts, whose unrivaled position as the world's leading manufacturers gave them a vested interest in that cause. Under the succession of governments dominated by France's leading politician of the period, François Guizot (1787–1874), the French expanded their educational system, thereby further underwriting their belief in the liberal doctrine of a meritocracy, or careers open to talent. A French law of 1833 provided for the establishment of elementary schools in every village. Children of indigent parents were to receive a free education; all others would pay a modest fee. In addition, larger towns were to provide training schools for trade and industry, and departments, schools for teacher training. As a result, the number of pupils in France increased from about 2 million in 1831, to about 3.25 million in 1846. Little else of lasting importance was accomplished during the regime of Louis Philippe. Guizot became more and more an apologist for the status quo. Everyone was free, he argued, to rise to the upper middle class and thus to a position of political and economic power. His advice to those who criticized his complacency was: "enrich yourselves." Politicians followed his advice, finding in schemes for the modernization of Paris and the expansion of the railway system ample opportunities for graft. Louis Philippe did little to counteract the lifelessness and corruption that characterized his regime. Although he had played a minor part in the first stage of the revolution of 1789, he was no revolutionary. He did not have the dash and glamor of a Napoleon. He was a paunchy, fussy, and undistinguished person, easily caricatured by his enemies. He appeared to most to be nothing more or less than a typically successful plutocrat. He amassed a fortune which, in characteristic bourgeois fashion, he claimed he had accumulated in order to provide for his five sons and three daughters. He enjoyed the company of bankers and businessmen, though he attempted to develop a reputation as the friend of the people. Rumor had it that when he stopped to shake hands with shopkeepers he wore a special pair of dirty gloves, which he would replace with white kid when hobnobbing with the rich. Louis Philippe was unable to rise above his stodgy public image. The German poet Heinrich Heine reported that the young people of France "yearned for great deeds and scorned the stingy small-mindedness and huckstering selfishness" that the king seemed to embody.

The slower pace of reform in France

Meanwhile radical members of the French and British lower middle and working classes who had assisted—if not propelled—the forces of liberalism to victory in 1830 and 1832 grew increasingly dissatisfied with the results of their efforts. In Britain they soon realized that the Reform Bill had done little to increase their chances for political participation. For a time they devoted their energies to the cause of trade unionism, believing that industrial, rather than political, action might bring them relief from the economic hardships they were suffering.

Growing dissatisfaction of radicals

Trade unionism

Trade union organization had been a goal of militant workers since the beginning of the century. Among the first workers' campaigns in the nineteenth century were those often-riotous revolts organized both in England and, later, on the Continent against the introduction of machinery. In some instances, factories were attacked by workers and machines smashed, in the belief that machines, by replacing skilled workers, were producing widespread unemployment. In England, the rioters were called Luddites, after "Ned Ludd," who was the mythical leader of the movement. In other instances, the hostility of trade unionists was not directed so much toward machinery as toward those workers who refused to join in unions against their masters. Yet nowhere in Europe were trade unions able to organize themselves into effective bargaining agents before 1850. They came closest in England. There, artisans and skilled workers had banded together in the mid-1820s to form both Friendly Societies, really mutual aid and insurance organizations, and cooperatives, communal stores that cut prices by eliminating the middleman between producer and consumer. By 1831, there were about 500 cooperative societies in England, with a membership of something like 20,000. These organizations encouraged the parallel growth of trade unions, which, in the early 1830s, reached the peak of their early power and effectiveness. The National Association for the Protection of Labour comprised about 150 separate local unions in the textile and mining industries of the north; the Operative Builder's Union, about 30,000 workers throughout the country. In 1834, a new and potentially far more radical organization, the Grand National Consolidated Trades Union of Great Britain and Ireland, was organized by a group of London artisans. Its leadership declared that only by bringing the country to a standstill with a general strike could workers compel the governing class to grant them a decent life. At that point, the government decided to put an end to unions. In 1834, six organizers for the Grand National were convicted of administering secret oaths (unions were not themselves illegal) and sentenced to transportation (forced emigration to penal colonies in Australia). Subsequently employers demanded that their workers sign a document pledging their refusal to join a union, thereby stifling opportunities for further organization.

Chartism

After the defeat of the Grand National, the efforts of radical democratic reformers in England turned back from trade union to political activity, centering on attempts to force further political reform upon the uninterested government through the device of the "People's Charter." This document, circulated across the country by committees of Chartists, as they were known, and signed by millions, contained six demands: universal manhood suffrage; institution of the secret ballot; abolition of property qualifications for membership in the House of Commons; annual parliamentary elections; payment of salaries to members of the House of Commons; and equal electoral districts.

The fortunes of the Chartist movement waxed and waned. In some areas its strength depended upon economic conditions: Chartism spread with unemployment and depression. There were arguments among its leaders as to both ends and means: Did Chartism imply a reorganization of industry or, instead, a return to preindustrial society? Were its goals to be accomplished by petition only, or by more violent means if necessary? The Chartist William Lovett, a cabinet-maker, for example, was as fervent a believer in self-improvement as any member of the middle class. He advocated a union of educated workers to acquire their fair share of the nation's increasing industrial bounty. The Chartist Feargus O'Connor, on the other hand, appealed to the more impoverished and desperate class of workers. He urged a rejection of industrialization, and the resettlement of the poor on agricultural allotments. These polarities and disagreements regarding the aims of the movement suggest the extent of the confusion within the working class, whose consciousness as a separate political force was only just beginning to develop. Events answered most of the Chartists' questions for them. In 1848, revolutionary outbreaks across the Continent inspired Chartist leaders to plan a major demonstration and show of force in London. A procession of 500,000 workers was called, to bear to Parliament a petition containing 6,000,000 signatures demanding the six points. Confronted, once again, with the spectre of open class conflict, special constables and contingents of the regular army were marshaled under the now-aged duke of Wellington to resist

The Great Chartist Rally of April 10, 1848. Undiscovered in the royal archives until the 1970s, this early photograph draws attention to the respectable attire of working-class radicals and to the decidedly male character of mid-century radicalism.

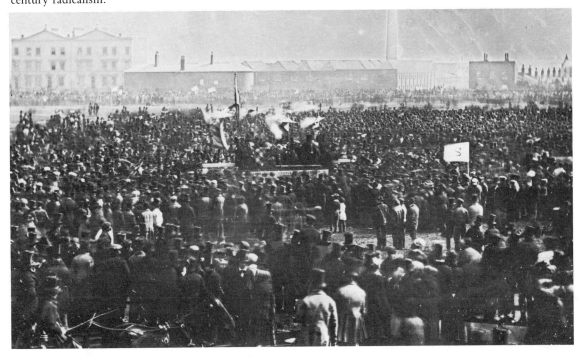

this threat to order. In the end, fewer than 50,000 made the march to Parliament, however. Rain, poor management, and unwillingness on the part of many to do battle with the well-armed constabulary put an end to the Chartists' campaign. Increased prosperity among skilled workers disarmed the movement after mid-century.

In France, radical agitation produced very different results. There, as well, those who had manned the barricades in 1830 soon grew disgusted with the liberalism for which they had risked their lives. In their minds they carried memories or myths of the years of the first French Republic—its domestic accomplishments, its foreign victories, if not its Reign of Terror. They were opposed to constitutional monarchy, and unenthusiastic about parliamentary government, especially by a *nouveau riche* upper middle class. They were prepared, if necessary, to use force in order to achieve their ends. Centered in an increasingly industrialized Paris, they were for the most part either writers, students, or working-class leaders. They met in secret, studied the works of the radical theorist, Gracchus Babeuf (see above, p. 710), whose socialist *Conspiracy of Equals,* written during the French Revolution, became their Bible, and succeeded in making constant trouble for the liberal, middle-class governments of Louis Philippe. Their leading spokesman was the socialist Auguste Blanqui (1805–1881). He decried the victimization of the workers by the middle class, and helped organize secret societies that were to become the instruments of eventual insurrection. Radicals waged some of their most successful campaigns in the press. Honoré Daumier's savage caricatures of Louis Philippe landed him in prison more than once. But campaigners took to the streets as well. In retaliation, the government in 1834 declared radical political organizations illegal. Rioting broke

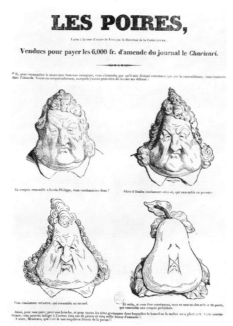

Louis Philippe in Caricature. In contrast to the portrait of Louis Philippe on page 794 as he wanted to appear, these 1833 caricatures by Charles Philipon depict the king as he increasingly appeared to his subjects and suggest the degree to which Louis Philippe failed in his attempt to celebrate the supposed virtues of the bourgeoisie.

Rue Transnomain. A drawing by Daumier to commemorate the victims of government repression in 1834.

out in Lyon and Paris in protest, where for two days government troops massacred hundreds of insurgents, and arrested some 2,000 republican leaders. In 1835, following an attempt to assassinate Louis Philippe, the government passed a censorship law, which forbade the publication of articles attempting to inspire contempt for the king and which prohibited the printing of any drawing or emblem without prior governmental approval.

These repressive measures served only to increase dissatisfaction with the regime. Guizot was advised by more progressive members of the legislature to extend the franchise to professionals whose lack of wealth now denied them the vote, but whose general adherence to the doctrines of liberalism was unquestioned. Guizot unwisely refused, thereby driving these moderates into the camp of the more radical republicans. By 1847, various elements within the opposition were disaffected enough to instigate a general campaign of agitation throughout France. At political banquets, republicans such as the poet Alphonse de Lamartine (1790–1869) and socialist republicans such as Louis Blanc (see above, p. 780) preached drastic reform, though not outright revolution. Contrary to the expressed wishes of the king, a giant protest meeting was announced for February 22, 1848. The day before, the government forbade the meeting. Rioting and barricading during the following two days ended in the abdication of Louis Philippe and increased demands for a republic.

A Caricature of Louis Philippe by Daumier. The inscription reads "Louis Philippe, the Last King of the French." It reflects a popular sentiment of the time.

4. THE REVOLUTION OF 1848 IN FRANCE

The February revolution in France was a catalyst which, as we shall see, helped to produce uprisings in the succeeding months throughout much of Europe. Meanwhile, in Paris, a provisional government was

A National Workshop. When few could read, newspapers were heard rather than scanned. Under government auspices, these workshops achieved a good deal less than Louis Blanc had envisioned.

Republican-socialist split: Blanc's workshops

established consisting of ten men, seven of whom, including Lamartine, were middle-of-the-road republicans; three of whom, including Blanc, were socialists. The tensions between middle-class republicans and radical socialists, which had been masked by a common disgust with the government of Louis Philippe, now emerged to shape the political events of the ensuing months in several specific ways. Blanc insisted upon the establishment of national workshops, institutions he had championed as a writer, which were to be organized by trades as producers' cooperatives, where men and women workers would be trained if necessary, put to work, and paid two francs a day when employed and a smaller stipend when unemployed. Instead, the government established what it called workshops, but what amounted to nothing more than a program of public works in and around Paris, where economic conditions had resulted in widespread unemployment. Initially, plans had called for the employment of no more than ten or twelve thousand in projects throughout the city. But with unemployment running as high as 65 percent in construction trades and 51 percent in textiles and clothing, workers began to flood into the government's so-called workshops, as many as 66,000 by April, and 120,000 by June.

Paris meanwhile attracted numbers of radical writers, organizers, and agitators. The provisional government had removed all restrictions upon the formation of political clubs and the dissemination of political literature. As a result, 170 new journals and more than 200 clubs formed within weeks; the club headed by the socialist Auguste Blanqui boasted a membership of some 3,000. Delegations claiming to represent the oppressed of all European countries—Chartists, Hungarians, Poles—moved freely about the city, attracting attention, if not devoted followings, and contributing to tension which was convincing more and more members of the middle class that stern measures were needed to forestall further insurrectionary outbreaks. This sentiment was fortified as a result of elections held at the end of April.

Continuing agitation

Apotheosis of Homer, Jean Auguste Ingres (1780–1867). Though he painted during the Romantic period, Ingres did not desert the neoclassical themes and style that dominated art during the Revolutionary and Napoleonic eras. (Louvre)

Beatrice and Dante, William Blake (1757–1827). Blake was a mystical Romantic whose work possesses a compelling uniqueness that defies exact categorization. This painting is from his series for *The Divine Comedy.* (The Tate Gallery, London)

Execution of the Rioters, Francisco Goya (1746–1828). Unlike most artists of his time, Goya dealt unflinchingly with suffering, violence, fear, and death. Depicted here is the execution of Spanish rebels by Napoleon's soldiers in 1808. This harshness caused the rebellion to spread over the whole peninsula. (Prado)

Liberty Leading the People, Eugène Delacroix (1798–1863). Delacroix was a romantic painter of dramatic and emotional scenes. In this painting he celebrates the triumph of the revolutionary principle of liberty in a tempestuous allegory. (Louvre)

The Massacre of Chios, Eugène Delacroix. Here Delacroix again puts his brush to work for the cause of liberty, eulogizing the more than 20,000 Greeks slain by the Turks during the Greek war of independence in 1822. (Louvre)

The Movings by Louis Léopold Boilly (1761–1845). Dating from 1822, this realist-allegorical painting depicts Parisians of various classes in the process of moving their household goods. By juxtaposing the buildings of contemporary Paris with the Church of Santa Maria de' Miracoli of Rome, the artist appears to suggest that for some, including the peasants in their wagon leaving the city and the corpse in the horse-drawn hearse heading for its grave, the idea of the metropolis as a place of promise and prosperity is an illusion. (Art Institute of Chicago)

The Last of England, Ford Madox Brown (1821–1893). A haunting scene of a couple emigrating from England by one of the most noted pre-Raphaelites. (The City Museum and Art Gallery, Birmingham, England)

Valley of Aosta—Snowstorm, Avalanche, and Thunderstorm, Joseph M. W. Turner (1775–1851). Turner's complete absorption in light, color, and atmosphere helped to prepare the way for the French Impressionists. (MMA)

A Woman Reading, Camille Corot (1796–1875). Corot was a Naturalist whose interest in the effects of light prefigured to a degree the work of the Impressionists. Sentimentality and a preference for scenes of innocence and simplicity distinguished him from the Realists. (MMA)

Public Notary Eltz and His Family by Ferdinand Georg Waldmüller (1793–1865). A portrait that celebrates the rise to power and influence of the bourgeois bureaucrat. (Österreichische Galerie, Vienna)

The Gleaners, Jean François Millet (1814–1875). A Realist, Millet remained fascinated with color and setting to a degree that often made his paintings something other than a record of social change. (Louvre)

Funeral at Ornans, Gustave Courbet (1819–1877). Though a less strident Realist than his contemporary Daumier, Courbet was concerned to express human nature as he found it—neither more handsome nor more ugly. This painting, in which he used men and women from his village as models, reflects his commitment to personal, as opposed to social, Realism. (Louvre)

The provisional government had been pressured by Parisian radicals into decreeing universal manhood suffrage. Yet the election returned only a small proportion of radical socialists. The largest blocs consisted of "true," or moderate, republicans and monarchists—this latter group divided, however, between supporters of the Bourbon dynasty and the Orleanist Louis Philippe. The generally conservative tenor of the newly elected assembly strengthened the hand of those who pressed for the repession of the socialists. It also, naturally, convinced the socialists that once again, as in the 1790s, a potentially radical revolution had been betrayed by the timid, self-serving middle class.

By late spring, a majority of the assembly believed that the workshop system represented both an unbearable financial drain and a serious threat to social order. At the end of May, the workshops were closed to new enrollment as a first step toward barring membership to all who had resided for less than six months in Paris and sending all members between the ages of eighteen and twenty-five to the army. Thousands of workers lost their state-financed jobs, and with them their best chance for survival. Desperate, they and their supporters once more threw up barricades across Paris. For four days, June 23–26, they defended themselves in an ultimately hopeless military battle against armed forces recruited, in part, from willing provincials eager enough to assist in the repression of the urban working class. Whether or not the Parisian insurrectionists were fighting as members of a beleaguered class, or simply as men and women on the brink of starvation, is a matter that historians continue to debate. That they were taken seriously as a revolutionary threat can be seen by the ferocity with which they were hunted out once the street fighting had ceased. About 3,000 were killed and 12,000 more arrested, the majority of whom were deported to Algerian labor camps.

The "June Days"

In the aftermath of the "June Days," the French government moved

The Revolution of 1848 in France. A contemporary broadside celebrating the triumph of the people.

quickly to bring order to the country. The assembly, faced with the task of drafting a republican constitution, contained a large number of men to whom the idea of a republic was anathema. Assembly members therefore arranged for the immediate election of a president. Their hope was that a strong leader might assist in bringing dissidents to heel. Four candidates stood: Lamartine, the moderate republican; General Eugène Cavaignac, who had commanded the troops in June; Alexander Ledru-Rollin, a socialist; and Louis Napoleon Bonaparte, nephew of the emperor, who polled more than twice as many votes as the other three candidates combined.

The astonishing upstart Louis Napoleon had spent most of his life in exile. Returning to France after the Revolution of 1830, he was imprisoned a few years later for attempting to provoke a local uprising. But in 1846 he escaped to England, where he was supplied with funds by both British and French reactionaries. By the summer of 1848 the situation in France was such that he knew it was safe to return. In fact, he was welcomed by members of all classes. Conservatives were looking for a savior to protect their property against the onslaughts of the radicals. Workers were beguiled by his glittering schemes for prosperity in his book, *The Extinction of Pauperism,* and by the fact that he had corresponded with Louis Blanc and with Pierre Proudhon, the anarchist. In between these two classes was a multitude of patriots and hero-worshipers to whom the name Napoleon was a symbol of glory and greatness. It was chiefly to this multitude that the nephew of the Corsican owed his astounding triumph. As one old peasant expressed it: "How could I help voting for this gentleman—I whose nose was frozen at Moscow?"

With dreams of emulating his uncle, Louis Napoleon was not long content to remain president of France. Almost from the first he used the power he already had to achieve the further power he desired. He enlisted the support of the Catholics by permitting them to regain control over the schools and by sending an expedition to Rome to restore to the pope the temporal power denied him during the revolutionary struggles of 1848. He courted the workers and the middle class by introducing old-age insurance and laws for the encouragement of business. In 1851, alleging the need for extraordinary measures to protect the rights of the masses, he proclaimed a temporary dictatorship and invited the people to grant him the power to draw up a new constitution. In the plebiscite held on December 21, 1851, he was authorized by an overwhelming majority (7,500,000 to 640,000) to proceed as he liked. The new constitution, which he put into effect in January 1852, made the president an actual dictator. After one year Louis Napoleon Bonaparte ordered another plebiscite and, with the approval of over 95 percent of the voters, assumed the title of Napoleon III, emperor of the French.[2]

[2] Napoleon I's son, Napoleon II, had died in Vienna in 1832.

AU NOM DU PEUPLE FRANÇAIS.

LE PRÉSIDENT DE LA RÉPUBLIQUE
DÉCRÈTE:

Art. 1.
L'Assemblée nationale est dissoute.

Art. 2.
Le Suffrage universel est rétabli. La loi du 31 mai est abrogée.

Art. 3.
Le Peuple français est convoqué dans ses comices à partir du 14 décembre jusqu'au 21 décembre suivant.

Art. 4.
L'état de siége est décrété dans l'étendue de la 1ʳ division militaire.

Art. 5.
Le Conseil d'État est dissous.

Art. 6.
Le Ministre de l'intérieur est chargé de l'exécution du présent décret.

Fait au Palais de l'Élysée, le 2 décembre 1851.

LOUIS-NAPOLÉON BONAPARTE.

Le Ministre de l'Intérieur.
DE MORNY.

Napoleon III's Decree Dissolving the National Assembly

What is the significance of the French Revolution of 1848 and its political aftermath in the history of middle-class liberalism, which is our subject? Two points need particular emphasis. First, we must recognize the pivotal role of the liberal middle class. Under Louis Philippe, it increasingly perceived itself and its particular interests as neglected. Denied a direct political voice because of a severely limited franchise, it swung to the left, allying itself with radicals who, by themselves, would probably have stood no chance of permanent success. Yet no sooner had Louis Philippe abdicated than the liberal middle class began to wonder if "success" was not about to bring disaster upon its heels. And so it swung again, this time to the right, where it found itself confronting the mysterious and yet not entirely unattractive prospect of Louis Napoleon. He, in turn, was clever enough to understand this first lesson of 1848, that in France no government could survive that did not cater to the interests of the middle class. By assisting it to achieve its liberal economic goals, the emperor helped it forget just how heavily he was trampling on its political liberties.

The implications of the French Revolution of 1848

Yet 1848 proved that there was now in France another element—class consciousness may, at this point, not yet be the correct term—that governments ignored at their peril. If mid–nineteenth-century Europe saw the middle class closer than ever to the center of power, it saw the workers moving rapidly in from the edge. Their barricades could, if necessary, be destroyed, and their demands ignored, but only at an increasingly grave risk to the fabric of the state. Middle-class liberalism, if it was to thrive, would not only have to pay lip service to working-class demands, but in some measure accommodate to them as well.

Napoleon III

Napoleon III's constitution

Napoleon III and the middle class

Napoleon III recognized the vital role that public opinion had now assumed in the management of affairs of state. He labored hard and successfully to sell his empire to the people of France. He argued that legislative assemblies only served to divide a nation along class lines. With power residing in him, he would unite the country as it had not been for generations. The French, who craved order following their recent political misadventures, bought the program he was selling willingly enough. Napoleon III modeled his constitution upon that of his uncle. An assembly, elected by universal manhood suffrage, in fact possessed almost no power. It could do no more than approve legislation drafted at the emperor's direction by a Council of State. Elections were manipulated by the government to ensure the return of politically docile representatives. Control of finance, the army, and foreign affairs rested exclusively with the emperor. France was a democracy only in the sense that its people were periodically afforded a chance, through elections, to express their approval of Napoleon's regime.

In return for the gift of almost absolute power, Napoleon III gave the French what they appeared to want. For the middle class, he provided a chance to make a great deal of money. The device of the *Crédit Mobilier,* an investment banking institution, facilitated the expansion of industry by selling its shares to the public and using its income to underwrite various entrepreneurial schemes. In 1863 a limited liability law encouraged further investment by guaranteeing that stockholders could lose no more than the par value of their stock no matter how indebted the company in which they had invested. Railways, owned by the state, spread across the country, and spurred further industrial expansion. So prosperous did the French economy appear that Napoleon was prepared to follow Britain's lead in pressing for tariff-free trade between the two countries. A treaty was signed in 1860. Though funds were set aside to compensate French industries for any loss they might suffer, they were never completely expended, suggesting that French manufacturers were now well enough established to meet the threat of British competition. The apparent satisfaction of the middle class with Napoleon's regime provides a measure with which to assess the state of liberalism in France after 1850. The fact that the country no longer enjoyed a free press, that universities were politically controlled, and that political opposition was repressed seemed to matter very little to most. Liberalism, if it existed at all, existed as the freedom to have one's own economic way.

Napoleon III, though he catered to the middle class, did not fail to court the favor of the workers as well. He encouraged the establishment of hospitals and instituted a program of free medical assistance. More important, he permitted, if he did nothing to encourage, the existence of trade unions and in 1864 introduced legislation to legalize

Paris under the Second Empire. The Avenue de l'Imperatrice was designed for the enjoyment of the middle class.

strikes. Ultimately, he appealed to the workers much as he appealed to the middle class, as a glamorous, if not heroic symbol of his country's reemergence as a leading world power. The activities of his court, and of his stylish empress, Eugénie, were well publicized. The reconstruction of Paris into a city of broad boulevards and grand open spaces was calculated to provide appropriate scenery for the theater of empire—as well as to lessen the chances for successful proletarian barricade-building across narrow streets.

Grandeur, however, appeared to Napoleon III to demand an aggressive foreign policy. Although early in his regime he declared himself in favor of that central liberal tenet—international peace—he was soon at war: first against Russia in the Crimea; then in Italy; then in Mexico, where he attempted to assist in the establishment of another empire; and finally and disastrously with Prussia. The details of these adventures are part of the subject of the following chapter. It is enough at this point to remark that Napoleon III's foreign policy reflects clearly how far he—and the rest of France with him—had subordinated the liberal heritage of the first French Revolution to that of another of its legacies: national glory.

What, meanwhile, of the liberal tradition in Britain? There the course of liberalism was altered by changes occurring within the working class. Industrialization had, by this time, begun to foster and sustain a growing stratum of labor "aristocrats," men whose particular skills, and the increasing demand for them, allowed them to demand wages high enough to ensure them a fairly comfortable standard

Empress Eugénie

of living. These workers—concentrated for the most part within the building, engineering, and textile industries—turned from the tradition of militant radicalism that had characterized the so-called hungry forties. Having succeeded within the liberal economic system imposed upon Britain by the middle class, they were now prepared to accept many liberal, middle-class principles as their own. They believed in self-help, achieved by means of cooperative societies or through trade unions, whose major function was the accumulation of funds to be used as insurance against old age and unemployment. They believed in education as a tool for advancement, and patronized the Mechanics Institutes and other similar institutions either founded by them or on their behalf.

Yet the labor aristocracy, as it came to appreciate its ability to achieve a decent life for itself within the capitalist system, grew all the more dissatisfied with a political system that excluded it from any direct participation in the governmental process. Although some pressed for extension of the franchise as democrats, as many argued for it on the same grounds the middle class had used in 1832. They were responsible workers, whose loyalty to the state could not be questioned. As such, they were a bona fide "interest," as worthy of the vote and of direct representation as the middle class. They were joined in their campaign by many middle-class reformers who continued to chafe at the privileged position of national institutions that they associated with the landed society and the old order. Many middle-class men and women, for example, were dissenters from the Church of England; yet they were forced to pay taxes to support a church which was staffed, in the main, by sons of the gentry. Their sons were denied the facilities of the nation's ancient universities, Oxford and Cambridge, unless those sons subscribed to the articles of faith of the Anglican church.

Together with working-class leaders, these middle-class dissidents organized a Reform League to campaign across the country for a new reform bill and a House of Commons responsive to their interests. Though by no means revolutionary, the reformers made it clear by their actions that they were determined to press their case to the utmost. Politicians in Britain in the 1860s were confronted by a situation not unlike that which had faced Guizot in France in 1848: middle class, lower middle class, and skilled workers discontented and demanding reform. Unlike Guizot, however, the leaders of both British political parties, Conservative (formerly Tory) and Liberal (formerly Whig), were prepared to concede what they recognized it would be dangerous to withhold. Once convinced of this need, the Conservative leader of the House of Commons and future prime minister, Benjamin Disraeli, seized upon reform as an issue with which to belabor the Liberals. In 1867 he steered a bill through Parliament more far-reaching than anything proposed by his political opponents. It doubled the franchise by extending the vote to any males who paid poor rates or rent of ten pounds or more a year in urban areas (this would mean, in general, the skilled workers), and to tenants paying rent of twelve pounds or more in the counties. Seats were again redistributed as in 1832, with large northern cities gaining representation at the expense of the rural south. The "responsible" working class had been deemed worthy to participate in the affairs of state. For the next twenty years it showed its appreciation by accepting its apprentice position without demur, and by following the lead prescribed by the middle class.

The decade or so following the passage of the Reform Bill of 1867 marked the high point of British liberalism. The labor aristocracy was accommodated with an Education Act, virtually guaranteeing a primary education to all, with legalization of strikes, and with a series of measures designed to improve living conditions in the great cities; yet it was the middle class that set the governmental tone. Under Disraeli and his Liberal counterpart William Gladstone, and with the cooperation of the newly enfranchised skilled workers, Britain celebrated the triumph of the liberal principles of free trade, representative—but not democratic—government, and general prosperity.

The triumph of British liberalism

SELECTED READINGS

• *Items so designated are available in paperback editions.*

Anderson, R. D., *Education in France, 1848–1870,* New York, 1975. Covers every level of formal education and its practical and theoretical relationship to state and society.
• Artz, Frederick B., *Reaction and Revolution, 1814–1832,* New York, 1834. A European survey, dated but still useful.
• Blake, Robert, *Disraeli,* London, 1966. A masterful biography.
• Briggs, Asa, *The Age of Improvement, 1783 to 1867.* New York, 1959. A survey of England from 1780 to 1870, particularly strong on Victorian attitudes.
• Duveau, Georges, *1848: The Making of a Revolution,* New York, 1967. Focuses on the working class during the revolution in Paris: their unity at the outset, their division in the "June Days."
Finer, Samuel E., *The Life and Times of Edwin Chadwick,* London, 1952. An excellent biography of the great English Benthamite reformer.
Halévy, Elie, *A History of the English People, 1905–1914,* Vols. II–IV, London, 1949–1952. The best survey of nineteenth-century England, comprehensive and analytical.
• Harrison, Royden, *Before the Socialists: Studies in Labour and Politics, 1861–1881,* London, 1965. Examines the social and political background of franchise extension in Britain.
Johnson, Douglas, *Guizot: Aspects of French History, 1787–1874,* London, 1963. Analytical essays about the leading politician of the July monarchy.

- Kissinger, Henry, *A World Restored: Metternich, Castlereagh, and the Problem of Peace, 1812–1822,* Boston, 1957. By an admirer of Metternich.
- Langer, William L., *Political and Social Upheaval, 1832–1852,* New York, 1969. (Several chapters have been published separately under the title *The Revolutions of 1848.*) A thorough general survey.

Magnus, Philip, *Gladstone: A Biography,* London, 1955. A readable and reliable biography.

Merriman, John M., ed., *1830 in France,* New York, 1975. Recent scholarship emphasizing the nature of revolution and examining events outside of Paris.

- Pinkney, David, *Napoleon III and the Rebuilding of Paris,* Princeton, 1972. An interesting account of the creation of Modern Paris during the Second Empire.

———, *The French Revolution of 1830,* Princeton, 1972. A reinterpretation, now the best history of the revolution.

Raeff, Marc, *The Decembrist Movement,* New York, 1966. Examines the uprising; contains documents.

Roberts, David, *Victorian Origins of the British Welfare State,* New Haven, 1960. Examines various nineteenth-century reforms in England.

- Robertson, Priscilla, *Revolutions of 1848: A Social History,* Princeton, 1960. Surveys the revolutions across Europe.

de Sauvigny, G. de Bertier, *The Bourbon Restoration,* New York, 1967. An outstanding work; the best history of a neglected period.

- Stearns, Peter N., *1848: The Revolutionary Tide in Europe,* New York, 1974. Stresses the social background of the revolutions.
- Thompson, J. L. *Louis Napoleon and the Second Empire,* Oxford, 1954. A good biography. Presents Louis Napoleon as a modern Hamlet.

Woodward, E. L., *The Age of Reform,* Oxford, 1962. An excellent survey from the Oxford History of England series.

- Wright, Gordon, *France in Modern Times: 1760 to the Present,* 4th ed., New York, 1987. The best textbook on modern France.
- Zeldin, Theodore, *The Political System of Napoleon III,* New York, 1958. Examines the processes by which Napoleon maintained power as the first modern dictator.
- ———, *France, 1848–1945,* 2 vols., Oxford, 1973–77.

SOURCE MATERIALS

- Flaubert, Gustave, *L'Education Sentimentale,* London, 1961. Contains an unsympathetic but memorable portrait of the Revolution of 1848 and of the bourgeois style of life that contributed to its outbreak.
- Greville, Charles Fulke, *Memoirs,* ed. by Roger Fulford, New York, 1963. Originally published in seven volumes in 1875, these comprise the diaries of the secretary to the Privy Council for the years 1821–1861. An excellent source for the court and politics of the period.
- Price, Roger, ed., *1848 in France,* Ithaca, N.Y., 1975. An excellent collection of eyewitness accounts, annotated.

Stewart, John Hall, *The Restoration Era in France, 1814–1830,* Princeton, 1968. A brief narrative and a good collection of documents.

Chapter 23

NATIONALISM AND NATION-BUILDING (1815–1870)

The present problem, the first task . . . is simply to preserve the existence and continuance of what is German.

—Johann Fichte, *Addresses to the German Nation*

The great questions of the day will not be decided by speeches or by majority decisions—that was the mistake of 1848 and 1849—but by blood and iron.

—Otto von Bismarck, speech, 1862

If the history of nineteenth-century Britain and France can be studied against a general background of middle-class liberalism, that of much of the rest of Europe during the same period must be understood in terms of a more complex combination of the forces of liberalism, nationalism, and nation-building. We shall define nationalism as a sentiment rooted in broad historical, geographical, linguistic, or cultural circumstances. It is characterized by a consciousness of belonging, in a group, to a tradition derived from those circumstances, which differs from the traditions of other groups. Nation-building is the political implementation of nationalism, the translation of sentiment into power.

Nationalism and nation-building defined

Men and women in Britain and France during the nineteenth century entertained national as well as liberal sentiments. When Britain's prime minister, Lord Palmerston, declared in 1850 that any British citizen, in any part of the world, had but to proclaim, like a citizen of the Roman Empire, "civis Romanus sum" ("I am a citizen of Rome") to summon up whatever force might be necessary to protect him from foreign depradations, he was echoing his countrymen's pride in the powers of their nationhood. When the French rejoiced in 1840 at the return of the Emperor Napoleon's remains from St. Helena to an elaborate shrine in Paris, they were reliving triumphs that had become

Nationalism in Britain and France

part of their nation's heritage. Palmerston's boast and Napoleon's bones were both artifacts of national traditions and sentiments bound up in the life of the English and the French.

Nineteenth-century nationalism in other areas of Europe was to be a more assertive phenomenon than it was in Britain and France, which had for centuries existed as particular geographical, cultural, and political entities. Elsewhere, common traditions and assumptions were less clearly articulated, because the political unity that might have helped define them did not exist. East Prussians or Venetians had no difficulty in perceiving of themselves as such; history had provided them with those identities. But history had not provided them, except in the most general way, with identities as Germans or Italians. They had to make a deliberate effort to think of themselves in those terms before the terms could have any political reality.

Neither nationalism nor nation-building stood in necessary opposition to liberalism. Indeed, to the extent that nationalism celebrated the achievements of a particular common people over those of a cosmopolitan aristocratic elite, it reflected liberalism's abhorrence of traditional privilege. Yet to liberalism's readiness to accept the new, nationalism responded with an appreciation, if not veneration, of the past. And to the liberals' insistence upon the value and importance of individualism, nation-builders replied that their vital task might require the sacrifice of some measure of each citizen's freedom. The success of nation-building rested upon the foundation of a general balance of international power, achieved by the European states during the half century after 1815. The emergence of new nations—a unified Italy and Germany—would require readjustments to that balance. But accommodation remained possible, with only minor skirmishes marring the stability of the settlement achieved at the Congress of Vienna.

1. ROMANTICISM AND NATIONALISM

As we noted in the preceding chapter, nationalism was in part a child of the French Revolution. It was closely related, as well, to the intellectual movement that has been called "romanticism." Romanticism was so broad and so varied that it all but defies definition, if not analysis. Perhaps as much as anything, romanticism represented a reaction against the rationalism of the eighteenth-century Enlightenment. Where the eighteenth century relied on reason, the romantics put their faith in emotion. The eighteenth century understood the mind as a blank tablet, which received knowledge from impressions imprinted upon it through the senses by the external world. Romantics also believed in the importance of sense experience. But they insisted that innate sensibility—that which constituted a person's own particular personality—was inherited, and therefore present in the mind from birth. Knowledge, then, for the romantic, was the product of both innate feelings *and* external perceptions. Romanticism thus stressed individualism, and the individual creativity that resulted from the interaction of unique personality with external experience. At the same time, by stressing the inheritance of attitudes, it also celebrated the past. And that celebration was its link with nationalism.

Romanticism and nationalism were connected by their common belief that the past should be made to function as a means of understanding the present and planning for the future. It was in Germany that this notion received its fullest airing and most enthusiastic reception. One of the earliest and most influential German romantics was Johann von Herder (1744–1803). A Protestant pastor and theologian, his interest in past cultures led him, in the 1780s, to set out his reflections in a lengthy and detailed treatise, *Ideas for a Philosophy of Human History*. Herder traced what he perceived to be the progressive development of European society from the time of the Greeks through the Renaissance. He believed that civilization was not the product of an artificial, international elite—a criticism of Enlightenment thinking—but of the genuine culture of the common people, the *Volk*. No civilization could be considered sound which did not continue to express its own unique historical character, its *Volksgeist*. Herder did not argue that one *Volksgeist* was either better or worse than any other. He insisted only that each nation must be true to its own particular heritage. He broke dramatically with the Enlightenment idea that human beings could be expected to respond to human situations in more or less the same fashion, and with the assumption that the value of history was simply to teach by example.

Johann von Herder

Herder's intellectual heirs, men like the conservative German romantics Friedrich Schlegel (1772–1829) and Friedrich von Savigny (1779–1861) condemned the implantation of democratic and liberal ideas—"foreign" to Germany—in German cultural soil. History, they argued, taught that institutions must evolve organically—a favorite word of the political romantics, and that proper laws were the product of historical growth, not simply deductions from universal first principles. This idea was not peculiar to German romantics. The English romantic poet and philosopher Samuel Taylor Coleridge (1772–1834) argued against the utilitarian state and in favor of giving that ancient institution, the national church, a larger role in the shaping of society. The French conservative Chateaubriand (1768–1848) made much the same case in his treatise, *The Genius of Christianity,* published in 1802. The past, and in particular the religious experiences of the past, are woven into the present, he declared. They cannot be unwoven without destroying the fabric of a nation's society.

The role of history and religion

The theory of the organic evolution of society and the state received its fullest exposition in the writings of the German metaphysician Georg Wilhelm Hegel (1770–1831), a professor of philosophy at the

Georg Wilhelm Hegel

Fichte

University of Berlin. Hegel wrote of history as development. Social and political institutions grew to maturity, achieved their purposes, and then gave way to others. Yet the new never entirely replaced the old, for the pattern of change was a "dialectic." When new institutions challenged established ones, there was a clash between what had been and what was becoming, producing a "synthesis," a reordering of society that retained elements from the past while adapting to the present. Hegel expected, for example, that the present disunity among the German states, which generated the idea of unity, would inevitably result in the creation of a nation-state. Hegel had no use for the theory of a state of nature, so popular with philosophers like Rousseau and Hobbes. Men and women have always lived within some society or other, Hegel argued. The institution of the state was itself a natural historic organism; only within that institution, protected by its laws and customs from personal depradations, could men and women enjoy freedom, which Hegel defined not as the absence of restraint but as the absence of social disorder.

These theories of history and of historical development articulated by the romantics relate directly to the idea of nationalism formulated during the same period. The French Revolution provided an example of what a nation could achieve. Nationhood had encouraged the French to raise themselves to the level of citizenship; it had also allowed them to sustain attacks from the rest of Europe. Applying the historical lessons of the French Revolution and the theories of romantics, Germans, in particular, were roused to a sense of their own historical destiny. The works of the philosopher J. G. Fichte (1762–1814) are an example of this reawakening. As a young professor at the University of Jena, Fichte had at first advanced a belief in the importance of an individual's inner spirit, the creator of its own moral universe. Devoid of national feeling, he welcomed the French Revolution as an emancipator of the human spirit. Yet when France conquered much of Germany, Fichte's attitude changed dramatically. He adopted Herder's notion of a *Volksgeist;* what mattered was no longer the individual spirit, but the spirit of a whole people, expressed in its customs, traditions, and history. In 1808, Fichte delivered a series of *Addresses to the German Nation,* in which he declared the existence of a German spirit to be, not just one among many such spirits, but superior to the rest. The world had not yet heard from that spirit; he predicted it soon would. Although the French military commander in Berlin, where Fichte spoke, believed the addresses to be too academic to warrant censorship, they expressed a sentiment that aided the Prussians in their conscious attempt to rally themselves and, as a political *Volk,* to drive out the French.

Nationalism, derived from romantic notions of historical development and destiny, manifested itself in a variety of ways. The brothers Grimm, editors of *Grimm's Fairy Tales* (1812), traveled across Germany to study native dialects, and collected folktales that were published as part of a national heritage. The poet Friedrich Schiller's (1759–1805) drama of *William Tell,* the Swiss hero (1804), became a rallying cry for German national consciousness. In Britain, Sir Walter Scott (1771–1832) retold in many of his novels the popular history of Scotland, while the poet William Wordsworth (1770–1850) consciously strove to express the simplicity and virtue of the English people in collections such as his *Lyrical Ballads* (1798). Throughout Europe, countries assiduously catalogued the relics of their historical past as in the society for publishing the *Monumenta Germaniae Historica* (Monuments of German History), founded in 1819; the French École des Chartes (1821); and the English Public Records Office (1838). In France, the neoclassical style, typified by the paintings of David, and used by Napoleon to exalt his image, gave way to the turbulent romanticism of painters like Eugène Delacroix, whose *Liberty Leading the People* (1830) was a proclamation not only of liberty, but of the courage of the French nation. Music, too, reflected national themes, though not until a generation or so after 1815. Many of Giuseppe Verdi's (1813–1901) operas, *Don Carlo,* for example, contained musical declarations of faith in the possibility of an Italian *risorgimento:* a resurrection of the Italian spirit. The operas of Richard Wagner (1813–1883)—in particular, those based on the German epic, *Song of the Nibelung*—managed to raise veneration for the myths of Nordic gods and goddesses to the level of pious exaltation. Architects, though they found it difficult to escape entirely from the neoclassicism of the eighteenth century, often tried to resurrect a "national" style in their designs. Sir Charles Barry, assigned the task of redesigning the British Houses of Parliament following their destruction by

Giuseppe Verdi

See color plates following page 800 for *Liberty Leading the People* and *The Massacre of Chios* by Delacroix

Houses of Parliament, London. Redesigned by Sir Charles Barry with a Gothic facade after the earlier structure was destroyed by fire.

A William Blake Etching for a Children's Book Written by Mary Wollstonecraft

See color plates following page 800 for *Beatrice and Dante* by Blake, *Execution of Rioters* by Goya, and *Valley of Aosta— Snowstorm, Avalanche, and Thunderstorm* by Turner

George Sand

fire in 1836, managed to mask a straightforward and symmetrical classical plan behind a Gothic screen, intended to acknowledge the country's debt to its own past. All this creative activity was the spontaneous result of artists' and writers' enthusiastic response to the romantic movement. Yet politicians soon perceived how historical romanticism might serve their nationalist ends. They understood how an individual work of art, whether a painting, a song, a drama, or a building, could translate into a national symbol. And they did not hesitate to assist in that translation when they deemed it useful.

Though romanticism and nationalism shared a common devotion to the past, romantics were not necessarily nationalists. Indeed, romanticism was explicitly international in its celebration of nature, and above all, of individual creativity. The romantics declared that nature was best perceived not by reason, but by the senses. And they respected those elements of nature that appeared to be the product of chance, not rational order. Whether as a single flower or a mountain range, nature was welcomed as it impressed itself directly on the senses. Men and women were declared free to interpret nature—and life as well—in terms of their individual reactions to it, not simply as it might reflect a set of general rational precepts. The English poet Percy Shelley (1792–1822), the German poet Heinrich Heine (1797–1856), the French novelist Victor Hugo (1802–1885), the Spanish painter Francisco Goya (1746–1828)—all characteristic figures of the romantic movement—expressed in their works romanticism's concern for the experiences of human individuals, a concern that transcended national boundaries. Human experience, romantics believed, was not linked to any one national tradition or *Volksgeist*, but rather to transcendent nature. The paintings of the Englishmen William Blake (1757–1827) and J. M. W. Turner (1775–1851), although they often reflect "Englishness," transcend nationalism by recording a communion with the fundamental elements of nature.

Romantics were internationalists because they enjoyed freedom from the confinement of any boundary—metaphysical or political—which tended to restrict a person's ability to realize his or her potential. In this way romanticism encouraged women to make themselves heard. The Englishwoman Mary Wollstonecraft (1759–1797), author of *A Vindication of the Rights of Woman;* Madame de Staël (1766–1817), an emigré from France to Germany during the revolutionary period, whose essay *De l'Allemagne* (On Germany) was steeped in romanticism; George Sand (1804–1876), whose novels, and whose life, proclaimed allegiance to the standards of radical individualism—these women exemplify romanticism's readiness to break with the past, and its assumptions and stereotypes, if they stood in the path of individual expression.

Romantics, as worshipers of individuality, worshiped "genius." The genius was possessed of a spirit that could not be analyzed and must be allowed to make its own rules. (It was the particular genius of an entire people, of course, that Herder extolled as the *Volksgeist*.) And the human spirit must never allow itself to be fettered by national prescriptions, any more than by social conventions, in such a way as to prevent enjoyment of its most precious possession, its freedom.

Freedom and the problem of self-recognition were major themes in the works of two of the giants of the romantic movement, the composer Ludwig van Beethoven (1770–1827) and the writer Johann Wolfgang von Goethe (1749–1832). The most remarkable quality about Beethoven's compositions is their uniqueness and individuality. In the Fifth Symphony Beethoven reaches the summit of symphonic logic, the Sixth is a glorification of nature, the Seventh a Dionysian revelry, the Eighth a genial conjuring up of the spirit of the eighteenth-century symphony. The deafness that afflicted Beethoven in his later years seems to have encouraged him in his determination to speak out through his music as one extraordinarily powerful, and at times distressed, human being. Five piano sonatas, five string quartets, the Ninth Symphony, and the great Mass, *Missa Solemnis,* constitute his final legacy. They fill the listener with awe not so much because of their unusual form or their vast proportions, but because they express boundless individual will and power.

Ludwig van Beethoven

Goethe's dedication to the idea of individual freedom was, in part, the product of his having been born and raised in the free imperial city of Frankfurt. Frankfurt was an international center, a trading place open to intellectual winds from all quarters. Goethe was, in terms of his environment, free from the particularist, nationalist influences that directed the work of other German romantics. Goethe's own "genius" drove him first to the study of law, then medicine, then the fine arts and natural sciences. In 1775 he took up residence at the court of the young duke of Weimar. Weimar was a tiny German principality with a population of no more than half a million, another cosmopolitan community and in this respect not unlike Frankfurt. Influenced by Herder, Goethe had already published various romantically inclined works, including the immensely popular *Sorrows of Werther,* a novel expressive of Goethe's early restlessness and emotionalism. The almost excessive sensitivity characteristic of Goethe's earlier writings gave way, in his middle years, to the search for a new spirit, equally free and yet more ordered. This mode derived from his experiences in Italy and from his study of the ancient Romans and Greeks. In 1790 Goethe published the first part of his masterpiece, *Faust,* a drama in verse, which he completed a year before his death in 1832. The play, in its retelling of the German legend of the man who sold his soul to the devil in return for universal knowledge, reflects the romantic unwillingness to restrain the spirit; it also expresses Goethe's own recognition of the magnitude of humanity's daring in its desire for unlimited knowledge and its own fulfillment.

Goethe

An Illustration from Goethe's Sorrows of Werther

Romanticism and nationalism bear much the same relationship to each other in the history of nineteenth-century Europe as they do in the thought of the men and women we have just surveyed. At some points, as in England, they appear to run separate courses. At others they join together, as they did in Germany, whose own history lies at the center of the history of both romanticism and nationalism.

2. NATIONALISM AND NATION-BUILDING: 1800–1848

Nationalism and reform in Prussia, 1806–1815

The humiliating French occupation of Prussia, combined with the growing sense of national destiny exemplified in Fichte's *Addresses,* resulted in a drive on the part of Prussian intellectuals and political reformers to bring their country once more to its former position among European powers. Prussia's crushing defeat by the French in 1806 had been the logical outcome of the inertia that had gripped the country during the half century or so since the aggressive achievements of Frederick the Great. Unlike the rest of the German states, however, allied directly with France in the Confederation of the Rhine, the separate kingdom of Prussia consciously avoided French "contamination," participating unwillingly in the Continental System, and otherwise holding itself aloof.

Military reforms

Its major task was to rebuild its armies, since only by that means could Prussia reassert itself against Napoleon. To that end, two generals, Gerhard von Scharnhorst and August Gneisenau, instituted changes based on an essential lesson in nation-building they had learned from the French Revolution: that men were far more effective fighters if they believed themselves to have some direct stake in the wars they fought. A reconstituted national army, eventually based upon a system of universal military service, involved the country as a whole in its own defense and grew to become a far more consciously "Prussian" force than it had been heretofore. Officers were recruited and promoted on the basis of merit, not birth, although the large majority continued to come from the Junker (aristocratic) class. This breach with tradition encouraged the Prussian middle class to take a more active and enthusiastic interest in its country's affairs. Old or inefficient officers, despite their social standing, were removed from positions of command; training at the royal cadet school in Berlin was modernized.

These reforms, which illustrate the way in which a liberal desire for modernization might combine with nationalism, paralleled similar changes instituted during the same period under the direction of Prussia's principal minister, Baron Heinrich Friedrich Karl vom Stein (1757–1831), and his successor, Prince Karl von Hardenberg (1750–1822). Stein was not himself a Prussian; he was initially less interested in achieving a Prussian nation-state than in uniting by some means

Baron Heinrich Friedrich Karl vom Stein

or other all the various principalities of Germany. He had read Hegel and Fichte, and was convinced that a state must somehow make its citizens aware of their obligations to the national interest. A sense of duty to the state could hardly be kindled, however, without first convincing men and women that loyalty meant reward as well as obligation. Stein therefore labored to dismantle the caste system which had until that time characterized Prussia, in order to permit individuals to rise within society. Stein's Municipal Ordinance of 1808 was a conscious attempt to increase the middle-class Germans' sense of themselves as citizens—again, a goal shared by both liberals and nationalists. Cities and towns were henceforth required to elect their councilmen, while local justice and security continued to be administered by the central government in Berlin; all other matters, including finance, were left to individual communities. Education played a vital role in nation-building. Schools were ideal agencies for the dissemination of the doctrines of national duty. Recognizing this fact, the Prussian reformers expanded facilities for both primary and secondary education. The University of Berlin, founded in 1810, numbered among its faculty such ardent nationalists as Fichte and Savigny, and was the institutional embodiment of the new spirit that contributed to Prussia's eventual victory over the French.

Stein's governmental reforms

The history of Prussia between 1815 and 1850 can most easily be understood in terms of its continuing struggle to establish itself as the leading independent national power among the thirty-nine states that comprised Germany after 1806, and as a successful rival to Austrian domination. The most important Prussian victory in this respect was the establishment of the *Zollverein,* or customs union. By the 1840s, the union included almost all of Germany except German Austria, and offered manufacturers a market of almost 34 million people. But the writings of the economist Friedrich List (1789–1846) inspired a nationalist response to the internationalism of the liberal free-trade economists. List wrote that while free trade might suit the British, it did not suit a nation such as Prussia. Economics, he argued, far from being an abstract science equally applicable everywhere, was a discipline that must be grounded in the particular national experience of individual countries. Germany's, and therefore Prussia's, experience demanded not free trade but high tariffs. Only when sheltered behind a protectionist system could Prussia build the factories and manufacture the goods that would guarantee its economic health.

Economic nationalism

The events that had altered the political shape of Britain and France in the early 1830s—revolution in the latter and liberal reforms in both—had their counterparts in Germany. Liberals had resented both Prussian nationalism and Austrian conservatism. They hoped for the achievement of both unity and freedom, avoiding the particularism that had haunted Germany's political past and the domination by either Austria or Prussia that promised to blight its future. Student

German liberalism thwarted

societies—*Burschenschaften*—had sprung up throughout Germany following the Napoleonic wars. At an assembly in 1817 at Wartburg Castle, where Martin Luther had three hundred years before proclaimed his ninety-five theses, these modern protestants on behalf of "the holy cause of union and freedom" marched to a bonfire upon which they placed the works of reactionary writers. Repressed for a time by Metternich, the *Burschenschaften* reappeared in the late 1820s, and welcomed the 1830 revolution in France. Minor revolts occurred in Brunswick, Saxony, and Hesse-Cassel; unpopular monarchs were replaced by royal relatives more sympathetic to reform. In 1832 at an all-German festival held at Hambach, on the French border, 25,000 men and women toasted Lafayette and denounced the Holy Alliance. Once again, Metternich imposed a series of repressive reforms upon the German Confederation, which effectively stifled protest and thwarted liberal aspirations.

The politics of Frederick William IV

Prussia avoided revolution as a result of the reforms instituted a generation before by Stein and Hardenberg. In 1840 Frederick William IV succeeded to the Prussian throne. Apparently devoted to liberal principles, he relaxed censorship laws and encouraged participation in the central government by provincial diets. It soon became apparent, however, that the king was no liberal, but some sort of romantic-nationalist, and an authoritarian as well. He crushed the revolt of thousands of Silesian weavers in 1844, when they protested the importation of English yarn and cotton goods and their consequent unemployment and poverty. He further declared himself opposed to constitutionalism, that central doctrine in the liberal canon of beliefs. When Prussian liberals pressed, in 1847, for control over legislative and budgetary matters in the recently convened assembly of diets (the *Landtag*) the king saw to it that their request was denied. Frederick William then turned his attention to a scheme whereby Prussia might play a far larger role in the German Confederation. But before his plan could receive a hearing, it was overtaken by the revolutionary movement of 1848, which, as we shall see, engulfed central Europe as it had western Europe, though with different results.

Nationalism in the Austrian Empire

National sentiment, the spirit that served to unite the Prussians, was at the same time operating to divide the heterogeneous elements within the Austrian Empire. Its people, who lived within three major geographical areas—Austria, Bohemia, and Hungary—were composed of a considerable number of different ethnic and language groups: Germans, Czechs, Magyars, Poles, Slovaks, Serbs, and Italians, to name the most prominent. In some parts of the empire, these people lived in isolation; elsewhere they dwelt in direct proximity, if not much harmony, with others. The Austrian Empire attempted to unite these groups by means of a reigning house, the Habsburgs, and a supposedly benevolent bureaucracy. These devices failed increasingly to satisfy the various groups, in whom a spirit of cultural, if not political, nationalism grew persistently stronger in the years after 1815. In the Polish territories of the empire, where the gentry had for generations been conscious of themselves as Poles, the imperial government succeeded in stifling the sentiment by playing off the serfs against their masters, encouraging a class war as a means of preventing an ethnic one. Elsewhere within the empire they were less adroit. In Hungary, nationalism expressed itself in both cultural and political forms. In 1827, a Hungarian national theater was established at Budapest. The year before, Magyar was substituted for Latin as the official language of government. A political movement, whose most formidable leader was the radical nationalist Louis Kossuth (1802–1894), was at the same time seeking independence and a parliamentary government for Hungary.

The most widespread of the eastern European cultural nationalist movements was Pan-Slavism. Slavs included Russians, Poles, Czechs, Slovaks, Slovenes, Croats, Serbs, and Bulgars. Before 1848 Pan-Slavism was an almost exclusively cultural movement, united by a generalized anti-Western sentiment, yet divided by a tendency to quarrel as to the primacy of this or that particular language or tradition. These divisions did not substantially lessen the effect of Pan-Slavism as a further problem of the Austrian Empire. The literature of the movement—for example, the historian Francis Palacky's (1798–1876) *History of the Bohemian People* and the poetry of the revolutionary Pole Adam Mickiewiez (1798–1855)—fed the desires of those who wished to rid themselves of what they considered a foreign yoke. In Russia, slavophilism had been held in check by the Western-looking Alexander I. After his death, however, the notion that the Russian people possessed its particular *Volksgeist* increased in general popularity.

Pan-Slavism

Two other national movements were growing beyond infancy during the years before 1848: one in Italy, the other in Ireland. Italy, at the beginning of the nineteenth century, was a peninsula divided into a multitude of states, most of them poor and ineffectually governed. The most efficient governments in Italy after 1815 were those imposed by Austria on the northern territories of Lombardy and Venetia (see map, p. 832) and by the introverted, visionary, yet intensely reform-minded king of Sardinia, Charles Albert (1831–1849). At the opposite pole were the Kingdom of the Two Sicilies and the Papal States, governed by equally obscurantist rulers, Francis I (1825–1830), a Bourbon, and thereafter by his son, Ferdinand II (1830–1859), and Pope Gregory XVI (1831–1846). Popular uprisings in Modena, Parma, and Bologna occurred in 1830, but with no lasting consequences, either for the initiation of local liberal reforms or for the cause of unification of the various disparate states into some sort of national whole. Among the pan-Italian organizations formed in the confused period at the end of the Napoleonic wars, none was louder in its nationalist proclamations than the Italian *Carbonari*. One member

Nationalism in Italy

Joseph Mazzini

Nationalism in Ireland

of that group, Joseph Mazzini (1805–1872), founded a society of his own in 1831, Young Italy, which was dedicated to the cause of uniting the peninsula. In 1834, from Switzerland, Mazzini launched a totally unsuccessful verbal assault against the Kingdom of Sardinia, in the hope that the rest of Italy would join with him. Mazzini subsequently contented himself with propagandizing for the cause of Italian nationalism and republicanism, attracting a devoted following, particularly among British liberals. Liberals in Italy, however, mistrusted him. Although they too wished to see a united Italy, they were dismayed, as "good" liberals, and members of the middle class, by Mazzini's insistence upon a republic, hoping instead to merge existing principalities together into some sort of constitutional monarchy.

If Italian nationalism was primarily a middle-class liberal phenomenon at this time, the same was not true of the Irish movement to repeal the union with England. Headed by Daniel O'Connell (1775–1847), it derived its strength from the support of Irish peasants. O'Connell's remarkably successful appeal was based on the hatred all Irish felt for the English, because of the centuries of oppression Irish Catholics had suffered under English Protestant rule. Both before and after the official union of 1801, the English had imposed on the Irish a foreign rule that had brought with it little but poverty and persecution. O'Connell's campaign for the repeal of the union was grounded in the hope that he would be able to negotiate some sort of moderate agreement with the English ruling class. The desires of his followers exceeded him in being far more radical in nature. Neither the separatist hopes of O'Connell, called by the Irish the "Liberator," nor the more genuinely nationalist hopes of his followers, however, were to achieve realization. Unlike the nationalist movements of central Europe, nationalism in Ireland faced a powerful and determined adversary— England—which would for a century deny it victory.

3. NATIONALISM, LIBERALISM, AND REVOLUTION, 1848

The history of the revolutions of 1848 in central Europe can most easily be understood in terms of two major themes: the first, the struggle of various nationalities, particularly within the Austrian Empire, to assert their own autonomy; the second, the contention between the forces of liberalism and nationalism in Germany.

The "March Days" in Austria

News of the February revolution in France traveled quickly eastward. By the end of March the Austrian Empire was split apart. Hungary, with Kossuth in the lead, severed all but the most tenuous of links with the House of Habsburg and prepared to draft its own constitution. In Vienna, workers and students imitated their counterparts in Paris, erecting barricades and invading the imperial palace. A measure of the political chaos was the fact that Metternich, veteran of a score of threats to the precarious stability he had crafted, found the pressure this time too great, and fled in disguise to Britain. The feeble Habsburg emperor, Ferdinand, once he had been deserted by Metternich, yielded to nationalist demands from Bohemia and granted that kingdom its own constitution as well. To the south, Italians launched attacks against the Austrian-held territories in Milan, Naples, Venetia, and Lombardy, where the forces of the Sardinian ruler, King Charles Albert, routed the Austrians.

Yet the forces of national sentiment that had brought Austria to its knees then succeeded in allowing the empire to recoup its fortunes. The paradox of nationalism, as it manifested itself in central Europe, was that as soon as a cultural majority had declared itself an independent or semi-independent state, other cultural minorities within that new state complained bitterly about their newly institutionalized inferiority. This is precisely what happened in Bohemia. There the anti-German Czech majority refused to send delegates to an all-German assembly, which was meeting at Frankfurt to draft a German constitution. Instead, they summoned a confederation of Slavs to Prague. The delegates, most of them from within the boundaries of the old Austrian Empire, immediately recognized that the idea of a united Germany represented a far greater threat to their political and cultural autonomy than the fact of the empire ever had. The German minority in Bohemia, however, was naturally anxious to participate in discussions that might result in closer union with their ethnic counterparts. They resented the Bohemian government's refusal to do so. The resulting animosities made it all the easier for the Austrians to take advantage of a May 1848 insurrection in Prague, subdue the city, send the Slav congress packing, and reassert control in Bohemia. Although the Austrian government was at this time a liberal one, the product of the March revolution in Vienna, it was no less determined than its predecessor had been to prevent the total dismemberment of the empire, for economic as well as political reasons. Hence it was quick to restore Lombardy and Venetia to its realm when quarrels among the heretofore united Italian allies had sufficiently weakened their common stand against the Austrians.

Nationalism and counternationalism in Hungary set the stage for the final act of the restoration of Austrian hegemony. Kossuth's radical party was, above all, a Magyar nationalist party. Once in power, in early 1849 it moved the capital from Pressburg, near the Austrian border, to Budapest, and again proclaimed Magyar as the country's official language. These actions offended national minorities within Hungary, particularly the Croats, who prior to the revolution had enjoyed certain liberties under Austrian rule. The Croatians raised an insurgent army and launched a civil war. The Austrains, once more encouraging division along nationalist lines, named the Croatian rebel Josef von Jellachich their military commander against the Magyars. By this time the Viennese liberals began to recognize—too late—that their turn might come next. They were right. Despite a second uprising in Vienna in October, the revolution was spent. Forces loyal to the emperor descended upon Vienna from Bohemia. On October 31, the liberal government capitulated.

Imperial nation-building

Once the imperial government had reasserted itself, it labored to suppress nationalist impulses as thoroughly as possible. Austria's ministers recognized that, though tactically advantageous at times, nationalist movements operated generally to the detriment of the empire's political and economic unity. The emperor's chief minister, Prince Felix von Schwarzenberg, and the minister of the interior, Alexander Bach, both nation-builders, together centralized the state within one united political system. Hungary and Bohemia no longer enjoyed separate rights. Peasants of all ethnic groups, liberated from serfdom as part of the general reform movement, were permitted to retain their freedom, on the grounds of their loyalty to the empire. The law was reformed, again to achieve uniformity, and railways and roads were constructed to link the empire. Economic nationalism was encouraged through tariffs designed to exclude foreign manufactures, while a free trade area within the empire encouraged domestic industries. Having done all it could to eradicate separatist movements, the Austrian government thus moved to secure its advantage by engaging in a vigorous campaign of nation-building.

The failure of revolution in Prussia

In Prussia, revolution ran a similar course. In March, King Frederick William found himself compelled to yield to demands for a popularly elected legislative assembly. When it met, the body proved particularly sympathetic to the plight of the Polish minority within Prussia, and antagonistic toward the Russians, whom radical legislators saw as the major threat to the spread of enlightened political ideas in central Europe. When the assembly's sympathy with Polish nationalism extended to the granting of self-government to Prussian Poland, however, it generated the same feelings among the German minority there that we have seen arousing minorities within the Austrian Empire. In so doing, it precipitated the same eventual results. Germans in Posen, the major city of Prussian Poland, revolted against the newly established Polish government; not surprisingly, Prussian army units on duty sided with the Germans and helped them crush the new government. Power, it now became clear, lay with the army, professionalized since the days of Gneisenau and Scharnhorst, yet still dominated by the Junkers. Against the armed authority of the military, the radical legislators of Berlin were no match; revolution ended in Prussia as quickly as it had begun.

The Frankfurt Assembly

Meanwhile, at Frankfurt, Germans engaged in the debate that provides the history of central Europe in these revolutionary years with its second theme: liberalism vs. nationalism. Delegates had been chosen from across Germany and Austria to attend the Frankfurt Assembly. They were largely from the professional classes—professors, lawyers, administrators—and generally devoted to the cause of

Procession of the German National Assembly to Its Opening Session at St. Paul's Church, Frankfurt, May 1848

middle-class liberalism. Many had assumed that their task would resemble that of the assembly that had met in 1789 to draft a constitution for the French: i.e., they would draft a constitution for a liberal, unified Germany. That former convocation, however, had been grounded in the simple but all-important fact that a French nation-state already existed. The French assembly had been elected to give the nation a new shape and new direction. But a centralized sovereign power was there to reshape; there was an authority that could be either commandeered or, if necessary, usurped. The Frankfurt Assembly, in contrast, was grounded upon nothing but its own words. It was a collection of thoughtful, well-intentioned middle-class liberals, committed to a belief that a liberal-national German state could somehow be constituted out of abstract principles.

Almost from the start, the assembly found itself tangled in the problems of nationality. Who, they asked, were the Germans? A majority of the delegates argued that they were all those who, by language, culture, or geography, felt themselves bound to the enterprise now underway at Frankfurt. The German nation that was to be constituted must include as many of those "Germans" as possible. This

Great Germans vs. Little Germans

point of view came to be known as the "Great German" position. Great Germans found themselves stymied, however, by the unwillingness of other nationalities to be included in their fold. The Czechs in Bohemia, as we have seen, wanted no part of Great Germany. In the end the Great Germans settled that the nation for which they were drafting a constitution should include, among other territories, all Austrian lands except Hungary. This decision meant that the crown of their new country might most logically be offered to the Habsburg emperor. At this point the voice of the "Little Germans" began to be heard. Prussian nationalism took precedence over German nationalism; a minority argued that Austria should be excluded altogether and the crown instead offered to King Frederick William of Prussia.

Liberalism vs. nationalism

The liberalism of the assembly was put to the test by events in Austria and Poland in the fall of 1848. When the imperial forces crushed the Czech and Hungarian rebellions, when the Prussian Junkers put an end to Polish self-government, liberals found themselves forced to cheer. They were compelled to support the suppression of minority nationalities; otherwise there would be no new Germany. But their cheers were for the forces not only of German nationalism but of antiliberal authoritarianism. The assembly's most embarrassing moment occurred when it found itself compelled to take shelter behind the Prussian army. Riots broke out in Frankfurt protesting the assembly's willingness to withdraw from a confrontation with the Danes over the future of Germans in Schleswig, a Danish province. That particular area, which many considered to be part of Germany, had been annexed by the Danes in March 1848. The Frankfurters had been unable to do more than ask the Prussians to win Schleswig back

Fighting in Frankfurt, September 18, 1848. Note the contrast between the disciplined maneuvers of the troops and the guerilla tactics of the rioting populace.

for them; and the Prussians had refused. Hence the riots; hence a second request, this time heeded, for Prussian assistance.

Reduced to the status of dependents, the Frankfurt delegates nevertheless, in the spring of 1849, produced a constitution. By this time Austria, fearing its Prussian rival, had decided to have no more to do with Frankfurt. The Little Germans thus won by default and offered their constitutional monarchy to Frederick William of Prussia. Though tempted, he turned them down, arguing that their constitution was too liberal, embodying as it did the revolutionary notion that a crown could be offered to a monarch. Frederick wanted the crown, but on his own terms. The delegates went home, disillusioned by their experience, many of them convinced that their dual goal of liberalism and nationalism was an impossible one. Some, who refused to surrender that goal, emigrated to the United States, where they believed the goal had already been achieved. Many of those who stayed behind convinced themselves that half the goal was better than none, and sacrificed their liberalism to nationalism.

One German exile who took hope for the future from the events of the revolutions of 1848 was the young Karl Marx (1818–1883), whose radical ideas and activities had compelled his emigration to England. Like his friend and collaborator Friedrich Engels (1820–1895), Marx was the son of middle-class parents. After study at the university of Berlin, in 1842 he took a job as editor of the *Rhineland Gazette,* hoping to use that position to argue for the transformation of a society he was growing to despise. His radical policies soon put him at odds with his publishers, however. He moved first to Paris and then to Brussels, where he helped found the Communist League, a body whose declared aim was the overthrow of the middle class. While in Paris, Marx had renewed a former friendship with Engels. Together, during the late 1840s, they produced a theory of revolutionary change that was published by Marx at the request of the League in 1848, at the height of the struggles on the Continent, as *The Communist Manifesto.*

In the *Manifesto* Marx outlined a theory of history that owed a good deal to the German philosopher Hegel (see above, p. 811). Hegel, it will be recalled, had argued that ideas, the motive force of history, were in constant conflict with each other, and that this clash between ideas in turn would produce an eventual synthesis, representing an advance in the history of the human race. Marx adapted this particular progressive notion of history to his own uses. Whereas Hegel perceived conflict and resolution (a dialectic) in terms of ideas, Marx saw them in terms of economic forces. Society, he argued, was at any time no more than the reflection of a hierarchy of classes dictated by those who own the means of production and control the distribution of its material goods. As history had progressed, so had the means changed. Feudalism and manorialism were vanquished by capitalism. And capitalism, Marx declared, would be vanquished in

The end of the assembly

Karl Marx

The Communist Manifesto

turn by communism. That process, however, would first involve the concentration of capitalist economic power into the hands of fewer and fewer members of the middle class (the bourgeoisie), and the consequent opposition of an ever-increasing and ever-debased working class (the proletariat). Once the proletariat overthrew the bourgeoisie by revolution, as it was bound to do eventually, society as a whole would be emancipated. An interim period in which a "dictatorship of the proletariat" rid the world of the last vestiges of bourgeois society would be followed by an end of the dialectical process and the emergence of a truly classless civilization.

The Manifesto's *appeal*

Marx insisted that the *Manifesto* was not just another theory. His declaration that the proletariat together could consciously participate in the revolutionary process he described—could actually advance history through its own efforts—and that the revolutions of 1848 were part of that process, helps explain the document's eventual appeal. The writings of Marx and Engels did not bring about an immediate proletarian revolution. Few paid much attention to the *Manifesto* when it was published. Indeed, though the *Manifesto,* in its famous declaration, called upon the workers of the world to unite, Marx and Engels realized that this goal would not be achieved quickly. Marx and Engels, however, more than any other political thinkers of the 1830s and 1840s, provided workers with a potential sense of their worth as human beings and of their vital role in the historical process.

4. NATION-BUILDING, 1850–1870

Bismarck

The twenty years between 1850 and 1870 were years of intense nation-building in the Western world. Of the master-builders, none was more accomplished than the man who brought Germany under Prussian rule, Otto von Bismarck (1815–1898). Born into the Junker class, Bismarck had emerged during the revolutionary period of 1848 and 1849, as a defender of the monarchy. Bismarck was really neither a liberal nor a nationalist; he was before all else a Prussian. When he instituted domestic reforms, he did so not because he favored the "rights" of this or that particular group but because he thought that his policies would result in a more united, and hence more powerful, Prussia. When he maneuvered to bring other German states under Prussian domination, he did so not in conformity with a grand Germanic design but because he believed that some sort of union was almost inevitable and, if so, that it must come about at Prussia's behest. He prided himself on being a realist; and he became a first-rate practitioner of what has come to be called *Realpolitik*—the politics of what its practitioners claim to be hardheaded reality. Bismarck readily acknowledged his admiration of power. He at one point had considered a career in the military—not at all surprising considering his Junker origins. He once wrote the emperor William I that he regretted that he was compelled to serve his country from behind a desk rather than at the front. But whatever his post, he intended to command. "I want to play the tune the way it sounds good to me or not at all," he declared. "Pride, the desire to command. . . . I confess I am not free from these passions." Nor did he consider those passions unworthy of the man who was to undertake the task of shaping the fortunes of the German state.

When Bismarck came to power as minister-president of Prussia in 1862, he was confronted by a liberal parliamentary majority that, since 1859, had opposed a campaign to increase military expenditures despite pressure from the king. This majority had been produced by an electoral system that was part of the constitution granted by Frederick William to Prussia in 1850, following the collapse of the assembly. The parliament was divided into two houses, the lower one elected by universal male suffrage. Votes were apportioned according to one's ability to pay taxes, however; those few who together paid one-third of the country's taxes elected one-third of the legislators. A large landowner or industrialist exercised about a hundred times the voting power of a poor man. Contrary to the king's expectations, however, under this constitution a liberal majority was succeeding in thwarting the plans of the sovereign and his advisors. It was to break this deadlock that King William I, who succeeded his brother Frederick William in 1861, summoned Bismarck. In Bismarck the liberals more than met their match. When they refused to levy taxes, he collected them anyway, claiming that the constitution, whatever its purposes, had not been designed to subvert the state. When liberals argued that Prussia was setting a poor example for the rest of Germany, Bismarck replied that Prussia was admired not for its liberalism but for its power.

Bismarck and the liberals

Whether or not the Germans—or the rest of Europe—admired Prussia's power, they soon found themselves confronted by it. Bismarck proceeded to build a nation that in the short space of eight years came into being as the German Empire. Bismarck was assisted in his task by his readiness to take advantage of international situations as they presented themselves, without concerning himself particularly with the ideological or moral implications of his actions. He was aided as well by developments over which he had no initial control but which he was able to turn to his advantage. The first of these, the Crimean War, had occurred in 1854–1856, prior to his taking office. Russia and Turkey, perennial European squabblers, had precipitated the hostilities. Russia invaded the territories of Moldavia and Wallachia (later Rumania) in an attempt to take advantage of the continuing political rot that made the Ottoman Empire an easy prey. In 1854 France and then Britain came to the aid of the Turks by invading Russia's Crimean peninsula. These allies were soon joined by Sardinia. The quarrel had by this time enlarged to include the question of who

The Crimean War

British Encampment near Sebastopol, 1854–1855. Photograph taken by Roger Fenton. The Crimean War was the first to be reported to the world by photograph as well as by news dispatch.

was to protect the Christians in Jerusalem from the Turks; it was fueled from the start as well by Britain's continuing determination to prohibit a strong Russian presence in the Near East. The allies' eventual victory was primarily the result of a British blockade of Russia. The peace settlement was a severe setback for Russia, whose influence in the Balkans was drastically curbed. Moldavia and Wallachia were united as Rumania, which, along with Serbia, was granted power as a self-governing principality. Austrian military resources were severely taxed during the invasion and occupation of Moldavia and Wallachia. And Austria's failure to come to the aid of Russia lost her the support of that powerful erstwhile ally. It was the subsequent weakness of both Russia and Austria, the result of the Crimean War, that Bismarck used to his advantage in the 1860s.

Steps to German unification: (1) weakening of Austria

In consolidating the German states into a union controlled by Prussia, Bismarck first moved to eliminate Austria from its commanding position in the German Confederation. As a means to this end he inflamed the long-smoldering dispute with Denmark over the possession of Schleswig and Holstein. Inhabited by Germans and Danes, these two provinces had an anomalous status. Since 1815 Holstein had been included in the German Confederation, but both were subject to the personal overlordship of the king of Denmark. When, in 1864, the Danish king attempted to annex them, Bismarck invited Austria to participate in a war against Denmark. A brief struggle followed, at the end of which the Danish ruler was compelled to renounce all his claims to Schleswig and Holstein in favor of Austria and Prussia. Then the sequel for which Bismarck had ardently hoped occurred: a quarrel between the victors over division of the spoils. The conflict that followed in 1866, known as the Seven Weeks' War, ended in

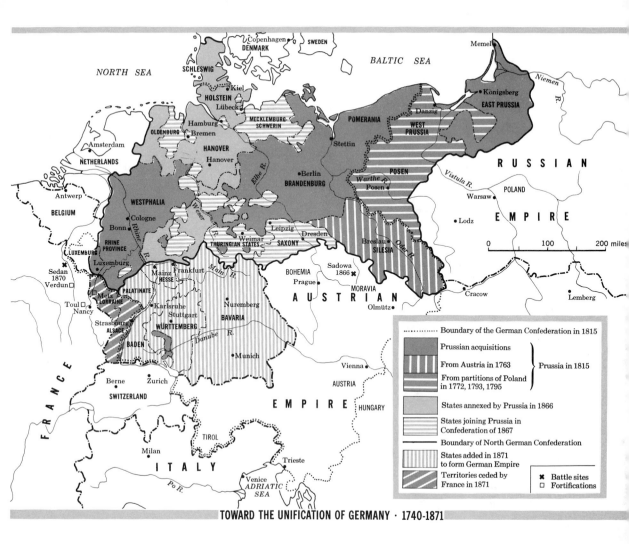

Legend:

.... Boundary of the German Confederation in 1815

Prussian acquisitions
From Austria in 1763 } Prussia in 1815
From partitions of Poland in 1772, 1793, 1795

States annexed by Prussia in 1866

States joining Prussia in Confederation of 1867

——— Boundary of North German Confederation

States added in 1871 to form German Empire

Territories ceded by France in 1871

✖ Battle sites
□ Fortifications

an easy triumph for Prussia. Austria was forced to give up all claims to Schleswig and Holstein, to surrender Venetia, and to acquiesce in the dissolution of the German Confederation. Immediately following the war Bismarck proceeded to isolate Austria by uniting all of the German states north of the Main River into the North German Confederation.

To achieve the confederation Bismarck willingly turned himself into a democrat. He saw that if he was to attain his end, which was a strong union with Prussia at its head, he would need to cultivate a constituency hitherto untapped by any German politicians: the masses. He appreciated the manner by which Napoleon III had reinforced his regime through plebiscites. And Bismarck understood that the majority of Germans were not particularly enthusiastic supporters of capitalist liberals, of the bureaucracies of their own small states, or

(2) courting the masses

of the Austrian Habsburgs. The constitution he devised for his confederation provided for two chambers: the upper chamber represented the individual states within the union, though not equally; the lower chamber was elected by universal manhood suffrage. The liberal middle class, to say nothing of the Junkerdom, was astonished and dismayed, as well they might be. Bismarck's intention was to use popular support to strengthen the hand of the central government against the interests of both landlords and capitalists.

(3) the Franco-Prussian War

Bismarck's final step in the completion of German unity was the Franco-Prussian War of 1870–1871. He hoped that a conflict with France would kindle the spirit of German nationalism in Bavaria, Würtemberg, and other southern states still outside the confederation. Taking advantage of a diplomatic tempest concerning the right of the Hohenzollerns (Prussia's ruling family) to occupy the Spanish throne, Bismarck worked hard to force a Franco–German misunderstanding. King William agreed to meet with the French ambassador at the resort spa of Ems in Prussia to discuss the Spanish succession. When William telegraphed Bismarck that the demands of the French for perpetual exclusion of the Hohenzollern family from the Spanish throne had been refused, Bismarck released portions of the message to the press so as to make it appear that King William had insulted the ambassador—which he had not done. Once the garbled report of what happened at Ems was received in France, the nation reacted with a call for war. The call was echoed in Prussia, where Bismarck published evidence that he claimed proved French designs upon the Rhineland. Upon the declaration of war, the south German states rallied to Prussia's side in the belief that it was the victim of aggression. The war was quickly fought. The French were no match for Prussia's professionally trained and superbly equipped forces. Nor did other European powers come to France's assistance. Austria, the most likely candidate, remained weakened by its recent war with Prussia. The Magyars, who at this time had assumed positions of influence within the Austrian government, were quite prepared to welcome a strengthened Prussia; Prussia's growing strength in Germany would further increase Austria's weakness there. And the weaker Austria was as a German power, the stronger would be the claims of the Magyars to predominance. Once more one nationalist consciousness was grinding against another. The war began in July; it ended in September with the defeat of the French and the capture of Napoleon III himself at Sedan in France.

The German Empire

Following the collapse of the French imperial government, insurrectionary forces in Paris continued to hold out against the Germans until the winter of 1871. Bismarck meanwhile proceeded to consummate the German union toward which he had worked so assiduously. On January 18, 1871, in the great Hall of Mirrors at Versailles the German Empire was proclaimed. All those states, except Austria, which had not already been absorbed into Prussia declared their allegiance to William I, henceforth emperor or kaiser. Four months later, at Frankfurt, a treaty between the French and Germans ceded the border region of Alsace to the new empire, condemned the French to an indemnity of five billion francs, and thereby broadcast to the world the remarkable success of Bismarck's nation-building.

Events in Italy ran a course almost parallel to that which had led to the unification of Germany. Italy before 1848, it will be recalled, was a patchwork of petty states. The most important of those possessing independence were the Kingdom of Sardinia in the north, the Papal States in the central region, and the Kingdom of the Two Sicilies in the south. The former republics of Lombardy and Venetia were held by Austria, while Habsburg dependents ruled in Tuscany, Parma, and Modena. As the revolutionary fervor of 1848 swept across the peninsula, one ruler after another granted democratic reforms. Charles Albert of Sardinia outdistanced all the others by guaranteeing civil liberties and granting a parliamentary form of government. It soon became evident, however, that the Italians were as determined nationalists as they were liberals. For some years romantic patriots had been dreaming of a *Risorgimento,* which would restore the nation to the position of glorious leadership it had held in Roman times and during the Renaissance. To achieve this, it was universally agreed that Italy must be welded into a single state. But opinions differed as to the form the new government should take. Young idealists followed the leadership of Mazzini. Religious-minded patriots believed that the most practicable solution would be to federate the state of Italy under the presidency of the pope. The majority of the more moderate nationalists advocated a constitutional monarchy built upon the foundations of the Kingdom of Sardinia. The aims of this third group gradually crystallized under the leadership of a shrewd Sardinian nobleman, Count Camillo di Cavour (1810–1861). In 1850 he was appointed minister of commerce and agriculture of his native state and in 1852 prime minister.

The campaign for unification of the Italian peninsula began with efforts to expel the Austrians. In 1848 revolts were organized in the territories under Habsburg domination, and an army of liberation marched from Sardinia to aid the rebels; but the movement ended in failure. It was then that Cavour, as the new leader of the campaign, turned to less heroic but more practical methods. In 1858 he held a secret meeting with Napoleon III and prepared the stage for an Italian War of Liberation. Napoleon agreed to cooperate in driving the Austrians from Italy for the price of the cession of Savoy and Nice by Sardinia to France. A war with Austria was duly provoked in 1859, for a time all went well for the Franco-Italian allies. After the conquest of Lombardy, however, Napoleon III suddenly withdrew, fearful of ultimate defeat and afraid of antagonizing the Catholics in his own country by aiding the avowedly anticlerical government of Cavour. Thus deserted by its ally, Sardinia was unable to expel the Austrians from Venetia. Nevertheless, extensive gains were made; Sardinia an-

Camillo di Cavour

THE UNIFICATION OF ITALY

Map legend:
- The Kingdom of Sardinia at the time of the Congress of Vienna, 1815
- Territories acquired, 1859-1860
- Territories acquired, 1860-1870

nexed Lombardy, and acquired by various means the duchies of Tuscany, Parma, and Modena, and the northern portion of the Papal States. Sardinia was now more than twice its original size and by far the most powerful state in Italy.

The second step in consolidating Italy was the conquest of the kingdom of the Two Sicilies. This kingdom was ruled by a Bourbon, Francis II, who was thoroughly hated by his Italian subjects. In May 1860 a romantic adventurer, Giuseppe Garibaldi, set out with a regiment of one thousand "red shirts" to rescue his fellow Italians from oppression. Within three months he had conquered the island of Sicily and had then marched to the deliverance of Naples, where the people were already in revolt. By November the whole kingdom of Francis II had fallen to Garibaldi. He at first intended to convert the territory into an independent republic but was finally persuaded to surrender it to the Kingdom of Sardinia. With most of the peninsula now united under a single rule, Victor Emmanuel II, king of Sardinia, assumed the title of king of Italy (March 17, 1861). Venetia was still in the hands of the Austrians, but in 1866, following their defeat in the Seven Weeks' War, they were forced by the Prussians to cede it to Italy. All that remained to complete the unification of Italy was the annexation of Rome. The Eternal City had resisted conquest thus far, largely because of the military protection accorded the pope by Napoleon III. But in 1870 the outbreak of the Franco–Prussian War compelled Napoleon to withdraw his troops. In September 1870 Italian soldiers occupied Rome, and in July of the following year it was made the capital of the by now united kingdom.

The occupation of Rome brought the kingdom of Italy into conflict with the papacy. During the first years of his reign, which began in 1846, Pope Pius IX instituted a series of "modern" improvements: gaslight, railways, vaccination. Yet Pius, who, like his reactionary predecessor, Gregory XVI, continued to rule over the Papal States in the manner of a secular prince, was no friend to either liberalism or nationalism. And no wonder: the movement that had brought Italian troops to Rome had from its inception expressed hostility to the Church as an impediment to unification. Following the occupation of Rome in 1870, an attempt was made to solve the problem of relations between the state and the papacy. In 1871 the Italian parliament enacted the Law of Papal Guaranties, purporting to define the status of the pope as a reigning sovereign. The reigning pontiff, Pius IX, promptly denounced this law on the ground that issues affecting the pope could be settled only by an international treaty to which he himself was a party. Whereupon he shut himself up in the Vatican and refused to have anything to do with a government that had so shamefully treated Christ's vicar on earth. His successors continued this practice of voluntary imprisonment until 1929, when a series of agreements between the Italian government and Pius XI effected settlement of the dispute.

Nation-building was the preoccupation of another major country in the first half of the nineteenth century: the United States. The history of the expansion and consolidation of this newly born country into a nation of remarkable economic potential in little over half a century can best be understood in terms of several major factors. The first is the growth of political democracy.

The United States did not begin its history as a democracy. No more than a few of the country's leaders professed genuine democratic ideals. The authors of the Constitution were not interested in the rule

Giuseppe Garibaldi

Pope Pius IX. This contemporary cartoon lampoons the pope, shown as a conniving, worldly politician hiding behind the mask of Jesus. Pius IX, though in his early years something of a liberal, took an extreme reactionary political position in the wake of the revolutionary upheaval of 1848.

Thomas Jefferson by Gilbert Stuart

Jeffersonian principles

Jacksonian democracy

of the masses. The primary aim of the founders of the United States was to establish a *republic* that would promote stability and protect the rights of private property against the leveling tendencies of majorities. For this reason they adopted checks and balances between the branches of government, devised the Electoral College for choosing the president, created a powerful judiciary, and entrusted the selection of senators to the legislatures of the several states.

Following the establishment of a new and more firmly united government under the Constitution of 1787, democratic ideals began to win acceptance in the United States. Until 1801 the Federalists, the party of large landowners and successful merchant capitalists, held power. In 1801 the Democratic-Republicans gained control as a result of the election of Thomas Jefferson (1743–1826) to the presidency. Although this event is often referred to as the Jeffersonian Revolution, on the supposition that Jefferson was the champion of the masses and of the political power of the underprivileged, there is danger in carrying this interpretation too far. Jefferson strenuously opposed the unlimited sovereignty of the majority. His conception of an ideal political system was an aristocracy of "virtue and talent," in which respect for personal liberty would be the guiding principle.

Yet the Jeffersonian movement had a number of ultimately democratic objectives. Its leaders were vigorous opponents of special privilege, whether of birth or of wealth. They worked for the abolition of established churches. They led the campaign for the addition of a Bill of Rights to the Constitution and were almost exclusively responsible for its success. Although professing devotion to the principle of the separation of powers, they actually believed in the supremacy of the representatives of the people and viewed with abhorrence the attempts of the executive and judicial branches to increase their power.

By 1820, these notions were being expressed in more direct and forceful terms. Urban populations grew increasingly conscious of their political importance and demanded attention to their interests. The predominance of the agricultural Old South (the South of the original thirteen colonies) had declined. As a result of the Louisiana Purchase (a vast tract bought from the French in 1803) and of increased settlement in the area known as the Northwest Territory (western New York State and Ohio), a new frontier had come into existence. Life there was characterized by a rugged freedom that left little room for class distinctions. In the struggle to survive, hard work and sharp wits counted for more than birth and education. As a consequence a new democratic spirit, which eventually found its leader in Andrew Jackson (1767–1845), took shape around the principle of equality. The Jacksonian Democrats transformed the doctrines of liberalism into a more radical creed. They pronounced all (excluding slaves, American Indians, and women) politically equal, not merely in rights but in privileges. They were devoted adherents to the causes of suffrage for all white males; the election, rather than appointment, of all governmental office-holders; and the frequent rotation of men in positions of political power—a doctrine that served to put more Democratic politicians into federal office. These democratic beliefs helped encourage a spirit of unity within the United States during a period of rapid territorial expansion.

As the United States continued to acquire more territories in the West (the most notable addition resulting from the conquest of lands in the Southwest from Mexico in 1846), it not only faced the task of binding those areas and their settlers into the nation. There was, as well, the problem of assimilating the thousands of immigrants who came to America from Europe in the first half of the century. Many were Scottish and English; for them the difficulties of adjusting to a new life in a new country were generally not difficult since they spoke a common language with their fellow-citizens. For others the problems were far greater. For the Irish, who immigrated in great numbers, particularly during the 1840s, there was the fact of their alien religion, Roman Catholicism. For Germans and others from the Continent, there was the language barrier. The United States's policy toward its immigrants was directed against the creation of any foreign nationalist enclaves apart from the main body of its citizenry. Although foreign-language newspapers were tolerated, and immigrants were free to attend churches and social gatherings as they chose, English remained the language of the public schools, the police, the law courts, and the government. To hold a job, a person was almost always forced to learn at least some English. In this way, the

Immigration

"Meal Time." Between the decks on an immigrant ship to the United States in the mid–nineteenth century.

Slavery in the American South. Left: Slave pens at Pine, Birch & Co., a Virginia slave broker. Right: Cotton being prepared by slaves for the gin on a South Carolina plantation.

United States encouraged immigrants to shed their "foreign" ways and to commit themselves to their adopted nation.

If there were enclaves in the United States, they existed in the South, where the institution of slavery and the economic dependence of the planters upon England produced two distinct minorities, neither of which was to be assimilated without resort to war. During the nineteenth century, slavery had been abolished throughout much of the Western world, for both economic and humanitarian reasons. Southern planters continued to insist that without the slave system they would go bankrupt. To humanitarians they responded with arguments based upon theories of racial inferiority and upon their self-professed reputation as benevolent masters. The position of these Southern spokesmen grew increasingly distasteful and unconvincing to the North. As the country opened to the west, North and South engaged in a protracted tug-of-war as to which new states were to be "free" and which "slave." Northerners were motivated by more than concern for the well-being of blacks. The North was industrializing fast. Capitalists there were demanding protective tariffs to assist them in their enterprises. Southerners favored free trade, since they wished to import British goods in return for the cotton they sold to the manufacturers of Lancashire.

The American Civil War, when it came in 1861, was a war not about the issue of slavery so much as it was about preserving the union of American states and territories. President Abraham Lincoln under-

(3) slavery and the South

took the war to defend the unity of the United States. European governments, while never recognizing the Confederacy officially, nevertheless remained sympathetic to its cause. They hoped that the fragmentation of the United States would result in the opening up of markets for their manufactured goods, much as the dissolution of the Spanish Empire had proved a boon to European commercial interests. The victory of the North in 1865, however, ensured the continued growth of the United States as a nation. The Fourteenth Amendment to the Constitution stated specifically that all were citizens of the United States, and not of an individual state or territory. In declaring that no citizen was to be deprived of life, liberty, or property without due process of law, it established that "due process" was to be defined by the national, and not the state or territorial governments.

The Civil War

The years following the American Civil War witnessed the binding together of the nation economically under the direction of Northern private enterprise. The symbol of the North's triumph as a nation-builder came with the driving of the final spike of the transcontinental Union Pacific railroad in 1869. Nation-building in Europe and the United States helped ensure the continuing expansion of capitalism. Liberalism had provided a general climate of opinion and a set of attitudes toward government that encouraged industrialization. Nation-building, in its turn, produced the necessary economic units— large enough to generate the wherewithal to sustain economic growth; confident enough to enter into competition with the British Goliath.

Nation-building in the West

SELECTED READINGS

• *Items so designated are available in paperback editions.*

Artz, Frederick B., *France under the Bourbon Restoration, 1814–1830*, New York, 1963. A basic survey with a good treatment of romanticism.
• Beales, Derek, *The Risorgimento and the Unification of Italy*, New York, 1971. Objective, concise survey of Italian unification.
• Berlin, Isaiah, *Karl Marx: His Life and Environment*, New York, 1948. The best short account.
• Binkley, Robert C., *Realism and Nationalism, 1852–1871*, New York, 1935. An excellent synthesis despite some dated passages.
• Craig, Gordon, *The Politics of the Prussian Army, 1640–1945*, Oxford, 1964. Much more than the title implies. An excellent analysis of Prussian social structure and the role of the army in social reform and unification.
Deak, Istvan, *The Lawful Revolution: Louis Kossuth and the Hungarians, 1848–1849*, New York, 1979.
• Epstein, Klaus, *The Genesis of German Conservatism*, Princeton, 1966. Provides excellent early-nineteenth-century background.
• Eyck, Erich, *Bismarck and the German Empire*, London, 1958. The best one-volume study of Bismarck.

Eyck, Frank, *The Frankfurt Parliament, 1848–49,* New York, 1968. A detailed study of its composition and procedure.

Ford, Guy Stanton, *Stein: The Era of Reform in Prussia, 1807–1815,* New York, 1922. An old but still valuable work on a leading Prussian reformer.

• Hamerow, Theodore, *Restoration, Revolution, Reaction,* Princeton, 1966. An excellent social and economic history of Germany between 1815 and 1871.

• ———, *The Social Foundations of German Unification, 1858–1871,* 2 vols., Princeton, 1972. Concentrates on economic factors which determined the solution to the unification question. An impressive synthesis.

Hayes, C. J. H., *The Historical Evolution of Modern Nationalism,* rev. ed., New York, 1968. A valuable survey.

• Hobsbawm, Eric J., *The Age of Revolution, 1789–1848,* New York, 1962. An unrigidly Marxist interpretation, good for the entire period it covers.

• Holborn, Hajo, *History of Modern Germany,* Vols. II and III, Princeton, 1964. The best survey of German history in English.

• Howard, Michael, *The Franco-Prussian War,* New York, 1969. The war's effect on society.

• Kohn, Hans, *The Idea of Nationalism,* New York, 1944. A perceptive analysis.

• Krieger, Leonard, *The German Idea of Freedom,* Boston, 1957. A difficult but rewarding study of German political thought.

Macartney, C. A., *The Hapsburg Empire, 1790–1918,* London, 1968. A worthwhile survey.

Mack Smith, Denis, *Garibaldi: A Great Life in Brief,* New York, 1956.

———, *The Making of Italy, 1796–1870,* New York, 1968. A narrative with documents.

• Mehring, Franz, *Karl Marx: The Story of His Life,* New York, 1976. A good, recent life.

Namier, Lewis B., *1848: The Revolution of the Intellectuals,* London, 1964. A controversial analysis, highly critical of the Frankfurt Assembly.

Noyes, P. H., *Organization and Revolution: Working-Class Associations in the German Revolutions of 1848–49,* Princeton, 1966. An important monograph analyzing the degree of working-class consciousness at the time of the revolution.

• Pflanze, Otto, *Bismarck and the Development of Germany, 1815–1871,* Princeton, 1963. An impressive analysis of Bismarck's aims and policies.

Rosenberg, Hans, *Bureaucracy, Aristocracy, and Autocracy: The Prussian Experience, 1660–1815,* Cambridge, Mass., 1958. A difficult but valuable book explaining the forces that molded the modern Prussian state.

Salvemini, Gaetano, *Mazzini,* London, 1956. Biography with excerpts from Mazzini's writings.

Snyder, Louis L., *Roots of German Nationalism,* Bloomington, Ind., 1978.

• Taylor, A. J. P., *The Habsburg Monarchy, 1809–1918,* rev. ed., London, 1965. An idiosyncratic account by an eminent historian.

SOURCE MATERIALS

Bismarck, Otto von, *Bismarck, the Man and the Statesman, Written and Dictated by Himself,* London, 1899. Bismarck's memoirs, written after his fall from power.

Clausewitz, Karl von, *On War,* London, 1968. Published posthumously, this work, in reality a philosophy of war, was perceived by the Prussian military bureaucracy as a mandate for total war—for the subjugation of all interests of the state to war.

Fichte, Johann Gottlieb, *Addresses to the German Nation,* New York, 1968. Presented in 1808 while French armies occupied Prussia, these lectures helped stir a German nationalist spirit.

• Marx, Karl, and Friedrich Engels, *The Marx-Engels Reader,* 2nd ed., by R. C. Tucker, New York, 1978. Reprints the basic texts.

Schurz, Carl, *The Reminiscences of Carl Schurz,* 3 vols., New York, 1907–1908. Especially valuable is Vol. I. A young German liberal in 1848 and a delegate to the Frankfurt Assembly, Schurz spent the rest of his life as an exile in the United States.

Part Six

THE WEST AT THE
WORLD'S CENTER

The years between 1870 and 1945 found the West at the center of global af-
fairs. The industrial supremacy of western Europe and the United States
gave them a combined power greater than that possessed by any nation or
empire in previous times. Yet world domination was by no means accom-
panied by any sense of general world order. The economic might of the
Western nations, while it resulted in their ability to dominate the less de-
veloped quarters of the globe, resulted, as well, in their concern lest one of
their number overpower the others. The old system of the balance of
power, designed to preserve peace by ensuring that no one country achieved
overwhelming predominance at the expense of its neighbors, was strained to
the breaking point by economic rivalries that stretched around the world.
Meanwhile, tensions mounted within each nation, as landed and middle
classes, threatened by the possibility of social turmoil, tried to balance the
mounting clamor for political concessions against their desire to retain power
in their own hands. Twice during the period, in 1914 and 1939, interna-
tional and domestic pressures exploded into global wars. Those wars and
their results, generated by the rivalries and miscalculations of the Western
nations, so sapped the strength of those nations as to depose them thereafter
as the sole arbiters of the world's destinies.

	POLITICS	SCIENCE & INDUSTRY
1870		First commercially practical electrical generator, 1870
		Gilcrist-Thomas steel process, 1870s
	Paris Commune, 1871	
	Kulturkampf, Germany, 1872	
	League of Three Emperors, 1873	
	Constitution for Third French Republic, 1875	Germ theory of disease, 1875
	End of First International, 1876	Invention of telephone, 1876
	Congress of Berlin, 1878	
	Triple Alliance, 1882	
	Berlin conference on imperialism, 1885	
	Second International formed, 1889	
	Pan-Slavism, 1890–1914	
	Dreyfus affair, 1894–1899	
		Discovery of the X ray, 1895
	Spanish-American War, 1898	Marie Curie, discovery of radium, 1898
	Boer War, 1899–1902	Invention of wireless telegraph, 1899
1900		
	N. Lenin, *What Is to Be Done?,* 1902	
		First airplane flight, 1903
	Russo-Japanese War, 1904–1905	Ivan Pavlov, Nobel Prize for physiology, 1904
	Revolution in Russia, 1905	Albert Einstein, development of relativity theory, 1905–1910
	Triple Entente, 1907	
	Bosnian Crisis, 1908	Model T Ford, 1908
	Revolt of the Young Turks, 1908	
	Balkan Wars, 1912–1913	
	First World War, 1914–1918	
	Russian Revolution, 1917	
	Treaty of Versailles, 1919	
	Socialist revolution, Germany, 1919	
1920	League of Nations, 1920–1946	
	NEP, Russia, 1921	
	Mussolini's March on Rome, 1922	
	Hitler's beer-hall putsch, 1923	
	New constitution, Soviet Union, 1924	
	Locarno agreements, 1925	
		Discovery of viruses, sulfa drugs, and penicillin, 1930s
	Hitler, chancellor of Germany, 1933	World economic conference, 1933
	New Deal, United States, 1933–1940	
	Italy conquers Ethiopia, 1935–1936	National rearmament programs, 1935
	Rome-Berlin Axis, 1936	
	Spanish Civil War, 1936–1939	
	Germany annexes Austria, 1938	
	Munich conference, 1938	
	Nazi-Soviet pact, 1939	Discovery of atomic fission, 1939
1940	Second World War, 1939–1945	
	United States enters war, 1941	
	Allied invasion of Normandy, 1944	
	Bombing of Hiroshima and Nagasaki, 1945	First atomic bomb test, 1945
	United Nations founded, 1945	

ECONOMICS & SOCIETY	ARTS & LETTERS	
		1870
	Impressionism in art, 1870–1900	
Growth of finance capitalism, 1880s		
Social welfare legislation, Germany, 1882–1884		
	Émile Zola, *Germinal*, 1885	
Sherman Anti-Trust Act, United States, 1890	Henrik Ibsen, *Hedda Gabler*, 1890	
	Paul Cézanne, *The Card Players*, 1890–1892	
Meline tariff, 1892		
	George Bernard Shaw, *Plays Pleasant* and *Unpleasant*, 1898	
Women's suffrage movement, England, 1900–1914	Sigmund Freud, *The Interpretation of Dreams*, 1900	1900
Social welfare legislation, France, 1904; 1910		
	Cubism in art 1905–1930	
Social welfare legislation, England, 1906–1912		
	Marcel Proust, *Remembrance of Things Past*, 1913–1918	
	Oswald Spengler, *The Decline of the West*, 1918	
	Bauhaus established, 1919	
German inflation, 1920s	Writers of the "Lost Generation," 1920–1930	1920
	Surrealism and Dadaism, 1920s	
	Ludwig Wittgenstein, *Tractatus Logico-philosophicus*, 1921	
	T. S. Eliot, *The Waste Land*, 1922	
	James Joyce, *Ulysses*, 1922	
Great Depression, 1929–1940	Neo-realism in art, 1930s	
J. M. Keynes, *General Theory of Employment, Interest, and Money*, 1936		
		1940
	Jean-Paul Sartre, *Being and Nothingness*, 1943	

Chapter 24

THE PROGRESS OF INTERNATIONAL INDUSTRIALIZATION AND COMPETITION (1870-1914)

We have conquered for ourselves a place in the sun. It will now be my task to see to it that this place in the sun shall remain our undisputed possession. . . .

—Kaiser William II, speech, 1901

I f most historians now speak of a second industrial revolution oc-curring during the years after 1870, they are quick to qualify the term. Whatever the changes in technique and in scope—and they were significant—they do not compare to those which characterized the first revolution—*the* Industrial Revolution. There is, however, good reason to distinguish a second period of industrial development and advance from the first. Successful nation-building meant that the years 1870–1914 would be characterized by sharply increased interna-tional political and economic rivalries, culminating in a scramble after imperial territories in Africa and Asia. Britain, if it did not actually surrender its industrial primacy during this period, failed to counter with any real success the energetic and determined challenges from Germany and the United States to its constantly decreasing lead. New technology, particularly in the fields of metals, chemicals, and elec-tricity, resulted in new products. Larger populations and improving standards of living produced greater demand, which, in turn, increased the volume of production. And the need for increased production called forth significant reorganization to provide a freer supply of capital and to ensure a more efficient labor force. It is these changes that distin-guish the second stage of industrialization from the first, and therefore warrant its separate treatment. Yet they must be perceived as stem-ming not only from those economic conditions that were the result of the first stage, but also from the more general political, social, and cultural climate whose history we have been tracing.

A second industrial revolution

In analyzing the progress of industrialization, we shall deal with changes in three major areas: in technology, in scope and scale of production, and in the reorganization of the capitalist system. Finally we shall examine the phenomenon of late–nineteenth-century imperialism, and consider the extent to which that phenomenon can be attributed to increasing economic and industrial rivalries.

1. NEW TECHNOLOGIES

Technology in steel

A most important technological change in this period resulted in the mass production of steel. The advantages of steel over iron—a result of steel's lower carbon content—are its hardness, its malleability, and its strength. Steel can keep its cutting edge, where iron cannot; it can be worked more easily than iron, which is brittle and which, if it is to be used industrially, must almost always be cast (that is, poured into molds). And steel, because of its strength in proportion to its weight and volume, makes a particularly adaptable construction material. These advantages had been recognized by craftsmen for centuries. Until steel could be produced both cheaply and in mass, however, the advantages remained more theoretical than real. Two inventions, during the earlier years of the Industrial Revolution, had reduced the price and increased the output of steel to some degree. The crucible technique, discovered in the eighteenth century in England, called for the heating of relatively small amounts of iron ore to a point at which foreign matter could be removed by skimming, the carbon content reduced, and a proper proportion of carbon distributed evenly throughout the finished product. Although individual crucibles were not large, holding on the average no more than forty-five to sixty pounds, they could be poured together to produce steel ingots of several tons. A century later, in the early 1840s, two Germans adapted the puddling process, used in the production of iron, to the manufacture of steel. While it did not produce steel as hard as that made in crucibles, it reduced its price considerably.

*Bessemer, Siemens-
Martin, and Gilchrist-
Thomas systems*

Not until the invention of the Bessemer and Siemens-Martin processes, however, could steel begin to compete with iron. In the 1850s, an Englishman, Henry Bessemer, discovered that by blowing air into and through the molten metal he could achieve a more exact degree of decarbonization in much shorter time, and with far larger quantities of ore, than was possible with either the crucible or puddling methods. Bessemer soon found, however, that his "converters" were incapable of burning off sufficient quantities of phosphorous; and phosphorous in anything but the smallest quantities made the metal unworkable. A partial solution was achieved with the introduction of nonphosphoric hematite ores. Yet this was of little long-term use in most European countries, where supplies of hematite ore were not

The Rise of the Steel Industry. Bristling with massive machinery such as this steam-hammer, the Krupp Works in Essen, Germany, was already a major force in steel production by the 1870s.

abundant. This same problem plagued the German inventors Frederick and William Siemens, whose furnace made use of waste gases to increase heat. Not until Pierre Martin, a Frenchman, discovered that the introduction of scrap iron into the mix would induce proper decarbonization, could the Siemens furnace be used to make steel commercially. And not until the late 1870s was the problem of phosphoreting solved for both the Bessemer and the Siemens-Martin processes. The solution was a simple one, discovered by two Englishmen, a clerk and a chemist: Sidney Gilchrist Thomas and his cousin Sidney Gilchrist. They introduced limestone into the molten iron to combine with the phosphorus, which was then siphoned from the mix. And they lined the converter in such a way that the slag was prevented from eating away the walls and releasing phosphorus back into the molten metal.

Together, these three processes revolutionized the production of steel. Although the use of iron did not end overnight, steel soon moved into the lead. In the British shipbuilding industry, for example, steel had overtaken iron by 1890. In part because Siemens-Martin was particularly suited to the manufacture of steel plates used in shipbuilding, that process dominated the manufacture of steel in Britain, where shipbuilding was a major industry. Bessemer steel, which could be manufactured more cheaply and in larger plants, was

Increased steel production

more commonly produced on the Continent and in America. The result was a particular increase in the production of German steel: by 1901, German converters were capable of pouring annually an average of 34,000 tons, compared to Britain's 21,750. By 1914 Germany was producing twice as much steel as Britain, and the United States twice as much as Germany.

Electricity

A second and equally important technological development resulted in the availability of electric power for industrial, commercial, and domestic use. Electricity's particular advantages result from the facts that it can be easily transmitted as energy over long distances, and that it can be converted into other forms of energy—heat and light, for example. Although electricity had, of course, been discovered prior to the first Industrial Revolution, its advantages could not have been put to general use without a series of inventions which occurred during the nineteenth century. Of these, some of the most important were the invention of the chemical battery by the Italian Alessandro Volta in 1800; of electromagnetic induction by the Englishman Michael Faraday in 1831; of the electromagnetic generator in 1866; of the first commercially practical generator of direct current in 1870; and of alternators and transformers capable of producing high-voltage alternating current in the 1880s. These inventions meant that by the end of the century it was possible to send electric current from large power stations over comparatively long distances. Electric power could be manufactured by water—hence cheaply—and delivered from its source to the place where it was needed.

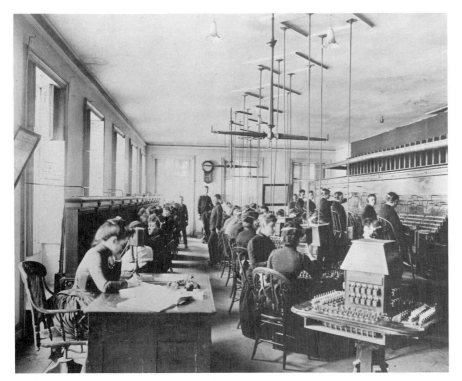

New Technology: The Telephone. This 1885 photograph of a New York City telephone exchange bears witness to the transformation wrought by the dramatic expansion of the electrical industry. Note also the extent to which the position of operator has become the province of female employees.

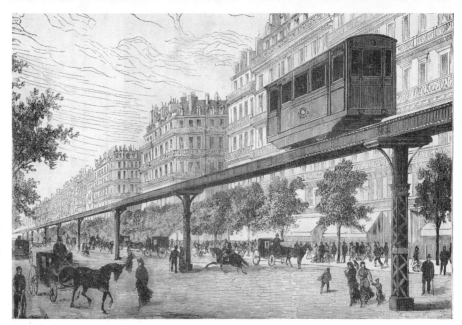

New Technology: The Elevated Train. This electric railway was erected in Paris in the 1880s.

Once it had been delivered to its destination, the power was converted and put to use in myriad ways. Households quickly became one of the major users of electrical power. The invention by Thomas Edison of the incandescent filament lamp—or light bulb—was crucial in this regard. As individual houses were electrified to receive the power that was to be transformed into light, consumer demand for electricity resulted in further expansion of the electrical industry. Demand for electrical power was increasing in the industrial sector as well. Electric motors soon began to power subways, tramways, and, eventually, long-distance railways. Electricity made possible the development of new techniques in the chemical and metallurgical industries. Most important, electricity helped to transform the work patterns of the factory. Heavy steam engines had made equipment and machinery stationery; electric motors meant that comparatively lightweight power tools could be moved—often by hand—to the site of a particular piece of work. The result was far greater flexibility in terms of factory organization. Smaller workshop industries benefited as well; they could accommodate themselves to electrically powered motors and tools in a way they could not to steam.

The uses of electricity

Steel and electricity were only two of the most important areas where technological changes were taking place. The chemical industry was significantly advanced by developments in the manufacture of alkali and organic compounds. Demand for alkali had increased with the demand for soaps and textiles, and with the changes in the manufacturing process of paper, which required large amounts of bleach. An older, more expensive and wasteful technique used extensively by the British was superseded after 1880 by a new process perfected by the Belgian Ernest Solvay. The result was, again, a rapid overtaking of

Other technological advances

The First Successful Airplane Flight

the British by the Germans in the production not only of alkalis but of sulfuric acid, a by-product recoverable in the Solvay process, and used in the manufacture of fertilizers, petroleum refining, iron, steel, and textiles. In the field of organic compounds, the impetus for further discovery came as a result of demand for synthetic dyes. Although the British and French were the first successful pioneers in this area, the Germans once more moved ahead to a commanding lead by 1900. At the turn of the century German firms controlled about 90 percent of the world market.

Improved engines

The need for more and more power to meet increasing industrial demands resulted not only in developments in the field of electricity, already noted, but in the improved design and expanded capacity of steam engines. The most noteworthy invention in this area was the steam turbine, which permitted engines to run at speeds heretofore unobtainable. Internal combustion engines made their appearance during this period as well. Their major advantage lay in their efficiency; i.e., they could be powered automatically, and did not need to be stoked by hand like steam engines. Once liquid fuels—petroleum and distilled gasoline—became available, as they did increasingly with the discovery of oil fields in Russia, Borneo, and Texas about 1900, the internal combustion engine took hold as a serious competitor to steam. By 1914 most navies had converted from coal to oil, as had domestic steamship companies. The automobile and the airplane, both still in their infancies, made little impact upon the industrial world, however, before 1914.

2. CHANGES IN SCOPE AND SCALE

These technological changes must be understood as occurring against a background of—indeed in part as a result of—a constantly growing population and a generally increased standard of living for the majority of men and women in the Western world. Between 1870 and 1914, *Population increases* Europe's population increased from 295 million to 450 million. This was the case despite a declining birth rate in the more industrially advanced countries of western Europe, where more and more middle- and working-class men and women were postponing marriage and limiting the number of their children, confident that those children they did have stood a fairly decent chance of survival. Population growth was primarily the result of a sharp decline in infant mortality, caused by improved sanitation and diet, and by the virtual elimination of diseases such as cholera and typhus. Increases were greatest in the areas of central and eastern Europe, where the birth rate did not drop as dramatically as in the West. Britain's population grew from 34.9 to 45.2 million between 1881 and 1911; France's from 37.4 to 39.1. But Germany's advanced during the same period from 45.2 to 64.9 million, and Russia's from 94 to an estimated 129 million.

Declining death rates were an indicator of generally increasing prosperity. There were, of course, still a great many very poor people, both in cities and in the country: casual laborers, the unemployed, *Higher living standards* those in declining industries and trades. Those skilled workers and their families whose real incomes did rise as a result of deflation and higher wage rates did not experience anything like the rate of increase enjoyed by most of the middle class. Nor could they expect to avoid altogether the stretches of unemployment that made life so chaotic for so many of their unskilled co-workers. Yet despite these qualifications, it is fair to say that more people enjoyed a higher standard of living than ever before. And a higher standard of living produced the demand for an increase in consumer goods.

Increased consumption of manufactured goods was by no means uniform; it was higher in urban and industrialized areas than in the country. But even in the country, traditional thrift was challenged as *New consumers* farmers and their wives journeyed by train into the cities, saw what they had not imagined they could have, and then decided they must spend their savings to have it. To accommodate the new and largely middle-class consumers, department stores and chain stores designed their products and their advertising to make shopping as easy and inviting as possible. Behind large plate-glass windows, goods were displayed attractively and temptingly; periodic sales encouraged householders to purchase "bargains"; catalogues and charge accounts made it easy for customers to spend money without leaving home. The result was an enormous increase in the volume of manufactured goods

The Triumph of Middle-Class Consumerism. The interior of the Galeries Lafayette department store in Paris, c. 1890.

produced for this rapidly expanding consumer market. Bicycles, clocks, appliances, furnishings—these and a great many other things were were being made in large quantities, and with new materials (cheap steel) and new techniques (electrical power). Many of these products were designed according to the correct assumption that women were more and more responsible for household purchases. Therefore, goods were fashioned to appeal directly to women, or to the children for whom women were responsible. The foot-powered sewing machine was a particular case in point—the first domestic appliance. Isaac Singer, the American responsible for the development of the treadle and straight needle in the 1850s, was as much an entrepreneur as an inventor. He was a pioneer in the field of advertising and promotion, encouraging purchase on the installment plan and providing courses for would-be domestic seamstresses.

Sewing machines changed far more than the sewing habits of

housewives, however. They were inexpensive, lightweight tools, easily installed and easily operated. Workshop masters could set up several, employ a handful of young women at very low wages, and make a profit turning out cheap ready-made clothing in response to increasing markets. This was just one of the ways in which the scale of manufacturing was altered during the latter part of the nineteenth century, with both demand and technology conspiring to produce the change. The sewing machine also led to the development of other new tools that helped cut costs in the clothing industry: button-holers, lace-makers, leather-stitchers. Whereas it took one cobbler ten hours to make a pair of shoes in 1850 by hand, by the end of the century it took a team of cobblers but a few hours to produce ten pairs using machinery. In metal-working, hard-edged steel allowed for the rapid cutting of patterns, which reduced price, in turn encouraging the manufacture of a variety of inexpensive metal goods—kitchenware, for example. In textiles, improved engines doubled the pace of mules and looms. In heavy industry, steam hammers performed the work of many men more precisely and with greater speed than before. New equipment of this sort was expensive. As a result, in heavy industry, it was the larger companies that prospered, and in the course of their prosperity, they grew even larger.

In all the countries of Europe, and in the United States, the pattern was one of expansion and consolidation. This was especially the case in Germany, where in the iron and steel industry nearly 75 percent

The web of industrial change

Left: *Advertisement for a German Sewing Machine.* The company proclaims the machine's versatility: unsurpassed for use in the home as well as in the workshop or factory. Right: *Sweated Industry.* This English family is "manufacturing" cheap toys at home. While the scale of some industrial enterprises increased, others remained profitable through the employment of badly paid home workers.

of those employed worked in factories of a thousand or more, and where over 90 percent of the electrical equipment manufactured was made in factories with over fifty employees. Machinery was thus altering the scale of manufacturing in two directions at once. In the clothing industry, entrepreneurs could use inexpensive machines to make small workshops turn a profit. In steel foundries, the cost of new equipment forced small competitors to the wall, with the result that the foundries grew very much bigger.

The increase in the scale of manufacturing had important and often disturbing consequences for workers. The most obvious was the need for men and women to relearn their trades. They were compelled to adapt their older skills to the new machines. Very often this adaptation resulted in a loss of either pay or prestige, or both. Most machine work was not skilled work. A trainee could "pick up" a trade in a week or so. Workers who had prided themselves on a particular skill and had been paid according to their ability to perform it, had to face the fact that industrial change was not only forcing them to relearn, but was compelling them to tell themselves that their new "skills"—if they could be called that—did not amount to very much. For example, when the machine itself could cut metal with infinitesimal accuracy, there was far less need than there had been previously for the skills of a human "fitter." Even if workers were not forced to relearn in these ways in order to accommodate to increased scale, they often had at least to accommodate to factory reorganization and rationalization. In workplaces where the hand-carrying of materials had been a major factor in their final cost, mechanization to reduce that cost would produce a bewildering series of changes. Electric cranes, used together with huge magnets in the iron and steel industries, increased the speed with which goods could be moved, and demanded that workers defer to whatever changes their introduction might entail.

A second—and even more important—effect of the change in scale was the constant demand for further efficiency. The greater the scale of the operation, the more important it became to eliminate waste. One minute lost in the production of every ten pairs of shoes might not make much difference if only fifty pairs were produced in a day. But if hundreds were being made, it became crucial, in the eyes of management, to see that those minutes were no longer lost. In factories where capital had been spent on new machinery, the owners, conscious of the cost of their investment, increased output in order to realize a profit on that investment. In factories where older machinery was still in use, owners believed that the only way they could remain competitive with modernized operations was by extracting all they could from their less productive equipment. In both cases, workers were pressed to produce more and more. One result of this drive for efficiency was a restructuring of wage scales. Prior to this period, although there had been serious wage disputes, both management and

Technological Change and Production Speed-up. An early assembly line of the Ford Motor Company, United States, 1913. Car bodies slid down the ramp and were attached to the chassis as they passed through the line below. One thousand cars were produced each day.

labor appeared content to bargain from the traditional notion of "a fair day's wage for a fair day's work." Definitions of what was fair naturally varied. But the level of individual performance was generally set by custom. What workers produced in the course of a day continued to determine what they were expected to produce. From about 1870 onward, however, expectations and procedures began to change. Periodic economic depressions in the last quarter of the nineteenth century saw profits fall before wages. This pattern caused employers to insist on greater individual productivity from their employees. It was no longer enough to work at a job with customary speed. Workers were now asked to produce as much as the owners thought they were potentially capable of producing.

But who was to determine that potential? That question plagued industrial relations during these years. Employers, who were adopting precision tools in order to increase production, grew more and more convinced that worker output could be gauged with precision as well. The foremost theoretician of worker efficiency and what was called scientific management of labor was the American Frederick W. Taylor (1865–1915). Taylor devised a three-step system whereby a worker's output could be "scientifically" measured, a system which, he argued, would provide a precise method for the determination of wage scales. First, he observed, timed, and analyzed workers' movements on the job, in order to determine how long a particular task should take. Second, he figured the labor costs of these movements. Third, he produced "norms," or general standards, which all workers were expected to maintain. These norms were invariably higher than those which had prevailed under traditional conditions.

Scientific management

In order to encourage workers to accept these increased standards, Taylor urged all factory-owners to adopt piece rates (i.e., payment to workers according to the specific amount produced) rather than hourly or daily wages. Payment by piece rate was already a growing practice in many European and American factories. In theory, at least, workers were not opposed to this method of payment; they reasoned that their only hope for a share in increasing output lay in their chance to be paid directly for what they made. But when they were told that their pay would not increase unless they measured up to predetermined—and, to their mind, unrealistic—norms, they objected. They argued that rates were set according to the performance of the speediest workers. Even though workers might earn more money if they agreed to the new rates, they resented the intrusion of management upon the pace of their working lives. Despite this opposition, scientific management spread throughout the industrialized West. In England, the United States, and on the Continent, particularly in the engineering trades, factory after factory subscribed to the new gospel. Where it could not entirely succeed in introducing "efficiency" on the shop floor, management proceeded to rationalize its own procedures. Accounting departments were expanded, and encouraged to attend closely to the problem of cost control in all areas of production and distribution. These reforms were no more than a reflection of the general move in the direction of greater efficiency. They were brought on by the vastly increased scale of production, the need to reduce waste wherever possible, and the desire to derive maximum profits from the elimination of unnecessary motions and unproductive habits.

3. THE NEW CAPITALISM

Responding to the increased scope of production and to the consequent pressures for further efficiency, the institutions of capitalism began to reorganize toward the end of the nineteenth century. Hitherto, most firms had been small or at most middle-sized; now, as firms grew and their need for capital increased, they began to incorporate. Limited liability laws, enacted by most countries in the course of the century, worked to encourage this incorporation. "Limited liability" meant that an individual owning stock in a particular corporation could be held liable only for the amount of his or her shares, should that corporation bankrupt itself. Once insured in this way, many thousands of middle-class men and women considered corporate investment a safe and financially promising way of making money for themselves. A stockholding, "rentier" class emerged, brought into existence by the willingness of governments to encourage capitalism through friendly legislation, and by the desire of capitalist businessmen to expand their industrial undertakings to meet increased de-

The New York Stock Exchange, 1893

mands. More and more companies incorporated. In doing so, their management tended to be removed from the direct control of family founders or of company-based boards of directors. The influence of bankers and financiers, often situated in cities far removed from the factories they invested in, grew accordingly. These men were not investing their own money but the money of their clients; their power to stimulate or to discourage the growth of particular industries and enterprises encouraged a kind of impersonal "finance" capital.

Corporate organization on a large scale facilitated the spread of industrial unification. Some industries—steel, for example—combined vertically. Steel companies, to ensure uninterrupted production, acquired their own coal and iron mines. By doing so, they could guarantee themselves a supply of raw materials at attractive prices. Often the same steel companies would obtain control of companies whose products were made of steel: for example, shipyards or railway factories. Now they would not only possess a ready stock of raw materials but an equally ready market for their manufactured products—steel plates, steel rails, whatever they might be. Such vertical integration was only possible as a result of the money available for investment through the institutions of finance capital.

Vertical organization

A second form of corporate organization was a horizontal formation: the cartel. These were combinations of individual companies producing the same kind of goods, joined for the purpose of controlling, if not eliminating, competition. Since their products were iden-

Horizontal organization: cartels

J. P. Morgan

Opposition to cartels

Business and government

tical, an identical price could be charged. Companies involved in the production of coal and steel were especially suited to the organization of cartels because of the costs of initial capitalization. It is very expensive to build, equip, and man a steel foundry; thus there were relatively few of them. And because there were few, they were the more easily organized into a combine. Cartels were particularly strong in Germany; less so in France, where there was not as much heavy industry, where the tradition of the small family firm was particularly entrenched, and where there was longstanding opposition to competition in the form of price-cutting and general intra-industrial warfare. In Britain, though some cartels were formed, continuing subscription to the policy of free trade meant that companies would find it difficult to maintain fixed prices. How could they do so if they could not exclude, by means of a tariff, foreign competitors who wanted to undersell them? Germany had abandoned the policy of free trade in 1879; the United States, where cartels were known as trusts, did the same after the Civil War, though not all at once. Britain, however, clung to free trade until well into the twentieth century.

Defenders of the cartel argued that the elimination of competition brought more stable prices and more continuous employment. They pointed out as well that cartels almost always reduced the cost of production. Opponents questioned, however, whether those reduced costs were reflected in lower prices, or, as they charged, in higher stockholder profits. Critics of cartels were vocal in the United States, where the so-called captains of industry, most prominently the financier J. P. Morgan (1837–1913), were attacked as a new breed of feudal barons. The Sherman Anti-Trust Act was passed by Congress in 1890 to curb the practice of industrial combination. It had little effect in retarding the process, however, until the trust-busting presidency of Theodore Roosevelt (1901–1908).

Elsewhere in the West at the end of the nineteenth century, governments and big business tended to develop close working relationships contrary to the laissez-faire theories of early industrial entrepreneurs. A significant manifestation of this new partnership was the appearance of businessmen and financiers as officers of state. Joseph Chamberlain, a Birmingham manufacturer, served as Britain's colonial secretary; the German banker Bernhard Dernberg was German secretary of state for colonies; the Frenchman Charles Jonnart, president of the Suez Canal Company and the Saint-Étienne steel works, was later governor-general of Algeria; Guilio Prinetti, a north Italian industrialist, was his country's foreign minister from 1901 to 1903. The interrelationship between government and industry, like the growth of cartels and combines, was seen as a natural development in the capitalist system which, its defenders argued, was showering its benefits on all classes of society.

4. INTERNATIONAL COMPETITION: BRITAIN VS. GERMANY

Throughout the period we have been examining, Britain and Germany were locked in industrial competition. By 1914, both the United States and Germany were outproducing Britain in a number of areas. Yet the German challenge was, for the British, the more significant. Industrial competition with Germany helped reshape international political alliances at the end of the century. Britain, moving to align itself with its ancient enemy France against the Germans, found itself engaged in a contest of naval superiority with the latter, determined that in that field the British would not lose their age-old advantage to the upstart challenger.

To what degree did the Germans succeed in overtaking the British? By 1914, Britain's industrial-commercial day was by no means over. The volume of German trade at the turn of the century was no more than 60 percent as great. Because Britain was more mature industrially than Germany, the service sector of its economy was now expanding faster than its manufacturing sector. A greater proportion of the work force was involved in the business of distributing and selling goods than of making them. If Britain's output of manufactured goods did no more than double between 1870 and 1913, as compared to Germany's sixfold increase, it was in part for this reason. Nor should one suppose that all areas of German industry were functioning as efficient, modernized, and technologically advanced units. For every up-to-date chemical plant, for every thriving steel mill, there were many smaller workshops where manufacturing took place on little more than a domestic scale. Having said this, however, the fact remains that the Germans *were* a powerful threat to the British. Even before 1870, Germany had ceased to provide a ready market for British manufactures; the Germans were supplying their own needs. After 1870, Germany began to export to the rest of the world. Moving into markets that the British had considered exclusively their own, German salesmen promoted German goods in Australia, South America, China, and in Britain itself. In fields such as the manufacture of organic chemicals and electrical equipment, Germany outsold Britain across the globe.

The extent of Germany's achievement

How can Germany's success and, perhaps more important, Britain's inability to counter it be explained? To begin with, Britain was handicapped because it had been the first nation to industrialize. Because of the capital they had invested in older factories and equipment, the British were reluctant to enter new fields or to exploit new methods. For example, because the British had constructed plants to manufacture alkali by an earlier, less efficient process, they found themselves trapped into continuing to produce in that way after the Solvay process had

*Reasons for Britain's lag:
(1) the problem of priority*

been discovered. Rather than make the expensive switch, British manufacturers attempted to make their alkali more competitive by cutting costs and improving worker efficiency. But when further refinements were introduced in the 1890s, British output not only failed to keep pace with German and also American increases but actually decreased. The same difficulties arose with steel. Here again Britain was hampered by the problem of priority. Because the British were the first to industrialize, their manufacturing centers took shape in accordance with the scale of early– and mid–nineteenth-century production. Now there was need for large tracts of land, close to transportation, to accommodate steel mills. Because of the cramped layout of Britain's industrial cities, it could not build mills as large as those in Germany or the United States. The result was that by 1900 the largest British steel mills were no bigger than the average-sized mills in Germany. Even new plants built for other manufacturing purposes in Britain were only a third as large as those constructed by its major rival. Because German plants were big, and because, therefore, they represented a large investment of capital, those who managed them did all they could to ensure their efficient operation. They rationalized design and standardized parts to an extent the British, with their smaller plants, continued to believe unnecessary. Smaller firms tended to receive smaller and more specialized orders which did not encourage standardization. Although standardization was accomplished by 1914 in Britain in some industries—notably iron and steel—in many others it remained more the exception than the rule.

(2) attitudes

Britain's industrial lead, which froze its urban areas into obsolete patterns and thus prevented growth, froze British attitudes as well. Because they had come so far so fast, the British had grown complacent. Nowhere is this fact more clearly reflected than in the British attitude toward education. If the achievements of the first Industrial Revolution—for example, the steam engine, the spinning jenny—were the result of what might be called creative tinkering, those of the second revolution were the product of a close and fruitful union of pure science with technology. Achievement now depended on a generally literate workforce, a trained body of mechanics, a scientifically grounded body of technicians, and a corps of highly trained, creative scientists. Germany was producing these cadres; Britain was not. Only in 1870 was a system of public elementary education instituted in Britain, and not until ten years later was it made compulsory. In Germany, compulsory education dated from the eighteenth century. The British governing class believed the primary purpose of working-class education was control: teaching a boy or girl not only how to read and write, but to accept his or her particular place within the social structure. Though German elementary education was authoritarian in many respects as well, the fact that it had begun earlier and was directly joined to systems of secondary education encouraged the development of abilities; it was in this respect far less wasteful than that of the British. As Britain lagged in the area of elementary education, it lagged in the development of scientific and technological laboratories and training centers. In Germany, the state established an elaborate network of such technical institutions; in Britain there were almost none before the First World War.

Complacency was the major reason for this lack. The British tended to believe, wrongly, that practical experience and on-the-job training would produce the skills necessary to keep abreast of change. In addition, the British upper middle class convinced itself that the goal of education was not the production of creative technologists but of "gentlemen." Fathers who had made their fortunes as entrepreneurs during the first Industrial Revolution sent their sons to private boarding schools and to the ancient universities of Oxford and Cambridge to receive a "gentleman's" education—training in Greek and Latin, primarily. Those sons, whose creative talents might otherwise have been channeled into science and technology, chose careers in politics, or in the imperial or domestic bureaucracies instead. The result was a severe narrowing of the pool of creative technologists and dynamic entrepreneurs. There were fewer men than in either Germany or the United States interested in organizing the increasingly large amounts of capital necessary to engage in industrial expansion. It was easier to invest money overseas than to undertake the revitalization of various enterprises at home. A suspicion of what was new, encouraged by the British tendency to rely upon practical experience of the past, prevented Britain from rising in more than a fitful way to the German challenge.

Complacency

5. INTERNATIONAL COMPETITION: IMPERIALISM

The rivalry between Britain and Germany was only the most intense aspect of international competitiveness during the last decades of the nineteenth century. As nations proceeded with the business of industrialization, their search for markets brought them into direct opposition with one another. One result was that the dogma of free trade was abandoned by all save Britain. As we have seen, the Germans rejected the policy of low tariffs in 1879. Austria and Russia had already done so. Spain instituted new scales of import duties in 1877 and again in 1891. In France, two decades of gradual abandonment were climaxed by the passage of the Méline Tariff in 1892. Although individual nations attempted to isolate themselves from each other in this way, developments in international economics mandated the continuing growth and development of an interlocking, worldwide system of manufacturing, trade, and finance. The general adoption by western Europe and the United States of the gold standard meant that the

A global economy

currencies of the so-called civilized world could be readily exchanged with each other against the measure of a common standard—the international price of gold. Hence countries needing to import from the United States, for example, did not have to sell goods directly to that country. They could sell to South America, exchange the money they received for gold, and then buy from America.

Almost all European countries, dependent on vast supplies of raw materials to sustain their rate of industrial production, imported more than they exported. To avoid the mounting deficits that would otherwise have resulted from this practice, they relied upon "invisible" exports: i.e., shipping, insurance, and interest on money lent or invested. The extent of Britain's exports in these areas was far greater than that of any other country. London was the money market of the world, to which would-be borrowers looked for assistance before turning elsewhere. By 1914, Britain had $20 billion invested overseas, compared with the $8.7 of the French and the $6 billion of the Germans. The insurance firm of Lloyds of London served clients around the world. The British merchant fleet transported the manufactured goods and raw materials of every trading nation. It was the volume of its "invisible" exports that permitted Britain to remain faithful to the doctrine of free trade while other European nations were forced to institute tariffs.

The competition between the principal economic powers of this worldwide marketplace affected not only their relationships with each other but also with those less developed areas upon which they were increasingly dependent for both raw materials and markets. Some of those areas, such as India and China, were the seats of ancient empires. Others, such as central Africa, sheltered equally complex though less geographically expansive cultures. No matter what the nature of the indigenous civilization, the intrusion upon it of modern science and technology, systematic wage labor, financial and legal institutions caused enormous disruption. Though drawn into the world economy, these areas did not draw from it the benefits that the West did. Native industries such as Indian textile spinning and weaving stood no chance in competition with the factory-made products of Manchester. African herdsmen and hunters endured the disruption of their living habits by the activities of European ranchers and miners. Men who had made their living as boatmen and carters lost their livelihood to the railways constructed by Western nations. New jobs there might be; but they were jobs worked according to a Western style, dictated by Western economic demands, and threatened by Western economic disorders. In great measure the workers of this emerging world were assuming the role of a global unskilled working class under the hegemony of Western capitalism.

With this global background in mind, we can better understand the history of late-nineteenth-century imperialism—the subjugation by the European powers of vast tracts of land and indigenous populations, primarily on the continents of Africa and Asia. Imperialism was by no means a new phenomenon. During the eighteenth century, the French had penetrated Algeria and the British, India. In other parts of the world, where Western powers did not govern directly, they often exercised an indirect influence so powerful as to shape the policies and dictate the activities of indigenous authorities. When the West "opened" China beginning in 1834, it left the Chinese in nominal charge of their state. But it ensured that affairs would be conducted to its advantage and within its "sphere of influence." Britain added in this way to its "informal" empire, expanding into South America, Africa, and south and east Asia.

Earlier imperialism

As international rivalries increased, European powers moved with greater frequency and determination to control both the government and economy of underdeveloped nations and territories. French politicians supported imperialism as a means of restoring national prestige and honor, lost in the humiliating defeat by the Germans in the Franco-Prussian War of 1870–1871. The British, on the other hand, looked with alarm at the accelerating pace of industrialization in Germany and France and feared losing their existing and potential world markets. The Germans, recently unified in a modern nation, viewed overseas empire as a "national" possession and as a way of entering the "club" of great powers.

European views of overseas empire

The West's stunning inventions of the late eighteenth and nineteenth centuries provided the very tools of imperialism. Metal-hulled steamships, widely used in Africa from the 1850s, provided faster, cheaper transportation and allowed for the shipment of bulk cargoes such as unprocessed crops and heavy ores. Travel time between Liverpool and Cape Town was reduced from an average of three months to three weeks. Sail power quickly lost out to steam. By the same token, river and lake steamers overcame the problem of transportation in the African interior. Submarine telegraph cables also brought Africa closer to Europe. By 1885, West and South Africa were linked to London and Paris. With the use of quinine, malaria became less threatening and Europeans were emboldened to penetrate the tropical rain forests. In military technology, the shift in Africa from muzzle-loading rifles to fast-firing breechloaders was completed by 1878. European armies gained an even greater advantage with the introduction in 1884 of the Maxim gun, a prototype of the modern machine gun, capable of firing eleven bullets a second. These and other inventions and scientific breakthroughs made imperialist conquest and resource exploitation vastly cheaper and eminently more viable.

Technology as a tool of imperialism

The scope, intensity, and long-range consequences of this so-called new imperialism of the late nineteenth century have generated a debate about its causes as heated as that which surrounds the first Industrial Revolution. One influential group of social critics and historians has

Technology and Empire. A traction engine hauling an army road train in South Africa during the Boer War.

argued that the causes were predominantly, if not exclusively, economic. As early as 1902, the English social reformer and theorist, J. A. Hobson, charged that what he called "the scramble for Africa" had occurred as a result of the economic interests of a small group of extremely rich and influential financiers throughout western Europe. Hobson declared that the colonization of Africa had produced little economic gain for the taxpayers whose countries had dispatched armies of conquest and occupation at the behest of international capitalists. Profits went only to the rich, who ventured beyond the bounds of economically stagnant western Europe in search of a higher return on their investments than could be realized at home. Hobson concluded that late–nineteenth-century imperialism was "a depraved choice of national life," appealing primarily to "the lusts of self-seeking acquisitiveness and forceful domination."

Imperialism as economics: Hobson

Hobson's analysis inspired a more influential critique of imperialism by the Russian communist and future revolutionary leader, N. Lenin. Lenin agreed with Hobson that imperialism was an economic phenomenon. But, unlike Hobson, he saw it as an integral and inevitable phase of the capitalist system, as the title of his 1916 treatise, *Imperialism: The Last Stage of Capitalism,* explicitly declared. Capitalist competition, Lenin argued, and the consequent monopolies that it had produced, had lowered domestic profits, and thus compelled the owners of surplus capital to invest it overseas. The alternative, enlarging home markets by raising wages, would serve only to further decrease profits. Imperialism was thus the creature of the internal contradictions of industrial capitalism.

Lenin

While most historians would agree that economic pressures were one important cause of imperialism, they have remained uncomfortable with analyses that ignore other factors they consider equally important. They remain prepared to acknowledge the role of economics when it seems to make sense to do so: in the case of Great Britain, for example, where about half its total of £4 billion in foreign investments was at work within its empire. In all western European countries, demand for raw materials made colonies a necessary investment and helped persuade governments that imperialism was a worthwhile policy. Yet the economic explanation begins to break down when one considers facts like the following: that colonial markets were generally too poor to answer the needs of European manufacturers; that Africa, the continent over which there was the greatest "scramble," was also the poorest and least profitable to investors; that only a very small portion of German capital was invested in German colonies before 1914; that only one-fifth of French capital was so invested; that, indeed, the French had more capital invested in Russia, hoping to stabilize that ally against the Germans, than in all their colonial possessions.

Those in charge of the imperial building process decided policy in response to a combination of political and economic considerations, and as a corollary to the process of nation-building. National security and the preservation of a general balance of power were issues never far from the forefront of politicians' thinking and planning. Great-power interest in the eastern Mediterranean grew with the demise of the Ottoman Empire. At the Berlin Conference of 1878, France secured from Great Britain and Germany the assurance of a free hand in Tunisia as compensation for its acquiescence in British annexation of Cyprus. This understanding breathed new life into the principle that remuneration of territorial claims in one region must be compensated for by concessions elsewhere.

Britain's domination of Egypt in the 1880s was the result, in large measure, of its fear of what might occur in the Near East should large portions of the decaying Ottoman Empire fall into Russian hands. Britain had purchased 44 percent of the shares in the Suez Canal Company in 1875, and considered the waterway a strategic lifeline to the East. The canal had been built by the French under the direction of the engineer Ferdinand de Lesseps. Begun in 1859 and completed in 1869, it was expected to assist France in its bid for commercial expansion to the East. Britain obtained its shares from the spendthrift khedive (viceroy) of Egypt at a time when he was threatened with bankruptcy. When, in 1882, nationalist rebels protested continuing British intervention in the internal affairs of Egypt, the British claimed they had no choice but to bombard the port of Alexandria and place the Egyptian ruler under their protection. A continuing British presence in Egypt, and the willingness of the British government to support

Dredges and Elevators at Work on the Construction of the Suez Canal, 1869

Egyptian claims to the Upper Nile, worried the French, who were growing to fear Britain's political domination of the entire African continent. Moving to correct what they perceived as a severe political imbalance, the French challenged the British and at Fashoda, in the Sudan, came close to war in 1898. The British called the French bluff, however, and war was averted.

Imperial policy-making

The power struggle over Suez, Egypt, and the Sudan provides an excellent example of the manner in which international politics was directly related to imperial advance. It suggests, as well, that what passed for "imperial policy" was less a matter of long-range planning than of a series of pragmatic and often spontaneous responses to particular colonial political and economic situations. Often those in charge of policy-making found themselves led beyond their original ambitions, not only by the demands of international rivalries, but by the actions of individual explorers and entrepreneurs who established claims to hitherto unknown territories which home governments then felt compelled to recognize and defend.

"The white man's burden"

Imperialism must also be understood as something more than official policy, whether carefully conceived or accidental. A French diplomat once described the dynamic English imperial adventurer Cecil Rhodes as "a force cast in an idea"; the same might be said of imperialism itself. Imperialism as an idea excited the minds of explorers like the English missionary David Livingstone, who believed that his country's conquest of Africa would put an end to the East African slave trade, and "introduce the Negro family into the body of corporate nations." Rudyard Kipling, the English poet and novelist, wrote of "the white man's burden," of his mission to civilize the "half devil, half child" races that inhabited what most Europeans considered the "barbaric" and "heathen" quarters of the globe. To combat slave-trading, famine, filth, and illiteracy seemed to many a legitimate reason for invading the jungles of Africa and Asia.

Imperialism as an idea was also of use to European governments at home. A populace could be encouraged to forget domestic hardships as it celebrated its country's triumphs overseas. Patriotism—a not always attractive corollary to nation-building—was stimulated by arguments such as that expressed by the German historian Heinrich von Treitschke in 1887: that "the colonizing impulse has become a vital question for a great nation"—the implication clearly being that a nation was not great unless it possessed colonies. Associations with a

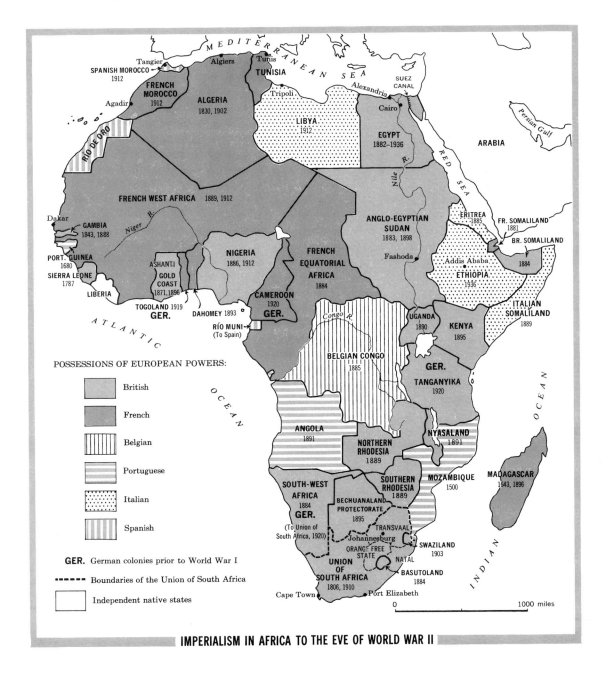

POSSESSIONS OF EUROPEAN POWERS:

British

French

Belgian

Portuguese

Italian

Spanish

GER. German colonies prior to World War I

- - - - - Boundaries of the Union of South Africa

Independent native states

0   1000 miles

IMPERIALISM IN AFRICA TO THE EVE OF WORLD WAR II

semi-official standing—the Deutsche Kolonialgesellschaft, the Comité de l'Afrique Française, the Royal Colonial Institute—propagandized on behalf of empire, as did newspapers, which recognized in sensational stories of overseas conquest a means of attracting a newly literate clientele.

The colonization of Africa

Imperial competition centered in Africa. In 1875, 11 percent of the continent was in European hands; by 1902, 90 percent. Germans pressed inward from the east; Frenchmen from the west. The Portuguese schemed to connect the ancient colonies of Angola, on the west, with Mozambique, on the east. Most active among the European powers during this initial period of late–nineteenth-century colonization was a privately financed group of Belgians under the leadership of that country's king, Leopold II. In association with H. M. Stanley, an American newspaperman and explorer, Leopold and a group of financiers founded the International Congo Association in 1878, which negotiated treaties with chieftains that opened the Congo River basin to commercial exploitation. A conference, called in Berlin in 1885 and attended by most European nations and the United States, attempted to establish certain ground rules for the game of imperial acquisition. The Congo was declared a Free State, under the trusteeship of Leopold (the first example of this later familiar device of protecting "backward" peoples). A European nation with holdings on the African coast was declared to have first rights to territory in the interior behind those coastal regions. Those rights, however, could be sustained only by what was termed "real" occupation—that is, the presence of either administrators or troops. The scramble was on! Occupation was accompanied by the exploitation of native labor. Agreements reached with local chieftains, whom the Europeans courted, authorized the employment of men and women as laborers under conditions little better than slavery. Often compelled to live in compounds apart from their families, Africans were victimized by a system which rooted out prevailing custom without attempting to establish anything like a new civilization in its place. In the Congo, the Arab slave trade was suppressed, replaced by a system of forced labor. Tribal lands were confiscated and rebellions brutally crushed.

The scramble for territory

The division of the geographical spoils accelerated after 1885. The Portuguese increased their hold in Angola and Mozambique. The Italians invaded Somaliland and Eritrea. They attempted to extend their controls to Ethiopia, but were repulsed by an army of 80,000 Ethiopians, the first instance of a major victory by native Africans over whites. Germany came relatively late to the game. Bismarck was reluctant to engage in an enterprise which, he believed, would do little to profit the empire either politically or economically. Eventually concluding, however, that they could not afford to let other powers divide the continent among them, the Germans established colonies in German East Africa, in the Cameroons and Togo on the west coast, and in the desertlike territory of South-West Africa. The French con-

Left: *"The Rhodes Colossus."* The ambitions of Cecil Rhodes, the driving force behind British imperialism in South Africa, are satirized in this cartoon, which appeared in *Punch.* Right: *"Now We Shant Be Long to Cairo."* So read the banner across Engine No. 1 taking the first train from Umtali to Salisbury, Rhodesia, reflecting Cecil Rhodes's vision of a Capetown to Cairo railway as a symbol of British domination of the African continent.

trolled large areas in West Africa and, in the Red Sea, the port of Djibouti. It was to further their plan for an east-west link that the French risked challenging the British at Fashoda. That scheme, however, fell afoul of Britain's need to dominate Egypt, and of its plans for a north-south connection through the African continent.

Cecil Rhodes, the English entrepreneur and imperial visionary, promoted the notion of a Capetown to Cairo railway both before and after his assumption of the prime-ministership of the Cape Colony in 1890. His plans were thwarted in the south, however, by the presence of two independent neighboring republics, the Transvaal and the Orange Free State, both inhabited by descendents of the original Dutch settlers in South Africa. These Boers—the Dutch word for "farmers"—had fled from the British in the Cape Colony and established themselves in their agricultural states in defiant opposition to the freebooting and exploitationist spirit of the British economic adventurers who had driven them from their original settlements. When diamonds and gold were discovered in the Transvaal in 1886, the tension between the British and the Boers grew. As British prospectors and entrepreneurs moved in, the Boers refused to pass laws permitting the exploitation of their resources by foreign firms. They also taxed the interlopers heavily. Rhodes retaliated by attempting to force a war

The Boer War

Boer Commandos under Louis Botha. Botha became the first prime minister of the Union of South Africa following the Boer War.

"The Execution of 'John Company.'" This 1857 *Punch* cartoon graphically depicts the abolition of the East India Company in the wake of the "Indian Mutiny."

with the republics. His first try, the dispatching of a force of irregular volunteers under the command of Dr. L. S. Jameson in 1895, failed to provoke a conflict, but precipitated general censure on the British for harassing a peaceful neighbor. Rhodes was forced to resign as prime minister of the Cape Colony in 1896. War broke out in 1899. Its course, however, did not run according to British plans. The Boers proved tough fighters. It took three years to secure an armistice; it took further long months and resort to brutal policies such as detention camps and farm-burning to bring the resilient republicans to heel. The war's consequences were British loss of international prestige, and a heightening of the Anglo-German rivalry, the kaiser having publicly pronounced his sympathy with the Boer cause.

Britain managed to increase its hold on its prize imperial possession—India—throughout the nineteenth century. The "informal" rule of the commercially motivated East India Company had proved ineffective in 1857, when native Indian troops and a large number of other disaffected elements within the subcontinent rebelled in what the British chose to call "The Indian Mutiny," but which was in fact a far more serious and deep-seated challenge to foreign control. Henceforth the British government administered the subcontinent. But at the same time, they decided to rule through the Indian upper classes, and not, as in the past, in opposition to them. Although instruction in British-sponsored schools continued in English, Indian customs were tolerated as they had not been before, and princes and their bureaucracies were incorporated as protectorates into the general scheme of government. A class of westernized, and yet devotedly Indian, civil servants and businessmen thus emerged by the end of the nineteenth century, trained by the British yet burdened by no sense of obligation to their

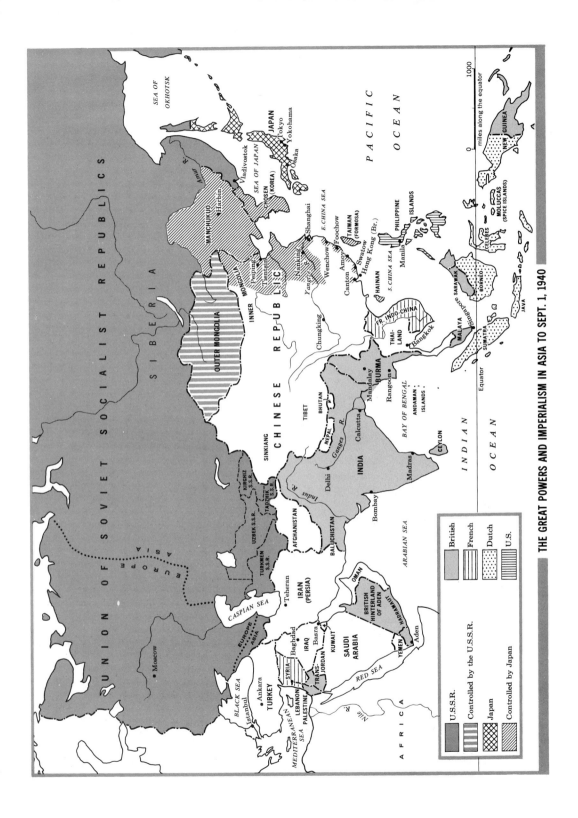

THE GREAT POWERS AND IMPERIALISM IN ASIA TO SEPT. 1, 1940

Imperialism. Left: Germans traveling in East Africa, 1907. Right: A British officer in India, c. 1900.

tutors. This group provided the leadership for the nationalist movement that was to challenge British rule in India during the mid–
Britain in India twentieth century. Britain's aim in India was to promote order and
stability. Civil servants administered justice even-handedly; they
promoted improved sanitation, which, ironically, helped to increase
the country's population beyond the point where it could sustain itself.
The vast majority of Indians remained desperately poor, victims in
many cases of the importation of cheap manufactured goods which
threatened indigenous industries and testified to Britain's willingness
to subordinate its colonies' economic well-being to its own.

The pattern of British imperialism differed throughout the world.
In areas dominated by white settlers, home rule was introduced in
British colonial rule hopes of preventing the sort of disaffection that had produced the
American Revolution. Australia was granted self-government in the
1850s, New Zealand in 1876. In 1867, a united Dominion of Canada,
with its own federal governments and legislatures, was established.

Elsewhere in the world, Western nations hastened to plant their colors upon those territories that promised rewards, either economic or
Imperialism elsewhere strategic. Britain, France, Germany, and the Netherlands all staked
claims in the East Indies, the Dutch achieving an overall hegemony
there by 1900. China allowed itself to be victimized by a series of commercial treaties; among the predators was China's neighbor Japan, the
only non-Western nation able to modernize in the nineteenth century.
The United States played a double game. It acted as champion of the
underdeveloped countries in the Western Hemisphere when they were
threatened from Europe. Yet the Americans were willing, whenever it
suited them, to prey on their neighbors, either "informally" or formally. When, at the end of the century, Spain's feeble hold on its Caribbean and Pacific colonies encouraged talk of rebellion, the United

States stepped in to protect its investments and guarantee its maritime security. It declared and won the Spanish-American War in 1898 on trumped-up grounds. In the same year, the United States annexed Puerto Rico and the Philippines, and established a "protectorate" over Cuba. When Colombia's colony, Panama, threatened to rebel in 1903, the Americans quickly backed the rebels, recognized Panama as a republic, and then proceeded to grant it protection while Americans built the Panama Canal on land leased from the new government. Intervention in Santo Domingo and in Hawaii proved that the United States was no less an imperial power than the nations of western Europe. Together, by the end of the century, those countries had succeeded in binding the world together as it had never been before. The military and economic power with which they had accomplished that achievement meant that, for the time being at any rate, they would be the world's masters.

SELECTED READINGS

- *Items so designated are available in paperback editions.*
- Ashworth, W., *A Short History of the International Economy since 1850*, rev. ed., London, 1975. A good introduction.

  Barkin, Kenneth D., *The Controversy over German Industrialization, 1890–1902*, Chicago, 1970. The political and social struggles between agricultural and industrial interests.

  Cameron, Rondo E., *France and the Economic Development of Europe, 1800–1914*, Princeton, 1961. Emphasizes the export of French capital and skill in the economic growth of Europe.
- Fieldhouse, D. K., *The Colonial Experience: A Comparative Study from the Eighteenth Century*, London, 1966. A general survey from the eighteenth to the twentieth centuries.

  ———, *Economics and Empire, 1830–1914*, London, 1973. Argues against the primacy of economic factors in the spread of imperialism.
- Gollwitzer, Heinz, *Europe in the Age of Imperialism, 1880–1914*, London, 1969. A brief survey with excellent illustrations.
- Headrick, Daniel R., *The Tools of Empire: Technology and European Imperialism in the Nineteenth Century*, Oxford, 1981. A study of the relationship between technological innovation and imperialism.
- Hobsbawm, Eric, *Industry and Empire: The Making of Modern English Society, 1750 to the Present Day*, New York, 1968. Emphasizes the economic background of imperialism.

  Kieran, V. G., *Marxism and Imperialism*, New York, 1975. Argues the Marxist position effectively.
- Kindleberger, C. P., *Economic Growth in France and Britain, 1851–1950*, Cambridge, Mass., 1963. A technical account.
- Landes, David S., *The Unbound Prometheus*, London, 1969. Particularly good on the Anglo–German rivalry.

  Langer, William L., *The Diplomacy of Imperialism, 1890–1902*, New York, 1960. A thorough, standard work, useful for its analysis of the intellectual as well as political origins of imperialism

Louis, William Roger, ed., *Imperialism: The Robinson and Gallagher Controversy*, New York, 1976. The best introduction to recent debate over the nature and causes of imperialism.

Miller, Michael B., *The Bon Marché: Bourgeois Culture and the Department Store, 1869–1920,* Princeton, 1981. Explores the revolution in merchandising of the late nineteenth century.

Milward, Alan S., and S. B. Saul, *The Development of the Economies of Continental Europe, 1850–1914,* Cambridge, Mass., 1977. An excellent, comprehensive text, particularly good on the smaller European nations.

• Moorehead, Alan, *The White Nile,* London, 1971. Captures much of the excitement of imperial exploration.

Price, Roger, *The Economic Modernization of France, 1730–1880,* New York, 1975. Rejects conventional periodizations; stresses the advent of railroads, which transformed the market structure of France.

Robinson, Ronald, and J. Gallagher, *Africa and the Victorians: The Official Mind of Imperialism,* London, 1961. Contains their famous thesis that imperialism was not deliberately pursued as a policy of state, but rather was a response to events in colonial areas. The modern debate over imperialism begins with this work.

• Shannon, Richard, *The Crisis of Imperialism, 1865–1915,* St. Albans, England, 1976. An excellent survey of the transformation of British society in the wake of modern industrialization.

Stolper, Gustav, et al., *The German Economy, 1870 to 1940,* New York, 1967. A good introduction.

SOURCE MATERIALS

• Court, W. H. B., *British Economic History, 1870–1914; Commentary and Documents,* Cambridge, 1965. An excellent collection of documents.

• Hobson, J. A., *Imperialism: A Study,* London, 1902.

• Lenin, Vladimir, *Imperialism: The Highest Stage of Capitalism,* 1916. (Many English editions.) Lenin's most significant contribution to Marxist ideology. He saw the essence of imperialism as the export of capital rather than goods, which led to worldwide competition, of which World War I was an inevitable result.

• Reitz, Deneys, *Commando: A Boer Journal of the Boer War,* London, 1929. A superb memoir of the Boer War.

Chapter 25

THE MIDDLE CLASS
CHALLENGED

The time of surprise attacks, of revolutions carried through by small conscious minorities at the head of unconscious masses, is past. Where it is a question of a complete transformation of the social organization, the masses themselves must also be in it, must themselves already have grasped what is at stake, what they are going in for, with body and soul.

—Friedrich Engels, Introduction to Karl Marx, *The Class Struggles in France, 1848–50*

C apitalism's continuing expansion encouraged middle-class men and women at the end of the nineteenth century to believe themselves the necessary key to the progress of the human race. At the same time, however, that belief was being challenged from several directions. In each case, the challenges called into question assumptions close to the core of middle-class consciousness. Socialist doctrine, which was for the first time receiving a widespread hearing, pronounced capitalism a threat, rather than a boon, to society. New scientific theories—particularly the theory of evolution— declared that the key to progress was not the well-laid schemes of humanity, but chance. Psychologists discovered the irrationality of human beings and philosophers their ultimate helplessness. Paintings, poetry, and music proclaimed an artists' revolution on behalf of the idea of art for its own sake, not for the edification of a middle-class public. Together, these various intellectual and cultural currents threatened the notion that society would most successfully advance under middle-class auspices, setting its course in accordance with middle-class moral and economic precepts, and placing its faith in a belief in the importance and inevitability of continued material progress.

The dimensions of the challenge

1. THE CHALLENGE OF SOCIALISM

Marx in England

The history of socialism in the latter half of the nineteenth century is, to a great degree, the biography of its most famous propagandist and theoretician, Karl Marx (1818–1883). Marx was both a social thinker and a political leader. At certain times theory dictated his actions; at others, political events led him to alter doctrine. But always he was at the center of the socialist movement, his moral passion, as much as his scholarly research, shaping the course of its events. The fact of his continuing influence is particularly remarkable for two reasons. First, although a German, he lived from 1849 until his death in London, an exile from the mainstream of continental socialism, in a country whose toleration of socialists was a mark of its comparative immunity from their doctrines. Second, Marx was not a leader who readily took others into his confidence. His antisocial nature was due, in part, to the poverty in which he was forced to live. He and his family were kept alive by gifts of money from his faithful friend and collaborator, Friedrich Engels, and by occasional stints as a political journalist—for a time Marx was a correspondent for the *New York Tribune*.

Capital

During the 1850s and 1860s Marx labored to produce his definitive analysis of capitalist economics, *Capital,* the first volume of which was published in 1867. The argument of *Capital* owed a great deal to that dialectical idealism and economic materialism which, as we have seen, shaped Marx's earlier thinking and writing. In *Capital* he synthesized ideas he and Engels had enunciated in their previous tracts. He described in detail the processes of production, exchange, and distribution as they operated within the capitalist system. He argued that under capitalism, workers were denied their rightful share of profits. The value of any manufactured item, Marx claimed, was determined by the amount of labor necessary to produce it. Yet workers were hired at wages whose value was far less than the value of the goods they produced. The difference between the value of workers' wages and the value of their work as sold was pocketed by members of the capitalist class, who, according to Marx, made off with far more than a justifiable portion of the sale price. This so-called labor theory of value, borrowed from a somewhat similar doctrine held by Ricardo and other classical economists, was the basis for Marx's claim that the working class was compelled to suffer under the capitalist system. Because workers were forced to sell their labor they became nothing more than commodities in the economic market.

So long as capitalists refused to pay wages more nearly equal to the labor value of their employees' work, those employees would remain exploited. Marx preached that the only class which, under capitalism, produced more wealth than it enjoyed was the working class, the proletariat. The bourgeoisie, which owned the means of production and

Karl Marx

was therefore able to appropriate that which was rightfully the workers', had a vested interest in maintaining the status quo; hence its willingness to make use of political, social, religious, and legal institutions to keep the proletariat in its place.

Marx predicted that capitalism would eventually do itself in. He argued that as time passed, market competition would compel the formation of ever-larger industrial and financial combinations. As the smaller enterpreneurial class—the petty bourgeoisie—was squeezed out by more powerful combines, its members would join with the proletariat, until society resembled a vast pyramid, with a much-enlarged proletariat at its base and an opposing force of a few powerful capitalists at its tip. At this point, Marx declared, the proletariat would rise in revolution against what was left of the bourgeoisie.

Marx as prophet

After capitalism had received its death blow at the hands of the workers, it would be followed by a socialist stage, characterized by the dictatorship of the proletariat; payment in accordance with work performed; and ownership and operation by the state of all means of production, distribution, and exchange. In time socialism would be succeeded by communism, the goal of historical evolution. Communism would bring with it a classless society. No one would live by owning, but solely by working. The state would now disappear, relegated to the museum of antiquities, "along with the bronze ax and the spinning wheel." Nothing would replace it except voluntary associations to operate the means of production and provide for social necessities. The essence of communism was payment in accordance with needs. The wage system would be abolished, and citizens would be expected to work in accordance with their abilities, entitled to receive from the total fund of wealth produced an amount in proportion to their needs.

The advent of communism

In the ten years after its publication, *Capital* was translated into English (Marx had written it in German), French, Russian, and Italian. The book's widespread appeal was the result of its compelling deterministic certainty and of its vigorous crusading temper. Though much that *Capital* predicted has failed to occur, middle- and working-class socialists reading it soon after its publication and measuring its pronouncements against the capitalistic world they knew had little difficulty in accepting Marx's reasoning. It seemed to them that he had constructed an objective science of society out of their own experiences. The book became the theoretical rallying point for a growing band of socialists who stood opposed to the world the middle class had made. For a time it breathed life into an organization of continental and British workers that had been founded in London in 1864: the International Workingmen's Association, usually referred to as the International. This body had been formed with the declared purpose of forging an international working-class alliance to overthrow capitalism and abolish private property. Marx delivered its inaugural address, in which he preached that workers must win political power

The First International

for themselves if they were ever to escape their industrial bondage. Various difficulties had prevented the formation of a radically oriented workers' organization prior to this time. There was, first of all, fear of official reprisal. Second, the irregular pace of industrialization across Europe meant that workers in one country could have little understanding of the particular plight of their fellow workers elsewhere. Finally, the period after 1850 had witnessed an increase in general prosperity which encouraged the more highly skilled—and more politically conscious—workers to forsake revolutionary goals and to pursue the more immediate end of accommodation with middle-class politicians. The German socialists' dealings with Bismarck (see below, p. 906), were a case in point. Meanwhile, however, the determination of a small band of dedicated radical socialists temporarily surmounted these problems to permit the formation of the first international workers' association.

Lassalle and Bakunin

Marx immediately assumed the direction of the International. He labored to exclude moderates from its councils and denounced the German socialists, and their leader Ferdinand Lassalle (1825–1864), for their failure to oppose Bismarck. The duty of socialists, Marx argued, was not partnership with the state, but rather its overthrow. At the same time Marx battled the doctrines of the Russian anarchist Michael Bakunin (1814–1876), who challenged the socialist notion that social evil was the product of capitalism. Bakunin argued that the state was the ultimate villain, and preached its immediate destruction through isolated acts of terrorism. He also opposed centralization within the International, urging instead a kind of federal autonomy for each national workers' group. To Marx, these individualist notions represented nothing more than reversion to a kind of primitive rebellion, heroic but ultimately fruitless. He succeeded in having Bakunin banished from the International in 1872. The International prospered for a time during the 1860s. Individual trade unions in various countries were persuaded to join in its united campaign, which preached revolution and, through the application of pressure both at the ballot box and in the factory, seemed to promise at least higher wages and shorter hours. Under Marx's direction the International was a highly organized and tightly controlled body, far more effective in this respect than any previous socialist organization.

The troubled International

Yet by 1876 it had faded from existence. Despite Marx's abilities as an authoritarian chief of staff, the International throughout its existence had to battle those same circumstances that had delayed its foundation. In addition, Marx's insistence upon control from the center thwarted a growing desire on the part of individual socialist organizations to pursue programs of immediate benefit to themselves. These factors weakened the International. What probably brought about its demise was its association with events occurring in Paris after the defeat of France by Germany in 1870 in the Franco-Prussian War.

Following the collapse of Napoleon III, a new republic, generally conservative in tone, had been established by the French. In March 1871, the government attempted to disarm the Paris National Guard, a volunteer citizen army with radical political sympathies. The guard refused to surrender, declared its autonomy, deposed officials of the new government, and proclaimed a revolutionary committee—the Commune—as the true government of France. Though this movement is commonly described as a rebellion of dangerous radicals intent upon the destruction of law and order, most of its members resembled the Jacobins of the first French Revolution and belonged largely to the lower middle class. They did not advocate the abolition of private property but rather its wider distribution. Their respect for the deposits in the Bank of France was as scrupulous as any bourgeois financier might have wished. Their most radical political action was a symbolic one: the toppling of a statue of Napoleon I in the Place Vendôme. The movement was precipitated by bitterness over the defeat of Napoleon III and exhaustion by the long siege of Paris that followed. There were fears as well that the central government would be dominated by the rural population to the disadvantage of the urban masses in the capital. After several weeks of frustrating disputation, the conflict turned into a bloody civil war. The Communards killed about sixty hostages, including the archbishop of Paris. The government numbered its victims by the thousands. The courts-martial which were set up executed twenty-six. Thousands of others were sentenced to imprisonment or banishment in New Caledonia, in the South Pacific.

While middle-class Europe reacted in horror at what it mistakenly perceived as a second Reign of Terror, Marx, in the name of the International, extolled the courage of the Communards, who, he wrote, had fought the first pitched battle in the class war he had predicted. In

A Symbol of the Paris Commune. The statue of Napoleon I in Roman garb, a symbol of imperial absolutism, is toppled from its base by the Communards.

Propaganda and the Paris Commune. This photograph, purporting to record the assassination of hostages by the radical Communards, was actually faked by their enemies in an effort to arouse anti-Communard sympathies.

The Commune and the International

a pamphlet entitled *The Civil War in France* (1871), Marx claimed that the Commune was an example of the transitional form of government through which the working class would have to pass on its way to emancipation. Yet many of the less radical members of the International were frightened and disturbed, not only by the events of the Commune itself, but by the possibility of reprisals against members of an organization that openly praised men and women who were considered by the middle class to be little more than murderers. In 1872 Marx acknowledged defeat by moving the seat of the International's council to the United States, a country far removed from the organization's affairs and from the criticisms that had begun to be heaped upon Marx for his misdirection. In 1876, the First International expired.

The spread of socialism

Although the International collapsed, socialism continued to gain ground as both a theory and a program. The German Social Democratic party was founded in 1875; a Belgian Socialist party in 1879; and in France, despite the disasters of the Commune, a Socialist party was established in 1905. In England, although socialism was much debated and discussed, no party proclaiming itself socialist emerged. When the Labour party came into being in 1901, however, various socialist societies were represented on its executive council, along with less radical, nonsocialist trade union groups. On the periphery of Europe—in Spain, Italy, and Russia—socialism made less headway. There the absence of widespread industrialization and the educational backwardness of large elements within the population retarded the development of a working-class consciousness, and of socialism as its political expression.

During the years before the First World War, socialists continuously and often bitterly debated the course they should follow as they attempted to achieve their goal of radical change. One group, led by Marx himself until his death, urged socialists to avoid collaboration with other parties to achieve such immediate ends as higher wages, shorter working hours, and unemployment insurance. These reforms, the "purists" declared, were the means by which the bourgeoisie could buy off the proletariat and hence indefinitely postpone revolution. On the other hand, "revisionists" urged their followers to take advantage of the fact that many of them now could vote for socialist candidates in elections. They argued that those candidates, if elected, could help them obtain a better life in the immediate future. Socialist theory might proclaim a worldwide struggle of the proletariat against the bourgeoisie, but was this any reason to turn one's back on a chance to make real headway through the ballot box in achieving reforms that would put a better life within reach of workers and their families?

"Purists" vs. "revisionists"

Revisionism spread despite efforts of the "purists" to put a stop to it. In Germany its most eloquent spokesman was Eduard Bernstein (1850–1932), a Social Democrat and a member of the German parliament, the Reichstag. Bernstein was among the first to question the predictions Marx had made in *Capital*. In his appropriately titled book, *Evolutionary Socialism*, published in 1899, Bernstein pointed out that for most European workers the standard of living had risen since 1850, and that the lower middle class showed no evidence that it wished to identify its interests with those of the proletariat. At the same time, increasingly wider franchises meant that workers had an excellent chance of achieving reform by means of the ballot box. The program of the future was not revolution, but democratic social reform. Bernstein's most outspoken opponent in Germany was his fellow socialist Karl Kautsky (1854–1938), an orthodox Marxist who warned that collaboration would end in the total corruption and demoralization of the proletariat. In France, the same battle was waged by the "purist" Jules Guesde, who preached that the Socialist party's primary goal should be the development of proletarian class consciousness, and Jean Jaurès, socialist leader in the Chamber of Deputies, who advocated a revisionist course. In both Germany and France, revisionists outnumbered purists by a wide margin. This was, to an even greater degree, the case in Britain. There, Fabian socialists—so named from their policy of delay, in imitation of the tactics of Fabius, a Roman general—preached what they called "the inevitability of gradualism." They believed their country would evolve toward socialism by means of parliamentary democracy. Prominent among the Fabians were the social investigators Sidney and Beatrice Webb, the novelist H. G. Wells, and the playwright George Bernard Shaw.

Revisionist gains

Jean Jaurès

The continued success of revisionism led its opponents to sharpen their attack and to advocate increasingly violent means to achieve their ends. Their campaigns, though they never managed to convince a majority of the working class, nevertheless attracted an increasing number of adherents. Some who had originally supported the revisionists grew disappointed when reforms did not come as quickly as expected. At the same time, in much of Europe, the cost of living began to rise for many workers. The comparative prosperity that some members of the working class had experienced vanished in the face of price rises that were not matched by wage increases. The result was a frustration which encouraged the adoption of a more militant stance. Germans rallied to the side of the radical socialists Rosa Luxemburg and Karl Liebknecht, while in France a new revolutionary socialist party disowned the reformist leader Alexandre Millerand after he agreed to serve as cabinet member in a nonsocialist government. The Second International, which had been founded in 1889, demanded at a conference in 1906 that affiliated parties declare their goal to be the destruction of the bourgeois order and the state that served its interests.

This militant mood encouraged acceptance of the doctrines of anarchists and syndicalists. Anarchists preached the overthrow of capitalism by violence. They differed from socialists, however, in their hatred of the machinery of the state or any government based upon coercion. Socialists argued that until the communist millennium promised by Marx, the state would remain a necessary means to the achievement of that eventual end. Anarchists worked to see the immediate abolition of a state bureaucracy which, no matter who controlled it, they believed would result in tyranny. Bakunin, whom Marx had succeeded in expelling from the First International, was anarchism's most popular propagandist. Syndicalism, like anarchism, demanded the abolition of both capitalism and the state. It resembled socialism in its demand that workers share in the ownership of the means of production. Instead of making the state the owner and operator of the means of production, however, the syndicalist would delegate these functions to syndicates of producers. The steel mills would be owned and operated by the workers in the steel industry, the coal mines by the workers in the coal industry, and so on. These associations would take the place of the state, each one governing its own members in their activities as producers.

Georges Sorel

Syndicalism received its most sympathetic hearing in France, where a General Confederation of Labour, after 1902, resolved to seek solutions to economic problems outside the legally constituted framework of French politics. The most effective spokesman for syndicalism was the Frenchman Georges Sorel (1847–1922). Sorel, in his *Reflections on Violence,* published in 1908, argued that workers should be made to believe in the possibility of a general strike by the proletariat which

The Haymarket Riots, Chicago, 1886. A contemporary illustration depicting the results of attempts to unionize workers at the McCormick Harvester works.

would result in the end of bourgeois civilization. The general strike might be nothing more than myth, Sorel acknowledged. Yet, as myth, it remained a powerful weapon in the hands of those whose goal was the destruction of society and who must not shy from the employment of violent means to achieve that end.

Socialism before the First World War, then, was not a unified force. It was divided by quarrels between purists and revisionists, and challenged by the even more radical proposals of anarchists and syndicalists. Socialists, intent on their goal of international solidarity among working classes, ignored the appeal that nationalism and imperialism might make to workers in France, Germany, and Britain. Yet despite its divisions and weaknesses, socialism appeared to the middle classes of Europe as a real threat to their continued prosperity. Capitalism had provided the machinery by which the bourgeoisie had achieved power. Socialism attacked capitalism and hence those who were its direct beneficiaries. Although most socialists disapproved of violence, violent acts were attributed by middle-class men and women to an amorphous, anticapitalist body easily labeled "socialist." Riots by trade unionists in Chicago's Haymarket Square in 1886 and in London's Trafalgar Square in 1887; the assassinations of President Sadi Carnot of France in 1894, of King Humbert of Italy in 1900, and of President William McKinley of the United States in 1901; strikes which grew in number and violence throughout Europe and America after 1900—all these events were perceived by members of the middle class as part of a larger movement whose professed goal was to tear from them their economic, political, and social security.

Socialism as a threat to the middle class

2. THE CHALLENGE OF SCIENCE AND PHILOSOPHY

Science and progress

Louis Pasteur

Marie Curie

While socialism challenged middle-class self-confidence from one quarter, science and philosophy threatened from another. The fact that science might undermine, rather than sustain, certainty was all the more difficult to comprehend, given the manner in which science and technology had together assisted in the birth and continued development of industrialization. This is not to say that science abandoned its role as an instrument for the solving of human problems and as a vital aid to continuing progress. There were striking improvements in the field of medicine, for example. The Frenchman Louis Pasteur (1822–1895) proved that all forms of life, no matter how small, are reproduced only by living beings. Hitherto, according to the theory of spontaneous generation, it had commonly been supposed that bacteria and other microscopic organisms originated from water or from other decaying vegetable and animal matter. By locating the source of bacteria, Pasteur's discovery opened the way for major improvements in the areas of public sanitation and health: among others, the process of ridding food of objectionable bacteria by sterilization—pasteurization—that was named for him. Pasteur, along with the German Robert Koch (1843–1910), also proved conclusively that germs were not, as was commonly supposed, the result but rather the cause of disease. The discovery of the X ray by the German Wilhelm von Röntgen in 1895 and of radium by the Polish scientist Marie Curie in 1898, not only altered perceptions as to the nature of energy, but suggested ways in which energy could be put to use for medical purposes. These discoveries—along with similarly important ones in the areas of cell theory, anesthetics, and antiseptics—worked to convince the educated public that science was a friend of humanity. They reinforced as well a belief in the predictability of the universe and in its essential timelessness, the sense that the passage of time brought with it no fundamental change.

Against this psychologically reassuring fortress of a harmonious universe, biological scientists hurled the bomb of evolutionary theory. We have seen that this theory was at least as old as Anaximander in the sixth century B.C., and that it was accepted by many of the great minds of antiquity. We have learned also that it was revived in the eighteenth century by the scientists Buffon and Linnaeus. But neither of these men offered much proof or explained how the process of evolution might work. The first to develop a systematic hypothesis of evolution was the French biologist, Jean Lamarck (1744–1829). The essential principle in Lamarck's hypothesis, published in 1809, was the inheritance of acquired characteristics. He maintained that an animal, subjected to a change in environment, acquired new habits, which in turn were reflected in structural changes. These acquired characteristics of body structure, he believed, were transmissible to the offspring, with the result that after a series of generations a new species of animal was eventually produced. Though Lamarck's successors found little evidence to confirm this hypothesis, it nonetheless dominated biological thought for nearly fifty years.

A much more convincing hypothesis of organic evolution was that of the English naturalist Charles Darwin (1809–1882), published in 1859. The son of a small-town physician, Darwin began the study of medicine at the University of Edinburgh, but soon withdrew and entered Cambridge to prepare for the ministry. Here he instead devoted most of his time to natural history. In 1831 Darwin obtained an appointment as naturalist without pay with a government-sponsored expedition aboard H.M.S. *Beagle,* which had been chartered for scientific exploration on a trip around the world. The voyage lasted nearly five years and gave Darwin an unparalleled opportunity to become acquainted at first hand with the manifold variations of animal life. He noted the differences between animals inhabiting islands and related species on nearby continents, and observed the resemblances between living animals and the fossilized remains of extinct species in the same locality. It was a magnificent preparation for his life's work. Upon returning from the voyage he read Malthus's essay on population, and was struck by the author's contention that throughout the world of nature many more individuals are born than can survive, and that consequently the weaker ones must perish in the struggle for food. The fruits of his observations, research, and hypothesizing were eventually published in 1859, in the *Origin of Species.*

Darwin's hypothesis was that of natural selection. He argued that it is nature, or the environment, which selects those variants among offspring that are to survive and reproduce. Darwin pointed out, first of all, that the parents of every species beget more offspring than can possibly survive. He maintained that, consequently, a struggle takes place among these offspring for food, shelter, warmth, and other conditions necessary for life. In this struggle for existence certain individuals have the advantage because of the factor of *variation,* which means that no two of the offspring are exactly alike. Some are born stronger than others; some have longer horns or sharper claws or perhaps a body coloration that enables them better to blend with their surroundings and thus to evade their enemies. It is these favored members of the species that win out in the struggle for existence and survive as the "fittest" of their generation; the others are eliminated generally before they have lived long enough to reproduce. Darwin regarded variation and natural selection as the primary factors in the origin of new species. In other words, he taught that individual plants and animals with favorable characteristics would transmit their inherited qualities to their descendants through countless generations, and that successive eliminations of the least fit would eventually produce a new species. Darwin applied his concept of evolution not only to plant and animal species but also to humans. In his second great work,

Charles Darwin

Illustrations from Darwin's First Edition of The Descent of Man. *The drawings were used to point up the similarities between a human embryo (top) and that of a dog (bottom).*

The Descent of Man (1871), he attempted to show that the human race originally sprang from some apelike ancestor, long since extinct, but probably a common forebear of the existing anthropoid apes and humans.

The Darwinian hypothesis was elaborated and improved by several later biologists. The German August Weismann (1834–1914) flatly rejected the idea that acquired characteristics could be inherited. He conducted experiments to show that body cells and reproductive cells are entirely distinct, and that there is no way in which changes in the former can affect the latter. He concluded, therefore, that the only qualities transmissible to the offspring are those that have always been present in the reproductive cells of the parents. In 1901 the Dutch botanist Hugo De Vries (1848–1935) published his celebrated mutation hypothesis, based upon Darwin's original hypothesis and, in large part, upon laws of heredity discovered by the Austrian monk Gregor Mendel (1822–1884). De Vries asserted that evolution results not from minor variations, as Darwin had assumed, but from radical differences or mutations, which appear in more or less definite ratio among the offspring. When any of these mutations are favorable to survival in a given environment, the individuals possessing them naturally emerge triumphant in the struggle for existence. Not only do their descendants inherit these qualities, but from time to time new mutants appear, some of which are even better adapted for survival than their parents. Thus in a limited number of generations a new species may be brought into existence. The mutation theory of De Vries corrected one of the chief weaknesses in the Darwinian hypothesis. The variations that Darwin assumed to be the source of evolutionary changes are so small that an incredibly long time would be necessary to produce a new species. De Vries made it possible to conceive of evolution as proceeding by sudden leaps.

Clearly, the implications of this new theory were deeply disturbing for those who had until now believed in an orderly universe, or had taken as literal the words of the Bible. For the latter the task of reconciling Darwin's account of creation with the first chapter of Genesis, though troublesome, was often not insuperable. Outside fundamentalist sects, the Bible was, at this time, perceived by growing numbers as containing a combination of myths, legends, history, and profoundly important moral truths. The work of the German theologian David Friedrich Strauss (1808–1874) and of the French historian Ernest Renan (1832–1892) had cast doubt on the historical accuracy of the Bible, and dealt with its inconsistencies. These writers had defended the intentions of the Bible's various authors, while firmly insisting upon their human fallibilities. Their searching yet nevertheless sensitive critiques helped people understand that they need not abandon their Christian faith simply because Darwin insisted that the world and all that lived within it had been created over millions of years and not in six days. Far more difficult to deal with was the notion, explicit in Darwin, that nature was not a changeless harmony, but instead a constant and apparently undirected struggle. Chance, and not order, ruled the universe. Nothing was fixed, nothing perfect; all was in a state of flux. Good and bad were defined only in terms of an ability to survive. The "best" of a species were those that triumphed over their weaker rivals. All of a sudden, the universe had become a harsh and uncompromising place, deprived of pre-Darwinian certainties; belief in a benevolent God was now much harder to sustain.

Darwin's most vigorous defender, the philosopher Thomas Henry Huxley (1825–1895), was one of those who could no longer reconcile science with a belief in God. While he did not reject the possibility of a supernatural power, Huxley averred that "there is no evidence of the existence of such a being as the God of the theologians." He pronounced Christianity to be "a compound of some of the best and some of the worst elements of Paganism and Judaism, moulded in practice by the innate character of certain people of the Western World." Huxley coined the word *agnosticism* to express his contempt for the attitude of dogmatic certainty symbolized by the beliefs of the ancient Gnostics. As propounded by Huxley, agnosticism was the doctrine that neither the existence nor the nature of God nor the ultimate character of the universe is knowable. Huxley earned himself the nickname of "Darwin's bulldog" because of his stout attacks upon orthodox Christians who refused to accept the implications of Darwinian theory. In a famous debate between Huxley and Samuel Wilberforce, the bishop of Oxford, in 1860, the bishop made the mistake of trying to turn Darwin into a joke, inquiring of the audience if anyone were willing to trace his descent from an ape, whether it was through his grandmother or grandfather. Huxley rejoined that the only ancestor of which he would feel ashamed was a man like the bishop, who so misused his talents to make light of such a serious issue. The sustained applause with which his remarks were greeted suggest the degree to which religious orthodoxy could now be safely challenged in public discussion.

The middle classes of western Europe and the United States, disoriented by the antireligious implications of evolutionary theory, received some comfort from the writings of those who adapted Darwinian thought to the analysis of society—the so-called Social Darwinists. These thinkers argued that the apparent "success" of Western civilization was the result of its special fitness. The white race, they boasted, had proved itself superior to the black; non-Jews superior to Jews; rich superior to poor; the British Empire superior to the subject territories it controlled. If nature was a matter of competition, so was society,

Thomas Henry Huxley

The Social Darwinists

Herbert Spencer

Anthropology

Friedrich Nietzsche

with the victory going to that race or nation that could demonstrate its fitness to survive by subduing others.

Though he never expressed his ideas that crudely, the English philosopher Herbert Spencer (1820–1903) extolled the virtues of competition in a way that made it easier for others to do so. Spencer grounded his philosophy upon evolutionary theory. He insisted upon the idea of evolution as a universal law. He was deeply impressed by Darwin's *Origin of Species* and enriched the hypothesis of natural selection with a phrase that has clung to it ever since—"the survival of the fittest." He contended that not only species and individuals are subject to evolutionary change, but also planets, solar systems, customs, institutions, and religious and ethical ideas. Everything in the universe completes a cycle of origin, development, decay, and extinction. When the end of the cycle has been reached, the process begins once more and is repeated eternally. As a political philosopher, Spencer was a vigorous champion of individualism. He condemned collectivism as a relic of primitive society, as a feature of the earliest stage of social evolution. Any so-called assistance individuals might receive from the state, Spencer argued, would result not only in their own degeneration, but in that of society as well.

If Social Darwinists could reassure some by implying the biological right of Western civilization to survive as the "fittest" within the contemporary world, anthropologists—pioneers in what was essentially a new scientific discipline—argued, on the contrary, that no culture could be perceived as "better" than any other. All societies were adaptations to a particular environment. Each society produced its own customs, which could not be declared "good" or "bad," but only successful or unsuccessful, according to the degree to which they helped that society survive. This notion of cultural "relativism" was a theme in the influential work of the English anthropologist Sir James Frazer (1854–1941). In his masterpiece, *The Golden Bough,* he demonstrated the relationship of Christianity to primitive practices and magical rites. Christianity was nothing more or less than one society's response to the craving for an explanation of the apparently inexplicable.

Christianity was challenged far more directly in the writings of the German philosopher Friedrich Nietzsche (1844–1900). Nietzsche was not a scientist, nor was he interested in the nature of matter or in the problem of religious truth. He was essentially a romantic poet glorifying the struggle for existence to compensate for his own life of weakness and misery. Born in 1844, the son of a Lutheran minister, he was educated in the classics at Leipzig and Bonn and at the age of twenty-five was appointed professor of philology at the University of Basel. Ten years later repeated and severe attacks of nerves forced his retirement. He spent the next decade of his life in agony, wandering from one resort to another in a fruitless quest for relief. If we can believe his own statement, each year was made up of two hundred days of pain. In 1888 he lapsed into hopeless insanity, which continued until his death in 1900.

Nietzsche's philosophy is contained in such works as *Thus Spake Zarathustra, A Genealogy of Morals,* and *The Will to Power.* His cardinal idea was the notion that natural selection should be permitted to operate unhindered in the case of human beings as it does with plants and animals. Yet he did not accept the deterministic worldview upon which the theories of Darwin—and of Marx as well—ultimately rested. He asserted the possibility of a triumph of human will over external circumstance, a triumph that he believed could eventually produce a race of supermen—not a race of physical giants but men distinguished above all for their moral courage, for their strength of character. Those who would perish in the struggle were the moral weaklings, who had neither the strength nor the courage to battle nobly for a place in the sun. Before any such process of natural selection could operate, however, religious obstacles would have to be removed. Nietzsche therefore demanded that the moral supremacy of Christianity and Judaism be overthrown. Both of these religions, he alleged, glorified the virtues of the downtrodden. They exalted into virtues qualities that ought to be considered vices—humility, nonresistance, mortification of the flesh, and pity for the weak and incompetent. The enthronement of these qualities prevented the elimination of the unfit and preserved them to pour their degenerate blood into the veins of the race.

Nietzsche's philosophy

Scientists and philosophers, as they continued to explore the various and sometimes contradictory implications of evolutionary theory, helped to undermine the comforting notion of humankind's essential superiority to the rest of the animal kingdom. The work of the Russian psychologist Ivan Pavlov (1849–1936) resulted in the discovery of the conditioned reflex. Although Pavlov experimented with animals, he insisted that his conclusions applied equally to human beings. The conditioned reflex is a form of behavior in which natural reactions are produced by an artificial stimulus. Pavlov showed that if dogs were fed immediately following the ringing of a bell, they would eventually respond to the sound of the bell alone and secrete saliva exactly as if confronted by the sight and smell of the food. This discovery suggested the conclusion that the conditioned reflex is an important element in human behavior and encouraged psychologists to center their attention upon physiological experiment as a key to understanding the mind.

Pavlov

Pavlovians inaugurated a type of physiological psychology known as behaviorism. Behaviorism is an attempt to study the human being as a purely physiological organism—to reduce all human behavior to a series of physical responses. Such concepts as *mind* and *consciousness* are dismissed as vague and meaningless terms. For the behaviorist noth-

Behaviorism

Sigmund Freud

ing is important except the reactions of muscles, nerves, glands, and visceral organs. There is no such thing as an independent psychic behavior; all that humans do is physical. Thinking is essentially a form of talking to oneself. Every complex emotion and idea is simply a group of physiological responses produced by some stimulus in the environment. Such was the mechanistic interpretation of human actions offered by followers of Pavlov.

The other important school of psychology to make its appearance after the turn of the century was psychoanalysis, founded by Sigmund Freud (1856–1939), an Austrian physician. Psychoanalysis interprets human behavior mainly in terms of the unconscious mind. Freud admitted the existence of the conscious mind (the ego), but he avowed that the unconscious (the id) is much more important in determining the actions of the individual. He considered humans as egoistic creatures propelled by basic urges of power, self-preservation, and sex. These urges are much too strong to be overcome; but inasmuch as society (the superego) has branded their unrestrained fulfillment as sinful, they are commonly driven into the unconscious, where they linger indefinitely as suppressed desires. Yet they are seldom completely submerged; they rise to the surface in dreams, or they manifest themselves in lapses of memory, in fears and obsessions, and in various forms of abnormal behavior. Freud believed that most cases of mental and nervous disorder result from violent conflicts between natural instincts and the restraints imposed by an unfortunate environment. Freud hoped that by elucidating his theory of the unconscious he could impose predictable patterns upon the irrationality that seemed to characterize so much human activity. His search for order, however, resembled that of the behaviorists by continuing to stress the extent to which men and women, like animals, were prey to drives, impulses, and reflexes over which they could exercise at best only minimal control.

Under the impact of these various scientific and philosophical challenges, the institutions responsible for the maintenance of traditional faith found themselves hard pressed. Protestantism had based its revolt against Roman Catholic orthodoxy upon the belief that men and women should seek to understand God with the aid of not much more than the Bible and a willing conscience. In consequence, Protestants had little in the way of authoritarian doctrine to support them when their faith was challenged. Some—the fundamentalists—chose to ignore the implications of scientific and philosophical inquiry altogether, and continued to believe in the literal truth of the Bible. Some were willing to agree with the school of American philosophers known as Pragmatists (Charles Pierce, William James), that if belief in a personal God produced mental peace or spiritual satisfaction, that belief must therefore be true. Truth, for the Pragmatists, was whatever provided useful, practical results. Other Protestants sought solace from religious doubt in religious activity, founding missions, and laboring among the poor. Many adherents to this "Social Gospel" were also "Modernists," determined to accept the ethical teachings of Christianity while discarding belief in miracles and the doctrines of original sin and the Incarnation.

The Roman Catholic Church was compelled by its tradition of dogmatic assertion to assist its followers in their response to the modern world. In 1864 Pope Pius IX issued a *Syllabus of Errors* condemning what he regarded as the principal religious and philosophical "errors" of the time. Among them were materialism, free thought, and "indifferentism," or the idea that one religion is as good as another. The *Syllabus* was condemned by critics as a "crusade against civilization." While heated discussions continued over the *Syllabus of Errors,* Pope Pius convoked a Church council in 1869, the first to be summoned since the Catholic Reformation. The most notable pronouncement of the Vatican Council was the dogma of papal infallibility. In the language of this dogma the pope, when he speaks *ex cathedra*—that is, in his capacity "as pastor and doctor of all Christians"—is infallible in regard to all matters of faith and morals. Though generally accepted by pious Catholics, the dogma of papal infallibility evoked a storm of protest in many circles. Governments of several Catholic countries denounced it, including France, Spain, and Italy. The death of Pius IX in 1878 and the accession of Pope Leo XIII brought a more accommodating climate to the Church. The new pope was ready to concede that there was "good" as well as "evil" in modern civilization. He added a scientific staff to the Vatican and opened archives and observatories. However, he made no concessions to "liberalism" or "anticlericalism" in the political sphere. He would go no farther than to urge capitalists and employers to be more generous in recognizing the rights of organized labor.

Pope Pius IX

The effect of various scientific and philosophical challenges upon the men and women who lived at the end of the nineteenth century cannot be measured in any exact way. Millions undoubtedly went about the business of life untroubled by the implications of evolutionary theory, content to believe as they had believed. Certainly, for most members of the middle class, the challenge of socialism was understood as "real" in a way that the challenge of science and philosophy probably was not. Socialism was a threat to livelihood. Darwinism, relativism, materialism, and behaviorism, though "in the air" and troublesome to those who breathed that air, did not impinge upon consciousness to the same degree. Men and women can postpone thoughts about their origins and ultimate destiny in a way that they cannot postpone thoughts about their daily bread. And yet the impact of the changes we have been discussing was eventually profound. Darwin's theory was not so complicated as to prevent its popularization. If educated men and women had neither the time nor inclination to read the *Origin of Species,* they read magazines and newspapers which spelled out for them its implications. Those implications in-

Pope Leo XIII

duced an uncertainty that tempered the optimism of capitalist expansion.

Men and women who had never read the German philosopher Arthur Schopenhauer (1788–1860) might well have agreed with his assessment of this world as one condemned to witness the devouring of the weak by the strong. Yet their commitment to the ways of the world prevented their acceptance of Schopenhauer's particular remedy: an escape into a life of personal asceticism and self-denial. Like the English poet and essayist Matthew Arnold, sensitive men and women might feel themselves trapped in a world resembling no more than "a darkling plain," where there was "neither joy, nor love, nor light, nor certitude, nor peace, nor help for pain."

3. THE CHALLENGE OF LITERATURE AND THE ARTS

After 1850 a handful of artists and a greater number of writers continued to challenge the middle-class worldview, as had their predecessors, by drawing attention to the shortcomings of industrial society. As the century drew to a close, however, one of the major problems these critics now faced was the question of audience: not merely what to say, but whom to say it to. Before the middle of the eighteenth century, that audience had been primarily aristocratic. Between 1750 and 1870 it was both aristocratic and upper middle class. Now, thanks to the fact of an increasingly literate general population, the potential audience appeared to have increased enormously. In 1850 approximately half the population of Europe had been illiterate. In subsequent decades, country after country introduced state-financed elementary and secondary education—in part as an attempt to provide citizens with an opportunity for social mobility, in part as a means of control and as a preventive to the establishment of schools run by workers for workers, and in part as a measure to keep pace with changing technological knowledge. Britain instituted elementary education in 1870, Switzerland in 1874, Italy in 1877. France expanded its existing system between 1878 and 1881. After 1871 Germany instituted a state system modeled on Prussia's. By 1900, approximately 85 percent of the population in Britain, France, Belgium, the Netherlands, Scandinavia, and Germany could read. Elsewhere, however, the percentages were far lower, ranging between 30 and 60 percent.

In those countries where literacy rates were highest, capitalist publishers such as Alfred Harmsworth in England and William Randolph Hearst in the United States hastened to serve the new reading public. Middle-class readers had for some time been well supplied by newspapers catering to their interests and point of view. *The Times* of London had a readership of well over 50,000 by 1850; the *Presse* and *Siècle* in France, a circulation of 70,000. By 1900, however, other newspa-

The New Power of the Press. With the spread of literacy, newspapers adapted to the needs and desires of the new mass audience. Here English railway passengers scramble for the latest edition.

pers were appealing to a different mass market—the newly literate—and doing so by means of sensational journalism and spicy, easy-to-read serials.

These new developments encouraged writers and artists to distance themselves more and more from what seemed to them a vulgar, materialistic culture. They agreed with writers of the mid-century who had insisted that the purpose of art and literature was not to pander or sentimentalize. They went further, however, by declaring that art had no business preaching morality to a public that, in any event, had proved itself unwilling to heed the sermon. This generation of artists and writers argued that one did not look at a painting or read a poem to be instructed in the difference between good and evil, but to understand what was eternally true and beautiful—to appreciate art for its own sake. They were not so much interested in reaching a wider audience, whose standards of taste they generally deplored, as they were in addressing each other. This self-conscious desire not only to live apart but to think apart from society was reflected in their work. In 1850, educated men and women could read a Dickens novel or examine a Daumier print and understand it, even if they did not admire it or agree with its message. In 1900, men and women found it much harder to understand, let alone admire, a painting by Paul Cézanne or a poem by Paul Valéry. Artists and public were ceasing to speak the same language, a fact that contributed, as did the ideas of Darwin and Nietzsche, Pavlov and Freud, to the further confusion and fragmentation of Western culture.

The distancing of art and literature from the public

These new perceptions of the artist's relationship to society did not surface to any measurable degree before the very end of the century. Until that time, the arts were dominated by what has come to be called *realism*. Realists were predominantly critics of contemporary society. Swayed by a fervor for social reform, they depicted the inequities of the human condition against the sordid background of indus-

Realism

trial society. Like the romantics, the realists affirmed the possibility of human freedom, although realists emphasized more than romantics the obstacles that prevented its achievement. Realists differed most markedly from romantics in their disdain of sentiment and emotional extravagance. Adopting from natural science the idea of life as a struggle for survival, they tried to portray human existence in accordance with hard facts, often insisting that their characters were the irresponsible victims of heredity, environment, or their own animal passions.

Literary realism in France

Realism as a literary movement made its initial appearance in France. Its leading exponents included the novelists Honoré de Balzac and Gustave Flaubert,[1] whose work, as we have already noted, contained a stinging assessment of the dullness and greed of modern life. Émile Zola (1840–1902), another Frenchman, is often called a naturalist rather than a realist, to convey the idea that he was interested in an exact, scientific presentation of the facts of nature without the intrusion of personal philosophy. Naturalism was expected to dismiss moral values in a way that realism was not. Zola did have a definite moral viewpoint, however. His early years of wretched poverty imbued him with a deep sympathy for the common people and with a passion for social justice. Though he portrayed human nature as weak and prone to vice and crime, he was not without hope that a decided improvement might come from the creation of a better society. Many of his novels dealt with such social problems as alcoholism, poverty, and disease.

Realism in England

Realism in the writings of the Englishman Charles Dickens was overlaid with layers of sentimentality. Dickens was a master at depicting the evils of industrial society, but the invariable happy endings of his novels testify to his determined—and unrealistic—unwillingness to allow wrong to triumph over right. No such ambivalence marked the works of the later English novelist Thomas Hardy (1840–1928), however. In such well-known novels as *The Return of the Native, Jude the Obscure,* and *Tess of the D'Urbervilles,* he expressed his conception that humans are the playthings of an inexorable fate. The universe, though beautiful, was depicted as in no sense friendly, and the struggle of individuals with nature was a pitiable battle against almost impossible odds. If God existed, he watched with indifference while the helpless denizens of the human ant-heap crawled toward suffering and death. Yet Hardy pitied his fellow creatures, regarding them not as depraved animals but as the victims of cosmic forces beyond their control.

Realism in Germany and Scandinavia

Pity for humanity was a central theme in the work of the German Gerhard Hauptmann (1862–1946). Calling himself a naturalist, Hauptmann nevertheless reflected the realists' concern for suffering. His plays show the influence of Darwin in their emphasis upon determinism and environment. *The Weavers,* which depicts the suffering of Silesian weavers in the 1840s, is probably his most outstanding work.

[1] See above, p. 777.

Doubtless the most eminent playwright among realists and naturalists was the Norwegian Henrik Ibsen (1828–1906). The stark message of Ibsen's early dramas was not favorably received, and while still a young man he decided to abandon his native country. Residing first in Italy and then in Germany, he did not return permanently to Norway until 1891. His writings were characterized most of all by bitter rebellion against the tyranny and ignorance of society. In such plays as *The Wild Duck, A Doll's House, Hedda Gabler,* and *An Enemy of the People,* he satirized the conventions and institutions of respectable life, and showed, with great insight, how these oppressed women in particular. Along with his scorn for hypocrisy and social tyranny went a profound distrust of majority rule. Ibsen despised democracy as the enthronement of unprincipled leaders who would do anything for the sake of votes to perpetuate themselves in power. As one of his characters in *An Enemy of the People* says: "A minority may be right—a majority is always wrong."

Henrik Ibsen

The literature of the Russians, which flourished during the period of realism, includes within it themes that are both romantic and idealist as well. Russia's three outstanding novelists of the late nineteenth century were Ivan Turgenev (1818–1883), Feodor Dostoevsky (1821–1881), and Leo Tolstoy (1828–1910). They were preceded by the equally talented Alexander Pushkin (1799–1837) who, between 1820 and his death in a duel seventeen years later, established himself as one of Russia's greatest writers. Though his early work was romantic in tone, his epic verse *Eugene Onegin* demonstrated his sympathy with realistic themes.

Turgenev, who spent much of his life in France, was the first of the Russian novelists to become known to western Europe. His chief work, *Fathers and Sons,* describes in brooding terms the struggle between the older and younger generations. The hero is a nihilist (a term first used by Turgenev), who is convinced that the whole social order has nothing in it worth preserving. Dostoevsky was almost as tragic a figure as any he projected in his novels. Condemned at the age of twenty-eight on a charge of revolutionary activity, he was exiled to Siberia, where he endured four horrible years of imprisonment. His later life was harrowed by poverty, family troubles, and epileptic fits. As a novelist, he chose to explore the anguish of people driven to shameful deeds by their raw emotions and by the intolerable meanness of their lives. He was a master of psychological analysis, probing into the motives of distorted minds with an intensity that was almost morbid. At the same time he filled his novels with a broad sympathy and with a mystic conviction that humanity can be purified only through suffering. His best known works are *Crime and Punishment* and *The Brothers Karamazov.*

Russian literature: Turgenev and Dostoevsky

As an earnest champion of the simple life of the peasant, Tolstoy was somewhat less deterministic than the author of *Crime and Punishment.* Yet in *War and Peace,* a majestic epic of Russian conditions

Tolstoy

Leo Tolstoy in His Study Dictating to His Secretary

Victor Hugo by Auguste Rodin. The artist's realism enhances his ability to impart human character to his work.

From realism to impressionism

during the period of the Napoleonic invasion, he expounds the theme that individuals are at the mercy of fate when powerful elemental forces are unleashed. His *Anna Karenina* is a study of the tragedy that lurks in the pursuit of individual desire. As Tolstoy grew older he became more and more an evangelist preaching a social gospel. In such novels as *The Kreutzer Sonata* and *Resurrection* he condemned most of the institutions of civilized society and called upon men and women to renounce selfishness and greed, to earn their living by manual toil, and to cultivate the virtues of poverty, meekness, and nonresistance. His last years were devoted to attacks upon such evils as war and capital punishment and to the defense of victims of political persecution.

The works of all these realists and naturalists, whatever their individual differences, shared two things in common: they contained vigorous moral criticism of present-day middle-class society, and they were written in direct and forceful language that the middle class could understand, if it chose to read or listen. The same can be said of realist painters such as Courbet and Daumier, discussed previously, and of the sculptor Auguste Rodin (1840–1917), whose style and message were neither difficult to comprehend nor easy to ignore. Realist artists were still anxious to address the public, if only to attack its members for their shallowness and insensitivity. The advent of the impressionist movement in painting in the 1870s marks the first significant break in this tradition. At this point artists began to turn away from the public and toward each other. The movement started in France, among a group of young artists whose work had been refused a place in the annual exhibitions of the traditionally minded French Royal Academy. They had been labeled "impressionists" in derision by critics who took them to task for painting not an object

Above: *The Birth of Venus,* Alexandre Cabanel (1823–1889). Below: *Luncheon on the Grass,* Edouard Manet (1823–1883). Cabanel's painting is a typical product of the fashionable French Salon, and was at one time owned by Napoleon III. It won the Salon prize in 1863 and was copied several times by the artist (as were other Salon paintings), emphasizing the fact that it was considered as much a piece of "decoration" as a piece of art. This sort of "bestseller" was exceedingly popular with upper-middle-class collectors, who felt no need to apologize for its semi-pornographic nature because of its classical subject matter. Manet's painting, done in the same year, created an enormous furor. Its style broke with the soft, painterly techniques of the Salon school; instead it was painted with broad, flat strokes that presaged the coming of Impressionism. Its subject matter caused a sensation as well. Whereas voluptuous classical nudes were respectable art, a painting of a young woman seated without her clothing at a picnic with fully clothed gentlemen friends conveyed a sense of serious social impropriety to bourgeois viewers. (Louvre)

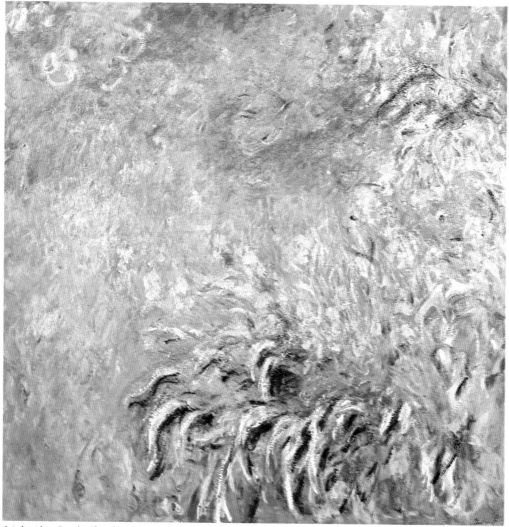

Iris beside a Pond, Claude Monet (1840–1926). Monet called some of his paintings Impressions, and the name soon came to designate a school. (Art Institute of Chicago)

Pink and Green, Edgar Degas (1834–1917). Degas was an Impressionist to the extent of his interest in fleeting motion. But as an admirer of the classicist Ingres, he emphasized line and careful composition. (MMA)

A Woman with Chrysanthemums, Degas. In his portraits, Degas sought to capture his subjects in familiar, informal positions. Avoiding traditional formal sittings, he frequently brought together an assortment of discrete observations first in his imagination, and then on canvas. When this painting was completed in 1858 it was a still life of flowers bearing the imprint of Delacroix; the woman was added in 1865. (MMA)

Luncheon of the Boating Party, Auguste Renoir (1841–1919). The impressionists enjoyed employing their revolutionary artistic techniques to portray the commonplace occasions of everyday life. (Phillips Memorial Gallery)

Montagne Sainte-Victoire with Aqueduct, Paul Cézanne (1839–1906). Cézanne's insistence upon the reduction of the landscape to patterns of form and planes of color illustrates the manner in which his genius created the vital link between impressionism and cubism. (Museum of Modern Art)

The Card Players, Cézanne. Here are exemplified Cézanne's skill in composition, his discriminating sense of color, and the sculptured qualities of solidity and depth he gave to his figures. (Stephen C. Clark)

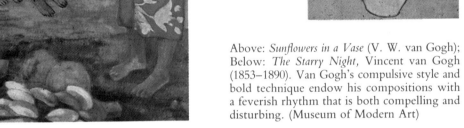

Above: *Sunflowers in a Vase* (V. W. van Gogh); Below: *The Starry Night,* Vincent van Gogh (1853–1890). Van Gogh's compulsive style and bold technique endow his compositions with a feverish rhythm that is both compelling and disturbing. (Museum of Modern Art)

Ia Orana Maria, Paul Gauguin (1848–1903). Gauguin's dissatisfaction with European life compelled his escape to Tahiti, where striking colors, bold patterns of light and shade, and local artistic tradition affected his "fauvist" style of painting. (Museum of Modern Art)

Portrait of Gertrude Stein, Pablo Picasso (1881–1973). Picasso seems to have given this portrait of the great experimenter in poetry some elements of the distortion of form characteristic of the work of both. (Museum of Modern Art)

The Piano Lesson, Henri Matisse (1869–1954). Matisse conveyed a freshness of approach and a vitality of line and color. (Museum of Modern Art)

Three Musicians, Pablo Picasso. This painting, regarded by many as the masterpiece of Cubism, sums up the final stage of the movement. (Museum of Modern Art)

itself, but only their impression of that object. The name in fact suited the personal, private nature of their work. They were painting to please themselves, to realize their own potential as artists.

In a sense, impressionists were realists, for they were determined to paint only what they saw, and they were vitally interested in the scientific interpretation of nature. But impressionist technique was different from that of the older realist painters. Scenes from the world around them were not depicted as if the result of careful study. On the contrary, the works of impressionists sought to reveal immediate sense impressions, leaving it to the mind of the observer to fill in additional details. This often resulted in a type of work appearing at first glance to be nonnaturalistic. Figures were commonly distorted; a few significant details were made to represent an entire object; and dabs of primary color were placed side by side without a trace of blending. Convinced that light is the principal factor in determining the appearance of objects, the impressionists left the studio for the woods and fields in an attempt to capture the fleeting alterations of a natural scene with each transistory shift of sunlight and shadow. From science they had learned that light is composed of a fusion of primary colors visible in the spectrum. Accordingly, they decided to use these colors almost exclusively. They chose, for example, to achieve the effect of the green in nature by placing daubs of pure blue and yellow side by side, allowing the eye to mix them.

Impressionism differed from realism in one other important respect. In these new paintings artists remained detached from their subject. They did not paint to evoke pity, or to teach a lesson. They painted to proclaim the value and importance of painting *as painting*. In doing so, the artist was not deliberately setting out to exclude the viewers. It was clear, however, that the viewer must not expect to understand a painting except on the artist's terms. Probably the greatest of the impressionists were the Frenchmen Claude Monet (1840–1926) and

The Monarch of the Glen by Sir Edwin Landseer. This was the sort of conventional, easy to comprehend art that appealed to the middle class and that brought forth the revolutionary impressionist movement.

See color plates following page 896 for *Iris Beside a Pond* by Monet and *Luncheon of the Boating Party* by Renoir

Expressionism: Cézanne

See color plates following page 896 for *Montagne Sainte-Victoire with Aqueduct* and *The Card Players* by Cézanne

Auguste Renoir (1841–1919). Monet was perhaps the leading exponent of the new mode of interpreting landscapes. His paintings have little structure or design in the conventional sense; they suggest, rather than depict, the outlines of cliffs, trees, mountains, and fields. Intensely interested in the problem of light, Monet would go out at sunrise with an armful of canvases in order to paint the same subject in a dozen momentary appearances. It has been said of one of his masterpieces that "light is the only important person in the picture." Renoir's subjects include not only landscapes but portraits and scenes from contemporary life. He is famous for his pink and ivory nudes, which, as expressions of frank sexuality, represented an additional threat to middle-class sensibilities.

The freedom explicit in the work of the impressionists encouraged other painters to pursue fresh techniques and to define different goals. The expressionists turned upon the impressionists, objecting to their preoccupation with the momentary aspects of nature and their indifference to meaning. Expressionists were not arguing for a return to meaning in the sense of "message." They were instead insisting that a painting must represent the artist's particular intellect. Here again, they were making art a private matter, removing it yet another step from the public. The artist who laid the foundations of expressionism was Paul Cézanne (1839–1906), now recognized as one of the world's greatest painters. A native of southern France, Cézanne labored to express a sense of order in nature that he believed the impressionists had ignored. To achieve this end, he painted objects as a series of planes, each plane expressed in terms of a color change. While Cézanne was in this way equating form with color, he also began to reduce natural forms to their geometrical equivalents, hoping thereby to express the basic shapes of existence itself. He distorted form into geomet-

The Joy of Life, by Henri Matisse. The sensuous use of line and boldness of composition celebrate not only life but the artist's freedom to break from past convention.

Girl Before a Mirror by Pablo
Picasso

rical regularity until abstraction became reality. In all this Cézanne
was declaring the painter's right to recreate nature in such a way as
to express an intensely personal vision.

Art as personal expression was the hallmark of two other painters in
the so-called post-impressionist period, the Frenchman Paul Gauguin
(1848–1903) and the Dutchman Vincent Van Gogh (1853–1890).
Both, by their life as well as their art, declared war on traditional nineteenth-century values. Dismayed by the artificiality and complexity of
civilization, Gauguin fled to the South Sea Islands and spent the last
decade of his life painting the hot and luscious colors of an unspoiled,
primitive society. Van Gogh, whose passionate sympathy for the sufferings of his fellow humans led him to attempt the life of a minister to
poor mining families and undoubtedly contributed to his eventual insanity and ultimate suicide, poured out the full intensity of his feelings
in paintings such as *The Starry Night,* which seem to swirl off the canvas.

In the years between 1900 and the First World War, art underwent
still further revolutionary development. Henri Matisse (1869–1954)
greatly extended Cézanne's use of distortion, thereby declaring once
again the painter's right to create according to an individual definition
of aesthetic merit. This declaration was given its most ringing prewar
endorsement by Pablo Picasso (1881–1973). Picasso, a Catalan Spaniard who came to Paris in 1903, developed a style, cubism, that takes
its name from an attempt to carry Cézanne's fascination with geometrical form to its logical conclusion. Influenced both by the work of

Self-Portrait by Paul Gauguin

See color plates
following page 896 for
representative works by
Gauguin, Matisse,
Picasso, and van Gogh

Cézanne and by African sculpture, cubism results not only in distortion but in some cases in actual dismemberment. The artist may separate the various parts of a figure and rearrange them in other than their natural pattern. The purpose is to express defiance of traditional notions of form—to repudiate once and for all the conception of art as representational prettiness.

New directions in literature and music

The artistic declaration of independence from middle-class society was enunciated most dramatically by painters, but was heard also in the realms of literature and music. In France, the work of a group calling itself the symbolists, and centered upon the poetry of Paul Verlaine, Arthur Rimbaud, Stéphane Mallarmé, and Paul Valéry attempted to intensify the personal while transcending reality in a way reminiscent of the impressionists, expressionists, and cubists. In music, as well, there was a break from the romantic tradition that had dominated the nineteenth century and that had been expressed in the works of composers such as Robert Schumann (1810–1856), Felix Mendelssohn (1809–1847), and Franz Liszt (1811–1886). Already the late romantic operas of Richard Wagner had taken vast liberties with harmony and departed from stereotypical melodic patterns, producing music that was not subject to the tyranny of form but was sensitive to personal expression. Now in the works of composers such as the Austrian Richard Strauss (1864–1949) and the Frenchman Claude Debussy (1862–1918) music moved even further in the direction of the intensely personal. Strauss's opera *Der Rosenkavalier* (1911), although based externally on the conventions of late–eighteenth-century plot, is nevertheless a musical expression of the inner realities of its characters, written to express those realities more directly than heretofore. Both Strauss and Debussy were, like the impressionists, determined to convey atmosphere; Debussy's piano compositions, and his symphonic sketch, *La Mer,* are musical manifestations of the impressionists' regard for association rather than formal structure.

Self-imposed isolation

Whether in painting, in literature, or in music, artists sought to escape to a position from which they could learn and then express what was closest to their own consciousness. Their direct, calculated dismissal of conventional form and content declared their fundamental disdain for—more important, their complete lack of interest in—the problems of the world at large. Their self-imposed isolation served only to increase the general sense of a fragmented world that, despite its material prosperity, was at war with itself.

SELECTED READINGS

• *Items so designated are available in paperback editions.*

SOCIALISM

• Avineri, S., *The Social and Political Thought of Karl Marx,* London, 1968.
• Cole, G. D. H., *A History of Socialist Thought,* Vols. I–III, London, 1953–1956. A comprehensive treatment of the period 1789–1914.

- Derfler, Leslie, *Socialism since Marx: A Century of the European Left*, New York, 1973. Survey and analysis of continental socialist movements.

  Edwards, Stewart, *The Paris Commune of 1871*, London, 1971. Straightforward analysis.

  Gay, Peter, *The Dilemma of Democratic Socialism: Eduard Bernstein's Challenge to Marx*, New York, 1952. A good study of German revisionism.

  Goldberg, Harvey, *A Life of Jean Jaurès*, Madison, Wisc., 1962. A fine biography of the eminent French socialist.

- Joll, James, *The Anarchists*, London, 1964. Survey of various radical European groups.

  Lichtheim, G., *A Short History of Socialism*, New York, 1970. Provides a useful overview.

  Lidtke, Vernon, *The Outlawed Party, Social Democracy in Germany*, Charlotte, N.C. 1966. Deals with German socialists from 1878 to 1890.

- McBriar, A. M., *Fabian Socialism and English Politics, 1884–1918*, Cambridge, 1966. An extensive study of this important circle: their composition, their ideology, their methods.

  Noland, Aaron, *The Founding of the French Socialist Party, 1893–1905*, Cambridge, Mass., 1956. Primarily a narrative account of the translation of ideology into political reality.

- Schorske, Carl E., *German Social Democracy, 1905–1918*, Cambridge, Mass., 1955. A magnificent study of the problems of the Social Democrats in a time of imperialism and war.

SCIENTIFIC THOUGHT

- Butterfield, Herbert B., *The Origins of Modern Science*, rev. ed., New York, 1957. A standard survey.
- Eiseley, Loren C., *Darwin's Century: Evolution and the Men Who Discovered It*, New York, 1961. The history of evolution after Darwin.
- Gay, Peter, *Freud, Jews, and Other Germans: Masters and Victims in Modernist Culture*, New York, 1978. Essays on end-of-the-century German culture.

  Gillespie, C. C., *The Edge of Objectivity*, Princeton, 1960. A history of scientific ideas.

- Hughes, H. Stuart, *Consciousness and Society*, New York, 1958. Examines the reaction to Positivism and the growing interest in the irrational by considering the work of Freud, Max Weber, and others.
- Jones, Ernest, *The Life and Work of Sigmund Freud*, 3 vols., New York, 1953–1957. The official biography, by a close collaborator and eminent psychoanalyst.
- Rieff, P., *Freud: The Mind of the Moralist*, New York, 1959. A useful, one-volume discussion.

THE ARTS AND PHILOSOPHY

- Barzun, Jacques, *Darwin, Marx, and Wagner*, Boston, 1941. Argues that these men were not so much originators of new ideas as founders of systems that are mechanistic and pseudoscientific, and therefore threatening to the human cultural heritage.

  Kaufmann, Walter A., *Nietzsche: Philosopher, Psychologist, Anti-Christ*, Princeton, 1974. A superb intellectual biography.

Lang, Paul, *Music in Western Civilization,* New York, 1941. Useful survey and reference.

• Masur, Gerhard, *Prophets of Yesterday,* New York, 1961. A broad survey of nineteenth-century European thinkers.

Mosse, G. L., *The Culture of Western Europe: The Nineteenth and Twentieth Centuries,* Chicago, 1961. Thoughtful analysis and overview.

• Schorske, Carl, *Fin-de-Siecle Vienna: Politics and Culture,* New York, 1980. Essays on Vienna's cultural impact on the West.

• Shattuck, Roger, *The Banquet Years: The Arts in France, 1885–1918,* New York, 1958. The emergence of modernism in French art, literature, and music.

SOURCE MATERIALS

• Arnold, Matthew, *Culture and Anarchy,* New York, 1971. Originally published in 1867. A perceptive criticism of English society and a call for an authoritarian principle in an increasingly democratic society.

• Darwin, Charles, *The Descent of Man,* Cambridge, Mass., 1964. See especially Chapter XXI.

• ———, *Origin of Species,* Cambridge, Mass., 1964. See especially Chapters IX, XV.

• Edwards, Stewart, ed., *The Communards of Paris, 1871,* New York, 1976. Annotated eyewitness reports, documents, and accounts of the Paris Commune.

• Gosse, Edmund, *Father and Son,* New York, 1963. A moving autobiography by a distinguished Victorian literary critic, this work reveals the conflict between the religious fundamentalism of the father and the skepticism of the son in the wake of Darwinian theory.

Kohn, Hans, *The Mind of Russia,* New Brunswick, N.J., 1955. An edited collection of historical, literary, and philosophical works of nineteenth- and twentieth-century Russian authors, designed to reveal the conflict between traditional and Western thought in Russia.

Marx, Karl, *Capital,* intro. by G. D. H. Cole, New York, 1974. A good edition of the classic.

• Webb, Beatrice, *My Apprenticeship,* London, 1926. Beatrice Webb was one of the leading Fabian Socialists, and in this first volume of her autobiography she explains how she, as a member of one of England's wealthier families, was converted to a socialist creed.

• Zola, Émile, *L'Assommoir,* London, 1970. Written in 1877 and set in the Paris of the 1860s, this bitterly realistic novel portrays the brutalization of the French working class by the forces of industrial change, poverty, and alcohol.

Chapter 26

THE SEARCH FOR STABILITY
(1870–1914)

Ah! What a seething there has been, . . . customs worthy of the inquisition and despotism, the pleasure of a few gold-braided individuals setting their heels on the nation, and stifling its cry for truth and justice, under the mendacious and sacrilegious pretext of the interest of the State!

—Émile Zola, "J'accuse"

Between 1870 and 1914, the major powers of Europe worked to maintain both domestic and international stability. Accomplishment of this goal was facilitated by continuing industrialization. Despite periodic trade depressions, general prosperity increased for almost all classes of society at least until 1900. And prosperity, in its turn, helped to produce stability, allowing for the establishment in many countries of social welfare systems designed to benefit workers and their families, and thus to gain their political allegiance.

Continuing prosperity

At the same time, various factors operated to make the achievement of a generally stable Western world difficult, and ultimately impossible. First, the process of nation-building, which had resulted in the dramatic creation of a modern Germany and Italy, left potential conflict in its wake. Second, although the majority of citizens in most western European countries participated at least indirectly in the governance of their country and enjoyed certain guaranteed rights, heated debate continued as to the political usefulness of such arrangements. In France, monarchists threatened the republic; in Germany, democrats battled imperial and bureaucratic oligarchy; in Russia, liberals rose against tsarist autocracy. And across Europe, socialists contended against the political strength of the middle classes.

The roots of instability

Internal tension was resulting as well from shifts in class structure and class consciousness. One of the most dramatic occupational changes to occur in late-nineteenth-century Europe was the rapid growth of a lower- to middle-level, "white-collar" class of bureaucrats, employed in commerce and industry and in expanding government departments. The post office, the railways, the police, and the bureaus charged with the task of administering various social welfare and insurance programs, all demanded growing numbers of recruits. In Germany, for example, by 1914 there were over two million white-collar employees in private firms and two million lower- or middle-range civil servants. Members of this new class were particularly anxious to give sharp definition to the line separating them from skilled "labor aristocrats," who might earn as much money as they did, but whose blue collars were, in the eyes of the white-collar brigades, a badge of their inferior status. Those same "aristocrats," as we have seen, however, often found their skills made obsolete by technological change, with the result that they showed themselves more willing than in the past to make common cause with their unskilled fellow workers against the middle class.

One further important source of European instability during this period lay in the international rivalries that grew between nations as they reached out to build empires. Nations grouped into alliances, hoping that a balance between power blocs might continue to provide the international stability that Europe had enjoyed since 1815, and that had prevented general war. Instead, the alliances produced only further tensions, and ultimately general world conflict.

1. GERMANY: THE SEARCH FOR IMPERIAL UNITY

During the years immediately following the foundation of the German Empire, Bismarck was particularly anxious to achieve imperial unity under Prussian domination. In this he was aided by the economic and military predominance of the Prussian state, and by the organizational framework upon which the empire had been constructed. All powers not granted to the central government were reserved to the individual states. Each had control over its own form of government, public education, highways, police, and other local agencies. Even the enforcement of the laws was left primarily in the hands of the state governments, since the empire had no machinery for applying its laws against individuals. Despite their apparent autonomy, however, the states were in fact subordinate to the empire, and to the emperor himself, the Prussian William I. The German imperial units were once described as comprised of "a lion, a half-dozen foxes, and a score of mice." The Prussian "lion" exercised authority through the person of the emperor and his chancellor. The empire was not governed by a cabinet system, in which ministers of state were responsible to a popularly elected legislature. Instead, ministers were responsible to the chancellor, and the chancellor was responsible solely to the emperor.

William was no mere figurehead; the emperor was vested with extensive authority over the army and navy, over foreign relations, and over the general enactment and execution of imperial laws. He had the authority to declare war if the coasts or territory of the empire were attacked. And as king of Prussia, he controlled that country's delegation in the generally conservative upper house, or Bundesrat, of the imperial parliament, commanding enough votes to veto any bill submitted. The chairman of the Bundesrat, charged with the control and supervision of the federal administration, was also the Prussian prime minister, appointed by the king of Prussia.

William I of Germany

The parliament was no rubber stamp, however. Money for the imperial treasury had to be voted by the lower house, the Reichstag, which was elected by universal manhood suffrage, and whose membership was primarily middle class. Yet the Reichstag's powers were essentially negative. Although the parliament could veto proposals of the kaiser (emperor) and his ministers, it could not initiate legislation on its own. Hence, although Bismarck often found himself temporarily stymied by the activities of an unsympathetic legislature, he could expect, in the end, to have his way. That way was directed toward the goal of a unified Germany under Prussian domination: essentially conservative; antisocialist, though not necessarily opposed to social welfare schemes; protectionist, and thus sympathetic to the interests of German industrialists; and, in foreign affairs, anti-French, standing firm against any threat from that longtime antagonist.

Bismarck's first campaign on behalf of imperial unity was launched against the Roman Catholic Church. Called the *Kulturkampf,* or "struggle for civilization," the attack was initiated, with some help from intellectual liberals, in 1872. Bismarck's motives were almost exclusively nationalistic. He perceived in some Catholic activities a threat to the power and stability of the empire he had just created. He resented, first of all, the support Catholic priests continued to give to the states'-rights movement in southern Germany and to the grievances of Alsatians and Poles. He was alarmed also by recent assertions of the authority of the pope to intervene in secular matters and by the promulgation in 1870 of the dogma of papal infallibility. For these reasons he resolved to deal such a blow to Catholic influence in Germany that it would never again be a major factor in national or local politics. His weapons were a series of laws and decrees issued between 1872 and 1875, designed to curb the independent power of the Church. Bismarck's campaign backfired, however. The Catholic Center party appealed to the electorate so effectively on behalf of the persecuted clergy, while adopting an economic policy attractive to the upper middle class, that it won fully one-quarter of the seats in the Reichstag in 1874. Recognizing that he needed Catholic support for other elements of his program, Bismarck took the occasion of the election of the more conciliatory Pope Leo XIII to make his peace with the Vatican and to negotiate an alliance of convenience with the Catholic

The Kulturkampf

Center party. By 1886 almost all of his anticlerical legislation either had been permitted to lapse or had been repealed.

Having forged a new political combination in 1878, Bismarck shifted the focus of his attacks to German socialism, now perceived by him as a far more immediate threat to the empire than Catholicism. The Social Democratic party, under the reformist leadership of the politician Wilhelm Liebknecht (1829–1900), successor to Ferdinand Lassalle, was building a substantial following. Bismarck, his memory of the Paris Commune (see above, pp. 879–80) still fresh, feared socialism as anarchy, and therefore as a direct challenge to the stability and unity he was attempting to achieve within the empire. Forgetting for the moment the manner in which he had courted the socialists when he needed their support in the 1860s, Bismarck now appeared determined to extinguish them. His attack was motivated not only by his personal perception of the socialist threat but also by his continuing need to secure the favor of industrialists whom he had won to his side by his policy of protective tariffs. In 1878, two separate attempts were made by unbalanced zealots on the life of the emperor. Although neither would-be assassin had anything but the most tenuous connection with the socialists, Bismarck used their actions as an excuse to secure legislation abolishing workers' rights to meet and to publish. The legislature also agreed to a law that gave the government the right to expel socialists from major cities, as was later done in Berlin, Breslau, and Leipzig. These laws in effect dissolved the Social Democratic party until after 1890, although individual socialist candidates continued to be elected to the Reichstag.

Bismarck was too clever a politician to suppose that he could abolish socialism solely by means of repression. He was prepared to steal at least a portion of the socialists' thunder by adopting parts of their legislative program as his own. In a speech in the Reichstag he frankly avowed his purpose of insuring the worker against sickness and old age so that "these gentlemen [the Social Democrats] will sound their bird call in vain." In addition, he had military purposes in mind. He hoped to make the German worker an effective potential soldier by safeguarding his health in some measure from the debilitating effects of factory labor. Bismarck's program of social legislation was initiated in 1883–1884 with the adoption of laws insuring workers against sickness and accidents. These acts were followed by others providing for rigid factory inspection, limiting the employment of women and children, fixing maximum hours of labor, establishing public employment agencies, and insuring workers against incapacity on account of old age. By 1890, Germany had adopted nearly all the elements, with the exception of unemployment insurance, in the matrix of social legislation that later became familiar in the majority of Western nations.

In that same year the Iron Chancellor was dismissed by the young emperor, William II (1888–1918), following the less-than-year-long

Bismarck and the socialists

Social welfare legislation

reign of his father Frederick III. Bismarck's loss of power was to a degree the result of a personality clash between the two men. William's father had remarked that his son had "a tendency to overestimate himself"; his tutor noted that he "imagined he knew everything— without having learned anything." William's arrogance was encouraged by the cult of imperial family worship which had by this time become part of the patriotic creed that was imposed by the state upon its citizens. Yet the quarrel between the young kaiser and his chancellor was a matter of substance as well as personality, involving policies directed at curbing the activities and popularity of the socialists. Bismarck's dismissal came in part over William's insistence that the antisocialist legislation of the past decade had achieved very little, and his mistaken belief that socialists would respond positively to his determination to rule in his own right and to create a more unified, stable, and powerful reich. Within a few years, however, William was arguing a line that appealed to the landowners, military leaders, and industrialists, whom he continued to court throughout his reign. He wooed the landowners by embarking on a policy of agricultural protection. And he wooed the military and the industrialists with a vast program of naval rearmament. Meanwhile, despite his decision to end the ban against the Social Democrats, he did all he could to undermine their growing political strength.

State schools were instructed to teach the dangers of socialism by

Left: *William II of Germany and Bismarck.* Right: *Dropping the Pilot.* This cartoon appeared in the British magazine *Punch* on March 29, 1890, after the inexperienced but ambitious young emperor dismissed Bismarck as chancellor and personally assumed the helm of the ship of state. Note that Bismarck appears stripped of the insignia of office.

stressing the virtues of patriotism and piety. Admission to the civil service was almost impossible unless one was an officer in the military reserve; and admission to that very influential body was not open to socialists—or to Jews. Stealing a leaf from Bismarck's text, William authorized the extension of earlier programs of social insurance, hoping to dampen enthusiasm for the Social Democrats by granting some of the reforms for which they continued to campaign. But William steadfastly refused to extend any sort of meaningful political participation beyond the powerful industrial, military, and agricultural classes. The country was administered efficiently, but not democratically. With the exception of Count Leo von Caprivi, a military officer, all his chancellors were civil servants, a fact that underscored his determination to keep the administration of the country as far removed as possible from democratic control.

Combating the socialists

Growing opposition to these policies brought the Social Democrats increasingly impressive electoral victories. In 1912 they polled a third of the votes cast, and elected 110 members—the largest single bloc—to the Reichstag. Yet they were thwarted, not only by William's determination to ignore his parliament, but by their inability to resolve the conflict within their own ranks between purist and revisionist theory (see above, pp. 881–82). The party continued to profess itself devoted to the principles of socialist purity. Yet its increasingly large following tended to push it in the direction of piecemeal reformist legislation. And even with their large bloc of Reichstag votes, the Social Democrats could not command a majority there unless they formed a coalition with center parties far less reformist—let alone revolutionary—than they were. By 1914, German politics were approaching stalemate. The country was spared a domestic constitutional crisis only by the infinitely more profound international crisis of the First World War.

Social Democrats and the political stalemate

2. FRANCE: THE EMBATTLED THIRD REPUBLIC

Although in 1870 France, was not a newly constructed nation like the German Empire, it was a nation sorely in need of reunification and dedication to a common set of political purposes. Its history for the past century had left it torn between various factions. The conflicts it suffered after 1870 tended to be more ideological than social, a reflection not only of France's tumultuous political past, but of its comparatively slow rate of industrialization. Monarchists were divided between supporters of the Bourbon and Orleanist dynasties, their allegiance sustained by loyalties either to the descendants of Louis XVIII or of Louis Philippe. Bonapartists looked for political salvation to Napoleon III's son and heir Louis Napoleon. Republicans recalled the short-lived triumphs of their revolutionary ancestors. Socialists called down plagues on all political houses but their own. The result of this

Politically divided France

deep division was that not until 1875 did France have a constitution under which it could function.

Following the collapse of Napoleon III's empire a provisional government was organized to rule the country until a new constitution could be drafted. Elections held in 1871 for a national constituent assembly resulted in the choice of some 500 monarchists and only about 200 republicans. Conservative political sentiment was further reinforced by the events of the Paris Commune, which occurred during the period immediately following the elections. But the apparent winners, the monarchists, could not agree among themselves as to whether their king should be a Bourbon or an Orleanist. This stalemate led to the eventual passage in 1875—by one vote—of a series of constitutive laws which made France a republic. These laws established a parliament with a lower house elected by universal manhood suffrage (the Chamber of Deputies) and an upper house elected indirectly (the Senate); a cabinet of ministers presided over by a premier; and a president. Although at first the relative powers of president and premier were not clearly established, within two years the nation had declared itself in favor of a premier at the head of a government answerable to the Chamber of Deputies. An early president, Marshal Marie-Edmé MacMahon, attempted in 1877 to dismiss a premier with whom he disagreed but who was supported by a majority in the chamber. When new elections were held, MacMahon's policy was repudiated. Henceforth, premiers of the Third Republic were answerable to the chamber and not to the president, who became a figurehead. Yet the resolution of this constitutional question failed to produce political stability, since the premier had no authority to dissolve the legislature. This meant that members of the chamber could vote a premier and his fellow ministers out of office at will, with no risk of being forced to stand for reelection. If defeated on a vote, the premier and his colleagues had no alternative but to resign. The result was no fewer than fifty ministries in the years between 1870 and 1914. The Third Republic, for all its constitutional shortcomings, nevertheless managed to last until 1940—far longer than any system of French government since 1789. Its longevity was due, as much as anything, to the stability of other French institutions—the family, the law courts, and the police, for example. And its stability was attested to by the willingness of French men and women to invest their savings in state loans, rather than in industrial enterprises that appeared far less secure to them.

In the years after 1875, the republicans, who had been feared at first as dangerous radicals, proved themselves to be generally moderate. It was the discontented monarchists and authoritarian sympathizers within the army, the Roman Catholic Church, and among the families of the aristocracy who took to plotting the overthrow of duly constituted governmental authority. Much of the time of successive republican governments was taken up defending the country from these reac-

Left: *The Avenue de l'Opéra, c. 1880.* During the era of the Third Republic official Paris declared itself in favor of architecture that bespoke middle-class opulence and respectability as manifested here by the broad street lined with elegant shops and dominated by the unimpeded view of the facade of the Paris Opéra. Right: *The Rue Mouffeta, 1910.* Conditions in this working-class street remained meanwhile much as they had been throughout most of the preceding century.

tionary radicals. In the late 1880s, a general, Georges Boulanger, gathered about him a following not only of Bonapartists, monarchists, and aristocrats, but of workingmen who were disgruntled with their lot and who believed, with Boulanger, that a war of revenge against Germany would put an end to all their troubles. Thanks to the general's own indecisiveness, the threatened coup d'état came to nothing. But the attempt was a symptom of deep discontents; Boulanger appealed, like Napoleon III, to disparate groups of disenchanted citizens, promising quick, dramatic solutions to tedious problems.

One further symptom of the divisions that plagued the republic during the later years of the nineteenth century was the campaign of anti-Semitism that the reactionaries adopted to advance their aims. The fact that certain Jewish bankers were involved in scandalous dealings with politicians lent color to the monarchist insistence that the government was shot through with corruption and that Jews were largely to blame. An anti-Semitic journalist, Edmond Drumont, insisted that "Jews in the army" were subverting the national interest. In 1889 he and others founded the Anti-Semitic League. This ugly and heated campaign furnished the background of the famous Dreyfus affair. In 1894 a Jewish captain of artillery, Alfred Dreyfus, was accused by a clique of monarchist officers of selling military secrets to Germany. Tried by court-martial, he was convicted and sentenced for

The Dreyfus affair

life to Devil's Island, a ghastly prison camp in the Caribbean. At first the verdict was accepted as the merited punishment of a traitor; but in 1897 Major Picquart, a new head of the Intelligence Division, announced his conclusion that the documents upon which Dreyfus had been convicted were forgeries. A movement was launched for a new trial, which the War Department promptly refused. Soon the whole nation was divided into friends and opponents of Dreyfus. On his side were the radical republicans, socialists, people of liberal and humanitarian sympathies, and such prominent literary figures as Émile Zola and Anatole France. The anti-Dreyfusards included monarchists, clerics, anti-Semites, militarists, and a considerable number of conservative workingmen. A Roman Catholic newspaper insisted that the question was not whether Dreyfus was guilty or innocent, but whether Jews and unbelievers were not the secret masters of France. Dreyfus was finally set free by executive order in 1899, and six years later was cleared of all guilt by the Supreme Court and restored to the army. He was immediately promoted to the rank of major and decorated with the emblem of the Legion of Honor.

The history of the Dreyfus affair gave the republicans the solid ground they had lacked in order to end the plottings of the radical reactionaries once and for all. The leaders of the republic chose to attack their enemies by effectively destroying the political power of the Roman Catholic Church in France. The anticlericalism expressed in this campaign was probably in part the product of a materialistic age, and of a longstanding mistrust by French republicans of the institution of the Church. Its main source, however, was the nationalism which we have already seen fueling Bismarck's *Kulturkampf*.

Anticlericalism

The great majority of the leaders of the Third Republic were hostile to the Church; and naturally so, for the Catholic hierarchy was aiding the monarchists at every turn. Clerics had conspired with monarch-

*Alfred Dreyfus Leaving His
Court Martial*

Legislation to curb the Church

Pressure from the Left

Socialist debate

ists, militarists, and anti-Semites in attempting to discredit the republic during the Dreyfus affair. But in the end they had overreached themselves. In 1901 the government passed a series of acts prohibiting the existence of religious orders not authorized by the state, forbidding members of religious orders to teach in either public or private schools, and finally, in 1905, dissolving the union of church and state, thereby prohibiting payment of the clergy from public funds. For the first time since 1801 the adherents of all creeds were placed on an equal basis.

The republic was, during these years, pressed from the Left as well as the Right. Socialism was a political force in France, as it was in Germany. Yet the response of republicans in France to socialist pressure differed markedly from that of Bismarck. There was no antisocialist legislation. Indeed, a law was passed in 1881 abolishing "crimes of opinion," thereby extending the freedom of the press considerably. In the same year, another law authorized public meetings without prior official approval. But if there was no attempt at repression, there was little positive social reform. The largest single party in the republic, the Radicals or Radical Socialists, was really a party representing small shopkeepers and lesser propertied interests. The Radicals were willing to found and maintain a democratic compulsory educational system, but they were reluctant to respond to demands for social legislation such as had been instituted in Germany. Those laws which were passed—establishing a ten-hour workday in 1904 and old-age pensions in 1910—were passed grudgingly and only after socialist pressure. The result was a growing belief among socialists and other workers that parliamentary democracy was worthless, that progress, if it was to be made, would be made only as a result of direct industrial action: the strike.

This attitude was reinforced by the same debate—revisionism vs. purism—that we have seen dividing the Social Democrats in Germany. Purists had called it "opportunism" when the socialist Alexandre Millerand had joined the nonsocialist cabinet of Prime Minister René Waldeck-Rousseau in 1899. Millerand had insisted that his cooperation would help heal the wounds inflicted on French politics by the Dreyfus affair. His opponents charged that such collaboration was a sellout. Their successors pointed to the lack of anything more than occasional and very mild social legislation in succeeding parliaments to prove their point. In response to this growing sentiment came a wave of strikes, which swept the country for several years before 1914, including one by postal workers in 1909 and by teachers and railwaymen in 1910. The government suppressed these actions by ruthless intervention. Tension increased after 1910 during debates over the extension of military conscription from two to three years, opposed by the socialists, and over the institution of an income tax, favored by the socialists as a way of financing social programs threatened as a result of increased military spending. By 1914, the republic, though hardly

Conflicts and Contrasts in Working-Class Life. Left: In this cartoon illustrating the tension that existed throughout Europe as a result of tighter work controls a working-class French woman complains to her father that "all day long, it's against the rules to sit down." He responds: "Do as we do! Ditch them." Right: At the same time, as this scene of workers on day-holiday at Yarmouth Sands in England suggests, workers enjoyed greater opportunities for a least some leisure-time than ever before. These contrasts helped to produce the class conflicts that characterized European politics before the First World War.

on the brink of revolution, remained divided and uncertain. If the threat from the radical Right had been quelled, the challenge from the Left was only just being faced.

3. GREAT BRITAIN: FROM MODERATION TO MILITANCE

Benjamin Disraeli

During the half-century before 1914, the British prided themselves on what they believed to be a reasonable, orderly, and workable system of government. Following the passage of the Second Reform Bill in 1867, which extended suffrage to over a third of the nation's adult males, the two major political parties, Liberal and Conservative, vied with each other in adopting legislation designed to provide an increasingly larger proportion of the population the chance to lead fuller and healthier lives. Laws that recognized the legality of trade unions, allowed male religious dissenters to participate fully in the life of the ancient universities of Oxford and Cambridge, provided elementary education for the first time to all children, and facilitated the clearance and rebuilding of large urban areas, were among those placed on the

William E. Gladstone Campaigning, 1885. Perhaps the first politician to make effective use of the railway in his campaigns, Gladstone took advantage of the mobility it provided to reach out to the electorate.

books during the administrations of the two leading politicians of the period, the Conservative Benjamin Disraeli (1804–1881) and the Liberal William Gladstone (1809–1898). In 1884, suffrage was once more widened, to include over three-fourths of the adult males, and to allow rural workingmen the chance to vote for the first time. Coupled with a previous act which instituted the secret ballot, this electoral reform bill brought Britain nearer to representative democracy.

Gladstone and Disraeli

Gladstone and Disraeli were remarkably different men. The former was a devout member of the Church of England, so dedicated to the cause of personal moral reform that he was willing to risk his political career by accosting prostitutes in the hope of persuading them to change their way of life. He devised his political programs—his long and ultimately unsuccessful campaign for Irish Home Rule, for example—on the basis of his moral convictions. Disraeli, on the other hand, was a pragmatist, willing to acknowledge the degree to which politics is an opportunistic game. When he became prime minister he celebrated the fact by declaring delightedly that he had at last climbed to "the top of the greasy pole." He thought Gladstone's morality a pose, and declared that he wouldn't mind the fact that his opponent had an extra ace up his sleeve, if only he didn't insist that God had put it there. Disraeli was probably correct, however, when he observed that Britain, "subject as it is to fogs and a middle class," preferred its statesmen to be properly grave. He was the exception, a converted Jew and former novelist, whose remarkably compelling political style had enabled him to overcome his unorthodox background.

Despite the personal differences between Gladstone and Disraeli, the political parties over which they presided were managed by a small ruling class of similar men drawn either from landed society or from the upper reaches of the middle class. As members of successive governmental cabinets they recognized their responsibility to Parliament and, in particular, to its lower House of Commons. It was their task, as cabinet ministers, to impose a legislative program upon the Commons. And if the House refused to agree to that program, they recognized, as well, their obligation either to resign forthwith—to make way for a cabinet of opposing party members—or to "go to the country," that is, to dissolve Parliament and order a new election to test the opinion of the voters. This system of "ministerial responsibility" meant that the cabinet retained full responsibility for the management of public affairs, subject, however, to the will of the people as represented by the House of Commons. It produced a generally stable government: although ministries had to answer to Parliament, Parliament would think twice before voting a ministry out of office when it knew that the ministry might well appeal to the voters for support in a general election. (The lack of this particular feature was what had condemned the French Third Republic to its succession of short-lived governments.) Political stability was ensured by more than the device of ministerial responsibility, however. Since both the Conservative and Liberal political leadership was drawn in large part from similar social and economic strata, there was little chance for violent change during these years. One party might espouse a particular cause—the Conservatives imperialism, the Liberals more self-government for Ireland, for example. But both parties generally agreed upon a course steered by men whose similar background and temperament promised programs that were neither radical nor reactionary. This moderation suited the electorate, which was content to defer to politicians whose leadership was secured by the undoubted fact of Britain's general prosperity.

*"Ministerial
responsibility"*

Not everyone was content, however. Prosperity, though widespread enough, did not extend to the unskilled: dock workers, transport workers, and the like. These groups formed trade unions to press their claims. Their determination encouraged other unions to assume a more militant and demanding stance. In the 1890s this activity produced a reaction in the form of anti-trade union employers' associations and a series of legal decisions limiting the right of unions to strike. Workers, in turn, reacted by associating with middle-class socialist societies to form an independent Labour party, which was born in 1901 and five years later managed to send twenty-nine members to the House of Commons. Sensitive to this pressure from the Left, the Liberals, during their ministry, which began in 1906, passed a series of reforms they hoped would ensure a minimum standard of living for those who had heretofore known little security. Sickness, accident, old-age, and unemployment insurance schemes were adopted. A minimum wage was decreed in certain industries. Labor exchanges, designed to help unemployed men and women find new

*Liberal reforms, 1906–
1914*

Lloyd George and Winston Churchill on Their Way to the House of Commons on Budget Day, 1910

jobs, were established. Restrictions on strikes and on the right of trade unions to raise money for political purposes were relaxed.

Much of this legislation was the work of David Lloyd George (1863–1945), a radical middle-class lawyer from Wales, much feared by many within the political establishment. Lloyd George was chancellor of the exchequer (finance minister) in the Liberal cabinet of Prime Minister Herbert Asquith, and together with another young Liberal, Winston Churchill (1874–1965), he hammered together legislation that was both a reflection of his own political philosophy and a practical response to the growing political power of the working class. To pay for these programs—and for a larger navy to counter the German buildup—Lloyd George proposed a budget in 1909 that included progressive income and inheritance taxes, designed to make wealthier taxpayers pay at higher rates. His proposals so enraged the aristocratic members of the House of Lords that they declared themselves prepared to throw out the budget, an action contrary to constitutional precedent. Asquith countered with a threat to create enough new peers (titled noblemen) sympathetic to the budget to ensure its passage.[1] The House of Lords eventually surrendered; the result of the crisis was an act of Parliament which provided that the House of Lords could not veto legislation passed by the House of Commons.

The rancor aroused by this constitutional conflict was intense. Self-

Lloyd George's budget

[1]In Britain the monarch had the authority to elevate an unlimited number of men to the peerage. But since the crown acts only on the advice of the prime minister, it is this official who had the actual power to create new members of the House of Lords. If necessary, he could use this power to pack the upper house with his own followers.

proclaimed defenders of the House of Lords screamed threats in a chamber unused to anything but gentlemanly debate. Angry threats were by no means confined to the Houses of Parliament during these years, however. Throughout Britain, men and women threw moderation to the winds as they disputed issues in an atmosphere little short of anarchic. The reasons for this continued agitation were various. A decline in real wages after 1900 kept the working class in a militant mood despite Liberal reforms and produced an unusually severe series of strikes in 1911 and 1912. A liberal plan to grant Home Rule (self-government) to Ireland produced not only panic in the Protestant minority counties of the north (Ulster) but arming and drilling of private militias with an intensity that seemed to forecast civil war.

Perhaps the most alarming—because the most unexpected—of the militant revolts that seized Britain in the years before 1914 was the campaign for women's suffrage. The middle-class women who engaged in this struggle enjoyed more freedom of opportunity than their mothers had known. Laws had been passed easing the process of divorce and permitting married women control of their own property. Some universities had started to grant degrees to women. Contraceptive devices—and feminist propaganda defending their use—had begun to result in changed attitudes toward sexuality within the middle class. Perhaps because of these gains, many women felt their lack of the vote all the more acutely. Although the movement began among middle-class women, it soon included some female members of the working class and the aristocracy. Agitation reached a peak after 1900, when militant suffragettes—under the leadership of Emmeline

Increased militance

Suffragettes

London Dock Strike, 1911. Police move to clear demonstrators from shops where they have taken refuge after having been fired upon.

Violent Suffragette Protest. Suffragette leader Emmeline Pankhurst is arrested during a violent demonstration at Buckingham Palace in 1911.

Pankhurst, her daughters Christabel and Sylvia, and others—resorted to violence in order to impress upon the nation the seriousness of their commitment. Women chained themselves to the visitors' gallery in the House of Commons; slashed paintings in museums; invaded that male sanctum, the golf course, and inscribed VOTES FOR WOMEN in acid on the greens; disrupted political meetings; burned politicians' houses; and smashed department store windows. The government countered violence with repression. When women, arrested for their disruptive activities, went on hunger strikes in prisons, wardens proceeded to feed them forcibly, tying them down, holding their mouths open with wooden and metal clamps, and running tubes down their throats. When hunger strikes threatened to produce deaths and thus martyrs for the cause, the government passed the constitutionally dubious Cat and Mouse Act, which sanctioned the freeing of prisoners to halt their starvation and then, once they had regained their health, authorized their rearrest. The movement was not to see the achievement of its goal until after the First World War, when reform came largely because of women's contributions to the war effort.

Whether Britain's militant mood might have led to some sort of general conflict if the war had not begun in 1914 is a question historians continue to debate. Suffice it to say that national sentiment in the last few years before the outbreak of general hostilities was far different from that of the 1870s. Britain, so confident of itself and of its moderation, was proving no less a prey to instability than other European nations.

4. RUSSIA: THE ROAD TO REVOLUTION

In only one European country, Russia, did conditions pass from instability to insurrection during these prewar years. The early-twentieth-century Russian revolutionary movement had numerous forerunners. Waves of discontent broke out several times during the nineteenth century. Threatened uprisings between 1850 and 1860, partly a consequence of Russia's defeat in the Crimean War, persuaded Tsar Alexander II, who came to the throne in 1855, to liberate the serfs, to modernize the military establishment, to reform the judicial system, and to grant local self-government.

Reform and reaction in nineteenth-century Russia

The law of 1861 granted legal rights to some 22 million serfs, and authorized their title to at least a portion of the land they had worked. Yet the pattern of rural life in Russia did not change drastically. Large-scale landowners managed to retain the most profitable acreage for themselves. Newly liberated serfs faced the need to pay the state for the land they held (the state, in turn, recompensing the former owners). This expense, plus the fact that peasants were often left with less than enough land to sustain themselves and their families, and without adequate pasturage, water, and forest rights, meant that

Liberation of the serfs

they were compelled to return to work as agricultural laborers for their previous masters.

The military reform of 1874 was designed to broaden the ranks to include all males, not just the peasantry. Military service was now to be determined by lot. The period of active duty was reduced from twenty-five to six years. Schooling was provided for draftees and corporal punishment was abolished.

Russia's judicial system, heretofore secret, corrupt, and tied to a rigid class system that ensured legal inequality, was reformed so as to make the courts for the first time independent of the central administration. All Russians were declared equal before the law; trial by jury was introduced for most criminal cases. Whereas formerly evidence could be presented only in written form, oral testimony was now permitted, thereby making trials far more public in character. A tiered system of courts, rising from local justices of the peace, provided the right to appeal.

The structure of local government instituted in 1861 placed responsibility in the hands of the *mir,* or village commune. Its officials regulated the assignment of land and collected taxes. They were also able to restrict the movement of residents in and out of their community, a regulation designed to ensure that peasants could not escape their obligation to pay for the land they now occupied as free men. At a higher level, district councils were authorized to administer their own courts and tax collection. In 1864, indirectly elected provincial councils—*zemstvos*—were empowered to manage local welfare and educational programs.

Though only moderately reformist, these *zemstvos* provided forums for the debate of political issues and, along with the extension of educational opportunities, encouraged middle-class Russians to suppose themselves on the way to some sort of liberalized state. The government, however, grown fearful of the path it was treading, called a halt to reform and substituted repression in its place. By 1875, censorship had been extended not only to the *zemstvos*, which were forbidden to discuss general political issues, but to the press and to schools as well. The result of suppression was, not surprisingly, further discontent and active subversion. Middle-class Russians argued privately the virtues of utopian socialism, liberal parliamentarianism, and Pan-Slavism. A growing number, calling themselves nihilists, espoused the doctrines of the anarchist Bakunin (see above, p. 878). Terrorists, believing that assassination of the tsar was the only solution to oppression, achieved their goal in 1881, when a bomb killed Alexander II.

The most important radical political element in late-nineteenth-century Russia was a large, loosely knit group of men and women who called themselves populists. They believed that although their country must Westernize, it could not expect to do so according to examples set elsewhere. They proclaimed a new Russia, yet one based upon the ancient institution of the village commune, which was to serve as a model for the socialist society they hoped to create. Populism sprang primarily from the middle class; a majority of its adherents were young, many of them students; and about 15 percent were women, a significantly large proportion for the period. They formed secret cadres, plotting the overthrow of tsarism by terror and insurrection. They dedicated their lives to "the people" (hence their name), attempting wherever possible to live among common laborers so as to understand and express the popular will. Populism's historical importance lies not so much in what it accomplished, which was little, but in what it promised for the future. A movement that marked the beginning of organized revolutionary agitation in Russia, it was the seedbed for thought and action that would in time produce general revolution. Populists read Marx's *Capital* before it was translated into Russian; they tested and revised his ideas and those of other major revolutionaries of the nineteenth century so as to produce a doctrine suited to Russia's particular destiny.

The activities of populists and anarchists, however, triggered a floodtide of reaction against the entire policy of reform. Alexander III (1881–1894), governed under the theory that Russia had nothing in common with western Europe, that its people had been nurtured on despotism and mystical piety for centuries and would be utterly lost without them. He believed that Western ideals such as rationalism and individualism would undermine the deferential faith of the Russian masses and would plunge the nation into anarchy and crime, and that in like manner, Western institutions could never bear fruit if planted in Russian soil. With these doctrines as his guiding principles, Alexander III enforced a regime of stern repression. He curtailed in

Autocracy and Russification

A Railroad Yard in Eastern Russia, 1896

every way possible the powers of the local assemblies, increased the authority of the secret police, and subjected villages to government by wealthy nobles selected by the state. These policies were continued, though in somewhat less rigorous form, by his son, Nicholas II (1894–1917), a much less effective ruler. Both tsars were ardent proponents of Russification, a more ruthless counterpart of similar nationalistic movements in various countries. Its purpose was to extend the language, religion, and culture of Great Russia, or Russia proper, over all of the subjects of the tsar and thereby to simplify the problem of governing them. It was aimed primarily at the Poles, Finns, and Jews, since these were the nationalities considered most dangerous to the stability of the state. Russification meant repression. The Finns were deprived of their constitution; the Poles were compelled to study their own literature in Russian translations; and high officials in the tsar's government connived at *pogroms,* i.e., wholesale massacres, against the Jews.

Westernization

Despite these attempts to turn Russia's back to the West, however, the nation was being drawn more closely than it had ever been before into the European orbit. Russia was industrializing, and making use of European capital to do so. Economic policies during the 1890s, when Count Sergei Witte was the tsar's leading minister, resulted in the adoption of the gold standard, which made Russian currency easily convertible. Railways and telegraph lines were constructed; exports and imports multiplied by factors of seven and five respectively from 1880 to 1913. In addition, Russian writers and musicians contributed in a major way to the enriching of Western culture. We have already noted the singular contributions of Tolstoy, Turgenev, and Dostoevsky. The musical works of Peter Tchaikovsky (1840–1893) and Nikolai Rimsky-Korsakov (1844–1908), while expressing a peculiarly Russian temperament and tradition, were recognized as important additions to the general body of first-rate contemporary composition.

A new working class

With Westernization came the growth of a new wage-earning class. Most of Russia's workers were recruited from the countryside. We have seen that regulations made migration outside the *mir* difficult if not impossible. To live permanently in cities meant surrendering all claim to one's land. The result was that peasant factory workers lived away from their villages only temporarily, returning to attend to farming's seasonal demands. Consequently, these workers could not easily master a trade, and were forced to take unskilled jobs at extremely low wages. They lived in large barracks; they were marched to and from factories, where conditions were as unsafe and unhealthy as they had been in British factories in the early years of industrialization. An average working day in a textile mill was from twelve to fourteen hours. This sudden and extremely harsh transition from country to city living instilled deep discontent and a militant class consciousness in Russian workers.

Worker's Quarters in St. Petersburg, c. 1900. These buildings, in which workers from the country were housed temporarily while they labored in factories, were breeding grounds for class consciousness.

Growth of political parties

The increase in class consciousness brought with it the emergence of new political parties. Middle-class businessmen and professionals combined with enterprising landowners in 1903 to form a Constitutional Democratic party, whose program included the creation of a nationally elected parliament or Duma to determine and carry out policies that would further the twin goals of liberalization and Westernization. Meanwhile, two essentially working-class parties, the Social Revolutionaries and the Social Democrats, began to agitate for far more radical solutions to the problems of Russian autocracy. The Social Revolutionaries concerned themselves with the onerous plight of the peasants, burdened with land purchase and high taxes. The Social Revolutionaries wanted to equalize the landholdings of peasants within their *mirs,* and to increase the power of the *mirs* in their continuing competition with large landowners. The Social Democrats were Marxists, who saw themselves as westerners and as part of the international working-class movement. In 1903 the leadership of the Social Democratic party split in an important disagreement over revolutionary strategy. One group, which achieved a temporary majority (and thus called itself the Bolsheviks—"Majority Group") favored a strongly centralized party of active revolutionaries, and opposed the notion of a postrevolutionary transitional bourgeois state, insisting instead that revolution be succeeded immediately by a socialist regime. The Mensheviks ("Minority Group"), whose position resembled that of other

European revisionist socialists, soon managed to regain control of the party. The Bolshevik splinter party remained in existence, however, under the leadership of the young, dedicated revolutionary Vladimir Ulanov (1870–1924), who wrote under the pseudonym of N. Lenin.

Lenin was a member of the middle class, his father having served as an inspector of schools and minor political functionary. He had been expelled from the University of Kazan for engaging in radical activity, following the execution of his elder brother for his involvement in a plot to assassinate Alexander III. Lenin spent three years as a political prisoner in Siberia; from 1900 until 1917 he lived as an exile in western Europe. His zeal and abilities as both a theoretician and a political activist are evidenced by the fact that he retained leadership of the Social Democrats even while residing abroad. Lenin continued to preach the gospel of Marxism and of a relentless class struggle. His treatise *What Is to Be Done?* was a stinging response to revisionists who were urging collaboration with less radical parties. Revolution was what was to be done, Lenin argued, revolution "made" as soon as possible by an elitist group of agitators working through the agency of a disciplined party. Lenin and his followers, by merging the tradition of Russian revolutionism with Western Marxism, and by endowing the result with a sense of immediate possibility, fused the Russian situation in such a way as to make eventual explosion almost inevitable.

The Young Lenin, 1897

The revolution that came in 1905, however, took even the Bolsheviks by surprise. Its unexpected occurrence was the result of a war between Russia and Japan, which broke out in 1904, and in which the Russians were soundly beaten. Both countries had conflicting interests in Manchuria and Korea; this fact was the immediate cause of the conflict. On land and sea the Japanese proved themselves the military superiors of the Russians. As dispatches continued to report the defeats of the tsar's army and navy, the Russian people were presented with dramatic evidence of the inefficiency of autocracy.

The Russo-Japanese War

Just as defeat in the Crimean War had spurred the movement for reform, so now members of the middle class who had hitherto refrained from association with the revolutionists joined in the clamor for change. Radical workers organized strikes and held demonstrations in every important city. Led by a priest, Father Gapon, a group of 200,000 workers and their families went to demonstrate their grievances at the tsar's winter palace in St. Petersburg on January 22, 1905—known ever after as Bloody Sunday. The demonstrators were met by guard troops and many of them were shot dead. By the autumn of 1905 nearly the entire urban population had enlisted in a strike of protest. Merchants closed their stores, factory-owners shut down their plants, lawyers refused to plead cases in court, even valets and cooks deserted their wealthy employers. It was soon evident to Tsar Nicholas that the government would have to yield. On October 30, he issued a manifesto, pledging guarantees of individual liberties, promising a

The Revolution of 1905

Bloody Sunday. Demonstrating workers who sought to bring their grievances to the attention of the tsar were met and gunned down by government troops, January 1905.

moderately liberal franchise for the election of a Duma, and affirming that henceforth no law would be valid unless it had the Duma's approval. This was the high-water mark of the revolutionary movement. During the next two years Nicholas issued a series of sweeping decrees which negated most of the promises made in the October Manifesto. He deprived the Duma of many of its powers, and decreed that it be elected indirectly on a class basis by a number of electoral colleges. Thereafter the legislative body contained a majority of obedient followers of the tsar.

The reasons for setback

There were several reasons for the setback to this movement for major political reform. In the first place, the army remained loyal to its commander-in-chief. Consequently, after the termination of the war with Japan in 1905, the tsar had a large body of troops that could be counted upon if necessary to decimate the ranks of the revolutionists. An even more important reason was the split in the ranks of the revolutionists themselves. After the issuance of the October Manifesto, large numbers of the bourgeoisie became frightened at threats of the radicals and declared their conviction that the revolution had gone far enough. Withdrawing their support altogether, they became known henceforth as Octobrists. The more radical merchants and professional men, organized into the Constitutional Democratic party, maintained that opposition should continue until the tsar had been forced to establish a government modeled after that of Great Britain. This fatal division rendered the middle class politically impotent. Finally, disaffection appeared within the ranks of the workers. Further attempts to employ the general strike as a weapon against the government ended in disaster.

But the Russian revolutionary movement of 1905 was not a total failure. The vengeance taken by the tsar convinced many people that their government was not a benevolent autocracy, as they had been led to believe, but a stubborn and brutal tyranny. The uprising revealed the ability of working-class leaders to control the destiny of Russia. The general strike had proved a valuable revolutionary tool, as had workers' councils, elected from the factory floor and briefly operating as the only effective government in some areas. In addition, the revolt of 1905 persuaded some of the more sagacious advisors of the tsar that last-ditch conservatism was none too safe. The result was the enactment of a number of conciliatory reforms. Among the most significant were the agrarian programs sponsored by the government's leading minister, Peter Stolypin, between 1906 and 1911. These included transfer of five million acres of royal land to the peasants for a price; the granting of permission to peasants to withdraw from the *mir* and set up as independent farmers; and cancellation of the remaining installments owed by the peasants for their land. Decrees were issued permitting the formation of labor unions, providing for a reduction of the working day (to not more than ten hours in most cases), and establishing sickness and accident insurance. Yet the hopes of some liberals that Russia was on the way to becoming a progressive nation on the Western model proved illusory. The tsar remained stubbornly autocratic. Few peasants had enough money to buy the lands offered for purchase. In view of the rising cost of living, the factory workers considered their modest gains insufficient. A new revolutionary outbreak merely awaited a convenient spark.

*Gains from the
revolutionary movement*

5. THE SEARCH FOR STABILITY ELSEWHERE IN THE WEST

Other European countries generally found it just as difficult to attain internal stability in the early twentieth century as did those whose history we have surveyed. Italy was burdened with the problems of a rapidly increasing population, the need to industrialize quickly, and a stark disparity between a relatively prosperous industrial north and an impoverished agricultural south. As the population increased, so did the stream of rural migration into cities, where there were few jobs available. In its drive to create jobs and to industrialize, the government intervened directly in the economy by placing large orders for military equipment and by undertaking an ambitious program of railway construction. By the First World War the share of industrial production in the national economy had risen to 25 percent.

Problems in Italy

These strides were largely the result of policies instituted by Gio-

Trasformismo

Socialist split

Nationalism in Austria-Hungary

Nationalist tensions in Austria

vanni Giolitti (1842–1928), who was prime minister for almost the entire period between 1900 and 1914. Yet his efforts to spur industrialization widened the division between north and south. Relying on opportunistic maneuvering which he called *trasformismo,* and which argued the pointlessness of party politics, Giolitti rewarded the support of southern politicians for his program of industrial expansion by allowing the south to remain under the domination of the great landowners, the Church, and—in Sicily—the Mafia, none of which were interested in furthering the economic well-being or political consciousness of the average citizen. Thus whereas illiteracy was reduced in northern Italy to about 11 percent, in the south it remained at 90 percent. By failing to address the desperate economic conditions in the south, *trasformismo* denied the country an opportunity to develop a much needed internal market for its goods.

Hoping to gain support for his program from the socialists, Giolitti engineered passage of laws legalizing trade unions, improving factory conditions, and extending the suffrage to virtually all males over thirty. But attempts to satisfy the Left did not sit well with more conservative elements in Italian society, who remembered bread riots in Milan in 1896, the assassination of King Humbert by radicals in 1900, and widespread strikes in 1902 and 1904. Meanwhile, socialists in Italy were as divided on the matter of strategy as they were elsewhere in Europe. Reformists competed with radicals, organized into chambers of labor—local trade union councils with a revolutionary outlook—which assisted in the takeover of the Socialist party by a militant left wing in 1912.

Nationalist aspirations continued to be a major problem in eastern Europe. In 1867 an attempt had been made to resolve national differences in Austria by dividing the empire in two—an Austrian empire west of the river Leith, and a kingdom of Hungary to its east. Each of the two components in this so-called Dual Monarchy was to be the equal of the other, though the two were joined by the same Habsburg monarch, by several common ministries, and by a kind of superparliament. This solution failed to put an end to nationalist divisions, however.

The Austrian portion of the monarchy was comprised not only of a German-speaking majority, but of Czechs, Slovaks, Slovenes, and Ruthenians as well. Without concessions to these nationalities the government could expect little peace. Yet to give in to their aspirations was to antagonize the German majority, a group constantly wary of any move that appeared to threaten its predominance. During the 1890s, an attempt to pacify the Czechs by requiring all officials in areas of mixed German and Czech populations to speak both languages infuriated the Germans, who staged violent demonstrations proclaiming the superiority of their culture and forced the government to back down. Anxious to promote industrial development, the bureaucracy recognized that to introduce the requisite economic and financial

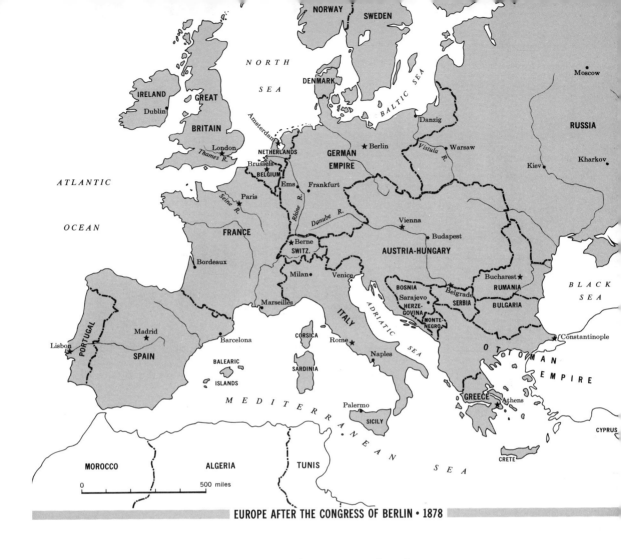

EUROPE AFTER THE CONGRESS OF BERLIN · 1878

measures, a Reichstag more sympathetic to modernization and to the needs of diverse imperial constituencies would be necessary. To that end, the Austrians introduced universal male suffrage in 1907, in the belief that newly enfranchised peasants recognized a primary allegiance to the emperor, rather than to any one particular nationality. Because the new electoral laws continued to specify quotas for each ethnic minority in the parliament, however, they strengthened the hand of the various national groups in the legislature, encouraging them to demand still further autonomy.

The major issue in the Hungarian half of the monarchy was a proposal to separate out the Hungarian regiments in the imperial army, allowing them their own insignia and requiring that they be commanded in their native language. The emperor, Francis Joseph, rejected these demands countering with a threat to introduce imperial male suffrage, a move the Magyars correctly saw as a challenge to their supremacy,

Nationalist tensions in Hungary

Vienna, 1873. Despite the fact that Vienna was the capital of an empire that straddled eastern and western Europe, it was by this date clearly a stylish and westernized metropolis.

as it had been to the Germans in Austria. The result was a standoff, part of the continuing desperate attempt on the part of the central government to play one side off against the other in order to maintain a shaky *status quo*.

The Ottoman Empire

In southeastern Europe nationalist agitation continued to rend the ever-disintegrating Ottoman Empire. Before 1829 the entire Balkan peninsula—bounded by the Aegean, Black, and Adriatic Seas—was controlled by the Turks. But during the next eighty-five years a gradual dismemberment of the Turkish Empire occurred. In some instances the slicing away of territories had been perpetrated by rival European powers, especially by Russia and Austria; but generally it was the result of nationalist revolts by the sultan's Christian subjects. In 1829, at the conclusion of a war between Russia and Turkey, the Ottoman Empire was compelled to acknowledge the independence of Greece and to grant autonomy to Serbia and to the provinces that later became Rumania. As the years passed, resentment against Ottoman rule spread through other Balkan territories. In 1875–1876 there were uprisings in Bosnia, Herzegovina, and Bulgaria, which the sultan suppressed with effective ferocity. Reports of atrocities against Christians gave Russia an excuse for renewal of its age-long struggle for domination of the Balkans. In this second Russo-Turkish War (1877–1878) the armies of the tsar won a smashing victory. The Treaty of San Stefano, which terminated the conflict, provided that the sultan surrender nearly all of his territory in Europe, except for a

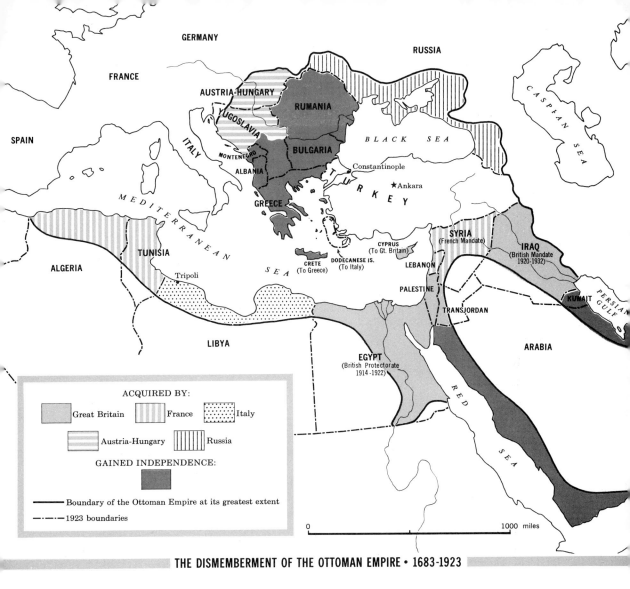

GERMANY

FRANCE

RUSSIA

AUSTRIA-HUNGARY

RUMANIA

YUGOSLAVIA

SPAIN

C A S P I A N   S E A

B L A C K   S E A

MONTENEGRO

BULGARIA

ALBANIA

Constantinople

★Ankara

T U R K E Y

GREECE

ITALY

M E D I T E R R A N E A N

TUNISIA

CYPRUS
(To Gt. Britain)

SYRIA
(French Mandate)

IRAQ
(British Mandate
1920-1932)

ALGERIA

Tripoli

CRETE
(To Greece)

DODECANESE IS.
(To Italy)

S E A

LEBANON

PALESTINE

PERSIAN GULF

KUWAIT

TRANSJORDAN

LIBYA

EGYPT
(British Protectorate
1914-1922)

ARABIA

R E D

S E A

ACQUIRED BY:

Great Britain   France   Italy

Austria-Hungary   Russia

GAINED INDEPENDENCE:

——— Boundary of the Ottoman Empire at its greatest extent

—·—·— 1923 boundaries

0   1000 miles

THE DISMEMBERMENT OF THE OTTOMAN EMPIRE · 1683-1923

remnant around Constantinople. But at this juncture the great powers
intervened. Austria and Great Britain, especially, were opposed to
granting Russia jurisdiction over so large a portion of the Near East.
In 1878 a congress of the great powers, meeting in Berlin, transferred
Bessarabia to Russia, Thessaly to Greece, and Bosnia and Herzegovina
to the control of Austria. Seven years later the Bulgars, who had been
granted some degree of autonomy by the Congress of Berlin, seized
the province of Eastern Rumelia from Turkey. In 1908 they established the independent Kingdom of Bulgaria.

In the very year when this last dismemberment occurred, Turkey
itself was engulfed by a tidal wave of nationalism. For some time the
more enlightened Turks had grown increasingly disgusted with the

weakness and incompetence of the sultan's government. Those who had been educated in European universities were convinced that their country should be rejuvenated by the introduction of Western ideas of science, patriotism, and democracy. Organizing themselves into a society known as the Young Turks, they forced the sultan in 1908 to establish constitutional government. The following year, in the face of a reactionary movement, they deposed the reigning sultan, Abdul Hamid II, and placed on the throne his brother, Mohammed V, as a titular sovereign. The real powers of government were now entrusted to a grand vizier and ministers responsible to an elected parliament. This revolution did not mean increased liberty for the non-Turkish inhabitants of the empire. Instead, the Young Turks launched a vigorous movement to Ottomanize all of the Christian subjects of the sultan. At the same time the disturbances preceding and accompanying the revolution opened the way for still further dismemberment. In 1908 Austria annexed the provinces of Bosnia and Herzegovina, which the Treaty of Berlin had allowed it merely to administer, and in 1911–1912 Italy entered into war with Turkey for the conquest of Tripoli.

The Young Turk revolution

Of all the major nations of the West, the United States probably underwent the least domestic turmoil during the several decades before 1914. The Civil War had exhausted the country; until the end of the century the ever-expanding frontier provided an alternative for those discontented with their present lot. Yet the United States also felt, to some degree, the pressures that made stability so hard to sustain in Europe. Though the Civil War had ended, the complex moral problem of racism remained to block all attempts to truly heal the nation. Severe economic crises, particularly an economic depression in the 1890s, accompanied by the collapse of agricultural prices and the closing of factories, caused great suffering and aroused anger at capitalist adventurers who seemed to be profiting at the expense of the country as a whole. Many grew convinced that a restricted money supply had produced the depression. Demand for the issuance of paper money and the increased coinage of silver were at the heart of the programs of the Greenback and the Populist parties, which attracted large followings, and which campaigned as well for an income tax and government ownership of railways, and telephone and telegraph lines. Socialism of a reformist brand was espoused by Eugene V. Debs (1855–1926), leader of a mildly Marxist Socialist party. It failed to appeal to the generally un–class-conscious American worker, who continued to have faith in the dream of economic mobility. More radical was the membership of the Industrial Workers of the World, a general union whose goal was to organize the unskilled and immigrant worker. Perceived as a device of foreign agitators, the IWW was repressed both by the government and by industrial management. Characteristic of the generally moderate tone of American reformism, the Progressive movement captured both the imagination and votes of a vocal minority of middle-class Americans whose hostility over

Unrest in the United States

Eugene Debs

the accumulation of private economic power and the political corruption of urban "bosses" was balanced by its belief in the democratic process and in the possibility of continuing progress. The movement, many of whose ideas were embodied in the programs of Presidents Theodore Roosevelt and Woodrow Wilson, was curtailed by the new realities that emerged with the advent of the First World War.

6. INTERNATIONAL RIVALRIES: THE ROAD TO THE FIRST WORLD WAR

Despite the domestic instabilities and uncertainties that characterized the Western world in the years before 1914, a great many men and women retained a faith in the notion of peaceful progress. There had been an absence of multinational armed conflict—with the exception of the Crimean War—for a century. European countries—even autocratic Russia—had been moving gradually toward what most agreed was the worthy goal of democracy. Indeed, instability could be understood as the result of either an overzealous or an overdelayed movement in that direction. Above all, industrialization seemed to be providing a better standard of living for all—or at least all within the Western world. There is little wonder, therefore, that men and women reacted with disbelief as they saw their world crumbling during the days of frantic diplomatic maneuvering just prior to the outbreak of war in August 1914.

The end of a century of peace

The key to an understanding of the coming of the First World War lies in an analysis of international diplomacy during the years after 1870. Europe had prided itself on the establishment of a balance of power, which had kept any one nation from assuming so predominating a position as to threaten the general peace. During his years as chancellor, Bismarck played a diplomatic variation upon this general theme, in order to ensure that France would not engage in a war of revenge against the German victors of 1870. There was little prospect that the French would attempt war singlehanded. Therefore, Bismarck determined to isolate France by attaching all of its potential allies to Germany. In 1873 he managed to form an alliance with both Austria and Russia, the so-called League of the Three Emperors, a precarious combination that soon foundered. Bismarck then cemented a new and much stronger alliance with Austria. In 1882 this partnership was expanded into a Triple Alliance with Italy. The Italians joined out of fear of the French. They resented the French occupation of Tunisia (1881), a territory which they regarded as properly theirs. Moreover, Italian politicians, still at odds with the Roman Catholic Church, feared that supporters of the papacy in France might gain the upper hand and send a French army to defend the pope. In the meantime, the Three Emperors' League had been revived. Though it lasted officially for only six years (1881–1887), Germany managed to hold the friendship of Russia until 1890, by means of a Reinsurance

The balance of power

Treaty (1887) providing for the neutrality of either power if the other went to war.

Thus after more than a decade of diplomatic maneuvering, Bismarck had achieved his ambition. By 1882 France was cut off from nearly every possibility of obtaining aid from powerful friends. Austria and Italy were united with Germany in the Triple Alliance, and Russia after a three-year lapse was back once more in the Bismarckian camp. The only conceivable quarter from which help might come to the French was Great Britain; but, with respect to continental affairs, the British were maintaining a policy of "splendid isolation." Therefore, so far as the danger of a war of revenge was concerned, Germany had little to fear. Bismarck's complicated structure of alliances appeared to answer the purpose for which he claimed it had been built—to keep the peace. But the alliance system was a weapon that could cut two ways. In Bismarck's hands, it kept the peace. In hands less diplomatically capable, it might become less an asset than a liability, as was the case after 1890.

Bismarck's diplomatic success

During the years between 1890 and 1907, European nations, competing across the globe for trade and territory, became more suspicious of each other. This general international insecurity produced a diplomatic revolution that obliterated Bismarck's handiwork, resulting in a new alignment that threatened the Germans. The Germans retained the support of Austria, but they lost the friendship of both Russia and Italy, while Britain abandoned its isolation to enter into agreements with Russia and France. This shift in the balance of power had fateful results. It helped convince the Germans that they were surrounded by a ring of enemies, and that consequently they must do everything in their power to retain the loyalty of Austria-Hungary.

A diplomatic revolution

The first of the major results of this diplomatic revolution was the formation of the Triple Entente between Russia, France, and Great Britain. William II of Germany, mistrustful of Russian ambitions in the Balkans, refused to renew the Reinsurance Treaty following Bismarck's dismissal in 1890. A growing coolness between the two countries led to Russia's political flirtation with France. Secret military conventions signed by the two countries in 1894 provided that each would come to the aid of the other in case of an attack by Germany, or by Austria or Italy supported by Germany. This Dual Alliance of Russia and France was followed by an Entente Cordiale between France and Great Britain. During the last two decades of the nineteenth century, the British and the French had been involved in frequent altercations over colonies and trade, as in the Sudan. By 1904, however, France, fearing Germany, had buried its differences with Britain and in that year signed the Entente. This was not a formal alliance but a friendly agreement, covering a variety of subjects. The final step in the formation of the Triple Entente was the conclusion of a mutual understanding between Great Britain and Russia in 1907. Again there

The Triple Entente

was no formal alliance, but the ability of the two powers to reconcile their ambitions in Asia suggested a willingness to ally in case of war.

Thus by 1907 the great powers of Europe were arrayed in two opposing combinations, the Triple Alliance of Germany, Italy, and Austria-Hungary, and the Triple Entente of Britain, France, and Russia. Nevertheless, these new groupings were not without internal strains. Italy and Austria, though allied, were bitterly at odds over the disposition of territory in the Adriatic region—Trieste in particular, which the Austrians held and which the Italians claimed as *Italia Irredenta* (unredeemed Italy). The Italians had designs on portions of Africa as well. In the 1890s, under the premiership of Francesco Crispi, a hero of the Risorgimento, they had attempted to establish a protectorate over the Ethiopians, only to suffer a devastating loss at Aduwa in 1896. Now the Italians coveted Tripoli in North Africa, which they believed they might more easily obtain, over the objections of Turkey, if they supported the Moroccan claims of their French adversaries. Strains within the Entente were equally apparent. Britain viewed Russia's growing determination to control the Dardenelles as a threat to its supply routes to the East.

The generally fragile state of international relations was certainly one of the important causes of the First World War. Yet it was by no means the only one. Recent scholars—most notably the German historian Fritz Fischer—ignited a controversy by insisting that the paramount reason was Germany's internally generated drive to power, its compulsion to aggrandize itself at the expense of the rest of Europe—not simply to achieve what the emperor had called its "place in the sun," but to see to it that the sun shone no more than fitfully on anyone else. Scholars of this persuasion, reacting to a more conventional view that has all nations sharing the blame, point to Germany's rapid commercial expansion, the growth, in particular, of its coal and steel industries, and its dockyards and overseas shipping as indications of its intentions. German capitalists financed the construction of a

The Baghdad Railroad. German and Turkish officials celebrate the launching of the enterprise.

Berlin to Baghdad railway, as part of a concerted *drang nach osten* (drive to the East). At the same time, the Germans launched a massive campaign to increase the size of their navy, a prospect particularly pleasing to the industrial bourgeoisie, who would profit directly from the new construction, and whose sons, excluded from the aristocratically based army, manned the naval officer corps. The naval buildup was accompanied by a brash and effective propaganda campaign—perhaps the first of its kind—directed by the secretary of the navy, Admiral Alfred von Tirpitz, and concerted through "navy leagues," organizations devoted to trumpeting Germany's intention of matching the strength of the British navy.

Others' responsibility

Others have taken issue with the notion that Germany faced the prospect of a preemptive war with equanimity, as it ignores the fact that many German industrialists did not want war since they had heavy investments in the economies of both Russia and France. They further argue that it is a mistake to view the problem of the war's outbreak through the single lens of Germany. They maintain that Britain's rapprochement with Russia and France, for example, reflected the demands of its own imperial policies and not simply a response to overweening German ambition.

Proliferation of "war machines"

Certainly the spirit of militarism extended beyond the borders of Germany, as all major European countries came to deploy massive "war machines." Serbia and Rumania, two very real threats to Austro-Hungarian security, possessed armies of over 400,000 each. In 1913, Russia embarked on a program of military expansion that bolstered its army by 500,000, to over 2,000,000 men, making it roughly equivalent in size to that of Germany. Nation after nation followed the German example by establishing a general staff, an institution one historian has called "the greatest military innovation of the nineteenth century." Problems of supplying and deploying mass armies had compelled governments to create a cadre of high-level planners, professional military advisors who were increasingly heeded by the civilian politicians to whom they reported. General staffs made it their particular business to deal with conscription, mobilization, the laying out of strategic railway lines—all complex technical issues demanding a high level of expertise.

Social impact of militarism

Reliance upon mass armies fostered a preoccupation with national birth rates, public health, and literacy. France regarded its declining birth rate after 1870 with alarm partly because it foretold a diminishing capacity to field a modern world-class army. If birth rates reflected a nation's long-term prospects for military manpower, the physical well-being of draft-age civilians was of immediate concern and encouraged reforms in health care and housing. A report on "physical deterioration" in Britain after the Boer War profoundly disturbed both military and civilian planners by demonstrating that in industrial cities such as Manchester as many as 8,000 out of 11,000 volunteers had been turned away by the army as unfit for military service. And, of course, with the introduction of increasingly sophisticated weaponry that required mastery of technological detail, noncommissioned officers and enlisted men could not function without the ability to read and to figure. The new armies had to be literate armies.

General European militarism was fed by notions of war as a therapeutic exercise. The French historian Ernest Renan had justified armed conflict as a condition of progress, "the sting which prevents a country from going to sleep." Middle-class citizens, anxious to prove themselves as patriotically aggressive as aristocrats, joined in the clamor to establish that the counting house was as much the seat of national fervor as the country estate. People began to speak increasingly of the "just" war. The British politician David Lloyd George praised the formation of a Balkan Alliance to fight the Turks in 1912 as "enlarging the boundaries of freedom." *Notions of the therapeutic
value of war*

We have seen that in all the major countries of Europe clashes between the political forces of Left and Right threatened internal stability. The notion that revolution and counterrevolution were on the prowl heightened a mood that seemed to proclaim the inevitability of conflict. "Almost one might think the world wished to suffer," Winston Churchill wrote after the war was over. "Certainly men were everywhere eager to dare." *Growing sense of the
inevitability of conflict*

Nationalism, too, fed the prevailing mood. From the beginning of the twentieth century, Serbia moved to extend its jurisdiction over all those alleged to be similar to its own citizens in race and in culture. Some of these peoples inhabited what were then the two Turkish provinces of Bosnia and Herzegovina. Others included Croatians and Slovenes in the southern provinces of Austria-Hungary. After 1908, when Austria suddenly annexed Bosnia and Herzegovina, Serbian activity was directed exclusively against the Habsburg Empire. It took the form of agitation to provoke discontent among the Slav subjects of Austria, in the hope of drawing them away and uniting the territories they inhabited with Serbia. It resulted in a series of dangerous plots against the peace and integrity of the Dual Monarchy. *Nationalism*

In many of their activities the Serbian nationalists were aided and abetted by the Pan-Slavists in Russia. The Pan-Slav movement was founded upon the theory that all of the Slavs of eastern Europe constituted one cultural nation. Therefore, it was argued that Russia, as the most powerful Slavic state, should act as the protector of the smaller Slavic nations of the Balkans. Pan-Slavism was not merely the wishful sentiment of a few ardent nationalists; it was a part of the official policy of the Russian government, and went far toward explaining Russia's aggressive stand in every quarrel that arose between Serbia and Austria. *Pan-Slavism*

All these factors—diplomatic instability, international militarism, domestic unrest, and nationalism—combined to produce a series of crises between 1905 and 1913. They were not so much causes as they were symptoms of international animosity. Yet each left a heritage of *Moroccan crises*

The Iron Fist of the Kaiser Strikes Agadir. This British cartoon depicts the Germans' use of gunboat diplomacy in Morocco in 1911 to secure colonial concessions from the French as an overtly hostile and sinister act. In precipitating this Second Moroccan Crisis the Germans hoped to drive a wedge between Britain and France but succeeded only in driving the Entente powers closer together.

Balkan Wars

A world at war

suspicion and bitterness that made war all the more probable. In some cases hostilities were averted only because one of the parties was too weak at the time to offer resistance. The result was a sense of humiliation, a smoldering resentment that was almost bound to burst into flame in the future. Two of the crises were generated by disputes over Morocco. Both Germany and France wanted to control Morocco; in 1905 and 1911 the two powers stood on the brink of war. Each time the dispute was smoothed over, but not without the usual legacy of suspicion.

In addition to the clash over Morocco, two flare-ups occurred in the Near East, the first in Bosnia in 1908. At the Congress of Berlin in 1878 the two Turkish provinces of Bosnia and Herzegovina had been placed under the administrative control of Austria, though actual sovereignty was still to be vested in the Ottoman Empire. Serbia also coveted the territories; they would double the size of its kingdom and place it within striking distance of the Adriatic. Suddenly, in October 1908, as we have seen, Austria annexed the two provinces, in flat violation of the Treaty of Berlin. The Serbs were furious and appealed to Russia. The tsar's government threatened war, until Germany addressed a sharp note to St. Petersburg announcing its firm intention to back Austria. Since Russia had not yet fully recovered from its war with Japan and was plagued by internal troubles, Russian intervention was postponed but not renounced. The Tsar's government resolved never to let itself be humiliated again.

Still more bad blood between the nations of eastern Europe was created by the Balkan Wars. In 1912 Serbia, Bulgaria, Montenegro, and Greece, with encouragement from Russia, joined in a Balkan alliance for the conquest of the Turkish province of Macedonia. The war started in October 1912; in less than two months the resistance of the Turks was shattered. Then came the problem of dividing the spoils. In secret treaties negotiated before hostilities began, Serbia had been promised Albania, in addition to a generous slice of Macedonia. But now Austria, fearful as always of any increase in Serbian power, intervened at the peace conference and obtained the establishment of Albania as an independent state. For the Serbs this was the last straw. It seemed to them that at every turn their path to western expansion was certain to be blocked by the Habsburg government. From this time on, anti-Austrian agitation in Serbia and in the neighboring province of Bosnia became ever more venomous.

It was the assassination of the Austrian Archduke Francis Ferdinand by a Serbian sympathizer on June 28, 1914, that ignited the conflict. The four-year war that ensued altered the Western world immeasurably. Yet many changes that came either during or after the First World War were the result, not of the war itself, but of pressures and forces we have seen at work during the prewar years, when European power, at its height, was challenged by forces which that power had unleased and which it proved unable to contain.

SELECTED READINGS

• *Items so designated are available in paperback editions.*

Barrows, Susanna, *Distorting Mirrors: Visions of the Crowd in Late Nineteenth-Century France,* New Haven, 1981. A study of crowd psychology.

• Berghahn, Victor, *Germany and the Approach of War in 1914,* New York, 1973. Examines the domestic background of German foreign policy, especially the naval program.

Blum, J., *Lord and Peasant in Russia from the Ninth to the Nineteenth Century,* Princeton, 1961. Contains a thorough discussion of emancipation.

Brogan, D. W., *France under the Republic, 1870–1930,* New York, 1940. An excellent survey, comprehensive and analytical.

• Dangerfield, George, *The Strange Death of Liberal England,* New York, 1961. Examines England's three major crises of the prewar period: women's suffrage, labor unrest, and Irish home rule.

• Emmons, Terence, *The Russian Landed Gentry and the Peasant Emancipation of 1861,* Charlotte, N.C., 1968.

• Fischer, Fritz, *Germany's Aims in the First World War,* New York, 1967. An extremely controversial study which seeks to lay major blame for the coming of the First World War on Germany.

• Haimson, L., *The Russian Marxists and the Origins of Bolshevism,* Cambridge, Mass., 1955. Analyzes the revolutionaries as part of the Russian radical tradition.

• Hale, Oron J., *The Great Illusion, 1900–1914,* New York, 1971. A general synthetic treatment of the period that is particularly concerned with mood and spirit.

Jenks, William A., *Austria under the Iron Ring, 1879–1893,* Charlottesville, Va., 1965. An examination of Austria's attempts at political and social reform, set in the context of a struggle for autonomy from German domination.

Johnson, Douglas, *France and the Dreyfus Affair,* London, 1966. A good survey, with breadth.

• Jones, Gareth Stedman, *Outcast London,* Oxford, 1971. A remarkable book which examines the breakdown in the relationship between classes in London during the latter half of the nineteenth century.

Mack Smith, Denis, *Italy: A Modern History,* rev. ed., Ann Arbor, Mich., 1969. An excellent survey.

• McManners, John, *Church and State in France, 1870–1914,* New York, 1972. Particularly good on the question of education and the final separation of church and state.

• May, Arthur J., *The Hapsburg Monarchy, 1867–1914,* Cambridge, Mass., 1951. A detailed narrative of the period.

• Mosse, W. E., *Alexander II and the Modernization of Russia,* New York, 1958. Brief but useful biography.

• Pulzer, Peter, *The Rise of Political Anti-Semitism in Germany and Austria,* New York, 1964. An excellent study of the roots of anti-Semitism and the part it played in shaping politics.

Ralston, David B., *The Army of the Republic: The Place of the Military in the Political Evolution of France, 1871–1914,* Cambridge, Mass., 1967. Useful for background to the Dreyfus affair.

Rémond, René, *The Right Wing in France: From 1815 to De Gaulle,* Philadelphia, 1969. Traces the survival of royalism and Bonapartism in French thought and politics.

Seton-Watson, Hugh, *The Russian Empire, 1801–1917,* Oxford, 1967. Standard survey.

Stavrianos, L. S., *The Balkans, 1815–1914,* New York, 1963. Surveys domestic and international affairs within the entire, troubled region.

• Taylor, A. J. P., *The Struggle for Mastery in Europe, 1848–1918,* Oxford, 1971. An excellent diplomatic history.

Thayer, John A., *Italy and the Great War: Politics and Culture, 1870–1914,* Madison, Wisc., 1964. Written to explain Italian policy and its origins in the prewar period.

Ulam, Adam, *Russia's Failed Revolutions: From the Decembrists to the Dissidents,* New York, 1981. Activities of revolutionary societies before 1917.

• Vicinus, Martha, ed., *A Widening Sphere: Changing Roles of Victorian Women,* Bloomington, Ind., 1977. Essays that trace the slow emancipation of Victorian women.

• Weber, Eugen, *Peasants into Frenchmen: The Modernization of Rural France, 1870–1914,* Stanford, 1917. Argues that the great achievement of the Third Republic was the consolidation of France, accomplished by bringing rural areas into the mainstream of modern life.

• Williams, Roger L., *The French Revolution of 1870–1871,* New York, 1969. A good narrative account.

Zelnik, R. E., *Labor and Society in Tsarist Russia: The Factory Workers of St. Petersburg, 1855–1870,* Stanford, 1971. The growth of class consciousness in Tsarist Russia.

SOURCE MATERIALS

• Childers, Erskine, *The Riddle of the Sands,* New York, 1978. A bestseller in England in 1903, this novel concerns a future war between England and Germany. Its reception gives evidence of the rise of anti-German sentiment prior to the First World War.

• Hamerow, Theodore S., ed., *The Age of Bismarck: Documents and Interpretations,* New York, 1973.

• Lenin, Nikolai, *What Is To Be Done?* London, 1918. Written in 1902, this is Lenin's most famous pamphlet. In it he called for the proletarian revolution to be led by elite cadres of bourgeois intellectuals, like himself.

• Mackenzie, Midge, ed., *Shoulder to Shoulder,* New York, 1975. A richly illustrated documentary history of the British movement for women's suffrage.

Pankhurst, Emmeline, *My Own Story,* New York, 1914. The memoirs of one of the leaders of England's militant suffragettes.

• Turgenev, Ivan, *Fathers and Sons,* New York, 1966. Turgenev's greatest novel is set in Russia in the 1860s and portrays the ideological conflict between generations at the time of the emancipation of the serfs and the rise of nihilism.

• Zola, Émile, *Germinal,* New York, 1964. Zola's realistic novel describes class conflict in France's coal-mining region.

Chapter 27

THE FIRST WORLD WAR

Nevertheless, except you share
With them in hell the sorrowful dark of hell,
Whose world is but the trembling of a flare,
And heaven but as the highway for a shell,

You shall not hear their mirth:
You shall not think them well content
By any jest of mine. These men are worth
Your tears. You are not worth their merriment.

—Wilfred Owen, "Apologia Pro Poemate Meo"

The war that broke out in 1914 was not really the "first world war." The wars against Napoleon at the beginning of the nineteenth century had extended beyond the European continent. Yet the war that took place between 1914 and 1918 had an impact that far exceeded any ever fought before. It quickly became a "people's war," to which civilians as well as soldiers and sailors were directly and totally committed. It bore fruit in revolution, and sowed the seeds of new and even more deadly conflicts in the future. It set the pattern for an age of violence that has continued through most of the twentieth century.

The world at war

1. PRELUDE TO WAR

The assassination of the Austrian archduke was the immediate cause of the First World War. Francis Ferdinand was soon to become emperor of Austria-Hungary. The reigning monarch, Francis Joseph, had reached his eighty-fourth year, and his death was expected momentarily. The murder of the heir to the throne was therefore considered in a very real sense as an attack upon the state. The actual murderer of Francis

The assassination of Francis Ferdinand

The Assassination at Sarajevo. Left: The Archduke Francis Ferdinand greets Bosnian notables a few hours before his death. Right: The police seize Princip after he had killed the heir to the Habsburg monarchy.

Ferdinand was a Bosnian student, Gavrilo Princip, the tool of Serbian nationalists. The murder, though committed in Sarajevo, the capital of Bosnia, was the result of a plot hatched in Belgrade, the Serbian capital. The conspirators were members of a secret society officially known as Union or Death, but commonly called the Black Hand. Their opposition to Francis Ferdinand stemmed from his support for a plan which would have resulted in the reorganization of the Habsburg Empire. This plan, designated as *trialism,* entailed changing the Dual Monarchy into a triple monarchy. In addition to German Austria and Magyar Hungary, already virtually autonomous, there was to be a third semi-independent region to accommodate the Slavs. Serbian national extremists opposed this scheme, fearing that if it were put into effect, their Slovene and Croatian kinsmen would be content to remain under Habsburg rule. They therefore determined to assassinate Francis Ferdinand before he could become emperor and press ahead with his reform.

See color map of Europe on the Eve of the First World War following page 992

The Austrians were immediately convinced that the Serbian government was behind this violent act. Austria waited for more than three weeks before acting on its suspicions and seizing the opportunity to extract a high price from Serbia for its transgressions. The delay was due in part to Austria's inability to decide how to proceed and in part to its unwillingness to mobilize its forces until after the harvest. On July 23 the Austrian government dispatched a severe ultimatum

Austrian ultimatum to Serbia

to the Serbians consisting of eleven demands: among them Serbia was to suppress anti-Austrian newspapers; to crush secret patriotic societies; to eliminate from the government and from the army all persons guilty of anti-Austrian propaganda; and to accept the collaboration of Austrian officials in stamping out the subversive movement against the Habsburg Empire. Two days later the Serbian government transmitted its reply. Of the total of eleven demands, only one was emphatically refused, and five were accepted without reservations. The Austrians, however, pronounced the Serbian reply unsatisfactory, severed diplomatic relations, and mobilized parts of their army. The Serbs themselves had been under no illusions about pleasing Austria, since, three hours before transmitting their reply, they had issued an order to mobilize their troops.

The Austrian intransigence vis-à-vis the Serbian response was actually the culmination of a belligerence that had been growing among European nations prior to the events that followed the assassination. As early as July 18 Sergei Sazonov, the Russian foreign minister, warned Austria that Russia would not tolerate any effort to humiliate Serbia. On July 24 Sazonov informed the German ambassador: "I do not hate Austria; I despise her. Austria is seeking a pretext to gobble up Serbia; but in that case Russia will make war on Austria." Russia had the support of France; on the twentieth of July, Raymond Poincaré, president of France, paid a visit to St. Petersburg to strengthen the Russian resolve to "be firm" and to avoid any compromise that might result in a loss of prestige for the Triple Entente. He warned the Austrian ambassador that "Serbia has very warm friends in the Russian people. And Russia has an ally, France."

The attitude of Germany in these critical days was ambiguous. Al-

Russia and France

Nicholas II and Raymond Poincaré, the President of the French Republic, in St. Petersburg on July 23, 1914

The attitude of Germany

though the kaiser was shocked and infuriated by the assassination, his government did not make any threats until after the actions of Russia gave cause for alarm. Yet both William II and the chancellor, Theobald von Bethmann Hollweg, adopted the premise that stern punishment must be meted out to Serbia without delay. They hoped in this way to confront the other powers with an accomplished fact. The kaiser declared on June 30: "Now or never! Matters must be cleared up with the Serbs, *and that soon."* On July 6 Bethmann Hollweg gave a commitment to the Austrian foreign minister which was interpreted by the latter as a blank check. The Austrian government was informed that the emperor would "stand true by Austria's side in accordance with his treaty obligations and old friendship." The Germans apparently hoped that by taking quick punitive action against Serbia, the Austrians would be able to counter a very real Serbian threat before Russia and its allies could recover from the shock of the assassination and mobilize either diplomatically or militarily.

Mobilizations begin

Austria declared war against Serbia on July 28, 1914. For a fleeting, anxious moment there was a possibility that the conflict might be contained. But it was quickly transformed into a war of larger scope by the action of Russia. On July 24 the Russian government decided to respond to any Austrian military initiative against Serbia with a partial mobilization. By July 30, however, Sazonov and a prowar military clique persuaded Tsar Nicholas II to issue an order mobilizing all troops, not only against Austria but against Germany as well, on the grounds that such a vast country as Russia would require considerable time to get its military machine into operation.

The German ultimatums to Russia and France

There was now no drawing back from the abyss. The Germans were alarmed by Russian preparations for war. The latest action by the tsar's government made the situation far more critical, since in German military circles, and also in French and Russian, general mobilization meant war. Upon learning that the tsar's decree had gone into effect, William II's government sent an ultimatum to St. Petersburg demanding that mobilization cease within twelve hours. On the afternoon of August 1, the German ambassador requested an interview with the Russian foreign minister. He appealed to Sazonov for a favorable answer to the German ultimatum. Sazonov replied that mobilization could not be halted, but that Russia was willing to continue negotiations. The ambassador repeated his question a second and a third time, emphasizing the terrible consequences of a negative answer. Sazonov finally replied: "I have no other answer to give you." The ambassador then handed the foreign minister a declaration of war and, bursting into tears, left the room. In the meantime, the kaiser's ministers had also dispatched an ultimatum to France demanding that its leaders make known their intentions. Premier René Viviani replied on August 1 that France would act "in accordance with her interests," and immediately ordered a general mobilization of the army. On August 3 Germany declared war upon France.

August 1, 1914. A German officer reads the declaration of war in the streets of Berlin.

These grim timetables had doomed the efforts of Britain's foreign secretary, Sir Edward Grey, to convene a conference to settle the Austro-Serbian dispute. Perhaps if Britain had declared its readiness to go to war on the side of France and Russia earlier, that declaration would have compelled Germany and Austria to draw back. Yet Grey was not certain enough of his country's willingness to fight to make such a commitment. Although military conversations between the British and French had bound the former to an expeditionary force on French soil in case of war, the British public did not know this. Opinion was divided: Conservatives generally favored war; the Liberals, still in power, disagreed among themselves; Labour was opposed.

The British position

Fortunately for Grey and the prime minister, Herbert Asquith, both of whom wanted a British declaration of war, Germany's invasion of neutral Belgium brought together parliamentary and public support for intervention. In 1839, along with the other great powers, Britain had signed a treaty guaranteeing the neutrality of Belgium. Moreover, it had been British policy for a century or more to try to prevent domination of the Low Countries, lying directly across the Channel, by any powerful continental nation. The Germans planned to attack France through Belgium. Accordingly, they demanded of the Belgian government permission to send troops across its territory, promising to respect the independence of the nation and to pay for any damage

Britain enters the war

to property. When Belgium refused, the kaiser's legions began pouring across the frontier. The British foreign secretary immediately went before Parliament and urged that his country rally to the defense of international law and to the protection of small nations. The next day, August 4, 1914, the cabinet sent an ultimatum to Berlin demanding that Germany respect Belgian neutrality, and that the Germans give a satisfactory reply by midnight. The kaiser's ministers offered no answer save military necessity, arguing that it was a matter of life and death for Germany that its soldiers reach France by the quickest route. As the clock struck twelve, Great Britain and Germany were at war.

The conflagration spreads

Other nations were quickly drawn into the struggle. On August 7 the Montenegrins joined with their kinsmen, the Serbs, in fighting Austria. Two weeks later the Japanese declared war upon Germany, partly because of their alliance with Great Britain, but mainly for the purpose of conquering German possessions in the Far East. On August 1 Turkey negotiated an alliance with Germany, and in October began the bombardment of Russian ports on the Black Sea. Italy, though still technically a member of the Triple Alliance, proclaimed neutrality. The Italians insisted that the Germans were not fighting a defensive war, and that consequently they were not bound to go to their aid. Italy remained neutral until May 1915, when it entered the war on the side of the Triple Entente.

Diplomacy and the question of guilt

The diplomatic maneuvers during the five weeks that followed the assassination at Sarajevo have probably best been characterized as "a tragedy of miscalculation." Because the war brought such disaster in its train, debate about immediate responsibility for its outbreak has been continual and often acrimonious. The eventual victors—Britain, France, the United States, and their allies—insisted at the war's end that Germany assume that responsibility, and wrote German war "guilt" into the postwar settlement. Historians during the 1920s and 1930s challenged that harsh assessment, arguing instead that all the major European nations—and the alliance systems they had constructed—had driven the world into conflict in those fatal weeks during the summer of 1914. More recently, Fritz Fischer has insisted that William II and Bethmann Hollweg did everything they could to encourage the Austrians to go to war against Serbia, knowing that such a war would almost certainly engage the Russians on the side of the Serbians and the French on the side of the Russians. Undoubtedly there were those in positions of power in Germany arguing that war was inevitable, that to wait until Russia had fully recovered from its war with Japan, and until France's armies had been strengthened by its three-year conscription law, was to invite defeat. Better to do battle now, from a position of strength. It is now clear that Bethmann Hollweg, had, indeed, succumbed to such fatalism by July 1914.

2. THE ORDEAL OF BATTLE

Because the war soon demanded the wholehearted support of entire civilian populations, national leaders felt compelled to depict it as a noble conflict rather than a widespread quarrel between imperialist powers or the unexpected outcome of nationalist jealousies. The socialist Second International had declared that workers should respond to a call to arms with a general strike. Although none of the European socialist parties heeded that call, governments continued to fear subversion of the war effort from "below," and attempted to head off any such movement by ceaseless appeals to patriotism. Propaganda became as important a weapon as the machine gun. The task of the Allies was at first made easier by Germany's treatment of the neutral Belgians: their execution of civilian hostages, destruction of the ancient library at Louvain, and massacre of over six hundred civilians at Dinant.

A "patriotic" war

On August 6, 1914, Prime Minister Asquith declared that Britain had entered the conflict to vindicate "the principle that smaller nationalities are not to be crushed by the arbitrary will of a strong and overmastering Power." Across the Channel, President Poincaré was assuring his fellow citizens that France had no other purpose than to stand "before the universe for Liberty, Justice and Reason." Later, as a consequence of the writings of individuals such as H. G. Wells and Gilbert Murray, and the pronouncements of the American president, Woodrow Wilson, the crusade of the Entente powers became a war to redeem mankind from the curse of militarism. In the opposing camp, the subordinates of the kaiser were doing all in their power to justify Germany's military efforts. The struggle against the Entente powers was represented to the German people as a crusade on behalf of a superior *Kultur* and as a battle to protect the fatherland against the wicked encirclement policy of the Entente nations. German socialist politicians were persuaded to vote for the war on the grounds that a German war with Russia would help liberate the Russian people from the tsarist yoke.

Propaganda efforts

The First World War fooled military experts who believed it would end quickly. Open warfare soon disappeared from the Western Front—the battle line that stretched across France from Switzerland to the North Sea, where the fighting was concentrated for four years. Germany's initially successful advance into France followed war plans drawn up by General Alfred von Schlieffen and adopted in 1905. Schlieffen's strategy called for Austria to hold against the Russians while Germany dealt a quick blow to the French, knocking them out of the war. Germany was then to turn, with Austria, to the major task of defeating the Russians. Contrary to expectation, however, the advance to the west, which brought German troops to within thirty

British Propaganda Poster. During the war governments, confronted with the bitter fruit of prewar militarism and nationalist rivalry, resorted to using any image that seemed likely to stir the passions of their populations against their foes.

miles of Paris, was halted. A series of flanking maneuvers by both sides ended in the extension of the battle lines in a vast network of trenches. Attacks to dislodge the enemy from their positions on the line failed to achieve more than very limited gains. Protected by barbed wire and machine guns—both making their first major appearance in a European war—defenders had the advantage. The one weapon with the potential to break the stalemate, the tank, was not introduced into battle until 1916, and then with such reluctance by tradition-bound commanders that its half-hearted employment made almost no difference. Airplanes were used almost exclusively for reconnaissance, though occasional "dog-fights" did occur between German and Allied pilots. The Germans sent Zeppelins to raid London, but they did little significant damage. Commanding officers continued to believe that the war would have to be won on the ground. Only by battering their enemies first with artillery and then with thousands of men armed with rifles, grenades, and bayonets, did they believe they could achieve the always-elusive "breakthrough." On more than one occasion those in charge of the war attempted to end the stalemate by opening military fronts in other areas of the world. In 1915, Britain and France attempted a landing at Gallipoli, in Asia Minor, in the hope of driving Turkey from the war. The campaign was a disaster for the Entente powers, however, failing, as did others, to refocus the fighting or to free it from the immobility of the trenches.

Life for the common soldier on the Western Front alternated between the daily boredom and extreme unpleasantness of weeks spent in muddy and vermin-ridden trench communities, and the occasional and horrifying experience of battle, a nightmare not only of artillery,

Trench Warfare. After the first few battles, the war on the Western Front settled into static or position warfare. During the four-year period, veritable cities of mud, stone, and timber sprang up behind the trenches.

Inside the British Trenches during the Battle of the Somme, 1916

machine guns, and barbed wire, but of exploding bullets, liquid fire, and poison gas. Morale among most troops remained remarkably steady, given the dreadful conditions in the trenches and the endless series of battles fought without significant gain to either side. Mutinies did occur among French troops in 1917, when soldiers moved forward in attack bleating like sheep, their pathetic way of protesting their commanders' continued willingness to lead them like lambs to the slaughter.

By 1916 the war, which appeared to have settled into an interminable stalemate, had extracted a fearful cost. Over 600,000 were killed and wounded when the Germans unsuccessfully besieged the French stronghold of Verdun, near France's eastern border, in the spring of that year. The Germans acknowledged that their aim was not so much to take the fortified city, which they knew the French would defend with desperation, but to "bleed France white of all able-bodied men"; yet the Germans lost as many men as the French. In August 1916 the British launched an enormous attack along the Somme River to ease the pressure on Verdun. Lasting from July to October, the battle cost the Germans 500,000, the British 400,000, and the French 200,000 in return for an Allied advance of seven miles across the front. On the first day of fighting alone, over 57,000 British troops were killed or wounded. Meanwhile, conditions within Germany worsened, as an Allied blockade slowly reduced the country's raw materials and food supply.

The enormous human cost

In time such losses fueled an unsuccessful move on the part of a minority on both sides to press for a negotiated peace. But in the minds of those who were making decisions, both military and civil-

Changes in leadership

ian, the immediate effect of the carnage was to reinforce determination to press ahead for total victory. This intransigence led, in turn, to changes in leadership. In Britain, the ineffectual prime minister Asquith was replaced by Lloyd George, a buccaneer politician who, if he had little new to propose, nevertheless projected a properly fervent public image. In France, the following year, Georges Clemenceau assumed the premiership, again with a mandate to counter a growing defeatist attitude within the military high command. And in Germany, control continued to pass into the hands of Generals Paul von Hindenburg and Erich Ludendorff, the men responsible as well for the overall military strategy of the Central Powers.

As the conflict dragged on, other countries were drawn into the war. Italy was bribed by the Allies with a promise of Austrian terri-

The expansion of the conflict

tories and a generous slice of the eastern shore of the Adriatic. Bulgaria joined the Central Powers in September 1915, and Rumania sided with the Allies a year later. It was the intervention of the United States on the Allied side, however, in April 1917, that tipped the balance. The United States entered the war vowing, in the words of its president, Woodrow Wilson, to "make the world safe for democracy," to banish autocracy and militarism, and to establish a league or society of nations in place of the old diplomatic maneuvering. Undoubtedly the primary reason for the American decision to enter the war, though, was the government's concern to maintain the international balance of power. For years it had been a cardinal doctrine in American diplomatic and military circles that the security of the United States depended upon a balance of forces in Europe. So long as Great Britain was strong enough to prevent any one nation from achieving suprem-

Wartime Leaders. Left: Allied Generals Haig and Joffre, and Prime Minister Lloyd George discuss strategy. Right: Reviewing a map are Hindenburg, William II, and Ludendorff, members of the German high command.

The Lusitania *Leaving New York Harbor.* In February 1915 the *Lusitania* was torpedoed and sunk by a German U-boat. Among the 1,200 people drowned were 119 Americans. The disaster was one step in the chain of events which led to the entry of the United States into the war on the side of Britain and France.

acy in Europe, the United States was safe. American officials had grown so accustomed to thinking of the British navy as the shield of American security that they found it difficult to contemplate any different situation. Germany, however, presented not merely a challenge to British naval supremacy; it threatened to starve the British nation into surrender and to establish a hegemony over all of Europe.

The direct cause of United States participation in the First World War was the U-boat, or submarine, warfare of the Germans. Once it became clear that the war would be one of attrition, the Germans recognized that unless they could break the Entente's stranglehold on their shipping, they would be defeated. In February 1915, the kaiser's government announced that neutral vessels headed for British ports would be torpedoed without warning. President Wilson replied by declaring that the United States would hold Germany to a "strict accountability" if any harm should come to American lives or property. The warning caused Germany to discontinue the campaign, but only temporarily. The Germans were convinced that the U-boat was one of their most valuable weapons, and they considered themselves justified in using it against the British blockade. They also believed, correctly, that the British were receiving war matériel clandestinely shipped aboard passenger ships from the United States, and continued to sink them, thus appearing to violate United States neutrality. When the kaiser's ministers announced that, on February 1, 1917, they would launch a campaign of unrestricted submarine warfare, Wilson cut off diplomatic relations with the Berlin government. On April 2 he went before Congress and requested and received a declaration of war.

The immediate result of U.S. entry was an increase in the amount of war matériel and food—later, in the number of troops—shipped unmolested in armed convoys across the Atlantic. New ship construction overcame earlier losses; submarine warfare, Germany's most effective weapon against the Allies, had been neutralized.

Submarine warfare

The success of the Atlantic convoys

3. REVOLUTION IN THE MIDST OF WAR

In the midst of world war came revolution. Russia, already severely weakened by internal conflicts before 1914, found itself unable to sustain the additional burden of continuous warfare. In a nation ruled as autocratically as was Russia, a successful war effort depended greatly on the determination and talents of its ruler, the tsar. Nicholas II was, by nature, irresolute and weak. His limited capabilities were further undermined by the irrationality of his wife, Alexandra, a religious fanatic, and of her spiritual mentor, the monk Rasputin. The latter had gained the tsarina's sympathy by his ability to alleviate the sufferings of her hemophiliac son, and used his influence over her to shape policy to his own self-aggrandizing ends. Russia's armies proved incapable of sustained success in the field. Although they managed to advance against the Austrians into Galicia in the south, they suffered two stunning defeats in 1914, at Tannenberg and the Masurian lakes in the north, losing almost 250,000 men in the process. In some instances soldiers were sent to the front without rifles; their clothing supplies were inadequate. Medical facilities were scarce. The railway system broke down, producing a shortage of food not only in the army but in cities as well. By the end of 1916, Russia's power to resist had all but collapsed.

Gregory Rasputin

The revolution in Russia followed a pattern of successive radicalization not unlike that of the French Revolution. It began in March 1917 with the forced abdication of the tsar. For this the immediate cause was disgust with the conduct of the war. The Russians had

The March 1917 revolution

Tsar Nicholas II and His Family on the Eve of the Revolution

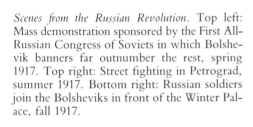

Scenes from the Russian Revolution. Top left: Mass demonstration sponsored by the First All-Russian Congress of Soviets in which Bolshevik banners far outnumber the rest, spring 1917. Top right: Street fighting in Petrograd, summer 1917. Bottom right: Russian soldiers join the Bolsheviks in front of the Winter Palace, fall 1917.

attempted a major offensive in the summer of 1916, to coincide with the campaign along the Somme in the west. The offensive, though initially successful, turned into a humiliating retreat, however, thanks to transportation breakdowns and a lack of ammunition. In addition to military disasters, inflation and consequent high prices, and shortages of food and fuel had produced a rebellious urban population. Demands for a popularly elected, broad-based government were met by the tsar's determination to retain power in his own hands until bread riots in Petrograd precipitated the abdication. (The city had abandoned its supposedly Germanic name of St. Petersburg at the beginning of the war.) Troops summoned to quell the fighting broke ranks and joined the protesters, further evidence of the collapse of both civilian and military order. With the overthrow of the tsar, the authority of the government passed into the hands of a provisional ministry organized by leaders in the Duma in conjunction with representatives of workers in Petrograd, calling themselves a *soviet* or government council. With the exception of Alexander Kerensky (1881–1970), who was a member of the rurally based Social Revolutionary party, nearly all of the ministers were middle-of-the-road bourgeois liberals. Their hope was to transform the Russian autocracy into a constitutional monarchy modeled after that of Great Britain. In accordance with this aim, they issued a proclamation of civil liberties, released thousands of prisoners, and made plans for the election of a constituent assembly.

The Kerensky government

The increasingly powerful soviets of workers and soldiers pressed for social reform, the redistribution of land, and a negotiated settlement with the Central Powers. Yet ministers of the provisional government insisted that demands for domestic change must be subordinated to the war effort, which they defined in terms of previously declared imperialistic aims. They argued that basic governmental and economic reform should await the convening of the constituent assembly. Because the provisional ministers could not govern without the cooperation of the soviets, Kerensky, vice-president of the Petrograd soviet by the summer of 1917, became prime minister. He organized a government which managed to retain power for several months. Meanwhile, opposition to the growing radicalization of the ministry—reflected in Kerensky's elevation—encouraged conservatives and liberals to make common cause, and to mount a military action led by General Lavr Kornilov, the commander-in-chief of the army, against the government. The attempted coup was crushed. Yet

Kerensky (second from right) *and His Aides in the Winter Palace.* This is the last known photograph of Kerensky in Petrograd.

Kerensky's own position had been undermined, his enemies on the Left arguing that Kornilov's ability to mount a counterrevolutionary effort was a sign of Kerensky's ineffectual leadership and willingness to compromise revolutionary aims.

On April 3, 1917, Lenin, who had been living in exile in Switzerland, was smuggled into Russia by the Germans, who recognized his potential as a revolutionary, and hence his value to them as a troublemaker. They correctly reasoned that his opposition to Russia's participation in the war would further weaken their enemy to the east. Throughout the spring and summer of 1917, while Kerensky was struggling to hold his government together, Lenin led the Bolsheviks on a bolder course which shunned all collaboration with the bourgeoisie and condemned their war policies. He soon became the leader of a vast popular uprising of workers, soldiers, and peasants; the Bolsheviks at this time clearly spoke to the people's needs as no other party did. Lenin, determined to sieze power from Kerensky, after Kornilov's failure waited on the advice of his fellow Bolsheviks until the convening of the All-Russian Congress of Soviets on November 7. The preceding day, a coup d'état, centered in Petrograd and directed by Lenin's ally Leon Trotsky (1879–1940), succeeded in overturning the provisional government.

Lenin and the Bolsheviks

Lenin immediately proceeded to issue decrees that would give substance to the Bolsheviks' slogan of "Peace, Bread, and Land." The "People's Commissars" (ministers) ordered the partition of land and its distribution to peasants, without compensation to former owners; nationalized banks, confiscating private accounts in the process; handed factory control over to workers; and began to negotiate a treaty with the Germans. The resulting agreement, signed at Brest-Litovsk in March 1918, surrendered Poland, Finland, and the Ukraine to the Germans. The treaty aroused the fury of Lenin's political enemies, both moderates and reactionaries, who were still a force to be reckoned with and who were prepared to plunge Russia into civil war rather than accept the revolution.

Revolutionary changes

Yet another outbreak of revolution in this period was the so-called Easter Rebellion in Ireland. At the beginning of the world war, Irish nationalists, who resented the rule of their country by the British, were ripe for revolt. They had been promised self-rule on the eve of the war, but the British later reneged on the grounds that a national emergency must take preeminence over everything else. This greatly angered the Roman Catholic majority of southern Ireland. They scheduled Easter Monday, 1916, as a day for revolt. British forces quelled the uprising, but not until a hundred people had been killed. Sporadic outbreaks kept the island in turmoil for years thereafter, but were finally brought to a temporary end by an agreement constituting southern Ireland as a free republic. The northern counties, or the province of Ulster, were to continue subject to the British crown.

The Easter Rebellion in Ireland

Strife in Ireland, 1916. British troops raiding the office of a Dublin printer who supported the rebellion.

4. ARMISTICE AND PEACE

Peace proposals

While the fighting raged on for four years, various attempts were made to bring about peace negotiations. In the spring of 1917, Dutch and Scandinavian socialists summoned an international socialist conference to meet at Stockholm to draft plans to end the fighting which would be acceptable to all the belligerents. The Petrograd soviet embraced the idea and on May 15 issued an appeal to socialists of all nations to send delegates to the conference and to induce their governments to agree to a peace "without annexations and indemnities, on the basis of the self-determination of peoples." The socialist parties in all the principal countries on both sides of the war accepted this formula and were eager to send delegates to the conference, but when the British and French governments refused to permit any of their subjects to attend, the project was abandoned. The rulers of the Entente states did not reject these proposals because they emanated from socialists. Indeed, a similar formula suggested by the pope was just as emphatically rejected. Nowhere was there a disposition to take peace proposals seriously. Woodrow Wilson, as spokesman for the Allies, declared that negotiation of peace under any conditions was impossible so long as Germany was ruled by the kaiser. The Central Powers regarded the general import of the papal suggestions with favor, but they refused to commit themselves on indemnities and restorations, especially the restoration of Belgium.

The Fourteen Points

The best known of all the peace proposals was President Wilson's program of Fourteen Points, which he incorporated in an address to Congress on January 8, 1918. Summarized as briefly as possible, this program included: (1) "open covenants openly arrived at," i.e., the abolition of secret diplomacy; (2) freedom of the seas; (3) removal of economic barriers between nations; (4) reduction of national armaments "to the lowest point consistent with safety"; (5) impartial adjustment of colonial claims, with consideration for the interests of the peoples involved; (6) evacuation of Russia by foreign armies; (7) restoration of the independence of Belgium; (8) restoration of Alsace and Lorraine to France; (9) a readjustment of Italian frontiers "along clearly recognizable lines of nationality"; (10) autonomous development for the peoples of Austria-Hungary; (11) restoration of Rumania, Serbia, and Montenegro, with access to the sea for Serbia; (12) autonomous development for the peoples of Turkey, with the straits from the Black Sea to the Mediterranean "permanently opened"; (13) an independent Poland, "inhabited by indisputably Polish populations," and with access to the sea; (14) establishment of a League of Nations. On several other occasions Wilson reiterated in public addresses that his program would be the basis of the peace for which he would work. Thousands of copies of the Fourteen Points were scattered by Allied planes over the German trenches and behind the lines, in an effort to convince both soldiers and civilians that the Entente nations were striving for a just and durable peace.

With Russia now no longer a combattant, Germany appeared to have gained an advantage that would almost guarantee ultimate victory. Yet by the late spring of 1918 the Germans were suffering acutely, not only because of the continued effectiveness of the Allied blockade, but because of a growing domestic conflict over war aims. German socialists attacked expansionist goals—control of the steel- and coal-producing areas of Belgium and of the agricultural regions in eastern Europe—which conservatives continued to urge and which the government endorsed. Socialists were alarmed as well by the reactionary administration imposed upon the territories taken from Russia at Brest-Litovsk. By the fall of 1918, Germany was a country on the verge of civil war.

Domestic conflict in Germany

German Supplies Moving toward the Somme during the Last German Offensive in 1918

The collapse of the
Central Powers

The signing of the
armistice

Meanwhile, fighting continued as it had for four years on the Western Front. A great offensive launched by the British, French, and United States forces in July dealt one shattering blow after another to the German battalions and forced them back almost to the Belgian frontier. By the end of September the cause of the Central Powers appeared hopeless. Bulgaria withdrew from the war on September 30. Early in October the new chancellor of Germany, the liberal Prince Max of Baden, appealed to President Wilson for a negotiated peace on the basis of the Fourteen Points. But the fighting went on, Wilson now demanding that Germany agree to depose the kaiser. Germany's remaining allies tottered on the verge of collapse. Turkey surrendered at the end of October. The Habsburg Empire was cracked open by rebellions on the part of the empire's subject nationalities. A German-Austrian offensive in Italy in October 1917 had gained them a major victory at Caporetto, where Italian military police were ordered to shoot their own soldiers, if necessary, to stem the retreat. Yet a year later, the Italians responded to a similar attack with a counteroffensive that cost Austria the city of Trieste and 300,000 prisoners. On November 3 Emperor Charles, who had succeeded Francis Joseph in 1916, signed an armistice which took Austria out of the war.

Germany was now left with the impossible task of carrying on the struggle alone. The morale of its troops was rapidly breaking. The blockade was causing such a shortage of food that there was real danger of starvation. Revolutionary tremors that had been felt for some-time swelled into an earthquake. On November 8 a republic was proclaimed in Bavaria. The next day nearly all of Germany was in the throes of revolution. A decree was published in Berlin announcing the kaiser's abdication, and early the next morning he was moved across the frontier into Holland. In the meantime, the government of the nation had passed into the hands of a provisional council headed by Friedrich Ebert, leader of the socialists in the Reichstag. Ebert and his colleagues immediately took steps to conclude negotiations for an armistice. The terms as now laid down by the Entente powers provided for acceptance of the Fourteen Points with three amendments. First, the item on freedom of the seas was to be stricken (in accordance with the request of the British). Second, restoration of invaded areas was to be interpreted in such a way as to include reparations, that is, payment to the victors to compensate them for their losses. Third, the demand for autonomy for the subject peoples of Austria-Hungary was to be changed to a demand for independence. In addition, troops of the Entente nations were to occupy cities in the Rhine valley; the blockade was to be continued in force; and Germany was to hand over 5,000 locomotives, 150,000 railway cars, and 5,000 trucks, all in good condition. The Germans could do nothing but accept these terms. At five o'clock in the morning of November 11, two delegates of the defeated nation met with the commander of the Entente armies, Marshal Foch, in the dark Compiègne forest and signed the papers officially ending the war. Six hours later the order "cease fire" was given to the troops. That night thousands of people danced through the streets of London, Paris, and Rome in the same delirium of excitement with which they had greeted the declarations of war four years before.

The peace concluded at the various conferences in 1919 and 1920 more closely resembled a sentence from a court than a negotiated settlement. Propaganda had encouraged victorious soldiers and civilians to suppose that their sacrifices to the war effort would be compensated for by payments extracted from the "wicked" Germans. The British prime minister, David Lloyd George, campaigned during the election of 1918 on the slogan "Hang the Kaiser!", while one of his partisans demanded "Squeeze the German lemon until the pips squeak!" In all the Allied countries nationalism and democracy combined to make compromise impossible and to reassert the claim that the war was a crusade of good against evil. The peace settlement drafted by the victors inevitably reflected these feelings.

A harsh peace

The conference convoked in Paris[1] to draft a peace with Germany was technically in session from January until June of 1919, but only six plenary meetings were held. All of the important business of the conference was transacted by small committees. At first a Council of Ten was made up of the president and secretary of state of the United States, and the premiers and foreign ministers of Great Britain, France, Italy, and Japan. By the middle of March this body had been found too unwieldy and was reduced to the Council of Four, consisting of the American president and the English, Italian, and French premiers. A month later the Council of Four became the Council of Three when Premier Vittorio Orlando withdrew from the conference in a huff because Wilson refused to give Italy all it demanded.

The Paris Conference

The final character of the Treaty of Versailles was determined almost entirely by the so-called Big Three—Wilson, Lloyd George, and Clemenceau. These men were as different in personality as any three rulers who have ever come together for a common purpose. Wilson was an inflexible idealist, accustomed to dictating to subordinates and convinced that the hosts of righteousness were on his side. When confronted with unpleasant realities, such as secret treaties among the Entente governments for division of the spoils, he had a habit of dismissing them as unimportant and eventually forgetting that he had ever heard of them. Though he knew little of the devious maneuvers of European diplomacy, his unbending temperament made it difficult for him to take advice or to adjust his views to those of his colleagues. Lloyd George, the canny Welshman, possessed cleverness and Celtic humor that enabled him to succeed, on occasions, where Wilson failed;

The Big Three: Wilson, Clemenceau, and Lloyd George

[1] The conference did most of its work in Paris. The treaty of peace with Germany, however, takes its name from Versailles, the suburb of Paris in which it was signed.

The Council of Four. Meeting to draft a peace treaty in Paris were Orlando of Italy, Lloyd George of Britain, Clemenceau of France, and Wilson of the United States.

but he was above all a politician—shifty, and not particularly sympathetic to particular European problems such as nationalism.

The third member of the great triumvirate was the aged and cynical French premier, Georges Clemenceau. Born in 1841, Clemenceau had been a journalist in the United States just after the Civil War. Later he had won his nickname of "the Tiger" as a relentless foe of clericals and monarchists. He had fought for the republic during the stormy days of the Boulangist episode, the Dreyfus affair, and the struggle for separation of church and state. Twice in his lifetime he had seen France invaded and its existence gravely imperiled. Now the tables were turned, and the French, he believed, should take full advantage of their opportunity. Only by keeping a strict control over a prostrate Germany could the security of France be preserved.

Emasculating the Fourteen Points

From the beginning a number of embarrassing problems confronted the chief architects of the Versailles treaty. The most important was what to do about the Fourteen Points. There could be no doubt that they had been the basis of the German surrender on November 11. It was beyond question also that Wilson had represented them as the Entente program for a permanent peace. Consequently there was every reason for the peoples of the world to expect that the Fourteen Points would be the model for the Versailles settlement—subject only to the three amendments made before the armistice was signed. In actuality, however, no one among the highest dignitaries at the conference, with the exception of Wilson himself, gave more than lip service to the Fourteen Points. In the end, the American president was able to salvage, in unmodified form, only four parts of his famous program: point seven, requiring the restoration of Belgium; point eight, demanding the return of Alsace and Lorraine to France; point ten, providing for independence for the peoples of Austria-Hungary; and the final provision calling for a League of Nations. The others were ignored or modified to such an extent as to change their original meanings.

By the end of April 1919 the terms of the Versailles treaty were ready for submission to the enemy, and Germany was ordered to send delegates to receive them. On April 29, a delegation headed by Count von Brockdorff-Rantzau, foreign minister of the provisional republic, arrived in Versailles. When Brockdorff-Rantzau protested that the terms were too harsh, he was informed by Clemenceau that Germany would have three weeks to decide whether or not to sign. Eventually the time had to be extended, for the heads of the German government resigned their positions rather than accept the treaty. Their attitude was summed up by Chancellor Philip Scheidemann in the pointed statement: "What hand would not wither that sought to lay itself and us in those chains?" The Big Three now made a few minor adjustments, mainly at the insistence of Lloyd George, and Germany was notified that seven o'clock on the evening of June 23 must bring either acceptance or invasion. Shortly after five a new government of the provisional republic announced that it would yield to "overwhelming force" and accede to the victors' terms. On June 28, the fifth anniversary of the murder of the Austrian archduke, representatives of the German and Allied governments assembled in the Hall of Mirrors at Versailles and affixed their signatures to the treaty.

Germany sentenced

Crowds Greet President Wilson in Paris after the War. Despite public demonstrations of this sort, Wilson's attempt to shape the peace was a failure.

The provisions of the Treaty of Versailles can be outlined briefly. Germany was required to surrender Alsace and Lorraine to France, northern Schleswig to Denmark, and most of Posen and West Prussia to Poland. The coal mines of the Saar Basin were to be ceded to France, to be exploited by the French for fifteen years. At the end of this time the German government would be permitted to buy them back. The Saar territory itself was to be administered by the League of Nations until 1935, when a plebiscite would be held to determine whether it should remain under the league, be returned to Germany, or be awarded to France. Germany's province of East Prussia was cut off from the rest of its territory, and the port of Danzig, almost wholly German, was subjected to the political control of the League of Nations and the economic domination of Poland. Germany was disarmed, surrendering all its submarines and navy of surface vessels, with the exception of six small battleships, six light cruisers, six destroyers, and twelve torpedo boats. The Germans were forbidden to possess an air force, and their army was limited to 100,000 officers and men, to be recruited by voluntary enlistment. To make sure that Germany would not launch any new attack upon France or Belgium, it was forbidden to keep soldiers or maintain fortifications in the Rhine valley. Last, Germany and its allies were held responsible for all the loss and damage suffered by the Entente governments and their citizens, "as a consequence of the war imposed upon them by the aggression of Germany and her allies." This was the so-called war-guilt provision of the treaty (Article 231), and also the basis for German reparations. The exact amount that Germany should pay was left to a Reparations Commission. In 1921 the total was set at $33 billion.

For the most part, the Treaty of Versailles applied only to Germany. Separate pacts were drawn up to settle accounts with Germany's allies—Austria-Hungary, Bulgaria, and Turkey. The final form of these treaties was determined primarily by a Council of Five, composed of Clemenceau as chairman and one delegate each from the United States, Great Britain, France, and Italy. The treaties reflected a desire on the part of their drafters to recognize the principle of national self-determination. The experience of the prewar years convinced diplomats that they must draw national boundaries to conform as closely as possible to the ethnic, linguistic, and historical traditions of the people they were to contain. Yet practical, political difficulties made such divisions impossible.

*The treaty with Austria:
the compromising of
national self-determination*

The settlement with Austria, completed in September 1919, was known as the Treaty of St. Germain. Austria was required to recognize the independence of Hungary, Czechoslovakia, Yugoslavia, and Poland, and to cede to them large portions of its territory. In addition, Austria had to surrender Trieste, the south Tyrol, and the Istrian peninsula to Italy. Altogether the Austrian portion of the Dual Monarchy was deprived of three-fourths of its area and three-fourths of its people. Contrary to the principles of self-determination, in several of the territories surrendered the inhabitants were largely German-speaking—for example, in the Tyrol, and the region of the Sudeten mountains awarded to Czechoslovakia. The Austrian nation itself was reduced to a small, land-locked state, with nearly one-third of its population concentrated in the city of Vienna.

The second of the treaties with lesser belligerents was that with Bulgaria, which was signed in November 1919 and called the Treaty of Neuilly. Bulgaria was forced to give up nearly all of the territory it had gained since the First Balkan War. Land was ceded to Rumania, to the new kingdom of Yugoslavia, and to Greece. Here again, self-determination was compromised. All of these regions were inhabited by large Bulgarian minorities. Since Hungary was now an independent state, it was necessary that a separate treaty be imposed upon it. This was the Treaty of the Trianon Palace, signed in June 1920. It required that Slovakia be ceded to Czechoslovakia, Transylvania to Rumania, and Croatia-Slovenia to Yugoslavia. Nowhere was the principle of self-determination of peoples more flagrantly violated. Numerous sections of Transylvania had populations that were more than half Hungarian. Included in the region of Slovakia were not only Slovaks but almost a million Magyars and about 500,000 Ruthenians. As a consequence, a fanatical irredentist movement flourished in Hungary after the war, directed toward the recovery of these lost provinces. The Treaty of the Trianon Palace slashed the area of Hungary from 125,000 square miles to 35,000, and its population from 22 million to 8 million.

The settlement with Turkey was a product of unusual circumstances. The secret treaties had contemplated the transfer of Constantinople and Armenia to Russia and the division of most of the remainder of Turkey between Britain and France. But Russia's withdrawal from the war after the Bolshevik Revolution, together with insistence by Italy and Greece upon fulfillment of promises made to them, necessitated considerable revision of the original scheme. Finally, in August 1920, a treaty was signed at Sèvres, near Paris, and submitted to the government of the sultan. It provided that Armenia be organized as a Christian republic; that most of Turkey in Europe be given to Greece; that Palestine and Mesopotamia become British "mandates," i.e., to remain under League of Nations control but to be administered by Britain; that Syria become a mandate of France; and that southern Anatolia be set apart as a sphere of influence for Italy. About all that would be left of the Ottoman Empire would be the city of Constantinople and the northern and central portions of Asia Minor. The decrepit government of the sultan, overawed by Allied military forces, agreed to accept this treaty. But a revolutionary government of Turkish nationalists, which had been organized at Ankara under the leadership of Mustapha Kemal (later called Atatürk), deter-

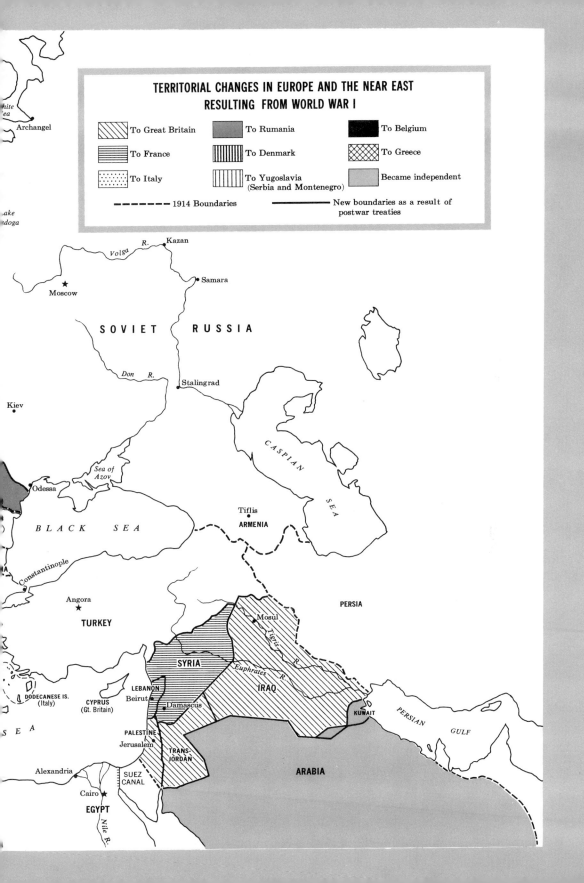

TERRITORIAL CHANGES IN EUROPE AND THE NEAR EAST RESULTING FROM WORLD WAR I

To Great Britain	To Rumania	To Belgium
To France	To Denmark	To Greece
To Italy	To Yugoslavia (Serbia and Montenegro)	Became independent

----- 1914 Boundaries ——— New boundaries as a result of postwar treaties

White Sea
Archangel

Lake Ladoga

Volga R.
Kazan

Samara

★ Moscow

SOVIET RUSSIA

Don R.

Stalingrad

Kiev

CASPIAN SEA

Sea of Azov

Odessa

BLACK SEA

Tiflis
ARMENIA

Constantinople

Angora
★
TURKEY

PERSIA

Mosul

SYRIA

Tigris R.

Euphrates R.

LEBANON
Beirut
Damascus

IRAQ

DODECANESE IS.
(Italy)

CYPRUS
(Gt. Britain)

KUWAIT

PERSIAN GULF

SEA

PALESTINE
Jerusalem

TRANS-
JORDAN

Alexandria

SUEZ
CANAL

ARABIA

Cairo ★

EGYPT

Nile R.

Kemal Atatürk

mined to prevent acceptance of the settlement of Sèvres. The forces of Kemal obliterated the republic of Armenia, frightened the Italians into withdrawing from Anatolia, and conquered most of the territory in Europe which had been given to Greece. At last, in November 1922, they occupied Constantinople, deposed the sultan, and proclaimed Turkey a republic. The Allies now consented to a revision of the peace. A new treaty was concluded at Lausanne in Switzerland in 1923, which permitted the Turks to retain practically all of the territory they had conquered. Though much reduced in size compared with the old Ottoman Empire, the Turkish republic still had an area of about 300,000 square miles and a population of 13 million.

Incorporated in each of the five treaties which liquidated the war with the Central Powers was the Covenant of the League of Nations. The establishment of a league in which the states of the world, both great and small, would cooperate for the preservation of peace had long been the cherished dream of President Wilson. Indeed, that had been one of his chief reasons for taking the United States into the war. He believed that the defeat of Germany would mean the deathblow of militarism, and that the road would thenceforth be clear for setting up the control of international relations by a community of nations instead of by the cumbersome and ineffective balance of power. But to get the league accepted he found himself compelled to make numerous compromises. He permitted his original idea of providing for a reduction of armaments "to the lowest point consistent with domestic safety" to be changed into the altogether different phrasing of "consistent with national safety." To induce the Japanese to accept the league he allowed them to keep former German concessions in China. To please the French, he sanctioned the exclusion of both Germany and Russia from his proposed federation, despite his long insistence that it should be a league of *all* nations. These handicaps were serious enough. But the league received an even more deadly blow when it was repudiated by the very nation whose president had proposed it.

Established under such unfavorable auspices, the league never achieved the aims of its founder. In only a few cases did it succeed in allaying the threat of war, and in each of these the parties to the dispute were small nations. But in every dispute involving one or more major powers, the league failed. It did nothing about the seizure of Vilna by Poland in 1920, because Lithuania, the victimized nation, was friendless, while Poland had the powerful backing of France. When, in 1923, war threatened between Italy and Greece, the Italians refused to submit to the intervention of the league, and the dispute was settled by direct mediation of Great Britain and France. Thereafter, in every great crisis the league was either defied or ignored. Its authority was flouted by Japan in seizing Manchuria in 1931 and by Italy in conquering Ethiopia in 1936. By September 1938, when the Czechoslovakian crisis arose, the prestige of the league had sunk so low that scarcely anyone thought of appealing to it. Yet the league justified its existence in other, less spectacular, ways. It reduced the international opium traffic and aided poor and backward countries in controlling the spread of disease. Its agencies collected invaluable statistics on labor and business conditions throughout the world. It conducted plebiscites in disputed areas, supervised the administration of internationalized cities, helped find homes for racial and political refugees, and made a notable beginning in codifying international law. Such achievements may well be regarded as providing a substantial groundwork for a later effort at international organization, the United Nations, formed after the Second World War.

The league, with all its failings, was seen as the one promising result of the war that many soon recognized as a hideously wasteful carnage. The price would have been enormous even if all the results which were supposed to flow from an Entente victory had really been achieved. Altogether 8.5 million men died and more than twice that number were wounded. The total casualties—killed, wounded, and missing—numbered over 37 million. Germany lost 6 million and France almost as many, a larger proportion, indeed, of its total population. But despite these appalling losses, almost nothing was gained. The war which was to "end all wars" sowed the seeds of a new and more terrible conflict in the future. The autocracy of the kaiser was destroyed, but the ground was prepared for new despotisms. The First World War did nothing to abate either militarism or nationalism. Twenty years after the fighting had ended, there were nearly twice as many men under arms as in 1913; and national and ethnic rivalries and hatreds were as deeply ingrained as ever.

A war of waste

If the war failed to make the world less of an armed camp, it nevertheless altered it drastically in other ways. In the first place, it strengthened a belief in the efficacy of central planning and coordination. To sustain the war effort, the governments of all the major belligerents were forced to manage their economies by regulating industrial output, exercising a close control over imports and exports, and making the most effective use of manpower—both civilian and military. Second, the war upset the world trade balance. With few manufactured goods coming from Europe, Japanese, Indian, and South American capitalists were free to develop industries in their own countries. When the war was over, Europe found it had lost many of its previously guaranteed markets, and that it had become a debtor to the United States which, throughout the war, had lent large sums to the Allies. Third, while war was altering the patterns of world trade, it was also producing worldwide inflation. To finance their fighting, governments resorted to policies of deficit financing (spending above their income) and increased paper money which, with the shortage of goods, inflated their price. Inflation hit hardest at the middle class, those men and women who had lived on their income from invested

Changes brought by the war

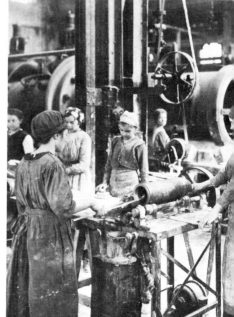

Women at Work. The all-out war effort combined with a manpower shortage at home brought women into factories across Europe in unparalleled numbers. On the left, men and women work side-by-side in a British shell factory. At the right, women toil in a German gun factory.

money, and now saw that money worth far less than it once had been. Fourth, the war, while it brought hardships to most, brought freedom to many. Women were emancipated by their governments' need for them in factories and on farms. The contribution of women to the war effort undoubtedly explains the granting of female suffrage in both Great Britain and the United States in 1918 and 1920. Finally, despite this legacy of liberation, the war's most permanent contribution to the spirit of the postwar years was disillusion—particularly within the middle classes. A generation of men had been sacrificed—"lost"—to no apparent end. Many of those left alive were sickened by the useless slaughter, to which they knew they had contributed and for which they believed they must share at least part of the guilt. They were disgusted by the greedy abandonment of principles by the politicians at Versailles. Hatred and mistrust of the "old men" who had dragged the world into an unnecessary conflict, who had then mismanaged its direction with such ghastly results, and who had betrayed the cause of international peace for national gain soured the minds of many younger men and women in the postwar period. The British poet Edmund Blunden expressed this profound disillusionment when he took as the title for a poem, written to celebrate New Year's Day 1921, the biblical verse: "The dog is turned to his own vomit again, and the sow that was washed to her wallowing in the mire."

SELECTED READINGS

• *Items so designated are available in paperback editions.*

THE WORLD WAR AND THE PEACE SETTLEMENT

Albertini, Luigi, *The Origins of the War of 1914*, 3 vols., New York, 1952–1957. An exhaustive, valuable study.

Albrecht-Carré, Rene, ed., *The Meaning of the First World War*, Englewood Cliffs, N.J., 1965. The war's consequences for both soldiers and civilians.

• Balfour, Michael, *The Kaiser and His Times*, London, 1964. An excellent biography of William II.

• Falls, Cyril, *The Great War*, New York, 1961. A military history.

Feldman, Gerald D., *Army, Industry, and Labor in Germany, 1914–1918*, Princeton, 1966. The effect of war on the domestic economy.

• Ferro, Marc, *The Great War, 1914–1918*, London, 1973. Social and economic developments receive particular treatment.

Fischer, Fritz, *War of Illusions*, New York, 1975. Deals with Germany within the context of internal social and economic trends. See also his *Germany's Aims in the First World War*, mentioned in the preceding chapter.

• Fussell, Paul, *The Great War and Modern Memory*, New York, 1975. A brilliant examination of British intellectuals' attitudes toward the war.

• Hardach, Gerd, *The First World War, 1914–1918*, Berkeley, 1977. An excellent economic history of the war.

Horne, Alastair, *The Price of Glory: Verdun, 1916*, New York, 1963.

Lafore, Laurence D., *The Long Fuse: An Interpretation of the Origins of World War I*, Philadelphia, 1971. Argues that the war was the result of obsolete institutions and ideas.

Laqueur, Walter, and G. L. Mosse, eds., *1914: The Coming of the First World War*, New York, 1969. An excellent series of essays by modern scholars.

• Marwick, Arthur, *The Deluge: British Society and the First World War*, Boston, 1965. The war's impact on the home front.

Mayer, Arno, *Politics and Diplomacy of Peacemaking: Containment and Counterrevolution at Versailles, 1918–1919*, New York, 1967. Emphasizes the role of the Russian Revolution in the peacemaking process.

• Moorehead, Alan, *Gallipoli*, London, 1956. A study of the British campaign.

Nicolson, Harold, *Peacemaking, 1919*, Boston, 1933. Written by a participant, provides a good account of the atmosphere of Versailles.

• Steiner, Zara S., *Britain and the Origins of the First World War*, New York, 1977. Argues that external rather than internal strains brought Britain into the war.

• Taylor, A. J. P., *English History, 1914–1945*, New York, 1965. An excellent treatment of the war and its impact on British society.

• Turner, L. C. F., *Origins of the First World War*, New York, 1970. Stresses Russia's role in the prewar diplomatic situation.

• Tuchman, Barbara, *The Guns of August*, New York, 1962. A popular account of the outbreak of war.

• Wheeler-Bennett, J. W., *Brest-Litovsk: The Forgotten Peace, March 1918*, London, 1939. An excellent study of personalities involved in the Russo-German peace treaty.

Williams, John, *The Home Fronts: Britain, France and Germany, 1914–1918*, London, 1972. A survey of life away from the battlefield and the impact of the war on domestic life.

• Wohl, Robert, *The Generation of 1914*, Cambridge, Mass., 1979. Uses generational analysis to explain attitudes toward the war.

Zeeman, Z. A. B., *The Break-up of the Hapsburg Empire, 1914–1918*, New York, 1961.

THE RUSSIAN REVOLUTION

• Deutscher, Isaac, *The Prophet Armed: Trotsky*, New York, 1954. The first volume of a magnificent biography of Trotsky; covers the years 1879–1921.

Fischer, Louis, *The Life of Lenin*, New York, 1964. A lengthy, somewhat popularized biography by a journalist who was present during the revolution.

Keep, John L. H., *The Russian Revolution*, New York, 1977.

Pares, Bernard, *A History of Russia*, rev. ed., New York, 1953. A useful, straightforward survey.

• Pipes, Richard, *The Formation of the Soviet Union*, New York, 1964. A solid, reliable study.

• Rabinowitch, Alexander, *The Bolsheviks Come to Power*, New York, 1976. A well-researched and carefully documented account.

Ulam, Adam, *The Bolsheviks*, New York, 1965. Analysis of both ideas and events.

• Wolfe, Bertram D., *Three Who Made a Revolution*, rev. ed., New York, 1964. A study of Lenin, Trotsky, and Stalin.

SOURCE MATERIALS

Carnegie Foundation, Endowment for International Peace, *The Treaties of Peace, 1919–1923*, 2 vols., New York, 1924.

Gooch, G. P., and H. Temperley, eds., *British Documents on the Origins of the War, 1898–1914*, London, 1927.

Keynes, John Maynard, *The Economic Consequences of the Peace*, London, 1919. A contemporary attack upon the peace settlement, particularly the reparations agreements, by the brilliant economist who served on the British delegation to the peace conference.

• Owen, Wilfred, *Collected Poems*, London, 1963. Moving evidence of the horror of life at the front by Britain's most talented war poet.

• Reed, John, *Ten Days That Shook the World*, New York, 1919. (Many editions.) A contemporary account by a sympathetic American journalist of the Bolshevik revolution.

• Remarque, Erich Maria, *All Quiet on the Western Front*, 1929. (Many editions.) A famous novel describing the war on the Western Front.

Chapter 28

THE WEST BETWEEN THE WARS

Democracy of the West today is the forerunner of Marxism, which would
be inconceivable without it. It is democracy alone which furnishes this
universal plague with the soil in which it spreads. In parliamentarianism,
its outward form of expression, democracy created a monstrosity of filth
and fire. . . .

—Adolf Hitler, *Mein Kampf*

A mong the claims made by the Allied Powers during the First
World War was that an Allied victory would make the world
"safe for democracy." The boast was grounded in a belief in
the inevitability of progress, fostered by a century of growing material
prosperity and by a habit of mind that found it all but impossible to
equate the events of history with something other than the "advance"
of civilization. The history of Europe in the 1920s and 1930s, however, would make it increasingly difficult for men and women to
believe in progress as they had, or to assume that war might prove of
ultimate benefit to mankind. These were decades of disillusionment
and desperation, a circumstance brought about not only by the war
itself but by the events that followed in the wake of war. Rather
than encourage the growth of democracy, those events were often
the direct cause of its decline and fall. A number of Western nations
remained democracies—Great Britain, France, and the United States
being the most notable cases—yet they nevertheless experienced the
same pressures and strains which in other countries resulted in the
demise of democracy altogether.

Decline of democracy

Although the reasons for the decline of democracy in the West varied according to particular national circumstances, its failure can be
attributed to several major causes. First, class conflict increased in many
countries during the interwar years. The real issue in most parts of
continental Europe was whether control of the government and economic system would continue in the possession of aristocracies,
industrialists, and financiers, or some combination of these elements.

Reasons for the decline

None of them were willing to surrender more than a fraction of their considerable power to the less privileged majorities which, at great sacrifice, had made major contributions to the war effort. The common people expected and had been promised that those contributions would be rewarded by greater attention to their political rights and economic needs. When they were ignored, they were naturally embittered, and hence prey to the blandishments of political extremists. Second, economic conditions worked against the establishment of stable democracies. The creation of new nations encouraged debilitating economic rivalries. War had disoriented the world's economy, leaving in its wake first inflation and then depression. Finally, nationalist sentiment encouraged discontent among minorities in the newly established states of central Europe. Countries weakened by conflicts between national minorities were an unlikely proving ground for democracy, a political system that functions best in an atmosphere of unified national purpose.

Rise of totalitarianism

The political history of the interwar years must be understood not only in terms of the decline of democracy, however, but also against the background of the rise of the totalitarian state. Totalitarianism, whatever it promised, preached the destruction of the political systems that had failed to grapple successfully with the problems of class conflict, economic chaos, and nationalism. Although there were significant differences between the communism of the Soviet Union under Joseph Stalin, the fascism of Italy under Benito Mussolini, and the National Socialism—or, as it was called, Nazism—of Germany under Adolph Hitler, all three systems can be defined as totalitarian.

Totalitarianism defined

These systems demanded the total subordination of individuals and classes to the greater good of the state as defined and directed by an all-powerful single political party. To this end, violent force, intimidation, and propaganda were employed to divert men and women from the pursuit of their individual interests, to deny them their freedom as citizens, and to compel them to labor on behalf of goals defined as useful to the nation. Churches, trade unions, even parliamentary government were either subverted or suppressed completely. The state, through the party, imposed its will on the total life of society.

Its ideology and appeal

Totalitarian governments framed their programs in ideology. In the case of Soviet Russia, the ideology was a nationalistic version of Marxist socialism. In the case of Italy and Germany, it was a peculiar concoction of nineteenth-century nationalism and socialism. These ideologies proclaimed the necessity of revolutionary change and encouraged belief in the ability of the party and its leader to effect that change. They thus appealed to those who saw themselves dispossessed by the system as it was, or as it had become, and who believed that nothing but desperate measures would suffice to bring society to rights. During the interwar years the ranks of those people in Europe were legion.

1. THE RISE OF TOTALITARIANISM IN COMMUNIST RUSSIA

Soon after the 1917 revolution in Russia, the country's desperate plight—a result of wartime devastation and governmental corruption and mismanagement—compelled the Bolshevik leaders to undertake a drastic program of authoritarian centralization. During this transformation, Lenin showed himself as capable a revolutionary administrator and politician as he had been a strategist. He commanded the respect and loyalty of his fellow Bolshevik ministers. His dedication to his own theory of revolution and his readiness to apply that theory with a ruthless disregard for human lives, if necessary, was combined with a willingness to heed the opinions of his close adherents. He welcomed free discussion during the decision-making process. Once a decision had been reached, however, discussion gave way to unquestioning implementation. Lenin won the confidence of the Russian people by speaking frankly to them of the dangers and difficulties inherent in a revolution as bold and all-consuming as theirs was. He was what he appeared to be: a selfless man, unwilling to claim special privileges for himself, wholly dedicated to the revolution which he had done so much to bring about. He cared nothing for luxury or personal glory, living an almost monklike existence in two rooms in the Kremlin, and dressing little better than an ordinary worker.

Lenin

Lenin's ablest and most prominent lieutenant was Leon Trotsky (1879–1940). Originally named Lev Bronstein, Trotsky was born of middle-class Jewish parents in the Ukraine. Before the revolution he had refused to identify himself with any particular faction, preferring to remain an independent Marxist. For his part in the revolutionary movement of 1905 he was exiled to Siberia; he escaped, and for some

Trotsky

Lenin Speaking to Crowds in Moscow. To the right of the platform, in uniform, is Trotsky.

years led a roving existence in various European capitals. He was expelled from Paris in 1916 for pacifist activity and took refuge in the United States. Upon learning of the overthrow of the tsar, he attempted to return to Russia. Captured by British agents at Halifax, Nova Scotia, he was eventually released through the intervention of Kerensky. He arrived in Russia in April 1917 and immediately began plotting the overthrow of the provisional government and later of Kerensky himself. He became minister of foreign affairs in the government headed by Lenin, and later, commissar for war.

The civil war

Scarcely had the Bolsheviks concluded the war with the Central Powers than they were confronted with a desperate civil war at home. Landlords and capitalists did not take kindly to the loss of their property. The result was a prolonged and bloody combat between the Reds, or Bolsheviks, and the Whites, including not only reactionary tsarists but also disaffected liberals, Social Revolutionaries, Mensheviks, and peasants. The Whites were assisted for a time by expeditionary forces of British, French, American, and Japanese troops—hoping to defeat the Bolsheviks in order to bring Russia back into the war against Germany—and later by the armies of the newly created republic of Poland.

See color map of the Soviet Union following page 992

Under the direction of Trotsky, who appealed to the Russian people both in the name of revolution and the fatherland, the Red army was mobilized to a degree that allowed it to withstand both the foreign invaders and the Russian insurgents. By 1922, the Bolsheviks had managed to stabilize their boundaries, although to do so they were forced to cede former Russian territory to the Finns, to the Baltic states of Latvia and Estonia, to Poland, and to Rumania. Internally, the Bolsheviks responded to the White counterrevolution by instituting a "terror" far more extensive than the repression that had earned that name during the French Revolution. A secret police force shot thousands as suspects or merely as hostages. The tsar and tsarina and

The Red Army, 1919. This scene near the southern front was the celebration of the victory over the counterrevolutionary forces.

their children were executed by local Bolsheviks in July 1918 as White forces advanced on the town of Ekaterinburg, where the family was held prisoner. That same year "enemies of the state" were hunted down in large numbers following the attempted assassination of Lenin. The terror abated when the regime had satisfied itself that it had destroyed its internal opposition.

The civil war was accompanied by an appalling economic breakdown. In 1920 total industrial production was only 13 percent of what it had been in 1913. To alleviate the shortage of goods, the government abolished the payment of wages and distributed supplies among urban workers in proportion to their need. All private trade was prohibited; everything produced by the peasants above what they required to subsist was requisitioned by the state. This system was an expedient to crush burgeois opposition to the revolutionary regime and to obtain as much food as possible for the army in the field. In 1921 it was superseded by the New Economic Policy (NEP), which Lenin described as "one step backward in order to take two steps forward." The NEP authorized private manufacturing and private trade on a small scale, reintroduced the payment of wages, and permitted peasants to sell their grain in the open market. In 1924 a constitution was adopted, replacing imperial Russia with the Union of Soviet Socialist Republics. The union represented an attempt to unite the various nationalities and territories that had constituted the old empire. Each separate republic was, in theory, granted certain autonomous rights. In fact, government remained centralized in the hands of a few leaders. Further, central authority was maintained by means of the one legal political party—the Communist party—whose Central Committee was the directing force behind both politics and government, and whose organizational apparatus reached out into all areas of the vast country.

The philosophy of Bolshevism, now known as communism, was developed primarily by Lenin during these years. It was proclaimed not as a new body of thought, but as a strict interpretation of Marx's writings. Nevertheless, from the beginning it departed at several important points from Marx's teachings. These changes were the necessary result of the fact that Marx had expected revolution to occur first in highly industrialized countries, whereas it had in fact broken out and succeeded in one of the least industrialized nations in Europe. Marx had assumed that a capitalist stage must prepare the way for socialism; Lenin denied that this was necessary, insisting rather that Russia could leap directly from a feudal to a socialist economy. In the second place, Lenin emphasized the revolutionary character of socialism much more than did its original founder. Marx did believe that in most cases revolution would be necessary, but he was inclined to deplore the fact rather than to welcome it. Finally, communism differed from Marxism in its conception of proletarian rule. When Marx spoke of the "dictatorship of the proletariat," he meant by this a dic-

Left: *Lenin's Casket Is Carried through the Streets of Moscow.* It was not known with certainty until 1956 that, prior to his death, Lenin had discredited Stalin. Right: *Lenin and Stalin.* Under Stalin this picture was used to show his close relationship with Lenin. In fact, the photograph has been doctored.

tatorship of the whole working class over the remnants of the bourgeoisie. Within the ranks of this class, democratic forms would prevail. Lenin, however, was persuaded by the desperate circumstances attendant upon the birth of the Soviet Union to proclaim the need for a dictatorship by the party elite, wielding supremacy not only over the bourgeoisie but over the bulk of the proletarians themselves.

The struggles between Trotsky and Stalin

The death of Lenin in January 1924 precipitated a struggle between two of his lieutenants to inherit his mantle of power. Outside of Russia it was generally assumed that Trotsky would succeed the fallen leader. But the fiery commander of the Red army had a formidable rival in the tough and mysterious Joseph Stalin (1879–1953). The son of a peasant shoemaker in the province of Georgia, Stalin received part of his education in a theological seminary. Expelled at the age of seventeen for "lack of religious vocation," he thereafter dedicated his career to revolutionary activity.

Stalin and the party

In 1917 Stalin assumed the secretary-generalship of the Communist party which, in the years that followed, became the heart of the government. Theoretically, Soviet Russia was ruled by a Central Executive Committee, which in turn represented local, provincial, and regional Councils of Workers and Peasants. Because the Central Executive did not remain in continuous session, however, power increasingly fell into the hands of that body responsible for day-to-day operations and decisions: the Council of the People's Commissars—that is, the various departmental ministers. These commissars were nominated by, and were themselves members of, the Communist party. In his position as the party's secretary-general, Stalin was able to control nominations to the Council of Commissars, and thus to fill the government with party members loyal to him. When the commissars picked Lenin's successor, they perceived Trotsky as brilliant but erratic; Stalin as predictable and safe.

The battle beween Stalin and Trotsky was not simply a struggle for personal power; fundamental issues of political policy were also involved. Trotsky maintained that socialism in Russia could never be entirely successful until capitalism was overthrown in surrounding countries. Therefore, he insisted upon a continuous crusade for world revolution. Stalin was willing to abandon the program of world revolution, for the time being, in order to concentrate on building socialism in Russia itself. His strategy for the immediate future was essentially nationalist. The outcome of the duel was a complete triumph for Stalin. In 1927 Trotsky was expelled from the Communist party, and two years later he was driven from the country. In 1940 he was murdered in Mexico City by Stalinist agents. Lenin did not hold either Stalin or Trotsky in lofty esteem. In a "testament" to the Council written shortly before his death, he criticized Trotsky for "far-reaching self-confidence" and for being too preoccupied with administrative detail. But he dealt far less gently with Stalin, condemning him as "too rough" and "capricious" and urging that the commissars remove him from his position at the head of the party.

Stalin, Trotsky, and world revolution

Once Stalin consolidated his power, he reinforced the role of the party as a state within a state, with its own bureaucrats—the *apparatchiki*—assuming ever-increasing influence in the administration of the country and in the determination of its fortunes. He insisted that Russia's first priority was economic well-being. His major reform was the introduction of the so-called Five-Year Plan, based on the conviction that the Soviet Union had to take drastic steps to industrialize and thereby achieve economic parity among the nations of the world. The plan instituted an elaborate system of priorities. It decreed how much of each major industrial and agricultural commodity the nation should produce, the wages workers should receive, and the prices that should be charged for goods sold at home and abroad. The first plan, instituted in 1928, was succeeded by others during the 1930s. In some areas goals were met, in a few they were exceeded, in some they fell short. One of the major results of the Five-Year Plans was the creation of an extensive state bureaucracy, charged with the task of organization and supervision at all levels.

The party and the state: Five-Year Plan

Included in the first plan was a program for agricultural collectivization. The scheme was designed to bring rural farms together into larger units of several thousand acres, under the communal proprietorship of peasants. Only with this sort of reorganization, Russia's rulers declared, could the new and expensive processes of mechanization be introduced, and the country's agricultural yield thereby increased. Not surprisingly, the argument failed to win the support of the more

Collectivization

СО ЗНАМЕНЕМ ЛЕНИНА ПОБЕДИЛИ МЫ В БОЯХ ЗА ОКТЯБРЬСКУЮ РЕВОЛЮЦИЮ.
СО ЗНАМЕНЕМ ЛЕНИНА ДОБИЛИСЬ МЫ РЕШАЮЩИХ УСПЕХОВ В БОРЬБЕ ЗА ПОБЕДУ
СОЦИАЛИСТИЧЕСКОГО СТРОИТЕЛЬСТВА.
С ЭТИМ ЖЕ ЗНАМЕНЕМ ПОБЕДИМ В ПРОЛЕТАРСКОЙ РЕВОЛЮЦИИ ВО ВСЕМ МИРЕ.
(Сталин. Политический отчет ЦК. XVI съезду ВКП(б).)

"The Five-Year Plan in Four Years." Stalin faces down reactionary capitalist enemies in this Soviet propaganda poster of the 1930s.

prosperous farmers—the kulaks—who had been allowed to retain ownership of their land. Their opposition led to another terror, made all the more deadly by a famine which occurred in southeastern Russia in 1932. The kulaks were liquidated, either killed or transported to distant labor camps: the rural bourgeoisie was eliminated, to be replaced by a rural proletariat. Collectivization was an accomplished fact by 1939. To a vast number of Russians it represented a revolution far more immediate than that of 1917. Twenty million people were moved off the land, which, once it had been reorganized into larger units, and production had been mechanized, required fewer laborers. They were sent to cities, where most went to work in factories. Although agricultural output did not increase during the early years of collectivization, the scheme was nevertheless of benefit to the government. By controlling production, the central bureaucracy was able to regulate the distribution of agricultural products, allocating them for export, where necessary, to pay for the importation of much-needed industrial machinery.

The Third International

As part of Stalin's campaign to put the interests of Russia ahead of those of international communism, the Bolshevik regime adopted a new and more conservative foreign policy during the 1930s. Its international goals contradicted the militant socialist internationalism of the 1920s. Lenin had supported revolutionary leftist movements in Europe, sending money and lending moral support to the radical German Marxists Karl Liebknecht and Rosa Luxemburg in 1919, and to the short-lived Soviet regime of the Bolshevik Béla Kun in Hungary in the same year. Shortly thereafter, the Third International—later called the Comintern—was formed. It declared its allegiance to international communism; its policy was to oppose cooperation or collaboration with the capitalist governments of the West and to work for their overthrow.

With Stalin's suppression of the internationalism advocated by Lenin and Trotsky, however, came a change in tactics and the revival of an interest in playing the game of power politics. The Russian army was more than doubled in size and was reorganized in accordance with the western European model. Patriotism, which strict Marxists despised as a form of capitalist propaganda, was exalted into a Soviet virtue, a symptom of totalitarianism. When Germany once again appeared to threaten Russian security, as it did in the 1930s, the Soviet leadership looked abroad for allies. Along with their efforts to build up a great army and to make their own country self-sufficient, they adopted a policy of cooperation with the western European powers. In 1934 they entered the League of Nations, and in 1934 they ratified a military alliance with France.

In June 1936, the Soviets adopted a new constitution, some of whose provisions suggested the possibility of a more liberal regime. Power continued to reside in a governing body (the Presidium) and an administrative agency (the Council of Ministers), both of which were chosen by a two-chamber parliament, the Supreme Soviet, which was elected, in turn, by universal suffrage. This pyramidal structure was not unlike that which it superseded and which, because of the dominant position of the Communist party, had resulted in the concentration of power in the person of Stalin. Now, however, the constitution provided citizens with a bill of rights guaranteeing freedom of speech, of assembly, and of religion. In addition, they were promised the right to employment, the right to leisure, and the right to maintenance at the expense of the state in case of old age or disability.

These guarantees meant very little, however, so long as all aspects of life in the Soviet Union continued to be dominated by the Communist party, whose membership of about 1 million in 1930 was but a small fraction of the total population of 150 million. That the new "bill of rights" was a sham was quickly proved by a series of purges which began shortly after the constitution was adopted. In August 1936, the first of several "show trials" occurred, at which persons alleged to be "Trotskyites" and spies were publicly condemned and either imprisoned, executed, or exiled to Siberia. Although the accused for the most part confessed to their "crimes," those confessions were obtained by physical and psychological torture.

Stalin's victims were people at all levels who had opposed his personal rule, men such as Nikolai Bukharin, editor of the newspaper *Izvestia,* who had spoken out against the elimination of the kulaks; Karl Radek, a leading political theorist; and a number of "old" Bolsheviks, who had been unwilling to acquiesce in Stalin's refusal to debate policy, who had opposed his increasingly nationalistic foreign policy, or who had hoped that revolution did not mean the complete suppression of personal liberty. The purges were the result of Stalin's own psychological instability and pathological distrust. They were as well, however, the logical result of totalitarianism's inability to tolerate any dissent whatsoever. Whatever their cause, the purges took a toll of almost nine million imprisoned, banished, or killed. By ridding the country of his opposition Stalin forestalled further revolution—not an unlikely possibility, given discontent with his policies—and solidified his position as dictator of Russia.

Revolutionary accomplishments

The results of the Soviet revolution were profound. No other regime in the history of western Europe had ever attempted to reorder completely the politics, economy, and society of a vast nation as the Russians had in the short space of twenty years. By 1939 private manufacturing and trade had been almost entirely abolished. Factories, mines, railroads, and public utilities were exclusively owned by the state. Stores were either government enterprises or cooperatives in which consumers owned shares. Agriculture had been almost completely socialized. At the same time, the nation had been industrialized. By 1932 over 70 percent of Russia's national product was industrial in origin. In the area of social reform, illiteracy was reduced from at least 50 percent to about 20 percent, and higher education was made available to increasingly large numbers. Government assistance for working mothers and free hospitalization did a great deal to raise the national standard of health.

The price of revolution

But, as we have seen, those achievements were purchased at a very high price. In addition to the liquidation of millions of kulaks and political dissidents and the internment of millions of others in slave-labor camps, the Russian people were subjected to an unrelenting campaign of indoctrination that encompassed every aspect of their lives. The Soviet leadership set out to shatter those prevailing belief systems which threatened to impede the achievement of its goals. Subtle forms of persecution were implemented to discourage religious orthodoxy while the nation's youth were inculcated with the new Soviet ideals of steadfast loyalty to the Soviet state and unquestioning obedience to the Communist party. Over time, experiments in the arts and literature, which had been promoted during the early years of the revolution under Lenin, gave way to the culture of totalitarian bureaucracy. Education became a tool of the revolution, much as violence and intimidation had. Control of the minds of the populace was regarded as a prerequisite to building a new society in which individual interests would be sacrificed to those of the state. After two decades of revolutionary change, the Stalinist regime had fastened upon the Russian people a tyranny as heavy as any imposed by the tsars.

2. THE EMERGENCE OF TOTALITARIAN FASCISM IN ITALY

That Italy turned to totalitarianism may at first seem surprising, in view of the fact that the Italians emerged as victors after the First World War. Yet Italy's difficulties were rooted in longstanding problems that the war had done little to resolve. Italy continued to be divided into two sharply contrasting halves: a relatively prosperous industrialized north, and a wretchedly poor agrarian south. In addition to the problems the country faced as a result of that unhealthy economic split, it was also the victim of an unrequited imperialist impulse which had existed since the 1890s. Its unsuccessful attempts to establish itself as a power in North Africa had left the country with a sense of frustration and humiliation. Before the war, the ruling class was held in public contempt by a younger generation anxious to cleanse the nation of rulers widely perceived to be at once cynical and corrupt, vaccilating and defeatist.

Italy's long-term problems

But the establishment of a dictatorship in Italy would never have been possible without the demoralizing and humiliating effects of the First World War. The chief business of the Italian armies had been to keep the Austrians occupied on the Southern Front while the British, French, and Americans hammered Germany into submission along the battle lines in the west. To accomplish this assignment, Italy had mobilized more than 5,500,000 men; of these nearly 700,000 were killed. The direct financial cost of Italian participation in the struggle was over $15 billion. These sacrifices were no greater than those made by the British and the French; but Italy was a poor country. Moreover, in the division of the spoils after the fighting, the Italians got less than they expected. While Italy did receive most of the Austrian territories promised in the secret treaties, the Italians maintained that these were inadequate rewards for their sacrifices and for their valuable contribution to an Entente victory. At first the nationalists vented their spleen for the "humiliation of Versailles" upon President Wilson, but after a short time they returned to castigating their own rulers. They alleged Premier Orlando had been so cravenly weak and inept that he and those who governed with him had allowed their country to be cheated of its just deserts.

*The demoralizing and
humiliating effects of the
war*

The war contributed to the revolutionary mood in a multitude of other ways. It resulted in inflation of the currency, with consequent high prices, speculation, and profiteering. Normally wages would have risen also, but the postwar labor market was glutted by the return to civilian life of millions of soldiers. Furthermore, business was demoralized, owing to extensive and frequent strikes and to the closing of foreign markets. In the minds of the upper and middle classes the most ominous consequence of the war was the growth of socialism. As

*Inflation, radicalism, and
economic chaos*

hardship and chaos increased, the Italian socialists embraced a philosophy akin to Bolshevism. They voted as a party to join the Third International. In the elections of November 1919, they won about a third of the seats in the Chamber of Deputies. During the following winter socialist workers took over about a hundred factories and attempted to run them for the benefit of the workers. Radicalism also spread through rural areas, where so-called Red Leagues organized to break up large estates and to force landlords to reduce their rents. Two large political parties with mass appeal, the Socialists and the Catholic People's party, drained strength from other parties of the Center and moderate Left. Neither preached revolution; yet both urged far-reaching social and economic reforms. Industrialists and landowners were badly frightened and were therefore ready to accept totalitarianism as a less dangerous form of radicalism that might save at least part of their property from confiscation.

The career of Mussolini

How much the Fascist movement depended for its success upon the leadership of Benito Mussolini is difficult to say. Mussolini was born in 1883, the son of a socialist blacksmith. His mother was a schoolteacher, and in deference to her wishes he eventually became a teacher. But he was restless and dissatisfied, soon leaving Italy for further study in Switzerland. Here he gave part of his time to his books and the rest to writing articles for socialist newspapers. He was eventually expelled from the country for fomenting strikes. Returning to Italy, he became a journalist, and eventually editor of *Avanti,* the leading socialist daily. His ideas in the years before the war were a contradictory mixture of radicalisms. He professed to be a Marxist socialist, but he mingled his socialism with doctrines of corporatism, adapted from the French syndicalists.

Mussolini's contradictory ideas

Mussolini in fact believed in no particular set of doctrines. No man with a definite philosophy could have reversed himself so often. When war broke out in August 1914, Mussolini insisted that Italy should remain neutral. He had scarcely adopted this position when he began urging participation on the Entente side. Deprived of his position as editor of *Avanti,* he founded a new paper, *Il Popolo d'Italia,* and dedicated its columns to arousing enthusiasm for war. He regarded the decision of the government the following spring to go in on the side of the Entente allies as a personal victory.

The evolution of fascism

The word *fascism* derives from the Latin *fasces,* the ax surrounded by a bundle of sticks representing the authority of the Roman state; the Italian *fascio* means group or band. *Fasci* were organized as early as October 1914, as units of agitation to drive Italy into the war. Their members were young idealists, fanatical nationalists, and frustrated white-collar workers. The original platform of the Fascist party was drafted by Mussolini in 1919. It was a surprisingly radical document, which demanded universal suffrage, abolition of the conservative Senate, the establishment by law of an eight-hour day, a heavy capital levy, a heavy tax on inheritances, confiscation of 85 percent of war profits, acceptance of the League of Nations, and "opposition to all imperialisms." This platform was accepted more or less officially by the movement until May 1920, when it was supplanted by another of a more conservative character. Indeed, the new program omitted all reference to economic reform. On neither of these platforms did the fascists achieve much political success.

The fascists made up for their initial lack of numbers by disciplined aggressiveness and strong determination. As the old regime crumbled, they prepared to take over the government. In September 1922, Mussolini began to talk openly of revolution. On October 28 an army of about 50,000 fascist militia, in blackshirted uniforms, marched into Rome and occupied the capital. The premier resigned, and the following day the king, Victor Emmanuel III, invited Mussolini to form a cabinet. Without firing a shot the blackshirts had gained control of the Italian government. The explanation of their success is to be found not in the strength of fascism, but in the chaos created by the war and in the weakness and irresolution of the old ruling classes. By the end of the next three years Mussolini's revolution was virtually complete.

The march on Rome

Italian fascism embodied a variety of doctrines that were an expression of its totalitarian nature:

(1) Statism. The state was declared to incorporate every interest and every loyalty of its members. There was to be "nothing above the state, nothing outside the state, nothing against the state."

Major doctrines of fascism

(2) Nationalism. Nationhood was the highest form of society. It had a life and a soul of its own apart from the lives and souls of the individuals who composed it. Yet there could be no real harmony of

Left: *Mussolini Reviews a Fascist Youth Parade.* Totalitarianism demanded the capture of youthful minds. Right: *Mussolini Addressing a Crowd of his Followers from the Balcony of the Palazzo Venezia in Rome.*

interests between two or more distinct nations. Hence internationalism was a perversion of human progress.

(3) Militarism. Strife was the origin of all things. Nations which did not expand would eventually wither and die. War exalted and ennobled man and regenerated sluggish and decadent peoples.

Declaring his allegiance to these principles, Mussolini began to rebuild Italy in accordance with them. He abolished the cabinet system and all but extinguished the powers of the Parliament. In characteristic totalitarian fashion, he made the Fascist party an integral part of the Italian constitution. The king was compelled to select a prime minister from a list compiled by the party's Great Council. Voters, as well, were left with no real choice; they were forced to select their candidates from lists prepared by the party. Within a few years, there were no other political parties left in Italy. Mussolini assumed the dual position of prime minister and party leader (*duce*). A potent and effective mechanism of political discipline was the party's militia, which Mussolini used to eliminate his enemies by violent means. Police supervision, censorship of the press and of academic life—the hallmarks of totalitarian regimes—were soon fastened upon the Italian people by the party.

Mussolini's fascist state

Mussolini reorganized the economy while preaching the end of class conflict as fascist doctrine. He secured worker support by instituting massive public works and building projects, along with state-sponsored programs of library-building, vacations, and social security. He won further popular acclaim when, in 1929, he settled Italy's sixty-year-old conflict with the Roman Catholic Church by a treaty granting independence to the papal residence in the Vatican City and establishing Roman Catholicism as the official religion of the nation's schools.

His bid for worker support

At the same time that Mussolini was attempting to pacify the Italian working class, he was pulling the teeth of the country's labor movement. The Italian economy was placed under the management of twenty-two corporations, each responsible for a major industrial enterprise. In each corporation were representatives of trade unions, whose members were organized by the Fascist party, the employers, and the government. Together, the members of these corporations were given the task of determining working conditions, wages, and prices. In fact, however, the decisions of these bodies were closely managed by the government and favored the position of management.

Corporatism

Although Mussolini's fascism was totalitarian in nature, it did not revolutionize government, economy, and society as did Soviet communism. Party officers exercised a degree of political supervision over bureaucrats, yet did not infiltrate the bureaucracy in significant numbers. Party and state were kept apart in Italy as they were not in the Soviet Union. Mussolini remained on friendly terms with the wealthy industrialists and bankers who had assisted his rise to power, insuring that whatever he might proclaim about the distinctions between fascism

Differences between Italian and Soviet totalitarianism

and capitalism, the economy of Italy would remain dependent upon private enterprise. Further evidence of Mussolini's conservatism was his concordat with the Church—this despite his earlier declarations of allegiance to atheism.

The Italian dictator enjoyed boasting that fascism had pulled the country back from economic chaos. The economy did improve some-what—along with the economies of other European countries—in the late 1920s, yet fascism did little to lessen Italy's plight during the years of worldwide depression which occurred in the 1930s. Although he managed to make his country appear more efficient—his admirers often bragged that he had at last "made the trains run on time"—Mussolini failed to solve its major problems, particularly those of the peasantry, whose standard of living remained desperately low. Mussolini's fascism was little more than illusion. It is a measure of the Italians' disgust with their past leaders that they were so ready to be taken in by him.

3. THE RISE OF NAZI GERMANY

Germany succumbed to totalitarianism later than Italy. For a brief period following the First World War, events seemed to be moving the country to the Left. Most of the leading politicians in the imme-diate post-armistice government were socialists, members of the Social Democratic party. Their reformist policies, which had seemed radical enough to many prior to the war, now appeared too mild to a group of extreme Marxists who had been encouraged by the revolution in Russia. Calling themselves Spartacists,[1] and led by the able Rosa Luxemburg and Karl Liebknecht, they attempted an uprising in 1919 designed to bring the proletarian revolution to Germany. Despite assistance from the Russian Bolsheviks, the rebellion was crushed; Liebknecht and Luxemburg were killed by soldiers while being taken to prison. In engineering the Spartacists' defeat, the German government had recourse to private vigilante groups headed by disillusioned former army officers, men whose true sympathies lay no more with democratic socialism than with Russian communism, and whose dis-content would soon focus on the government they had helped to sal-vage.

With the Spartacist revolt only just behind them, the leaders of a co-alition of socialists, Catholic centrists, and liberal democrats in 1919 drafted a constitution for the new German republic reflecting a gener-ally progressive political and social philosophy. It provided for uni-versal suffrage, for women as well as men; the cabinet system of gov-ernment; and for a bill of rights, guaranteeing not only civil liberties but the right of the citizen to employment, to an education, and to

[1] After the Roman, Spartacus, who led a slave revolt.

Left: *Karl Liebknecht and Rosa Luxemburg.* Right: *The German Election of 1919.* Here women line up to vote for the first time.

protection against the hazards of an industrial society. But the republic established under this constitution was beset with troubles from the start. Reactionaries and other extremists plotted against it. Moreover, the German people had had little experience with democratic government. The Weimar Republic (named for the city where its constitution was drafted) did not spring from the desires of a majority of the nation. It was born of change forced upon Germany in its hour of defeat. Its instability made it a likely victim of the forces it was desperately attempting to tame.

Various factors led to the eventual triumph of German totalitarianism. First was the sense of humiliation arising from defeat in the war.

Causes of German totalitarianism: (1) *defeat in war*

Between 1871 and 1914 Germany had risen to lofty heights of political and cultural prestige. German universities, science, philosophy, and music were known and admired all over the world. The country had likewise attained a remarkable prosperity, by 1914 surpassing Britain and the United States in several fields of industrial production. Then came the defeat of 1918, with Germany left to the mercy of its powerful enemies. It was too much for the German people to understand. They found it difficult to believe that their invincible armies had really been worsted in battle. Quickly the legend grew that the nation had been "stabbed in the back" by socialists and Jews in the government. Though there was no truth in this charge, it helped to salve the wounded pride of German patriots. Those in search of a scapegoat also blamed the laxity and irresponsibility that appeared to distinguish the republican regime. It was alleged that Berlin had displaced Paris as the most frivolous and decadent city of Europe. What the country seemed to need was authoritative leadership to spearhead a campaign to regain the world's respect.

The sense of humiliation was increased by two of the provisions imposed on the Germans in the Versailles treaty. First, Germany was compelled to reduce its army to 100,000 men, a requirement that produced bitter discontent among the politically powerful corps of officers that remained at the head of its ranks. Second, the enormous burden of reparations payments continued to arouse the anger of the Germans. Opponents of the reparations settlement urged an obstructionist policy of nonpayment, arguing that the sum of $33 billion demanded would doom the German economy for the foreseeable future. German politicians of all persuasions agreed that the sum was impossibly large. Yet Weimar's foreign minister in the early 1920s, Walter Rathenau, opposed the obstructionists, and attempted to reach a compromise with the former Allied powers. Rathenau's assassination in 1922, by a secret organization of obstructionist army officers, produced a reaction that led to the German government's refusal to make further payments. The result was French occupation of the Ruhr valley in early 1923, in a fruitless attempt to compel German miners there to produce for France. The ensuing stalemate, which lasted for several months, was ended by the German chancellor, Gustav Stresemann, who recognized the futility of obstructionist tactics. His success in persuading the Germans to accept his point of view was aided by an international agreement to renegotiate reparations under the guidance of a committee of experts headed by the American Charles G. Dawes. Crisis was temporarily averted, but the psychological wounds caused by the reparations controversy did not heal.

Another major reason for totalitarianism's appeal in Germany was the inflation the country suffered in the 1920s. The German government increased the supply of money in the early 1920s in a desperate effort to finance social welfare programs in the face of rising unemployment and to buy gold with which to make reparations payments. The result was a period of wild inflation, particularly demoralizing to the middle class. Salaries could not keep up with the vast increase in the cost of living. Farmers were angered by the collapse of agricultural prices and by their burden of debts and taxes. University students saw little prospect of gaining a place in already overcrowded professions. Those who existed on fixed incomes—pensioners, stockholders—saw their security vanish. As they lost their faith in the ability of the government to come to their aid, these men and women began, as well, to lose whatever faith they may have had in the republic. The middle class, traumatized by inflation, continued its search for a government that promised attention to its needs and sympathy with its problems. That search intensified with the advent of the Great Depression of 1929. As we shall see, the depression was a major

Inflation and the German Mark. As German inflation gained momentum and the value of the mark plummeted, every imaginable kind of container was pressed into service to transport money from place to place.

*Weimar's later
years*

*Parties
polarized*

*The early career of Hitler;
the early days of the Nazi
party*

disaster for most of the world. In few countries, however, were its effects more keenly felt than in Germany. Six million workers were unemployed. Once again the middle class saw its savings vanish.

For a brief period in the late 1920s, however, it had appeared that the German economy, and the Weimar Republic with it, might recover. Borrowed money meant that the country was able to make its reparations payments, scaled down in accordance with the Dawes Committee recommendations, and to earn money abroad with cheaply priced exports. Building programs, sponsored by socialist municipal governments in large cities such as Frankfurt, Düsseldorf, and Berlin—schools, hospitals, and low-cost worker housing—suggested that the country was both politically and economically healthier than it actually was. In fact the Dawes Plan, by stressing the need for immediate increases in production, ensured that the economy would remain in the hands of the country's leading industrialists whose tendency to overcapitalize their enterprises impaired their ability to cut costs once the Depression struck. These were very conservative men, some of whom sympathized with the restoration of a more authoritarian form of government than Weimar represented. They were allied with equally conservative landowners, bound together by their mutual desire for a protective economic policy that would stimulate the sale of domestically produced goods and foodstuffs. These conservative forces were augmented by the army and civil service, staffed with men opposed to the traditions of parliamentary democracy and international cooperation embodied in the republic.

By the end of the decade, party politics had polarized much as they had in Italy. The moderate parties attracted diminishing support while candidates for the Communist party on the Left and the monarchist German People's party on the Right were enjoying increased success. In 1932 discontent with the republic manifested itself in the national elections, which resulted in the continued presidency of the war hero Marshall von Hindenburg. What was significant, however, was not Hindenburg's return to power, but the fact that the Communists polled about five million votes, and that the candidate of the radical Right, Adolph Hitler, received over eleven million votes, more than one-third of those cast. The Weimar Republic was doomed. And Hitler was its logical nemesis.

Hitler was born in 1889, the son of a petty customs official in the Austrian civil service. Hitler's early life was unhappy and maladjusted. Rebellious and undisciplined from childhood, he seems always to have been burdened with a sense of frustration. He was a failure in school, decided that he would become an artist, and went to Vienna in 1909, hoping to enter the Academy. But he failed the required examinations. After squandering not one, but two good-sized inheritances, he eked out a dismal existence as a casual laborer and a painter of watercolors during his last eighteen months in Vienna. Meanwhile he developed violent political prejudices. He became an ardent admirer of certain vociferously anti-Semitic politicians in Vienna; and since he associated Judaism with Marxism, he learned to hate that philosophy as well. When war broke out, Hitler was living in Munich. Though an Austrian citizen, he immediately enlisted in the German army. Following the war, he joined with other disaffected Germans to denounce the Weimar Republic, choosing as the vehicle to express his alienation the newly formed National Socialist Workers' Party.[2] Originally a party of the Left, addressing itself primarily to working-class discontents, the Nazis under Hitler's direction in the mid-twenties broadened their appeal to attract disaffected members of the middle class as well. Nazism's doctrines derived in large part from a rambling treatise by Hitler entitled *Mein Kampf* (My Struggle), which he wrote while in prison following an attempt by the Nazis' private army to stage a "putsch," or sudden overthrow of the government, in Munich in 1923. In *Mein Kampf,* Hitler expressed his hatred of Jews and communists, his sense of Germany's betrayal by its enemies, and his belief that only with strong leadership could the country regain its rightful place within the European concert of nations.

Hitler's message appealed to an ever-growing number of his disillusioned and economically threatened countrymen and women. In the election of 1928 the Nazis won 12 seats in the Reichstag. In 1930 they won 107 seats, their popular vote increasing from 800,000 to 6,500,000. During the summer of 1932 the parliamentary system broke down. No chancellor could retain a majority in the Reichstag; the Nazis declined to support any cabinet not headed by Hitler, and the communists refused to collaborate with the socialists. In January 1933, a group of reactionaries prevailed upon President Hindenburg to designate Hitler as chancellor, in the mistaken belief that they could control him. It was arranged that there should be only three Nazis in the cabinet, and that Franz von Papen, a Catholic aristocrat, should hold the position of vice-chancellor. The sponsors of this plan failed to appreciate the tremendous popularity of the Nazi movement, however. Hitler was not slow to make the most of his new opportunity. He persuaded Hindenburg to dissolve the Reichstag and to order a new election on March 5. When the new Reichstag assembled, it voted to confer upon Hitler practically unlimited powers. Soon afterward the flag of the Weimar Republic was lowered and replaced by the swastika banner of the National Socialists. The new Germany was proclaimed to be the Third Reich, the successor of the Hohenstaufen Empire of the Middle Ages and of the Hohenzollern Empire of the kaisers.

During the next few months, other sweeping changes converted Germany from Bismark's federalized state into a highly centralized totalitarian regime. As both chancellor and leader of the Nazi party, Hitler was in a unique position to put the powers of the state to the

One Step Away from Power. President Hindenburg followed by Hitler.

An Anti-Nazi Poster Employed by the Social Democrats in 1932

[2] The name of the party was soon abbreviated in popular usage to Nazi.

Nazi rule

purposes of the party. To this end, all other political parties were declared illegal. Nazi party luminaries were appointed heads of various government departments, and party *gauleiters,* or regional directors, assumed administrative responsibility throughout the country. Hitler made use of paramilitary Nazi "storm troopers" (the S.A.) to maintain discipline within the party and to impose order on the populace through calculated intimidation and violence. Not even the S.A. itself was immune to the imperatives of totalitarian terror: when the aspirations of the S.A. leadership to supplant the established army hierarchy threatened to undermine Hitler's support within the military at a critical moment, he unleashed a bloody purge in which more than a thousand high-ranking S.A. officials were summarily executed. Hitler and his associates would brook no interference with their plans to achieve absolute power. During the late 1930s, a second paramilitary organization, the *Schutzstaffel* (bodyguard) or S.S. became the most dreaded arm of Nazi oppression and terror. Headed by the fanatical Heinrich Himmler, who answered to Hitler himself, the S.S. exercised sovereign power over the lives of all Germans, arresting, detaining, imprisoning, and murdering any who appeared to stand in the path of Nazi domination.

Nazi ideology and ruralism

Although Germany was one of the most highly industrialized countries in the world, National Socialist ideology had a peculiar peasant flavor. The key to Nazi theory was contained in the phrase *Blut und Boden* (blood and soil). The word *soil* reflected not only a deep reverence for the homeland but an abiding affection for the peasants, who were said to embody the finest qualities of the German race. This high

The Nazi Party Congress in Nuremburg, 1934. The Nazis were masters of the use of humanity *en masse* as propaganda. Hitler stands at attention in the center.

Nazism and the Rural Myth. Left and center: During the 1930s the Nazi artist W. Willrich painted sober, healthy peasant-types, the ideal Hitler professed to admire and to cultivate. Right: To stress the rural strength of Aryan Germany, Hitler appeared in lederhosen in the 1920s.

regard for country folk came partly, no doubt, from the fact that they had the highest birth rate of the nation's citizens and therefore were most valuable for military reasons. It was explainable also by the reaction of the Nazi leaders against everything that the city stood for—not only intellectualism and radicalism but high finance and the complicated problems of industrial society.

Despite these sentiments, however, the Nazis did little to restructure the economy of Germany. Although they came to power promising to tax chain stores heavily so as to benefit the small shopkeeper, they succumbed to pressure from bankers to mitigate those plans. Indeed, they encouraged heavy industry as part of their program of rearmament, forming what amounted to partnerships with such giants as I. G. Farben, the chemical concern, which worked closely with the government on the development of synthetic fuels. Like other Western nations, the Germans battled unemployment with large state-financed construction projects: highways, public housing, and reforestation. Late in the decade, rearmament and a substantial increase in the size of the military establishment all but ended the German unemployment problem—much as the same policies and programs were ending it elsewhere.

Germany's social structure remained relatively untouched by Nazi

Rearmament and pro-industrial economic policy

Social structure

rule. Government policy encouraged women to withdraw from the labor force, both to ease unemployment and to conform to Nazi notions of a woman's proper role. "Can woman," one propagandist asked, "conceive of anything more beautiful than to sit with her husband in her cozy home and listen inwardly to the loom of time weaving the weft and warp of motherhood . . .?" Like Mussolini, Hitler moved to abolish class conflict by robbing working-class institutions of their power. He outlawed trade unions and strikes, froze wages, and organized workers and employers into a National Labor Front, while at the same time increasing workers' welfare benefits. Class distinctions were to some degree blurred by the regime's insistence on infusing a new national "spirit" into the entire society. Organizations like the Hitler Youth, a sinister variant on the Boy Scout movement, and National Labor Service, which drafted students and others for a term to work on various state-sponsored building and reclamation projects, cut across, but did not abolish, class lines.

Anti-Semitism in nineteenth-century Europe

For the National Socialists, the great social dividing line was race. In this Nazism differed from other forms of totalitarianism, particularly in its single-minded persecution of the Jews. Anti-Semitism is a centuries-old phenomenon. It had manifested itself in nineteenth-century Europe: in the Russian pogroms; in the Dreyfus affair in France; and in the politics of Germany, where in 1893 sixteen avowed anti-Semites were elected to the Reichstag, and the Conservative Party made anti-Semitism part of its official program. Jews were a threat to those who feared urbanization and reform. The majority of Jews lived in cities, where they had advanced themselves in business and finance. They were in the forefront of scientific, cultural, and political innovation. Sigmund Freud was a Jew, as, of course, was Karl Marx. By attacking Jews, Anti-Semites could as well attack the modern institutions which they despised and which they associated with a "conspiracy" to deprive civilization of its reassuring base in tradition and authority. They perverted evolutionary theory to suit their arguments. Jews were declared "outsiders," without roots in any particular national culture, and therefore destructive of the racial "purity" necessary for the survival of the race. "The Jews are our national misfortune," the German historian Heinrich von Treitschke wrote in 1879. By that he meant that they were an alien force, subversive to the future of a triumphant German reich.

Nazi persecution of the Jews

Hitler was a fanatical believer in the anti-Semitic dogmas of the Right. The Nazis argued that the so-called Aryan race, which was supposed to include the Nordics as its most perfect specimens, was the only one ever to have made any notable contributions to human progress. They contended further that the accomplishments and mental qualities of a people were determined by blood. Thus the achievements of the Jew forever remained Jewish, no matter how long he or she might live in a Western country. It followed that no Jewish science or Jewish literature or Jewish music could ever truly represent the

German nation. A series of laws passed in 1935 deprived Jews and people of Jewish blood of their German citizenship, and prohibited marriage between Jews and other Germans. Eventually, millions of Jews were rounded up, tortured, and murdered in concentration camps. Other representatives of "imperfect" racial and social groups—homosexuals, gypsies, and anti-Nazi intellectuals—met a similar fate. The extremism of Hitler's anti-Semitic campaigns underscores the fact that National Socialism was more fanatical than Italian fascism. It was a new religion, not only in its dogmatism and its ritual, but in its fierce intolerance and its zeal for expansion.

If Nazism was a form of perverted religion, Hitler was its high priest. His appeal was based in part on his ability to give the German people what they wanted: jobs for workers, a productive economy for industrialists, a bulwark against communism for the still-influential Junker class. But more important, he preached what the German people wished to hear. His power lay not so much in the programs he championed, many of which were ill-thought out or contradictory, but in his talent for responding to the sentiments of his fellow-Germans, and for turning those sentiments into holy writ. As one of his early followers remarked: "Hitler responds to the vibrations of the human heart with the delicacy of a seismograph. . . . His words go like an arrow to their target; he touches each private wound on the raw, liberating the mass unconscious, expressing its innermost aspirations, telling it what it most wants to hear." That so many wanted most to listen to the poisonous dogmas of Adolph Hitler is a depressing commentary on the state of the Western world in the 1930s.

The power of Adolph Hitler

The significance of German and Italian totalitarianism remains a subject of controversy among students of modern history. Some argue that it reflected the enthronement of force by capitalists in an effort to save their dying system from destruction. And it is true that the success of both movements in gaining control of the government depended on support from great landowners and captains of industry. Others explain German and Italian totalitarianism as a reaction of debtors against creditors, of farmers against bankers and manufacturers, and of small businessmen against high finance and monopolistic practices. Still others interpret it as a reaction to communist threat, a reversion to primitivism, a result of the despair of the masses, a protest against the weaknesses of democracy, or a supreme manifestation of nationalism. Undoubtedly it was all of these things combined. One further argument holds that fascism and Nazism were extreme expressions of tendencies prevalent in all industrialized countries. If official policies in most Western countries in the 1930s took on more and more of an authoritarian semblance—a tightly controlled economy, limitation of production to maintain prices, and expansion of armaments to promote prosperity—it was because nearly all nations in that period were beset with similar problems and, in varying degrees, frightened of their implications.

The significance of German and Italian totalitarianism

4. THE DEMOCRACIES BETWEEN THE WARS

Class conflict in France

The histories of the three major Western democracies—Great Britain, France, and the United States—run roughly parallel during the years after the First World War. In all three countries there was an attempt by governments to trust to policies and assumptions that had prevailed before the war. The French, not surprisingly, continued to fear Germany and to take whatever steps they could to keep their traditional enemy as weak as possible. Under the leadership of the moderate conservative, Raymond Poincaré, who held office from 1922 to 1924, and again from 1926 to 1929, the French pursued a policy of deflation, which attempted to keep the price of manufactured goods low, by restraining wages. This policy pleased businessmen, but was hard on the working class. Edouard Herriot, a Radical Socialist who served as premier from 1924 to 1926 was, despite his party's name, a spokesman for the small businessman, farmer, and lower middle class. Herriot declared himself in favor of social reform, but refused to raise taxes in order to pay for it. Class conflict lay close to the surface of French national affairs throughout the 1920s. While industries prospered, employers rejected trade unionists' demands to bargain collectively. A period of major strikes immediately after the war was followed by a sharp decline in union activity. Workers remained dissatisfied, even after the government passed a modified social insurance program in 1930, insuring against sickness, old age, and death.

Britain's economic difficulties

Class conflict flared in Britain as well. Anxious to regain its now irretrievably lost position as the major industrial and financial power in the world, Britain, like France, pursued a policy of deflation, designed to lower the price of manufactured goods and thus make them more attractive on the world market. The result was a reduction in wages which undermined the standard of living of many British workers. Their resentment helped to elect a Labour party government in 1924

Labor Troubles in Britain. Mounted police escorting delivery wagons through a mob of angry strikers during the general strike of 1926.

Panel (3), Wassily Kandinsky (1866–1944). The Expressionist painters carried their explorations of the psychological properties of color and line to the point where subject matter was deemed unnecessary and even undesirable. (Museum of Modern Art)

Nude Descending a Staircase, Marcel Duchamp (1887–1968). An example of the impact of film on painting. The effect is that of a series of closely spaced photographs coalescing to create motion. (Philadelphia Museum of Art)

The Funeral Procession, George Grosz (1893–1959). Painted in the late stages of the First World War, this portrayal of a funeral procession gone mad shows death triumphant as humanity is swept into a hell of its own making. The work expressed an anger and a loathing felt by an entire generation. (Reproduced by Permission of the Estate of George Grosz, Princeton, New Jersey)

The Table, Georges Braque (1881–1963). An example of later Cubism showing the predominance of curvilinear form and line instead of geometric structure. (Museum of Modern Art)

I and the Village, Marc Chagall (1889–). The subject refers to the artist's childhood and youth in Vitebsk, Russia. The profile on the right is probably that of the artist himself. (Museum of Modern Art)

The Persistence of Memory, Salvador Dali (1904–). The Spaniard Dali is the outstanding representative of the Surrealist school. Many objects in his paintings are Freudian images. (Museum of Modern Art)

Barricade, José Clemente Orozco (1883–1949). The Mexican muralist Orozco was one of the most celebrated of contemporary painters with a social message. His themes were revolutionary fervor, satire of aristocracy and the Church, and deification of the common man. (Museum of Modern Art)

Around the Fish, Paul Klee (1879–1940). Klee is recognized as the most subtle humorist of twentieth-century art. The central motif of a fish on a platter suggests a banquet, but many of the surrounding objects appear to be products of fantasy. (Museum of Modern Art

Mystery and Melancholy of a Street, Giorgio de Chirico (1888-1978). Employing perspective to fashion familiar components into dreamscapes fraught with anxiety and loneliness, de Chirico had a profound effect on the surrealists. (Lee Boltin)

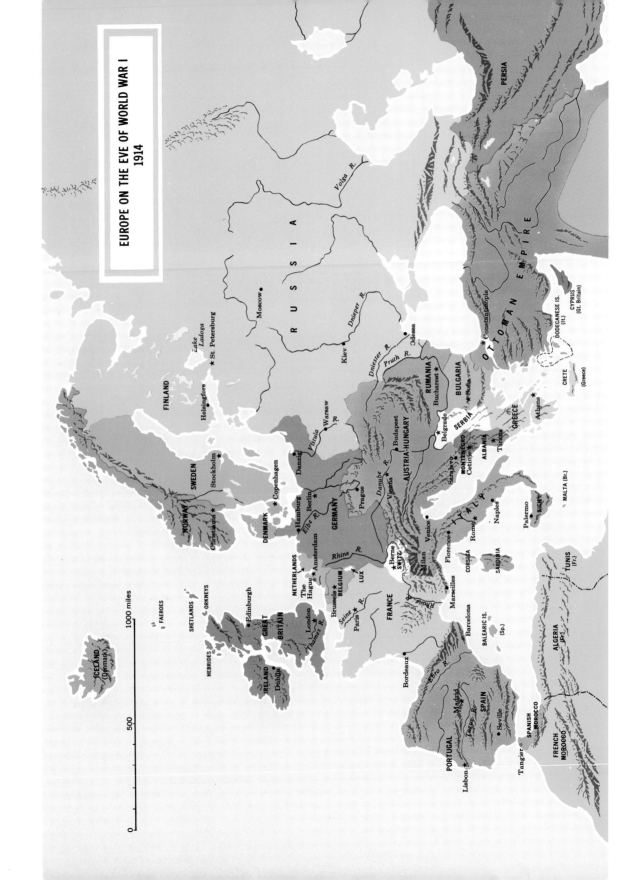

EUROPE ON THE EVE OF WORLD WAR I
1914

THE SOVIET UNION • 1918-1945

The Union of Soviet Socialist
Republics in 1939

Annexed 1940-45

JAPAN

KOREA

SEA OF JAPAN

Vladivostock

MANCHURIA

SEA OF OKHOTSK

SAKHALIN I.

Khabarovsk

Amur R.

Chita

Ulan-Bator

MONGOLIA

Lake Baikal

Irkhutsk

CHINA

1000 miles

0

SINKIANG

Yakutsk

Lena R.

RUSSIAN   SOVIET   FEDERATED   SOCIALIST   REPUBLIC

Yenisei R.

Krasnoyarsk

Novosibirsk

Omsk

Ob R.

URAL MTS.

Chelyabinsk

Sverdlovsk

Perm

KAZAKH S.S.R.

Alma-Ata

Tashkent

Frunze

KIRGIZ S.S.R.

Dushanbe

TADZHIK S.S.R.

AFGHANISTAN

UZBEK S.S.R.

TURKMEN S.S.R.

Ashkabad

Aral Sea

Orenburg

Kuibyshev

Kazan

Volga R.

Saratov

Stalingrad

Magnitogorsk

Don R.

Rostov

Kharkov

Krasnodar

Novorossisk

Pyatigorsk

CAUCASUS MTS.

CASPIAN SEA

Baku

AZERBAIDZHAN S.S.R.

GEORGIAN S.S.R.

Tiflis

ARMENIAN S.S.R.

Erivan

TURKEY

IRAN

IRAQ

SYRIA

ARCTIC   OCEAN

Murmansk

Archangel

Yaroslavl

Ivanovo

Orekhovo

Gorki

Moscow

Gomel

Minsk

WHITE RUSSIAN S.S.R.

Bobruisk

Kiev

UKRAINIAN S.S.R.

Odessa

Nikolaev

Kishinev

MOLDAVIAN S.S.R.

RUMANIA

HUNGARY

CZECHOSLOVAKIA

POLAND

Warsaw

Brest-Litovsk

Grodno

Danzig

Kaunas

LITHUANIAN S.S.R.

LATVIAN S.S.R.

Riga

Kalinin

ESTONIAN S.S.R.

Tallinn

Kronstadt

Leningrad

Helsinki

FINLAND

Gulf of Bothnia

SWEDEN

NORWAY

BLACK SEA

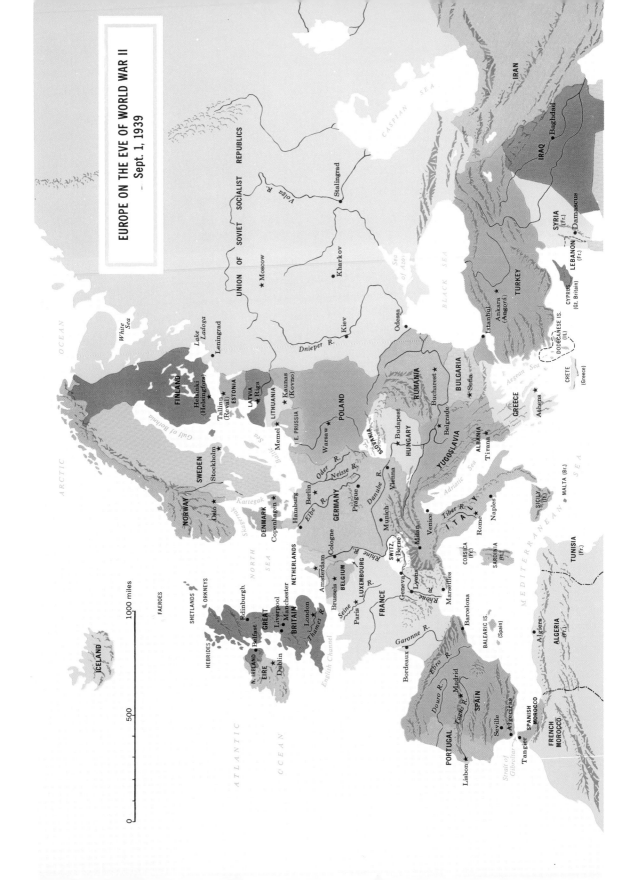

EUROPE ON THE EVE OF WORLD WAR II
- Sept. 1, 1939

Left: *U.S. Farmers on Their Way West in the 1930s*. Forced from their land by depression debts and by drought, thousands of farmers and their families headed to California, Oregon, and Washington in search of employment. Right: *The Stock Market Crash, October 24, 1929*. Crowds milling outside the New York Stock Exchange on the day of the big crash.

and 1929. But its minority position in Parliament left it little chance to accomplish much of consequence, even had its leader, Prime Minister J. Ramsay MacDonald, been a more adventurous socialist than he was. In 1926 British trade unions grew increasingly militant because of the particularly distressing wage levels in the coal mining industry, and because the Conservative government, returned to power under Stanley Baldwin in 1925, refused to be deflected from its deflationary stance. The unions staged a nationwide general strike which, though it failed as an industrial strategy, turned the middle class more than ever against the workers.

The United States was undoubtedly the most impregnable fortress of conservative power among the democracies. The presidents elected during the 1920s—Warren G. Harding, Calvin Coolidge, and Herbert Hoover—upheld a social philosophy formulated by the barons of big business in the nineteenth century, and the Supreme Court used its power of judicial review to nullify progressive legislation enacted by state governments and occasionally by Congress.

Conservatism in the U.S.

The course of Western history was dramatically altered by the advent of worldwide depression in 1929. We have already seen the way in which depression contributed to the rise of Nazism. But all countries were forced to come to terms with the economic and social devastation it produced. The Great Depression had its roots in a general agricultural slump in the 1920s, the result of increased postwar production which drove down the price of grain and other commodities to the point of bankrupting farmers, though not far enough to benefit

The Great Depression

the urban poor. To chronic agricultural distress was added the financial crisis that began with the collapse of prices on the New York Stock Exchange in 1929. With a drop in the value of stocks, banks found themselves short of capital and forced to close. International investors called in their debts. Industries, unable to sell their products, stopped manufacturing and started laying off workers. Unemployment further contracted markets—fewer people had money with which to buy goods or services—and that contraction led to more unemployment.

The results of the depression took varied forms throughout the West. In 1931 Great Britain abandoned the gold standard; the government of the United States followed suit in 1933. By no longer pegging their currencies to the price of gold, these countries hoped to make money cheaper, and thus more available for programs of public and private economic recovery. This action was the forerunner of a broad program of currency management, which became an important element in a general policy of economic nationalism. As early as 1932 Great Britain abandoned its time-honored policy of free trade. Protective tariffs were raised in some instances as high as 100 percent.

Results of depression: economic nationalism

Domestically, Britain moved cautiously to alleviate the effects of the depression. A national government, which came to power in 1931 with a ministry composed of members from the Conservative, Liberal, and Labour parties, was reluctant to spend beyond its income, as it would have to in order to underwrite effective programs of public assistance. Of the European democracies, France adopted the most advanced set of policies to combat the inequalities and distress that followed in the wake of the depression. In 1936, responding to a threat from ultraconservatives to overthrow the republic, a Popular Front government, under the leadership of the socialist Léon Blum (1872–1950), was formed by the Radical, Radical Socialist, and Communist parties, and lasted for two years. The Popular Front nationalized the munitions industry and reorganized the Bank of France so as to deprive the 200 largest stockholders of their monopolistic control over credit. In addition, it decreed a forty-hour week for all urban workers and initiated a program of public works. For the benefit of the farmers it established a wheat office to fix the price and regulate the distribution of grain. Although the threat from the political Right was for a time quelled by the Popular Front, conservatives were generally uncooperative and unimpressed by its attempts to ameliorate the conditions of the French working class. The anti-Semitism that had appeared at the time of the Dreyfus affair resurfaced; Blum was both a socialist and a Jew. Businessmen saw him as the forerunner of a French Lenin, and were heard to opine, "better Hitler than Blum." They got their wish before the decade was out.

Léon Blum

The most dramatic changes in policy occurred not in Europe but in the United States. The explanation was twofold. The United States had clung longer to the economic philosophy of the nineteenth cen-

tury. Prior to the depression the business classes had adhered firmly
to the dogma of freedom of contract and insisted upon their right to
form monopolies and to use the government as their agent in frustrating the demands of both workers and consumers. The depression in
the United States was also more severe than in the European democracies. Industrial production shrank by about two-thirds. The structure of agricultural prices and of common stocks collapsed. Thousands
of banks were forced to close their doors. Unemployment rose to one-
third of the total labor force. An attempt to alleviate distress was contained in a program of reform and reconstruction known as the New
Deal. The chief architect and motivator of this program was Franklin
D. Roosevelt (1882–1945), who succeeded Herbert Hoover in the
presidency on March 4, 1933.

The aim of the New Deal was to preserve the capitalist system, by
managing the economy and undertaking programs of relief and public
works to increase mass purchasing power. Although the New Deal
did assist in the recovery both of individual citizens and of the country, through programs of currency management and social security, it
left the crucial problem of unemployment unsolved. In 1939, after six
years of the New Deal, the United States still had more than nine
million jobless workers—a figure which exceeded the combined
unemployment of the rest of the world. Ironically, only the outbreak
of a new world war could provide the full recovery that the New Deal
had failed to assure, by directing millions from the labor market into
the army and by creating jobs in the countless factories that turned to
the manufacture of war matériel.

5. INTELLECTUAL AND CULTURAL TRENDS IN THE INTERWAR YEARS

The First World War, which proved so disillusioning to so many, and
the generally dispiriting political events which followed in its train,
made it difficult to hold fast to any notion of a purposeful universe.
Philosophers, to a greater degree than their predecessors, declared that
there was little point in attempting to discover answers to questions
about the nature of ultimate reality. These antimetaphysicians broke
dramatically with the philosophers of the past century, who had
grounded their speculations in a belief in progress and in a search for
all-encompassing explanations of human behavior. Probably the most
influential of these new thinkers was the Viennese Ludwig Wittgenstein (1889–1951), founder, with the Englishman Bertrand Russell
(1872–1970), of the school of Logical Positivism. Developed further
by the so-called Vienna Circle, whose leader was Rudolf Carnap,
Logical Positivism emerged as an uncompromisingly scientific philosophy. It is not concerned with values or ideals except to the extent
that they may be demonstrable by mathematics or physics. In general,

Bertrand Russell

the Logical Positivists reject as "meaningless" everything that cannot be reduced to a "one-to-one correspondence" with something in the physical universe. They reduce philosophy to a mere instrument for the discovery of truth in harmony with the facts of the physical environment. They divest it almost entirely of its traditional content and use it as a medium for answering questions and solving problems. They are concerned especially to attack political theory, regarding that subject as particularly burdened with unproved assumptions and questionable dogmas.

Religion as a cultural force

Sociologists reinforced philosophers in denying the value of metaphysics. One of the most important was the German Max Weber (1864–1920), who, in his book *The Protestant Ethic and the Spirit of Capitalism* (1905), argued that religion must be understood as a cultural force, in this case assisting directly in the spread of capitalism. By making work a cardinal virtue and idleness a supreme vice, Protestantism had encouraged the work ethic, which, in turn, had fueled the energies of early capitalist entrepreneurs. When he turned to a study of the contemporary world, Weber concluded that societies would inevitably fall more and more under the sway of ever-expanding and potentially totalitarian bureaucracies. Recognizing the extent to which such a development might threaten human freedom, Weber posited the notion of "charismatic" leadership as a means of escaping the deadening tyranny of state control. A term derived from the Greek word for gift, "charisma" was, according to Weber, an almost magic quality which could induce hero worship and which, if properly directed by its possessor, might produce an authority to challenge bureaucracy. Weber himself recognized the dangers as well as the attractions of charismatic authority, dangers which the careers of Stalin, Hitler, and Mussolini soon made all too apparent. Another thinker who treated religion as a powerful social and psychological force, rather than as a branch of metaphysics, was the Swiss psychologist Carl Jung (1875–1961). Originally a student and disciple of Freud, Jung broke with his intellectual mentor by proclaiming the existence of a force behind individual id, ego, and superego: the "collective unconscious." Jung's literary background and his personal penchant for mysticism helped persuade him of the enduring psychological and therapeutic value of myth and religion, something Freud refused to acknowledge.

Antirationalist and antidemocratic philosophies

The writings of some philosophers during the interwar years not only reflected a sense of crisis and despair but, because of the influence of those works, contributed to it as well. Foremost among these were the Italian Vilfredo Pareto (1848–1923) and the German Oswald Spengler (1880–1936), who agreed in their contempt for the masses, in their belief that democracy was impossible, in their anti-intellectual viewpoint, and in their admiration for strong and aggressive leaders. Spengler was, in many respects, more extreme than Pareto. In his *Decline of the West,* completed in 1918, and even more in his later writings, he gave vent to attitudes that reflect the extent to which totalitarianism might appeal to an "anti–intellectual" intellectual. In his *Hour of Decision,* published in 1933, he fulminated against democracy, pacifism, internationalism, the lower classes, and nonwhite peoples. He sang the praises of those "who feel themselves born and called to be masters," of "healthy instincts, race, the will to possession and power." Spengler despised the analytical reasoning of urban intellectuals and called upon men to admire the "deep wisdom of old peasant families." Human beings, he maintained, are "beasts of prey," and those who deny this conclusion are simply "beasts of prey with broken teeth."

Further confusion and uncertainty were encouraged by the pioneering work of the German physicist Albert Einstein (1879–1955), whose theorizing and experiments were revolutionizing the way in which men and women perceived the universe. In 1905 Einstein began to challenge not merely the older conceptions of matter but practically the entire structure of traditional physics. The doctrine for which he is most noted is his principle of relativity. During the greater part of the nineteenth century, physicists had assumed that space and motion were absolute. Space was supposed to be filled with an intangible substance known as *ether,* which provided the medium for the undulations of light. But experiments performed by English and American physicists near the end of the century exploded the ether hypothesis. Einstein then set to work to reconstruct the scheme of the universe in accordance with a different pattern. He maintained that space and motion, instead of being absolute, are relative to each other. Objects have not merely three dimensions but four. To the familiar length, breadth, and thickness, Einstein added a new dimension of *time* and represented all four as fused in a synthesis which he called the *space-time continuum.* In this way he sought to explain the idea that mass is dependent upon motion. Bodies traveling at high velocity have proportions of extension and mass different from those they would have at rest. Einstein also posited the conception of a finite universe—that is, finite in space. The region of matter does not extend into infinity; the universe has limits. While these are by no means definite boundaries, there is at least a region beyond which nothing exists. Space curves back upon itself so as to make of the universe a gigantic sphere within which are contained galaxies, solar systems, stars, and planets.

Einstein's theories

Albert Einstein

The Einstein theories had a major influence in precipitating another revolutionary development in physics: the splitting of the atom to release the energy contained within it. As early as 1905 Einstein became convinced of the equivalence of mass and energy and worked out a formula for the conversion of one into the other, which he expressed as $E = mc^2$. E represents the energy in ergs, m the mass in grams, and c the velocity of light in centimeters per second. In other words, the amount of energy locked within the atom is equal to the mass multiplied by the square of the velocity of light. But no practical application of this formula was possible until after the discovery of the neutron by the Englishman Sir James Chadwick in 1932. Since

*Releasing the energy
within the atom*

the neutron carries no charge of electricity, it is an ideal weapon for bombarding the atom. It is neither repulsed by the positively charged protons nor absorbed by the negatively charged electrons. Moreover, in the process of bombardment it produces more neutrons, which hit other atoms and cause them in turn to split and create neutrons. In this way the original reaction is repeated in an almost unending series.

Laying the groundwork for the atomic bomb

In 1939 two German physicists, Otto Hahn and Fritz Strassman, succeeded in splitting atoms of uranium by bombarding them with neutrons. The initial reaction produced a chain of reactions, in much the same way that a fire burning at the edge of a piece of paper raises the temperature of adjoining portions of the paper high enough to cause them to ignite. Scientists in Germany, Great Britain, and the United States were spurred on by governments anxious to make use of these discoveries for military purposes during the Second World War. The first use made of the knowledge of atomic fission was in the preparation of an atomic bomb—a device that would further heighten and perpetuate the anxieties of the era.

Literary disillusion

Literary movements during the interwar period showed tendencies similar to those in philosophy. Like the philosophers, the major novelists, poets, and dramatists were disillusioned by the brute facts of world war and by the failure of victory to fulfill its promises. Many were profoundly affected also by revolutionary developments in science, such as the theories of Einstein, and especially by the probings of the new science of psychoanalysis into the hidden secrets of the mind. Much of the literature of the interwar period reflected themes of frustration, cynicism, and disenchantment. The general mood of the era was expressed individually by different writers; for example, by the early novels of the American Ernest Hemingway (1899–1961), by the poetry of the Anglo-American T. S. Eliot (1888–1965), and by the plays of the German Bertolt Brecht (1898–1956). In *The Sun Also Rises,* Hemingway gave the public a powerful description of the essential tragedy of the so-called lost generation and set a pattern that other writers, like the American F. Scott Fitzgerald, were soon to follow. In his poem *The Waste Land* (1922), T. S. Eliot presented a philosophy that was close to despair. Once you are born, he seemed to be saying, life is a living death, to be endured as boredom and frustration. Brecht, in plays written to be performed before the proletarian patrons of cabarets, proclaimed the corruption of the bourgeois state and the pointlessness of war.

T. S. Eliot

The works of many writers in the interwar period reflected to an increasing extent the isolation of self-conscious intellectuals and the constricting of their audience that characterized the years before the First World War. While Brecht carried his revolutionary messages into the streets of Berlin, others wrote primarily for each other or for the small elite group who could understand what they were saying. Eliot crammed his poetry with esoteric allusions. The Irishman James Joyce (1882–1941), whose ability to enter his characters' minds and to reproduce their "stream-of-consciousness" on paper made him a writer of the very first order, nevertheless wrote with a complexity that only few could appreciate. The same was true, though to a lesser extent, of the novels of the Frenchman Marcel Proust (1871–1922) and the Englishwoman Virginia Woolf (1882–1941). In her novels and essays, Woolf was, as well, an eloquent and biting critic of the ruling class of Britain, focusing in part on the enforced oppression of women even in that class.

Virginia Woolf

The depression of the 1930s forced a reexamination of the methods and purposes of literature. In the midst of economic stagnation and threats of totalitarianism and war, literature was politicized. Authors came to believe that their work must indict meanness, cruelty, and barbarism, and point the way to a more just society, that it should also be a literature addressed not to fellow intellectuals, but to common men and women. The American John Steinbeck (1902–1968), in *The Grapes of Wrath,* depicted the sorry plight of impoverished farmers fleeing from the "dust bowl" to California only to find that all the land had been monopolized by companies that exploited their workers. Pervading the novels of the Frenchman André Malraux (1901–1976) was the strong suggestion that the human struggle against tyranny and injustice is that which gives meaning and value to life. Young British writers such as W. H. Auden, Stephen Spender, and Christopher Isherwood declared, as communist sympathizers, that artists had an obligation to politicize their art for the benefit of the revolution. They rejected the pessimism of their immediate literary forebears for the optimism of political commitment to a common cause.

Influence of the depression

In this they differed radically from their French contemporary, Jean-Paul Sartre (1905–1980), whose pessimistic philosophy of Existentialism was receiving its first hearing at this time. Sartre was a teacher of philosophy in a Paris *lycée* and subsequently a leader of the French Resistance movement against the Germans during the Second World War. His philosophy takes its name from its doctrine that the *existence* of human beings as free individuals is the fundamental fact of life. But this freedom is of no help to humanity; instead it is a source of anguish and terror. Realizing, however vaguely, that they are free agents, morally responsible for all their acts, individuals feel themselves strangers in an alien world. They can have no confidence in a benevolent God or in a universe guided by purpose, for, according to Sartre, all such ideas have been reduced to fictions by modern science. The only way of escape from despair is the path of "involvement," or active participation in human affairs. It should be noted that in addition to the atheistic Existentialism of Sartre, there was also a prior Christian version, which had its origin in the teachings of Søren Kierkegaard (1813–1855), a Danish theologian of the mid–nineteenth cen-

Jean-Paul Sartre

George Orwell

John Maynard Keynes

tury. Like its atheistic counterpart, Christian Existentialism also teaches that the chief cause of human agony and terror is freedom, but it finds the source of its freedom in original sin.

Another writer who refused to allow himself the luxury of political optimism was the Englishman George Orwell (1903–1950). Although sympathetic to the cause of international socialism, Orwell continued to insist that all political movements were to some degree corrupted. He urged writers to recognize a duty to write only on the basis of what they had themselves experienced. Above all, writers should never simply parrot party propaganda. Orwell's last two novels, *Animal Farm* and *1984,* written during and immediately after the Second World War, are powerful expressions of his mistrust of political regimes—whether of the Left or the Right—that profess democracy but in fact destroy human freedom.

Optimism during the 1930s was generally the property of those writers who were prepared to advocate a violent change in the social order, most notably men and women sympathetic to the doctrines of communism and the achievements of Soviet Russia. An exception to this rule was the British economist John Maynard Keynes (1883–1946), who argued that capitalism could be made to work if governments would play a part in its management, and whose theories helped shape the economic policies of the New Deal. Keynes had served as an economic advisor to the British government during the 1919 treaty-making at Paris. He was disgusted with the harsh terms imposed upon the Germans, recognizing that they would serve only to keep alive the hatreds and uncertainties that breed war. Keynes believed that capitalism with its inner faults corrected could provide a just and efficient economy. First, Keynes abandoned the sacred cow of balanced budgets. He did not advocate continuous deficit financing. He would have the government deliberately operate in the red whenever private investment was too scanty to provide for the economic needs of the country. When depression gave way to recovery, private financing could take the place of deficit spending for most purposes. He favored the accumulation and investment of large amounts of venture capital, which he declared to be the only socially productive form of capital. Finally, Keynes recommended monetary control as a means of promoting prosperity and full employment. He would establish what is commonly called a "managed currency," regulating its value by a process of contraction or expansion in accordance with the needs of the economy. Prosperity would thus be assured in terms of the condition of the home market, and no nation would be tempted to "beggar its neighbor" in the foolish pursuit of a favorable balance of trade.

Trends in art tended to parallel those in literature. For much of the period, visual artists continued to explore aesthetic frontiers far removed from the conventional taste of average men and women. Picasso followed his particular genius as it led him further into cubist

John Maynard Keynes

variations and inventions. So did others, such as the Frenchman Fernand Léger (1881–1955), who combined devotion to cubist principles and a fascination with the artifacts of industrial civilization. A group more advanced, perhaps, than the cubists, the expressionists argued that since color and line express inherent psychological qualities which can be represented without reference to subject matter, a painting need not have a "subject" at all. The Russian Wassily Kandinsky (1866–1944) carried the logic of this position to its conclusion by calling his untitled paintings "improvisations," and insisting that they meant nothing. A second group of expressionists rejected intellectuality for what they called "objectivity," by which they meant a candid appraisal of the state of the human mind. Their analysis took the form of an attack upon the greed and decadence of postwar Europe. Chief among this group was the German George Grosz (1893–1959), whose cruel, satiric line has been likened to a "razor lancing a carbuncle." Another school expressed its disgust with the world by declaring that there was in fact no such thing as aesthetic principle, since aesthetic principle was based on reason and the world had conclusively proved by fighting itself to death that reason did not exist. Calling themselves dada-ists (after a name picked at random, allegedly, from the dictionary) these artists, led by the Frenchman Marcel Duchamp (1887–1968), the German Max Ernst (1891–1976), and the Alsatian Jean Hans Arp (1887–1966), concocted "fabrications" from cutouts and juxtapositions of wood, glass, and metal, and gave them bizarre names: *The Bride stripped bare by her Bachelors, even* (Duchamp), for example. These works were declared by critics, however, to belie their professed meaninglessness, to be, in fact, expressions of the subconscious. Such certainly were the paintings of the surrealists, artists such

Trends in art

See color plates following page 992 for representative works by Kandinsky, Grosz, Duchamp, de Chirico, Dali, and Orozco

Big Julie by Fernand Léger. Note the artist's fascination with industrial shapes and images.

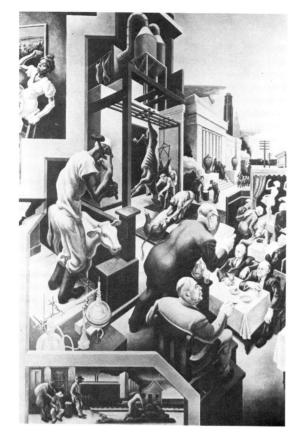

Left: *Mural of Kansas City, Missouri* by Thomas Hart Benton. The mural protests the corruption of American politics and the Depression misery and degradation of farm workers and industrial laborers. The man in the armchair is the political boss of Kansas City in the 1930s, Tom Pendergast. Right: *"Tie Yourself to the Fatherland, Dear Fatherland"* by George Grosz. Grosz's attacks on unfeeling capitalism during the Weimar years undoubtedly served to weaken the political center during the 1930s.

as the Italian Giorgio de Chirico (1888–1978) and the Spaniard Salvador Dali (1904–   ), whose explorations of the interior of the mind produced irrational, fantastic, and generally melancholy images.

Art as social commentary

For a time in the 1930s artists, like writers, responded to the sense of international crisis by painting to express their pain and outrage directly to a mass audience. Among the chief representatives of the new movement were the Mexicans Diego Rivera and Jose Clemente Orozco, and the Americans Thomas Hart Benton, Reginald Marsh, and Edward Hopper. The fundamental aim of these artists was to depict the social conditions of the modern world and to present in graphic detail the hopes and struggles of peasants and workers. While they scarcely adhered to the conventions of the past, there was nothing unintelligible about their work; it was intended to be art that anyone could understand. Much of it bore the sting or thrust of social satire. Orozco, in particular, delighted in pillorying the hypocrisy of the Church and the greed and cruelty of plutocrats and plunderers.

Music, along with the rest of the arts, continued its movement away from nineteenth-century form and intentions. Impressionists, such as Debussy, were succeeded by expressionists, whose work is concerned more with form than with sensuous effects and tends toward abstraction. Expressionism, more radical and more influential than impressionism, comprises two main schools: atonality, founded by the

Viennese Arnold Schoenberg (1874–1951), and polytonality, best typified by the Russian Igor Stravinsky (1882–1971). Atonality abolishes key. In this type of music, dissonances are the rule rather than the exception, and the melodic line commonly alternates between chromatic manipulation and strange unsingable leaps. In short, the ordinary principles of composition are reversed. The atonalists attempt, with some success, to let musical sound become a vehicle for expressing the inner meaning and elemental structure of things.

Polytonality is essentially a radical kind of counterpoint, deriving its inspiration partly from baroque practices of counterpoint that were placed in the service of new ideas. However, it does not simply interweave independent melodies which together form concord, but undertakes to combine separate keys and unrelated harmonic systems, with results that are highly discordant. While the atonalists have retained elements of romanticism, the polytonalists have tried to resurrect the architectural qualities of pure form, movement, and rhythm, stripping away all sentimentality and sensuous connotations.

Architects during this period were also intent upon denying sentimentality. Between 1880 and 1890 designers in Europe and America announced that the prevailing styles of building construction were out of harmony with the facts of modern civilization, and declared as well their intention of restoring that harmony. The chief pioneers of this "functionalism" were Otto Wagner (1841–1918) in Germany and Louis Sullivan (1856–1924) and Frank Lloyd Wright (1869–1959) in the United States. The basic principle of functionalism is the idea that the appearance of a building should proclaim its actual use and purpose. There must be no addition of friezes, columns, tracery, or battlements merely because some people consider such ornaments beautiful. True beauty consists in an honest adaptation of materials to the purpose they are intended to serve. Functionalism also embodies the notion that architecture should express either directly or symbolically the distinguishing features of contemporary culture. Ornamentation must therefore be restricted to such elements as will reflect an age of science

Igor Stravinsky

Development of functional architecture

Taliesin East by Frank Lloyd Wright. A famous example of the functional style, with the pattern of the house conforming to the natural surroundings.

Contrasting Architectural Styles in Germany between the Wars. Left: The Bauhaus by Walter Gropius. This school in Dessau, Germany, is a starkly functional prototype of the interwar "international style." Right: The Chancellery in Berlin by Albert Speer. Note the massive qualities of the Nazi state style.

and machines. A leading European practitioner of functionalism was the German, Walter Gropius (1883–1969), who in 1919 established a school—the *Bauhaus*—in Dessau to serve as a center for the theory and practice of modern architecture. Gropius and his followers declared that their style of design, which in time came to be called "international," was the only one which permitted an honest application of new material—chromium, glass, steel, and concrete.

The arts under Hitler

Gropius was one of the multitude of German intellectuals—both Jewish and non-Jewish—to leave their country after Hitler's rise to power. Totalitarianism had its own cultural aesthetic. Functionalism, which celebrated the qualities of material, line, and proportion, had no place in a totalitarian regime, where the arts were obliged to advertise the virtues of the state, its tradition, and the aspirations of its people. Instead of Gropius, Hitler had Albert Speer, an architect of unimpressive talents, who produced for him grandiose designs whose vacuous pretentiousness was an unconscious parody of Nazi ideology. Atonality in music was banished along with functionalism in architecture, to be replaced by a state-sponsored revival of the mystical and heroic nationalism of Wagner.

Art was an important part of the new and cultural arm of totalitarianism: propaganda, the practice of indoctrinating populations to believe only what governments wished them to believe. It mattered not at all that belief was based on falsehood, as in the "superiority of the Aryan race," for example. If it served the interest of the state, it was disseminated as truth. Never before had so many of the world's people been able to read. Nineteenth- and twentieth-century governments had encouraged literacy, fearing an ignorant working class as a revolutionary threat. Now totalitarian regimes used education unashamedly as a means of propagating a party line. "All effective propaganda has to limit itself to a very few points and to use them like slogans," Hitler wrote in *Mein Kampf*. "It has to confine itself to little and to repeat this eternally." Books critical of the state were banned, their places on school and library shelves taken by others specifically written to glorify the present leadership. Youth programs instructed children in the virtues of discipline and loyalty to the state. Mass gymnastic displays suggested the ease with which well-trained bodies could be made to respond to the military needs of the nation. Propagandizing was made more effective by the advent of mass-circulation publishing, the radio, and the motion picture. Newspapers which printed only what the state wanted printed reached a wider audience than ever before. Party political broadcasts, beamed into homes or blared through loudspeakers in town squares, by their constant repetitiveness made people begin to accept—if not believe—what they knew to be untrue. Films could transform German youths into Aryan gods and goddesses, as they could Russian collective farms into a worker's paradise. Sergei Eisenstein (1898–1948), the Russian director, rewrote Russian history on film to serve the ends of the Soviet state. Hitler commissioned the filmmaker Leni Riefenstahl to record a political rally staged by herself and Speer. The film, entitled *Triumph of the Will,* was a visual hymn to the Nordic race and the Nazi regime. (And the comedian Charlie Chaplin riposted in his celebrated lampoon, *The Great Dictator,* an enormously successful parody of totalitarian pomposities.)

In Western democracies, although the media were not manipulated by the state as they were elsewhere, their effectiveness as propagandizers was nevertheless recognized and exploited. Advertising became an industry when manufacturers realized the mass markets that newspapers, magazines, and radio represented. Much that was printed and aired was trivialized by writers and editors who feared that serious or difficult material would antagonize the readers or listeners upon whom they depended for their livelihood. This is not to say that the new media were uniformly banal, or that artists and performers were unable to use them to make thoughtful protests. The film version of Steinbeck's *Grapes of Wrath,* directed by John Ford, though an exception to the normal run of escapist Hollywood comedies and adventures, was perhaps as stinging an indictment of capitalism as the novel, and it reached far more people. During these years popular culture, whatever else it was, remained a powerful and alarming new fact of life:

powerful in terms of its vast audience; alarming because of its particular applicability as a means of controlling the minds of men and women.

SELECTED READINGS

• *Items so designated are available in paperback editions.*

GENERAL

Carsten, F. L., *Revolution in Central Europe, 1918–1919*, London, 1972. A useful treatment of the postwar revolts.

• Collaer, P., *A History of Modern Music*, Cleveland, Ohio, 1961. Useful introduction.

• Galbraith, John Kenneth, *The Great Crash, 1929*, Boston, 1955. An entertaining and informative account by the celebrated economist.

• Gamow, George, *Thirty Years That Shook Physics*, Mineola, N.Y., 1966. An erudite yet readable account.

• Hamilton, George Heard, *Painting and Sculpture in Europe, 1880–1940*, Baltimore, 1967. An excellent survey.

• Hartnack, Justus, *Wittgenstein and Modern Philosophy*, Garden City, N.Y., 1965. Clear introduction to a difficult subject.

• Hitchcock, H.R., *Architecture: 19th and 20th Centuries*, London, 1958. Thorough and well-written survey.

• Kahler, Erich, *The Tower and the Abyss*, New York, 1957. A survey of the arts in the context of contemporary culture.

• Kindleberger, C. P., *The World in Depression, 1929–1939*, Berkeley, 1973. A first-rate study of the worldwide aspects of the slump.

Laqueur, W., and G. L. Mosse, eds., *the Left-Wing Intellectuals between the Wars, 1919–1939*, New York, 1966. Recent essays by modern historians.

Masur, Gerhard, *Prophets of Yesterday*, New York, 1961. A useful intellectual history of the interwar period.

Mosse, George L., *The Naturalization of the Masses: Political Symbolism and Mass Movements in Germany from the Napoleonic Wars through the Third Reich*, New York, 1975. Attempts to trace the roots of Nazism in naturalist movements.

• Payne, Stanley G., *Fascism: A Comparative Approach toward a Definition*, Madison, Wisc., 1980. A review of various European fascist movements, written with balance and careful thought.

• Rothschild, Joseph, *East Central Europe between the Two World Wars*, Seattle, 1975. An authoritative survey; does not include Austria.

Shapiro, Theda, *Painters and Politics: The European Avant-Garde and Society, 1900–1925*, New York, 1976. An analysis of the political and social attitudes of a revolutionary generation in the arts.

• Sontag, Raymond V., *A Broken World, 1919–1939*, New York, 1971. A fine detailed survey of interwar Europe.

THE SOVIET UNION

Carr, E. H., *The Russian Revolution: From Lenin to Stalin*, New York, 1979. A distillation from his ten-volume *History of Soviet Russia*. A fine starting point for the general reader.

Conquest, Robert, *The Great Terror*, New York, 1968. An analysis of the Stalin purges.

• Daniels, Robert V., *The Conscience of the Revolution*, Cambridge, Mass., 1960. Discusses the opposition to Bolshevism in the 1920s.

• Deutscher, Isaac, *The Prophet Armed*, London, 1954; *The Prophet Unarmed*, London, 1959; *The Prophet Outcast*, London, 1963. A superb, three-volume biography of Leon Trotsky.

• Fitzpatrick, Sheila, ed., *Cultural Revolution in Russia, 1928–1931*, Bloomington, Ind., 1978. A first-rate analysis of the cultural effect of Bolshevik rule.

• Tucker, Robert C., *Stalin as Revolutionary, 1879–1929: A Study in History and Personality*, New York, 1973. An excellent account of Stalin's rise to power, and of the change from revolution to dictatorship in Russia.

GERMANY AND ITALY

• Bracher, Karl Dietrich, *The German Dictatorship: The Origins, Structure, and Effects of National Socialism*, New York, 1970. A penetrating and exhaustive study of the Nazi state by a political scientist.

• Bullock, Alan, *Hitler: A Study in Tyranny*, rev. ed., New York, 1971. The standard biography.

• Eyck, Erich, *History of the Weimar Republic*, 2 vols., Cambridge, Mass., 1962. A sympathetic account by a prominent German liberal.

• Gay, Peter, *Weimar Culture: The Outsider as Insider*, New York, 1970. Examines the failure of commitment to the Weimar Republic by German intellectuals.

• Hale, Oron J., *The Captive Press in the Third Reich*, Princeton, 1964. Examines the manner in which totalitarianism invades journalism.

Lyttelton, Adrian, *The Seizure of Power: Fascism in Italy, 1919–1929*, London, 1973. An excellent introduction.

Mack Smith, Denis, *Mussolini's Roman Empire*, New York, 1976. An able treatment of Italian fascism by the foremost English scholar of Italy.

• Nolte, Ernst, *The Three Faces of Fascism*, New York, 1966. A difficult but rewarding study of Germany, Italy, and France, from a philosophical perspective.

Rogger, Hans, and Eugen Weber, eds., *The European Right: A Historical Profile*, 1965. A country-by-country survey.

• Schoenbaum, David, *Hitler's Social Revolution: Class and Status in Nazi Germany, 1933–39*, Garden City, N.Y., 1966. Hitler's impact upon the various social and economic classes in Germany.

• Stern, Fritz, *The Politics of Cultural Despair: A Study in the Rise of Germanic Ideology*, Berkeley, 1961. Assesses the way in which cultural beliefs influence politics.

• Zeman, Z. A. B., *Nazi Propaganda*, New York, 1973. Examines an important bulwark of the authoritarian state.

THE DEMOCRACIES

Bullock, Alan, *The Life and Times of Ernest Bevin: Trade Union Leader, 1881–1940*, London, 1960. An excellent study of the British trade unionist and the political and social history of Britain between the wars.

• Burns, James M., *Roosevelt: The Lion and the Fox*, New York, 1956. A readable analysis.

Colton, Joel, *Léon Blum: Humanist in Politics,* New York, 1966. A first-rate biography that illuminates the history of the Popular Front.

• Graves, Robert, and Alan Hodge, *The Long Weekend: A Social History of Great Britain, 1918–1939,* London, 1940. A striking portrait of England in the interwar years.

• Greene, Nathanael, *From Versailles to Vichy: The Third Republic, 1919–1940,* Arlington Heights, Ill., 1970. Valuable survey.

Harrod, R. F., *The Life of John Maynard Keynes,* New York, 1951. A solid biography by an admirer of Keynes.

Hughes, H. Stuart, *The Obstructed Path: French Social Thought in the Years of Desperation, 1930–1960,* New York, 1968. Detailed analysis of major French thinkers.

• Leuchtenburg, W. E., *Franklin Roosevelt and the New Deal, 1932–1940,* New York, 1964. A good introduction.

• Mowat, Charles L., *Britain between the Wars, 1918–1940,* Chicago, 1955. A detailed political and social history, especially valuable for its extensive bibliographical footnotes.

• Taylor, A. J. P., *English History, 1914–1945,* New York, 1965. The best survey of the period; witty, provocative, insightful.

Weber, Eugen, *Action Française: Royalism and Reaction in Twentieth Century France,* Stanford, 1962. The best study of this protofascist movement.

SOURCE MATERIALS

Cole, G. D. H., and M. I. Cole, *The Condition of Britain,* London, 1937. A contemporary analysis by English socialists.

• Ehrenburg, Ilya, *Memoirs, 1921–1941,* New York, 1964. The intellectual at work within the Stalinist regime.

• Greene, Nathanael, comp., *European Socialism Since World War I,* Chicago, 1971. A collection of contemporary accounts.

Gruber, H., *International Communism in the Era of Lenin: A Documentary History,* Greenwich, Conn., 1967. A very useful collection of primary materials.

• Hitler, Adolf, *Mein Kampf,* New York, 1962. Hitler's autobiography, written in 1925. Contains his version of history and his vision for the future. Especially important for his insight into the nature of the masses and the use of propaganda.

Noakes, Jeremy, and Geoffrey Pridham, *Documents on Nazism, 1919–1945,* New York, 1975. An excellent sourcebook; comprehensive and annotated.

• Orwell, George, *The Road to Wigan Pier,* New York, 1972. Vivid description of Britain's interwar poverty and class system by an independently minded socialist.

• Silone, Ignazio, *Bread and Wine,* rev. ed., tr. H. Ferguson, New York, 1965. A moving account of the effects of Italian fascism.

• Speer, Albert, *Inside the Third Reich,* New York, 1964. The self-serving but informative memoirs of one of the leaders of Nazi Germany.

Tucker, Robert C., ed., *The Great Purge Trial,* New York, 1965. An annotated edition of the transcript of one of the Soviet "show-trials" that so puzzled Western observers.

Chapter 29

THE SECOND WORLD WAR

The President [Roosevelt] and the Prime Minister [Churchill], after a complete survey of the world situation, are more than ever determined that peace can come to the world only by a total elimination of German and Japanese war power. This involves the simple formula of placing the objective of this war in terms of an unconditional surrender by Germany, Italy, and Japan.

—Franklin D. Roosevelt, Casablanca, January 24, 1943

In September 1939, Europe was drawn again into a general war. The peace of 1919–1920 proved to be no more than an armistice; once more millions of people were locked in a conflict whose devastation surpassed any that had occurred heretofore. As had happened in 1914–1918, the new struggle soon became worldwide. Although the Second World War was not merely a continuation of, or a sequel to, the First, the similarity in causes and characteristics was more than superficial. Both were precipitated by threats to the balance of power, and both were conflicts between peoples, entire nations, rather than between governments. On the other hand, there were notable differences between the two conflicts. The methods of warfare in the Second World War had little in common with those of the earlier conflict. Trench warfare was superseded by bombing and by sudden aerial (Blitzkrieg) attacks, with highly mobile armies, on both civilian populations and military installations. Because so many were now vulnerable to the ravages of warfare, the distinction between those on the battlefield and those at home was more completely obliterated in the second war than it had been in the first. Finally, this war was not greeted with the almost universal, naïve enthusiasm that had marked the outbreak of the other. Men and women still remembered the horrors of the First World War. They entered the Second with determination, but also with a keener appreciation of the frightful devastation that war could bring than their predecessors had possessed.

A comparison of the two world wars

The causes of the Second World War related to the failure of the peace terms of 1919–1920. Those terms, while understandable in view of the passions and hatreds engendered by the First World War, created almost as many problems as they solved. By yielding to the demands of the victors for annexation of territory and the creation of satellite states, the peacemakers sowed new seeds of bitterness and conflict. By proclaiming the principle of self-determination while acquiescing in the distribution of national minorities behind alien frontiers, the treaties raised expectations while at the same time frustrating them. Perhaps most important, by imposing harsh terms on Germany, the treatymakers gave the Germans what seemed to many to be legitimate grievances, by depriving them of their rightful share of international power and saddling them with the entire burden of war "guilt."

Defects of the peace treaties

Power politics were a second cause of war. Although Woodrow Wilson and other sponsors of the League of Nations had acclaimed the league as a means of eliminating power struggles, it did nothing of the sort. It merely substituted a new and more precarious balance for the old. The signatures on the peace treaties had scarcely dried when the victors began the construction of new alliances to maintain their supremacy. A neutralized zone consisting of the Baltic states, Poland, and Rumania was created as a buffer against Soviet Russia. A "Little Entente" composed of Czechoslovakia, Yugoslavia, and Rumania was established to prevent a revival of Austrian power. These combinations, together with a Franco-Belgian alliance and a Franco-Polish alliance, would also serve to isolate Germany. Even the league itself was fundamentally an alliance of the victors against the vanquished. That there would be fears and anxieties over a disturbance of the new power arrangement was natural. The first sign of such a disturbance appeared in 1922 when Germany and Russia negotiated the Treaty of Rapallo. Though disguised as a mere trade agreement, it opened the way for political and, according to some accounts, even military collaboration between the two states.

Power politics

Diplomats made various attempts to preserve or restore international amity during the 1920s and 1930s. Some saw in disarmament the most promising means of achieving their purpose. Accordingly, a succession of conferences was called in the hope of at least limiting a race to rearm. In 1925 representatives of the chief European powers met at Locarno and acted on the suggestion of the German and French foreign ministers, Gustav Stresemann and Aristide Briand, that Germany and France pledge themselves to respect the Rhine frontiers as established in the Versailles treaty. They agreed also that they would never go to war against each other except in "legitimate defense." More widely celebrated than the Locarno Agreements was the Pact of Paris, or Kellogg-Briand Pact of 1928. Its purpose was to outlaw war as an international crime. Eventually, nearly all the nations of the world

Attempts to preserve international amity

Members of the Council of the League of Nations. In the front row, from the right, are Chamberlain of Britain, Vandervelde of Belgium, Stresemann of Germany, and Briand of France.

signed this agreement renouncing war as "an instrument of national policy" and providing that the settlement of international disputes "of whatever nature or of whatever origin" should never be sought "except by peaceful means." Neither the Locarno Agreements nor the Pact of Paris was much more than a pious gesture. The signatory nations adopted them with so many reservations and exceptions in favor of "vital interests" that they could never be effective instruments for preserving peace. Had the League of Nations been better organized, it might have relieved some of the tensions and prevented clashes between nations still unwilling to relinquish their absolute sovereignty. Yet it was not a league of all nations, since both Germany and Russia were excluded for much of the interwar period.

Economic conditions were a third important cause of the outbreak of war. The huge reparations imposed upon the Germans, and the French occupation of much of Germany's industrial heartland, helped, as we have seen, to retard Germany's economic recovery and bring on the debilitating inflation of the 1920s. The depression of the 1930s contributed to the coming of the war in several ways. It intensified economic nationalism. Baffled by problems of unemployment and business stagnation, governments resorted to high tariffs in an attempt to preserve the home market for their own producers. The depression was also responsible for a marked increase in armaments production, which was seen as a means of reducing unemployment. Despite the misgivings of some within the governments of Britain and France, Germany was allowed to rearm. Armaments expansion, on a large scale, was first undertaken by Germany about 1935, with the result that unemployment was substantially reduced and business boomed. Other nations followed the German example, not simply as a way of boosting their economies, but in response to Nazi military power. The depression helped as well to produce a new wave of militant expansionism directed toward the conquest of neighboring territories

Economic conditions

The Krupp Shipworks in Germany. Seen here are German submarines in the final stages of assembly.

as a means of solving economic problems. Japan took the lead in 1931 with the invasion of Manchuria. The decline of Japanese exports of raw silk and cotton cloth meant that the nation as a consequence was unable to pay for needed imports of coal, iron, and other minerals. Japanese militarists were thus furnished with a convenient pretext for seizing Manchuria, where supplies of these commodities could then be purchased for Japanese currency. Mussolini, in part to distract the Italians from the domestic problems brought on by economic depression, invaded and annexed Ethiopia in 1936. Finally, the depression was primarily responsible for the triumph of Nazism, whose expansionist policies contributed directly to the outbreak of war.

Nationalism was a further cause of the general discontent that helped increase the chances for world war. In eastern Europe, national and ethnic minorities remained alienated from the sovereign states into which the treaty-makers had placed them. This was particularly the case of the Sudetenland Germans, who had been included in the newly created state of Czechoslovakia. That country could in fact boast no national majority, including as it did Czechs, Slovaks, Poles, Ruthenians, and Hungarians, as well as Germans. Although it possessed an enlightened policy of minority self-government, the patchwork state of Czechoslovakia remained unstable. And its instability was to prove a key factor as the tensions mounted in the late 1930s.

A final cause of war was the policy of "appeasement" which was pursued by the Western democracies in the face of German, Italian, and Japanese aggression. The appeasers' strategy was grounded in three commonly held assumptions. The first was that the outbreak of another war was unthinkable. With the memory of the slaughter of 1914–1918 fresh in their minds, many in the West embraced pacifism, or at any rate adopted an attitude that kept them from realistically addressing the implications of Nazi and fascist policies and programs. Second, many in Britain and the United States argued that Germany had been mistreated in the Versailles treaty, that the Germans had legitimate grievances which should be acknowledged and resolved. Finally, the appeasers were, for the most part, staunch anti-Communists. They believed that by assisting Germany to regain its former military and economic power, they were constructing a bulwark to halt the westward advance of Soviet communism. When Japan invaded Manchuria, the West refused to impose sanctions against the Japanese through the League of Nations, arguing that Japan, too, could serve as a counterweight to Russia.

Hitler took advantage of this generally tolerant attitude to advance the expansionist ambitions of Germany. As the country rearmed, Hitler played upon his people's sense of shame and betrayal, proclaiming their right to regain their former power within the world. In 1933, he removed Germany from the League of Nations—and thus from any obligation to adhere to its declarations. In 1935 Hitler tore up the disarmament provisions of the Treaty of Versailles, announcing the revival of conscription and the return to universal military training. In 1936 he repudiated the Locarno Agreements and invaded the Rhineland. Britain and France did nothing to stop him, as they had done nothing to prevent Mussolini's invasion and conquest of Ethiopia the previous year. Hitler's move tipped the balance of power in Germany's favor. While the Rhineland remained demilitarized and German industry in the Ruhr valley unprotected, France had held the upper hand. Now it no longer did so.

In 1936 civil war broke out in Spain; a series of weak republican governments had proved unable to prevent the country's political disintegration. Although they had signed a pact of nonintervention with the other Western powers, Hitler and Mussolini both sent troops and equipment to assist the forces of the rebel fascist commander, Fran-

Guernica by Pablo Picasso. This painting, a protest against the bombing of an undefended city during the Spanish Civil War, has come to be recognized as one of the century's most profound antiwar statements.

The Munich Conference, 1938. Left: Prime Minister Chamberlain of Britain and Hitler during the Munich conference. Right: Chamberlain addressing a crowd on his return from the Munich conference.

cisco Franco. Russia countered with aid to the Communist troops serving under the banner of the Spanish republic. Again, Britain and France failed to act decisively. The Spanish Civil War lasted three years, with the forces of the fascists finally victorious over those of the republicans. The conflict engaged the commitment of many young European and American leftists and intellectuals, who saw it as a test of the West's determination to resist totalitarianism. The fighting was brutal; aerial bombardment of civilians and troops was employed for the first time on a large scale. Because of this, the Spanish war has often been seen as a "dress rehearsal" for the much larger struggle that was shortly to follow. The war also served to confirm Hitler's belief that if Britain, France, and Russia did decide to attempt to contain fascism, they would have a difficult time concerting their policies— another reason, indeed, why Britain and France did remain content to do nothing.

Munich and after

In March of 1938, Hitler annexed Austria, declaring it his intention to bring all Germans into his Reich. Once more, there was no official reaction from the West. Hitler's next target was the Sudetenland in Czechoslovakia. With Austria now a part of Germany, Czechoslovakia was almost entirely surrounded by its hostile expansionist neighbor. Hitler declared that the Sudetenland was a natural part of the Reich and that he intended to occupy it. The British prime minister, Neville Chamberlain, determined to negotiate, but on Hitler's terms. On September 28, Hitler agreed to meet with Chamberlain, Premier Édouard Daladier of France, and Mussolini in a four-power conference in Munich. The result was another capitulation by France and Britain. Ignoring the vital interests of a nation whose territory the Versailles treaty had guaranteed, the four negotiators bargained away a major slice of Czechoslovakia, while that country's representatives were left to await their fate outside the conference room. Chamberlain returned to England proclaiming "peace in our time." Hitler soon proved that fatuous boast untrue. In March 1939 he invaded what was left of Czechoslovakia and established a puppet regime in its capital, Prague. This action convinced British public opinion of the foolhardiness of appeasement. Chamberlain, compelled to shift his policies dramatically, guaranteed the sovereignty of the two states now directly in Hitler's path: Poland and Rumania. France followed suit.

Meanwhile, the appeasement policies of Britain and France had fueled Stalin's fears that the timid Western democracies might strike a bargain with Germany at Soviet expense by diverting Nazi expansion eastward. This, combined with the suspicion that they might make unreliable allies, convinced Stalin that he must look elsewhere for security. Tempted by the traditional Russian desire for territory in Poland, and promised a share of both Poland and the Baltic states by Hitler, Stalin signed a pact with the Nazis in August 1939. In going to Munich, Britain and France had put their interests first; Russia would now look after its own.

2. THE OUTBREAK OF HOSTILITIES

Following the extinction of Czechoslovakia, and despite Chamberlain's guarantee, Hitler demanded the abolition of the Polish Corridor, a narrow strip of territory connecting Poland with the Baltic Sea. The corridor contained a large German population, which Hitler declared must be reunited with the Fatherland. Judging Britain and France by past performance he believed their pledges to Poland worthless. With the Soviets now in his camp, he expected that Poland would quickly

See color map of Europe on the Eve of the Second World War facing page 993

Nazi-Soviet pact

Beginning of the war

The Beginning of the Second World War. A long line of German tanks crossing into Poland.

The blitzkrieg

capitulate, and that the Western allies would back down once more as they had done at Munich. When Poland stood firm, Hitler attacked. On September 1, 1939, German tanks crossed the Polish border. Britain and France sent a joint warning to Germany to cease its aggression. There was no reply; on September 3, Britain and France declared war against Germany.

The conflict with Poland proved to be a brief encounter. In less than three weeks the Polish armies had been routed, Warsaw had been captured, and the chiefs of the Polish government had fled to Rumania. For some months after that the war resolved itself into a kind of siege, a "phony war" or "sitzkrieg," as it was sometimes called. Such fighting as did occur was largely confined to submarine warfare, aerial raids on naval bases, and occasional battles between naval vessels. In the spring of 1940 the sitzkrieg was suddenly transformed into a blitzkrieg, or "lightning war." The Germans struck blows at Norway, Denmark, Belgium, the Netherlands, and France, conquering them in short order, and driving the British and French forces back against the English Channel at Dunkirk in Belgium. Despite heavy German air attacks, the British were able to evacuate over 300,000 troops, many of them in commercial and pleasure boats which had been pressed into emergency service. Northern France, including Paris, was occupied by the Germans. In the south, a puppet government loyal to the Germans was established at Vichy under the leadership of the aged First World War hero, Marshal Henri-Philippe Pétain.

Before launching an invasion across the Channel, the Nazis decided to attempt the reduction of Britain's military strength and civilian will

Left: *London during the Blitz*. This picture conveys a vivid impression of the agony which the British capital suffered during the Battle of Britain, which lasted from August 1940 to June 1941. Behind the tumbling ruins brought down by firebombs is St. Paul's Cathedral. Right: *French Refugees Driven from Their Homes during the Early Years of the Nazi Occupation.*

by air raids. From August 1940 to June 1941, in the so-called Battle of Britain, thousands of planes smashed at British ports, industrial centers, and air defenses throughout the country. Despite the fact that whole sections of cities were laid in ruins and more than 40,000 civilians killed, the British held firm. Winston Churchill had by this time succeeded Neville Chamberlain as prime minister of Britain. A maverick Conservative, who had served in Britain's First World War government as a Liberal, Churchill was not trusted by his party's leadership, particularly since he had been one of the few who had spoken out in favor of British rearmament during the years of appeasement. Now that his warnings had proved true, he was given direction of the war as head of a national government composed of ministers from the Conservative, Liberal, and Labour parties. Churchill, an exceedingly compelling orator, used the radio to persuade his countrymen and women—and the rest of the free world—that Britain must not, and would not, surrender to the Nazis. His friendship with President Roosevelt, and the latter's conviction that the United States must come to Britain's aid, resulted in the shipment of military equipment and ships to the British under the Lend-Lease Act passed by the U.S. Congress in 1941.

Meanwhile, Germany moved eastward into the Balkans, subduing the Rumanians, Hungarians, Bulgarians, and Yugoslavs. The Italians, less successful in their campaigns in Greece and North Africa, required German assistance to accomplish their missions. Scornful of Mussolini's military inadequacies, Churchill called him Hitler's "jackal." Frustrated in his attempt to subjugate Britain, Hitler broke with his erstwhile ally Russia, and turned eastward, on June 22, 1941, with a massive invasion. Before the end of the year his armies had smashed their way to the gates of Moscow but never actually succeeded in capturing it. The defense of Moscow by the Russian armies marked one of the war's important early turning points.

The war was converted into a global conflict when Japan struck at Pearl Harbor on December 7 of the same year. The Japanese had been involved in a costly war with China since 1937. To wage it successfully they needed the oil, rubber, and extensive food resources of the Netherlands Indies, the Malay Peninsula, and Southeast Asia. They had allied with Germany in 1940. (Germany, Italy, and Japan were together known as the Axis powers, a name derived from the Rome-Berlin diplomatic axis formed in the 1930s.) Now, before attacking south, they considered it necessary to secure their position to the rear by crushing American naval and air power on the base of Pearl Harbor. The next day the United States Congress recognized a state of war with Japan, and on December 11 Germany and its allies declared war upon the United States.

In the course of the next two and a half years, events turned slowly but inexorably against the forces of Germany, Italy, and Japan. Churchill and Roosevelt, meeting shortly after the United States's entry

Pearl Harbor, December 7, 1941. This photo shows American battleships sunk at their moorings, following the Japanese raid on what President Franklin D. Roosevelt declared was "the day that will live in infamy."

A German V-2 Rocket. Used in the later years of the war, it was the forerunner of the early space launch vehicles.

The battle of Stalingrad

into the war, agreed that victory in the West would be their first priority. As an initial step toward that goal, the British succeeded in turning the North African advance of Germany's brilliant tank commander, General Erwin Rommel, who had driven the British back across the Sahara to the Egyptian border. That victory was the prelude to a joint Anglo-American invasion of North Africa in November 1942. The success of this first major combined Allied offensive led in turn to further Mediterranean campaigns in the next year, first in Sicily and then in Italy. Mussolini's government was overthrown, and his successors sued for peace. The Germans, however, sent troops into Italy and resurrected Mussolini as the ruler of a puppet state in the north, where he remained a virtual prisoner of the Nazis until his death at the hands of his countrymen at the time of the general defeat of the Axis powers in Europe. Despite Allied attempts to break the German grip on the peninsula, the Nazi forces continued to hold central and northern Italy until the spring of 1945.

In eastern Europe, meanwhile, the Germans had continued to press the war against the Russians, turning in 1942 to the south and the rich agricultural and industrial areas of the Ukraine, the Donets Basin, and the Caucasus oilfields. The German advance was stopped at Stalingrad, in a military struggle of great strategic and symbolic importance for both sides. The battle saw 300,000 Germans for a time in control of the city, then enclosed by the counterattacking Russians in a pincers movement, and eventually, by the time of their surrender, reduced to fewer than half their original number. The loss of the battle of Stalingrad compelled the Germans to undertake a general retreat. By the spring of 1943, they were no further east than they had been the previous year.

Stalin continued to pressure his allies to open a second front in the west to relieve the concerted Nazi drive against Russia. The North African and Italian campaigns were a response to that plea. But not until June 1944 did Allied troops invade France. On June 6 (D-Day) a massive invasion force landed on the Normandy coast. Air superiority, plus a tremendous buildup of matériel and manpower, produced a series of successful advances and the liberation of Paris on August 25. Despite a final German assault in December 1944, the Allied armies penetrated deep into Germany itself by the early spring of 1945.

The D-Day invasion

At the same time, Soviet troops were approaching from the east. On April 21, 1945, they hammered their way into the suburbs of Berlin. During the next ten days a savage battle raged amid the ruins and heaps of rubble. On May 2 the heart of the city was captured, and the Soviet red banner flew from the Brandenburg Gate. A few hours earlier Adolf Hitler killed himself in the bomb-proof shelter of the Chancellery. On May 8 representatives of the German High Command signed a document of unconditional surrender.

End of the war in Europe

The war in the Pacific came to an end four months later. Important victories won by the United States Navy against the Japanese at the battles of the Coral Sea and Midway in the spring of 1942 forestalled Japanese attempts to capture Australia and the Hawaiian Islands so as to deprive the United States of advance bases for a counteroffensive against Japan. Final Allied victory followed further naval battles, island assaults, and land battles in Southeast Asia. In June 1945, the island of Okinawa was taken, after eighty-two days of desperate fighting. The American forces now had a foothold less than 500 miles from the Japanese homeland. The government in Tokyo was anticipating

The Pacific war

Left: *D-Day.* Cargo ships are seen pouring supplies ashore during the invasion of France. Balloon barrages float overhead to protect the ships from low-flying enemy planes. Right: *Signing the German Surrender, May 7, 1945*

The atomic bomb

an invasion and calling upon its citizens for supreme endeavors to meet the crisis.

On July 26 the heads of the United States, British, and Chinese governments issued a joint proclamation calling upon Japan to surrender or be destroyed. In the absence of a reply the United States resolved to make use of a new and revolutionary weapon to end the war quickly. This was the atomic bomb, which could destroy entire cities and their inhabitants, a weapon developed in secrecy in the United States by scientists from Europe and America, some of whom were exiles from Nazi or fascist oppression.

Many high military and naval officers contended that use of the bomb was not necessary, on the assumption that Japan was already beaten. Harry Truman, who had succeeded Roosevelt following the latter's death in April 1945, decided otherwise. On August 6, a single atomic bomb was dropped on Hiroshima, completely obliterating about 60 percent of the city. Three days later a second bomb was dropped, this time on Nagasaki. President Truman warned that the United States would continue to use the atom bomb as long as might be necessary to bring Japan to its knees. On August 14, Tokyo transmitted to Washington an unconditional acceptance of Allied demands.

Total war

To an even greater extent than was the case in the First World War, total populations were mobilized as part of the war effort. Governments imposed the rationing of food and clothing and the regulation of manpower. Production quotas demanded that factories produce around the clock. In Russia, all men between the ages of sixteen and fifty-five and all women between the ages of sixteen and forty-five were pressed into service, either in the armed forces or on the home

View of Hiroshima after the First Atom Bomb Was Dropped, August 6, 1945. This photo, taken one month later, shows the utter devastation of the city. Only a few steel and concrete buildings remained intact.

front. The Germans destroyed much of Russia's industrial plant and existing war matériel in the early months of the war—over 90 percent of Russia's tanks, for example. To produce what was necessary, factories were rebuilt in the security of the Ural mountain region, and whole populations moved there to work in them.

In countries conquered and occupied by the Germans and Italians, the Axis powers installed administrations willing to follow their commands without question. (Vidkun Quisling, the Norwegian Nazi leader, made his name synonymous with the word "traitor.") Life for civilians was harsh at best. Rations in occupied France, for example, were less than half the amount considered to be a healthy minimum. There and elsewhere, Resistance movements emerged, composed of men and women of various political persuasions united in their determination to assist the Allies in driving the Axis powers from their native lands. By transmitting intelligence reports, aiding prisoners to escape, distributing newspapers to counter official propaganda, and undertaking acts of direct sabotage to military and industrial targets, these groups helped the Allied cause immeasurably. The success of the Normandy invasion was in part the result of information concerning German military emplacements sent to Britain by the French Resistance.

The Resistance

The war brought devastation in the form of street fighting and air bombardment to most of the major urban centers of Europe. The Allies proved to be fully as ruthless and even more efficient than the Axis powers in this regard. After some debate, British and American strategists abandoned pinpoint bombing in favor of the nighttime aerial bombardment of entire cities. The result was the deliberate fire-bombing of civilian populations, climaxing in Europe in early 1945 with the brutal obliteration of Dresden, a German city without significant industry and filled with refugees. These attacks were equaled by the German bombing of French, Belgian, Dutch, Russian, and British cities and civilian populations. Such raids were, of course, dwarfed by the United States's atomic bomb attacks on the Japanese cities of Hiroshima and Nagasaki.

The war's devastation of cities

Ghastly as was the destruction meted out by the armed forces to each other and to civilians, none of it matched in premeditated, obscene horror the systematic persecution by the Nazis of whole Jewish populations, not only in Germany itself, but in occupied countries as well. When Allied armies opened the concentration camps in Germany and elsewhere in what had been German-occupied Europe, they found the starved, diseased, and brutalized survivors of the ghastly experience of Nazi persecutions that cost six million prisoners their lives. Most of the men, women, and children who had been imprisoned, tortured, and killed were Jews, although Poles, Russians, Gypsies, homosexuals, and other "traitors" to the Reich had been incarcerated, used for forced labor, and executed also.

The concentration camps

German Civilians Compelled to View the Bodies of Concentration Camp Victims at the Landesburg Camp in 1945 as an American army Officer Lectures Them on the Horrors of the Nazis' "Final Solution"

3. THE PEACE SETTLEMENT

Postwar plans

During the war the Allied leaders had come together on several occasions to discuss war aims and postwar goals. The public rhetoric of government propaganda spoke of the need for a world without conflict and of the right of all people to political self-determination, objectives expressed in the "Atlantic Charter" issued by Roosevelt and Churchill in August 1941, and in a declaration signed by twenty-six nations, including Britain, the United States, the Soviet Union, and China, the following year. Yet those worthy goals, like most of Wilson's Fourteen Points, fell eventual victim to the realities of international politics.

Allied conflicts

Stalin, Churchill, and Roosevelt convened in two conferences that were of major importance in determining the shape and political complexion of postwar Europe. In both cases, tensions between the three major participants were to some degree glossed over in their desire to present a united front to the world. Yet those tensions were real. The focus of disagreement was central Europe, and particularly the future of Germany and Poland. Stalin insisted that Russia retain the Polish territory annexed in 1939 at the time of the Nazi-Soviet pact, an expression of his understandable desire to build a bulwark against any future German aggression, and a reflection of his unwillingness to see postwar Western influence extended too far in Russia's direction. His memories of Anglo-American participation in the attempt by White Russians to overthrow the newly created communist regime in 1919 were matched by American perceptions of the Soviet Union as an expansionist and politically alien and dangerous regime. All three leaders were also confronted by conflicting plots and aspirations on the part of governments-in-exile from Nazi-occupied countries, and of extra-governmental Resistance groups—often led by Communists—whose struggles to retain or to assume leadership in their homelands were exceeded only by their determination to oust the Germans.

When the three leaders met in Teheran in December 1943, they managed to put forward a declaration of unified purpose only by postponing the really knotty problems that confronted them. The invasion of France was agreed to for the following year; Stalin undertook to enter the war against Japan following the defeat of Germany. But on the question of Poland, only the most tentative agreement was reached regarding boundary lines, and the nature of the postwar Polish government was left for further negotiation.

The Teheran conference

By the time Stalin, Churchill, and Roosevelt met again, in February 1945 at Yalta, the military situation favored Russia's position. Soviet troops had occupied Poland the previous spring; they now held part of Czechoslovakia as well, and were poised to invade Germany. Once more the matter of Poland's future arose, as well as that of the composition of postwar regimes. A general declaration outlined plans for Russian expansion westward into Poland, and the compensation of Poland with territory taken from the Germans. As to Poland's government, though communiqués spoke of the need for free elections there and elsewhere among the occupied countries, the fact remained that the Soviets had already established a communist government in Warsaw, and were unlikely to tolerate its replacement by an anti-communist faction still in London, whatever the results of an election. Yalta produced accord on several important issues: the establish-

The Yalta conference

The Yalta Conference. Churchill, Molotov, Secretary of State Stettinius, at the left, and Stalin, in the center, with glasses raised in a toast. Roosevelt is also to Stalin's left.

The Potsdam conference

ment of a United Nations organization to keep the peace; the terms for Russian entry into the Japanese war; the positioning of zones of Allied occupation in Germany and Austria; and agreement in principle to a policy of German reparation payments—though in goods and equipment rather than in gold, as had been the case after the First World War.

Little more than two months after Germany's surrender, the Allies met again, this time at Potsdam, a suburb of Berlin and the former residence of Prussian kings. Roosevelt had died the previous spring; his place at the conference was taken by his successor, President Harry Truman. Churchill represented Britain until replaced, as the result of elections at home, by the new prime minister and Labour party leader, Clement Attlee. Stalin remained to negotiate for the Soviets. As at past conferences, less was settled than was allowed to remain unresolved. Peace treaties were to be prepared with the "recognized democratic governments" of previously occupied lands. Yet the question as to whether those governments set up by the Soviets in Poland and—by this time—elsewhere in eastern Europe were truly democratic was not settled. Polish boundaries were redrawn to conform to the general agreement reached at Yalta. An inter-Allied war tribunal was established to try major Nazi leaders for "war crimes." In November 1945, the trials began in Nuremberg, Germany. The following September, eighteen of the twenty-two defendants were found guilty and received sentences ranging from ten-years' imprisonment to death.

The Potsdam conference was shadowed by the East-West conflict that had darkened all the wartime meetings and was to do the same to

The Potsdam Conference. Churchill, a cigar in his mouth, is seated in the back to the left; Stalin is at the right; Truman is seated with his back to the camera.

international politics in the immediate postwar years. The division of Germany into four occupied zones—American, British, French, and Soviet—and the agreement to structure reparations payments on the basis of those zones rather than on a united Germany, forecast the unwillingness of either the Soviet Union or the Western powers to trust each other, or to tolerate the extension of the other's influence in that country which, though devastated, still remained vital to the security and peace of Europe as a whole. *East-West tensions*

The treaty with Japan, though it too produced disagreement between Russia and the West, did not reflect conflicts as immediate as those that characterized the European negotiations. The treaty deprived the Japanese of all the territory they had acquired since 1854—their entire overseas empire. They surrendered the southern half of Sakhalin Island and the Kuril Islands to Soviet Russia, and the Bonins and Ryukyus to control by the United States. They also renounced all rights to Formosa, which was left in an undefined status. They yielded as well to the United States the right to continue maintaining military installations in Japan until the latter was able to defend itself. The treaty went into effect in April 1952 despite opposition from the Russians, who feared a United States military presence in the Far East. *The treaty with Japan*

As in the case of the Versailles treaty one of the most significant elements in the settlements was their provision for an international organization. The old League of Nations had failed to avert the outbreak of war in 1939, and in April 1946 it was formally dissolved. Yet Allied statesmen continued to recognize the need for some international organization. In February 1945, they agreed at Yalta that a conference to respond to that need should be convoked the following April. Despite the sudden death of Roosevelt two weeks earlier, the conference met as scheduled. A charter was adopted on June 26, providing for a world organization to be known as the United Nations and to be founded upon the principle of "the sovereign equality of all peace-loving states." Its important agencies were to be (1) a General Assembly composed of representatives of all the member states; (2) a Security Council composed of reresentatives of the United States, Great Britain, the Soviet Union, the Republic of China, and France, with permanent seats, and of six other states chosen by the General Assembly to fill the nonpermanent seats; (3) a Secretariat consisting of a secretary-general and a staff of subordinates; (4) an Economic and Social Council composed of eighteen members chosen by the General Assembly; (5) a Trusteeship Council, and (6) an International Court of Justice. *Establishment of the United Nations*

Although the United Nations has failed to live up to the hopes of its founders, it continues to function as the world's longest lived international assembly of nations. By far the most important functions of the new organization were assigned by the charter to the Security Council. This agency has the "primary responsibility for the maintenance of international peace and security." It has authority to investigate any *The Security Council*

The veto power of the Big Five

Other agencies of the U.N.

Record of the U.N.

dispute between nations, to recommend methods for settlement, and, if necessary to preserve the peace, to employ diplomatic or economic measures against an aggressor. If, in its judgment, these have proved, or are likely to prove, inadequate, it may "take such action by air, naval, or land forces" as may be required to maintain or restore international order. The member states are required by the charter to make available to the Security Council, on its call, armed forces for the maintenance of peace.

The Security Council was so organized as to give almost a monopoly of authority to its permanent members, since no action of any kind could be taken without the unanimous consent of Great Britain, France, the United States, the Republic of China, the Soviet Union, and two other members besides. This absolute veto given to each of the principal states, instead of bolstering the peace of the world, crippled the council and rendered it helpless in the face of emergencies.

The remaining agencies of the U.N. were given a wide variety of functions. The Secretariat, composed of a secretary-general and a numerous staff, is chiefly an administrative authority. Its duties, though, are by no means routine, for the secretary-general may bring to the attention of the Security Council any matter which, in his opinion, threatens international peace. The functions of the Economic and Social Council are the most varied of all. Composed of eighteen members elected by the General Assembly, it has authority to initiate studies and make recommendations with respect to international social, economic, health, educational, cultural, and related matters, and may perform services within such fields at the request of U.N. members.

During its first three decades the work of various U.N. agencies helped the organization achieve a modestly impressive record of accomplishment. But against its successes must be recorded major failures as well. The U.N. was unable to establish control of nuclear weapons. And it was powerless in the face of any determined effort by a major power to have its own way, as in the case of the Soviet suppression of a revolt in Hungary in 1956; or the massive intervention by the United States in Vietnam in the 1960s and early 1970s. If the United Nations acted upon occasion to defuse potentially explosive world situations, it failed to achieve the lofty peacemaking and peacekeeping goals set for it by its founders.

SELECTED READINGS

• *Items so designated are available in paperback editions.*

• Carr, E. H., *The Twenty-Years' Crisis, 1919–1939,* London, 1942. Stimulating, though somewhat dogmatic.
• Carr, Raymond, *The Spanish Tragedy: The Civil War in Perspective,* London, 1977. A thoughtful introduction to the Spanish Civil War and the evolution of Franco's Spain.

Collins, Larry, and Dominique, LaPierre, *Is Paris Burning?*, New York, 1965. A highly readable account of the liberation of Paris.

• Dawidowicz, Lucy S., *The War Against the Jews, 1933–1945*, New York, 1975. A full account of the Holocaust.

• Divine, Robert A., *Roosevelt and World War II*, Baltimore, 1969. A diplomatic history.

• Feis, Herbert, *Churchill-Roosevelt-Stalin: The War They Waged and the Peace They Sought*, Princeton, 1957. A standard survey.

Géraud, André, *The Gravediggers of France*, Garden City, N.Y., 1944. A critical and impassioned account of the fall of France.

Gilbert, Martin, and R. Gott, *The Appeasers*, Boston, 1963. Excellent study of British pro-German sentiment in the 1930s.

Holborn, Hajo, *The Political Collapse of Europe*, New York, 1951. Examines Europe's position in light of the rise of Russia and the United States as superpowers.

• Jackson, Gabriel, *The Spanish Republic and the Civil War, 1931–1939*, Princeton, 1965. A solid, useful account.

Michel, Henri, *The Shadow War: The European Resistance, 1939–1945*, New York, 1972. Thoroughly researched and compelling reading.

• Milward, Alan S., *War, Economy, and Society, 1939–1945*, Berkeley, 1977. Analyzes the impact of the war on the world economy and the ways in which economic resources of the belligerents determined strategies.

• Paxton, Robert O., *Vichy France: Old Guard and New Order, 1940–1944*, New York, 1972. A bitter account.

• Taylor, A. J. P., *The Origins of the Second World War*, New York, 1962. A controversial but provocative attempt to prove that Hitler did not want a world war.

Thomas, Hugh, *The Spanish Civil War*, New York, 1961. A thorough and balanced account.

Wheeler, Bennett, J. W., *Munich: Prologue to Tragedy*, London, 1966. A sensitive treatment of prewar diplomatic negotiations, outdated to some extent, but still evocative.

• Wright, Gordon, *The Ordeal of Total War, 1939–1945*, New York, 1968. Particularly good on the domestic response to war and the mobilization of the resources of the modern state.

SOURCE MATERIALS

• Bloch, Marc, *Strange Defeat: A Statement of Evidence Written in 1940*, London, 1949. An analysis of the fall of France, written by one of France's greatest historians, who later died fighting for the Resistance.

• Churchill, Winston S., *The Second World War*, 6 vols., London, 1948–1954. The war as Churchill saw it and as he wanted history to see it. Especially useful is the first volume on the 1930s, *The Gathering Storm*.

• De Gaulle, Charles, *The Complete War Memoirs*, New York, 1964. De Gaulle's apologia.

• Hershey, John, *Hiroshima*, New York, 1946. A moving account of the aftermath of the U.S. atomic bombing written very soon after the event.

Noakes, Jeremy, and Geoffrey Pridham, *Documents on Nazism, 1919–1945*, New York, 1975. A helpful collection.

Part Seven

THE EMERGENCE OF
WORLD CIVILIZATION

*Western civilization, as we have described and analyzed it, no longer
exists today. Instead, we speak in terms of a world civilization, one that
owes much of its history and many of its most perplexing problems to the
West, but one which is no longer shaped by those few nations that for so
many centuries dominated the globe.*

*The great powers of the nineteenth century—Britain, France, and Ger-
many—are powers now only insofar as they have agreed to pool their interests in an all-European Common Market. The mid–twentieth century
superpowers, the United States and the Soviet Union, after two decades of
confrontation, have begun to understand the limitations of their power and
to adjust their expectations accordingly. Power, and with it the attention of
the world, is shifting from the West to the emerging nations of Africa, the
Middle East, Asia, and Latin America. Their vast natural resources are
affording many of them the chance to play the old Western game of power politics, and in a world arena wider than ever before. The equally vast dimensions
of their internal problems—economic, racial, nutritional, and political—suggest that their solution will have to be worldwide as well. We are all,
as the American designer Buckminster Fuller has said, partners for better or
worse on "spaceship earth."*

The Emergence of World Civilization

POLITICS	SCIENCE & INDUSTRY

1945

Truman Doctrine, 1947
Independence of India, 1947
Communist regimes established in eastern Europe,
   1947–1948
Marshall Plan, 1948
Division of Germany, 1949
Victory of Chinese communists, 1949
NATO, 1949
Korean war, 1950–1953

Death of Stalin, 1953

Hydrogen bomb, 1952
Discovery of polio vaccine, 1953

Discovery of DNA, 1953

Hungarian revolt, 1956
Suez crisis, 1956

Sputnik launched, 1957

1960

Conflict in the Congo, 1960
Nigerian Civil War, 1960s
Berlin wall, 1961

Cuban missile crisis, 1962
Assassination of John F. Kennedy, 1963
War in Vietnam, 1964–1975
Assassination of Malcolm X, 1965
Civil war in Nigeria, 1966–1970
Arab-Israeli war, 1967
Assassination of Martin Luther King, Jr., 1968
Czechoslovakian revolt, 1968

Manned U.S. spacecraft lands on moon, 1969
Advent of automation, 1970s

1970

Civil war in India, 1971

First SALT agreements signed, 1972
Arab-Israeli war, 1973

Assassination of Aldo Moro, 1978
Egyptian-Israeli peace treaty, 1979
Iranian revolution, 1979
U.S.S.R. invasion of Afghanistan, 1979
Iran-Iraq war, 1980–
Zimbabwe established, 1980
Assassination of Anwar Sadat, 1981
U.S. rejection of SALT II agreement, 1981

1980

Solidarity movement in Poland, 1982–
War in Lebanon, 1982–

ECONOMICS & SOCIETY	ARTS & LETTERS	
	Richard Wright, *Native Son,* 1940	
	Abstract expressionism in art, mid-1940s	*1945*
	Albert Camus, *The Plague,* 1947	
	Norman Mailer, *The Naked and the Dead,* 1948	
	Simone de Beauvoir, *The Second Sex,* 1949–1950	
	James Jones, *From Here to Eternity,* 1951	
European Coal and Steel Community, 1952	Samuel Beckett, *Waiting for Godot,* 1952	
	Boris Pasternak, *Doctor Zhivago,* 1957	
European Common Market established, 1958		
Black civil rights movement, United States, 1960–1968	"Pop" art, 1960s	*1960*
Frantz Fanon, *Wretched of the Earth,* 1961	Francois Truffant, *Jules and Jim,* 1961	
Youth "revolution," 1960s	James Baldwin, *The Fire Next Time,* 1963	
Women's liberation movement, 1960s–1970s		
	Arthur Penn, *Bonnie and Clyde* (1967)	
	Günter Grass, *Local Anaesthetic,* 1970	*1970*
	Aleksandr Solzhenitsyn, *The Gulag Archipelago,* 1973	
Worldwide inflation and unemployment, late 1970s and early 1980s		*1980*

Chapter 30

NEW POWER RELATIONSHIPS AND THE NEW EUROPE

Not only the West but also the East is becoming aware of the importance of all-European cooperation. Slowly, and it is to be hoped not too late, it will become clear that the cooperation and unification of Europe is not directed against anyone. In a dangerous epoch and in a strife-divided world it could, rather, be an example of how nations and states, regardless of different kinds of governmental and social systems, can achieve prosperity and security by peacefully working together.

—Willy Brandt, *A Peace Policy for Europe*

In April 1945 European men and women, surveying the devastation that their countries had brought down upon each other during the past six years, found it all but impossible to imagine their continent arising from the ashes of total conflict. As in the First World War, both victors and vanquished had endured punishing destruction. Between 1914 and 1918, 8 million had died. Now the total was four times as great. Although France and Britain had suffered fewer casualties in the Second than in the First World War, loss of life elsewhere had been cataclysmic. Poland's population was reduced by 20 percent (in part as a consequence of the Nazis' ruthless destruction of the Jews); losses in the Soviet Union were close to 15 million; in Germany, they were 5 million.

The costs of war

Across Europe, cities lay in ruins. Hitler had boasted in 1935 that in ten years Berlin would be transformed so that no one could recognize it. His prophecy came true, though in a grisly fashion he had not intended. Industrial and commercial centers in France, the Low Countries, Italy, and in the wasted territories of central Europe and Russia were largely rubble. Housing was scarce everywhere—in some areas it was practically nonexistent. Six million houses had been destroyed in German-occupied Soviet Russia; 93 percent of the homes in Dusseldorf, Germany, were deemed uninhabitable. Food remained in dangerously short supply, a consequence of the violation of agricultural lands and people, the lack of farm machinery and fertilizer, and a severe

The extent of the destruction

Berlin, 1945. The rubble from which the German "miracle" was created.

drought in the summer of 1945. A year later, about 100 million people in Europe still existed on less than 1,500 calories per day—not enough to sustain working adults in a healthy state. Food rationing remained a dreary fact of life everywhere, for without it a large portion of the Continent's population would have starved to death. The food shortage was intensified by a general breakdown of transportation and communication. In the British and American zones of Germany 740 out of 958 major bridges had been destroyed. France had suffered the loss of about two-thirds of its railway stock and its merchant fleet. Canals had been bombed; harbors were choked with scuttled warships. During the winter of 1945–1946, many regions had little or no fuel for heat and what coal there was (less than half the prewar supply) could not be transported to those areas most in need of it.

No wonder Europeans were initially dazed by the trauma they had inflicted upon themselves. The wonder, indeed, was that the period of trauma lasted such a relatively short time. Ten years later, Europe had been transformed—though not restored. Two all-important changes had occurred by then. The first, reflecting an altered balance of international power, resulted in a dividend continent, the East under the control of the Soviet Union, the West dominated by the military and diplomatic presence of the United States. The second change, a consequence of human determination and favorable economic trends, produced in the West a buoyant, lively, and creative civilization, more expansive and up-to-date than even the most optimistic forecaster might have deemed possible in 1945.

Ten years later

1. A DIVIDED CONTINENT

During the decade after Second World War the world of nations assumed a bipolar character, in large measure the result of mutual mistrust and increasing hostility between the Soviet Union and the United States. The war had left these two nations the most powerful on earth. Germany, Italy, and Japan were destined for a time to play a subordinate international role as a consequence of their defeat. Britain and France possessed neither populations nor resources great enough to qualify as "superpowers." China, the remaining major victor in the conflict, was soon thereafter overwhelmed by a revolution that turned that nation in upon itself. Hence the dominance of the United States and the Soviet Union, both vying for world supremacy and both striving to draw the states of Europe into their orbits.

A bipolar world

The Soviet Union had insisted during the negotiations at Teheran and Yalta that it had a legitimate claim to hegemony over eastern Europe, a claim that Western leaders willingly acknowledged. When visiting Moscow in 1944, Churchill and Stalin had bargained like two Old World power brokers over the fate of several supposedly free nations. Churchill proposed a 90 percent preponderance of Soviet influence in Rumania, countered by 90 percent for the West in Greece; Yugoslavia, 50–50; and so on. Stalin, however, increasingly mistrustful of Western leadership, believed that bargains with the West, no matter how attractive they might appear on paper, were really worth little. "Churchill," he remarked, "is the kind who, if you don't watch him, will slip a kopek out of your pocket. . . . Roosevelt . . . dips in his hands only for bigger coins." Stalin's authoritarian domestic regime was motivated by a siege mentality that saw almost everyone as an enemy or, at best, a threat. Not surprisingly, his foreign policy was dictated by that same state of mind.

Soviet hegemony in the East

Yet Stalin's anti-Western policy was based upon more than personal paranoia. It was a reflection of traditional fears that had characterized Russia's attitudes toward its European neighbors for centuries, of ambivalences toward Western ways that had marked the regime of Peter the Great, for example, at the beginning of the eighteenth century, and of Alexander III at the end of the nineteenth. Stalin's mistrust of the United States in particular stemmed as well from the prewar years when the Americans had never hesitated to express their antagonism to Stalinist communism. U.S. mistrust was matched by escalating fear on the part of Russia's leaders of American-inspired military and economic encirclement.

Winston Churchill Denounces Soviet Tyranny. In a speech at Fulton, Missouri, in March 1946, Churchill coined the phrase "iron curtain" to characterize the Soviet's partitioning of eastern from western Europe.

From the standpoint of economic power, the United States far outdistanced the other nations of the world. Since 1939 Americans had doubled their national income and quadrupled their savings. Though they constituted only 7 percent of the world's population, they enjoyed over 30 percent of the world's estimated income. For the first time in its history the United States was in a position to be the economic and military arbiter of at least half the earth. The United States controlled both the Atlantic and Pacific Oceans, policed the Mediterranean, and shaped the development of international policy in western Europe. And until 1949, America had a monopoly of death-dealing atomic weapons.

Russia's strengths and weaknesses

Soviet Russia emerged from the Second World War as the second-strongest power on earth. Though its navy was small, its land army and possibly its air force by 1948 were the largest in the world. Soviet population was climbing rapidly toward 200 million, and this in spite of the loss of 7 million soldiers and about 8 million civilians during the war. In mineral wealth and petroleum resources Russia's position compared favorably with that of the richest countries. On the other hand, its industrial machine had been badly crippled by the war. No fewer than 1,700 Russian cities and towns had been totally destroyed along with 40,000 miles of railway and 31,000 factories. Stalin declared in 1946 that it would probably require at least six years to repair the damage and rebuild the devastated areas.

The Soviet Union in eastern Europe

In part because of the need to recoup their enormous industrial losses, the Soviets were particularly determined to maintain political, economic, and military control of those countries in eastern Europe which they had liberated from Nazi control. The Russians employed diplomatic pressure, political infiltration, and military terrorism to establish "people's republics" in eastern Europe sympathetic to the Soviet regime. In country after country the process repeated itself: at first, all-party coalition governments from which only fascists were excluded; then further coalitions, in which communists predominated; and finally, one-party states. By 1948, governments that owed allegiance to Moscow were established in Poland, Hungary, Rumania, Bulgaria, and Czechoslovakia. The nations of eastern Europe did not all succumb without a struggle. Greece, which the Russians wished to include within their sphere of influence, was torn by civil war until 1949, when with Western aid its monarchy was restored. A direct challenge to the Yalta guarantee of free, democratic elections occurred in Czechoslovakia, where in 1948 the Soviets crushed the coalition government of liberal leaders Eduard Beneš and Jan Masaryk.

See color map of Europe facing page 1057

Eastern European resistance

The most important check the Soviets received at this time to their campaign for eastern European hegemony also occurred in 1948, when the Yugoslavian government of the wartime hero Marshal Tito declared its independence of Moscow and its determination to steer a course unallied to either East or West. Tito, the only satellite communist leader who had risen to power on his own and not as a Soviet puppet, possessed political authority rooted within his own country that secured his position from reprisals once he had established Yugoslavia's freedom from Soviet hegemony. Events in Czechoslovakia and Yugoslavia inspired a series of Soviet-directed purges within the political hierarchies of the various satellite governments, a measure of the degree to which Stalin remained prey to the fear of opposition.

The United States countered these moves with massive programs of economic and military aid to western Europe. In 1947, President Truman proclaimed the Truman Doctrine, which provided assistance programs to prevent further communist infiltration into the governments of Greece and Turkey. The following year, the Marshall Plan, named for Secretary of State George Marshall who first proposed it, provided funds for the reconstruction of western European industry. The plan was notable in two respects: first, it represented an attempt by the United States to restore the strength of its most serious economic competitors, and of its former enemy Germany, in the belief that an economically independent Europe would be less likely to fall prey to Soviet domination. Second, it relied upon a willingness on the part of the western European nations to coordinate their economic efforts, substituting, at least to some degree, cooperation for competition.

The Marshall Plan

At the same time, the United States moved to shore up the military defenses of the West. In April 1949, a group of representatives of North Atlantic states together with Canada and the United States signed an agreement providing for the establishment of the North Atlantic Treaty Organization (NATO). Subsequently Greece, Turkey, and West Germany were added as members. The treaty declared that an armed attack against any one of the signatory parties would be regarded as an attack against all, and that they would combine their armed strength to whatever extent necessary to repel the aggressor. The joint military command, or NATO army, established in 1950, was increased from thirty to fifty divisions in 1953, with a rearmed West Germany contributing twelve of the divisions.

NATO

The Russians reacted with understandable alarm to the determination of the United States to strengthen western Europe economically and militarily. They organized an international political arm, the Cominform, responsible for the coordination of worldwide communist policy and programs. In addition the Soviets rejected an original offer of Marshall Plan aid, and instead organized an eastern European counterpart for economic recovery, the Council for Mutual Economic Assistance. They responded to NATO with the establishment of military alliances, confirmed by the Warsaw Pact of 1955. This agreement set up a joint armed forces command among its signatories, and more important, authorized the continued stationing of Russian troops in Albania, Czechoslovakia, Hungary, Poland, Rumania, and the eastern portion of Germany, which had remained under Soviet domination since the end of the war.

Russian response

Germany was, in fact, the focal point of East-West tensions during these years. After the war, the Russians had continued to insist on $10 billion worth of reparations from Germany in the form of industrial

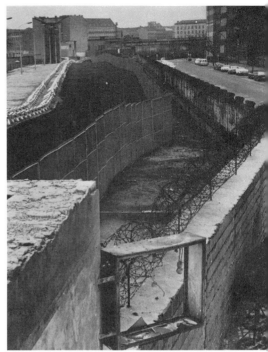

Crises in Berlin. Left: The Berlin Airlift, 1948. For fifteen months the United States, Britain, and France airlifted over two million tons of supplies into West Berlin, around which the Russians had imposed a land blockade. Right: The Berlin Wall, 1961. Thirteen years after the blockade, the East German government constructed a wall between East and West Berlin to stop the flow of escapees to the West. This manifestation of the "iron curtain" remains in place today.

Focus on Germany

production. Although the Soviets' desperate economic condition and fear of a revived Germany played a role in this posture, Britain and the United States read this demand as a reflection of a Soviet desire to keep Germany weak and therefore susceptible to political instability—specifically, to the spread of communism.

By 1946 the joint administration of Germany by the four former Allied powers had collapsed. The Soviet Union remained in control

The Berlin blockade

of its satellite, which eventually became the nominally independent German Democratic Republic (East Germany), while the Western powers continued to support the industrial recovery of the area under their control—in its turn to emerge as the Federal Republic of Germany (West Germany). A crisis arose in 1948 when, in retaliation for the reunification of the western zones of control under one authority, the Russians closed down road and rail access from the west to Berlin. Berlin, though within the territory of East Germany, was administered by all four powers. The Western powers countered with an airlift of food and other necessary supplies which prevented the collapse of the city into Soviet hands. After almost a year the Russians lifted the blockade. For many years to come, however, Berlin was to remain one of the hottest spots in the ongoing "Cold War," as it came to be called, between Russia and the West. The city symbolized opposition to a divided Germany, as well as the determination of the Western powers to ensure that nation's economic recovery.

The tensions that produced the Cold War were the result of a set of misconceptions on both sides. Americans, who had been persuaded by wartime government propaganda to admire the Russians as stalwart anti-fascists, were naïvely disillusioned when they discovered that their erstwhile allies were in fact not democrats. Concerned about the economic weakness throughout postwar western Europe, U.S. leaders allowed themselves to believe that the Russians were hatching a vast plan to take advantage of that weakness by establishing communist regimes throughout the West, as they had in the East.

The Cold War: U.S. attitudes

Scholars have recently argued convincingly that there was no grand Soviet strategy of this sort. The Russians were not willing to undertake any such campaign, primarily because they were economically and militarily incapable of doing so. However, since the Soviets had long feared encirclement by hostile capitalist powers, they saw the Truman and Marshall programs as a direct form of neoimperialism, an American plot to subject western Europe to the economic hegemony of the United States. Stalin found it useful to orchestrate his propaganda to this theme. As a result of wartime destruction, he needed to convince the Russian people that they must undergo a further series of rugged Five-Year Plans stressing the production of heavy industrial materials rather than consumer goods. He could demand sacrifices more convincingly if he could point to an international anti-Russian conspiracy.

Russian attitudes

Stalin himself remained deeply suspicious, not only of the West, but of any power or personality perceived by him as a threat to his dictatorial rule. He convened neither Central Committee nor party congress. He relied on a shrinking number of political henchmen to carry out the business of government, among them: Vyacheslav Molotov, the Soviet foreign minister; Lavrenty Beria, head of the powerful secret police; and Andrei Zhdanov, secretary of the party central committee. The latter was charged with the task of devising a new communist gospel, one prescribed by Stalin, which tended to ignore the earlier doctrines of Marx, Engels, and Lenin, and amounted to little more than an apologia for Stalin's repressive personal despotism. Party propaganda preached Soviet superiority to the West. Writers and artists were attacked for imitating their Western counterparts. Economists were taken to task for suggesting that European industry might succeed in recovering from the damages it had sustained. In the realm of science, accepted genetic theory was supplanted by that of the Russian Trofim Lysenko, whose work implied the inheritance of acquired characteristics; Einstein was vilified; and Freud was pronounced a decadent charlatan.

Stalinism

Only with Stalin's death in 1953 did this relentless barrage of anti-Western propaganda begin to abate somewhat. Although relations

After Stalin

Nikita Khrushchev, Premier (1958–1964) and First Secretary of the Communist Party (1956–1964) of the Soviet Union, Addressing the United Nations in 1958

Khrushchev's goals and policies

between East and West remained wary, tensions eased considerably during the late 1950s and 1960s. The United States, it is true, continued to adhere to a policy of Soviet "containment," seeking as allies those most willing to oppose by military force, if necessary, the spread of international communism. By the mid-1950s, however, western European nations had begun to wonder whether U.S. intervention in their affairs might not, in fact, represent as much an American power play as an attempt to protect the West from Soviet aggression. American claims to the role of "protector of the free world" began to sound hollow, particularly after U.S. Secretary of State John Foster Dulles negotiated a diplomatic and military understanding with the aging Spanish dictator Francisco Franco in 1955.

In the Soviet Union, a change of direction was signaled by the accession to power in that same year of Nikita Khrushchev (1894–1971). Khrushchev possessed a kind of earthy directness which, despite his hostility to the West, nevertheless helped for a time to ease tensions. Abandoning the seclusion of the Kremlin, where Stalin had immured himself, he traveled throughout the world. On visits to the United States in 1958 and 1960 he traded quips with Iowa farmers and was entertained at Disneyland. Attending a meeting of the United Nations in New York, he underscored his disagreement with the speaker by banging his desk with his shoe.

As testimony to his desire to reduce international conflict, Khrushchev soon agreed to the first of a series of summit meetings with the leaders of Britain, France, and the United States. This new Soviet determination to lower international tensions grew out of Khrushchev's need to consolidate his regime at home and to prevent the threatened crumbling of the communist bloc in eastern Europe. The harsh demands of the Stalin regime had generated discontent among the Russian people. Dissenters, their voices no longer silenced by the Stalinist police, began to demand a shift from the production of heavy machinery and armaments to the manufacture of consumer goods, and, in the arts, a return to at least a measure of intellectual freedom of expression. Their voices were heard in essays and in novels such as Ilya Ehrenburg's *The Thaw* (1954), which contributed its name to the period. The Russian leadership followed a tricky and not always successful line, on the one hand denouncing the excesses of the Stalinist regime and the "cult of personality" that Stalin had imposed upon his nation; on the other, as Stalin's heirs, loosening only partially their grip on the lives of their countrymen and women. When, in 1956, Khrushchev delivered a secret speech to the Communist party's twentieth congress on the crimes of the Stalin regime, he did so by describing Stalin himself as a bungler and, ultimately, a madman, but at the same time by defending the system of government that Stalin had created.

Meanwhile, throughout the other communist states, growing resentment of Soviet demands for rapid industrialization and collectivization generated arguments for an easing of the restrictions that Stalinism had imposed. In response to these pressures the Soviet leaders altered their economic goals and began preaching that there was more than one road to socialism. The Soviet Union's new posture toward its client states in eastern Europe received its severest test in 1956 when Poland and Hungary demanded greater autonomy in the management of their domestic affairs. In Poland, the government at first responded to major strikes with military repression and then with a promise of liberalization. The anti-Stalinist Polish leader Wladyslaw Gomulka was able to win Soviet permission for his country to pursue its own "ways of socialist development" by pledging Poland's continued loyalty to the terms of the Warsaw Pact. Events in Hungary produced a different result. There, protests against Stalinist policies developed into a much broader anti-communist struggle. If the Russians were prepared to entertain a liberalization of domestic policy, they would not tolerate a repudiation of the Warsaw Pact. On November 4, 1956, Russian troops occupied Budapest; leaders of the Hungarian liberation were taken prisoner and executed.

Challenges in eastern Europe: Poland and Hungary

Despite these events, Khrushchev did not abandon his policy of "peaceful coexistence" with the West. Though he did not renounce his ultimate belief in the triumph of communism, he argued that victory could be achieved by other than military means. Yet Soviet leaders remained unyielding in their determination to reduce any possible German military threat to eastern Europe. They continued to nurture the fear that Germany might launch a new war, abetted by its capitalist allies. For this reason, they staunchly opposed the reunification of the country. In 1961 the East German government built a high wall separating the two sectors of Berlin in order to cut off the

The limits of coexistence: The Berlin Wall

The Occupation of Czechoslovakia. In 1968 the liberalized regime of Alexander Dubček was suppressed by the Soviets. The violent response by the citizens was put down by military force.

The Czech revolt of 1968

Eurocommunism and independence from Soviet policy

Soviets relax their hold on the East

escape of thousands of East Germans to West Berlin and thence to western Germany. The wall remained as a symbol of Soviet determination to prevent the formation of a united Germany.

Khruschchev eventually fell prey to political rivals and was deposed in 1964, with the reins of Soviet power passing to Alexei Kosygin (1904–1980) as premier and Leonid Brezhnev (1906–1982) as secretary of the Communist party. The Soviets continued to hold the governments of eastern Europe in check. In 1968 they sent troops into Czechoslovakia after the leadership there had attempted to meet criticisms by decentralizing the administration, democratizing the Communist party, and permitting a brief flowering of intellectual life.

Throughout the 1960s and 1970s, politicians in western Europe responded in various ways to the fact of their divided continent. Following the events in Hungary and Czechoslovakia, leaders of Communist parties in France, Italy, and elsewhere recognized a need to separate themselves from Moscow's repressive line if they were to retain credibility with their memberships or attain political power. In 1975 the word "Eurocommunism" appeared for the first time in print. Eurocommunists declared their independence of Soviet foreign policy, while proclaiming their continuing adherence to the principles first espoused by Marx and Engels. The practice of yielding to Moscow on matters of foreign policy, so characteristic of western European Communist parties from the 1920s to the 1950s, was henceforth abandoned. "We, the communists of today," the Spanish leader Santiago Carillo remarked, "have no international discipline imposed upon us. What unites us today are the bonds of affinity, based on the theory of scientific socialism." Eurocommunists showed a new interest in participating as partners in coalition governments with noncommunist parties of the Left which they had heretofore shunned. In a joint statement in 1975, the French and Italian communists proclaimed that "socialism is democracy realized in the most complete manner, and the prerequisite in achieving this goal is a continuous democratization of economic, political and social life." The political division of Europe into Eastern and Western camps had compelled Western communists to cut their close ties to the Soviet Union. Moscow had been to them what Rome was to Catholic Christendom, Carillo declared. No longer, however. The great divide had fragmented an international movement into a collection of polycentric political entities.

At the same time, Western leaders remained concerned about a divided Europe and sought ways to bring the two halves into closer association with each other. Despite evidence to the contrary in Hungary and Czechoslovakia, Soviet leaders also perceived a need to relax their hold on the satellite nations of the East. Following the Czech invasion in 1968, they proclaimed the so-called Brezhnev Doctrine, which stated that while no socialist state should permit itself to adopt policies detrimental to the interests of international socialism, each state might proceed to determine the most appropriate path for its own development.

The politician most effective in bridging the gap between East and West was the West German Willy Brandt, chancellor of West Germany in the early 1970s. Brandt, in his youth an outspoken enemy of Hitler, had fled Germany in the 1930s to Norway, where he joined the anti-Nazi resistance movement in the Second World War. His wartime record increased his credibility with eastern Europeans, who, if they were not pleased to be subject to the Soviet Union, had as much historical reason to fear Germany as they did Russia. Brandt recognized the need to accept the division of Germany into two nations. Accordingly his government initiated a policy to regularize relations with West Germany's eastern neighbors (*Ostpolitic*). A complex series of diplomatic negotiations with the Soviet Union, East Germany, and Poland resulted in treaties that established East and West Germany as separate states within one nation, guaranteed unimpeded Western access to Berlin, and recognized Poland's claim to a western frontier along the Oder and Neisse Rivers as established originally after the Second World War.

Tensions between East and West, which eased during the 1960s and 1970s, arose once more in the next decade, in response to the Soviet Union's meddling in Poland's internal affairs. In 1980, calling their movement "Solidarity," Polish workers had organized strikes which brought the government of the country to a standstill. The strikers were objecting to working conditions imposed by the govern-

West German Chancellor Willy Brandt in Poland, 1970. This widely distributed photograph of Brandt kneeling before a memorial to Jewish victims of the Nazi Holocaust in Warsaw signalled both his determination to make amends for past German war crimes and to ease animosities between East and West.

Defiance in Poland. Thousands of striking workers take part in religious services in the Lenin Shipyards in Gdansk on August 24, 1980. This was the scene of the first in a series of strikes that paralyzed an already troubled economic and political system and challenged Soviet domination of Polish governmental policy.

ment to combat a severe economic crisis which had produced high prices. Again the Russians assisted a puppet military regime in reimposing authoritarian rule. Though the Soviet Union did not intervene directly, the implied threat that it might do so, reinforced by the presence of increasing numbers of Russian troops near the Polish border, reemphasized Soviet unwillingness to permit its eastern European neighbors autonomy over their internal affairs.

Gorbachev, the new self-criticism and bureaucratic resistance

With the accession to the party leadership of Mikhail Gorbachev in 1985, Soviet policy appeared to make a dramatic break with the patterns of past leadership. In his mid-fifties, Gorbachev was significantly younger than his immediate predecessors and therefore, perhaps, less prey to the habits of mind that had shaped Soviet domestic and foreign affairs. Frankly critical of aspects of repressive communist society and its sluggish economy, Gorbachev did not hesitate to voice those criticisms openly. He proclaimed a policy of freeing domestic dissidents, though the number released by mid-1987 was but a small portion of those imprisoned. He expressed a more tolerant attitude than past Soviet leaders toward deviant political behavior within the satellite states. And he advocated a degree of economic reorganization in the face of the Soviet Union's continuingly disappointing industrial performance. There remains, however, a sizable section of the Soviet populace, numbering perhaps in the millions, who will oppose any major reforms that threaten its privileges as a governing elite. These men and women, who hold key positions in the management of the economy, the army, the universities and, importantly, the nation's institutions of propaganda and coercion, can exercise great power on behalf of the status quo. Just what success Gorbachev will have in producing the changes he has proposed depends on the degree to which the massive Russian bureaucracy, bound for half a century to policies designed to thwart change, can be persuaded to respond positively to the challenges its leader is hurling in its direction.

Mikhail Gorbachev, General Secretary of the Central Committee of the Communist Party of the Soviet Union, 1985–

2. ECONOMIC RENAISSANCE

Reasons for postwar boom

Western Europeans, who likened their successful postwar economic recovery to a "miracle," ignored the degree to which human agencies and predictable economic forces precipitated the change. First, the war had encouraged a variety of technological innovations with direct and important peacetime applications: improved communications (the invention of radar, for example), the manufacture of synthetic materials, the increasing use of aluminum and alloy steels, and advances in the techniques of prefabrication. Secondly, nations had added significantly to the sum of their productive capital during the war. In Britain the total was in excess of one and half billion pounds and it was even greater in West Germany. Despite the apparent wartime devastation, capital invested in plants that were easily impaired but difficult to destroy completely survived to sustain a postwar boom. This boom was fueled by a third set of factors: the continued buoyancy of consumer demand and the consequent high level of employment throughout the 1950s and 1960s. These in turn encouraged continued capital investment and technological innovation. Finally, brisk foreign demand for goods convinced Europeans of the need to remove obstacles to international trade and payments. This fortuitous combination of circumstances made possible a remarkable period of dynamic economic growth.

The economic theories of John Maynard Keynes (see above, p. 1000), touting the power of governments to maintain high levels of consumption and investment by means of taxation and public spending, had a profound influence on planners throughout the West. As one economic historian has written of the period, "economic growth became a universal creed and a common expectation." The creed was a popular one because it met equally common expectations about rising standards of living that seemed just recompense for the suffering endured during the war. Europeans were also inspired by the example of the United States. They, too, craved the automobiles, washing machines, radios, and other domestic gadgets that Americans considered necessities but which Europeans had until now perceived as luxuries.

Governments resorted to a variety of devices to encourage economic expansion: West Germany provided tax breaks to encourage business investment; Britain and Italy offered investment allowances to their steel and petroleum industries. Virtually all of western Europe experimented with the nationalization of industry and services in an effort to enhance efficiency and productivity. The result was a series of "mixed" economies combining public and private ownership. France, Britain, Italy, and Austria took the lead in the move toward state-controlled enterprise. In France, where public ownership was already well advanced in the 1930s, railways, electricity and gas, banking, radio and television, and a large segment of the automobile industry were brought under state management. In Britain, the list was equally long: coal and utilities; road, railroad, and air transport; and banking. Though nationalization was less common in West Germany, the railway system—state-owned since the late nineteenth century; some electrical, chemical, and metallurgical concerns; and the Volkswagen company—the remains of Hitler's attempt to produce a "people's car"— were all in state hands, though the latter was largely returned to the private sector in 1963.

These government policies and programs contributed to astonishing growth rates. Between 1945 and 1963 the average yearly growth of Gross Domestic Product (Gross National Product minus income received from abroad) in West Germany was 7.6 percent; in Austria,

5.8 percent; in Italy, 6 percent; in Holland, 4.7 percent; and so on. This was a remarkable reversal of the economic patterns of an interwar period which had been beset by slack demand, overproduction, and insufficient investment. In the face of reconstruction and recovery, production facilities were hard pressed to keep up with soaring demand.

West German resurgence

West Germany's recovery was particularly noteworthy. Production increased sixfold between 1948 and 1964. Unemployment fell to record lows, reaching 0.4 percent in 1965, when there were six jobs for every unemployed person. Though prices rose initially, their subsequent leveling off provided an opportunity for most citizens to participate in a domestic buying spree that caused production to soar. In the 1950s, an average of half a million housing units were constructed annually to accommodate both those whose homes had been destroyed and an influx of new resident-refugees from East Germany and eastern Europe, and transient workers from Italy, Spain, Greece, and elsewhere who were attracted by West Germany's labor demands.

Explanations for West Germany's economic renaissance

The reasons for this remarkable economic renaissance were diverse. Certainly the presence of an army of highly skilled workers and a long tradition of industrial know-how counted for much. Other factors included: (1) the split from East Germany, which meant that the powerful and generally reactionary Junker class was no longer able to brake progress as it had since the mid-nineteenth century; (2) the crippling of much of Germany's industrial plant, entailing the opportunity to incorporate up-to-date equipment and techniques into rebuilt factories; and (3) the fact that initially West Germany was expressly forbidden by the occupying powers to spend money on defense.

France's program of national economic recovery

In France the major problem following the war centered on a perceived need to modernize the nation's industries, many of which remained small family enterprises resistant to technological change. Under the direction of a minister for planning, Jean Monnet, a special office—the General Commissariat for Planning—was established to initiate and execute a program for national economic recovery. Using money provided by the Marshall Plan, the French government played a direct and active role in the revival and reform, contributing not only capital but expert advice, and facilitating shifts in the national labor pool to place workers where they were most needed. The plan gave priority to basic industries, with the result that the amount of electricity produced doubled, the steel industry was thoroughly modernized, and the French railway system became the fastest and most efficient on the Continent. Other sectors of the economy tended to stagnate, however, while agriculture remained in the hands of a peasant class loathe to avail itself of government incentives intended to foster productivity through mechanization. Nevertheless, the French Gross National Product increased at the very creditable rate of about 5 percent per year in the 1950s.

Italy's industrial "miracle" was even more impressive than that of West Germany and France, given the woeful state of the nation's

The Porte Maillot, Paris. Construction on this expressway interchange at the site of the new Paris Convention Center and two new 1,000-room hotels (in the foreground) was begun in 1965. Viewed against an older Paris, it symbolized the degree to which Europe was prepared to commit itself to change during the economic boom of the 1950s and 1960s.

economy immediately following the war. Stimulated by infusions of capital from the government and from the Marshall Plan, Italian companies soon began to compete with other European international giants as the products of Olivetti, Fiat, and Pirelli became familiar in households across the world to an extent that no Italian goods had in the past. Electric power production—particularly important in Italy because of its lack of coal—had by 1953 increased 100 percent over that in 1938. By 1954 real wages were 50 percent higher than they had been in 1938. Yet Italy's success was marred by the enduring poverty of the country's southern regions, where illiteracy remained high and land continued to be held by a few rich families.

Italy's industrial "miracle"

Elsewhere on the Continent, nations with little in common in terms of political traditions or industrial patterns all shared in the general prosperity. Spain's economy changed markedly in the late 1950s, when a combination of rising foreign investment and the lifting of government controls spurred higher levels of production. Tourism was for Spain, as for all European countries, an increasingly important industry. Seventeen million visitors came to Spain in 1966, making it second only to Italy as a tourist attraction. Holland, Belgium, Austria, Greece, and the Scandinavian countries all enjoyed booms in the late 1950s. Though each country succeeded in increasing its GNP significantly, however, there remained marked differences in the levels of prosperity across the Continent. The per capita GNP in Sweden, for example, was almost ten times that of Turkey.

Shared prosperity elsewhere on the Continent

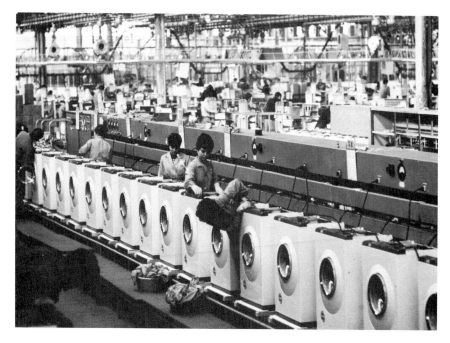

An Italian Washing-Machine Factory. Consumer goods once considered luxuries became commonly accepted necessities in postwar Europe.

Heating Fuel Shortage in Great Britain. This scene of British householders queuing for coal during the severely cold winter of 1948 provides a measure of the degree to which "winners" as well as "losers" suffered in the immediate aftermath of the Second World War.

Britain throughout remained a special case. Although it shared in the economic prosperity of the postwar years, it did so to a lesser extent than other European countries. The British rise in GNP averaged 2.5 percent per year between 1948 and 1962—a respectable enough figure when compared with past performance (2.2 percent between 1924 and 1937, for example), but nothing like the spectacular achievements recorded during the same period across the Channel. The Conservative party prime minister Harold Macmillan campaigned successfully for reelection in 1959 with the slogan "You've never had it so good"—an accurate-enough boast. Yet the British economy remained sluggish. The country was burdened with obsolete factories and techniques, the legacy of its early industralization. It was plagued as well by a series of balance-of-payments crises precipitated by an inability to sell more goods abroad than it imported.

Both trade unions and management share responsibility for Britain's poor performance. Unions refused to cooperate with management in schemes to increase productivity. A vigorous sense of "us against them," little different from the shop-floor antagonisms of the previous century, continued to prevail. Management remained uninterested in innovation and in devising effective ways to meet rising foreign competition. Industrial leadership suffered from an entrepreneurial failure of nerve. Neither government nor private investors were willing to gamble on the future of British industry in the way their continental counterparts did. Because shipbuilders refused to invest in new productive capacity, for example, tonnage built fell from 1.2 million in 1949 to 1 million in 1965, while in the same period it increased in Japan from 0.1 to 5 million. Finally, the country's worldwide defense commitments, its unwillingness to surrender its obligations to colonies and former colonies overseas, its position as an island dependent to a great degree upon imports in order to survive—in short its history and its geography—all helped dictate its economic position in the postwar world.

The western European renaissance was achieved by more than the efforts of individual nations. From the late 1940s on, they took steps to bind themselves together as an effective economic third force between the superpowers. In 1951 a European coal and steel community was created, which placed the management of those industries in France, West Germany, Belgium, Holland and Luxembourg (a small principality lying between the Low Countries and France) under a joint High Authority. Consisting of representative experts from each of the participating countries, the Authority possessed the power to regulate prices, to increase or limit production, and to impose administrative fees. Britain declared itself unwilling to participate, fearing the effects of European economic union on its declining coal industry and on its relationship with long-time trading partners such as Australia, New Zealand, and Canada.

Steps toward European economic integration

During the mid-1950s, further steps toward supernational economic integration were taken—the establishment of EURATOM, for example, a research organization in the field of nuclear development—culminating in 1957 with the founding of the European Economic Community, or Common Market. The EEC declared its goals to be the abolition of all trade barriers between the initial six members: France, West Germany, Italy, Belgium, Holland, and Luxembourg. In addition, the organization pledged itself to common external tariffs, the free movement of labor and capital, and the establishment of uniform wage structures and social security systems, so as to foster similar working conditions throughout the EEC. A commission with headquarters in Brussels was charged with the administration of this ambitious program.

The Common Market

Signatories of the Agreements Establishing the European Common Market. In the center are Adenauer of West Germany and de Gaulle of France.

Despite inevitable difficulties, particularly in the area of agricultural policy and prices, the European Economic Community was a remarkable success. By 1963, it had become the world's largest importer. Its steel production was second only to that of the United States, and total industrial production was over 70 percent higher than it had been in 1950. Even critics who complained about constant interference of EEC "Eurocrats"—over 3,000 in Brussels by 1962—conceded that centralized European planning and decision-making had brought the Continent extraordinary and unheralded prosperity. In addition, the Common Market operated increasingly as a semiautonomous political unit. In 1972 citizens of member nations voted directly for representatives to an EEC parliament, and its court of justice has ruled on a variety of different issues, both economic and social. Special aid programs to developing countries in Asia and Africa suggest that the EEC is a force to reckon with beyond the realm of economics and beyond the border of Europe.

Although economic development in eastern Europe was not nearly so dramatic as that of the West, significant advances occurred there as well. National income rose and output increased. Poland and Hungary, in particular, strengthened their economic connections with the West, primarily with France and West Germany. By the 1970s, commerce outside the Soviet bloc accounted for about 30 percent of eastern Europe's volume of trade. Nevertheless, the Soviet Union required its satellites to design their economic policies to serve more than their own national interests. Regulations governing the eastern equivalent of the Common Market—the Council of Mutual Economic Assistance, or COMECON—insured that Russia could sell its exports at prices well above the world level, while other members were compelled to trade with the Soviet Union to their disadvantage. Emphasis initially was on heavy industry and collectivized agriculture, though political tension in countries such as Hungary and Poland compelled the Soviets eventually to moderate their policies so as to permit the manufacture of more consumer goods and the development of a modest trade with the West. As with the Western nations, those in the East demonstrated a continuing determination to free themselves from economic dependence upon a single power.

Behind the drive for economic growth in western Europe lay the determination of individual men and women to improve their standard of living and quality of life. To this end, they demanded more from their governments in the form of social services. Governments, in turn, relied on their generally robust economies to provide for their citizens to a greater degree than ever before. State welfare programs had, of course, existed throughout the twentieth century, their roots extending back to the insurance schemes for old age, sickness, and invalidity introduced by Bismarck in Germany in the late 1880s. Postwar western Europe saw the expansion of such programs based on assumptions of state support that were hardly less compelling than the obligation to keep the peace, nowhere stated more clearly than in the preamble of the French constitution: "The nation guarantees the condition necessary for the development of the individual and the family. It guarantees every individual . . . the protection of health, material security, rest and leisure." A survey in 1957 found that public expenditure on health, pensions, family allowances and assistance, but excluding housing and education, accounted for 20.8 percent of the national income in West Germany, 18.9 percent in France, and 12.1 percent in Britain. In Sweden, money spent on social services was six times higher in 1957 than in 1930; in Italy, it was fourteen times higher.

3. THE POLITICS OF EUROPEAN RECOVERY

The governments responsible for these remarkable economic and social changes were ideologically almost uniformly middle-of-the-road. Yet unlike the situation after 1918, when the "old men" resumed power throughout Europe, new men who were unwilling to see Europe return to business as usual moved into positions of authority after 1945. In Britain the Labour party, led by middle-class, mild-mannered socialist Clement Attlee, enacted the social legislation that produced a welfare state. The Labour government gave way in 1951 to the Conservatives who, led most notably by Harold Macmillan (1894–1987) from 1957 to 1963, proved more than willing to enbrace the promise of economic growth and a continuation of welfare policies. The Labour party returned to power in the mid-sixties, under the prime ministership of Harold Wilson, who pledged to forge a more prosperous nation in the "white heat" of a new technological revolution. Although Labourites and Conservatives fought partisan campaigns, they appeared to agree upon fundamentals: a mixed economy and an extended program of welfare benefits. Labourites still called themselves socialists, but most defined socialism, as the party's mainstream always had, as centralization, rather than as worker control of the means of production.

New, moderate leadership: British politics

Moderates dominated the politics of continental Europe as well. In Germany, France, and Italy, centrist parties affiliated with the Roman Catholic Church held power throughout most of the two decades after 1945: the German Christian Democratic Union; the French *Mouvement Républicain Populaire* (the M.R.P., initially more popular than it would be in the mid-1950s); and the Italian Christian Democrats. The leaders responsible for the direction of European political affairs during the immediate postwar period were no-nonsense men, committed to the achievement of practical economic and social agendas: Robert Schuman (1886–1963), for a time the French premier and the man most responsible for the establishment of the European Coal and Steel Community; Alcide de Gasperi (1881–1954), Italian

Dominance of centrist parties on the Continent

Alcide de Gasperi of Italy Electioneering during His 1948 Campaign

French political fragmentation and de Gaulle

The Fifth Republic and De Gaulle's independent course

premier from 1949 to 1953; and Konrad Adenauer (1876–1967), West German chancellor from 1949 to 1963. The latter was a former mayor of Cologne, a devout Roman Catholic who, though he despised the traditions of Prussian militarism that had contributed to the rise of Hitler, was apprehensive about the consequences of parliamentary democracy for Germany, and thus tended to govern in a paternalistic if not authoritarian manner. His determination to see an end to the centuries-old hostility between France and Germany contributed significantly to the movement toward economic union. De Gasperi, too, was not particularly enamored of democracy and thwarted attempts by Italian socialists and communists immediately after the war to institute radical reforms.

Yet neither Adenauer nor de Gasperi aroused much real political enmity. Socialists throughout western Europe, recognizing the political popularity of economic prosperity, toned down their rhetoric and their demands, speaking far less about the inevitability of class war and more often about the contributions workers were making to the European postwar renaissance. The program adopted by the German Socialist party (the Social Democrats) in 1959, for example, abandoned orthodox Marxism by declaring the need to leave economic planning as much as possible to individual enterprise, rather than in the hands of the state.

France's political situation during the early 1950s was tangled in a way that West Germany's and Italy's were not. Party strength was fragmented. Twenty-five percent of the voting population regularly supported the French Communist party, not so much from commitment to its current policies as from a traditional proletarian habit of mind. Several conservative or reactionary parties of the Right existed as well. The political middle, strong in other countries and initially strong in France, gradually eroded after 1945. Matters reached a crisis when successive centrist governments found it increasingly difficult to resolve a seemingly intactable political problem borne of an independence movement in the French colony of Algeria. In May 1958 a revolt of French nationals in Algeria and disgruntled French army officers, both at home and in the colony, threatened to topple the government. In desperation, the political leadership stepped down in favor of the Resistance hero, General Charles de Gaulle (1890–1970), who had played a brief role in French politics immediately after the war and then retired.

De Gaulle accepted office on the condition that he be permitted to rule by decree for six months and to draft a new constitution for France. This document, adopted by referendum in September 1958 and ushering in France's Fifth Republic, strengthened the executive branch of the government as a means of avoiding the parliamentary deadlocks that had so weakened France earlier in the decade and, indeed, throughout much of the preceding century. The president was granted power to appoint the premier and dissolve the National

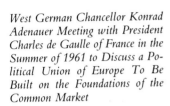

West German Chancellor Konrad Adenauer Meeting with President Charles de Gaulle of France in the Summer of 1961 to Discuss a Political Union of Europe To Be Built on the Foundations of the Common Market

Assembly. And the assembly's powers to dismiss a premier were considerably weakened. Thus armed with new authority, de Gaulle set out to restore France to power and prestige. "France is not really herself unless in the front rank," he wrote in his memoirs. "France cannot be France without greatness." De Gaulle assumed that Algeria would have to be granted independence, which in due course it was, in 1963. Concerned about U.S. influence in Europe, he withdrew French troops from NATO in 1966. He cultivated better relations with the Soviet Union and, with Adenauer, he worked toward closer cooperation between France and West Germany. He accelerated the pace of France's economic and industrial expansion by building a modern military establishment, complete with atomic weapons—a nuclear "force de frappe," an independent nuclear strike force whose objectives were primarily political and diplomatic, part of de Gaulle's effort to reclaim France's great power status. De Gaulle's independent stand was largely based upon his belief that invasion of the West was far from the minds of the Soviet leadership.

Though like de Gasperi and Adenauer, de Gaulle was not by nature a democrat, he was like them committed to a centrist course. Such a policy entailed avoiding extremism and working hard to produce "practical" solutions to vexing political problems, thereby undermining radical sentiments of the sort that had produced fascism in Italy and Nazism in Germany. Most other western European nations followed suit. Holland, Belgium, and the Scandinavian countries initiated economic and social policies and programs that echoed the concerns and desires of the British, French, Germans, and Italians. In Spain and Portugal, however, different political, economic, and social agendas were pursued under the dictatorships of General Francisco Franco and of António Salazar. And in Greece, political instability in the

Other countries and other courses

1950s and early 1960s opened the way for a coup by conservative right-wing generals in 1967. Yet these were exceptions to a two-decade history of domestic tranquility and economic prosperity—a sharp contrast to the tragic failures of the 1920s and 1930s.

4. PATTERNS OF SOCIAL CHANGE

Population growth

Clearly, economic change of this sort was bound to effect the lives of the men, women, and children who lived in Europe after the Second World War. Prosperity brought with it population shifts. The population of western Europe in 1940 was 264 million; in 1982 it was 320 million. This increase was the result of an increase in the birthrate. Population growth was sustained by social welfare policies, such as family allowances, which encouraged parents to have children and enabled them to care adequately for them, and by health programs, which extended longevity considerably. As populations increased they also shifted across the Continent. Both West Germany and France found it necessary to import workers in order to sustain their production booms. By the mid-1960s, there were 1.3 million foreign workers in West Germany and 1.8 million in France. Most came from the south, particularly from the agrarian areas of southern Italy, where unemployment remained high. Migrations of this sort, not to mention the movement of political refugees that occurred during and immediately after the war, contributed to a breaking down of national barriers that was accelerated by the advent of the Common Market.

The rise of a managerial class

Economic resurgence also altered patterns and perceptions of class. Commentators were quick to perceive a marked growth in the number of middle-class, white-collar employees, the result, in part, of the bureaucratic expansion of the state. By 1964, the total number of men and women employed in government service in most European states exceeded 40 percent of the labor force, significantly higher than the number in the 1920s and 1930s. In business and industry, the number of "middle-management" employees grew as well. This "managerial class" tended to be more innovative and adventurous than were the owner-managers of business in previous generations. More often than not, these managers possessed university degrees. In the mid-1950s, for example, over 72 percent of a sample of 5,000 French industrialists were university graduates, more than half of them with degrees in engineering. This was in marked contrast to the prewar situation, when managers far more frequently moved directly from secondary education into family-run concerns. What was true of the West was true of the Soviet Union as well where, following educational reforms instituted by Nikita Khrushchev in 1958, programs encouraged bright children to pursue a course of study leading eventually to managerial positions. This new class was not "bourgeois" in the Marxist sense of that term. The technocrats were not "owners of the means of production" or capitalist tycoons. To some degree they saw themselves less as the servants of the company that employed them than of the general public who purchased the goods or services they were providing.

If the nature of the middle class was changing, so was that of the working class. The introduction of complex machinery effectively altered the shape of the factory work force. The proportion of salaried employees—supervisors, inspectors, technicians, and draftsmen—grew significantly. In West Germany, for example, the number of such workers increased between 1950 and 1961 by 95 percent. And manual labor tended to mean something far different from what it had in the nineteenth century. Skills were specialized to a greater degree than ever, based on technological expertise rather than custom and routine. "Skill" meant the ability to monitor automatic controls, to interpret abstract signals, and to make precise, mathematically calculated adjustments.

The changing working class

All of these changes, suggesting a merging of the interests of working class and middle class, led some observers in the mid-1960s to declare class consciousness and its associated fierce antagonisms at an end. In fact, events in the late 1960s and 1970s reopened class conflicts, as we shall see. Although men and women earned more money than ever before, performing less physically yet more mentally demanding jobs and living more secure lives, they did not entirely lose their sense of themselves as workers. Trade unions throughout western Europe remained powerful institutions: the largest of the French general unions had a membership of 1.5 million; of the Italian, 3.5 million; of the German, 6.5 million. Britain's Trade Union Congress, an affiliation of separate unions, boasted close to 8 million members.

Continuing class consciousness

Unquestionably, workers tended to lead lives that more closely resembled those of the prewar middle class than of their own parents and grandparents. They and their children went to school longer. All European countries passed laws providing for the extension of compulsory secondary education—up to the age of sixteen in France, West Germany, and Britain. As a consequence of new legislation and increased birthrates, school populations increased dramatically. Secondary school enrollment in France, Holland, and Belgium doubled between 1950 and 1960. In England and West Germany it grew by more than 50 percent. Higher education was used in the Soviet Union as a means of unifying a nation that remained culturally heterogeneous. Turks and Slavs constitute sizable minorities in the U.S.S.R. Concern lest the pull of ethnic "nationality" tear at the none-too-solid fabric of the Soviet "union" increased the government's desire to impose one unifying culture by means of education.

The leveling effect of education

Educational reforms were accompanied by a communications revolution. In both western and eastern Europe the paperback book, the long-playing record, the radio and, above all, the television brought knowledge—of varying degrees of quality—to millions who heretofore had had neither the time nor the money to acquire it. Workers in the West for the first time found it possible to take inexpensive holidays, often in their own automobiles. Between 1948 and 1965 car ownership increased in western Europe from 5 million to 44 million. The work week contracted from forty-eight hours to about forty-two. In most countries, workers received over thirty days of paid vacation per year. Britain's prime minister Harold Macmillan was not alone in his belief that "we've never had it so good!"

5. PROBLEMS OF THE 1970s AND 1980s

While 1960 seemed both golden and full of promise, fifteen years later men and women were no longer so certain of their prosperity or of their leaders' abilities to provide them with the sort of life they had come to take for granted. From the mid-1960s, social and economic tensions ate away at the consensus that postwar prosperity had created. Societies fragmented in new and confusing ways Governments were baffled about how to deal with the demands of groups from whom little had been heard previously. Their problems were compounded after 1975 by a continuing economic crisis that threatened the security that a generation had labored so hard to achieve.

The years from 1965 to 1972 were marked by widespread protests and upheaval among youth in Europe and the United States. Young people had, of course, revolted in previous generations—indeed, revolt has always been considered a prerogative of youth. The Russian revolution of 1917 and the Nazi movement of the 1930s were both instances in point. Yet in those cases, leadership had come from an older generation. Now it was to come from men and women in their twenties.

Products of the baby boom of the immediate postwar period, youths were jammed into universities whose conservative, authoritarian traditions made intellectual as well as physical accommodation all but impossible. University enrollment tripled in France, Italy, and Britain between 1938 and 1960; in West Germany, the university population increased from 110,000 in 1950 to 280,000 in 1960. Members of this new generation, raised in a more permissive society where premarital sex and liberation from traditional patterns of middle-class behavior were becoming the norm and where in most countries the voting age had been lowered to eighteen, had little use for the disciplines of the past. Science antagonized them because of its association with warmaking—in particular with the unpopular war the United States was then waging in southeast Asia (see below, p. 1081). Knowledge that was not perceived as relevant to the world's problems was challenged as worthless.

The most serious outbreak of student unrest in Europe occurred in Paris in the spring of 1968. Inspired in part by the role youths had played in the revolt against Soviet oppression in Czechoslovakia

Student Uprising at the University of Paris, May 1968. Following demonstrations calling for sweeping reforms at the university, French students took to the streets to make their case more forcefully and violently at the barricades.

that same year, French students at the University of Paris demanded reforms that would modernize their university. Confrontation with authorities precipitated riots, which in turn brought police interference. Sympathy with the students' cause expanded to encompass opposition to de Gaulle's regime, leading to massive trade union strikes. By mid-May 10 million French workers had walked off their jobs. The government was able to satisfy the strikers by acquiescing to wage increases, thereby isolating the students, who grudgingly agreed to resume university life. De Gaulle had no sympathy for the students. "Reform, yes—bed messing, no," he is said to have declared at the height of the confrontation. Yet events of May and June 1968 undoubtedly helped weaken de Gaulle's position as president and contributed to his eventual retirement from office. Young people across Europe staged protests as well. Students in Berlin rioted at the appearance there of the shah of Iran and against newspapers critical of the revolt of the young. In Italy, undergraduates staged a lengthy series of riots to draw attention to university overcrowding. And in the United States, serious protests against the Vietnam War continued into the early 1970s.

Violent student protest

Women, like young people, began to assert themselves during the 1960s and 1970s. As was the case with the youth rebellion, the women's movement was first directed from within the middle class. By the mid-seventies the movement had spread worldwide, including the Third World nations, and was no longer limited to the middle class. Many of the early activists within the movement had been part of the youth rebellion during its most intense phase in the sixties. Their activism, in part, stemmed from a realization that even in a radical political atmosphere, women were relegated to second place.

The women's movement

Vietnam Protest, 1971. Veterans of the U.S. Armed Forces march on the Capitol to protest continued U.S. involvement in the war in Vietnam.

Women's position within society had changed dramatically since the nineteenth century. The assumption that the middle-class woman's place was in the home had been challenged by the ever-increasing demand for women workers and by the need experienced by more and more women to hold a job—either for financial reasons or because housework was for a growing number an unfulfilling occupation. The increased availability and social acceptance of birth-control devices meant that women were having fewer children, and that they could begin to exercise more control over the pattern of their lives.

Women's political action

Yet society seemed loath to acknowledge the implication of these changes: that women are equal to men. Women were paid less than men for similar work. Women with qualifications no different from men were turned down because of their gender when they applied for jobs. Women with excellent employment records were forced to rely on their husbands to establish credit. Political action helped alleviate some of these inequities in the late 1960s and the 1970s. The U.S. government instituted programs of "affirmative action" which mandated the hiring of qualified women as well as members of racial minority groups. In Britain an Equal Pay Act, passed in the late 1960s, established that wages for women should be equal to those of men holding the same job. In France, a ministry for the status of women was created in the mid-1970s.

The issue of abortion

The campaign for equality did not meet with universal approval, however. A particularly volatile subject was a woman's right to an abortion. Feminists argued that women must enjoy the freedom to plan for their future unencumbered by the responsibilities of motherhood if they choose, and that their bodies are theirs to govern. Their opponents, which included members of the so-called right-to-life movement, countered with the argument that abortion encouraged sexual irresponsibility; some declared that abortion is the equivalent of murder. By the mid-1980s, however, despite the failure in the

United States of passage of a constitutional Equal Rights Amendment, the campaigners for women's equality had a good many successes to their credit.

Economic as well as social problems plagued Europe in the 1970s. The stagnation that overtook the Continent was the product of trends that had their roots in the prosperous sixties. By the middle of that decade, for example, the West German growth rate had slowed. Demand for manufactured goods declined and in 1966 the country suffered its first postwar recession. Volkswagen, that mythic symbol of the German "miracle," introduced a shortened work week; almost 700,000 West Germans were thrown out of work. In France an inability to solve a long-standing housing shortage increased the cost of living. While new industries continued to prosper, the basics—coal, steel and railways—began to run up deficits. Unemployment was rising in tandem with prices. Prime Minister Harold Wilson's pledge to revive Britain's economy by the introduction of new technology foundered on balance-of-payment crises. The Common Market, expanded in 1973 to include Britain, Ireland, and Denmark, and again in the early 1980s to admit Greece, Spain, and Portugal, struggled to overcome problems stemming from the conflict between the domestic economic regulations characteristic of many European states and the free-market policies that prevailed among the EEC countries.

The 1960s as the source of economic stagnation in the 1970s

All these difficulties were compounded by the dramatic rise in the price of oil that occurred once the Arab-dominated Organization of Petroleum Exporting Countries (OPEC) instituted an oil embargo against the Western powers for economic and political reasons in 1973. By 1975 the cost per barrel of oil had risen to $10.46, as compared with $1.73 two years before, and continued to rise to over $30 in

OPEC, inflation, and competition

The Women's Movement in France. French women demand equal pay for equal work.

the early 1980s. This increase produced an inflationary spiral; interest rates rose and with them the price of almost everything else Western consumers were used to buying. Wage demands calculated to meet rising costs produced strikes. The placid industrial relations that had characterized the 1950s and early 1960s were a thing of the past. Meanwhile the U.S. economy, as a result of its commitment to the war in southeast Asia, began to absorb more capital than it exported, thus contributing further to international inflation. Finally, European manufacturers encountered serious competition, not only from highly developed countries like Japan but also from the increasingly active economies of Asia and Africa, in which the West had invested capital eagerly in the previous decades. By 1980 Japan had captured 10 percent of the automobile market in West Germany and 25 percent in Belgium. By 1984, unemployment in western Europe had reached about 19 million. The lean years had arrived.

Soviet economic stagnation

Meanwhile the Soviet Union and its satellites were also experiencing the stagnation that accompanies the maturing of an economy. The Soviet Communist party proclaimed in 1961 that by 1970 the U.S.S.R. would exceed the United States in per capita production. However, by the end of the seventies, Soviet per capita production was not much higher than in the less-industrialized countries of southern Europe. During the same period its rate of economic growth was on a sluggish par with that of other Western nations.

Eastern-European economic malaise in the 1970s

Following an impressive economic performance during the early 1970s, the eastern European nations encountered serious financial difficulties. Their success had rested in part on capital borrowed not from the Soviet Union but from the West. By 1980 those debts had become serious burdens to their national economies. Poland's hard-currency indebtedness to Western countries, for example, was almost four times as great as its annual exports. The solution to this problem attempted in Poland and elsewhere was to cut back on production for domestic consumption in order to increase exports. Yet this policy encountered strong popular opposition. Although there was virtually no unemployment in the East, men and women were by no means happy with their economic situation. Working hours were longer than in the West, and goods and services, even in prosperous times, remained far from abundant. The result of further cuts, therefore, was a degree of discontent that in Poland contributed significantly to the "Solidarity" movement of 1980, and generally put governments on the defensive.

Western governments also found it difficult to react effectively to the abrupt change in their economic circumstances. Politicians of both the Right and the Left struggled to rediscover the magic that had produced prosperity, but with little success. In England, the Labour and Conservative parties alternatively governed through the 1970s, unable to meet the demands of trade unionists, who were angry as they saw their real wages eroded by inflation, or of international bankers, who were impatient with Britain's inability to bring its trade

Margaret Thatcher, Prime Minister of Great Britain, 1979–

figures into balance. Twenty-four million individual workdays were lost in strikes in 1972, one of the worst years of industrial unrest on record. In the mid-seventies the rate of inflation increased alarmingly, reaching 26 percent in 1976; unemployment rose to 1.4 million that same year; and the value of the pound declined precipitously. The new, radically conservative leader of the Conservative party, Margaret Thatcher, claimed to have the answer, and was elected in 1979—and reelected in 1983 and 1987—on the basis of that claim. Yet despite massive cuts in public spending designed to stimulate the economy and the return of many publicly owned enterprises to private hands, the economy remained weak, with close to 15 percent of the work force unemployed by 1986. The standard of living in Britain had sunk below the level of all western European nations save Greece, Spain, and Portugal. Once the seat of an empire upon which the sun never set, Britain was reduced to the status of a tiny, economically sickly island state.

West Germany, like Britain, veered to the Right in the eighties. The Social Democratic party, headed in the late sixties and early seventies by Willy Brandt, had remained in power after Brandt's resignation as chancellor in 1974, under the leadership of his less charismatic successor, Helmut Schmidt. Schmidt's coalition government attempted in the early 1980s to combat economic recession with job-training programs and tax incentives, both financed by higher taxes. These programs did little to assist economic recovery, and Schmidt was replaced by the Christian Democrat Helmut Kohl, who, like Margaret Thatcher in Britain, proposed cuts in social programs and unemployment compensation.

France fared little better than its European neighbor in the struggle to maintain economic momentum. De Gaulle resigned in 1969, his prestige eroded by the outbreaks of the previous year. His successors in the 1970s, Georges Pompidou and Valéry Giscard d'Estaing, pursued a middle course that did no more than keep the country on an even keel. In 1981, Giscard was ousted by a socialist, François Mitterand, whose record as an escaped prisoner of war and Resistance fighter in the Second World War made him a popular figure, and whose visit to the tomb of the French Socialist hero Jean Jaurès was meant to symbolize his intention to govern in accordance with Marxist ideals. Among the array of reforms promptly undertaken by the new government was the further nationalization of major industries and private financial institutions, including the famed 150-year-old Rothschild bank, Pompidou's former employer. Yet these bold moves, bitterly opposed by conservative interests, did not resolve the nation's economic malaise. Inflation and unemployment rose, along with budget and balance-of-trade deficits. Newly nationalized enterprises drained government resources. Difficulties led to a devaluation of the franc, a temporary freeze on wages and prices, and in 1986 to a return to power of more conservative political forces committed to

Economic blight in the West: Great Britain

Helmut Kohl, Chancellor of the Federal Republic of Germany, 1982–

Newly Elected French President François Mitterand Lays a Symbolic Rose on the Tomb of French Socialist Jean Jaurès in 1981

a policy of "privatization" of companies and industries that had been nationalized under the socialists.

Spain and Italy moved Left in the early 1980s. Spain, freed from the rule of General Franco by his death in 1974, and under the nominal rule of his hand-picked successor King Juan Carlos, saw the Socialist Workers party score a major upset in 1982. Intent on modernizing rather than radicalizing Spain, the socialists eschewed widespread government ownership of industry in favor of selective nationalization, which included the nation's electric power grid. Similarly, Italy witnessed increasing victories by parties of the Left at the expense of the previously indomitable Christian Democratic party.

The fact that governments of neither Right nor Left were able to recreate the sort of economic climate that had characterized Europe's unprecedented postwar prosperity suggested the degree to which economic forces remain outside the control of individual states, prey to the far-from-predictable vagaries of international finance, trade cycles, and human miscalculation.

6. INTELLECTUAL AND CULTURAL PATTERNS

Intellectual life in the West after 1945 was patterned broadly as it had been in the interwar years. The gulf remained wide between the avant-garde and the generally educated public—now far larger than ever before thanks to burgeoning universities. If attendance at museums increased—as it did dramatically—more often than not it was because people were attracted by exhibits of treasures from the distant past—from King Tutankhamen's tomb or from the Renaissance collections of the Vatican Museum. Audiences who welcomed a chance to hear the works of long-dead composers—Mozart and Verdi—sung by internationally acclaimed "stars"—the soprano Maria Callas, the tenor Luciano Pavarotti—rejected as pointless the puzzling works of composers such as John Cage, whose "silent sonata" entitled "4.33" consisted of a pianist seated at the piano for precisely four minutes, thirty-three seconds, but who never once actually struck a note. Intellectuals, on the other hand, railed against the increasing vapidity of mass culture and in particular of television, the "idiot box" that by 1965 had found its way into 62 million homes in the United States, 13 million in Britain, 10 million in West Germany, 5 million each in France and Italy. They also objected to the promotion of art and music as big business, with jampacked "blockbuster" art exhibits attended by tens of thousands and opera tickets sold at prices approaching $100 apiece.

Despite this continuing alienation, the work of many of the West's leading writers did reflect the dilemmas of the human condition that prevailed throughout the years after 1945. During the immediate postwar period novelists concerned themselves with the horrors of war and of the totalitarian systems that had spawned the conflict of the 1940s. The Americans James Jones (1921–1977) and Norman Mailer (1923–   ), in *From Here to Eternity* and *The Naked and the Dead*, portrayed the coarseness and cruelty of military life with ruthless realism. The German Günter Grass's (1927–   ) first and probably most important novel, *The Tin Drum,* depicted the vicious and politically diseased life of Nazi Germany in the 1930s. In France Jean-Paul Sartre (1905–1980), as a result of his own and his country's wartime experiences, recommitted himself in his novels, plays, and other writings to a life of active political involvement as a Marxist. Whereas he had previously defined hell in terms of individual hostilities, he now defined it in terms of class inequality. Unlike Sartre, his compatriot Albert Camus (1913–1960) was unable to construct a secular faith from his own perceptions of the world and its apparent absurdities. Though idealist enough to participate in the French resistance movement against the German occupation in the Second World War, and though proclaiming the virtues of rebellion, Camus remained tortured in novels such as *The Fall, The Plague,* and *The Rebel* by the problem of humanity's responsibility for its own miserable dilemma and by the limitations placed upon the ability of men and women to help each other.

Marxism continued to attract European intellectuals, both as a recipe for changing the world and as a way of explaining it. Historians, economists, and sociologists focused their attention more frequently on the writings of the younger Marx, less on his economic theories, more on his perceptions of alienation and class consciousness. The writings of the Italian Antonio Gramsci (1891–1937) and the Hungarian Georg Lukacs (1885–1971), both concerned with these particular matters, attracted widespread attention. Claude Lévi-Strauss (1908–   ), a French sociologist who considers himself a Marxist in contemporary matters, nevertheless applied a different model than Marx's essentially idealist and value-laden dialectic to the study of society. A leading exponent of the so-called structuralist school, Lévi-Strauss subjected all elements of the primitive societies he studied—kinship, rituals, and traditions—to analysis in terms of thought structures, which though unconscious, were nevertheless said to possess an objective reality. He argued that his method proved the intrinsic value of every society and that there was rationality where many had previously seen only the irrational or the absurd.

Shifting focus on Marx in the West

It is worth noting that these reinterpretations of Marx came from outside the Soviet Union. Inside, genuine philosophical debate has been repressed by the government, although nothing like the grisly purges of the 1930 has occurred since the Stalin era. Soviet thinkers are encouraged to keep their thoughts to themselves. Most intellectuals pay lip service to Marxism's past achievements. But if they are attempting to recast Marxist ideology so as to accord with the facts of late twentieth-century history, they are not broadcasting these attempts,

The fate of Marx within the Soviet Union

Simone de Beauvoir

Boris Pasternak

Aleksandr Solzhenitsyn

content rather to remain within the "private sphere" of their own narrow professional specialities.

The specific issues that drove men and women in western Europe and America to committed action in the mid-1960s compelled writers to take sides as well. Günter Grass, in *Local Anaesthetic,* published in 1970, was only one of many who wrote of student unrest and political involvement. Women authors described not only the general loneliness of the human condition, but the particular plight of women trapped in a world not of their own making. The Frenchwoman Simone de Beauvoir (1908–1986) in *The Second Sex,* a germinal study of the female condition, denounced the male middle class for turning not only workers but also its own women into objects for its own ends. American writers like Germaine Greer, Tillie Olsen, and the philosopher Mary Daly helped define the politics and culture of the women's movement.

The theme of individual alienation and helplessness, a reflection of the problems arising from the growth of state power, was one to which writers addressed themselves with increasing frequency in the 1960s and 1970s. The Russian Boris Pasternak (1890–1960), in his novel *Dr. Zhivago,* indicted the Soviet campaign to shape all its citizens to the same mold. His countryman Aleksandr Solzhenitsyn (1918–   ) attacked the brutal methods employed by the Soviet Union in its rapid climb to world power. His *Gulag Archipelago,* published in 1973, is a fictionalized account of the fate of those whose willingness to stand in the way of Soviet "progress" sentenced them to life in Siberian labor camps. Although both Pasternak and Solzhenitsyn were awarded the Nobel Prize for literature, the former in 1958 and the latter in 1970, their works were condemned by the Soviet government and Solzhenitsyn was sent into exile. Herbert Marcuse, (1898–1979), an American, charged that authoritarianism was just as much a fact of life under capitalism as under communism. He argued that industrial capitalism had produced a "one-dimensional" society, in which the interests of individual citizens had been ruthlessly subordinated to those of the powerful corporate interests which were the true governors of the world.

Some authors, although they agreed with indictments of contemporary civilization, believed the human condition too hopeless to warrant direct attack. They expressed their despair by escaping into the absurd and fantastic. In the plays of Samuel Beckett (1906–1986), an Irishman who wrote in French, and of the Englishman Harold Pinter (1930–   ), nothing happens. Characters speak in the banalities that have become the hallmark of modern times. Words which are meaningless when spoken by human beings nevertheless take on a logic of their own; yet they explain nothing. Other authors, less willing, perhaps, to attempt to make a statement out of nothingness, have invaded the realms of hallucination, science fiction, and fantasy. The novels of the Americans William Burroughs and Kurt Vonnegut convey their readers from interior fantasizing to outer space. Significantly one of the most popular books among the youth of the sixties and seventies was *The Lord of the Rings,* a pseudo-saga set in the fantasy world of "Middle Earth," written before the Second World War by the Englishman J. R. R. Tolkien.

Film

Filmmakers, in the decades after the Second World War, made films which mirrored the problems and concerns of society, with a depth and artistic integrity seldom attempted or achieved previously. The Swede Ingmar Bergman, the Frenchmen Jean-Luc Godard and François Truffaut, the Italians Frederico Fellini and Michelangelo Antonioni, to name but a few of the most gifted directors, dealt in their films with the same themes that marked the literature of the period: loneliness, war, oppression, and corruption. One important factor facilitating the achievement of artistic quality was the general willingness on the part of censors—state or industry sponsored—to reflect public taste by permitting filmmakers great license in the handling of themes such as racism, violence, and sexuality. While there is no question that this relaxation led to exploitation, it cleared the way for extraordinarily powerful film statements, such as the American Arthur Penn's *Bonnie and Clyde* (1967) and the Italian Bernardo Bertolucci's *Last Tango in Paris* (1972), shocking declarations about humanity made possible by explicit depictions of violence and sex. Film, while gaining a general maturity it had heretofore lacked, did not desert its role as entertainment. The international popularity of the British rock-and-roll group, the Beatles, was translated, for example, into equally successful films—charming, slapstick escapism which nevertheless proclaimed the emancipation of youth from the confining formalities and conventions of their elders.

Fine arts

Unlike writers or filmmakers, the majority of postwar artists did not use their work as a vehicle to express either ideological commitment or a concern for the human situation. Following trends established by the impressionists and cubists, they spoke neither about the world nor to the world, but instead to each other and to the extremely small coterie of initiates who understood their artistic language. Foremost among the postwar schools of art was abstract expressionism, whose chief exponents were the American painters Jackson Pollock (1912–1956), Willem de Kooning (1904–   ), and Franz Kline (1910–1962). Their interests lay in further experimentation with the relationship between color, texture, and surface, to the total exclusion of "meaning" or "message" in the traditional sense. Jasper John's painting of the American flag demanded that the viewer see it not as *a* painting—that is, something to be interpreted—but instead as painting, the treatment of canvas with paint. Robert Rauschenberg, in revolt against the abstract expressionists, exhibited blank white panels, insisting that by so doing he was pressing art to the ultimate question

Composition (1955) by Willem de Kooning. A work representative of the abstract expressionists' desire to explore the varieties of light, texture, and surface.

Divorce of visual arts from social commentary

See color plates following page 1040 for representative works by Rothko, Rauschenberg, Johns, Hansen, and Stella

of a choice of medium. Painters fought the notion that their work in some way expressed disgust with an empty civilization. "My paintings are based on the fact that only what can be seen is there," declared the American Frank Stella, who painted stripes on irregularly shaped canvases. "Pop" art, a phenomenon of the late sixties which took as its subject everyday objects such as soup cans and comic-strip heroes, was likewise, according to its practitioners, not a protest against the banality of industrialism but another experiment in abstractions.

Even the remote and yet extraordinarily compelling abstractions of Mark Rothko (1903–1970), glowing or somber rectangles of color imposed upon other rectangles, were said by the artist himself to represent "nothing but content—no associations, only sensation." Only with the coming, in the 1970s, of the so-called hyper-realists, artists such as the American Duane Hansen, who recreates his invariably depressing human subjects in plastic down to the last eyelash, can we perhaps say that some artists are making a statement not only about technique but about what they perceive as the vacuity of life. Most artists, however, remained uninterested in commenting directly upon the elements of alienation, pain, and despair that were a part of Western life in the forty years after the Second World War or upon the generally positive, productive nature of society during that same exciting, if ultimately disappointing, period.

SELECTED READINGS

• *Items so designated are available in paperback editions.*

Ardagh, John, *The New French Revolution,* New York, 1969, The social impact of economic change.

• Aron, Raymond, *The Imperial Republic: The United States and the World, 1945–1973,* Lanham, Md., 1974. World analysis by a leading French political theorist.

Ash, Timothy, *The Polish Revolution: Solidarity,* New York, 1983. The best account.

• Beer, Samuel, *Britain Against Itself,* New York, 1982. A clear-headed analysis of the reasons for British decline.

Black, C. E., *The Dynamics of Modernization: A Study in Comparative History,* New York, 1966. Includes material on non-Western countries as well.

• Brzezinski, Z., *The Soviet Bloc: Unity and Conflict,* rev. and enl. ed., Cambridge, Mass., 1967. Eastern European politics analyzed by a former U.S. National Security Advisor.

• Crossman, Richard H., ed., *The God That Failed,* New York, 1950. Testimony from former Marxists about their loss of political faith.

• Crouzet, Maurice, *The European Renaissance Since 1945,* New York, 1971. Optimistic appraisal of Europe's postwar recovery.

• Dahrendorf, Ralf, *Society and Democracy in Germany,* New York, 1971. The extent of the change from fascism to democracy.

• DePorte, A. W., *Europe Between the Superpowers: The Enduring Balance,* New Haven, 1979.

• Ehrmann, Henry W., *Politics in France,* Boston, 1968. Detailed treatment of politics in the decade after 1958.

• Gaddis, John, *The United States and the Origins of the Cold War, 1942–1947,* New York, 1972. Focuses on the United States. A balanced account.

Hoffman, Stanley, et al., *In Search of France,* Cambridge, Mass., 1965. Essays providing perceptive analysis of postwar French politics and society.

Hough, Jerry, and Merle Fainsod, *How the Soviet Union Is Governed,* Cambridge, Mass., 1979.

Kolko, Gabriel, *The Politics of War: The World and United States Foreign Policy, 1943–1945,* New York, 1969. Argues that the blame for the Cold War rests with the Western Allies.

• LaFeber, Walter, *America, Russia and the Cold War,* 5th ed., New York, 1985. Another revisionist treatment.

• Laqueur, Walter, *Europe Since Hitler,* rev. ed., New York, 1982. A useful, thorough survey.

• Leslie, R. F., et al., *The History of Poland Since 1863,* New York, 1981. Useful background for current events.

Mayne, Richard, *The Recovery of Europe, 1945–1973,* Garden City, N.Y., 1973. Another reliable account.

Mowat, R. C., *Creating the European Community,* New York, 1973. A diplomatic historian's account of the merging of Europe's economic fortunes.

Parker, Geoffrey, *The Logic of Unity,* 3rd ed., London, 1981. Another study of the forces working for and against European community.

Postan, M. M., *An Economic History of Western Europe, 1945–1964,* London, 1967. A lively account of a lively period.

• Sampson, Anthony, *The Changing Anatomy of Britain,* New York, 1982. A sharp critical dissection of British society.

• Ulam, Adam, *Expansion and Coexistence: Soviet Foreign Policy, 1917–1973,* 2nd ed., New York, 1974.

Wright, Gordan, *Rural Revolution in France: The Peasantry in the Twentieth Century,* Stanford, 1964. The effect of social change on a firmly entrenched peasantry.

SOURCE MATERIALS

Adenauer, Konrad, *Memoirs, 1945–1953,* Chicago, 1966. Adenauer served as chancellor of the Federal Republic of Germany from 1949 to 1963 and sought both American support and the reunification of dismembered Germany.

• Barnes, Thomas G., and Gerald D. Feldman, eds., *Breakdown and Rebirth: 1914 to the Present,* Boston, 1972. An excellent documentary collection of contemporary history, primarily European.

De Gaulle, Charles, *Memoirs of Hope: Renewal and Endeavor,* New York, 1971.

Kennan, George F., *Memoirs, 1925–1950,* New York, 1967. Kennan, a career diplomat, was America's leading expert on Russia and instrumental in the formation of the containment policy.

• Servan-Schreiber, J. J., *The American Challenge,* New York, 1968. A Frenchman's assessment of the impact of American economy and technology on Europe.

Chapter 31

PROBLEMS OF WORLD CIVILIZATION

Africa, all I ask from you is the courage to know: to look about you and see what is happening in this old and tired world; to realize the extent and depth of its rebirth and the promise which glows on your hills.

—W. E. B. Du Bois, *Autobiography*

The nuclear accident at Chernobyl is a tragedy for those killed or injured by the fire and for the many more who must live with the fear that exposure to radiation may cause cancer and genetic defects in the future. Nevertheless we should remember that the danger from this accident is negligible compared with what would happen in a nuclear war.

—George Rathjens and Jerome Grossman, Council for a Livable World, 1986

The writing of a final chapter in a textbook of this sort is, for the authors, a difficult task. Not only are they called upon to attempt an instant analysis of their own society and time; they are expected as well to discern in present events patterns that will continue to be of some consequence five to ten years hence. In other words, they are called upon to pick historical winners, to decide not what *has* mattered, which is difficult enough, but what *will* matter. Historians, whose job it is to acknowledge the way in which human idiosyncrasies make prediction a tricky business, are particularly loath to single out this movement or that trend and to pronounce it "significant" in terms of the future. We shall therefore merely content ourselves with a discussion of some of the most serious problems confronting society in the 1970s and 1980s, calling attention at the outset to the fact that these problems are rooted in many of the historical developments—industrialization, urbanization, and international competition, for example—that we have traced in the preceding chapters.

The present as history

I. THE EMERGENCE OF THE THIRD WORLD AND ITS CONSEQUENCES

The emergence of an independent Third World

As significant as any trend in world politics since the end of the Second World War has been the decline of the Western imperial powers, and the concurrent emergence of what has come to be called the Third World—newly independent states in Africa and Asia, along with older nations there as well as in Latin America. Many of these countries have established themselves in territories which were formerly part of European empires. Others—China and the various nations of the Middle East and Latin America, for example—while nominally independent of the West before 1945, nevertheless existed under European hegemony and were forced to acquiesce to European demands. Such is the case no longer. Although many of these so-called emerging nations are poor, and although the people of the Third World are by no means a united bloc, they represent a new and increasingly independent factor in the world power equation.

Assets and liabilities

Many of these countries are rich in natural resources. Nations in the Middle East, Venezuela in South America, and Nigeria in Africa, possess oil in quantities sufficient to make their every move of vital importance to the West. Other African nations, Zaire and Angola, for example, are immensely rich in many mineral resources. Population is both a liability and an asset in the Third World. The people of China, by their sheer numbers, constitute an implicit threat to the balance of power at all times. The people of India, again by dint of their numbers, and lack of food, represent a perpetual threat to the stability of their own country and hence to all Asia. Every area in the Third World is a potential "trouble spot." This is so not only because the problems of racism, poverty, hunger, and overpopulation make them particularly vulnerable to violent civil conflicts. It is so, as well, because the superpowers—the United States, the Soviet Union, the European nations, and China itself—are prepared to engage each other through the medium of Third World adversaries, thus increasing the possibility of conflict by their willingness to encourage it. To protect themselves from direct confrontation with each other, these developed nations interfere in the civil wars of others, on opposite sides and with an intensity that frequently belies their declared interest in avoiding general world war.

A final general observation concerning the Third World: although the governments of most countries have pursued the twin goals of industrialization and urbanization, this policy has not gone unchallenged. In the spring of 1979, for example, the extremely repressive regime of one of the Third World's most devoted "westernizers," the shah of oil-rich Iran, was overthrown by the revolutionary forces of an equally repressive religious fanatic, the Ayatollah Khomeini, whose explicit policy was to turn his country's back not only on the

The Ayatollah Ruhollah Khomeini of Iran

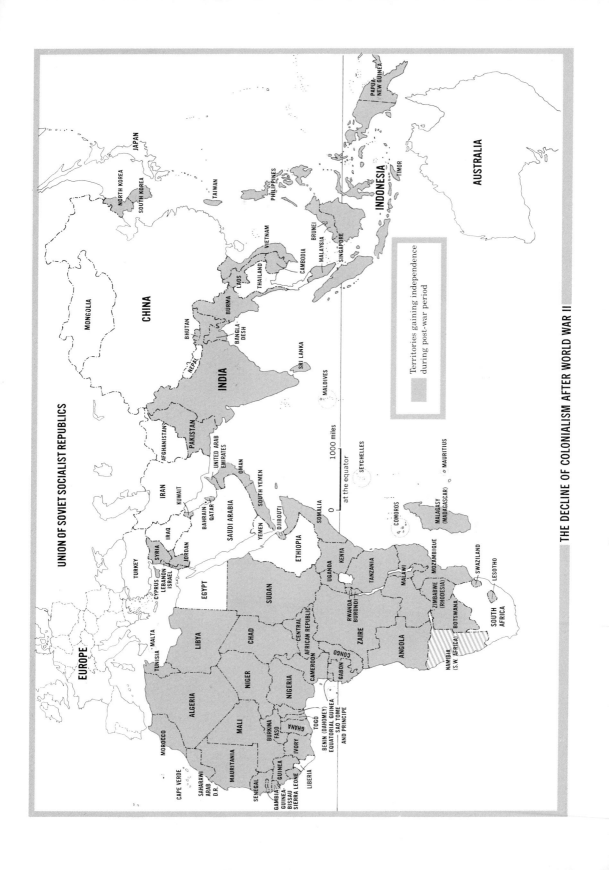

THE DECLINE OF COLONIALISM AFTER WORLD WAR II

Territories gaining independence during post-war period

UNION OF SOVIET SOCIALIST REPUBLICS

EUROPE

MONGOLIA

CHINA

JAPAN

NORTH KOREA

SOUTH KOREA

TAIWAN

TURKEY

CYPRUS

MALTA

TUNISIA

LEBANON

ISRAEL

SYRIA

IRAQ

JORDAN

IRAN

AFGHANISTAN

KUWAIT

BAHRAIN

QATAR

SAUDI ARABIA

UNITED ARAB EMIRATES

OMAN

YEMEN

SOUTH YEMEN

DJIBOUTI

PAKISTAN

NEPAL

BHUTAN

BANGLA-DESH

INDIA

BURMA

LAOS

THAILAND

VIETNAM

CAMBODIA

SRI LANKA

MALDIVES

MALAYSIA

SINGAPORE

BRUNEI

PHILIPPINES

INDONESIA

TIMOR

PAPUA NEW GUINEA

AUSTRALIA

MOROCCO

ALGERIA

LIBYA

EGYPT

MALI

NIGER

CHAD

SUDAN

ETHIOPIA

SOMALIA

MAURITANIA

SENEGAL

GAMBIA

GUINEA-BISSAU

GUINEA

SIERRA LEONE

LIBERIA

IVORY

BURKINA FASO

GHANA

TOGO

BENIN (DAHOMEY)

NIGERIA

CAMEROON

CENTRAL AFRICAN REPUBLIC

EQUATORIAL GUINEA

SAO TOME AND PRINCIPE

GABON

CONGO

ZAIRE

UGANDA

KENYA

RWANDA

BURUNDI

TANZANIA

MALAWI

ANGOLA

ZAMBIA

ZIMBABWE (RHODESIA)

MOZAMBIQUE

NAMIBIA (S.W. AFRICA)

BOTSWANA

SOUTH AFRICA

SWAZILAND

LESOTHO

MADAGASCAR (MALAGASY)

COMOROS

SEYCHELLES

MAURITIUS

CAPE VERDE

SAHRAWI ARAB D.R.

0   1000 miles

at the equator

*The Chinese Communist
Revolution*

Mao Zedong. A photograph taken in 1933 when he was the leader of the radical left opposition to the Kuomintang under Chiang Kai-shek.

Indian independence

West but on "progress" as the West had defined that term for the past two hundred years.

The most radical Third World change resulting from the events of the Second World War was the Chinese revolution. A civil war had raged in China since 1927, when the forces of the nationalists, under Chiang Kai-shek (1887–1975), had engaged in battle first in the south, then in the north with communist insurgents under the leadership of Mao Zedong (1893–1976), a former teacher and union organizer. A truce in 1937 had allowed both sides to wage common battle against the Japanese. At the end of the war, however, the communists, still led by Mao Zedong, refused to surrender the northern provinces under their control, and civil war broke out again. The United States intervened, first as mediator, then with massive military assistance, as an ally of Chiang—all to no avail. The nationalists, corrupt and unrepresentative of the people, surrendered in 1949 to the communists and decamped to the island of Taiwan. Intensely hostile to the capitalist West, the Chinese communists soon found themselves engaged, as well, in a series of skirmishes, verbal and otherwise, with their erstwhile Marxist co-revolutionaries, the Russians. The Sino-Soviet rivalry, the willingness of the United States in the 1970s to reach an accommodation with the Chinese in order to capitalize on that rivalry, and the more recent willingness of the Chinese guided by Deng Xiaoping to encourage Western capitalist investment in their country, suggest that however much power has shifted since the Second World War, power politics remains a game nations believe themselves compelled to play—if necessary, in opposition to their professed ideological commitments.

The Second World War, which had assisted the course of Chinese revolution by dissolving older power structures, served the same purpose within the colonial empires of the West. The first major British colony to establish self-government after the war was India. Rebel movements had harassed the representatives of Britain in that country throughout the nineteenth century. Flames of revolt burned more fiercely during the First World War and after; another world war added more tinder. By 1945 anti-British resentment had reached such a pitch that the country was ripe for revolution. Resolutions by nationalist bodies such as the Indian National Congress called upon Britain to "quit India." The congress had taken the position that India would fight only as a free nation without limitations imposed by the "mother country." The foremost Indian nationalist leader, Mohandas K. Gandhi (1869–1948) did not approve of armed attacks on rulers and their institutions, however. His methods were noncooperation and civil disobedience. By 1947 he and his comrade and disciple, Jawaharlal Nehru (1889–1964), had gained such widespread support that the British found it expedient to grant autonomy to India and its neighboring area, Pakistan. In 1950 both countries organized themselves as independent republics. Disorders continued to plague the two coun-

Four Darks in Red, Mark Rothko (1903–1970). Oil on canvas. Rothko became obsessed with the need to reduce both color and form, achieving thereby a kind of gloomy mysticism. (The Whitney Museum of American Art)

Summer Rental No. 2, Robert Rauschenberg (born 1925). Oil on canvas. Rauschenberg experiments with problems of dimensionality and painterly technique as he strives to achieve a total harmony out of disparate elements. (Collection Whitney Museum of American Art). Gift of the Friends of the Whitney Museum of American Art.

Three Flags, Jasper Johns (born 1930). Encaustic on canvas. Painted with absolute objectivity Johns' objects, in this case three American flags, cease to be mere reproductions and take on distinctive identities of their own. (The Whitney Museum of American Art)

Woman with Dog, Duane Hansen (born 1925). Polyvinyl, polychromed in oil, life size. Hansen recreates the human artifacts of Middle-American culture as symbols of a hollow society. (Collection Whitney Museum of American Art). Gift of Frances and Sydney Lewis.

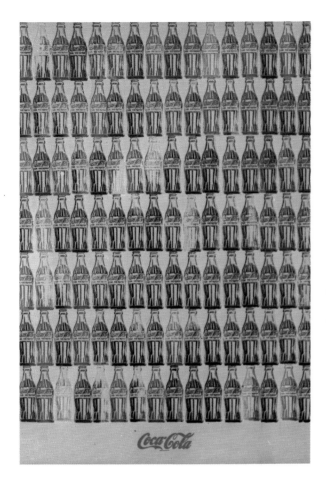

Green Coca Cola Bottles, Andy Warhol (born 1931). Oil on canvas. Warhol, who stands as the high priest of the "pop art" movement in the public imagination, turns mass production into art. Here he takes a commercial product and presents it in row after row, much as it might appear on a grocery store shelf. (Collection Whitney Museum of American Art). Gift of the Friends of the Whitney Museum of American Art.

Gran Cairo, Frank Stella (born 1936). Synthetic polymer paint on canvas. The artist employs absolute symmetry and a rectilinear pattern with compelling effect. (Collection Whitney Museum of American Art). Gift of the Friends of the Whitney Museum of American Art.

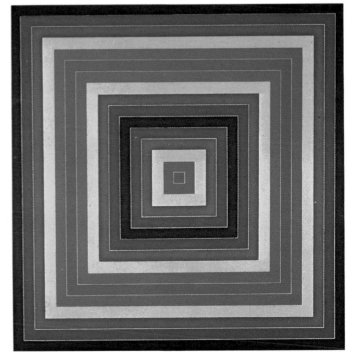

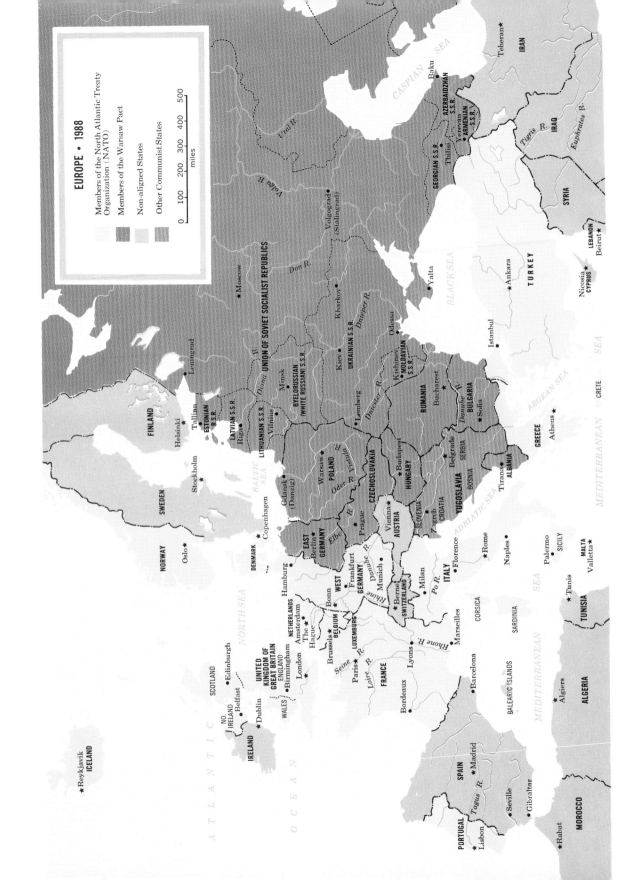

EUROPE · 1988

Members of the North Atlantic Treaty
Organization (NATO)

Members of the Warsaw Pact

Non-aligned States

Other Communist States

0   100   200   300   400   500

miles

Gandhi and Nehru at a Meeting of Indian Leaders in 1946

tries, however, finally resulting in a bloody war in 1971. An important outcome of this conflict was the establishment of the independent republic of Bangladesh, formerly East Pakistan.

In recent years India has struggled to maintain itself as a democracy in the face of mounting economic and social problems. In the mid-1970s, Prime Minister Indira Gandhi (1917–1984) (the daughter of Nehru) assumed authoritarian powers after declaring a state of emergency. Though defeated in 1977 in free elections that she sanctioned following more than a year of virtual dictatorship, she returned to power in early 1980, only to be felled by an assassin's attack in 1984. The succession of her son Rajiv Gandhi leaves unresolved the question of whether a country as dominated by the internal problems of poverty, illiteracy, overpopulation, and near-starvation as India can afford what many Third World leaders claim is the luxury of a slow-moving and comparatively inefficient democracy.

India's struggle to maintain itself as a democracy

Indira Gandhi Campaigning on the Eve of Her Return to Power in Early 1980

Important as India was to Great Britain, it was only the first and largest of the colonies surrendered by colonial powers following the war. Vast areas of Africa achieved independence as well after 1945. In 1951 Egyptian nationalists compelled the British to withdraw their troops from Egyptian territory. A year later a group of nationalist army officers seized control of the government. They deposed the playboy king, Farouk, alleged to be subservient to the British, and proclaimed the state a republic. Shortly thereafter an Egyptian colonel, Gamal Abdel Nasser (1918–1970), assumed the presidency of the country. The British misread Nasser's nationalist ambitions. Anthony Eden, prime minister at the time, called Nasser the Middle Eastern equivalent of Adolph Hitler, and accused him, without foundation, of widespread imperial designs. When Nasser nationalized the Suez Canal Company in 1956 in order to finance the construction of a high dam on the Nile at Aswan, the British and French, dependent

Independent Egypt and the Suez Canal

British withdrawal from sub-Saharan Africa

Jomo Kenyatta Addressing an All-Africa Congress in London

Algeria

on the canal as their major trade route to the East, interpreted the Egyptian action as a direct threat to their economic security. Together with Israel, the three countries launched an abortive, ill-fated invasion of the canal zone as a way not only of recovering control of the company but, as Eden put it, of "punishing" Nasser. World opinion turned against the invaders, who were forced to withdraw.

The British gradually departed from sub-Saharan Africa as well, beginning with Ghana (formerly called the Gold Coast), which was granted self-government in 1954 and independence in 1957. Apologists for British colonial rule claimed that by training indigenous elites and gradually transferring to them responsibility for local administration, British colonies would make the transition to independence more smoothly than would the colonies of other European states where self-government came with less preparation. Despite such protestations, the British colonies' emergence into independence and political and economic stability proved no less difficult than it was for their neighbors. Even in resource-rich Nigeria the euphoria of independence (gained in 1960) fell prey in 1966 to familiar charges of corruption and inefficiency, political assassinations, the overthrow of the government, the secession of the eastern region of the country, and a devastating thirty-one-month civil war in which more than 1 million people perished in battle and of starvation. Kenya, as poor as Nigeria was rich, was beset by the Mau Mau rebellion in 1952, more than a decade before independence. The Mau Mau, an offshoot of the Kikuyu tribe, conducted a six-year reign of terror against white colonists who took their lands, Indian merchants who excluded Africans from their trade, and their kinsmen who were deemed sympathetic to the colonial government. Although driven in part by racial and ethnic antipathies, the Mau Mau uprising was essentially a nationalist movement dedicated to achieving African self-determination over questions of land and governance, a goal realized with the election of Kikuyu tribesman and proponent of African socialism Jomo Kenyatta (1893–1978) as the first president of independent Kenya in 1963. In Rhodesia, however, race was the dominant issue. White Rhodesians had long denied the inevitability of black rule and in 1965 unilaterally declared their independence from Great Britain. The white government held firm in its determination to resist black rule until 1977 when the cumulative effect of U.S. and British pressure, economic sanctions, fierce guerrilla warfare, and the withdrawal of South African assistance caused the government to open negotiations that eventually led to the creation of a government dominated by black nationalists and presided over by Robert Mugabe.

The French were perhaps even less successful than the British in surrendering their colonial possessions without conflict. For France, the most painful and protracted withdrawal occurred in its North African colony of Algeria, inhabited by about one million immigrants, mainly French, in a total population of over ten million. The immi-

Anti-Imperialist Revolt in Algeria, 1960. At Dar-es-Saada, Muslims take furniture from the homes of Europeans and burn it in the streets.

grants occupied positions of economic and political power; Arabs and Berbers remained impoverished laborers. In 1954 nationalists' demands for equal status with the immigrants were denied, triggering a seven-year war during which, as we have seen (see above p. 1052), Algeria's European settlers grew to fear the French government—and its desire for a resolution of the conflict even at the cost of granting independence to Algeria—almost as much as they feared the Algerian nationalists. Charles de Gaulle's 1962 promise of self-determination put an end to the fighting and led to independence a year later. In the meantime the French extricated themselves from other portions of their North African empire with less difficulty. In 1955 they withdrew from their protectorate over Morocco, which was established as an independent kingdom, and a short time later they renounced their protectorate over Tunisia as well.

Britain, France, and other European countries that found themselves compelled to liquidate their empires after 1945 attempted to do so in ways that would enhance the prospects for an orderly transition and stable successor governments. Yet in almost no instance—except, perhaps in the islands of the Caribbean area—was the hope realized. In the wake of independence the unifying symbol of colonial oppression gave way to old ethnic and regional antagonisms dating from the precolonial as well as the colonial eras. These tensions resulted in bitter secessionist movements and devastating civil wars. Belgium's precipitous decision to grant independence to the Congo (later known as Zaire) in 1960 signaled the beginning of a civil war that raged for more than five years between the newly formed central government and the southeastern mineral-rich province of Katanga (later known as Shaba) and has continued to smolder into the 1980s with assistance

The post-independence resurgence of ethnic and regional antagonisms

Nelson Mandela. Imprisoned since 1964, Mandela is nevertheless considered the best-known and most popular African nationalist in South Africa. He has been the symbolic head of the African National Congress since 1967.

Pieter W. Botha, President of the Republic of South Africa since 1984 and Prime Minister from 1978 to 1984

from Angolan-based Katangan refugees. In addition to the struggle in Nigeria, similar conflicts erupted in the Sudan and Chad between a Muslim north and a Christian/animist south, in Ethiopia between the Marxist central government and the Islamic Eritreans, and in Angola and Zimbabwe between the government and ethnically and regionally based revolutionary movements that had participated in the struggle for independence but not in the subsequent regime. Many of these conflicts were spurred on by support from neighbors or non-African powers. While none of these breakaway resistance movements has yet succeeded, they have left a legacy of suspicion, violence, and instability.

Undoubtedly the most explosive area of conflict on the African continent was South Africa, whose all-white government continued to oppose appeals and pressures from all quarters to relax its racial policy of *apartheid,* which has formally decreed a separate and desperately inferior existence for its black and mixed-race population since the Nationalists, an Afrikaner party of the extreme right, began to enact a severe segregationist program affecting every aspect of life in South Africa in the 1950s. Initially, the nonwhite population led by the African National Congress responded with campaigns of passive resistance. Government-sponsored repression and violence, however, drove the leadership of the African National Congress, including Nelson Mandela, to adopt a more radical and violent strategy after 1960. The government responded by banning the African National Congress as a terrorist organization, hunting down and prosecuting militants, and legislating further curbs on the personal liberties of nonwhites. Racial tensions among the nation's 5 million whites, 3 million coloreds, and over 20 million blacks continued to worsen. South African whites grew even more fearful of the "black menace" when, in 1975, neighboring Angola and Mozambique were granted independence by Portugal and promptly installed Marxist, militantly anti-South African governments that fueled the expectations of black South Africans. Domestic violence erupted again in 1976 in the Johannesburg ghetto of Soweto where police killed more than 1,000 rioting blacks.

Seeking ways to defuse domestic tensions and improve their image abroad, the government of Pieter W. Botha took steps in the early 1980s to liberalize the country's social and economic policies toward the nonwhite population by authorizing African labor unions to bargain collectively, desegregating some public facilities, and raising wages. But at the same time nearly 3 million blacks were deprived of citizenship and sent to live in overcrowded "ethnic homelands." A new constitution adopted in 1984 conferred near-dictatorial powers on the president and, while creating a tricameral legislature with separate chambers for whites, coloreds, and Asians, totally excluded blacks from political participation. Angry blacks became more violent still in their opposition to the white regime and Botha declared a state of emergency in mid-1985. By 1986 a wide range of nations, fearing a cataclysmic

Apartheid in South Africa. Among the restrictions imposed upon blacks is the requirement that they carry passports. Here a policeman and an interpreter check the papers of an African bound for Johannesburg to work in the mines.

confrontation between the white minority and the black majority, joined in imposing severe economic sanctions upon South Africa in hopes of persuading the government to come to terms with the black population peacefully.

The prevailing political turmoil in Africa has been compounded by the onset of a massive economic decline in the 1970s after the global escalation of petroleum prices and the attendant inflation in prices for Western technology, seed, and fertilizer. Recurring droughts struck nearly every part of the continent impairing agricultural development and bringing starvation to many areas. African states were compelled to divert currency from development projects to import food for their swelling populations at the very time that falling world prices for agricultural commodities and metals diminished the market value of Africa's major exports and the sources of foreign currency. In the growing number of African states whose leaders espoused various brands of socialism many government-sponsored corporations were inefficiently managed and became financial liabilities. This made it all the more difficult for these nations to maintain payments to Western financial institutions on debts incurred for development projects during the boom years of the 1960s; and defaulting in turn limited their access to further loans.

Africa's political turmoil compounded by economic decline

The liberation of colonial peoples in the decades following the Second World War heightened racial consciousness and racial conflict, not only in Africa and Asia but in the West as well. Newly independent black nations, on guard against real or perceived threats of neocolonialism, remained understandably sensitive to the fact of their economic dependence upon the predominantly white nations of Western Europe and America. Black and Asian immigration into those nations produced

The Third World and racial conflict

tension and frequent violence. And indigenous black populations in the West, particularly in the United States, derived a sense of both their present social and economic inferiority and their potential strength as a political force from the independence movements occurring elsewhere in the world.

The growth of insurgency among American blacks paralleled the rise of black nations in Africa and the Caribbean. Through most of the years from the Civil War to 1900, black people were condemned, in the North as well as the South, to a subordinate role within a predominantly white culture. Black political consciousness and black leaders were not unknown before the turn of the century: Harriet Tubman, Sojourner Truth, Frederick Douglass, Nat Turner, and others, were eloquent and powerful spokespeople and activists. But with the twentieth century came a massive emigration of blacks from the South to the North. Although the North shared most of the attitudes of the South, there were more opportunities for blacks in the industrial cities than in the primarily agrarian South. Many thousands of black people emigrated to the North during the years of the First World War, when the lack of white labor created a need for their services.

U.S. blacks after the Civil War

In 1910 the National Association for the Advancement of Colored People was founded and contributed to the growing awareness among black people that they were an oppressed group and that this should be changed. The work of the NAACP was supplemented in 1911 with the founding of the National League on Urban Conditions Among Negroes (later known as the National Urban League). The work of black leaders of this time—for example, Ida Wells-Barnett (1862–1931), A. Philip Randolph (1889–1979), W. E. B. Du Bois (1868–1963), Mary McLeod Bethune (1875–1955)—who were visible and vocal opponents of lynching, promoters of educational opportunities for blacks, and of the organization of blacks into labor unions, kept the movement for equality alive.

Early twentieth-century civil rights movements

The Second World War saw another influx of blacks into northern cities and intensified their drive for dignity and independence. The Congress of Racial Equality (CORE) was founded by James Farmer in 1942. By 1960 CORE had combined its efforts with those of other political and civil rights organizations seeking the same goals. Together they helped to promote "freedom rides" on behalf of civil rights and boycotts directed at private businesses and public services that discriminated against blacks in the South. The leader of these protests, and the undoubted leader of the black movement in the United States in the 1960s, was Martin Luther King, Jr. (1929–1968), a Baptist minister. Like Farmer, King embraced the Gandhian philosophy of nonviolence. His personal participation in countless demonstrations, his willingness to go to jail for a cause that he believed to be just, and his ability as an orator to arouse both blacks and whites with his message led to his position as the most highly regarded—

Martin Luther King, Jr., American Civil Rights Activist

and widely feared—defender of black rights. His career was ended by assassination in 1968.

The goal of King and of organizations like CORE was a fully integrated nation. That of other charismatic black leaders was complete independence from white society. Marcus Garvey (1887–1940), a native of Jamaica who lived in the black New York City ghetto of Harlem, emphasized the African origins of black Americans. He claimed that his people were the descendants of the "greatest and proudest race who ever peopled the earth." In his campaign for black separatism he generated a movement of black emigration from America to Africa. Another black separatist was Malcolm X (1925–1965), who assumed the "X" after having discarded his "white" surname. For most of his adult life a spokesman for the Black Muslim movement, Malcolm X urged blacks to renew their commitment to their own heritage—the Muslim religion, for example—and to establish black businesses as a way of maintaining economic and psychological distance from white domination. Like King, he was assassinated, in 1965 while addressing a rally in Harlem.

*Black independence:
Garvey and Malcolm X*

Civil rights laws enacted under the administration of President Lyndon B. Johnson (1908–1973) in the 1960s brought American blacks some measure of equality with regard to voting rights—and, to a much lesser degree, school desegregation. In other areas, such as housing and job opportunities, blacks continue to suffer disadvantage and discrimination, as a result of white racism, which lies beneath arguments that blacks should be satisfied with the gains they have made, and the general recalcitrance of administrations following Johnson's domestically innovative one. These problems are not confined to the United States. In Great Britain, for example, where there has been a large immigration of blacks from former colonies, extreme discrimination in jobs and housing menaces the chances for early or satisfactory

*Blacks in the 1970s and
1980s*

British Police Arrest a Black Rioter in the London Suburb of Brixton, 1981. Deteriorating relations between police and black residents, along with high unemployment, were cited as causes of the violence.

integration. Because most black workers are "last hired, first fired," they are particular victims of Britain's rising unemployment. In the summer of 1981 and again in 1985 black frustrations resulted in serious rioting in London and other British cities. Disturbances broke out again in the United States in 1982 in Miami, where an influx of Latin American refugees, most of them Cuban, had created further tensions. Response to these outbreaks followed the pattern established in the 1960s: immediate concern and investigation, but little else, particularly in terms of solving the problems of economic inequality.

2. WARMAKING AND PEACEKEEPING IN THE NUCLEAR AGE

Frequency of conflicts

The violence attendant upon the emergence of new nations was but a part of the pattern of armed confrontations imposed across the globe after 1945 by international rivalries and tensions. The conflicts that have intruded with agonizing consistency upon the world were frequently the result of local circumstance. Yet almost always they produced far more than local consequences. As they unfolded, they proved not only how fragile were the processes of international peacekeeping, but also how vulnerable even the mightiest nations were to circumstances that frequently lay beyond their limited control.

The Korean War

The most serious clash between communist and noncommunist forces in the first postwar decade occurred not in Europe but in Korea, where armed conflict broke out in 1950. Treaties with Japan at the end of the Second World War had provided that Korea, under Japanese rule since 1910, would become an independent and united country. The United States and the Soviet Union left occupying forces there until 1949, the Americans to the south of the thirty-eighth parallel, the Russians to the north of it. During this period of occupation, the Soviets refused to cooperate with the United Nations–sponsored plan to hold free elections for the entire country. Instead, they established in the north a people's republic similar to those they had erected in eastern Europe. In June 1950, troops from North Korea crossed the thirty-eighth parallel and invaded the south. Taking advantage of a temporary Russian boycott of the United Nations, the United States was able to avoid a Soviet veto of its plan to counter this invasion by sending a contingent of troops to oppose it. The troops, though nominally under United Nations command, were largely American, directed and supplied by the United States. Initial military gains by this force were countered in November by the invasion into Korea of troops from the newly established People's Republic of China, sent to aid the North Koreans. A stalemate ensued, President Truman and his advisors being as unwilling to widen the conflict into China—fearing a third world war—as they were to abandon their South Korean allies. After two years of military and diplomatic deadlock, a peace was concluded, recognizing the existence of both North and South Korea and abandoning any scheme for their reunion. As in the case of Germany, the limited ability of major powers to achieve their goals completely resulted in a divided settlement—and a divided nation.

A decade later, another trouble spot, Vietnam, produced the same lesson, in a war far more devastating than that in Korea. After the defeat of Japan in 1945, France had sought to recover its lost empire in the Far East. The French were immediately confronted by a rebellion of Vietnamese nationalists, however, under the leadership of Ho Chi Minh (1890–1969). The rebels resorted to guerrilla warfare and inflicted such costly defeats upon the French that the latter decided to abandon the struggle. An agreement was signed at Geneva in 1954 providing for the division of Vietnam into two zones, pending elections to determine the future government of the entire country. Ho Chi Minh became president of North Vietnam and established his capital at Hanoi. His followers, the Viet Cong, were numerous in both halves of the country. Had elections been held as provided by the Geneva Agreement, Ho Chi Minh would probably have been elected president of all of Vietnam. But the government of South Vietnam, backed by the United States, refused to permit elections to be held.

Ho Chi Minh, President of North Vietnam, 1954–1969

From this point on, involvement by the United States in the Vietnamese civil war escalated steadily. President John F. Kennedy (1917–1963) was convinced that a Chinese communist juggernaut would soon roll over all of Southeast Asia: Vietnam, Laos, Cambodia, Malaysia, and Singapore; then Thailand, Burma, and India. How far Kennedy would have gone in his crusade to confront communism had he escaped assassination in 1963 is impossible to say. Kennedy's successor, Lyndon Johnson, hoped that a relatively small force of perhaps 100,000 men would be sufficient to defeat the Viet Cong and drive them back into their own country. Little consideration was given to the fact that the Viet Cong were solidly entrenched in both states of Vietnam, and that they had been waging a bitter national struggle for upward of eighteen years. They had succeeded in driving out the French in 1954 and were not likely to surrender to a new invader, as they conceived the Americans to be. The Viet Cong and the North Vietnam regulars, though less well equipped, nevertheless fought the South Vietnamese and their American allies to a standstill on several occasions.

Kennedy's intrusion into Vietnam

Exasperated by failure to win an easy victory in South Vietnam, the American civilian and military chiefs undertook a campaign of heavy aerial bombardment. A series of incidents in 1964 were contrived so as to provide them with justification. Reports, of doubtful veracity, indicated that North Vietnamese ships had attacked American naval vessels in the Tonkin Gulf. President Johnson pronounced these incidents acts of war and immediately obtained from Congress authorization to use whatever measures might prove necessary to repel communist aggression. Soon afterward the first American raids began.

President Johnson escalates the war

War in Vietnam. Confronted with a new kind of warfare, the American military sought to adapt its methods to the Vietnamese situation.

Although evidence accumulated which cast doubt on the efficacy of these raids, they continued. At least as much tonnage in nonnuclear bombs was dropped on tiny Vietnam as was unloaded by the Allied forces on all of Germany in the Second World War. As the struggle entered its fifth year, with no end in sight, disillusionment spread throughout the United States. Criticism of President Johnson was so harsh in 1968 that he was forced to abandon his plans to run for a second term.

The Nixon policies

Johnson's successor, Richard M. Nixon (1913–   ), elected on the strength of promises to end the war, instead continued its escalation. In May 1970 the United States invaded Cambodia and a few months later the kingdom of Laos. In April 1972, the North Vietnamese, with aid from Russia and China, launched a powerful counteroffensive with the objective of conquering South Vietnam and driving all foreign armies out of the country. A number of South Vietnamese strongholds were captured. Nixon countered with increased bombing of North Vietnam's factories and railroads and by mining its harbors. Savage raids continued while negotiations were underway in December 1972. A ceasefire, early in 1973, did no more than postpone the inevitable. Two years later, South Vietnam fell to the Viet Cong and the North Vietnamese. The massive intervention had proved a ghastly failure.

U.S. presence in the Caribbean

The lesson of Vietnam—that in a nuclear age there are limits to national power—was one that the United States, the Soviet Union, and other countries have continued to find hard to learn. Since the early 1960s, for example, the United States has found it increasingly difficult to maintain its accustomed hegemony over the Caribbean area and Central America. A revolution in Cuba in 1959 brought to power Fidel Castro, who declared himself a Marxist-Leninist shortly thereafter. His increasingly anti-American regime relied heavily on economic support from the Soviet Union. Castro's insistence on the right to assist revolutionary movements elsewhere in Latin America and in Angola made him, in the minds of U.S. policy-makers, a continuing yet apparently unavoidable threat to American interests. In the late 1970s, insurgents in Nicaragua toppled the regime of a pro-American dictator, Anastasio Somoza. The victorious rebels, calling themselves the Sandinista National Liberation Front (after a guerilla leader treacherously slain by Somoza's father), plotted a leftist course for Nicaragua, accepted Cuban and Soviet aid and declared their determination to avoid U.S. domination. The Sandinista regime was perceived by President Ronald Reagan as a creation of Soviet ideology and Cuban subversion and as a direct threat to U.S. security. The Reagan administration proceeded to commit the United States to the overthrow of the Sandinistas through a series of increasingly dangerous moves: pressuring financial institutions to withhold loans; supporting and arming a counterrevolutionary force (the Contras); mining Nicaraguan harbors; conducting air and naval maneuvers in nearby waters; building airstrips and camps for joint military exercises in Honduras; and declaring the United States above international law. The posture of the United States hardened the Sandinistas' determination to resist American aggression, inducing a siege mentality and resulting in an increasingly authoritarian regime. In El Salvador, a similar coup in 1979 expelled that country's hard-line dictator. Yet there, in contrast to Nicaragua, the revolutionary government moved to the Right with the support of the United States. State-backed death squads battled an insurgent Democratic Revolutionary Front as the country plunged into civil war. American intervention in both El Salvador and Nicaragua was limited by U.S. unwillingness to engage directly in the conflicts there, and to this extent expressed a realization that even a superpower could not expect to shape the world to its own ends.

Fidel Castro of Cuba

The Nicaraguan Revolution. Sandinista commandos celebrate the fall of the Somoza government by toppling a huge statue of Anastasio Somoza Garcia, the father of the ousted president, in Managua, Nicaragua.

The Cuban Missile Crisis

The Soviet involvement in Afghanistan

Palestine under British mandate

During the past three decades the Soviet Union has been forced to come to terms with this lesson as well. Having arranged to supply their Cuban ally Fidel Castro with "offensive" missiles and other war matériel, the Russians were confronted by a U.S. naval blockade of the island designed to prevent delivery of the promised equipment in October 1962. The Soviet government, alarmed by the threat of war, agreed to withdraw and to remove the bombers and missiles already on Cuban soil. The incident posed an extremely difficult question for the superpowers: How could one nation convince another of its determination to brook no further interference with its plans, if its adversary could be fairly certain that because of the fear of nuclear war the threat was no more than a bluff?

In deciding to invade Afghanistan in 1979 in support of a recently installed pro-Soviet regime, however, the U.S.S.R. seemed to repeat the experience of the French and the Americans in Vietnam. Eight years later, a force of 100,000 Russian troops had been unable to quell guerrilla opposition to this action. An ability to accommodate goals to limitations was a talent difficult for the superpowers to master.

Yet even to set goals was an almost impossible task in that part of the world that was the most persistent trouble spot in the post–Second World War era: the Middle East. Here the conflict centered on the presence of the Jewish state of Israel. At the end of the First World War, the country now known as Israel, then called Palestine, was a province of Turkey. Its population was about 70 percent Arab and 30 percent Jewish and Christian. Following Turkey's defeat, Palestine was mandated to the League of Nations as a protectorate of Britain.

Immigration to Palestine. Left: British soldiers guard the shore as a ship loaded with unauthorized refugees attempts to land in 1947. Right: A view of the unbearably crowded conditions aboard ships bringing refugees to Palestine.

Meanwhile, Zionist organizations in Europe and America worked to convert Palestine into a national home for the Jewish people.

For a time Palestine flourished under the British mandate. By 1929, however, tension between Arabs and Jews had become severe. The paramount cause of Arab concern was the increasing flow of Jews into Palestine. Arabs feared a relentless immigrant wave, backed by foreign capital and bearing a culture alien to the ways of the Muslim majority. This anxiety manifested itself in a series of armed attacks and terrorist raids by Arabs against the Jews in the late 1920s and early 1930s. As news spread of the Nazi persecution of the Jews, pressure increased on the British to allow more and more Jewish immigrants into Palestine. During the period from 1930 to 1933 more than 130,000 Jews were admitted; uncounted thousands more entered the country illegally. The Arabs rose in open rebellion. Guerilla attacks in rural areas and looting, burning, and sabotage in towns and cities kept the population in turmoil. By 1939, though the British had 20,000 troops in Palestine, they were unable to maintain order.

Little progress toward a lasting settlement had been achieved when, in April 1947, the British government referred the Palestine problem to the United Nations and announced that a year later it would terminate its mandate and withdraw all its troops from the country. On May 15, 1948, the British mandate came to an end; on the same day a Jewish provisional government proclaimed the establishment of an independent state of Israel. From the day of proclaimed independence until the spring of 1949, Israel and its Arab neighbor countries were at war. United Nations' efforts brought about temporary truces, but nothing lasting was achieved until Israel, Egypt, Jordan, and Syria signed general armistice agreements in early February 1949. The status of the ceasefire was regarded as a victory for Israel and a defeat for the Arab powers. Neither, however, accepted it as final. Violent incidents continued to occur, including retaliatory massacres.

Despite wars with the Arabs, Israel embarked on a concerted program of industrialization to strengthen the economy. Large sums of money flowed into the country, mainly from the United States, Britain, and West Germany, as restitution for the outrages of Nazi persecution. Yet Israel's conflict with its Arab neighbors continued unabated, fueled by Israel's inability to resolve the question of the rights of Palestinian Arabs who still claim the state of Israel as their home and by the Arabs' refusal to recognize Israel as a legitimate state. These tensions were exacerbated by Israeli participation in a poorly conceived action against Egypt in 1956. In 1967 President Nasser of Egypt, in alliance with Jordan and Syria, closed the port of Aqaba, Israel's only direct outlet to the Red Sea. The Israelis responded with a lightning war against Egypt and its allies, whose forces were routed in six days. An eventual ceasefire did nothing to ease regional animosities. New outbreaks flared sporadically for more than two years. The Arabs were tormented by loss of confidence and fearful of their own future

Uncertain prospects for peace in the Middle East

as a result of their defeat. The Israelis were obsessed with security and determined to preserve it regardless of cost.

Another war of longer duration in 1973 once again failed to resolve the impasse. In that conflict, the Arabs threatened to withhold their immense oil reserves from the West, in hopes that the West would in turn put pressure on the Israelis to negotiate. This tactic succeeded only to the extent of convincing Europe and America of their dependence on Arab oil, and of their need to escape from that dependence. Since that time, prospects for peace have waxed and waned. In 1978, President Anwar Sadat (1918–1981), Nasser's successor, traveled to Jerusalem in a dramatic bid to break the deadlock. And in the fall of that year U.S. President Jimmy Carter (1924–   ), having persuaded Sadat and Israeli Prime Minister Menachem Begin (1914–   ) to meet with him at Camp David outside Washington, engineered their agreement to a treaty draft, which was signed in final form by Israel and Egypt in Washington in 1979. Yet factors such as Israel's reluctance to surrender Arab territory in the Sinai peninsula and the continuing terrorist campaigns of non-Jewish Palestinians guaranteed that peace would not come easily or soon to the Middle East. Proof of that unhappy truth came yet again in 1982, when Israel launched a ferocious attack against Palestinian forces based in Lebanon. During the conflict the Israelis bombed suspected strongholds of the Palestine Liberation Organization (PLO) in the cities of Tyre, Sidon, and Beirut, whose civilian populations were used by the PLO as human shields for its military activities.

Further instability in the Middle East

The issue of Israel's place among the nations of the Middle East was by no means the sole cause of that area's political volatility. The revolutionary government of Iran, following the overthrow of the shah in 1979, charted an erratic and unpredictable course that further jeopardized the stability of the region. In 1980 war broke out between Iran and Iraq, ultimately spilling into the Persian Gulf, where it threatened to disrupt vital oil shipping lanes in international waters. In the face of

On the Path to Peace in the Middle East. From left to right, Egyptian President Anwar Sadat, U.S. President Jimmy Carter, and Israeli Prime Minister Menachem Begin shake hands at the announcement of the Camp David accord which laid the groundwork for a peace treaty between Egypt and Israel.

A Meeting of the Organization of Petroleum-Exporting Countries (OPEC) in Qatar, 1976

this danger the United States government in 1987 placed American flags on select foreign oil tankers, hoping by this gesture to discourage attack on those ships by the Iranians. The immediate result, however, was an increased number of Iranian mines in the Persian Gulf and an increased threat of general war.

Influencing the attitudes of United States and European governments toward Israel and its Arab enemies was the fact of Western dependence on the Arabs for oil. The Organization of Petroleum Exporting Countries (OPEC), formed in 1960 to regulate the production and pricing of crude oil, assumed an increasingly militant posture in the 1970s under the leadership of its Middle Eastern Arab members. For a time a majority appeared willing to follow the lead of militant Middle Eastern nationalists such as Muammar Qaddafi, Libyan chief of state, in attempting to extract a high price—both economic and political—from the West. Western powers tempered their support of Israel and designed their policies toward the PLO at least in part on the basis of their continuing need for oil. In the mid-1980s overproduction and a decrease in the demand for oil brought about by economic depression in western Europe and the United States made it far more difficult for the OPEC countries to keep the price of oil uniformly high. Yet the resulting price reductions were not an unalloyed boon to Western economies. Many oil-producing nations in the Third World had borrowed large sums of money from Western financial institutions in the 1970s using their "black gold" as collateral. When reduced oil prices resulted in financial crisis for some of those nations—as in Mexico, for example—Western lenders were threatened with default. The problems of oil production and pricing illustrate convincingly the way in which the problems of the world economy and of international peacekeeping are locked together.

Even without the dangerous conflicts that have scarred global trouble spots since 1945, the world would not be at peace. Terrorism, a plague of apparently senseless acts of human destruction, though often related to larger events and causes, has over the past decade emerged

The oil crisis

Terrorism

Former Italian Prime Minister Aldo Moro, victim of the terrorist Red Brigade, May 9, 1978

as a frightening and thus far insoluble threat to world stability. Terrorism has been employed by separatist or nationalist movements, the Palestinians (the PLO) in the Middle East, for example, the Basques in northern Spain, or the Catholic (Irish Republican Army, or IRA) and Protestant extremists in Northern Ireland. It has also been the tactic of radical national leaders such as the Ayatollah Khomeini of Iran or Muammar Qaddafi of Libya. The catalogue of terrorist outrages continues to grow: the incendiary attacks and bank robberies of the so-called "Red Army Faction" in Germany in the early 1970s, which were launched to arouse revolutionary sentiment among frustrated youth; the PLO attack against the quarters of Israeli athletes at the 1972 Olympics in Munich; the kidnapping and murder of the Italian politician Aldo Moro by the Italian "Red Brigade" in 1978; the murder of Israel-bound passengers in the Rome airport in 1985; the repeated hijacking of passenger planes, and indeed, on one occasion in 1985, of a Mediterranean cruise ship, the *Achille Lauro*. These and countless other incidents appear to have become a ghastly commonplace.

Looming above all the other issues and circumstances we have surveyed has been the continuing threat of nuclear destruction. During the 1960s and 1970s, both the United States and the Soviet Union vacillated in their willingness to discuss arms control, let alone to move toward actual reduction. Henry Kissinger, U.S. secretary of state under Presidents Richard Nixon and Gerald Ford in the 1970s, proclaimed détente with the Russians as his goal, and devoted much time to negotiations aimed at defusing potentially explosive areas of conflict between the two nations. Both countries were concerned to curb the spread of nuclear weapons and to limit, if possible, the apparently endless expansion of their own arsenals. The Strategic Arms Limitation Treaty (SALT) talks, in which the Russians and Americans

Antiwar Protest in London, 1983. Demonstrations such as this one directed against the installation of U.S. missiles with nuclear warheads in Europe were a factor influencing the superpowers to negotiate arms reductions.

engaged during the 1970s and early 1980s, were an indication of mutual willingness to recognize and tackle a problem of awesome dimensions. Yet the talks produced little in the way of concrete agreement. President Ronald Reagan, who took office in 1981, denounced a second stage of the SALT negotiations during his campaign and subsequently has continued to press for dramatic increases in his military budgets for sophisticated armaments, even as he proclaimed his devotion to the cause of disarmament. Changing leadership within the Soviet Union did not allow for new initiatives from that quarter until 1986, when Mikhail Gorbachev floated a series of proposals that met with mixed response from the Reagan administration, still publicly committed to increased missile deployment and to an elaborate and astronomically expensive space-based "defensive" system. In December 1987, however, despite continuing disagreement on other issues, Gorbachev and Reagan signed a treaty in Washington eliminating all short- and medium-range nuclear missiles from the European arsenals of both East and West. The agreement was reached partly as a result of vigorous public disarmament campaigns, partly as well in consequence of a realization by world leaders that the existing balance of terror threatened large portions of the world with total destruction.

3. THE PROBLEMS OF ECOLOGY AND POPULATION

Pessimism about the human condition in the 1980s stemmed from more than the problems of the present. It derived as well from a fear about the future, the future of the earth's human beings, of the earth itself, and of what is termed its ecology. The word *ecology* is often used to refer to human beings and their environment, but it is much broader than that. Ecologists think of humans as related to a vast chain of life which extends through mammals, amphibians, invertebrates, and the simplest microorganisms, either plants or animals. In popular usage ecology may be synonymous with pollution problems. Again this is an oversimplification. The causes and prevention of pollution make up important elements in the study of ecology, but they are not its whole subject. Equally important is the use of our environment in ways that will safeguard the heritage of fertile soil, pure air, fresh water, and forests for those who come after us.

The meaning of ecology

Ecological violations consist not merely of poisoning the atmosphere and contaminating oceans, rivers, and lakes by dumping wastes into them, but of any assault upon them that makes them less valuable for human survival. The excessive construction of dams, for example, causes the silting of rivers and the accumulating of nitrates at a faster rate than the surrounding soil can absorb. The use of insecticides, especially those containing DDT, may result in upsetting the balance of nature. An example in the recent history of Malaysia illustrates such an occurrence. The Malaysian government resorted to extensive spraying of remote areas with DDT in the hope of stamping out

Assaults upon nature

Disaster at the Chernobyl Nuclear Power Station, May 1986. The explosion at this Soviet nuclear power facility (the white arrow indicates the damaged unit surrounded by debris) near Kiev produced radioactive fallout that killed and injured numerous people close to the site, and threatened the health of thousands more as it spread across Europe. This accident fueled the continuing debate on the safety of nuclear power plants not only in the Soviet Union but around the earth.

malaria-carrying mosquitoes. The DDT killed the mosquitoes but also poisoned the flourishing cockroaches. The cockroaches in turn were eaten by the village cats. The cats died of the DDT poison. The net result was a multiplication of rats formerly kept from a population explosion by their natural enemies, the cats. So badly disturbed was the balance of nature that a fresh supply of cats had to be airlifted from other regions. Other assaults upon the balance of nature have been even more serious. The Aswan High Dam of Egypt, undoubtedly valuable for increasing the water supply of that country, has at the same time cut down the flow of algal nutrients to the Mediterranean, with damaging effects on the fishing industry of various countries. From the ecological standpoint the rapid development of industry in modern times is an almost unmitigated disaster. For thousands of years the human race introduced into the environment no more waste substances than could easily be absorbed by the environment. But modern technology has introduced a variety of wastes never abundant before. Among them are carbon monoxide, sulfur dioxide, and nitrogen oxide. And this is to say nothing of the discharge into nature of pesticides, the great host of synthetic products that are not biologically degradable, and the fallout of nuclear weapons testing. As the nature and gravity of these problems have become apparent, governments have been pressured to take preventive and remedial action. In late 1982 the United States government was actually compelled to purchase the entire town of Times Beach, Missouri, where a pesticide had been sprayed (with permanently damaging effects to the health of its citizens), before it could proceed with a detoxification program. In 1986, a nuclear power station at Chernobyl, near Kiev in the Soviet

Union, exploded, producing highly dangerous radioactive fallout not only in the vicinity of the accident but, because of prevailing winds, across the continent of Europe. Affected countries protested, while citizens increased the pressure on their governments to curtail the manufacture of such lethal industrial and military by-products.

Ecology and the population explosion

The ecological problem is caused not simply by the dumping of harmful and nondegradable products. It is also the result of wastage of land as our most valuable natural resource. In many parts of the world rivers run brown because they are filled with earth washed from the fields bordering them. In some of the largest American cities two-thirds to three-quarters of the land area is paved with streets and parking lots. A close link exists between the problems of ecology and the population explosion that is occurring throughout the world. Indeed, if population had not increased alarmingly in recent years, the problems of ecology might well have passed unnoticed. For example, New York City on the eve of the Civil War had a total population of 700,000. The area was not essentially smaller than it is now. Yet the inhabitants of the five boroughs constituting the city have multiplied ten times over. The example of New York City can be duplicated in many other overcrowded areas, not only in America but especially in Asia. Calcutta now has a population of 7.5 million, compared with 3 million in 1961. Tokyo has grown from 9 million to over 12 million in little more than twenty years. The total population of the earth at the beginning of the Christian era was about 250 million. More than sixteen centuries passed before another quarter-billion had been added to the total. Not until 1860 did the population of the globe approximate 1 billion. From then on the increase was vastly more rapid. The sixth half-billion, added about 1960, required scarcely more than ten years. By 1986 the earth's population was fast approaching 5 billion.

Causes of the demographic revolution

What have been the causes of this demographic revolution that overturned the ancient balance between births and deaths which had long kept the population on a stationary or slowly rising level? Fundamentally, what has happened has been the achievement of a twentieth-century death rate alongside a medieval birthrate. Infant mortality rates have markedly declined. Deaths of mothers in childbirth have also diminished. The great plagues, such as cholera, typhus, and tuberculosis, take a much smaller toll than they did in earlier centuries. Wars and famines still number their victims by the millions, yet such factors are insufficient to counteract an uncurbed rate of reproduction. Though the practice of contraception has been approved by the governments of such nations as India, China, and Japan, only in the last decade have the effects of that policy been noticeable. In some countries poverty, religion, and ignorance have made the widespread use of contraceptives difficult. Leaders in Third World countries charge that attempts by Western powers to encourage them to limit population growth, either by contraceptive devices or by sterilization, is a not-so-subtle form of genocide.

Its uneven effects

The demographic revolution has not affected all countries uniformly. Its incidence has been most conspicuous in the underdeveloped nations of Central and South America, Africa, and Asia. Whereas the population of the world as a whole will double, at present rates of increase, in thirty-five years, that of Central and South America will multiply twofold in only twenty-six years. An outstanding example is that of Brazil. In 1900 its population was estimated to be 17 million. By 1975 this total had grown to 98 million, and by 1986 to 143 million, a more than eightfold increase in less than one hundred years. The population of Asia (excluding the U.S.S.R.) grew from 813 million in 1900 to approximately 2.9 billion in 1986—approximately 60 percent of the world's population. A situation in which the poorest nations are also the most overpopulated does not augur well for the future of world stability.

4. THE ACHIEVEMENTS AND LIMITATIONS OF SCIENCE AND TECHNOLOGY

Science and technology: cause and cure of the world's problems

For solutions to many of these problems, men and women have, paradoxically, turned to those agencies responsible, in many cases, for the creation of the problems: science and technology. Scientists and technicians invented and perfected the internal combustion engine and the chemical DDT. Now other scientists and technicians are seeking ways to combat their deleterious effects. Scientific research has been responsible for the medical advances which have helped to produce worldwide population increase. No one would argue, of course, that the research should not have taken place, or that the continuing battle against disease is not one of humanity's most worthwhile engagements. Most would agree, however, that science must move as quickly as possible to come up with a safe and simple method of controlling birth, as it continues to fight to prolong life.

The discovery of viruses; DNA

The achievements of science in the field of health during the past half-century have been truly remarkable. Two discoveries of great importance have enabled scientists to understand more clearly the ways in which the human body receives and transmits disease. The discovery of viruses was the result of experimentation conducted chiefly by the American biochemist Wendell Stanley in the 1930s. Viruses are microscopic organisms which show signs of life—including the ability to reproduce—only when existing inside living cells. They are the cause of many human diseases, including measles, poliomyelitis (infantile paralysis), and rabies. Not until the nature of viruses was understood could scientists begin to develop means of treating and preventing the virus-produced illnesses in human beings. A second most important discovery that has increased our understanding of human life occurred in 1953, when the Englishman F. H. C. Crick and the American James D. Watson further unlocked the mysteries

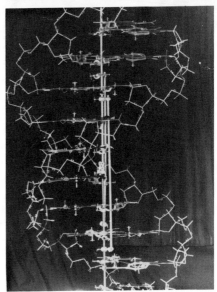

The Decoding of DNA. Left: F. H. C. Crick and James D. Watson discuss their efforts to analyze the molecular structure of DNA. Right: A model of the molecular structure of DNA. The dual spiral chains are called a double helix.

of genetic inheritance that had been explored by Gregor Mendel at the end of the nineteenth century. Crick and Watson successfully analyzed deoxyribonucleic acid, or DNA, the chemical molecular structure that occurs in the nuclei of gene cells. They discovered that DNA is composed of smaller molecules of four different kinds, linked together in spiral chains. The arrangement of these molecules in each cell forms a distinct chemical message which determines the character of the genes and therefore of the human organism of which they are a part. The knowledge gained through analysis of DNA has enabled scientists and doctors to understand the causes of hereditary disease and also, by altering a patient's body chemistry, to prevent it. Despite the great benefits that have resulted from this recent discovery, scientists and others have warned that an understanding of the workings of DNA could lead to dangerous tampering with the genetic processes, as, for example, in attempts to produce artificially a breed of more "perfect" human beings.

Experimentation based upon a fuller understanding of the causes of disease has led to the discovery of new medicines to treat it. In 1935 the German Gerhard Domagk discovered the first of the sulfa drugs, which he called sulfanilamide. Soon others were added to the list. Each was found to be marvelously effective in curing or checking such diseases as rheumatic fever, gonorrhea, scarlet fever, and meningitis. About 1930, the Englishman Sir Alexander Fleming discovered the first of the antibiotics, penicillin. Antibiotics are chemical agents produced by living organisms and possessing the power to check or kill bacteria. Many have their origin in molds, fungi, algae, and in

Medical advances: sulfa drugs, antibiotics, tranquilizers

simple organisms living in the soil. Penicillin was eventually found to be a drug that could produce spectacular results in the treatment of pneumonia, syphilis, peritonitis, tetanus, and numerous other maladies hitherto frequently fatal. Scientists used knowledge obtained through the analysis of DNA to strengthen the cultures used to develop penicillin. In the 1940s the second most famous of the antibiotics—streptomycin—was discovered by the American Dr. Selman W. Waksman. Streptomycin seems to hold its greatest promise in the treatment of tuberculosis, though it has been used for numerous other infections that do not yield to penicillin.

Preventative discoveries

As important as the discovery of new drugs to treat disease has been the development of new means of preventing it. Sir Edward Jenner discovered the first successful vaccine, used to prevent smallpox, in 1796. But not until the 1950s were vaccines found that could protect from diseases such as mumps, measles, and cholera. One of the most exciting breakthroughs occurred with the development of an inoculation against poliomyelitis by the American Dr. Jonas Salk, in 1953. Still to be discovered are effective agents for the successful treatment of two of the world's most deadly killers, heart disease and cancer, and of a recent and potentially more dangerous worldwide plague Anti-Immune Deficiency Syndrome (AIDS), a virus that attacks the body's immune system, thus making it prey to any number of deadly diseases and infections. Unlike the victims of heart disease and cancer, no AIDS patient has ever been cured.

Dr. Jonas Salk in His Laboratory

Few would today oppose continued campaigns by scientists intent upon eradicating disease. Governments have found it increasingly difficult, however, to justify the spending of vast sums of public money on programs designed to facilitate the exploration of outer space. From their inception, these "experiments" have resembled international competitions between the United States and the Soviet Union as much as they have scientific and technological investigations. On October 4, 1957, the government of the Soviet Union rocketed the first artificial satellite into space at a speed of about 18,000 miles an hour. Though it weighed nearly 200 pounds, it was propelled upward higher than 500 miles. This Russian achievement gave the English language a new word—Sputnik, the Russian for satellite or fellow traveler. In April 1961, the Russians succeeded in sending the first

Space exploration

man into orbit around the earth. Meanwhile, scientists and military specialists in the United States had been competing to match the Soviets' achievements. After a number of successes with animals and "uninhabited" capsules, and the suborbital journey of a manned capsule, they launched the first American manned spaceship into orbit around the earth on February 20, 1962. Their successes were climaxed in July 1969 when Neil Armstrong, a civilian astronaut, left his lunar landing module and became the first man on the moon's surface. These voyages and those that followed were hailed as events of capital importance. They did promise an extension of our knowledge of outer space and could doubtless prepare the way for exploration of the moon and eventually of distant planets. But by the mid-1970s, both the United States and the Soviet Union had drastically cut back their space programs in response to demands on their economies from other quarters. A space "shuttle" and laboratory, plus continuing experiments of a minor nature, kept the programs alive, despite an accident in 1986 that killed all the crew members of a U.S. space shuttle. But the value of these devices was being questioned, in view of the billions required to keep them operational.

Undoubtedly it was in the area of nuclear science that the largest and most troubling questions arose as to the capabilities, limitations, and implications of science and technology. Even more disturbing than the results of the nuclear bombs dropped on Japan at the end of the Second World War were the first tests of a hydrogen bomb by the U.S. Atomic Energy commission in November 1952. The tests were conducted at Eniwetok Atoll in the South Pacific; an entire island disappeared after burning brightly for several hours. The hydrogen bomb, or H-bomb, is based upon fusion of hydrogen atoms, a process which requires the enormous heat generated by the splitting of uranium atoms to start the reaction. The fusion results in the creation of a new element, helium, which actually weighs less than the sum of the hydrogen atoms. The "free" energy left over provides the tremendous explosive power of the H-bomb. The force of hydrogen bombs is measured in *megatons,* each of which represents 1,000,000 tons of TNT. Thus a 5-megaton H-bomb would equal 250 times the power of the A-bombs dropped on Hiroshima and Nagasaki.

Clearly the scientists had, at the behest of their government, unleashed a weapon of devastating proportions upon the world. By the 1970s, not only the United States, but the Soviet Union, China, Britain, France, India, Israel, and other nations either possessed atomic weapons or were in the process of developing the technology to do so. Science was once and for all proved to be something other than "pure," that is, without practical and political implications. The application of its discoveries had become a burdensome fact of life for humanity the world over.

Governments experimented with schemes to harness nuclear energy for peaceful purposes. Some progress has been made in the development of atomic power as an alternative source of domestic and industrial fuel. But the dangers of radiation as a by-product suggest that this scheme may prove of limited value. During the late 1970s, when the West's supplies of oil were threatened, heated debate continued between advocates of further construction of atomic power plants and those who argued in favor of other energy forms—among them solar—as safer and cheaper alternatives. Meanwhile, technologists working for private industry made use of discoveries in atomic physics

The First Lunar Landing. Astronaut Edwin E. Aldrin, Jr., is photographed walking near the lunar module of Apollo 11. Astronaut Neil Armstrong, who took the picture, and part of the lunar module are reflected in Aldrin's face plate.

Proliferation of nuclear weapons

The uses of atomic energy; electronics

to pioneer the field of electronics. Electronics derives from that branch of physics which deals with the behavior and effects of electrons, or negatively charged constituents within the atom. Electronic devices have multiplied in staggering profusion since the Second World War. Among them are devices to measure the trajectory of missiles, to give warnings of approaching missiles or aircraft, to make possible "blind" landings of airplanes, to store and release electrical signals, to amplify and regulate the transmission of light and sound images, and to provide the power for photoelectric cells that open doors, and operate various automatic machines. The spacecraft industry, which has made possible the exploration of outer space, is closely dependent upon electronics.

Automation

The use of electronic devices for radio reception led to initial progress in automation. Automation should not be confused with mechanization, though it may be considered the logical extension of that process. More correctly, automation means a close integration of four elements: (1) a processing system; (2) a mechanical handling system; (3) sensing equipment; and (4) a control system. Though all of these elements are necessary, the last two are the most significant. Sensing equipment performs a function similar to that of the human senses. It observes and measures what is happening and sends the information thus gained to the control unit. It employs such devices as photoelectric cells, infrared cells, high-frequency devices, and devices making use of X rays, isotopes, and resonance. It operates without fatigue and much faster and more accurately than do the human senses. Moreover, its observations can be made in places unsafe for, or inaccessible to, human beings. A control system receives information from a sensing element, compares this information with that required by the "program," and then makes the necessary adjustments. This series of operations is continuous, so that a desired state is constantly maintained without any human intervention, except for that initially involved in "programming." This revolution has been greatly extended by the invention of lasers. A laser is a device for amplifying the focus and intensity of light. High-energy atoms are stimulated by light to amplify a beam of light. Lasers have demonstrated their value recently in medicine. They have been used effectively in arresting hemorrhaging in the retina in eye afflictions. Through automation, expensive and complicated machines are constantly taking the place of much human labor. Data-processing machines and electronic computers are employed to control switching operations in railroad yards, to operate assembly lines, to operate machines that control other machines, and even to maintain blood pressure during critical operations in hospitals.

Technological unemployment

Electronic inventions have proved no more an unmixed blessing than have the other discoveries and developments of scientists and technicians. One obvious problem generated by devices that can do the work of humans is that they put humans out of work. Technological unemployment has become an important problem for the modern world. Though new industries absorbed many workers, others were bound to be displaced by automation. While the demand for skilled labor remained high, the so-called entry jobs performed by the unskilled were fast disappearing. They were being eliminated not by computers so much as by fork-lift trucks and motorized conveyors and sweepers. Mechanization of agriculture also eliminated thousands of jobs for unskilled and uneducated workers.

Science and technology provide no panaceas for the problems of the world. If those problems are to be solved, men and women, not machines, will have to do the work. They will be better equipped to do so if they possess some sense of their own past. The lesson of history is not that it repeats itself. The lesson is, rather, that the present can be clearly perceived, and the future intelligently planned for, only when those responsible for the world's destiny understand the workings of human nature. And for knowledge of that extraordinarily complicated and fascinating mechanism, there is no better source than history.

Science, technology, and an understanding of human nature

SELECTED READINGS

• *Items so designated are available in paperback editions.*

• American Friends Service Committee, *A Compassionate Peace: A Future for the Middle East,* New York, 1981. An examination of the problems and proposals for their solution.
• Barnett, A. Doak, *China and the Major Powers in East Asia,* Washington, D.C., 1977. A careful study of recent international relations.
  Bates, Robert H., *Essays on the Political Economy of Rural Africa,* Cambridge, 1983. An excellent study of the problems of food production in contemporary Africa.
  Bhatia, Krishan, *The Ordeal of Nationhood: A Social Study of India since Independence, 1947–1970,* New York, 1971. Informed and objective account of India's problems.
• Bianco, Lucien, *Origins of the Chinese Revolution, 1915–1949,* tr. Muriel Bell. Stanford, 1971. A brilliant interpretive summary.
  Brain, Robert, *Art and Society in Africa,* London, 1981.
• Butterfield, Fox, *China Alive in the Bitter Sea,* New York, 1982. Poignant and critical.
• Caputo, Philip, *A Rumor of War,* New York, 1977. The best memoir of the American experience in the Vietnam War.
• Coetzee, J. M., *Waiting for the Barbarians,* London, 1980. A searing critique of South Africa by a brilliant Afrikaner novelist.
• Cornish, Edward, *The Study of the Future: An Introduction to the Art and Science of Understanding and Shaping Tomorrow's World,* Washington, D.C., 1977. An introduction to the world of the "futurists."
• Erlich, Paul, *The Population Bomb,* New York, 1968. Discusses the threat of overpopulation.
• Fall, Bernard B., *The Two Vietnams: A Political and Military Analysis,* rev. ed., New York, 1967.

• Fanon, Frantz, *The Wretched of the Earth,* New York, 1968. The extraordinary and brilliant delineation of the oppression of Third World peoples.

• Fitzgerald, Frances, *Fire in the Lake: The Vietnamese and the Americans in Vietnam,* Boston, 1972. A detailed and moving account.

• Gamow, George, *Thirty Years That Shook Physics,* New York, 1966. A lucid account by a physicist.

• Heilbroner, Robert L., *An Inquiry into the Human Prospect,* New York, 1974, 1980. Optimistic assessment of the durability of Western cultural values.

Issawi, Charles, *Egypt in Revolution: An Economic Analysis,* New York, 1963.

• Khouri, Fred J., *The Arab-Israeli Dilemma,* Syracuse, N.Y., 1968.

• Myrdal, Alva, *The Game of Disarmament: How the United States and Russia Run the Arms Race,* New York, 1976.

Myrdal, Gunnar, *Against the Stream: Critical Essays on Economics,* New York, 1972. Offers pertinent comments on problems of the Third World.

Nattrass, Jill, *The South African Economy: Its Growth and Change,* Cape Town, 1981.

• Nelson, Nici, ed., *African Women in the Development Process,* London, 1981.

Ngugi wa Thiong'o, *Petals of Blood,* New York, 1977. A scathing critique of neocolonialism in Kenya by Africa's best-known novelist.

O'Connor, Anthony, *The African City,* London, 1983. Explores the various characteristics of tropical African cities in the postcolonial era.

• Rubin, Barry, *Paved with Good Intentions: The American Experience and Iran,* New York, 1980. Reliable account of U.S.-Iranian diplomacy.

Servan-Schreiber, J. J., *The World Challenge,* New York, 1981. Analyzes problems of distribution of world resources.

• Spence, Jonathan, *The Gate of Heavenly Peace: The Chinese and Their Revolution, 1895–1980,* New York, 1981. A penetrating account of the contributions and frustrations of China's intellectuals.

• Thompson, Leonard, and Andrew Prior, *South African Politics,* London, 1982. An excellent, well-balanced survey of contemporary South Africa.

• Toffler, Alvin, *Future Shock,* New York, 1971. An extended essay on the consequences of rapid change in modern industrial society.

• Tordoff, William, *Government and Politics in Africa,* Bloomington, 1984. Highly readable, wide-ranging, and up-to-date.

• Worsley, Peter, *The Third World,* 2d ed., Chicago, 1970.

RULERS OF PRINCIPAL EUROPEAN STATES SINCE 700 A.D.

The Carolingian Dynasty

Pepin, Mayor of the Palace, 714
Charles Martel, Mayor of the Palace, 715–741
Pepin I, Mayor of the Palace, 741; King, 751–768
Charlemagne, King, 768–814; Emperor, 800–814
Louis the Pious, Emperor, 814–840

MIDDLE KINGDOMS

Lothair, Emperor, 840–855
Louis (Italy), Emperor, 855–875
Charles (Provence), King, 855–863
Lothair II (Lorraine), King, 855–869

WEST FRANCIA

Charles the Bald, King, 840–877; Emperor, 875
Louis II, King, 877–879
Louis III, King, 879–882
Carloman, King, 879–884

EAST FRANCIA

Ludwig, King, 840–876
Carloman, King, 876–880
Ludwig, King, 876–882
Charles the Fat, Emperor, 876–887

Holy Roman Emperors

SAXON DYNASTY

Otto I, 962–973
Otto II, 973–983
Otto III, 983–1002
Henry II, 1002–1024

FRANCONIAN DYNASTY

Conrad II, 1024–1039
Henry III, 1039–1056
Henry IV, 1056–1106
Henry V, 1106–1125
Lothair II (of Saxony), King, 1125–1133; Emperor,
    1133–1137

HOHENSTAUFEN DYNASTY

Conrad III, 1138–1152
Frederick I (Barbarossa), 1152–1190
Henry VI, 1190–1197
Philip of Swabia, 1198–1208 ⎱ Rivals
Otto IV (Welf), 1198–1215 ⎰
Frederick II, 1220–1250
Conrad IV, 1250–1254

INTERREGNUM, 1254–1273

EMPERORS FROM VARIOUS DYNASTIES
Rudolf I (Habsburg), 1273–1291

Adolf (Nassau), 1292–1298
Albert I (Hapsburg), 1298–1308
Henry VII (Luxemburg), 1308–1313
Ludwig IV (Wittelsbach), 1314–1347
Charles IV (Luxemburg), 1347–1378
Wenceslas (Luxemburg), 1378–1400
Rupert (Wittelsbach), 1400–1410
Sigismund (Luxemburg), 1410–1437

HABSBURG DYNASTY

Albert II, 1438–1439
Frederick III, 1440–1493
Maximilian I, 1493–1519
Charles V, 1519–1556
Ferdinand I, 1556–1564
Maximilan II, 1564–1576
Rudolf II, 1576–1612
Matthias, 1612–1619
Ferdinand II, 1619–1637
Ferdinand III, 1637–1657
Leopold I, 1658–1705
Joseph I, 1705–1711
Charles VI, 1711–1740
Charles VII (not a Habsburg), 1742–1745
Francis I, 1745–1765
Joseph II, 1765–1790
Leopold II, 1790–1792
Francis II, 1792–1806

CAPETIAN KINGS

Hugh Capet, 987–996
Robert II, 996–1031
Henry I, 1031–1060
Philip I, 1060–1108
Louis VI, 1108–1137
Louis VII, 1137–1180
Philip II (Augustus), 1180–1223
Louis VIII, 1223–1226
Louis IX, 1226–1270
Philip III, 1270–1285
Philip IV, 1285–1314
Louis X, 1314–1316
Philip V, 1316–1322
Charles IV, 1322–1328

HOUSE OF VALOIS

Philip VI, 1328–1350
John, 1350–1364
Charles V, 1364–1380
Charles VI, 1380–1422
Charles VII, 1422–1461
Louis XI, 1461–1483
Charles VIII, 1483–1498
Louis XII, 1498–1515
Francis I, 1515–1547

Henry II, 1547–1559
Francis II, 1559–1560
Charles IX, 1560–1574
Henry III, 1574–1589

BOURBON DYNASTY

Henry IV, 1589–1610
Louis XIII, 1610–1643
Louis XIV, 1643–1715
Louis XV, 1715–1774
Louis XVI, 1774–1792

AFTER 1792

First Republic, 1792–1799
Napoleon Bonaparte, First Consul, 1799–1804
Napoleon I, Emperor, 1804–1814
Louis XVIII (Bourbon dynasty), 1814–1824
Charles X (Bourbon dynasty), 1824–1830
Louis Philippe, 1830–1848
Second Republic, 1848–1852
Napoleon III, Emperor, 1852–1870
Third Republic, 1870–1940
Pétain regime, 1940–1944
Provisional government, 1944–1946
Fourth Republic, 1946–1958
Fifth Republic, 1958–

Rulers of England

ANGLO-SAXON KINGS

Egbert, 802–839
Ethelwulf, 839–858
Ethelbald, 858–860
Ethelbert, 860–866
Ethelred, 866–871
Alfred the Great, 871–900
Edward the Elder, 900–924
Ethelstan, 924–940
Edmund I, 940–946
Edred, 946–955
Edwy, 955–959
Edgar, 959–975

Edward the Martyr, 975–978
Ethelred the Unready, 978–1016
Canute, 1016–1035 (Danish Nationality)
Harold I, 1035–1040
Hardicanute, 1040–1042
Edward the Confessor, 1042–1066
Harold II, 1066

HOUSE OF NORMANDY

William I (the Conqueror), 1066–1087
William II, 1087–1100
Henry I, 1100–1135
Stephen, 1135–1154

House of Plantagenet

Henry II, 1154–1189
Richard I, 1189–1199
John, 1199–1216
Henry III, 1216–1272
Edward I, 1272–1307
Edward II, 1307–1327
Edward III, 1327–1377
Richard II, 1377–1399

House of Lancaster

Henry IV, 1399–1413
Henry V, 1413–1422
Henry VI, 1422–1461

House of York

Edward IV, 1461–1483
Edward V, 1483
Richard III, 1483–1485

House of Tudor

Henry VII, 1485–1509
Henry VIII, 1509–1547
Edward VI, 1547–1553
Mary, 1553–1558
Elizabeth I, 1558–1603

House of Stuart

James I, 1603–1625
Charles I, 1625–1649

Commonwealth and Protectorate, 1649–1659

House of Stuart Restored

Charles II, 1660–1685
James II, 1685–1688
William III and Mary II, 1689–1694
William III alone, 1694–1702
Anne, 1702–1714

House of Hanover

George I, 1714–1727
George II, 1727–1760
George III, 1760–1820
George IV, 1820–1830
William IV, 1830–1837
Victoria, 1837–1901

House of Saxe-Coburg-Gotha

Edward VII, 1901–1910
George V, 1910–1917

House of Windsor

George V, 1917–1936
Edward VIII, 1936
George VI, 1936–1952
Elizabeth II, 1952–

Prominent Popes

Silvester I, 314–335
Leo I, 440–461
Gelasius I, 492–496
Gregory I, 590–604
Nicholas I, 858–867
Silvester II, 999–1003
Leo IX, 1049–1054
Nicholas II, 1058–1061
Gregory VII, 1073–1085
Urban II, 1088–1099
Paschal II, 1099–1118
Alexander III, 1159–1181

Innocent III, 1198–1216
Gregory IX, 1227–1241
Boniface VIII, 1294–1303
John XXII, 1316–1334
Nicholas V, 1447–1455
Pius II, 1458–1464
Alexander VI, 1492–1503
Julius II, 1503–1513
Leo X, 1513–1521
Adrian VI, 1522–1523
Clement VII, 1523–1534
Paul III, 1534–1549

Paul IV, 1555–1559
Gregory XIII, 1572–1585
Gregory XVI, 1831–1846
Pius IX, 1846–1878
Leo XIII, 1878–1903
Pius X, 1903–1914
Benedict XV, 1914–1922

Pius XI, 1922–1939
Pius XII, 1939–1958
John XXIII, 1958–1963
Paul VI, 1963–1978
John Paul I, 1978
John Paul II, 1978–

Rulers of Austria and Austria-Hungary

*Maximilian I (Archduke), 1493–1519
*Charles I (Charles V in the Holy Roman Empire), 1519–1556
*Ferdinand I, 1556–1564
*Maximilian II, 1564–1576
*Rudolph II, 1576–1612
*Matthias, 1612–1619
*Ferdinand II, 1619–1637
*Ferdinand III, 1637–1657
*Leopold I, 1658–1705
*Joseph I, 1705–1711
*Charles VI, 1711–1740
Maria Theresa, 1740–1780

*Joseph II, 1780–1790
*Leopold II, 1790–1792
*Francis II, 1792–1835 (Emperor of Austria as Francis I after 1804)
Ferdinand I, 1835–1848
Francis Joseph, 1848–1916 (after 1867 Emperor of Austria and King of Hungary)
Charles I, 1916–1918 (Emperor of Austria and King of Hungary)
Republic of Austria, 1918–1938 (dictatorship after 1934)
Republic restored, under Allied occupation, 1945–1956
Free Republic, 1956–

*Also bore title of Holy Roman Emperor.

Rulers of Prussia and Germany

*Frederick I, 1701–1713
*Frederick William I, 1713–1740
*Frederick II (the Great), 1740–1786
*Frederick William II, 1786–1797
*Frederick William III, 1797–1840
*Frederick William IV, 1840–1861
*William I, 1861–1888 (German Emperor after 1871)

Frederick III, 1888
William II, 1888–1918
Weimar Republic, 1918–1933
Third Reich (Nazi Dictatorship), 1933–1945
Allied occupation, 1945–1952
Division into Federal Republic of Germany in west and German Democratic Republic in east, 1949–

*Kings of Prussia.

Rulers of Russia

Ivan III, 1462–1505
Vasily III, 1505–1533
Ivan IV, 1533–1584
Theodore I, 1584–1598
Boris Godunov, 1598–1605

Theodore II, 1605
Vasily IV, 1606–1610
Michael, 1613–1645
Alexius, 1645–1676
Theodore III, 1676–1682

Ivan V and Peter I, 1682–1689
Peter I (the Great), 1689–1725
Catherine I, 1725–1727
Peter II, 1727–1730
Anna, 1730–1740
Ivan VI, 1740–1741
Elizabeth, 1741–1762
Peter III, 1762

Catherine II (the Great), 1762–1796
Paul, 1796–1801
Alexander I, 1801–1825
Nicholas I, 1825–1855
Alexander II, 1855–1881
Alexander III, 1881–1894
Nicholas II, 1894–1917
Soviet Republic, 1917–

Rulers of Italy

Victor Emmanuel II, 1861–1878
Humbert I, 1878–1900
Victor Emmanuel III, 1900–1946
Fascist Dictatorship, 1922–1943
   (maintained in northern Italy until 1945)

Humbert II, May 9–June 13, 1946
Republic, 1946–

Rulers of Spain

Ferdinand { and Isabella, 1479–1504
{ and Philip I, 1504–1506
{ and Charles I, 1506–1516
Charles I (Holy Roman Emperor Charles V),
   1516–1556
Philip II, 1556–1598
Philip III, 1598–1621
Philip IV, 1621–1665
Charles II, 1665–1700
Philip V, 1700–1746
Ferdinand VI, 1746–1759
Charles III, 1759–1788
Charles IV, 1788–1808

Ferdinand VII, 1808
Joseph Bonaparte, 1808–1813
Ferdinand VII (restored), 1814–1833
Isabella II, 1833–1868
Republic, 1868–1870
Amadeo, 1870–1873
Republic, 1873–1874
Alfonso XII, 1874–1885
Alfonso XIII, 1886–1931
Republic, 1931–1939
Fascist Dictatorship, 1939–1975
Juan Carlos I, 1975–

ILLUSTRATIONS IN COLOR

(Illustrations appear facing or following the pages indicated)

ILLUSTRATIONS IN THE TEXT

Index

Guide to Pronunciation

The sounds represented by the diacritical marks used in this Index are illustrated by the following common words:

āle	ēve	īce	ōld	ūse	b͞oot
ăt	ĕnd	ĭll	ŏf	ŭs	fŏŏt
fȧtality	év́ent		ȯbey	u̇ite	
câre			fôrm	ûrn	
ärm					
ȧsk					

Vowels that have no diacritical marks are to be pronounced "neutral," for example: Aegean = ê-je′an, Basel = bäz′el, Basil = bă′zil, common = kŏm′on, Alcaeus = ăl-sē′us. The combinations ou and oi are pronounced as in "out" and "oil."